Developing & Managing
Your School Guidance and Counseling Program
☙ Fourth Edition ❧

by

Norman C. Gysbers
Patricia Henderson

AMERICAN COUNSELING ASSOCIATION
5999 Stevenson Avenue
Alexandria, VA 22304
www.counseling.org

Developing & Managing
Your School Guidance and Counseling Program
⌒ Fourth Edition ⌒

10 9 8 7 6 5 4 3 2 1

American Counseling Association
5999 Stevenson Avenue
Alexandria, VA 22304

Director of Publications
Carolyn C. Baker

Production Manager
Bonny E. Gaston

Copy Editor
Elaine Dunn

Cover and text design by Bonny E. Gaston.

Library of Congress Cataloging-in-Publication Data
Gysbers, Norman C.
   Developing and managing your school guidance and counseling program / by Norman C. Gysbers and Patricia Henderson.—4th ed.
      p. cm.
   Includes bibliographical references.
   ISBN 1-55620-243-1 (alk. paper)
   1. Educational counseling—United States. I. Henderson, Patricia, Ed.D. II. Title.

LB1027.5.G9 2005
371.4—dc22   2005011771

To School Counselors and Their Leaders

summary of change 17

might use a time line to show changes in counseling

Table of Contents

☜ Part I ☞

Planning

☜ Part II ☞

Designing

☜ Part III ☞

Implementing

Preface

☞ In this first decade of the 21st century, the United States continues to undergo substantial changes in its occupational, social, and economic structures. Occupational and industrial specialization continue to increase dramatically. Increasing size and complexity are the rule rather than the exception, often creating job invisibility and making the transition from school to work and from work to further education and back again more complex and difficult.

Social structures and social and personal values also continue to change and become more diverse. Emerging social groups are challenging established groups, asking for equality. People are on the move, too, from rural to urban areas and back again and from one region of the country to another in search of economic, social, and psychological security. Our population is becoming increasingly diverse.

All of these changes are creating substantial challenges for our children and adolescents. A rapidly changing work world and labor force; violence in the home, school, and community; divorce; teenage suicide; substance abuse; and sexual experimentation are just a few examples. These challenges are not abstract aberrations. These challenges are real, and they are having and will have substantial impact on the personal/social, career, and academic development of our children and adolescents.

Responding to Challenges

In response to these and other continuing societal and individual needs and challenges, educational leaders and policymakers are in the midst of reforming the entire educational enterprise (National Association of Secondary School Principals, 2004; No Child Left Behind Act, 2001). Guidance and counseling in the schools also continues to undergo reform, changing from a position-services model to a comprehensive program firmly grounded in principles of human growth and development. This change places guidance and counseling in the schools as an integral part of education and as an equal partner with the instruction program, focusing on students' academic, career, and personal/social development.

Traditionally, however, guidance and counseling was not conceptualized and implemented in this manner because, as Aubrey (1973) suggested, guidance and counseling was seen as a support service lacking a content base of its own. Sprinthall (1971) made this same point when he stated that there is little content in the practice of guidance and counseling and that guidance and counseling textbooks usually avoided discussion of a subject-matter base for guidance and counseling programs.

If guidance and counseling is to become an equal partner in education and to meet the increasingly complex needs of individuals and society, it is our opinion that guidance and counseling must become a program conceptually and organizationally with its own content base and structure. The call for this is not new; many early pioneers had issued the same call. But the call was not loud enough during the early years, and guidance and counseling became a position and a service with an emphasis on duties, processes, and techniques.

The need and the call continued to emerge occasionally thereafter, however, but not until the late 1960s and early 1970s did it reemerge and become visible once more in the form of a developmental comprehensive program.

This is not to say that developmental guidance and counseling was not present before the late 1960s. What it does mean is that by the late 1960s the need for attention to aspects of human development other than "the time-honored cognitive aspect of learning-subject matter mastery" (Cottingham, 1973, p. 341) again had become apparent. Cottingham characterized these other aspects of human development as "personal adequacy learning" (p. 342). Kehas (1973) pointed to this same need by stating that an individual should have opportunities "to develop intelligence about his [or her] self—his [or her] personal, unique, idiosyncratic, individual self" (p. 110).

Reconceptualization of Guidance and Counseling

The next step in the evolution of guidance and counseling was to establish guidance and counseling as a comprehensive program—a program that is an integral part of education with a content base and organizational structure of its own. In response to this need, Gysbers and Moore (1981) published a book titled *Improving Guidance Programs*. It presented a content-based, K–12 comprehensive guidance and counseling program model and described the steps to implement the model. The first, second, and third editions of this current book built on the model and implementations steps presented in *Improving Guidance Programs* and substantially expanded and extended the model and implementation steps. This fourth edition expands and extends the model and steps even further, sharing what has been learned through various state and local adoption/adaptations since 2000.

Organization of the Book

Five phases of developing comprehensive guidance and counseling programs are used as organizers for this book. The five phases are planning (chapters 1 through 4), designing (chapters 5 and 6), implementing (chapters 7 through 9), evaluating (chapter 10), and enhancing (chapter 11). In several chapters, ways to attend to the increasing diversity of school populations and the roles and responsibilities of district- and building-level guidance and counseling leaders are highlighted. The appendixes offer examples of forms and procedures used by various states and school districts in the installation of comprehensive guidance and counseling programs. Also included as an appendix are the ethical standards of the American School Counselor Association (ASCA) and the Multicultural Competencies and Objectives of the American Counseling Association (ACA).

Part One: Planning. Chapter 1 traces the evolution of guidance and counseling in the schools from the beginning of the 20th century. The changing influences, emphases, and structures from then until now are described and discussed in detail. The emergence of comprehensive guidance and counseling programs is highlighted. To have an understanding of the evolution of guidance and counseling in the schools and the emergence of developmental comprehensive programs is the first step in improving your school's guidance and counseling program. Chapter 2 is based on this understanding and focuses on the issues and concerns in planning and organizing for guidance and counseling program improvement. Chapter 3 then presents a model guidance and counseling program based on the concept of life career development; it is organized around four basic elements. Chapter 4, the last chapter in the planning phase, discusses the steps involved in finding out how well your current program is working and where improvement is needed.

Part Two: Designing. Chapter 5 begins the designing phase of the program improvement process and focuses on designing the program of your choice. Issues and steps in selecting the desired program structure for your comprehensive program are presented. Chapter 6 describes the necessary tasks required to plan the transition to a comprehensive guidance and counseling program.

Part Three: Implementing. Chapter 7 presents the details of beginning a new program in a district, and chapter 8 emphasizes the details of managing and maintaining the program in a district. Chapter 9 first looks at how to ensure that school counselors have the necessary competence to develop, manage, and implement a comprehensive guidance and counseling program and then highlights counselor supervision procedures.

Part Four: Evaluating. Comprehensive guidance and counseling program evaluation is discussed in detail in chapter 10. Program evaluation, personnel evaluation, and results evaluation are featured, with attention given to procedures for each.

Part Five: Enhancing. Chapter 11 considers the use of data gathered from program, personnel, and results evaluation to redesign and enhance a comprehensive guidance and counseling program that has been in place for a number of years. The chapter uses actual data gathered in a school district and describes in detail the way this school district built on the guidance and counseling program foundation it had established in the early 1980s to update and enhance its program to meet continuing and changing student, school district, and community needs.

Who Should Read This Book

A goal of this book is to inform and involve all members of a guidance and counseling staff K–12 in the development and management of comprehensive school guidance and counseling programs. Although specific parts are highlighted for guidance and counseling program leaders (central or building-level directors, supervisors, coordinators, department heads) and school administrators, the information provided is important for all to know and use. In addition, the book is designed for practitioners already on the job as well as for the counselors-in-training and administrators-in-training. It can and should be used in preservice education as well as in-service education. If you are a guidance and counseling program leader or school administrator, you also will be interested in *Leading and Managing Your School Guidance Program Staff* (Henderson & Gysbers, 1998), a book that describes your roles and responsibilities in providing leadership to guidance and counseling program staff.

The Fourth Edition: What Is New?

All of the chapters in the fourth edition have been reorganized and updated to reflect current theory and practices. A more complete theory base for comprehensive guidance and counseling programs is provided along with updated examples of the contents of various components of comprehensive guidance and counseling programs drawn from many state models and from the ASCA National Model. New information and practical ideas and methods have been added to assist school counselors and school counselor leaders better understand the issues involved in developing and managing comprehensive school guidance and counseling programs. For examples, the timetable of tasks involved in the above phases that had been in the Preface of the third edition has been moved to chapter 2. This change places the sample timetable of tasks in the actual change phase (Planning), in which such a timetable would actually be constructed to guide the overall change process.

Increased attention is given in this fourth edition to the important topic of diversity. Increased attention is also given to expanded discussions of who school counselors' clients are and the range of issues they present. Also, increased attention is given to helping school counselors and their leaders be accountable for the work they do, for evaluating and reporting the impact of their programs' activities and services on students' academic, career, and personal and social development. In addition, increased attention is given to the issues and challenges that the leaders of comprehensive guidance and counseling programs face in an increasingly complex educational environment.

Finally, readers will note that the title of the book has been changed to *Developing and Managing Your School Guidance and Counseling Program*. The word *guidance* is maintained in the title to reflect the heritage of our profession and because of its use as a title of a program component, the guidance curriculum. The word *counseling* was added to reflect current usage in the ASCA National Model and in many new state models.

Concluding Thoughts

Some readers may think that guidance and counseling program improvement is a simple task requiring little staff time and few resources. This is not true. Substantial work can be completed during the first several years, but at least 4 to 5 years with the necessary resources available to ensure successful implementation are usually required. To carry the program through the enhancement phase may require an additional 5 years. Then we recommend an ongoing program improvement process.

Further, the chapter organization may lead some readers to think that guidance and counseling program improvement activities follow one another in a linear fashion. Although there is a progression involved, some of the activities described in chapters 2 through 10 may be carried on concurrently. This is true particularly for the evaluation procedures described in chapter 10, some of which are carried out from the beginning of the program improvement process throughout the life of the program. The program enhancement process follows evaluation and connects back to the beginning as program redesign unfolds, but at a higher level. Thus the process is spiral, not circular. Each time the redesign process unfolds, a new and more effective guidance and counseling program emerges.

Finally, it is important to understand that a comprehensive guidance and counseling program, as described in the chapters that follow, provides a common language for the program elements that enable students, parents, teachers, administrators, school board members, and school counselors in a school district to speak with a common voice when they describe what a program is. They all see the same thing and use the same language to describe the program's framework. This is the power of common language whether the program is in a small or large, rural or urban or suburban school district. Within the basic framework at the local district level, however, the guidance knowledge and skills (competencies) students are to learn, the activities and services to be provided, and the allocations of school counselor time are tailored specifically to student, school, and community needs and local resources. This provides the flexibility and opportunity for creativity for the personnel in every school district to develop and implement a comprehensive guidance and counseling program that makes sense for their districts. We are convinced that without the common language for the program elements and the obligation to tailor it to fit local school districts, guidance and counseling and the work of school counselors will be lost in the overall educational system and, as a result, will continue to be marginalized and seen as a supplemental activity that is nice to have but is not necessary.

References

Aubrey, R. F. (1973). Organizational victimization of school counselors. *The School Counselor, 20,* 346–354.

Cottingham, H. F. (1973). Psychological education, the guidance function, and the school counselor. *The School Counselor, 20,* 340–345.

Gysbers, N. C., & Moore, E. J. (1981). *Improving guidance programs.* Englewood Cliffs, NJ: Prentice-Hall.

Henderson, P., & Gysbers, N. C. (1998). *Leading and managing your school guidance program staff.* Alexandria, VA: American Counseling Association.

Kehas, C. D. (1973). Guidance and the process of schooling: Curriculum and career education. *The School Counselor, 20,* 109–115.

National Association of Secondary School Principals. (2004). *Breaking ranks II: Strategies for leading high school reform.* Reston, VA: Author.

No Child Left Behind Act of 2001, Pub. L. No. 107-110, 115, Stat. 1434 (2001).

Sprinthall, N. A. (1971). *Guidance for human growth.* New York: Van Nostrand Reinhold.

Acknowledgments

With this fourth edition we gratefully acknowledge the substantial contributions of school counselors as they work with the children, young people, parents, teachers, administrators, and community members throughout the United States. It is to school counselors and their leaders that we dedicate this book. At the same time we also gratefully acknowledge the assistance of those individuals who helped us make all four editions of this book possible. Unfortunately, it is impossible to list them all, but know that we appreciate their support and encouragement. We particularly acknowledge the work of the counselors, head counselors, and administrators from Northside Independent School District, San Antonio, Texas. We appreciate the district's willingness to host visitors who come to see a comprehensive guidance and counseling program at work. Thanks also to Linda Coats and Jennifer Price, who typed a number of the revised chapters as well as helped assemble the revised chapters into the final book form. Finally, thanks to Carolyn Baker, director of publications at the American Counseling Association, for all of her help.

About the Authors

✎ **Norman C. Gysbers** is a Professor With Distinction in the Department of Educational, School, and Counseling Psychology at the University of Missouri–Columbia. He received his BA (1954) from Hope College and his MA (1959) and PhD (1963) from the University of Michigan. He is a licensed school counselor in Missouri. He was a teacher in the public schools, a school counselor and director of guidance at the University Laboratory School, University of Missouri, and has served in the U.S. Army. He has been a visiting professor at the University of Nevada–Reno and Virginia Polytechnic Institute and State University. He was awarded a Franqui Professorship from the Université Libre de Bruxelles, Belgium, and lectured there in 1984. He was a visiting scholar at the University of Hong Kong in 2000, 2002, and 2004; the Chinese University of Hong Kong in 2001; and a scholar in residence at the University of British Columbia in 2000. In addition, he has given presentations in Canada, Germany, Indonesia, England, Portugal, Japan, Australia, Singapore, Israel, Romania, France, and China.

Gysbers's research and teaching interests are in career development, career counseling, and school guidance and counseling program development, management, and evaluation. He is author of 73 articles in 17 different professional journals, 30 chapters in published books, 14 monographs, and 17 books, including *Career Counseling: Skills and Techniques for Practitioners* (1987, with Earl J. Moore); *Counseling for Career Development: Theories, Resources, and Practice* (1992, with Carl McDaniels); *Comprehensive Guidance Programs That Work—II* (1997, with Patricia Henderson); *Leading and Managing Your School Guidance Program Staff* (1998, with Patricia Henderson); *Developing and Managing Your School Guidance Program* (3rd ed., 2000, with Patricia Henderson); and *Career Counseling: Process, Issues, and Techniques* (2nd ed., 2003, with Mary Heppner and Joseph Johnston). The first edition of *Career Counseling: Process, Issues, and Techniques* (1998) was published in Italian (2001), Japanese (2002), and Korean (2003).

In 1978 he received the American Vocational Association's Division Merit Award and the Missouri Guidance Association's Outstanding Service Award. In 1981 he was awarded the National Vocational Guidance Association's National Merit Award and in 1983 the American Counseling Association's Distinguished Professional Service Award and the Distinguished Professional Service Award from the Missouri Association of Counselor Education and Supervision. In 1984 he received the Franqui Foundation Medal, Université Libre de Bruxelles. In 1987 he was awarded the United States Air Force Recruiting Service's Spirit of America Award and the Distinguished Service Award of the Association of Computer-Based Systems for Career Information. In 1989 he received the National Career Development Association's Eminent Career Award, and in 2000 he received the National Career Development Association's President's Recognition Award. He was awarded the American School Counselor Association Postsecondary School Counselor of the Year Award in 2001. In 2004, he received the American School Counselor Association's Mary Gehrke Lifetime Achievement Award.

Gysbers was editor of the *The Career Development Quarterly,* 1962–1970; president of the National Career Development Association, 1972–1973; president of the American Counseling Association, 1977–1978; and vice president of the American Vocational Association, 1979–1982. Currently he is the editor of *The Journal of Career*

Development. Since 1967 he has served as director of numerous national and state projects on career development and career counseling, and school guidance program development, implementation, and evaluation.

☞ **Patricia Henderson** is a former director of guidance at the Northside Independent School District in San Antonio, Texas. She received her AB (1962) in English from Mount Holyoke College, her MA (1967) in guidance from California State University at San Jose, and her EdD (1986) in educational leadership from Nova University. She is certified as a school counselor and midmanagement administrator by California and Texas. She has been a teacher, counselor, and administrator in public schools—most notably as director of guidance in Northside Independent School District in San Antonio, Texas. She has been an adjunct professor at California State University at Fullerton, California State University at Long Beach, Our Lady of the Lake University in San Antonio, and is currently at the University of Texas at San Antonio. She consults with school districts and has conducted workshops in numerous states.

Henderson's professional interests are in school guidance and counseling; program development, management, implementation, evaluation, and improvement; enhancing roles of school counselors through supervision, staff leadership, and meaningful school counselor performance evaluation; creating systemic change through collaborative program development; and counselor supervision. She and Dr. Gysbers have also coauthored *Leading and Managing Your School Guidance Program Staff* (1998), *Comprehensive Guidance Programs That Work—II* (1997), and *Implementing Comprehensive School Guidance Programs: Critical Issues and Successful Responses* (2002). She has authored or coauthored 25 articles or chapters. She wrote *The Comprehensive Guidance Program for Texas Public Schools: A Guide for Program Development, Pre-K–12th Grade* (1990, 2004) under the auspices of the Texas Education Agency and the Texas Association for Counseling and Development, and *Guidelines for Developing Comprehensive Guidance Programs in California Public Schools* (1981) with D. Hays and L. Steinberg.

She has received awards from professional associations for her writing, research, and contributions to professional development, and recognition as an outstanding supervisor at the state and national levels. She received the Texas Association for Counseling and Development Presidential Award in 1990 and an Honorary Service Award from the California State PTA in 1978 and Lifetime Membership in the Texas PTA in 1999.

Henderson has been a member or chair of numerous committees within the California Counseling Association, Texas Counseling Association, American School Counselor Association, Association for Counselor Education and Supervision, and American Counseling Association. She has been president of the Texas Counseling Association (1992–1993), Texas Association for Counselor Education and Supervision (1988–1989), Texas Career Development Association (1995–1996), California Career Guidance Association (1981–1982), Orange County (California) Personnel and Guidance Association (1979–1981), and South Texas Counseling Association (2001–2002).

Planning

≈ Chapter 1 ≈

The Evolution of Comprehensive Guidance and Counseling Programs: From Position to Services to Program

Planning—Building a Foundation for Change

- Study the history of guidance and counseling in the schools.
- Learn about the people, events, and societal conditions that helped shape guidance and counseling in the schools.
- Understand the implications of the shift from position to services to program in the conceptualization and organization of guidance and counseling.

≈ By the beginning of the 20th century, the United States was deeply involved in the Industrial Revolution. It was a period of rapid industrial growth, social protest, social reform, and utopian idealism. Social protest and social reform were being carried out under the banner of the Progressive Movement, a movement that sought to change negative social conditions associated with the Industrial Revolution.

These conditions were the unanticipated effects of industrial growth. They included the emergence of cities with slums and immigrant-filled ghettos, the decline of puritan morality, the eclipse of the individual by organizations, corrupt political bossism, and the demise of the apprenticeship method of learning a vocation. (Stephens, 1970, pp. 148–149)

Guidance and counseling were born during the height of the Progressive Movement as "but one manifestation of the broader movement of progressive reform which occurred in this country in the late 19th and early 20th centuries" (Stephens, 1970, p. 5). Their beginnings can be traced to the work of a number of individuals and social institutions. People such as Charles Merrill, Frank Parsons, Meyer Bloomfield, Jessie Davis, Anna Reed, E. W. Weaver, and David Hill, working through a number of organizations and movements such as the settlement house movement, the National Society for the Promotion of Industrial Education, and schools in San Francisco, Detroit, Grand Rapids, Seattle, New York, and New Orleans, were all instrumental in formulating and implementing early conceptions of guidance and counseling.

This chapter traces the history of guidance and counseling in the schools from the beginning of the 20th century to the beginning years of the 21st century. It opens with a review of guidance and counseling during the first two decades of the 1900s, focusing on the work of Frank Parsons, the early purposes of guidance and counseling, the appointment of teachers to the position of vocational counselor, the spread of guidance and counseling, and early concerns about the efficiency of the position model. The chapter continues with a discussion of the challenges and changes for guidance and counseling that occurred in the 1920s and 1930s. The changing purposes of guidance and counseling, as well as the emergence of the service model, are described. Then, two important federal laws from the 1940s and 1950s are presented and described. This is followed by a focus on the 1960s, a time of new challenges and changes, a time when pupil personnel services provided a dominant organizational structure for guidance and counseling. It also was a time when elementary guidance and counseling emerged and a time when calls were heard about the need to change the then dominant organizational structure for guidance and counseling.

The next sections of the chapter focus on the emergence of comprehensive guidance and counseling programs in the 1960s and their implementations in the 1980s and 1990s across the United States. Attention is paid to the importance of federal and state legislation. The chapter continues with an emphasis on the promise of the 21st century: the full implementation of comprehensive guidance and counseling programs in every school district in the United States. State models as well as the American School Counselor Association (ASCA) National Model are described, along with pertinent state and federal legislation. The chapter closes with a presentation of five foundation premises that undergird comprehensive guidance and counseling programs.

The Beginnings of Guidance Counseling in the Schools: The First Two Decades of the 1900s

The Work of Frank Parsons

The implementation of one of the first systematic conceptions of guidance and counseling in the United States took place in Civic Service House, Boston, Massachusetts, when the Boston Vocation Bureau was established in January 1908 by Mrs. Quincy Agassiz Shaw based on plans drawn up by Frank Parsons, an American educator and reformer. The establishment of the Vocation Bureau was an outgrowth of Parsons's work with individuals at Civic Service House. Parsons issued his first report on the bureau on May 1, 1908, and according to H. V. Davis (1969, p. 113), "This was an important report because the term *vocational guidance* apparently appeared for the first time in print as the designation of an organized service." It also was an important report because it emphasized that vocational guidance should be provided by trained experts and become part of every public school system.

Parsons's conception of guidance stressed the scientific approach to choosing an occupation. The first paragraph in the first chapter of his book, *Choosing a Vocation* (1909), illustrated his concern:

No step in life, unless it may be the choice of a husband or wife, is more important than the choice of a vocation. The wise selection of the business, profession, trade, or occupation to which one's life is to be devoted and the development of full efficiency in the chosen field are matters of deepest movement to young men and to the public. These vital problems should be solved in a careful, scientific way, with due regard to each person's aptitudes, abilities, ambitions, resources, and limitations, and the relations of these elements to the conditions of success in different industries. (p. 3)

The basis for Parsons's conceptualization of guidance, stressing the scientific approach, was his concern about society's general lack of attention to the development of human resources.

It trains its horses, as a rule, better than men. It spends unlimited money to perfect the inanimate machinery of production but pays very little attention to the business of perfecting the human machinery, though it is by far the most important in production. (p. 160)

Parsons also was concerned about assisting young people in making the transition from school to work: "Yet there is no part of life where the need for guidance is more emphatic than in the transition from school to work—the choice of a vocation, adequate preparation for it, and the attainment of efficiency and success" (p. 4).

Early Purposes of Guidance and Counseling

In the beginning, the early 1900s, the term for school guidance and counseling was *vocational guidance*. It had a singular purpose. It was seen as a response to the economic, educational, and social problems of those times and was concerned about the entrance of young people into the work world and the conditions they might find there. Economic concerns focused on the need to better prepare workers for the workplace, whereas educational concerns arose from a need to increase efforts in schools to help students find purpose for their education as well as their employment. Social concerns emphasized the need for changing school methods and organization as well as exerting more control over conditions of labor in child-employing industries (U.S. Bureau of Education, 1914).

Two distinctly different perspectives concerning the initial purpose of vocational guidance were present from the very beginning. Wirth (1983) described one perspective, espoused by David Snedden and Charles Prosser, that followed the social efficiency philosophy. According to this perspective, "the task of education was to aid the economy to function as efficiently as possible" (Wirth, 1983, pp. 73–74). Schools were to be designed to prepare individuals for work with vocational guidance being a way to sort individuals according to their various capacities preparing them to obtain a job.

The other perspective of vocational guidance was based on principles of democratic philosophy that emphasized the need to change the conditions of industry as well as assist students to make educational and occupational choices. According to Wirth (1980), "The 'Chicago school'—[George Hubert] Mead, [John] Dewey, and [Frank] Leavitt—brought the perspective of democratic philosophy to the discussion of vocational guidance" (p. 114). Leavitt (1914), in a speech at the founding meeting of the National Vocational Guidance Association in 1913 in Grand Rapids, Michigan, stressed the need to modify the conditions and methods in industry. He stated, "It is well within the range of possibility that vocational guidance, when carried out in a comprehensive, purposeful, and scientific way, may force upon industry many modifications which will be good not only for children but equally for the industry" (p. 80).

The Position of Vocational Counselors

The work of Frank Parsons and the Vocation Bureau soon became known across the country. Out of it grew the first National Conference on Vocational Guidance, held in Boston in 1910, followed by a similar conference in New York in 1912 and the formation of the National Vocational Guidance Association in Grand Rapids in 1913 (W. C. Ryan, 1919). It also had a direct impact on the Boston public schools because in 1909 the Boston School Committee asked personnel in the Vocation Bureau to outline a program of vocational guidance for the public schools of Boston. On June 7, 1909, the Boston School Committee approved the bureau's suggestion and "instructed the Superintendent of Schools to appoint a committee of six to work with the director" (Bloomfield, 1915, p. 34). Upon completion of its work, the committee issued a report that identified three primary aims for vocational guidance in the Boston schools:

> Three aims have stood out above all others: first, to secure thoughtful consideration, on the part of parents, pupils, and teachers, of the importance of a life-career motive; second, to assist in every way possible in placing pupils in some remunerative work on leaving school; and third, to keep in touch with and help them thereafter, suggesting means of improvement and watching the advancement of those who need such aid. (Bloomfield, 1915, p. 36)

These aims were implemented by a central office staff and by appointed vocational counselors in each elementary and secondary school in Boston. Teachers were appointed to the position of vocational counselor often with no relief from their teaching duties and with no additional pay (Brewer, 1922; Ginn, 1924). The vocational counseling duties these teachers were asked to perform in addition to their regular teaching duties included the following:

1. To be the representative of the Department of Vocational Guidance in the district.
2. To attend all meetings of counselors called by the Director of Vocational Guidance.
3. To be responsible for all material sent out to the school by the Vocational Guidance Department.
4. To gather and keep on file occupational information.
5. To arrange with the local branch librarians about shelves of books bearing upon educational and vocational guidance.
6. To arrange for some lessons in occupations in connection with classes in Oral English and Vocational Civics, or wherever principal and counselor deem it wise.
7. To recommend that teachers show the relationship of their work to occupational problems.
8. To interview pupils in grades six and above who are failing, attempt to find the reason, and suggest a remedy.
9. To make use of the cumulative record card when advising children.
10. To consult records of intelligence tests when advising children.
11. To make a careful study with grades seven and eight of the bulletin A Guide to the Choice of Secondary School.
12. To urge children to remain in school.
13. To recommend conferences with parents of children who are failing or leaving school.
14. To interview and check cards of all children leaving school, making clear to them the requirements for obtaining working certificates.
15. To be responsible for the filling in of Blank 249, and communicate with recommendations to the Department of Vocational Guidance when children are in need of employment. (Ginn, 1924, pp. 5–7)

Vocational Guidance Spreads Across the Country

At about the same time that the Boston schools were establishing a vocational guidance program, a group of New York City teachers, called the Student Aid Committee of the High School Teachers' Association, under the leadership of E. W. Weaver, was active in establishing a program in the New York City schools. A report issued in 1909 by the committee indicated they had passed the experimental stage and were ready to request that

> (1) the vocational officers of the large high schools be allowed at least one extra period of unassigned time to attend to this work; (2) that they be provided with facilities for keeping records of

students and employment; and (3) that they have opportunities for holding conferences with students and employers. (W. C. Ryan, 1919, p. 25)

In Grand Rapids, Michigan, vocational guidance began first in the classroom and then was organized in a central office. Jessie B. Davis (1914) inaugurated a plan of teaching vocational guidance through the English curriculum. The following general topics were to be covered in each of the grades:

7th grade: Vocational ambition
8th grade: The value of education
9th grade: The elements of character that make for success
10th grade: The world's work—a call to service
11th grade: Choosing a vocation
12th grade: Preparation for one's life work

Vocational guidance also was being introduced into the public schools in other parts of the United States. In Chicago, it first took the form of a central office to serve students applying for employment certificates, to publish vocational bulletins, and for placement. In other cities such as Buffalo, New York; Cincinnati, Ohio; DeKalb, Illinois; Los Angeles; Milwaukee, Wisconsin; New York; Philadelphia; Rochester, New York; and San Jose, California, vocational guidance took several different forms but relied mostly on disseminating occupational information and on conducting occupational surveys, placement activities, and life career classes.

According to W. C. Ryan (1919, p. 26),

by April 1914, approximately 100 public high schools, representing some 40 cities, were reported to the U.S. Bureau of Education as having definitely organized conscious plans of vocational guidance, through vocation bureaus, consultation committees, trial vocational courses, or regular courses in vocations.

Titles of these offices varied and included, for example, the Division of Attendance and Vocational Guidance in Minneapolis. This expansion continued throughout the next 4 years, so that by 1918, 10 years after the establishment of the Vocation Bureau by Parsons in Boston, "932 four-year high schools reported vocation bureaus, employment departments, or similar devices for placing pupils" (W. C. Ryan, 1919, p. 36).

Early Concerns About the Position of Vocational Counselor

By the 1920s, as the guidance movement was spreading across the United States, concerns were already being expressed about the way guidance was organized, was being perceived by others, and was being practiced. In a review of the Boston School system, Brewer (1922) stated that the work was "commendable and promising" (p. 36). At the same time, he expressed concern about a lack of effective centralization and supervision. What was done and how well it was done were left up to individual principals and counselors. Myers (1923), in an article titled "A Critical Review of Present Developments in Vocational Guidance With Special Reference to Future Prospects," also expressed concern:

The first development to which I wish to call attention is a growing recognition of vocational guidance as an integral part of organized education, not as something different and apart from education that is being wished upon the schools by a group of enthusiasts because there is no other agency to handle it (p. 139). . . . Second, vocational guidance is becoming recognized as a specialized educational function requiring special natural qualifications and special training (p. 139). . . . A third development that claims attention is an increasing appreciation that a centralized, unified program of vocational guidance for the entire school system of a city is essential to the most effective work. We are rapidly passing out of the stage when each high school and junior high school can be left to organize and conduct vocational guidance as it sees fit. (pp. 139–140)

In expressing these concerns, Myers was calling attention to problems associated with the position model for guidance in which teachers were designated as vocational counselors with no structure to work in and little or no released time from their teaching duties. Apparently, the position model for guidance caused it to be seen as an ancillary activity that could be conducted by anybody. In contrast, he stressed the need to view guidance as an "integral part of education" that required "trained personnel" working in a "unified program" of guidance. Myers's words were prophetic. These are the same words we use today to describe the importance, personnel requirements, and structure of comprehensive guidance and counseling programs in our schools.

Myers (1923) made another astute observation about some unanticipated outcomes the prevailing way of organizing guidance and counseling (the position model) was causing in the schools:

Another tendency dangerous to the cause of vocational guidance is the tendency to load the vocational counselor with so many duties foreign to the office that little real counseling can be done. The principal, and often the counselor . . . [have] a very indefinite idea of the proper duties of this new officer. The counselor's time is more free from definite assignments with groups or classes of pupils than is that of the ordinary teacher. If well chosen he [or she] has administrative ability. It is perfectly natural, therefore, for the principal to assign one administrative duty after another to the counselor until he [or she] becomes practically assistant principal, with little time for the real work of a counselor. In order to prevent this tendency from crippling seriously the vocational guidance program it is important that the counselor shall be well trained, that the principal shall understand more clearly what counseling involves, and that there shall be efficient supervision from a central office. (p. 140)

Myers's words were again prophetic. They pointed directly at the heart of the problem with the position model, that is, the ease at which "other duties as assigned" can become part of guidance and counseling and the work of school counselors, a problem that continues to plague school counselors even today.

Guidance and Counseling in the 1920s and 1930s: Challenges and Changes

Changes in Purpose of Guidance and Counseling

The 1920s witnessed the continued expansion of guidance and counseling in the schools. During this period of time, the nature and structure of guidance and counseling were being influenced by the mental hygiene and measurement movements, developmental studies of children, the introduction of cumulative records, and progressive education. In effect, "Vocational guidance was taking on the new vocabulary present in the culture at large and in the educational subculture; the language of mental health, progressive education, child development, and measurement theory" (A. H. Johnson, 1972, p. 160). As a result, additional purposes for guidance and counseling were identified.

Educational Purposes

The addition of an educational purpose for guidance was a natural outgrowth of a change that was taking place in education itself. With the advent of the Cardinal Principles of Secondary Education (National Education Association [NEA], 1918), education, at least philosophically, began to shift from preparation for college alone to education for total life.

> This was a life to be characterized by an integration of health with command of fundamental processes, worthy home membership, vocational competence, civic responsibility, worthy use of leisure time and ethical character. . . . Given these Seven Cardinal Principles, an education now appeared equally vocationally relevant—from this one could construe that all of education is guidance into later vocational living. (A. H. Johnson, 1972, pp. 27–28)

This change occurred partly because the leadership of guidance and counseling, particularly on the part of people like John Brewer (1922), increasingly was more educationally oriented. It also occurred, according to Stephens (1970), because the NEA's Commission on the Reorganization of Secondary Education (CRSE) "had so broadened the definition of vocation as to soften it, if not to virtually eliminate it as a cardinal principle of secondary education" (p. 113). This move by the CRSE, together with the more educationally oriented leadership of guidance, served to separate what had been twin reform movements of education—vocational education and vocational guidance, as Stephens called them—leaving vocational guidance to struggle with its own identity. This point is made in a similar way by A. H. Johnson (1972):

> The 1918 report of the NEA's Commission on the Reorganization of Secondary Education construed almost all of the education as training for efficient vocational and avocational life. No element in the curriculum appeared salient after the CRSE report. This was no less true of vocational education. Thus, as a "cardinal principle" vocational education was virtually eliminated. The once-correlated responsibility of vocational guidance lost its historical anchorage to vocational education and was set adrift in the public school system to be redefined by the logic of the education subculture. (p. 204)

Personal Adjustment Purposes

During the 1920s it was clear that less attention was being focused on the social, industrial, and national/political aspects of individuals, whereas considerably more attention was being given to the personal, educational, and statistically measurable aspects of individuals. More specifically, at least within the school setting, there apparently was a "displacement of the traditional vocational, socioeconomic, and political concerns from the culture at large to the student of the educational subculture whose vocational socialization problems were reinterpreted as educational and psychological problems of personal adjustment" (A. H. Johnson, 1972, p. 221).

As a result of this displacement of concerns, vocational guidance practices began to emphasize a more personal, diagnostic, and clinical orientation to students, with an increasing emphasis on psychological measurement.

> Content to explore with yet greater precision the psychological dimensions of the student, and guaranteed a demand for testing services in the public school system, the guidance movement defined its professional role to meet the expectations of its institutional colleagues. Thus there developed a mutual role expectation that requires analysis and synthesis (gathering and organizing personal data), diagnosis (comparing personal data to test norms, and occupational or professional profiles), prognosis (indicating available career choices), and counseling (or treating, to effect

desired adjustment then or in the future). This formed the basis for the clinical model. Testing had created the demand for a unique technical skill around which the clinical model could develop, and around which vocational guidance had established a professional claim. (A. H. Johnson, 1972, p. 138)

Further evidence of this can be seen in the 1921 and 1924 statements of the Principles of Vocational Guidance of the National Vocational Guidance Association (Allen, 1927). These principles emphasized testing, the use of an extensive cumulative record system, information, the study of occupations, counseling, and case studies. Between 1925 and 1930, as the personal adjustment purpose of vocational guidance emerged, counseling became of primary concern. "Vocational guidance became problem oriented, centering on adjustable psychological, personal problems—not social, moral, religious, ethical, or political problems" (A. H. Johnson, 1972, p. 201).

What Should Be the Duties of the Counselor?

One of the tasks of the profession in the 1920s and early 1930s was to establish the preferred list of duties to be carried out by individuals filling the position of counselor. The task was to decide which duties would constitute a complete program, or as Procter (1930) stated, the "standard setup" for guidance and counseling. Myers (1931) prepared a list of actual counselor duties. There were 37 items on the list. After reviewing the list, Myers stated:

> Here is, indeed, a formidable list of things which counselors do. It is obvious that many of these are essential to an effective guidance program and may properly be expected of a counselor. It is equally obvious that some of them are routine administrative or clerical matters which have nothing whatever to do with counseling. Evidently, under the guise of setting up a counseling program, some junior and senior high school principals have unloaded a large number of their office duties upon the counselor. (p. 344)

In the same article, Myers (1931) classified the preferred duties into the following categories:

- Interviewing or conferring with individual pupils
- Meeting with pupils in groups
- Conferring with teachers and other members of the school staff
- Conferring with special officers of the school system
- Conferring with parents
- Conferring with representatives of industry, business, and the professions
- Working with social agencies of the community (pp. 345–347)

As guidance and counseling was becoming institutionalized in schools and was in the process of being defined and implemented, the expectations of other educational personnel concerning guidance and counseling also were being shaped. This seemed to be particularly true for school administrators. A. H. Johnson (1972) underlined this when he pointed out that administrative obligations were a substantial part of the new professional responsibilities. In fact, many suggested vocational guidance responsibilities delineated by the profession became administrative obligations when incorporated into the school settings. "Professional responsibilities became in fact administrative obligations for which guidance would be held accountable not to professionally determined values but values of the education subculture interpreted through its administrative structure" (A. H. Johnson, 1972, p. 191).

The Services Model of Guidance and Counseling

By the late 1920s and early 1930s, various specialists, in addition to counselors, had joined the staffs of schools. These specialists included personnel such as attendance officers, visiting teachers, school nurses, and school physicians. Myers (1935) suggested that the phrase *pupil personnel work* be used to coordinate the work of these specialists and that someone from central office be given the responsibility for overseeing their work. Myers (1935) went on to point out that "Probably no activity in the entire list suffers as much from lack of a coordinated program as does guidance, and especially the counseling aspect of it" (p. 87).

Given Myers's point about the lack of a coordinated program for guidance (remember that the prevailing organization for guidance and counseling at that time was a position with a list of duties), what would be the best way to provide a more coordinated program for guidance and counseling? The concept that emerged was *guidance services*. Five or more services were identified, including individual inventory, occupational and educational information, counseling, placement, follow-up, and sometimes orientation. According to Roeber, Walz, and Smith (1969):

> This conception of guidance services was developed during a period in the history of the guidance movement when it was necessary to have some definitive statement regarding the need for and nature of a more organized form of guidance. This delineation of guidance services generally served its purpose and gave the guidance movement something tangible to "sell" to state departments of education and to local schools. (p. 55)

Personal Counseling Becomes Prominent

By the beginning of the 1930s, as a result of the work of American psychologist and pediatrician Arnold Lucius Gesell, the mental health movement, and the emerging services model of guidance and counseling, personal counseling began to dominate professional theory and practice.

> Up to 1930, . . . not much progress had been made in differentiating this function [personal counseling] from the preexisting programs of vocational and educational guidance. After that date, more and more of a separation appeared as guidance workers in the high schools became aware of increasingly large numbers of students who were troubled by personal problems involving hostility to authority, sex relationships, unfortunate home situations, and financial stringencies. (Rudy, 1965, p. 25)

Bell (1939), in a book on personal counseling, stated that the goal of counseling was student adjustment through personal contact between counselor and student. Adjustment in his thinking included all phases of an individual's life: school, health, occupational, motor and mechanical, social, home, emotional, and religious.

The Focus of Vocational Guidance Narrows

By the 1930s, it was also clear that the term *guidance and counseling* was seen as an all-inclusive term including "problems of adjustment to health, religion, recreation, to family and friends, to school and to work" (M. E. Campbell, 1932, p. 4). Vocational guidance, however, was being defined more narrowly as the process of assisting the individual to choose an occupation, prepare for it, enter upon and progress in it. As preparation for an occupation involves decisions in the choice of studies, choice of curriculums, and the choice of schools and colleges, it becomes evident that vocational guidance cannot be separated from educational guidance. (M. E. Campbell, 1932, p. 4)

Interesting to note is that vocational guidance was seen as a process that helped individuals examine all occupations, not just those for which vocational education provided training.

As vocational guidance and vocational education are linked together in many minds, a statement about this relationship may clarify the situation. Vocational education is the giving of training to persons who desire to work in a specific occupation. Vocational guidance offers information and assistance which leads to the choice of an occupation and the training which precedes it. It does not give such training. The term *vocational* refers to any occupation, be it medicine, law, carpentry, or nursing. Preparation for many occupations and professions must be planned in the secondary school and in college by taking numerous courses, which are not usually known as vocational. Vocational guidance concerns itself, therefore, with pupils in the academic courses in high school or students of the liberal arts in college, as well as with the pupils in the trade and commercial courses, which have become known as vocational education. (M. E. Campbell, 1932, p. 4)

This distinction is important because, from the 1960s to the present, this was and is a point of contention in defining the focus and scope of guidance and counseling in career and technical education legislation. Some individuals contend that vocational guidance is guidance and counseling for career and technical education students only, and that if money were made available it should be spent only for the guidance and counseling of students in these programs.

Federal Initiatives Begin

Although the educational and personal adjustment themes for guidance continued to play a dominant role in guidance and counseling practice in the schools during the 1930s, the vocational emphasis also continued to show strength. In February 1933 the National Occupational Conference, funded by a Carnegie grant, opened its doors. The activities of the National Occupational Conference included studies and research related to the problems of occupational adjustment, book publication, and the development of a service that provided information and consultation about vocational guidance activities. The National Occupational Conference for a time also provided joint support for *Occupations,* the official journal of the National Vocational Guidance Association.

In 1938, a national advisory committee on education, originally appointed in 1936 by President Franklin D. Roosevelt, issued a report that pointed to the need for an occupational information service at the national level as well as for guidance and placement services as a part of a sound program of vocational education. As a result of these recommendations, and with funds from Vocational Education and from the Commissioner of Education (Studebaker, 1938), the Occupational Information and Guidance Service was established in 1938 in the Vocational Division of the U.S. Office of Education. Richard Allen served for a few months as the chief of the unit before Harry Jager assumed the post (Wellman, 1978). Although the service was located in the Vocational Division, it was not designed to be exclusively vocational in nature. This point was made clear in a document, "Principles Underlying the Organization and Administration of the Occupational Information and Guidance Service," issued by the U.S. Office of Education in 1940.

The functions to be performed by the Occupational Information and Guidance Service are to be as broad and complete as it is practicable for the Office to provide for at any given time within the limits of funds, cooperative assistance from various organizations, both within the government and outside, and other assets. The activities in which the service will be interested will include such phases of guidance as vocational guidance, personal guidance, educational guidance, and placement. While, with respect to personnel, no service in the Office can now be said to be complete, the various divisions or services go as far as possible in their respective fields in meeting needs or requests for service. Thus, for example, in the field of education for exceptional children, a service which would require 15 or 20 professional workers in the office if it were even to approximate completeness in numbers and types of persons needed, we have only one specialist. Yet this specialist is responsible for representing the Office in handling all problems and service in this particular field. (Smith, 1951, p. 66)

Of particular importance was the statement that "The activities in which the service will be interested will include such phases of guidance as vocational guidance, personal guidance, educational guidance, and placement." Not only did the statement clearly outline the broad mission of the service, and, as a result, of guidance and counseling in the schools, but it also described a currently popular way of describing guidance and counseling as having three phases: vocational, personal, and educational. Once the Occupational Information and Guidance Service was established at the federal level, it also became possible to establish guidance offices in state departments of education. Such funds could be used only for state offices, however. No funds could be used to support guidance and counseling at the local level.

Reimbursement was provided for state supervision under the George Dean Act [An Act to Provide for the Further Development of Vocational Education in the several states and territories; Public Law No. 673] and the number of states with a state guidance supervisor increased from 2 to 28 between 1938 and 1942. The Occupational Information and Guidance Service was instrumental in initiating conferences of state supervisors to consider issues in the field. This group subsequently became the NAGS (National Association of Guidance Supervisors), then NAGSCT (National Association of Guidance Supervisors and Counselor Trainers), and finally the current ACES (Association for Counselor Education and Supervision). (Wellman, 1978, p. 2)

A Growing Interest in Psychotherapy

As the 1930s ended, the services model of guidance and counseling with its position of counselor continued to evolve and flourish, assisted by a growing interest in psychotherapy. Of particular importance to guidance in the schools was the work of Carl Rogers, beginning with the publication of his book *Counseling and Psychotherapy* in 1942.

The years following its publication in 1942 saw a growth in interest in psychotherapeutic procedures, which soon became even greater than interest in psychometrics. This movement, and the numerous research and theoretical contributions which have accompanied it, has had its impact on vocational guidance. (Super, 1955, p. 5)

Aubrey (1982) used the expression "steamroller impact" to describe the full effect of this book as well as Rogers's later works on guidance in the schools.

The impact of psychotherapy on vocational guidance and the testing movement precipitated a new field: counseling psychology. This, in turn, had a substantial impact on the professional development of school guidance and counseling and the work of school counselors in the 1950s, 1960s, and 1970s, particularly in terms of the training counselors received and the role models and professional literature available to them.

> An important outcome of the merger of the vocational orientation, psychometric, and personality development movements has been a changed concept of the function and training of the person who does the counseling. He [or she] was first either a teacher who helped people explore the world of work or a psychologist who gave and interpreted tests. Then he [or she], who might or might not have been a psychologist, was a user of community resources, of occupational information, and of psychological tests. He [or she] has now emerged as a psychologist who uses varying combinations of exploratory experiences, psychometric techniques, and psychotherapeutic interviewing to assist people to grow and to develop. This is the counseling psychologist. (American Psychological Association, 1956, p. 284)

Important Federal Legislation in the 1940s and 1950s

Vocational Education Act of 1946 (P.L. 586)

In 1946, an event occurred that was to have substantial impact on the growth and development of guidance and counseling in the schools. The event was the passage of the Vocational Education Act of 1946 (P.L. 586), commonly referred to as the George–Barden Act after the two legislators who sponsored the legislation. As a result of the Act, funds could be used to support guidance and counseling activities in a variety of settings and situations. More specifically, the U.S. Commissioner of Education ruled that federal funds could be used for the following four purposes:

1. the maintenance of a state program of supervision
2. reimbursement of salaries of counselor-trainers
3. research in the field of guidance
4. reimbursement of salaries of local guidance supervisors and counselors. (Smith, 1951, pp. 67–68)

For the first time, because of the ruling of the U.S. Commissioner of Education, guidance and counseling received material, leadership, and financial support. The result of such support was a rapid growth of guidance and counseling at state and local levels. It also signaled to all concerned the need for attention to the preparation of counselors. This problem had been of concern for some time but had not been given extensive consideration. The passage of P.L. 586, which made it possible to use state funds to reimburse counselor training, made the constantly reoccurring question, What should constitute a counselor training program?, of extreme importance. How this question was answered set the pattern for the practice of guidance and counseling in the schools for many years to come.

In the spring of 1948 the Occupational Information and Guidance Service staff called a meeting of state guidance supervisors and counselor trainers in cooperation with the Division of Higher Education of the U.S. Office of Education. The question was, What should be the preparation of counselors? Eight major subtopics were identified, and subcommittees were established to study each subtopic. Reports were presented for consideration at the National Conference of State Supervisors of Guidance Services and Counselor Trainers held in Washington, DC, on September 13–18, 1948. These reports were then revised with others participating in the work. Six of the seven were then published between 1949 and 1950 by the Federal Security Agency, Office of Education. These reports (and the one not published) were as follows:

1. "Duties, Standards, and Qualifications for Counselors," February 1949, Cochairpersons, Eleanor Zeis and Dolph Camp
2. "The Basic Course" (never published)
3. "Counselor Competencies in Occupational Information," March 1949, Chairperson, Edward C. Roeber
4. "Counselor Competencies in the Analysis of the Individual," July 1949, Chairperson, Ralph C. Bedell
5. "Counselor Competencies in Counseling Techniques," July 1949, Chairperson, Stanley R. Ostrom
6. "Administrative Relationships of the Guidance Program," July 1949, Chairperson, Glenn Smith
7. "In-Service Preparation for Guidance Duties, Parts One and Two," May 1950, Chairperson, John G. Odgers

An additional report had been issued on supervised practice at the eighth National Conference but was referred back to committee. After revision it was considered at the ninth National Conference in Ames, Iowa, September 11–15, 1950, and with subsequent revision, was released as the eighth report in the series:

8. "Supervised Practice in Counselor Preparation," April 1952, Chairperson, Roy Bryan

All of the published reports were edited by Clifford P. Froehlich, Specialist for the Training of Guidance Personnel, under the general direction of Harry A. Jager, Chief, Guidance and Personnel Services Branch.

During the early and middle 1950s, a major change occurred in the organizational structure of guidance and counseling at the federal level. On May 16, 1952, the Guidance and Personnel Branch of the U.S. Office of Education was discontinued under the Division of Vocational Education. Then, on October 27, 1953, a Pupil Personnel Services Section was established in the Division of State and Local School Systems with Harry Jager designated as chief, but this work was halted with the death of Jager the following year. However, in 1955, a Guidance and Personnel Services Section was once again established, with Frank L. Sievers as the first chief (Miller, 1971).

These changes reflected the shift that had begun in the 1930s— the shift to guidance and counseling organized as a set of services within pupil personnel services with its continued emphasis on the position of counselor. As we will see, the pupil personnel services model was to become the dominant organizational framework for guidance and counseling in the 1950s and 1960s.

The National Defense Education Act of 1958 (P.L. 85–864)

In 1958 another important event occurred that had substantial impact on guidance and counseling in U.S. schools throughout the 1960s and 1970s. The event was the passage of the National Defense Education Act (NDEA) of 1958 (P.L. 85–864). Under Title V, the guidance and counseling title in the Act, funds were provided for two major programs: Part A provided funds in the form of grants to states to establish statewide testing programs; Part B provided funds for training institutes to prepare individuals to be counselors in secondary schools. In the 1960s, the provisions in Part B were expanded to include support for guidance programs, testing, and training at the elementary and junior high school levels as well.

Our purpose here is not to report fully on the overall impact of the NDEA but rather to focus briefly on the Act's impact on how school guidance and counseling and the work of school counselors were further conceptualized and institutionalized as a result of its implementation. Of particular importance was the nature of the training school counselors received and the major professional issues addressed during the courses provided for institute participants.

Pierson (1965) described five issues that seemed to be central to the training of school counselors in NDEA institutes:

1. determinism and a free society
2. mental health and individual responsibility
3. basic science and supervised practice
4. teaching and counseling
5. the role of the school counselor

Of these, Issues 4 and 5 related most directly to how counselors functioned in schools. The teaching and counseling issue was resolved according to Pierson (1965) by counselor educators who promoted the idea "that the services of the high school counselor are adjunct to the services of the classroom teacher" (p. 40). The role definition issue was handled by saying that the role of the counselor cannot be predetermined. Counselors were taught to develop their own role definition. "The adequately trained school counselor develops his [or her] own role, a role that tends to be unique with him [or her] and unique to the situation in which the role is developed" (p. 39).

Further analysis of NDEA institutes also makes it clear that there was a heavy emphasis on individual and group counseling through counseling practica and group procedures courses. Placement and traditional educational and occupational information procedures (collecting, classifying, and using information) as well as philosophy and principles received relatively less attention. Pierson (1965, p. 46) summarized curriculum offerings in institutes by pointing out that

> the curriculum in regular session institutes has placed great stress upon practicum; about one third of an enrollee's time has been spent in supervised practice in counseling. At the same time, institutes have strengthened their instruction in psychology, particularly in the areas of personality, learning, growth and development, and mental health.

Another aspect of the counselor role dilemma was identified by Tyler (1960) in her review of the first 50 institutes. She described it as follows:

> Before one can really define the role of the counselor, it will be necessary to clarify the roles of all workers who make up guidance staffs. It may be desirable to replace the ambiguous word *guidance* with the clearer term *pupil personnel work*. (p. 77)

New Challenges and Changes: Guidance and Counseling in the 1960s

Pupil Personnel Services Become Dominant

Concurrent with the influence of NDEA on the development of guidance and counseling in the schools was the influence of the pupil personnel services movement in the 1960s. What began in the 1930s, and was nurtured in the 1940s and 1950s, finally matured in the 1960s. What were those services? The Council of Chief State School Officers (1960) stated that pupil personnel services included "guidance, health, psychological services, school social work, and attendance" (p. 3). Thus guidance and the position of school counselors were conceptualized among several services that sought to "facilitate pupil learning through an interdisciplinary approach" (Stoughton, McKenna, & Cook, 1969, p. 1).

Of particular importance to the development of the pupil personnel services concept was the creation in 1962 of the Interprofessional Research Commission on Pupil Personnel Services (IRCOPPS). IRCOPPS was created by the U.S. Office of Education and financed by the National Institute of Mental Health. It was composed of 16 professional member associations. The aims of the Commission were threefold:

1. to provide through research a body of knowledge that will increase the effectiveness of all professions and services collaborating to provide the total learning experience
2. to demonstrate efficient programs of pupil personnel services for various sizes and types of communities
3. to carry on and stimulate research on preventative mental hygiene related to the schools. (Eckerson & Smith, 1966, p. 4)

In the IRCOPPS conception of pupil personnel services, guidance and counseling were viewed "as a lifetime service, from preschool to retirement, with the goal of increasing each individual's capacity for self-direction" (Eckerson & Smith, 1966, p. 24).

As the 1960s continued to unfold, the impact of the pupil personnel services movement on guidance and counseling became increasingly apparent. Many state departments of education and local school districts placed guidance and counseling and the positions of school counselors administratively under the pupil personnel services umbrella. In addition, textbooks written in the 1960s on the organization and administration of guidance and counseling adopted the pupil personnel services model as the way to organize guidance in the schools. This fitted nicely with the service model of guidance and counseling with its position orientation that had been evolving since the 1920s. As a result, guidance and counseling became a subset of services to be delivered by school counselors who occupied positions within the broader framework of pupil personnel services. The number of these guidance services varied depending on the authority quoted, but usually there were six, including orientation, individual inventory or appraisal, counseling, information, placement, and follow-up. Also, as a result of the services model of guidance and counseling and the focus on personal adjustment discussed earlier in this chapter, the counseling service emerged as the central service.

Stripling and Lane (1966) stressed the centrality of counseling—both individual and group. A second priority area was consultation with parents and teachers. Other traditional guidance functions such as appraisal, placement, and evaluation were seen as supplementary and supportive to counseling, group procedures, and consultation. Ferguson (1963) emphasized the same theme that counseling was the core service: "No longer is it viewed merely as a technique and limited to vocational and educational matters; counseling is regarded as the central service in the guidance program" (p. 40).

This emphasis on counseling during the 1960s had deep historical roots. It began to emerge in the 1920s under the services model and the intense interest in personal adjustment that followed. It was reinforced further, according to Hoyt (1974), by the NDEA Title V-B training institutes whose enrollees by law were either counselors or teachers and by the standards used by the U.S. Office of Education to judge whether or not a proposed training institute was acceptable for funding. These factors, Hoyt suggested, led the training institutes to place "a heavy emphasis on the counseling function. . . . The emphasis was on counseling and counselors, not on guidance and guidance programs" (p. 504).

17

A Focus on School Counselors, Not Guidance

During this time the services model for guidance and counseling, with its position orientation within pupil personnel services, focused heavily on the role and functions—the positions—of school counselors. In fact, to many individuals, what school counselors did became the program. Literally hundreds of articles were written about the role and functions of school counselors. The need for such statements was heightened considerably by competition from other pupil personnel workers as they too sought to establish themselves and their roles in the schools, particularly when the Commission on Guidance in American Schools proposed that

> the confusing term *guidance services* be abandoned and that pupil personnel services be seen as the activities of the school counselor, the school psychologist, the school social worker, the school health officer, and the school attendance officer. Pupil personnel services thus became broader than any so-called guidance services and yet a central function of such services is the work of the school counselor. (Wrenn, 1962, p. 142)

In his landmark work, *The Counselor in a Changing World* (1962), Wrenn also emphasized the work of the counselor. He delineated four major functions for the school counselor:

> It is recommended that the professional job description of a school counselor specify that he [or she] perform four major functions: (a) counsel with students; (b) consult with teachers, administrators, and parents as they in turn deal with students; (c) study the changing facts about the student population and interpret what is found to school committees and administrators; (d) coordinate counseling resources in school and between school and community. From two thirds to three fourths of the counselor's time, in either elementary or high school, should be committed to the first two of these functions. (p. 137)

In a similar fashion, Roeber (1963) outlined proposed school counselors' functions. He suggested that counselors engage in helping relationships, including individual counseling, group procedures, and consulting. In addition, the counselor should have supporting responsibilities, including pupil-environment studies, program development, and personal development. This emphasis on the counselor during the 1960s came at a time when some individuals were calling for "the abandonment of the term *guidance* as it is associated with services provided by a counselor" (Roeber, 1963, p. 22).

Elementary Guidance and Counseling

The 1960s also witnessed the birth of elementary school guidance and counseling, after a gestation period of over 50 years. Professional literature indicated that teachers were appointed as elementary counselors as early as 1910 in the Boston schools. Apparently, however, the secondary school emphasis was so strong during the early years that little attention was paid to the work of counselors in elementary schools. What attention there was proved to be heavily occupational in nature. Witness, for example, the publication of a book by McCracken and Lamb in 1923 titled *Occupational Information in the Elementary School*.

Faust (1968) divided the emergence of elementary school counselors into three time periods. The first period, which he titled *traditional,* stretched from the beginnings of the guidance and counseling movement in 1908 through the 1940s. During this period, elementary guidance and counseling borrowed methods and techniques extensively from secondary school guidance and counseling practice. For the next 15 years, from 1950 to

1965, elementary guidance and counseling began to change. Faust called this the *neotraditionalist* period. It was characterized by a deemphasis on traditional secondary methods coupled with more emphasis on group counseling and learning climates. In the middle 1960s, according to Faust, the *developmentalist* period emerged. Elementary school counselors had arrived and had an identity of their own. The emphasis now was developmental, not crisis-centered. Individual and group work were stressed.

The developmental emphasis was reinforced by a preliminary report of the Joint Association for Counselor Education and Supervision and American School Counselor Association (ACES–ASCA) Committee on the Elementary School Counselor that appeared in the February 1966 issue of the *Personnel and Guidance Journal*. Its central focus was "on the child and teacher in the educative process" (Faust, 1968, p. 74). Effective learning climates were to be central to the work of school counselors.

Calls for Change

Beginning in the 1960s, but particularly in the 1970s, the call came to reorient guidance and counseling from what had become an ancillary position organized around a set of services within pupil personnel services to a comprehensive developmental program. The call for reorientation came from a number of diverse sources. They included a renewed interest in vocational-career guidance and its theoretical base career development, concern about the efficacy of the then-prevailing approach to guidance and counseling in the schools, and a renewed interest in developmental guidance and counseling.

Vocational-Career Guidance

The resurgence of interest in vocational-career guidance that began in the 1960s was aided, in part, by a series of national conferences on the topic. These conferences were funded through the Vocational Education Act of 1963 (P.L. 88–210) and later amendments. It is clear from Hoyt's (1974) account of these conferences that they contributed substantially to the renewed interest in the term *guidance* and its practice in the schools.

The resurgence of interest in vocational-career guidance also was aided by a number of career guidance projects begun in the 1960s. Among them was the Developmental Career Guidance Project, begun in 1964 in Detroit to provide career guidance for disadvantaged youths. It was one of the early developmental career guidance programs, one that accumulated sufficient evaluative data to support the further development of comprehensive guidance programming in schools (Leonard & Vriend, 1975).

Concern About the Prevailing Position Service Model

Paralleling the resurgence of interest in vocational-career guidance was a growing concern about the efficacy of the services model with its emphasis on the role and function—or the position—of the school counselor. Particular concern was expressed about an overemphasis on the one-to-one relationship model of counseling and the tendency of counselors to focus mainly on crises and problems to justify their reason for being in a school.

> The traditional one-to-one relationship in counseling which we have cherished and perhaps overvalued will, of course, continue. But it is quite likely that the conception of the counselor as a room-bound agent of behavior change must be critically reappraised. The counselor of the future will likely serve as a social catalyst, interacting in a two-person relationship with the counselee part of the time, but also serving as a facilitator of the environmental and human conditions which are known to promote the counselee's total psychological development, including vocational development. (Borow, 1966, p. 88)

This same issue was discussed from a slightly different perspective in an exchange between Brammer (1968) and Felix (1968). Brammer proposed the abandonment of the guidance model for counselors and the adoption of a counseling psychologist model in its place. Felix, in a reply to Brammer, sharply disagreed with Brammer's recommendation, pointing out that the counseling psychologist model was not valid for a school setting. Felix instead recommended an educational model for guidance. Similarly, Aubrey (1969) recommended an educational model as opposed to a therapy model by pointing out that the therapy model was at odds or even frequently incongruent with educational objectives.

During the 1960s there were also expressions of concern about the potency of the guidance services model and the need for more meaningful reconceptualizations for guidance so that guidance could reach higher levels of development (Roeber et al., 1969). This same theme was echoed by Sprinthall (1971):

> It is probably not an understatement to say that the service concept has so dominated guidance and counseling that more basic and significant questions are not even acknowledged, let alone answered. Instead, the counselor assumes a service orientation that limits and defines his [or her] role to minor administrative procedures. (p. 20)

Developmental Guidance

In the 1960s, the term *developmental guidance* was heard with increasing frequency. Mathewson (1962), in discussing future trends for guidance, suggested that although adjustive guidance was popular, a long-term movement toward developmental forms of guidance would probably prevail:

> In spite of present tendencies, a long-term movement toward educative and developmental forms of guidance in schools may yet prevail for these reasons: the need to develop all human potentialities, the persistence and power of human individuality, the effects of dynamic educative experience, the necessity for educational adaptability, the comparative costs, and the urge to preserve human freedom. (p. 375)

Similarly, Zaccaria (1966) stressed the importance of and need for developmental guidance. He pointed out that developmental guidance was a concept in transition, that it was in tune with the times, but that it was still largely untried in practice.

Comprehensive Guidance and Counseling Programs Emerge: The 1970s

In the early 1970s interest in career development theory, research, and practice as well as in career guidance and career education, their educational manifestations, increased. Other educational movements, such as psychological education, moral education, and process education, emerged as well. In addition, interest in the development of comprehensive systematic approaches to guidance and counseling program development and management continued to increase. The convergence of these movements in the early 1970s served as a stimulus to continue the task of defining guidance and counseling developmentally in measurable student outcome terms—as a program in its own right rather than as services ancillary to other educational programs.

Basic Ideas, Vocabulary, and Systems Thinking

By 1970 a substantial amount of preliminary work had been done in developing the basic ideas, vocabulary, and constructs to define guidance and counseling in comprehensive-developmental-outcome terms. As early as 1961 Glanz identified and described four basic models for organizing guidance because of his concern about the lack of discernible patterns for implementing guidance in the schools. Tiedeman and Field (1962) issued a call to make guidance an integral part of the educational process, and they also stressed the need for a developmental, liberating perspective of guidance. Zaccaria (1965) stressed the need to examine developmental tasks as a basis for determining the goals of guidance. Shaw and Tuel (1966) developed a model for a guidance program designed to serve all students. At the elementary level, Dinkmeyer (1966) emphasized the need for developmental counseling by describing pertinent child development research that supported a developmental perspective.

Paralleling the preliminary work on ideas, vocabulary, and constructs was the application of systems thinking to guidance and counseling. Based on a nationwide survey of vocational guidance in 1968, a systems model for vocational guidance was developed at the Center for Vocational and Technical Education in Columbus, Ohio. This model focused on student behavioral objectives, alternative activities, program evaluation, and implementation strategies (R. E. Campbell et al., 1971). T. A. Ryan (1969), Thoresen (1969), and Hosford and T. A. Ryan (1970) also proposed the use of systems theory and systems techniques for the development and improvement of comprehensive guidance and counseling programs.

Beginning Models for Guidance and Counseling Programs

On the West Coast, McDaniel (1970) proposed a model for guidance called Youth Guidance Systems. It was organized around goals, objectives, programs, implementation plans, and designs for evaluation. The primary student outcome in this model was considered to be decision making. Closely related to this model was the Comprehensive Career Guidance System (CCGS) developed by personnel at the American Institutes for Research (Jones, Hamilton, Ganschow, Helliwell, & Wolff, 1972; Jones, Nelson, Ganschow, & Hamilton, 1971). The CCGS was designed to plan, implement, and evaluate guidance programs systematically. Systems thinking also undergirded T. A. Ryan and Zeran's (1972) approach to the organization and administration of guidance services. They stressed the need for a systems approach to guidance to ensure the development and implementation of an accountable program. A final systematic approach to guidance was advocated in the PLAN (Program of Learning in Accordance with Needs) System of Individualized Education (Dunn, 1972). Guidance was seen as a major component of PLAN and was treated as an integral part of the regular instructional program.

Integrating Career Development Into the Curriculum

The task of defining guidance and counseling in comprehensive-developmental-outcome terms received substantial support from these approaches that applied systems thinking to guidance. Additional support was provided by the development in a number of states in the early 1970s of state guides for integrating career development into the school curriculum. One such guide was developed in August 1970 by the state of Wisconsin (Drier, 1971) and another, the California Model for Career Development, in summer 1971 (California State Department of Education, 1971).

The idea of implementing career development through the curriculum did not, of course, originate with these models. As early as 1914 Davis had outlined such a curriculum. Of more immediate interest, however, are the work of Tennyson, Soldahl, and Mueller (1965) titled *The Teacher's Role in Career Development* and the Airlie House Conference in May 1966 on the topic "Implementing Career Development Theory and Research Through the Curriculum," which was sponsored by the National Vocational Guidance Association (Ashcroft, 1966). Later in the 1960s and early 1970s came the work of such theorists and practitioners as Gysbers (1969), Herr (1969), Hansen (1970), and Tennyson and Hansen (1971), all of whom spoke to the need to integrate career development concepts into the curriculum. Through these efforts and others like them, career development concepts began to be translated into individual outcomes and the resulting goals and objectives arranged sequentially, K–12.

A National Project to Develop State Models

Concurrent with these efforts, a national effort was begun to assist the states in developing and implementing state models or guides for career guidance, counseling, and placement. On July 1, 1971, the University of Missouri–Columbia was awarded a U.S. Office of Education grant, directed by Norman C. Gysbers, to assist each state, the District of Columbia, and Puerto Rico in developing models or guides for implementing career guidance, counseling, and placement programs in local schools. This project was the next step in a program of work begun as a result of a previous project at the university, a project that conducted a national conference on career guidance, counseling, and placement in October 1969 and regional conferences across the country during the spring of 1970. All 50 states, the District of Columbia, and Puerto Rico were involved in the 1971 project, and by the time the project ended in 1974, 44 states had developed some type of guide or model for career guidance, counseling, and placement. As a part of the assistance provided to the states, project staff conducted a national conference in January 1972 and developed a manual (Gysbers & Moore, 1974) to be used by the states as they developed their own guides.

Model Development Continues

As the movement toward planning and implementing systematic developmental and accountable guidance and counseling programs in the early 1970s became more sophisticated, theoretical models began to be translated into practical, workable models to be implemented in the schools. Many of these translations were based on an expanded conception of career guidance. For example, when the guidance staff in Mesa, Arizona, felt the need to reorient their guidance program to make it more accountable in 1972, they chose a comprehensive career guidance program that included needs assessment, goals, and objectives development and related guidance activities (McKinnon & Jones, 1975). To train the staff in program development and implementation methods and procedures for the new system, they wrote competency-based training packages in cooperation with the American Institutes for Research. For another example, guidance personnel at the Grossmont Union High School District in California chose the California Model for Career Development (California State Department of Education, 1971) to supply the content of their program and then proceeded to lay out a systematic, developmental career guidance program (Jacobson & Mitchell, 1975). For yet another example, the Georgia State Department of Education initiated a project funded by the U.S. Office of Education to coordinate the efforts of several Georgia school systems in planning and implementing comprehensive career guidance programs. The goal of the project was to develop a career guidance system that was based on student needs and focused on a team approach and curriculum-based strategies (Dagley, 1974).

On July 1, 1974, the American Institutes for Research began work on bringing together program planning efforts previously undertaken by the Pupil Personnel Division of the California State Department of Education and their own Youth Development Research Program in Mesa, Arizona, and elsewhere (Jones, Helliwell, & Ganschow, 1975). This resulted in the development of 12 competency-based staff development modules on developing comprehensive career guidance programs K–12. As a part of the project, the modules were field-tested in two school districts in California in the summer of 1975 and in a preservice class of guidance and counseling majors at the University of Missouri–Columbia in the fall of 1975. A final report of this project was issued by the American Institutes for Research in January 1976 (Dayton, 1976). Jones, Dayton, and Gelatt (1977) subsequently used the 12 modules as a point of departure to suggest a systematic approach in planning and evaluating human service programs.

The work that began in the early 1970s on various guidance program models was continued and expanded. "Career Development: Guidance and Education," a special issue of the *Personnel and Guidance Journal* edited by Hansen and Gysbers (1975), contained a number of articles describing program models and examples of programs in operation. The American College Testing Program (1976) published a programmatic model for guidance in *River City High School Guidance Services: A Conceptual Model*.

An Increasing Number of Publications

An increasing number of articles, monographs, and books on various aspects of comprehensive guidance programming were published in the late 1970s. Brown (1977) discussed the organization and evaluation of elementary school guidance services using the three-Cs approach (counseling, consulting, and coordinating). Upton, Lowery, Mitchell, Varenhorst, and Benvenuti (1978) described procedures for developing a career guidance curriculum and presented leadership strategies to teach the procedures to those who were to implement the curriculum. Ballast and Shoemaker (1978) described a step-by-step approach to developing a comprehensive K–12 guidance program. R. E. Campbell, Rodebaugh, and Shaltry (1978) edited a handbook that presented numerous examples of career guidance programs, practices, and models. Included in the handbook were descriptions (by Gysbers, 1978) of systematic approaches to comprehensive guidance programming, such as the Career Planning Support System (R. E. Campbell, 1977) and the Cooperative Rural Guidance System (Drier, 1976), both developed at the National Center for Research in Vocational Education, Columbus, Ohio. Peterson and Treichel (1978) wrote the *Programmatic Approach to Guidance Excellence: PAGE 2*, a similar systematic approach. Herr and Cramer (1979) described a further systematic planning approach for career guidance and delineated goals, objectives, and activities for elementary, junior, and high schools as well as for higher and adult education. Hilton (1979) provided a conceptual framework for career guidance in the secondary school. Mitchell (1978) and Mitchell and Gysbers (1978) described the need for comprehensive guidance programs and provided recommendations for how to develop and implement such programs. Halasz-Salster and Peterson (1979) presented descriptions of different guidance planning models.

Putting Comprehensive Guidance and Counseling Programs Into Practice in the 1980s and 1990s

Comprehensive Programs Gain Acceptance

As the 1970s ended, examinations of the traditional way of organizing and managing guidance and counseling in the nation's schools continued and recommendations for a new way increased (Herr, 1979). The idea of developmental, comprehensive guidance programs was gradually enveloping the services model and its position orientation. This movement was endorsed by ASCA first in a 1974 position statement, *The School Counselor and the Guidance and Counseling Program*, and then in a review and revision of the statement in 1980. The movement was further endorsed in ASCA's 1978 position statement, *The School Counselor and Developmental Guidance*, and in that statement's review and revision in 1984 (see ASCA, 1984). As Shaw and Goodyear (1984) noted, guidance specialists needed to "make concrete, written, and reasonable proposals for the delivery of primary preventive services so that some of their less professional and highly scattered responsibilities can be diminished" (p. 446).

The work of putting comprehensive guidance and counseling programs into place in the schools continued throughout the 1980s. Gysbers and Moore (1981) provided a theoretical base as well as a step-by-step process for developing and implementing comprehensive school guidance programs in a book titled *Improving Guidance Programs*. This publication grew out of earlier work (Gysbers & Moore, 1974) in the University of Missouri project to assist states in developing and implementing models or guides for career guidance, counseling, and placement. In addition, Hargens and Gysbers (1984) presented a case study of how one school district had remodeled and revitalized its school guidance and counseling program so that it was developmental and comprehensive.

The state of Missouri published a draft version of *Missouri Comprehensive Guidance* (1986) that presented the state's plan to help school districts to develop, implement, and evaluate comprehensive, systematic school guidance programs begun during the 1984–1985 school year. Wisconsin published *School Counseling Programs: A Resource and Planning Guide* (Wilson, 1986), the result of work begun in 1984 to reexamine the school counselor's role. The National School Boards Association (1986) passed a resolution that supported comprehensive programs of guidance and counseling in the schools. The College Entrance Examination Board (1986) issued *Keeping the Options Open: Recommendations*, a report with direct relevance to comprehensive guidance and counseling programs in the schools that was based on work of the Commission on Precollege Guidance and Counseling begun in 1984. Recommendations in the report urged schools to establish comprehensive and developmental guidance programs for kindergarten through the 12th grade. Henderson (1987), in "A Comprehensive School Guidance Program at Work" and "How One District Changed Its Program" (1989), described how a comprehensive guidance program was designed, the program's content, how the program was being implemented in a large school district in Texas, and the process used to implement it. Myrick (2003) discussed a developmental guidance and counseling model and its implementation in detail.

The 1980s also witnessed the development of an approach to comprehensive guidance and counseling programs called *competency-based guidance*. S. K. Johnson and Johnson (1991) described this approach as the new guidance, a concept they defined as

> a total pupil services program developed with the student as the primary client. The program is designed to guarantee that all students acquire the competencies to become successful in school and to make a successful transition from school to higher education, to employment or to a combination of higher education and work. (p. 6)

The Importance of Legislation

As described previously, in the 1940s and 1950s, the federal Congress passed the Vocational Education Act of 1946 (P.L. 586) and the National Defense Education Act of 1958 (P.L. 85–864). Each of these acts had substantial and long-lasting impact on the nature, structure, and availability of guidance and counseling in the schools. In addition to these two pieces of legislation in the 1940s and 1950s, the 1960s witnessed the passage of the Elementary and Secondary Education Act of 1965 and the Amendment to that Act in 1969, both of which provided some funding for school guidance and counseling (Herr, 2003).

Vocational education (career and technical education) legislation has continued to provide support for guidance and counseling in the schools through the reauthorization of such legislation in the 1930s, 1940s, 1950s, 1960s, and 1970s. Beginning in the 1980s, this legislation was named after Carl D. Perkins, a legislator from Kentucky, and was called the Carl D. Perkins Vocational Education Act of 1984 (P.L. 98–524). Subsequent reauthorizations occurred in 1990 (Carl D. Perkins Vocational Education and Applied Technology Education Act of 1990; P.L. 101-392) and in 1998 (Carl D. Perkins Vocational Technical Education Act Amendments of 1998; P.L. 105–332).

Several other federal laws are worth noting. In 1994, the School-to-Work Opportunities Act of 1994 (P.L. 103–239) was passed. It had the same definition of guidance and counseling as the 1990 Carl D. Perkins Act (P.L. 101–392). The same year the Elementary School Counseling Demonstration Act of 1994 (P.L. 103–382) was passed and provided funds for guidance and counseling in the schools.

State Models Are Developed

Several states developed and published, in the late 1980s, state guides for comprehensive school guidance programs generally patterned after the organizational framework described in the first edition of this book (Gysbers & Henderson, 1988). Examples include Missouri (Starr & Gysbers, 1986), Alaska (Southeast Regional Resource Center, 1989), Idaho (Idaho Department of Education, 1988), New Hampshire (Carr, Hayslip, & Randall, 1988), and Utah (Utah State Office of Education, 1989). The purpose of these guides was to assist local school district counselors and administrators in remodeling and revitalizing their local programs. The work of putting comprehensive guidance and counseling programs into practice, begun in the 1980s, continued into the 1990s. Additional states that developed guides in the early 1990s for local school districts to follow included Nebraska (Nebraska Department of Education, 1990), Nevada (Gribble, 1990), Texas (Texas Education Agency, 1990), Colorado (Developmental Guidance Committee, 1991), Massachusetts (Massachusetts School Counselors Association, 1991), and South Dakota (South Dakota Curriculum Center, 1991). How Missouri, Alaska, and New Hampshire, as well as several school districts across the country, undertook the planning, designing, implementing, and evaluating phases of installing their guidance and counseling programs was documented in *Comprehensive Guidance Programs That Work* (Gysbers, 1990).

Other states developed guides or updated previously published guides later in the 1990s. States that developed guides included Alabama (Alabama State Department of Education, 1996, 2003) and the state of Washington (Washington State Office of Public Instruction, Counseling and Guidance, 1998). States revising guides developed in the 1980s included Missouri (Gysbers, Starr, & Magnuson, 1998) and Utah (Utah State Office of Education, 1998). The ERIC Counseling and Student Services Clearinghouse published two books on comprehensive guidance programs. The first described a visit to the comprehensive guidance program at Northside Independent School District from the school counselors' point of view (Bailey, Henderson, Krueger, & Williams, 1995), and the second (*Comprehensive Guidance Programs That Work–II*; Gysbers & Henderson, 1997) featured the work of 10 school districts across the country as well as four states.

As the 1990s ended, comprehensive guidance and counseling programs increasingly were being developed and put into operation as a result of the work of guidance leaders at the state level and the work of counselors, administrators, and boards of education at the local level. A nationwide survey conducted by Sink and MacDonald (1998) revealed that approximately one half of the states had developed models for comprehensive guidance and counseling programs, and the authors speculated that by the end of the 1990s this number would increase to 34 or more states. With the increased recognition of guidance as a unique program within schools, and the advancement of supervision and administration in the counseling field, new models for providing leadership to school guidance programs and counselors were evolving (Gysbers & Henderson, 1997; Henderson & Gysbers, 1998).

Moving Toward Full Implementation of Guidance and Counseling Programs: The Promise of the 21st Century

As the beginning years of the 21st century began to unfold, the work of developing, implementing, and evaluating comprehensive guidance and counseling programs in the schools has intensified and been expanded. During this time period, a number of states developed or revised their state models. The ASCA developed a national model. Work on federal legislation for guidance and counseling has continued, and a number of states have passed legislation or rules that support the development, implementation, and evaluation of comprehensive guidance and counseling programs in their local school districts. Finally, models for leadership and management of school guidance and counseling programs and staff members continue to be refined.

State Model Development/Revisions Continues

In 2000 the Connecticut School Counselor Association (2000), in collaboration with the Connecticut Association for Counselor Education and Supervision and the Connecticut State Department of Education, developed the *Connecticut Comprehensive School Counseling Program*. In the same year the Nebraska Department of Education (2000) published the *Nebraska School Counseling Guide for Planning and Program Improvement*. Then, in 2004, the Nebraska Department of Education (2004) published the *Nebraska/ASCA School Counseling Model*. Two states published guides in 2001. The Florida Department of Education (2001) published *Florida's School Counseling and Guidance Frameworks: A Comprehensive Student Development Program Model*. In the same year the Iowa Department of Education (2001) developed the *Iowa Comprehensive Counseling and Guidance Program Development Model*. During the next year Missouri revised its model, the *Missouri Comprehensive Guidance Program* (Gysbers, Kosteck-Bunch, Maguson, & Starr, 2002). Two states published guides in 2003: The New York State School Counselor Association (2003) published the *New York State Comprehensive School Counseling Program*, and the Oregon Department of Education (2003) published *Oregon's Comprehensive Guidance and Counseling Framework*. In the next year (2004), Texas published the fourth edition of *A Model Comprehensive, Developmental Guidance and Counseling Program for Texas Public Schools* (Texas Education Agency, 2004), and the Montana School Counselor Association (2004) published the *Montana School Counseling Program*. Finally, in 2005, the Michigan School Counselor Association revised the *Michigan Comprehensive Guidance and Counseling Program*.

The ASCA National Model

In 1997, the ASCA published *Sharing the Vision: The National Standards for School Counseling Programs* (C. A. Campbell & Dahir, 1997). This was followed by the publication of *Vision Into Action: Implementing the National Standards for School Counseling*

Programs (Dahir, Sheldon, & Valiga, 1998). These national standards are now called content standards for students. In 2001, ASCA's Governing Board agreed that the development of a national school counseling program model was the next necessary step because what had been developed by ASCA up to this point had only been content standards for students' academic, career, and personal/social development. What was needed was a framework for a total school counseling program.

Based on ASCA's Governing Board's decision to move forward to develop a national model, a committee of national leaders and practicing school counselors met in Tucson, Arizona, in June 2001. A draft of the model was prepared in the fall of 2001. Two subsequent meetings of the committee took place in 2002, and the model was officially unveiled at the ASCA National Conference in Miami in June 2002. Additional revisions were undertaken, and in 2003, *The ASCA National Model* was officially released by the association (ASCA, 2003). The next year ASCA published a workbook to assist school counselors to implement the program in their schools (ASCA, 2004). Revisions of the manual were completed in 2005 (ASCA, 2005).

Federal and State Legislation

In 2001, the United States Congress passed the No Child Left Behind Act (P.L. 107–110). In it, Part D, Subpart 2 titled "Elementary and Secondary School Counseling Programs" provided for grants to local educational agencies to establish or expand elementary and secondary school counseling programs. However, the level of money actually appropriated was not sufficient to fund the secondary portion of the Act. Thus, only grants to local education agencies were available for elementary school counseling programs.

A number of states also have been active in passing legislation or rules for guidance and counseling in the schools. For example, Utah's State Board of Education passed a rule (R277–462) that defined a comprehensive guidance program as well as provided qualification criteria by which to distribute Comprehensive Guidance Funds. In another example, the Texas Legislature enacted SB 518, which made Education Code Sections 33.003–33.006 applicable to all school districts ("An Act Relating to Public School Counselors," 2001). These sections stated that Texas school counselors shall plan, implement, and evaluate developmental guidance and counseling programs. Similarly, in the state of West Virginia, the Board of Education enacted a legislative rule for comprehensive developmental guidance and counseling in 2002. Finally, as a last example, the state of Florida enacted a bill titled "An Act Relating to Career Education" in 2004. In Section 5, Section 1006.025, it states each district school board shall annually submit a district guidance report to the Commissioner of Education that includes the degree to which a district has adopted or implemented a guidance model program.

Leadership Models

With rules and guidelines for comprehensive guidance programs delineated in federal and state legislation, policy, and models, effective leadership of guidance programs and school counselors is recognized as necessary to ensure compliance. A growing number of school counseling leaders are being identified at the school district and building levels. Issues identified as critical to successful implementation of comprehensive guidance programs have been successfully resolved through effective leadership (Henderson & Gysbers, 2002). Models for guidance leadership, administration, supervision, and management are being refined. Leadership of school counselors is required to ensure competent performance by school counselors (Henderson & Gysbers, 1998; Lieberman, 2004; Schwallie-Giddis, ter Maat, & Pak, 2003). Management and accountability systems have been called for throughout the history of school guidance and counseling. It is finally clear that without proper leadership such systems cannot be implemented. Leadership by school counselors is called for not only to manage their own programs (Fitch & Marshall, 2004) but also to assist teachers and administrators better meet the needs of their students (ASCA, 2003; Education Trust, 2003).

Comprehensive Guidance and Counseling Programs: Five Foundation Premises

As the guidance and counseling movement (then called vocational guidance) began to unfold in the United States at the turn of the 20th century, teachers, often part time or with no reduced time, were appointed as counselors and given a list of duties to perform. By the 1920s the guidance and counseling movement had spread across the country. Educational guidance became a priority along with vocational guidance. During the late 1920s and early 1930s, efforts were made to identify what the activities of guidance and counseling should be, to establish "the standard setup" for guidance and counseling. During this same period of time, personal/social guidance and counseling emerged, as did the services model under the banner of pupil personnel work. Thus, by the 1930s, the three aspects of guidance and counseling (vocational, education, and personal/social) and the services model with the position of counselor had been established. With the aid of federal legislation in the 1940s and 1950s, guidance and counseling in the schools continued to expand and became a part of overall education in the Untied States.

In the 1960s and 1970s, owing to concerns about the efficacy of the position-services model of guidance and counseling, the program model began to emerge. While not a new concept, the program model has become, during the 1980s, 1990s, and the early years of the 21st century, the major way of organizing and managing guidance and counseling in the schools. The position-services model has been transformed and incorporated into a developmental, comprehensive program.

Why is an understanding of the history of guidance and counseling in the schools important? It helps us understand why and how the position-services model for guidance and counseling evolved. It also helps us understand why and how the comprehensive guidance and counseling model emerged in the 1960s and 1970s in response to dissatisfaction with the position-services model.

Just as we need to understand how guidance and counseling in our schools evolved, so too do we need to understand the five premises on which the program model is based. These premises undergird the organization and management of guidance and counseling in the schools. These premises are the point of departure for developing and managing your school guidance and counseling program.

1. *Guidance and counseling is a program.* Its characteristics are similar to other programs in education and includes the following:
   - student standards
   - activities and processes to assist students in achieving these standards
   - professionally certificated personnel
   - materials and resources
   - program, personnel, and results evaluation
2. *Guidance and counseling programs are developmental and comprehensive.* They are developmental in that guidance and counseling activities are conducted on a regular, planned, and systematic basis to assist students in their academic, career, and

personal/social development. Although immediate and crisis needs of students are to be met, a major focus of a developmental program is to provide all students with experiences to help them grow and develop. Guidance and counseling programs are comprehensive in that a full range of activities and services are provided.

3. *Guidance and counseling programs feature a team approach.* A comprehensive, developmental program of guidance and counseling is based on the assumption that all school staff are involved. At the same time, it is understood that professionally certified school counselors are central to the program. School counselors not only provide direct services to students but also work in consultative and collaborative relations with other members of the guidance team, members of the school staff, parents, and members of the community.

4. *Guidance and counseling programs are developed through a systematic process of planning, designing, implementing, evaluating, and enhancing.* This process assures intentional delivery of a program designed to address established priorities.

5. *Guidance and counseling programs have established leadership.* This ensures accountability for the program and for the quality of the performance of program staff.

Based on the understanding gained from this chapter's review of how guidance and counseling has been conceptualized and institutionalized in the schools over the years, we are now ready to examine a comprehensive program organization and management structure for guidance and counseling. The chapters that follow provide the philosophical foundation and practical specifics about organizing and managing guidance and counseling while using the concept of a comprehensive program. The issues involved, the procedures and methods to be used, and the resources and personnel required are presented in detail.

References

Alabama State Department of Education. (1996). *The revised comprehensive counseling and guidance state model for Alabama's public schools* (Bulletin 1996, No. 27). Montgomery, AL: Author.

Alabama State Department of Education. (2003). *Comprehensive counseling and guidance model for Alabama public schools* (Bulletin 2003, No. 89). Montgomery, AL: Author.

Allen, F. I. (1927). *Principles and problems in vocational guidance.* New York: McGraw-Hill.

American College Testing Program. (1976). *River City High School guidance services. A conceptual model.* Iowa City, IA: Author.

American Psychological Association, Division of Counseling Psychology, Committee on Definition. (1956). Counseling psychology as a specialty. *American Psychologist, 11,* 282–285.

American School Counselor Association. (1984). *The school counselor and developmental guidance: Position statement.* Alexandria, VA: Author.

American School Counselor Association. (2003). *The ASCA national model: A framework for school counseling programs.* Alexandria, VA: Author.

American School Counselor Association. (2004). *The ASCA national model workbook.* Alexandria, VA: Author.

American School Counselor Association. (2005). *The ASCA national model: A framework for school counseling programs,* (2nd ed.). Alexandria, VA: Author.

An Act Relating to Career Education, Florida H.B. 0769 (2004).

An Act Relating to Public School Counselors, SB 518, Amends Texas Education Code, Sections 33.001, 33.005–33.006 (2001).

Ashcroft, K. B. (1966). *A report of the invitational conference in implementing career development theory.* Washington, DC: National Vocational Guidance Association.

Aubrey, R. F. (1969). Misapplication of therapy models to school counseling. *Personnel and Guidance Journal, 48,* 273–278.

Aubrey, R. F. (1982). A house divided: Guidance and counseling in 20th century America. *Personnel and Guidance Journal, 61,* 198–204.

Bailey, M., Henderson, P., Krueger, D., & Williams, L. (1995). *A visit to a comprehensive guidance program that works.* Greensboro, NC: ERIC Counseling and Student Services Clearinghouse.

Ballast, D. L., & Shoemaker, R. L. (1978). *Guidance program development.* Springfield, IL: Charles C Thomas.

Bell, H. M. (1939). *Theory and practice of personal counseling.* Stanford, CA: Stanford University Press.

Bloomfield, M. (1915). *Youth, school, and vocation.* Boston: Houghton Mifflin.

Borow, H. (1966). Research in vocational development: Implications for the vocational aspects of counselor education. In C. McDaniels (Ed.), *Vocational aspects of counselor education* (pp. 70–92). Washington, DC: George Washington University.

Brammer, L. M. (1968). The counselor is a psychologist. *Personnel and Guidance Journal, 47,* 4–9.

Brewer, J. M. (1922). *The vocational-guidance movement.* New York: Macmillan.

Brown, J. A. (1977). *Organizing and evaluating elementary school guidance services: Why, what, and how.* Monterey, CA: Brooks/Cole.

California State Department of Education. (1971). *Career guidance: A California model for career development K–adult.* Sacramento, CA: Author.

Campbell, C. A., & Dahir, C. A. (1997). *Sharing the vision: Standards for school counseling programs.* Alexandria, VA: American School Counselor Association.

Campbell, M. E. (1932). *Vocational guidance committee on vocational guidance and child labor: Section III. Education and training* (White House Conference on Child Health and Protection). New York: Century.

Campbell, R. E. (1977). *The career planning support system.* Columbus, OH: National Center for Research in Vocational Education.

Campbell, R. E., Dworkin, E. P., Jackson, D. P., Hoeltzel, K. E., Parsons, G. E., & Lacey, D. W. (1971). *The systems approach: An emerging behavioral model for career guidance.* Columbus, OH: National Center for Research in Vocational Education.

Campbell, R. E., Rodebaugh, H. D., & Shaltry, P. E. (1978). *Building comprehensive career guidance programs for secondary schools.* Columbus, OH: National Center for Research in Vocational Education.

Carl D. Perkins Vocational Education Act of 1984, Pub. L. No. 98–524, Part 1, Stat. 2433 (1984).

Carl D. Perkins Vocational Education and Applied Technology Education Act Amendments of 1990, Pub. L. No. 101–392, 104, Part 2, Stat. 753 (1990).

Carl D. Perkins Vocational-Technical Education Act Amendments of 1998, Pub. L. No. 105–332, 112, Part 1, Stat. 3076 (1998).

Carr, J. V., Hayslip, J., & Randall, J. (1988). *New Hampshire comprehensive guidance and counseling program: A guide to an approved model for program development.* Plymouth, NH: Plymouth State College.

College Entrance Examination Board. (1986). *Keeping the options open: Recommendations.* New York: Author.

Connecticut School Counselor Association. (2000). *Connecticut Comprehensive School Counseling Program.* Hartford, CT: Author.

Council of Chief State School Officers. (1960). *Responsibilities of state departments of education for pupil personnel services.* Washington, DC: Author.

Dagley, J. C. (1974, December). *Georgia career guidance project newsletter.* Athens: University of Georgia.

Dahir, C. A., Sheldon, C. B., & Valiga, M. J. (1998). *Vision into action: Implementing the national standards for school counseling programs.* Alexandria, VA: American School Counselor Association.

Davis, H. V. (1969). *Frank Parsons: Prophet, innovator, counselor.* Carbondale: Southern Illinois University Press.

Davis, J. B. (1914). *Vocational and moral guidance.* Boston: Ginn.

Dayton, C. A. (1976). *A validated program development model and staff development prototype for comprehensive career guidance, counseling, placement, and follow-up* (Final Report, Grant No. OEG–0–74–1721). Palo Alto, CA: American Institutes for Research.

Developmental Guidance Committee. (1991). *A team approach to guiding students to excellence: A comprehensive school guidance program at work in Colorado.* Denver: Colorado School Counselor Association.

Dinkmeyer, D. (1966). Developmental counseling in the elementary school. *Personnel and Guidance Journal, 45,* 262–66.

Drier, H. N. (Ed.). (1971). *Guide to the integration of career development into local curriculum: Grades K–12.* Madison: Wisconsin Department of Public Instruction.

Drier, H. N. (1976). *Cooperative rural guidance system.* Columbus, OH: National Center for Research in Vocational Education.

Dunn, J. A. (1972). *The guidance program in the plan system of individualized education.* Palo Alto, CA: American Institutes for Research.

Eckerson, L. O., & Smith, H. M. (Eds.). (1966). *Scope of pupil personnel services* (Catalog No. FS5.223: 23045). Washington, DC: U.S. Government Printing Office.

The Education Trust. (2003). *Transforming school counseling.* Retrieved October 28, 2004, from http://ww.edtrust.org

Elementary and Secondary Education Act of 1965, Pub. L. No. 89–10, Stat. 27–58 (1965).

Elementary School Counseling Demonstration Act of 1994, Title X, Programs of National Significance, Fund for the Improvement of Education, Section 10102 of the Improving America's School Act of 1994, Pub. L. No. 103–382, 108 Stat. 3518–4062 (1994).

Faust, V. (1968). *History of elementary school counseling: Overview and critique.* Boston: Houghton Mifflin.

Felix, J. L. (1968). Who decided that? *Personnel and Guidance Journal, 47,* 9–11.

Ferguson, D. G. (1963). *Pupil personnel services.* Washington, DC: Center for Applied Research in Education.

Fitch, T. J., & Marshall, J. (2004). What counselors do in high-achieving schools: A study on the role of the school counselor. *Professional School Counseling, 7,* 172–178.

Florida Department of Education. (2001). *Florida's school counseling and guidance framework: A comprehensive student development program model.* Tallahassee, FL: Author.

Ginn, S. J. (1924). Vocational guidance in Boston public schools. *The Vocational Guidance Magazine, 3,* 3–7.

Glanz, E. C. (1961). Emerging concepts and patterns of guidance in American education. *Personnel and Guidance Journal, 40,* 259–65.

Gribble, C. (1990). *Nevada school and counseling: Grades K–12.* Carson City: Nevada State Department of Education.

Gysbers, N. C. (1969). *Elements of a model for promoting career development in elementary and junior high school.* Paper presented at the National Conference on Exemplary Programs and Projects, 1968 Amendments to the Vocational Education Act (ED045860), Atlanta, GA.

Gysbers, N. C. (1978). Comprehensive career guidance programs. In R. E. Campbell, H. D. Rodebaugh, & P. E. Shaltry (Eds.), *Building comprehensive career guidance programs for secondary schools* (pp. 3–24). Columbus, OH: National Center for Research in Vocational Education.

Gysbers, N. C., with Guidance Program Field Writers. (1990). *Comprehensive guidance programs that work.* Ann Arbor, MI: ERIC Counseling and Personnel Services Clearinghouse.

Gysbers, N. C., & Henderson, P. (1988). Developing and managing your school guidance program. Alexandra, VA: 1988.

Gysbers, N. C., & Henderson, P. (1997). *Comprehensive guidance programs that work— II.* Greensboro, NC: ERIC Counseling and Student Services Clearinghouse.

Gysbers, N. C., Kosteck-Bunch, L., Magruson, C. S., & Starr, M. F. (2002). *Missouri comprehensive guidance program.* Columbia, MO: Instructional Materials Laboratory.

Gysbers, N. C., & Moore, E. J. (Eds.). (1974). *Career guidance counseling and placement: Elements of an illustrative program guide.* Columbia: University of Missouri.

Gysbers, N. C., & Moore, E. J. (1981). *Improving guidance programs.* Englewood Cliffs, NJ: Prentice-Hall.

Gysbers, N. C., Starr, M. F., & Magnuson, C. S. (1998). *Missouri comprehensive guidance: A model for program development and implementation* (Rev. ed.). Jefferson City: Missouri Department of Elementary and Secondary Education.

Halasz-Salster, I., & Peterson, M. (1979). *Planning comprehensive career guidance programs: A catalog of alternatives.* Columbus, OH: National Center for Research in Vocational Education.

Hansen, L. S. (1970). *Career guidance practices in school and community.* Washington, DC: National Vocational Guidance Association.

Hansen, L. S., & Gysbers, N. C. (Eds.). (1975). Career development: Guidance and education [Special issue]. *Personnel and Guidance Journal, 53.*

Hargens, M., & Gysbers, N. C. (1984). How to remodel a guidance program while living in it: A case study. *The School Counselor, 32,* 119–125.

Henderson, P. (1987). A comprehensive school guidance program at work. *Texas Association for Counseling and Development Journal, 10,* 25–37.

Henderson, P. (1989). How one district changed its program. *The School Counselor, 37,* 31–40.

Henderson, P., & Gysbers, N. C. (1998). *Leading and managing your school guidance program staff.* Alexandria, VA: American Counseling Association.

Henderson, P., & Gysbers, N. (2002). *Implementing comprehensive school guidance programs: Critical leadership issues and successful responses.* Greensboro, NC: CAPS.

Herr, E. L. (1969). *Unifying an entire system of education around a career development theme.* Paper presented at the National Conference on Exemplary Programs and Projects, 1968 Amendments to the Vocational Education Act (ED045860), Atlanta, GA.

Herr, E. L. (1979). *Guidance and counseling in the schools: The past, present, and future.* Washington, DC: American Personnel and Guidance Association.

Herr, E. L. (2003). Historical roots and future issues. In B. T. Enford (Ed.), *Transforming the school counseling profession* (pp. 21–38). Upper Saddle River, NJ: Prentice-Hall.

Herr, E. L., & Cramer, S. H. (1979). *Career guidance through the life span.* Boston: Little, Brown.

Hilton, T. L. (1979). *Confronting the future: A conceptual framework for secondary school career guidance*. New York: College Entrance Examination Board.

Hosford, R. E., & Ryan, T. A. (1970). Systems design in the development of counseling and guidance programs. *Personnel and Guidance Journal, 49*, 221–230.

Hoyt, K. B. (1974). Professional preparation for vocational guidance. In E. L. Herr (Ed.), *Vocational guidance and human development* (pp. 502–527). Boston: Houghton Mifflin.

Idaho Department of Education. (1988). *Idaho comprehensive guidance and counseling program model*. Boise, ID: Author.

Iowa Department of Education. (2001). *Iowa comprehensive counseling and guidance program development model*. Des Moines, IA: Author.

Jacobson, T. J., & Mitchell, A. M. (1975). *Master plan for career guidance and counseling* (Final Report, Pupil Personnel Services). Grossmont, CA: Grossmont Union High School District.

Johnson, A. H. (1972). Changing conceptions of vocational guidance and concomitant value-orientations 1920–30. *Dissertation Abstracts International, 33*, 3292A. (University Microfilms No. 72-31,933)

Johnson, S. K., & Johnson, C. D. (1991). The new guidance: A system approach to pupil personnel programs. *CACD Journal, 11*, 5–14.

Jones, G. B., Dayton, C., & Gelatt, H. B. (1977). *New methods for delivering human services*. New York: Human Services Press.

Jones, G. B., Hamilton, J. A., Ganschow, L. H., Helliwell, C. B., & Wolff, J. M. (1972). *Planning, developing, and field testing career guidance programs: A manual and report*. Palo Alto, CA: American Institutes for Research.

Jones, G. B., Helliwell, C. B., & Ganschow, L. H. (1975). A planning model for career guidance. *Vocational Guidance Quarterly, 23*, 220–226.

Jones, G. B., Nelson, D. E., Ganschow, L. H., & Hamilton, J. A. (1971). *Development and evaluation of a comprehensive career guidance program*. Palo Alto, CA: American Institutes for Research.

Leonard, G. E., & Vriend, T. J. (1975). Update: The developmental career guidance project. *Personnel and Guidance Journal, 53*, 668–671.

Levitt, F. M. (1914). How shall we study the industries for the purposes of vocational guidance? In U.S. Bureau of Education, *Vocational guidance: Papers presented at the organization meeting of the Vocational Guidance Association, Grand Rapids, Michigan, October 21–24, 1913* (pp. 79–81) (Bulletin, 1914, No. 14, Whole Number 587). Washington, DC: U.S. Government Printing Office.

Lieberman, A. (2004, Spring). Confusion regarding school counselor functions: School leadership impacts role clarity. *Education, 124*, 522–529.

Massachusetts School Counselors Association. (1991). *Comprehensive developmental guidance and counseling curriculum guide and role statement revision*. Fitchburg, MA: Blanchard & Brown.

Mathewson, R. H. (1962). *Guidance policy and practice* (3rd ed.). New York: Harper & Row.

McCracken, T. C., & Lamb, H. E. (1923). *Occupational information in the elementary school*. Boston: Houghton Mifflin.

McKinnon, B. E., & Jones, G. B. (1975). Field testing a comprehensive career guidance program: K–12. *Personnel and Guidance Journal, 53*, 663–667.

Michigan School Counselor Association. (2005). *Michigan comprehensive guidance and counseling program*. East Grand Rapids, MI: Author.

Miller, C. H. (1971). *Foundations of guidance*. New York: Harper & Row.

Missouri comprehensive guidance. (1986). *The Counseling Interviewer, 18*(4), 6–17.

Mitchell, A. M. (1978). The design, development, and evaluation of systematic guidance programs. In G. Walz & L. Benjamin (Eds.), *New imperatives for guidance* (pp. 113–148). Ann Arbor, MI: ERIC Counseling and Personnel Services Clearinghouse.

Mitchell, A. M., & Gysbers, N. C. (1978). Comprehensive school guidance programs. In *The status of guidance and counseling in the nation's schools* (pp. 23–39). Washington, DC: American Personnel and Guidance Association.

Montana School Counselor Association. (2004). *Montana school counseling program.* Florence, MT: Author.

Myers, G. E. (1923). A critical review of present developments in vocational guidance with special reference to future prospects. *The Vocational Guidance Magazine, 2,* 139–142.

Myers, G. E. (1931). What should be the duties of the counselor? *Occupations, 9,* 343–347.

Myers, G. E. (1935). Coordinated guidance: Some suggestions for a program of pupil personnel work. *Occupations, 13,* 804–807.

Myrick, R. D. (2003). *Developmental guidance and counseling: A practical approach* (4th ed.). Minneapolis, MN: Educational Media Corporation.

National Defense Education Act of 1958, Pub. L. No. 85–864, 72, Part 1, Stat. 1580 (1958).

National Education Association. (1918). *Cardinal principles of secondary education: A report of the commission on the reorganization of secondary education.* Washington, DC: Author.

National School Boards Association. (1986). *Resolution on guidance and counseling.* Alexandria, VA: Author.

Nebraska Department of Education. (1990). *Nebraska school counseling program guide for planning and program improvement.* Lincoln, NE: Author.

Nebraska Department of Education. (2000). *Nebraska school counseling guide for planning and program improvement.* Lincoln, NE: Author.

Nebraska Department of Education. (2004). *Nebraska/ASCA school counseling model.* Lincoln, NE: Author.

New York State School Counselor Association. (2003). *New York State comprehensive school counseling program.* Leicester, NY: Author.

No Child Left Behind Act of 2001, Pub. L. No. 107–110, 115, Stat. 1434 (2001).

Oregon Department of Education. (2003). *Oregon's comprehensive guidance and counseling framework.* Salem, OR: Author.

Parsons, F. (1909). *Choosing a vocation.* Boston: Houghton Mifflin.

Peterson, M., & Treichel, J. (1978). *Programmatic approach to guidance excellence: PAGE 2* (Rev. ed.). McComb: Western Illinois University, Curriculum Publishing Clearinghouse.

Pierson, G. A. (1965). *An evaluation—Counselor education in regular session institutes.* Washington, DC: U.S. Department of Health, Education, and Welfare, Office of Education.

Proctor, W. M. (1930). Evaluating guidance activities in high schools. *The Vocational Guidance Magazine, 9,* 58–66.

Roeber, E. C. (1963). *The school counselor.* Washington, DC: Center for Applied Research in Education.

Roeber, E. C., Walz, G. R., & Smith, G. E. (1969). *A strategy for guidance.* New York: Macmillan.

Rogers, C. R. (1942). *Counseling and psychotherapy.* Boston: Houghton Mifflin.

Rudy, W. S. (1965). *Schools in an age of mass culture.* Englewood Cliffs, NJ: Prentice-Hall.

Ryan, T. A. (1969). Systems techniques for programs of counseling and counselor education. *Educational Technology, 9,* 7–17.

Ryan, T. A., & Zeran, F. R. (1972). *Organization and administration of guidance services*. Danville, IL: Interstate.

Ryan, W. C., Jr. (1919). *Vocational guidance and the public schools* (Bulletin 1918, No. 24). Washington, DC: U S. Department of the Interior, Bureau of Education.

School-to-Work Opportunities Act of 1994, Pub. L. No. 103-239, 108, Stat. 568 (1994).

Schwallie-Giddis, P., ter Maat, M., & Pak, M. (2003). Initiating leadership by introducing and implementing the ASCA National Model. *Professional School Counseling, 6,* 170–174.

Shaw, M. C., & Goodyear, R. K. (1984). Prologue to primary prevention in schools. *Personnel and Guidance Journal, 62,* 446–447.

Shaw, M. C., & Tuel, L. K. (1966). A focus for public school guidance programs: A model and proposal. *Personnel and Guidance Journal, 44,* 824–830.

Sink, C. A., & MacDonald, G. (1998). The status of comprehensive guidance and counseling in the United States. *Professional School Counseling, 2,* 88–94.

Smith, G. E. (1951). *Principles and practices of the guidance program*. New York: Macmillan.

South Dakota Curriculum Center. (1991). *South Dakota comprehensive guidance and counseling program model* (working document, 1st draft). Pierre: South Dakota Department of Education and Cultural Affairs.

Southeast Regional Resource Center. (1989). *Alaska school counseling program guide*. Juneau, AK: Author.

Sprinthall, N. A. (1971). *Guidance for human growth*. New York: Van Nostrand Reinhold.

Starr, M., & Gysbers, N. C. (1986). *Missouri comprehensive guidance: A model for program development, implementation, and evaluation*. Jefferson City: Missouri Department of Elementary and Secondary Education.

Stephens, W. R. (1970). *Social reform and the origins of vocational guidance*. Washington, DC: National Vocational Guidance Association.

Stoughton, R. W., McKenna, I. W., & Cook, R. P. (1969). *Pupil personnel services: A position statement*. National Association of Pupil Personnel Administrators.

Stripling, R. O., & Lane, D. (1966). Guidance services. In L. O. Eckerson & H. M. Smith (Eds.), *Scope of pupil personnel services* (pp. 25–35). Washington, DC: U.S. Government Printing Office (Catalog No. F5 5.223:23045).

Studebaker, J. W. (1938). The new national occupational information and guidance service. *Occupations, 16,* 101–105.

Super, D. E. (1955). Transition: From vocational guidance to counseling psychology. *Journal of Counseling Psychology, 2,* 3–9.

Tennyson, W. W., & Hansen, L. S. (1971). Guidance through the curriculum. In L. C. Deighton (Ed.), *The encyclopedia of education* (No. 4, pp. 248–254). New York: Macmillan.

Tennyson, W. W., Soldahl, T. A., & Mueller, C. (1965). *The teacher's role in career development*. Washington, DC: National Vocational Guidance Association.

Texas Education Agency. (1990). *The comprehensive guidance program for Texas public schools: A guide for program development, pre-K–12th grade*. Austin, TX: Author.

Texas Education Agency. (2004). *A model comprehensive, developmental guidance and counseling program for Texas public schools* (4th ed.). Austin, TX: Author.

Tiedman, D. V., & Field, F. C. (1962). Guidance: The science of purposeful action applied through education. *Harvard Educational Review, 32,* 483–501.

Tyler, L. E. (1960). *The vocational defense counseling and guidance training institutes program: A report of the first 50 institutes*. Washington, DC: U.S. Department of Health, Education, and Welfare, Office of Education.

U.S. Bureau of Education. (1914). *Vocational guidance: Papers presented at the organization meeting of the Vocational Guidance Association, Grand Rapids, Michigan, October 21–24, 1913, Prefatory Statement* (Bulletin, 1914, No. 14, Whole Number 587). Washington, DC: U.S. Government Printing Office.

Upton, A., Lowery, B., Mitchell, A. M., Varenhorst, B., & Benvenuti, J. (1978). *A planning model for developing career guidance curriculum.* Fullerton: California Personnel and Guidance Association.

Utah State Board of Education Rule R 277-462, Comprehensive Guidance Program, 1997.

Utah State Office of Education. (1989). *Utah comprehensive counseling and guidance program: A proposed model for program development.* Salt Lake City, UT: Author.

Utah State Office of Education. (1998). *Model for comprehensive counseling and guidance programs* (Rev. ed.). Salt Lake City, UT: Author.

Vocational Education Act of 1946, Pub. L. No. 79–586, 60, Part 1, Stat. 775–778 (1946).

Washington State Office of Public Instruction, Counseling and Guidance. (1998). *Washington State guidelines for comprehensive counseling and career guidance programs from kindergarten through community and technical college* (No. 360–753–0555). Olympia, WA: Author:

Wellman, F. E. (1978). *U.S. Office of Education Administrative Unit: Past, present, and future.* Unpublished manuscript, University of Missouri–Columbia.

Wellman, F. E., & Moore, E. J. (1975). *Pupil personnel services: A handbook for program development and evaluation.* Columbia: Missouri Evaluation Projects.

West Virginia Board of Education Legislative Rule, Series 67, Comprehensive Developmental Guidance and Counseling (2315), 2002.

Wilson, P. J. (1986). *School counseling programs: A resource and planning guide.* Madison: Wisconsin Department of Public Instruction.

Wirth, A. G. (1980). *Education in the technological society.* Lanham, MD: University Press of America.

Wirth, A. G. (1983). *Productive work in industry and schools.* Lanham, MD: University Press of America.

Wrenn, C. G. (1962). *The counselor in a changing world.* Washington, DC: American Personnel and Guidance Association.

Zaccaria, J. S. (1965). Developmental tasks: Implications for the goals of guidance. *Personnel and Guidance Journal, 44,* 372–375.

Zaccaria, J. S. (1966). Developmental guidance: A concept in transition. *The School Counselor, 13,* 226–229.

⌒ Chapter 2 ⌒

A Comprehensive School Guidance and Counseling Program: Getting Organized to Get There From Where You Are

Planning—Getting Organized to Get There From Where You Are

- Decide that you want to change.
- Understand the necessary conditions for effective change.
- Expect resistance to change.
- Develop trust among counselors, teachers, and administrators.
- Form committees and work groups.
- Meet with the administration/district board of education.
- Provide leadership for change.
- Be active.

⌒ The traditional way of organizing guidance and counseling in the schools, first as a position, and then as a position in a service, is continuing to give way to the organizational framework of a comprehensive guidance and counseling program. Comprehensive guidance and counseling programs are increasingly becoming a reality, not just a promise, in school districts across the United States. This change is not yet complete, however, because school counselors are often unable to spend 100% of their time carrying out a fully implemented comprehensive guidance and counseling program. They are still expected to fulfill multiple, often conflicting roles. They are expected to work in the curriculum, assist students with their educational and occupational planning, and do community outreach. They are expected to do crisis counseling, small-group counseling, and teacher and parent consultation as well as referral. In addition, they are expected to be the coordinators of the school district's testing program, develop master schedules, do assessment and case management work for special education, and be responsible for various administrative and clerical duties not connected with the guidance program.

School counselors want to respond to the needs and expectations of students, parents, and teachers. However, they often find that the press of some of their existing duties interferes with or actually prevents them from doing so. Thus they find themselves in a quandary, and role confusion, if not direct role conflict, is often the result.

How serious is the problem? Consider the findings from the following studies of how school counselors spend their time. In a 3-year study conducted in Arizona (Vandegrift, 1999), the question was asked, "Are Arizona public schools making the best use of school counselors?" The study revealed that school counselors in Arizona were spending up to 15% of their time in performing "nonguidance" activities. To put this percentage into perspective, Vandegrift (1999) conducted a cost–benefit analysis based on 1996 median salaries:

A simple cost–benefit analysis helps in beginning to answer these questions. The median counselor salary in Arizona is $27,000. The median salary of a school secretary is $20,600. Fifteen percent of a counselor's wages is $4,050, while 15% of a secretary's wages is $3,090—a difference of nearly $1000. If all 1,327 Arizona public school counselors (who comprise the state's counselor directory) are spending an average of 15% of their time on non-guidance activities, this represents an investment of some $5 million. Assuming non-guidance activities such as class scheduling could be performed by secretarial staff, Arizona taxpayers currently are paying 100 times more (or over $1 million) for these services to be performed by Master's-degreed professionals. Moreover, time spent on non-guidance activities clearly is time not spent working with students, faculty and staff. (p. 5)

In a similar study conducted in Texas (Rylander, 2002), the study revealed

that school counselors spend only about 60 percent of their time exclusively on counseling. A good portion of their time is spent on other administrative tasks. Counselors acknowledge they should not be relieved entirely of administrative duties, because all school staff must assume some measure of administrative responsibility. Most claimed, however, that excessive administrative duties hampered their effectiveness and their availability to students. One particular area of concern among counselors was their role in administering statewide tests. While counselors believe they have a role in test assessment, they argued that the role of coordinator of TAAS [Texas Assessment of Academic Skills] testing took too much time away from counseling. Many recommend shifting most or all of those duties to other staff. (Executive summary)

Why does the problem exist? One reason is that the organizational framework for guidance and counseling in many schools is still the position-services model with lists of duties. Guidance and counseling remains an undefined program in many school buildings even though there may be a written comprehensive program somewhere at the district level. As a result, school counselors continue to find themselves in mainly supportive remedial roles, roles that are not seen as mainstream by most people. And, what is worse, this organizational framework reinforces the practice of having counselors do many inappropriate tasks because such tasks can be justified as being of service to someone. The following duties list is typical. Most school counselors do not do all of them, but a lot of school counselors do some of them.

- Counselors register and schedule all new students.
- Counselors serve as coordinators for the schoolwide testing program.
- Counselors talk to new students concerning school rules.
- Counselors change students' schedules.
- Counselors are responsible for signing excuses for students who are tardy or absent.
- Counselors teach classes when teachers are absent.
- Counselors fill in for the principal when the principal is absent.
- Counselors do senior grade checks.
- Counselors are assigned lunchroom duty.

- Counselors arrange class schedules for students.
- Counselors are responsible for discipline cases.
- Counselors send students home who are not appropriately dressed.
- Counselors compute grade point averages.
- Counselors fill out student reports and records.
- Counselors are in charge of student records.
- Counselors supervise study halls.
- Counselors assist with duties in the principal's office.
- Counselors serve as case managers for special education.
- Counselors are responsible for all of the assessments for special education.

Another reason for this jumble of duties is that some counselors are unwilling to see others playing a role in the delivery of the guidance and counseling program. They feel that it is their job to carry out the total program. In addition, some counselors take their occupational title literally. They do individual counseling only and, as a result, are reluctant to take on the duties necessary to carry out the broader functions of a comprehensive guidance and counseling program. Given this situation, the challenge that we face as school counselors and program leaders is how to make the transition from the position-services model, with the wide variety of tasks involved, to a comprehensive program that is an equal partner with other programs in education. How do we take an undefined and fragmented program, improve it, and make it a clearly defined and fully operational comprehensive program K–12?

Making the transition is complex, difficult, but doable. It means for a time carrying out the duties required by the current position-services model while at the same time planning and beginning to carry out the new comprehensive guidance and counseling program and its tasks. The experience is similar to living in your home while you are remodeling it. It can be done, but it is exacting, time consuming, and often frustrating.

A number of issues and conditions need to be considered in planning the process of change, in making the transition to a comprehensive guidance and counseling program. Thus this chapter first gives attention to deciding that you want to change and to understanding the necessary general and specific conditions for change. Then, a sample timetable of tasks that may be involved in the change over process is presented. Possible resistance to change is discussed next, including appreciating the challenges involved in change. Developing trust among counselors, teachers, and administrators follows. Next, the need to form committees and works groups to carry out the tasks involved in change is described. The chapter ends with the issue of the leadership for change and the admonition that action is needed.

Decide That You Want to Change

The initial stimulus to move to a comprehensive guidance and counseling program may come from counselors, or it may come from parents, students, school administration, the school board, or community organizations. No matter where the initial stimulus comes from, however, the total K–12 guidance staff must be involved in responding, and the administration and board of education must be involved and provide support. The decision to change, we believe, must be made jointly by school counselors and administrators. Because this is a key decision that will change how guidance and counseling is delivered in the schools, it requires careful thought (Erickson, 1997).

In one school district, for example, the guidance and counseling staff met several times with the full endorsement of administration to assess the need to change. They compared and contrasted activities they thought they should be providing with those they actually were providing. On the basis of this comparison, they decided to take a detailed look at their program. Once consensus was obtained among the guidance and counseling staff, the decision was shared with the administration and support was obtained to proceed (Hargens & Fuston, 1997).

When the issue of changing has been fully discussed, consensus must be reached on how to respond. School counselors and administrators may decide to maintain the program as it is and not to change. Or, as in the school district just cited, the decision to change may be made jointly. If the decision to change is made, it is imperative that a majority of staff (counselors and administrators) agree to participate fully in whatever it takes to change their guidance and counseling program, to make it comprehensive K–12.

Understand the Necessary Conditions for Effective Change

As you are considering changing to a comprehensive guidance and counseling program, it is important to understand that there are general conditions that affect how changes are made in any setting as well as ones that are specific to school guidance and counseling and your school district. Identifying and appreciating the roles these conditions may play in the change process is indispensable in this first phase of the planning process.

Some General Conditions to Consider

Change Is a Process, Not an Event

Too often change is treated as a one-time event. Enthusiasm is generated about a possible change, an event is held to launch the change, but then, everyday events that follow smother any follow-through. People are good at holding "First Annuals" but often forget to finish the tasks. Make no mistake! Change is a process, not an event. Sufficient time must be built into the change schedule if the change is to be successful. Perseverance is a virtue.

The Diagnostic Approach to Change

Connor, Lake, and Stackman (2003) recommended that a diagnostic approach be used in the change process. Their approach begins with formulating the problem statement (We need to improve the way we organize and implement guidance and counseling activities and services in our school district). Then they recommended gathering information about the problem (How are we presently organized to provide guidance and counseling activities and services?). Next, they recommended analyzing the information (We are not reaching all students and their parents, our activities and services are disconnected K–12, and we are not accountable). Finally, they recommended developing suggestions for future actions (We need to improve what we do by adopting and implementing an accountable comprehensive guidance and counseling program K–12).

The Magnitude of Change

Waters, Marzano, and McNulty (2003) used the terms *first order* and *second order* to describe the magnitude of change. They defined first-order change as

> changes that are consistent with existing values and norms, create advantages for individuals or stakeholder groups with similar interests, can be implemented with existing knowledge and resources, and where agreement exists on what changes are needed and on how the changes should be implemented can be considered first order. (p. 7)

Second-order change, on the other hand, "requires individuals or groups of stakeholders to learn new approaches or it conflicts with prevailing values of norms" (p. 7).

What is the problem? The problem occurs when one group sees a change as first order, that is, it is simply an extension of the past and is consistent with current values, whereas another group sees the same change as second order, a break from the past that conflicts with current values. As Waters et al. (2003) pointed out, it is important to find out if the changes to be made are first- or second-order changes for which individuals or groups. Is the change to a comprehensive guidance and counseling program seen as a first-order change by school counselors but a second-order change by administrators? Or vice versa? It makes a difference and will affect whether change occurs smoothly, unevenly, or not at all.

Some Specific Conditions to Consider

Mitchell and Gysbers (1978) identified a list of conditions they felt were prerequisite for successful transition to a comprehensive guidance and counseling program in a local school district. We believe these conditions are as applicable to today's situations as they were in the 1970s and 1980s.

1. All staff members are involved.
2. All staff members are committed to the common objective: total, integrated development of individual students.
3. The administration is committed to the comprehensive approach and is willing to negotiate (trade off), helping staff members identify current activities that do not contribute to priority outcomes and supporting staff members' abandonment of such activities in favor of those that do contribute to priority outcomes.
4. All staff members see the comprehensive systematic counseling and guidance program as a function of the total staff rather than the exclusive responsibility of the counselors.
5. Counselors are willing to give up such "security blankets" as writing lengthy reports of their contacts with counselees or seeing counselees individually on matters better addressed in a group.
6. Counselors are interested in acquiring competencies.
7. Staff development activities to help staff members acquire competencies needed for successful implementation of a comprehensive program are provided.
8. Time is made available for planning and designing the program and the evaluation, with all interested groups participating (students, parents, teachers, counselors, administrators, and community).
9. Program developers design an incremental transition rather than an abrupt transition that ignores the need for continuing many current activities and thrusts. (p. 36)

From the perspective of a statewide implementation effort, Jensen and Petersen (1997) identified similar conditions in describing the state of Utah's plan to implement comprehensive guidance and counseling programs in the schools of Utah. They affirmed that the model for guidance and counseling must be endorsed and supported by school and community leaders, that time must be devoted to the change process, that change requires strong support from building administrators in local school districts, and that teams of school counselors and administrators must participate in the change process. In addition, they stressed that the change process must be adequately funded.

Making the transition from guidance and counseling organized around the position-services model to guidance and counseling as a comprehensive program is not easy, automatic, or rapid. It involves changing the behavior patterns of students, parents, the teaching staff, administration, the community, and the guidance staff. Because of this, Mitchell and Gysbers (1978) pointed out that although all nine conditions are important, none is more important than the 10th and last condition:

10. Abrupt change is difficult and anxiety-producing; it tends to cause participants in the change to build barriers against it. (p. 36)

This 10th item speaks to perceptions of change as first or second order. Thus the magnitude of change as perceived by the individuals and groups involved is important to assess as the planning phrase begins to unfold.

A Sample Timetable of Tasks Involved in the Change Process

Because modifying an existing school guidance and counseling program or planning and implementing a new program is complex and time consuming, it is important in the getting-organized phase of planning to understand fully the tasks involved in the change process from beginning to end as well as the amount of time that may be involved. To help you understand possible tasks and time, we have prepared a sample timetable of tasks. It is organized around the four phases of change suggested by Mitchell and Gysbers (1978): planning, designing, implementing, and evaluating. We added the fifth phase, enhancing.

The time periods and the tasks presented in the sample timetable that follows are illustrative only. Some school districts move through the phases of change more quickly than others, whereas other districts enter at different phases depending on the nature and structure of their current program. Some tasks as presented may not fit some school districts, so tasks may need to be added or subtracted depending on specific school district needs and resources.

Note that the sample timetable below focuses on evaluation over a period of 5 years (a period of time chosen only for purposes of illustration). This continuing evaluation through the 4th, 5th, 6th, 7th, and 8th years allows sufficient time for program, personnel, and results data to be gathered and analyzed. The 9th and 10th years begin the program enhancement process during which evaluation data are used to inform us about how to redesign the program. The sample timetable is designed to provide you with a clear picture, a road map, of what needs to be done during an example period of 10 years to fully install, evaluate, and enhance a comprehensive guidance and counseling program. Use it as a checklist to create your own timetable that meets your needs in the getting-organized phase of planning for your district to follow.

You will also note that in Year 1, the first two points of Planning include Building a Foundation for Change and Getting Organized to Get There From Where You Are. You have seen these titles with their example tasks already, because they appear at the beginning of chapters 1 and 2 as advance organizers for these chapters. All of the chapters that follow use this format as shown below.

Year 1

Planning—Building a Foundation for Change
- Study the history of guidance and counseling in the schools.
- Learn about the people, events, and societal conditions that helped shape guidance and counseling in the schools.
- Understand the implications of the shift from position to services to program in the conceptualization and organization of guidance and counseling.

Planning—Getting Organized to Get There From Where You Are
- Decide that you want to change.
- Understand the necessary conditions for effective change.
- Expect resistance to change.
- Develop trust among counselors, teachers, and administrators.
- Form committees and work groups.
- Meet with the administration/district board of education.
- Provide leadership for change.
- Be active.

Planning—Conceptualizing the Comprehensive Guidance and Counseling Program Model
- Understand the theoretical foundation of the program.
- Learn about a perspective of student development.
- Learn about the place of comprehensive guidance and counseling programs in the educational enterprise.
- Learn about the four comprehensive guidance and counseling program elements that constitute a comprehensive program.
- Understand the power of common language.
- Appreciate the flexibility and adaptability of a program.
- Learn about six program imperatives.

Years 1–2

Planning—Conducting a Thorough Assessment of the Current Program
- Gather student and community status information.
- Identify current resource availability and use.
- Study current guidance and counseling program delivery.
- Gather perceptions about the program.
- Present a report describing the current program.

Years 2–3

Designing—Adapting the Guidance and Counseling Program Model
- Define the basic structure of your program.
- Identify and list student competencies by content areas and school levels or grade groupings.
- Reaffirm policy support.
- Establish priorities for program delivery (qualitative design).
- Establish parameters for resource allocation (quantitative design).
- Write down and distribute the description of the desired program.

Designing—Planning the Transition
- Specify changes needed to implement a comprehensive guidance and counseling program districtwide.
- Develop a plan for accomplishing districtwide program improvement.
- Begin building-level program improvement efforts.
- Expand the leadership base.

Years 3–4

Implementing—Making the Transition
- Develop the personnel, financial, and political resources needed for full program implementation.
- Focus on special projects.

- Facilitate building-level changes.
- Implement public relations activities.

Years 4–5 (and Thereafter)

Implementing—Managing the New Program
- Improve program activities.
- Enhance the role of the professional school counselor.
- Develop the building program plan.
- Monitor program implementation.

Implementing—Ensuring School Counselor Competency
- Implement a counselor performance improvement system.
- Support professional development.
- Address incompetence.
- Bring new counselors into the program and to the proper roles.
- Clarify roles of building guidance and counseling program/staff leaders.

Years 4–8

Evaluating—Evaluating the Program, Its Personnel, and Its Results
- Evaluate school counselor performance.
- Conduct program evaluation.
- Conduct results evaluation.

Years 9–10

Enhancing—Redesigning Your Comprehensive Guidance and Counseling Program
- Commit to the redesign process.
- Begin the redesign process.
- Gather updated needs information
- Make redesign decisions based on evaluation data and new information.
- Implement the new design.
- Understand that revitalization follows redesign.

Expect Resistance to Change

What Is Resistance to Change?

Connor et al. (2003) defined resistance to change as "any attempt to maintain the status quo when there is pressure for change" (p. 151). According to Connor et al. (2003), some people resist by refusing to move. Others become spectators, sitting on the sidelines criticizing but not participating. Some may even try to keep others from participating in change.

Expressing Resistance to Change

Given the above definition of resistance, what kind of resistance have school counselors and administrators exhibited when faced with change from their current organizational structure for guidance and counseling to that of a comprehensive program? Goodloe (1990) described the following expressions of resistance:

Reluctance to change: Principals were used to a guidance service model that focused on student scheduling. Older counselors near retirement had a built-in bias for the tried and true of the "old time" service delivery model. Since many of these educators steadfastly denied that the old guidance services were "broken," they flatly refused to even consider listening to the "fixing organizers" of the CGCP [Comprehensive Guidance and Counseling Program].

Double duty: Despite the convincing logic demonstrating the need for a new and improved organized guidance program, counselors were paralyzed by the administrators' conflicting message: "Okay, establish the new program, but continue to maintain your present list of duty assignments." Schools failed to "streamline and displace" nonguidance functions to other paraprofessionals or clerical staff. "Add-ons" continually threatened the program's successful implementation.

Time and stress management: As the message of change worked its way through the system's tightly connected communications grapevine, and news came out that the new program demanded a greater time commitment and contributed to more job stress, the pilot expansion schools became more and more skeptical and resistant. The sentiment was, "Why trade a new model when the old one works fine?"

Killer statement: If given the chance to solidify, resistance to change blocked the road to innovation. Statements such as "Ain't it awful!" "If only . . . . ." "We've tried that!" "Yes, but . . . ." "THEM vs. US" "Let's wait until . . . ." had a debilitating effect on the will and energy to change. (pp. 72–73)

Appreciate the Challenges Involved

Behind these statements may lie fears of those faced with change. This human condition of some members of the school counseling and administrative staff must be understood. The failure of some staff members to embrace a program approach can be appreciated if their original justification for existence and their current functions and operational patterns are understood. Many school counselors, for example, maintain they are trapped and can react only minimally to change; they are victims of school rigidity and bureaucracy that place them in quasi-administrative and services functions that impede them from achieving guidance objectives (Aubrey, 1973).

It is easy to label those who resist as trouble makers and to dismiss resistance as negative and malicious acts. Connor et al. (2003) pointed out, however, that "a more constructive, and in the long run more effective, approach is to acknowledge the validity of the class of responses as a whole and respond from a position of understanding and respect" (p. 151). We need to appreciate the challenges involved in developing, implementing, and evaluating a comprehensive guidance and counseling program, and thus understand why some school counselors and administrators might resist.

The failure of some school counselors and administrators to readily embrace a comprehensive program approach to guidance and counseling can be better understood if the challenges of this approach to organizing guidance and counseling are known. Here are a few examples of these challenges:

- Guidance and counseling programs are developmental.
- Guidance and counseling programs serve all students and their parents.
- Guidance and counseling programs require school counselors to do large-group presentations, small-group counseling, individual student planning activities, consultation, and referral.
- Guidance and counseling programs facilitate students' academic, career, and personal/social development.
- Guidance and counseling program activities are aimed at explicitly stated expectations for student results.
- Guidance and counseling programs are intentionally delivered and are accountable.

Why do some school counselors and administrators consider these statements as challenges? They are challenges because they may require the school staff to change their work behavior. They also may require some counselors to acquire new skills to fulfill the responsibilities of new guidance program emphases. In addition, some counselors may fear the potential loss of status and power they enjoy from being associated with the authority of the principal. New relationships with teachers and students required by the program may make some counselors uncomfortable. New demands and the need to develop new counselor competencies threaten others. The most difficult challenge most counselors face, however, may be the prospect of accepting responsibility for helping students achieve success in school. Can counselors, working in a comprehensive program, deliver what they propose? Can they be accountable?

Another challenge counselors face in considering change is balancing the "costs" involved (the personal and professional time involved, the changes in day-by-day work behavior) with the benefits to be gained. Will the benefits outweigh the costs involved in working through the transition? One school district (Davis, 2002) faced this challenge and found that the hard work involved paid off in the following ways:

> The comprehensive guidance model provided the immediate structure to establish the program in every school. Administrators received comprehensive guidance training. A few had to be converted to a model that allocated considerable time for class curriculum. They thought a counseling program should be limited to individual and small-group counseling for identified students. Soon after the program began, principals and teachers observed positive behavior changes as students began applying the skills the counselors were teaching. They acknowledged the value of everyone receiving the curriculum. Skills were reinforced throughout the school. Siblings, friends, and school personnel reminded one another to apply the skills the counselor had taught. Data collected in each school gave evidence that violations of school rules and negative behavior were decreasing. Other districts using the curriculum also reported positive behavior changes. (p. 225)

Develop Trust Among Counselors, Teachers, and Administrators

Because of the tendency of people to resist change and because of the challenges and risks involved in making the transition to a comprehensive guidance and counseling program, guidance staff may require time and privacy as they deal with the issues involved. Time and privacy are necessary to work through possible resistance to change that may not emerge otherwise and to develop trust and working relationships as a total staff. This is true particularly for school districts with personnel at elementary, junior high or middle school, and high school levels. Current duties at these levels often do not provide time for full staff discussions about program direction and focus. Thus having time and privacy for open dialogue, confrontation, and the processing of attitudes and feelings during the planning process is a necessity.

Staff trust can be developed and nurtured through the full involvement of staff in the change process. In the earlier section, Decide That You Want to Change, an example was given about how the guidance staff of one school district met several times as a full staff to assess the need for change. One result of these discussions was the decision to change; to take charge of their own destiny (Hargens & Fuston, 1997). Another result, just as important, was the full involvement of the staff in the change process.

Having staff involved in the initial decision to make changes and then in the steps involved in the transition process can help bring about staff trust and commitment; we are all in this together. It also is important that staff members realize that their advice and counsel will be put to legitimate use. Going through the frustrations and joys of making the transition to a comprehensive program can bond staff into a full-fledged guidance and counseling team. As Maliszewski (1997) remarked, a person

> can't steal second with one foot on first. . . . Change implies risk taking and hard work. . . . Personal and professional growth are rewards for counselors who develop and implement "risk taking" approaches to ensure that guidance programs produce positive results for all students. (p. 217)

Form Committees and Work Groups

Once consensus to change has been reached, the next step is to form committees and work groups to accomplish the tasks involved. Only two committees are recommended throughout the entire process: a steering committee and a school–community advisory committee. The majority of improvement tasks can be handled by forming work groups. It is desirable that the superintendent of schools or the designee of the superintendent formally appoint the members of both committees.

Steering Committee

The steering committee should be large enough to reflect a cross-section of the ideas and interests of the staff but not so large as to be unwieldy and inefficient. Ordinarily, the steering committee is composed of guidance personnel or representatives from each grade level or building involved. Building administrators and the superintendent or a member of the cabinet are essential members, as are such individuals as the directors of vocational education and special education. Sometimes teachers, parents, school board members, or students also may serve. The chairperson of the steering committee is the guidance and counseling program leader. If no such title exists, then the person who is administratively responsible for the guidance and counseling program should be chairperson.

The steering committee is responsible for managing the efforts needed to plan, design, implement, evaluate, and enhance the district's guidance and counseling program. This committee is a decision-making body and is responsible for outlining the tasks involved and making certain that the resources needed to carry out these tasks are available. It monitors the activities of the work groups and coordinates their tasks. The steering committee not only makes process-change decisions but also program change decisions.

To carry out these responsibilities, one of the first tasks for the steering committee is to prepare a timetable of the steps it has chosen to take. Because it is the master timetable for program change, it requires careful thought and attention. Allow sufficient planning time for this phase of getting organized. Keep in mind that the timetable will probably be modified as the program improvement process unfolds. The master timetable is important because it provides those involved with an overview of the scope and sequence of the improvement process. It also shows the relationship of the steps and activities. Potential problems can be identified and therefore anticipated and dealt with in advance. Further, the master timetable provides those involved with an indication of the resources and materials required.

As your local timetable for tasks is being developed, consider the sample timetable for program installation presented in the first part of this chapter. This book is organized on the basis of this sample timetable so that the timetable can provide advice and counsel every step of the way as well as serve as a beginning point and as a checklist for all program planning, designing, implementing, evaluating, and enhancing processes.

In addition to being responsible for the steps, resources, and strategies needed to make the transition to a comprehensive program, the steering committee is responsible for developing a plan for public relations through advocacy. This may be done later in the program improvement process, but whenever it is done, careful planning is required. Effective public relations do not just happen, nor can they be separated from the basic comprehensive program. In fact, the best public relations begin with a sound, comprehensive guidance and counseling program. The best public relations in the world cannot cover up an ineffective guidance and counseling program that does not meet the needs of its consumers.

School–Community Advisory Committee

The school–community advisory committee is composed of representatives from the school and community. The membership of this committee will vary according to the size of the school district and the community and can include such individuals as an administrator (assistant superintendent, principal); the guidance program leader; a representative of the teaching staff; a representative of the student body; representatives from business, industry, and labor; a representative from the mental health community; a representative from the parent–teacher association; and a newspaper editor or other media representative. If any of these individuals are serving on the steering committee (with the exception of the guidance program leader), they probably should not serve here.

The school–community advisory committee acts as a liaison between the school and community and provides recommendations concerning the needs of students and the community. A primary duty of the committee is to advise those involved in the guidance program improvement effort. The committee is not a policy- or decision-making body; rather it is a source of advice, counsel, and support. It is a communication link between those involved in the guidance program improvement effort and the school and community. The committee meets throughout the transition period and continues as a permanent part of the improved guidance program. A community person should be chairperson. The use and involvement of a school–community advisory committee will vary according to the program and the community, but in all cases membership must be more than in name only. Community involvement and interaction are important, and advisory committee members can be particularly helpful in developing and implementing the public relations plans for the community.

Work Groups

To accomplish the work involved in making the transition to a comprehensive guidance and counseling program, we recommend the use of work groups. Work groups are small groups of staff members, usually counselors, but sometimes also including administrators, teachers, parents, and students who are assigned specific tasks that need to be completed as part of the transition process. Assignments to work groups will vary depending on the tasks involved. Work groups form and disband as needed.

Here are some suggestions concerning work groups:

1. Use as many work groups as possible because they reduce the overall workload and provide opportunities for as many people as possible to become involved and learn about remodeling and revitalizing the guidance and counseling program. Remember: Never use one person when two will do!

2. Some work groups should include counselors only; some should include administrators or others. Specific suggestions about work group membership are provided in subsequent chapters.
3. Work groups are responsible to the steering committee. Work group leadership is drawn from the steering committee. In fact, in the first phases of the improvement process, the steering committee's agenda will consist of work group reports.
4. Charges to work groups need to be specific and feasible. Each group exists for one purpose; when the purpose is accomplished, the work group disbands.
5. Work group membership should include cross-grade-level representation when appropriate. This enhances trust and builds knowledge among the members that will provide a foundation for the comprehensive guidance and counseling program.

Meet With the Administration/District Board of Education

Because the development and installation of a comprehensive guidance and counseling program is a school district issue as well as a building issue, the district's administration and board of education must be brought into the planning process at the very beginning. Early on it is important for the steering committee, working closely with the superintendent, to meet with the board and inform its members about the need for the shift from the position service model to a comprehensive program to meet the needs of students, parents, teachers, and the community more effectively. The goal of the initial meeting is to inform the board, gain its support, and secure its authorization to work toward improving the guidance and counseling program in the district.

At the initial meeting, sharing with the board the resolution concerning guidance passed by the National School Boards Association may be useful. The first part of the resolution states that the association "encourages local school boards to support comprehensive guidance and counseling programs, kindergarten through grade 12, staffed by professionally trained counseling personnel" (National School Boards Association, 1986). At the initial meeting it also is important to obtain in writing from the board assurances concerning its authorization of the improvement process. The assurances requested by the steering committee could include those listed in the state of Missouri:

- Provide time or district staff to develop, implement, and manage a quality, comprehensive guidance program.
- Receive periodic reports from administration and the advisory council.
- Take the action on decisions needed to ensure continued program development and progress.
- Use program evaluation findings in making funding decisions.
- With the assistance of the advisory council, direct the staff to publicize the program to the community.
- Provide adequate funding to assure continued program development, implementation, and evaluation. (Gysbers, Kosteck-Bunch, Magnuson, & Starr, 2002, p. 27)

Provide Leadership for Change

If you are the school district's guidance and counseling program leader, you will have the primary responsibility for organizing and managing the program improvement process. If you do not take the primary leadership role for these efforts, they will not get done. You must cause, lead, implement, and maintain the work accomplished during this important time of change in your school district. You are the manager of the improvement process as well as the program.

As the manager of the improvement process, you must develop and monitor the plan for change. Specifically, you must develop the proposal to change and the time frame you anticipate that will take. You must form the steering committee, chair it, and plan its agendas and meeting schedule. You must also form, or cause to form, the school–community advisory committee and the various work groups as needed. You should attend as many meetings of the work groups as feasible to keep them on task, and you must attend all steering and school–community advisory committee meetings. They are, after all, steering and advising the program for which you are accountable.

As the program leader, you not only continue your usual duties but also add the responsibilities of being the primary missionary for the improved program. You must be very clear about the model you and your district want to adopt or adapt. The success of this project is directly linked to your conceptualization of the guidance and counseling program. For a while you may be the only person who may grasp the new design, the student competencies, the comprehensive nature of the program, and the means for redirecting the activities of the guidance staff.

As the school district's guidance program leader, you have responsibility not only for improving and managing the program but also for assisting the staff involved. As explained in *Leading and Managing Your School Guidance Program Staff* (Henderson & Gysbers, 1998), we use the "generic title, 'guidance program staff leader,' to connote the interconnectedness of program and staff leadership responsibilities" (p. 21). At this point, the focus is on your staff leader responsibilities. You develop mechanisms for educating and involving counselors and administrators. You bring all of the members of the steering committee along as the process unfolds. Ultimately, the counselors on the steering committee provide peer leadership to their colleagues, under your direction.

You need to keep the purposes for changing the program in front of everyone for the duration of the change process. Remember that you are doing all this to better facilitate students' academic career and personal/social development and parent involvement by the more appropriate use of school counselors' unique talents and skills. We advise you to develop a support system for yourself. This might include committed school counselors in the district, your own supervisor(s) who is(are) eager for the change to come, and guidance and counseling program leaders from other districts who have embarked on similar projects. Involvement in state and national associations for school counselors and counselor educators provides useful assistance and affiliation as well.

Be Active

Make a Commitment to Action

It is important to remember that many systems grind along with much polarization; even some school counselors compose their worlds of grim problems to be worked through. You may be flooded with the destructive aspects of situations. You may find that some individuals with whom you work are impressed with the weaknesses of others and stereotype them with all the incompetencies they can uncover. Although you cannot ignore destructive forces, the positive prescription is to be alert for the constructive forces that are sometimes masked and suppressed in a problem-oriented system.

Some people have as great an innate capacity for joy as they have for resentment, but resentment causes them to overlook opportunities for joy. People who are locked into destructive situations often focus on their differences. As a leader, your job is to help them discover and build on their commonalities. Unhappy people tend to emphasize past wrongs, and as a result, use them to destroy the present and future. As a leader, your task is to help change the present so that there will be a new past on which to create the future (Shepard, 1974). Make a commitment to action!

Be Optimistic

The tasks in making the transition from an undefined program to a defined program are complex and difficult. They require time and perseverance. Although the time required may seem long, it does provide the opportunity for counselors (and everyone else) to learn how to master the new program. Thus the getting-organized phase of planning should be designed to assist those involved to develop a vision of what the comprehensive program will look like and to become committed to working to make it happen. Our belief is that staff development enables people to have vision and involvement and raises their level of commitment. Staff development begins during the getting organized phase and must be carried out throughout the entire program improvement and revitalizing process. Be optimistic!

References

Aubrey, R. F. (1973). Organizational victimization of school counselors. *The School Counselor, 20,* 346–354.

Connor, P. E., Lake, L. K., & Stackman, R. W. (2003). *Managing organizational change* (3rd ed.) Westport, CT: Proaeger.

Davis, D. (2002). Revising and enhancing the Davis School District comprehensive guidance program. In P. Henderson & N. C. Gysbers (Eds.), *Implementing comprehensive school guidance programs: Critical leadership issues and successful responses* (pp. 219–228). Greensboro, NC: CAPS.

Erickson, T. (1997). Box Elder comprehensive guidance program. In N. C. Gysbers & P. Henderson (Eds.), *Comprehensive guidance programs that work—II* (pp. 125–137). Greensboro, NC: ERIC Counseling and Student Services Clearinghouse.

Goodloe, J. P. (1990). Comprehensive guidance in Montgomery County, Maryland. In N. C. Gysbers (Ed.), *Comprehensive guidance programs that work* (pp 63–78) Ann Arbor, MI: ERIC Counseling and Personnel Service Clearinghouse.

Gysbers, N. C., Kosteck-Bunch, L., Magnuson, C. S., & Starr, M. F. (2002). *Missouri comprehensive guidance program. A manual for program development, implementation, evaluation, and enhancement.* Columbia: University of Missouri, Instructional Materials Laboratory.

Hargens, M., & Fuston, J. K. (1997). Comprehensive guidance program of the St. Joseph district. In N. C. Gysbers & P. Henderson (Eds.), *Comprehensive guidance programs that work—II* (pp. 61–74). Greensboro, NC: ERIC Counseling and Student Services Clearinghouse.

Henderson, P., & Gysbers, N. C. (1998). *Leading and managing your school guidance program staff.* Alexandria, VA: American Counseling Association.

Jensen, L., & Petersen, J. (1997). The comprehensive guidance program in Utah. In N. C. Gysbers & P. Henderson (Eds.), *Comprehensive guidance programs that work—II* (pp. 89–106). Greensboro, NC: ERIC Counseling and Student Services Clearinghouse.

Maliszewski, S. J. (1997). Developing a comprehensive guidance system in the Omaha Public Schools. In N. C. Gysbers & P. Henderson (Eds.), *Comprehensive guidance programs that work—II* (pp. 195–219). Greensboro, NC: ERIC Counseling and Student Services Clearinghouse.

Mitchell, A. M., & Gysbers, N. C. (1978). Comprehensive school guidance and counseling programs. In *The status of guidance and counseling in the nation's schools* (pp. 23–39). Washington, DC: American Personnel and Guidance Association.

National School Boards Association. (1986). *Resolution on guidance and counseling*. Alexandria, VA: Author.

Shepard, H. (1974). *Rules of thumb for change agents*. Unpublished manuscript.

Rylander, C. K. (2002). *Guiding our children toward success: How Texas school counselors spend their time*. Austin, TX: Texas Comptroller of Public Accounts.

Vandergrift, J. A. (1999). *Are Arizona public schools making the best use of school counselors? Results of a 3-year study of counselors' time use*. Phoenix, AZ: Morrison Institute for Public Policy.

Waters, T., Marzano, R. J., McNulty, B. (2003). *Balanced leadership: What 30 years of research tells us about the effect of leadership on student achievement*. Aurora, CO: Mid-Continent Research for Education and Learning.

Chapter 3

A Comprehensive Guidance and Counseling Program: Theoretical Foundations and Organizational Structure

Planning—Conceptualizing the Comprehensive Guidance and Counseling Program

- Understand the theoretical foundation of the program.
- Learn about a perspective of student development.
- Learn about the place of comprehensive guidance and counseling programs in the educational enterprise.
- Learn about the four guidance and counseling program elements that constitute a comprehensive program.
- Understand the power of common language.
- Appreciate the flexibility and adaptability of a program.
- Learn about six program imperatives.

 The second phase of planning consists of conceptualizing the comprehensive guidance and counseling program, of bringing together all of the necessary and appropriate guidance and counseling activities and services, and of arranging them into a program configuration. To accomplish this task, it is first necessary to have a firm understanding of the theoretical foundation of the program as well as a perspective of student development. It is also necessary to understand the place such a program has in the overall educational enterprise K–12.

To assist you in the conceptualization process, we begin this chapter with a presentation of a theoretical foundation for comprehensive guidance and counseling programs (Henderson, in press) and a perspective of student development called life career development (Gysbers, Heppner, & Johnston, 2003; Gysbers & Moore, 1975, 1981; McDaniels & Gysbers, 1992). Next we present the two major education systems: the instruction program and the guidance and counseling program. Then we describe the four program elements of a comprehensive guidance and counseling program, including (a) content, (b) organizational framework, (c) resources, and (d) development, management, and accountability.

Understand the Theoretical Foundation of the Program

According to *Random House Webster's Unabridged Dictionary* (2001), a theory "is a more or less verified or established explanation accounting for known facts or phenomena"

(p. 1968). It is "a coherent group of general propositions used as principles of explanation for a class of phenomena" (p. 1967). In keeping with this definition of theory, Henderson (2005) presented a brief history of school counseling theory, identified seven fundamental questions to be answered by theory, and then described 27 major principles that provide answers to the seven fundamental questions. These 27 principles become the "principles of explanation for a class of phenomena," in this case, comprehensive guidance and counseling programs K–12, and are presented below as follows:

Principle 1: As with other dimensions of their development, all children and adolescents benefit from assistance in accomplishing the age-appropriate tasks related to their academic, career, and personal/social development.

Principle 2: All children and adolescents can benefit from interventions designed to assist their academic, career, and personal/social development.

Principle 3: Some children/adolescents need more assistance in accomplishing the age-appropriate academic, career, and personal/social developmental tasks. These children/adolescents benefit from preventive or remedial interventions specially designed to assist them achieve tasks appropriate to their developmental level.

Principle 4: School counselors are qualified to make contributions to all children's and adolescents' development in the areas of academic (educational), career, and personal/social development.

Principle 5: School counselors can design and deliver interventions to meet students' developmental needs and design and deliver interventions to meet needs of students for prevention and remediation, thereby helping to close gaps between specific groups of students and their peers.

Principle 6: School counselors' interventions in students' academic, career, and personal/social development assist students to acquire and apply skills, attitudes, and knowledge that promote development in those three dimension of human growth and development.

Principle 7: School counselors can assist other adults to enhance their work with students' academic/educational, career, and personal/social development, and for the purpose of removing personal barriers to individual student's success.

Principle 8: School counselors work with others in the school system on behalf of students to support accomplishment of the system's mission and to assist in the removal of systemic barriers to student success.

Principle 9: The work of school counselors should be organized as a program.

Principle 10: The delivery system dividing program activities into the four program components of guidance curricula, individual student planning, responsive services, and system support is the most effective and efficient means for organizing the program.

Principle 11: The four program activity components described as the delivery system for the model school counseling program include all the means to impact students' academic, career, and personal/social development: guidance curricula, individual student planning, responsive services, and system support.

Principle 12: School counseling program activities can be designed that effectively impact all students' academic, career, and personal/social development and that help those students whose healthy academic, career, and/or personal/social development is threatened or interrupted.

Principle 13: Intentionally designed interventions targeting identified needs or specified goals and objectives are more effective than interventions that are not intentionally designed.

Principle 14: A systematic approach to developing the school counseling program (i.e., planning and building the foundation, designing the delivery system, implementing and monitoring the program, holding program staff accountable, and evaluating the program) ensures its effectiveness and relevancy.

Principle 15: Collaborative, cooperative planning with parents/guardians, teachers, administrators, staff, and community members in developing a school counseling program results in the program being effective and an integral part of the total school mission.

Principle 16: Effective local school counseling programs are designed with awareness of local demographics and political conditions and on needs assessments based on locally gathered data.

Principle 17: Establishing priorities for and recognizing parameters within the program are critical to effective management and implementation of school counseling programs.

Principle 18: There are organizational procedures that school counselors can use to manage implementation of their programs for effectiveness, efficiency, and relevancy to the school.

Principle 19: Accountability for student results, school counselor performance, and program completeness is essential to ensuring the effectiveness and relevance of school counseling programs, and it requires the collection and use of data.

Principle 20: Leadership for school counseling programs is a shared responsibility between schools counselors and school principals.

Principle 21: Having benefited from school counselors' interventions, children and adolescents are more ready to learn academically and to be successful in school.

Principle 22: Explicit statements of the results desired for students better ensure their achievement for those results.

Principle 23: Evaluation of student results, school counselor performance, and program completeness is essential to ensuring the effectiveness and relevance of school counseling programs, and it requires the collection and use of data.

Principle 24: Evaluation of student results is based on established standards for the measurement of student development, growth, and change.

Principle 25: Evaluation of school counselors' performance is based on established standards for school counseling practice.

Principle 26: Evaluation of program completeness is based on alignment with the American School Counselor Association (ASCA) National Model and the local program design.

Principle 27: The purpose of evaluation is improvement.

Individually, each principle describes a determining characteristic of a comprehensive guidance and counseling program. Taken together, they constitute the guiding principles that characterize and operationalize the total program. When viewed holistically, they represent the principles for guiding the overall planning, designing, implementing, evaluating, and enhancing of the program.

Learn About a Perspective of Student Development

Life Career Development

Life career development is defined as self-development over the life span through the integration of the roles, settings, and events in a person's life. The word *life* in the definition indicates that the focus of this conception of human growth and development is on the total person—the human career. The word *career* identifies and relates the many and often varied roles in which individuals are involved (student, worker, consumer, citizen, parent), the settings in which individuals find themselves (home, school, community), and the events that occur over their lifetimes (entry job, marriage, divorce, retirement). The word *development* is used to indicate that individuals are always in the process of becoming. When used in sequence, the words *life career development* bring these separate meanings together, but at the same time a greater meaning evolves. Life career development describes total individuals, each of whom is unique with his or her own lifestyle.

Added to the basic configuration of life career development are the influencing factors of gender, ethnic origin, spirituality, race, sexual orientation, and socioeconomic status. All of these factors play important roles in shaping the life roles, life settings, and life events of all ages and circumstances over the life span. These factors are important to the conception of life career development because we live in a nation that is part of a world economy; it is increasingly diverse racially, religiously, and ethnically, and yet has common themes that connect us all. Our nation continues to change its views on what it means to be female or male, educationally and occupationally. Socioeconomic status continues to play an important role in shaping an individual's socialization and current and future status (Gysbers et al., 2003).

Career Consciousness

A major goal in using the theoretical perspective of life career development is to assist individuals to identify, describe, and understand the dynamics of their own life career development, to create within them career consciousness, that is, the ability to visualize and plan their life careers. "Included within the idea of consciousness is a person's background, education, politics, insight, values, emotions, and philosophy" (Reich, 1971, p. 15). But consciousness, according to Reich, is more than this. It is the whole person. It is the person's way of creating his or her own life. Thus the challenge is to assist individuals to become career conscious. The challenge is to assist them to project themselves into future possible life roles, life settings, and life events; to realize the importance of gender, ethnic origin, spirituality, race, sexual orientation, and socioeconomic status on their development; and then to relate their projections to their present situations for consideration and incorporation into their plans to achieve their goals or resolve their problems.

Contained in the concept of career consciousness is the notion of *possible selves*. What are possible selves? According to Markus and Nurius (1986), "Possible selves represent individuals' ideas of what they might become, what they would like to become, and what they are afraid of becoming, and thus provide a conceptual link between cognition and motivation" (p. 954). Why are possible selves important? "Possible selves are important, first, because they function as incentives for future behavior (i.e., they are selves to be approached or avoided) and, second, because they provide an evaluative and interpretive context for the current view of self" (p. 954).

In the definition of life career development, the word *career* has a substantially different meaning from that in some other definitions. Here it focuses on all aspects of life, not as separate entities but as interrelated parts of the whole person. The term *career*, when viewed from this broad perspective, is not a new word for occupation. People have careers; the work world or marketplace has occupations. Unfortunately, too many people use the word *career* when they should use the word *occupation*. Further, the term *career* is not restricted to some people. All people have a career; their life is their career. Thus, the words *life career development* do not delineate and describe only one part of human growth and development.

Although it is useful to focus at times on different aspects of development—physical, emotional, and intellectual—there also is a need to integrate these aspects of development. Life career development is advocated as an organizing and integrating concept for understanding and facilitating human growth and development.

Wolfe and Kolb (1980) summed up the life view of career development as follows:

Career development involves one's whole life, not just occupation. As such, it concerns the whole person, needs and wants, capacities and potentials, excitements and anxieties, insights and blindspots, warts and all. More than that, it concerns him/her in the ever-changing contexts of his/her life. The environmental pressures and constraints, the bonds that tie him/her to significant others, responsibilities to children and aging parents, the total structure of one's circumstances are also factors that must be understood and reckoned with. In these terms, career development and personal development converge. Self and circumstance—evolving, changing, unfolding in mutual interaction—constitute the focus and the drama of career development. (pp. 1–2)

Goals of a Program From a Life Career Development Perspective

One goal of a comprehensive school guidance and counseling program, founded on the concept of life career development, is to assist students to acquire competencies to handle the here-and-now issues that affect their growth and development. These issues may include changes in the family structure, expanded social relationships, substance abuse, sexual experimentation, changes in physical and emotional maturation, and peer pressure. Another goal is to create career consciousness in students to assist them to project themselves into possible future life roles, settings, and events; analyze them; relate their findings to their present identity and situations; and make informed, personal, education, and career choices based on their findings.

Learn About the Place of Comprehensive Guidance and Counseling Programs in the Educational Enterprise

Over the decades of the past century, discussions have centered on the proper place of guidance and counseling in education. Early on writers stressed the point of view that guidance and counseling are an integral part of education, not something "being wished upon the schools by a group of enthusiasts because there was no other agency to handle it" (Myers, 1923, p. 139). Some writers, particularly Jones and Hand (1938), viewed guidance and counseling as an inseparable part of education. They emphasized that teaching involved both guidance and instruction.

What is the proper place of guidance and counseling? We support the position that guidance and counseling are an integral part of education. We envision education as having two interrelated systems, namely, the instruction program and the guidance and counseling program, as noted in Figure 3.1. The instruction program typically includes such disciplines as fine arts, career and technical education, science, physical education, mathematics, social studies, foreign language, and English (language arts). Each of these disciplines has standards that identify the knowledge and skills students are to learn as they progress throughout their school years. Similarly, comprehensive guidance and counseling programs have standards that identify the knowledge and skills students are to learn as they are involved in the activities and services of comprehensive programs. Typically, these knowledge and skills (standards) are grouped under titles such as academic, career, and personal/social development.

In a school setting, even though the instruction program is by far the largest in terms of numbers of student standards, it is not more important than the guidance and counseling program. That is why the circles in Figure 3.1, which depict the education systems, are equal in size. Figure 3.1 also illustrates the fact that separate learnings in each system (unshaded areas) require specific attention. At the same time, these learnings overlap (shaded area), requiring that at times the instruction program supports the guidance and counseling program, and that at other times the guidance and counseling program supports the instruction program. It is not a case of either/or but both/and.

Richardson and Baron (1975) outlined a similar schema but labeled their systems as two major purposes of education: social learnings and personal learnings. They pointed out that

Figure 3.1
Two Major Interrelated Education Systems

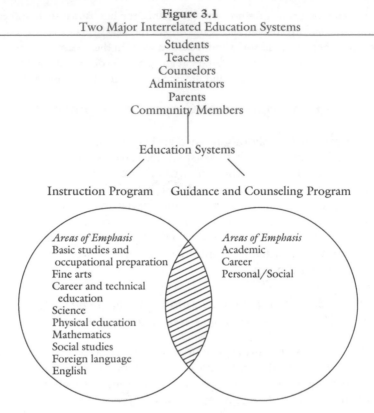

teachers were primarily responsible for the instructional function—that of "guiding and learning of developmental tasks in the area of 'social learnings'" (p. 21)—whereas counselors were primarily responsible for the counseling function—that of "guiding the learning of developmental tasks in the area of 'personal learnings'" (p. 21). They also pointed out that both the guidance and counseling program and the instruction program have developmental and remedial elements.

Learn About the Four Guidance and Counseling Program Elements That Constitute a Comprehensive Program

What is a comprehensive guidance and counseling program? We define a program as having a common language organizational framework with a specific configuration of planned, sequenced, and coordinated guidance and counseling activities and services based on student, school, and community needs and resources, designed to serve all students and their parents or guardians in a local school district. As the American School Counselor Association (2003) suggested, it is "comprehensive in scope, preventative in design, and developmental in nature" (p. 13).

The structure (see Figure 3.2) we recommend for a comprehensive guidance and counseling program has four elements: (a) program content; (b) organizational framework; (c) resources; and (d) development, management, and accountability. The content element identifies student competencies (cast as standards) considered important by a school district for students to master as a result of their participation in the district's comprehensive guidance and counseling program. The organizational framework element contains three structural components (definition, rationale, assumptions) and four program com-

Figure 3.2
Comprehensive Guidance and Counseling Program Elements

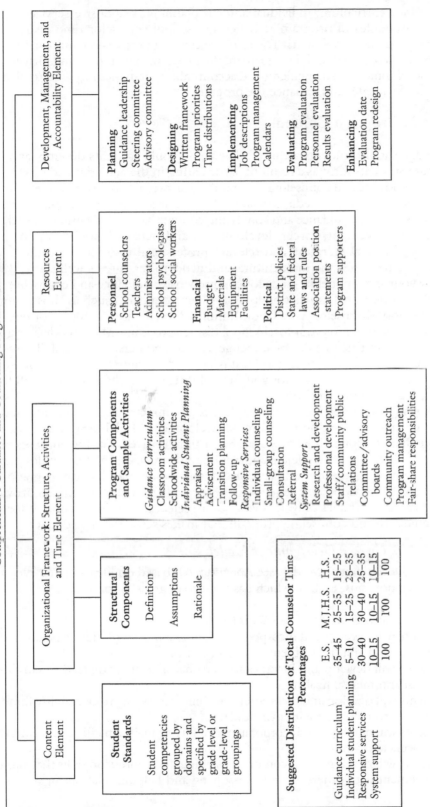

Content Element

Student Standards

Student competencies grouped by domains and specified by grade level or grade-level groupings

Organizational Framework: Structure, Activities, and Time Element

Structural Components

Definition

Assumptions

Rationale

Suggested Distribution of Total Counselor Time Percentages

	E.S.	M.J.H.S.	H.S.
Guidance curriculum	35–45	25–35	15–25
Individual student planning	5–10	15–25	25–35
Responsive services	30–40	30–40	25–35
System support	10–15	10–15	10–15
	100	100	100

Program Components and Sample Activities

Guidance Curriculum
Classroom activities
Schoolwide activities
Individual Student Planning
Appraisal
Advisement
Transition planning
Follow-up
Responsive Services
Individual counseling
Small-group counseling
Consultation
Referral
System Support
Research and development
Professional development
Staff/community public relations
Committee/advisory boards
Community outreach
Program management
Fair-share responsibilities

Resources Element

Personnel
School counselors
Teachers
Administrators
School psychologists
School social workers

Financial
Budget
Materials
Equipment
Facilities

Political
District policies
State and federal laws and rules
Association position statements
Program supporters

Development, Management, and Accountability Element

Planning
Guidance leadership
Steering committee
Advisory committee

Designing
Written framework
Program priorities
Time distributions

Implementing
Job descriptions
Program management
Calendars

Evaluating
Program evaluation
Personnel evaluation
Results evaluation

Enhancing
Evaluation date
Program redesign

Note. E.S. = elementary school; M.J.H.S. = middle/junior high school; H.S. = high school.

ponents (guidance curriculum, individual student planning, responsive services, system support), with examples of program activities and school counselor time distributions across the four program components. The resource element presents the human, financial, and policy resources required to fully implement the program. The fourth and final element contains the development, management, and accountability activities required to plan, design, implement, evaluate, and enhance the program.

Element 1: Program Content

What knowledge should students acquire, what skills should students develop, and what attitudes should students form as a result of participating in the activities and services of a comprehensive guidance and counseling program? To answer this question for your school district, begin by reviewing the educational goals of your school district and your state. Often such goals will have guidance and counseling content included focusing on such topics as academic achievement, career development, and personal/social development. Examine the professional literature and relevant professional association position statements. Make sure to review the multicultural and gender literature as well (Sink, 2002). Finally, review your state model or guide for comprehensive guidance and counseling programs as well as professional association lists of student standards such as those found in the American School Counselor Association National Model (ASCA, 2005) for ones that can be adopted or adapted for your local school district program. Many models or guides group standards under the domains of academic, career, and personal/social. These titles work well, but always consider state and local issues and circumstances when identifying the student standards that are right for your school district and the labels you will use to title the groupings of these standards.

In the following pages you will find example lists of competencies or student standards as they are often labeled from the Life Career Development Model, ASCA, and the state of Texas. Note the variation in how they are labeled and displayed. For the purposes of this chapter, we list only the broad student standards or competencies. In most guides they are further subdivided by grade or grade-level groupings (sometimes labeled as grade level expectations) so that a scope and sequence of expected student outcomes is provided. Remember, these are examples only. It is your job to select the program content for your local school guidance and counseling program that makes sense for your district.

Example: Life Career Development Model

The Life Career Development Model (see Appendix A), based on life career development theory, uses three domains, each of which has five broad goals as follows:

- *Self-Knowledge and Interpersonal Skills Goals*
  1. Students will develop and incorporate an understanding of unique personal characteristics and abilities of themselves and others.
  2. Students will develop and incorporate personal skills that will lead to satisfactory physical and mental health.
  3. Students will develop and incorporate an ability to assume responsibility for themselves and to manage their environment.
  4. Students will develop and incorporate the ability to maintain effective relationships with peers and adults.
  5. Students will develop and incorporate listening and expression skills that allow for involvement with others in problem-solving and helping relationships.

- *Life Roles, Settings, and Events Goals*
  1. Students will develop and incorporate those skills that lead to an effective role as a learner.
  2. Students will develop and incorporate an understanding of the legal and economic principles and practices that lead to responsible daily living.
  3. Students will develop and incorporate understanding of the interactive effects of lifestyles, life roles, settings, and events.
  4. Students will develop and incorporate an understanding of stereotypes and how they affect career identity.
  5. Students will develop and incorporate an ability to express future concerns and the ability to imagine themselves in these situations.
- *Life Career Planning Goals*
  1. Students will develop and incorporate an understanding of producer rights and responsibilities.
  2. Students will develop and incorporate an understanding of how attitudes and values affect decisions, actions, and lifestyles.
  3. Students will develop and incorporate an understanding of the decision-making process and how the decisions they make are influenced by previous decisions made by themselves and others.
  4. Students will develop and incorporate the ability to generate decision-making alternatives, gather necessary information, and assess the risks and consequences of alternatives.
  5. Students will develop and incorporate skills in clarifying values, expanding interests and capabilities, and evaluating progress toward goals.

For each of the goals in this model, competencies are listed by grade levels K–12. For example:

- *Domain:* Self-Knowledge and Interpersonal Skills
- *Goal:* Students will develop and incorporate an understanding of the unique personal characteristics and abilities of themselves and others.
- *Competencies for Grade K:*
  1. I can tell what I look like and some things I like to do.
  2. I can tell something special about myself.
  3. I can tell something special about other people I know.
  4. I can describe myself to someone who doesn't know me.
  5. I can tell how people are different and that they have different skills and abilities.
  6. I can tell how my special characteristics and abilities are important to me.
  7. I can tell how my characteristics and abilities change and how they can be expanded.
  8. I can compare the characteristics and abilities of others I know with my own and accept the differences.
  9. I can list the skills I already possess and those I hope to develop in the future.
  10. I can discuss the value of understanding my unique characteristics and abilities.
  11. I can describe and analyze how an individual's characteristics and abilities develop.
  12. I can explain which characteristics and abilities I appreciate most in myself and others.
  13. I can compare my characteristics and abilities with those of others and appreciate and encourage my uniqueness.

Example: American School Counselor Association

The American School Counselor Association (2005) recommended that guidance and counseling programs use three broad areas under which are student learnings stated as standards:

- *Academic Development Standards*
  1. Students will acquire the attitudes, knowledge, and skills that contribute to effective learning in school and across the life span.
  2. Students will complete school with the academic preparation essential to choose from a wide range of substantial postsecondary options, including college.
  3. Students will understand the relationship of academics to the world of work, and to life at home and in the community.
- *Career Development Standards*
  1. Students will acquire the skills to investigate the world of work in relation to knowledge of self and to make informed career decisions.
  2. Students will use strategies to achieve future career success and satisfaction.
  3. Students will understand the relationship between personal qualities, education and training, and the world of work.
- *Personal/Social Development Standards*
  1. Students will acquire the attitudes, knowledge, and interpersonal skills to help them understand and respect self and others.
  2. Students will make decisions, set goals, and take necessary action to achieve goals.
  3. Students will understand safety and survival skills.

Example: State of Texas

The state of Texas (Texas Education Agency, 2004) uses seven broad content domains, each having three skill levels as shown in Figure 3.3.

Element 2: Organizational Framework: Structural Components

Structural components are an important part of the organizational framework because they describe the nature of the program and provide a philosophical base for it. The structural components define the program, state the rationale for the program, and list the assumptions on which the program is based. Examples of language for each of these components follow; remember they are examples only. It is your job to make sure that the contents of these components fit your school district.

Definition

A definition of the guidance and counseling program identifies the centrality of guidance and counseling within the educational process and delineates, in broad terms, the competencies students will possess as a result of their involvement in the program. Two examples of a definition of guidance and counseling follow. The first is the definition of guidance and counseling used by the state of Missouri, and the second is from Northside Independent School District, San Antonio, Texas.

State of Missouri. The following is the state of Missouri's definition of guidance and counseling (Gysbers, Kosteck-Bunch, Magnuson, & Starr, 2002):

> The district's comprehensive guidance program is an integral part of the district's total educational program. It is developmental by design and includes sequential activities organized and imple-

Figure 3.3
Texts Skill Levels and Competency Domains

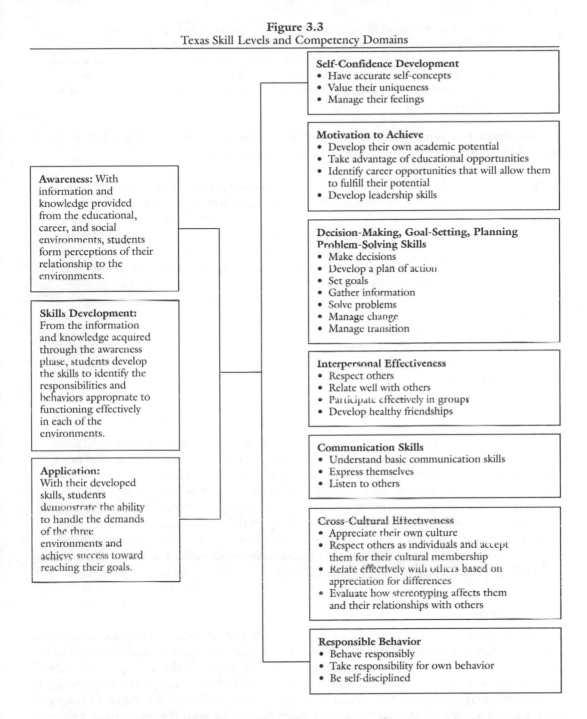

Self-Confidence Development
- Have accurate self-concepts
- Value their uniqueness
- Manage their feelings

Motivation to Achieve
- Develop their own academic potential
- Take advantage of educational opportunities
- Identify career opportunities that will allow them to fulfill their potential
- Develop leadership skills

Decision-Making, Goal-Setting, Planning Problem-Solving Skills
- Make decisions
- Develop a plan of action
- Set goals
- Gather information
- Solve problems
- Manage change
- Manage transition

Interpersonal Effectiveness
- Respect others
- Relate well with others
- Participate effectively in groups
- Develop healthy friendships

Communication Skills
- Understand basic communication skills
- Express themselves
- Listen to others

Cross-Cultural Effectiveness
- Appreciate their own culture
- Respect others as individuals and accept them for their cultural membership
- Relate effectively with others based on appreciation for differences
- Evaluate how stereotyping affects them and their relationships with others

Responsible Behavior
- Behave responsibly
- Take responsibility for own behavior
- Be self-disciplined

Awareness: With information and knowledge provided from the educational, career, and social environments, students form perceptions of their relationship to the environments.

Skills Development: From the information and knowledge acquired through the awareness phase, students develop the skills to identify the responsibilities and behaviors appropriate to functioning effectively in each of the environments.

Application: With their developed skills, students demonstrate the ability to handle the demands of the three environments and achieve success toward reaching their goals.

mented by professional school counselors with the active support of parents/guardians, teachers, administrators, and the community. As a developmental program, it addresses the needs of all students by facilitating their academic, personal/social, and career development as well as creating positive and safe learning climates in schools. At the same time, the program assists students as they face issues and resolve problems that prevent their healthy development. The program is delivered through the following four program components.

- Guidance Curriculum: structured group and classroom presentations
- Individual Planning: appraisal, educational and occupational planning, and placement
- Responsive Services: individual counseling, small-group counseling, consultation, and referral
- System Support: program management, fair-share responsibilities, professional development, staff and community relations, consultation, committee participation, community outreach, and research and development

Northside Independent School District. The following is the Northside Independent School District's (1994) definition of guidance and counseling:

The Northside Independent School District Comprehensive Guidance Program is based on individual, school, and community needs and organized around skill development goals. The program is delivered through the direct service program components of guidance curriculum, individual planning system, and responsive services and is implemented by certified school counselors. Additionally, the program provides indirect services supporting the total educational program. The program is a developmental educational program responsible for assisting students to acquire knowledge and skills needed to develop and maintain their

- self-esteem
- motivation to achieve
- decision-making and problem-solving skills
- interpersonal effectiveness
- communication skills
- cross-cultural effectiveness
- responsible behavior

The developmental perspective recognizes that every student needs sound emotional and social skills in order to achieve optimum benefit from the educational program. The comprehensive guidance program is designed to assist systematically all students in our schools. It is implemented with the assistance of administrators, teachers, and paraprofessionals. The program also assists students as they face issues and resolve problems that prevent their healthy development. Although other topics arise from time to time, recurrent issues in the 1990s included academics, attendance, behaviors, being at risk of dropping out, career choices, child abuse, cross-cultural effectiveness, educational choices, family, loss, peer relationships, relationships with adults, self-esteem, sexuality, stress, substance abuse, and suicide. (p. 6)

Rationale

A rationale presents the importance of the guidance and counseling program as an equal partner with other programs in education. It focuses on reasons why students need to acquire guidance and counseling competencies and have access to the assistance that school counselors, working in a comprehensive guidance and counseling program, provide. It should be based on the goals of your school, community, and state. Examples of areas and points you may wish to consider in writing the rationale for your comprehensive guidance and counseling program include student development, self-knowledge, decision making, changing environments, transition assistance, and relevant education.

Student Development. Students today face depersonalization in many facets of their lives as bureaucracies and impersonal relations are commonplace. They often feel powerless in the face of masses of people, mass communication, and mass everything else, and they need help in dealing with these feelings, not at the expense of society but in the context of society. Their feelings of control over their environment and their own destiny, and their relations with others and institutions, are of primary importance in guidance and counseling programs. Students must be viewed as totalities, as individuals. Their development can be best facilitated by comprehensive guidance and counseling programs that begin in kindergarten and continue to be available on a systematic basis through Grade 12.

Self-Knowledge. Formerly, students were brought up in a fairly stable society in which their roles were defined and relationships with others were fairly constant. Now they face an increasingly mobile society in which relationships with both people and things are becoming less and less enduring. Society is characterized by transience and impermanence. Traditional beliefs and ways of doing things no longer seem sufficient for coping with the environmental demands. As a result, many students have problems defining their roles and thus seek answers to questions such as Who am I? and Where do I fit in? Guidance and counseling programs can help individuals respond to such questions through the development of self-appraisal and self-improvement competencies. Through these learnings, students can become more aware of personal characteristics such as aptitudes, interests, goals, abilities, values, and physical traits and the influence these characteristics may have on the persons they are and can become. Being able to use self-knowledge in life career planning and interpersonal relationships and to assume responsibility for their own behavior are examples of needed competencies that students can acquire through participation in a comprehensive guidance and counseling program.

Decision Making. Students need help in decision making because planning for and making decisions are vital tasks in the lives of all individuals. Everyday decisions are made that influence each student's life career. Mastery of decision-making skills and the application of these skills to life career planning are central learnings in a guidance and counseling program. A preliminary task to effective decision making is the clarification of personal values. The degree of congruence between what individuals value and the outcomes of decisions individuals make contributes to personal satisfaction. Included in decision making are the skills for gathering and using relevant information. Understanding the influence of planning on the future and the responsibility each individual must take for planning are components of the life career planning process. Life career planning is ongoing. Change and time affect planning and decisions. A decision outcome that is satisfactory and appropriate for the present may become, with time or change, unsatisfactory or inappropriate. Thus the ability to evaluate decisions in view of new information or circumstances is vital. Being able to clarify personal values, identify steps needed to make personal decisions, gather relevant information, and apply decision-making skills to life career plans are examples of desired and needed outcomes for a guidance and counseling program.

Changing Environments. Increasing societal complexity affects not only interpersonal relationships and feelings of individuality but also other life roles, settings, and events, specifically including those associated with the worlds of education, work, and leisure. Changes resulting from advances in technology are perhaps more apparent as they affect the world of work. No longer are students well acquainted with the occupations of family and community members or their contributive roles to the common good of society. Parents' occupations are removed from the home and often from the immediate neighborhood. In addition, because students over their lifetimes will be assuming a number of roles, functioning in a variety of settings, and experiencing many events, learnings in this area emphasize their understanding of the various roles, settings, and events that interrelate to form their life careers. The roles of family member, citizen, worker, and leisure participant; settings such as home, school, community, and work; and events such as birthdays, educational milestones, job entry, and job change are identified and examined in terms of their influence on lifestyles. Guidance programs can help students develop an understanding of the structure of the family and education, work, and leisure requirements and characteristics. The effect of change—natural as well as unexpected, social as well as technological, in self as well as in others—is a needed major learning for students that a comprehensive guidance and counseling program can provide.

Transition Assistance. As students are and will be moving from one setting to another, they need specific knowledge and skills to make such moves as effectively as possible. They need help in making transitions. Although transitions are defined broadly, specific attention should be given to intra- and intereducational and occupational transitions and to the personal competencies needed to make such transitions. Personal competencies needed include knowledge of the spectrum of educational courses and programs, an understanding of the relationships they may have to personal and societal needs and goals, and skills in using a wide variety of information and resources. They also include an understanding of the pathways and linkages between those courses and programs and potential personal goals. Stress is placed on the need for employability skill development, including resume writing, job searching, and job interviewing.

Relevant Education. Some of the dissatisfaction of youths with education stems from the feeling that what they are doing in school is not relevant to their lives. A comprehensive guidance and counseling program is needed to seek to create relevance in the schools and to show individuals how the knowledge, understandings, and skills they are obtaining and the courses they are taking will help them as they progress through their life careers.

Example Rationale: Northside Independent School District

The following is an example rationale from the Northside Independent School District (1994, p. 3):

> The ever-increasing needs of children and the expectations of today's society impose growing demands on our educational system and its resources. Educators are challenged to educate students with diverse backgrounds at an ever higher level of literacy to meet the demands of an internationally competitive, technological marketplace. At the same time, societal and other factors cause some of our children to attend school ill equipped emotionally, physically, and/or socially to learn. Schools must respond by providing support for all students to learn effectively.
>
> Community influences and societal changes generate identifiable student needs that may not be met solely by classroom instructional programs. Meeting these needs is essential to individual growth, and can be accomplished through a planned educational program combining instruction and guidance. Northside Independent School District provides a comprehensive and balanced guidance program. The Framework describes the elements common to the program districtwide; however, each campus designs its program to meet the district minimum expectations and to meet the needs of the community it serves. As each school designs its guidance program, the rationale for the local design rests on an assessment of local student and community needs. Northside Independent School District educators identified student needs as follows:

- a sense of connection
- someone to listen
- support system
- advocacy
- personal management skills
- career skills, life skills
- goal-setting skills
- self-esteem

- valuing education as an investment in the future
- learning to give of oneself
- problem-solving skills

Assumptions

For the effective implementation of a comprehensive guidance and counseling program to occur, certain student, staff, and program conditions must exist. Assumptions are statements of these conditions. For example, the Northside Independent School District comprehensive guidance program is based on the following assumptions:

Students
- Every student in our schools has equal access to our guidance program.
- The services provided to all our students are equitable.

Staff
- Professional school counselors are essential in today's public schools.
- All school counselors adhere to the ethical standards of the profession.
- School counselors spend the majority of their time working directly with students.
- All school counselors are highly proficient in the seven school counselor roles.
- School administrators protect the professional integrity of the guidance program and the school counselors.

Program
- Guidance is a schoolwide responsibility.
- The essential goals of a school guidance program are to help students succeed academically.
- All students deserve assistance with their career development.
- The primary purposes of all guidance curriculum lessons and activities are directly related to or in direct support of one or more of the following three primary goals of the school:
  1. Academic success
  2. A safe, productive, and pleasant learning and working environment
  3. Helping each student develop and carry out an educational plan that matches with his or her abilities, interests, and future goals.

Element 2: Organizational Framework: Program Components

As we continue to learn more about the needs of students, the variety of new and traditional guidance and counseling methods, techniques, and the resources available, as well as the increased expectations of policymakers, consumers, and community members, it is clear that a comprehensive program is rapidly becoming the way to organize guidance and counseling activities and services in schools. The traditional formulation of guidance and counseling—a position with a number of services—once thought to be sufficient, is no longer adequate. When cast in the traditional way, guidance and counseling is often seen as ancillary and supportive, not as equal and complementary to the instruction program.

If the proposition that the traditional position-services formulation for guidance and counseling is no longer adequate is accepted, then the question is, What is an appropriate formulation? One way to answer this question is to ask what should be expected of a comprehensive guidance and counseling program:

1. Are there knowledge, skills, and attitudes (competencies) needed by all students that should be the instructional responsibility of guidance and counseling programs?
2. Do students and their parents or guardians have the right to have someone in the school system be sensitive to students' unique life career development needs, including their needs for planning, goal setting, making transitions, and follow-through?
3. Should school counselors be available and responsive to special or unexpected needs of students, staff, parents or guardians, and the community?
4. Does the guidance and counseling program, the educational programs of the district, and the staff of the school district require support that can be best supplied by school counselors?

The structure suggested by an affirmative answer to these four questions and by a review of the literature is a program of guidance and counseling techniques, methods, and resources containing four interactive components: guidance curriculum, individual student planning, responsive services, and system support (Gysbers & Henderson, 1988, 1994, 2000; Gysbers & Moore, 1981). The curriculum component was chosen because a curriculum provides a vehicle to impart to all students guidance and counseling content in a systematic way. The individual student planning component was included as a part of the program because of the need for all students, working closely with parents or guardians, to systematically plan, monitor, and manage their growth and development and to consider and take action on their next steps personally, educationally, and occupationally. The responsive services component was included because of the need in comprehensive guidance and counseling programs to respond to the direct, immediate concerns of students whether these concerns involve individual counseling, small-group counseling, referral, or consultation with parents, teachers, or other specialists. The system support component was included because it was recognized that, for the other guidance processes to be effective, a variety of guidance and counseling program support activities such as staff development, research and evaluation, and curriculum development are required. The system support component also was included because of the need for the guidance and counseling program to provide appropriate support to other programs in the school.

These components, then, serve as organizers for the many guidance and counseling methods, techniques, and resources required in a comprehensive guidance and counseling program. In addition, they also serve as a check on the comprehensiveness of the program. In our opinion, a program is not comprehensive unless it has activities in each of the components. We describe each of these components in detail in the following sections.

Guidance Curriculum

The Purpose of the Guidance Curriculum. One of the assumptions on which our conception of a comprehensive program is based is that there is guidance and counseling content that all students need to learn in a systematic, sequential way. This means school counselor involvement in the curriculum; it means a guidance curriculum. This is not a new idea. The notion of a guidance curriculum has deep, historical roots. What is new, however, is the array of guidance and counseling techniques, methods, and resources currently available that work best as a part of a curriculum. What is new, too, is the concept that a comprehensive guidance and counseling program has an organized and sequential curriculum (American School Counselor Association, 1984, 2005; Borders & Drury, 1992; Commission on Precollege Guidance and Counseling, 1986; ERIC Counseling and Personnel Services Clearinghouse, 1983).

Implementation Strategies. The guidance curriculum typically consists of student competencies chosen to fit the needs of your students (organized by domains and specified by grade levels) and structured activities, presented systematically, chosen to fit the needs of your students, schools, and community through such strategies as the following:

- *Classroom activities:* School counselors teach, team teach, or support the teaching of guidance curriculum learning activities or units in classrooms. Teachers also may teach such units. The guidance curriculum is not limited to being taught in one or two subjects but should include as many subjects as possible in the total school curriculum. These activities may be conducted in the classroom, guidance center, or other school facilities.
- *Schoolwide activities:* School counselors organize and conduct large group sessions such as career days and educational/college/vocational days. Other members of the guidance and counseling team, including teachers and administrators, also may be involved in organizing and conducting such sessions.

Although school counselors' responsibilities include organizing and implementing the guidance curriculum, the cooperation and support of the entire faculty and staff are necessary for its successful implementation. Also critical is that parents or guardians be invited to provide input to the guidance curriculum that is taught in the school their children attend, that they be aware of what is taught, and that they be encouraged to reinforce learnings from the guidance curriculum at home.

Guidance Curriculum Scope and Sequence Design: A Learning Theory Perspective. As you select the domains you will use in the guidance curriculum and identify the competencies to be included in each domain, keep in mind the following assumptions about human growth and development:

1. Individual development is a process of continuous and sequential (but not necessarily uninterrupted or uniform) progress toward increased effectiveness in the management and mastery of the environment for the satisfaction of psychological and social needs.
2. The stage, or level, of individuals' development at any given point is related to the nature and accuracy of their perceptions, the level of complexity of their conceptualizations, and the subsequent development rate and direction. No individual in an educational setting is at a zero point in development; hence change must be measured from some relative point rather than from an absolute.
3. Positive developmental changes are potential steps toward the achievement of higher level purposive goals. This interlocking relationship dictates that achievement at a particular growth stage be viewed as a means to further development rather than as an end result.
4. Environmental or situational variables provide the external dimension of individual development. Knowledge, understanding, skills, attitudes, values, and aspirations are the product of the interaction of these external variables with the internal variables that characterize the individual.
5. The developmental learning process moves from a beginning level of awareness and differentiation (perceptualization), to the next level of conceptualizing relationships and meanings (conceptualization), to the highest level of behavioral consistency and effectiveness by both internal and external evaluation (generalization). (Wellman & Moore, 1975, pp. 55–56)

A major task in the development of the guidance curriculum is to organize and lay out student competencies so that they follow a theoretically sound scope and sequence. Note the concepts perceptualization, conceptualization, and generalization discussed in Assumption 5. These concepts can serve as guidelines for this very important task. What follows is a detailed discussion of these concepts and how they function in making decisions about the scope and sequence of student competencies K–12 (Wellman & Moore, 1975).

Perceptualization level. Competencies at this level emphasize the acquisition of knowledge and skills and focus attention on selected aspects of the environment and self. The knowledge and skills most relevant are those that individuals need in making appropriate life role decisions and in responding to the demands of the school and social environment. Attention is the first step toward the development and maturation of interests, attitudes, and values. Competencies at the perceptualization level reflect accuracy of perceptions, ability to differentiate, and elemental skills in performing functions appropriate to the individual's level of development. Competencies at this level are classified under two major categories: *environmental orientation* and *self-orientation.*

Environmental orientation competencies emphasize the individual's awareness and acquisition of knowledge and skills needed to make life role decisions and to master the demands of life career settings and events. The competencies at this level are essentially cognitive in nature and have not necessarily been internalized to the extent that the individual attaches personal meaning to the acquired knowledge and skills. For example, individuals may acquire appropriate study skills and knowledge, but it does not necessarily follow that they will use these skills and knowledge in their study behavior. However, such knowledge and skills are considered to be prerequisites to behavior requiring them. Thus the acquisition of knowledge and skills required to make growth-oriented decisions and to cope with environmental expectations is viewed as the first step in individuals' development, regardless of whether subsequent implementation emerges. A primary and universally applicable goal of guidance is the development of knowledge and skills to enable individuals to understand and meet the expectations of their school and social environment and to recognize the values underlying social limits.

Self-orientation competencies focus on the development of accurate self-perceptions. One aspect of an accurate awareness of self is the knowledge of one's abilities, aptitudes, interests, and values. An integral part of identity is individuals' ability to understand and accept the ways that they are alike and different from other individuals. Attention to life career decisions and demands relevant to immediate adjustment and future development is considered a prerequisite to an understanding of the relationships between self and environment. An awareness, and perhaps an understanding, of feelings and motivations is closely associated with self-evaluation of behavior, with the formation of attitudes and values, and with voluntary, rationally based modification of behavior.

The goal of guidance at this level is to help individuals make accurate assessments of self so that they can relate realistically to their environment in their decisions and actions. Thus the goal of guidance at this level is also individuals' development of self-awareness and differentiation so as to enable appropriate decision making and mastery of behavior in the roles, settings, and events of their lives.

Conceptualization level. Individual competencies at the conceptualization level emphasize action based on the relationships between perceptions of self and perceptions of environment. The types of action sought are categorized into personally meaningful growth decisions and adaptive and adjustive behavior. The general goal at this level of development is to help individuals (a) make appropriate choices, decisions, and plans that will move them toward personally satisfying and socially acceptable development; (b) take action necessary to progress within developmental plans; and (c) develop behavior to master their school and social environment as judged by peers, teachers, and parents. The two major classifications of conceptualization objectives are *directional tendencies* and *adaptive and adjustive behavior.*

Directional tendencies relate to individuals' movement toward socially desirable goals consistent with their potential for development. These competencies are indicators of directional tendencies as reflected in the choices, decisions, and plans that individuals are expected to make in ordering the course of their educational, occupational, and social growth. The acquisition of knowledge and skills covered by competencies at the perceptual level is a prerequisite to the pursuit of competencies in this category, although the need to make choices and decisions may provide the initial stimulus for considering perceptual competencies. For example, a ninth grader may be required to make curricular choices that have a bearing on post-high-school education and occupational aspirations. The need to make an immediate choice at this point may stimulate an examination of both environmental perceptions and self-perceptions as well as a careful analysis of the relationships between the two. To this extent, then, the interrelationship and interdependence of perceptual and conceptual competencies preclude the establishment of mutually exclusive categories. Furthermore, the concept of a developmental sequence suggests this type of interrelationship. Any choice that may determine the direction of future development is considered to represent a directional tendency on the part of individuals, and competencies related to such choices are so classified.

The expected emergence of increasingly stable interests and the strengthening and clarification of value patterns constitute additional indicators of directional tendencies. Persistent attention to particular persons, activities, or objects in the environment to the exclusion of others (selective attention) is an indication of the development of interests through an evaluation of the relationships of self to differentiated aspects of the environment. Objectives that relate to value conceptualization, or the internalization of social values, complement interest development. Here individuals are expected to show increased consistency in giving priority to particular behavior that is valued personally and socially. In a sense, the maturation of interests represents the development of educational and occupational individuality, whereas the formation of value patterns represents the recognition of social values and the normative tolerances of behavior.

Competencies in these subcategories include consistency in the expression of interests and values and the manifestation of behavior compatible with the emerging interests and value patterns. For example, high school students may be expected to manifest increasing and persistent interest (measured or expressed) in particular persons, activities, and objects. They may be expected to develop a concept of self that is consistent with these interests and to place increasing importance, or value, on behaviors, such as educational achievement, that will lead to the development of related knowledge and skills and to the ultimate achievement of occupational aspirations. The directional tendency emphasis is on achieving increased consistency and strength of interests and values over a period of time. The incidental or occasional expression of an immediate interest or value with little or no long-range impact on the behavior of individuals should not be interpreted as an indication of a directional tendency.

Adaptive and adjustive behaviors at the conceptualization level include competencies related to the application of self-environment concepts in coping with environmental pressures and in solving problems arising from the interaction of individuals and their environment. Adaptive behavior refers to individuals' ability and skill to manage their school and social environment (with normative tolerances) to satisfy self-needs, to meet environmental demands, and to solve problems. There are two types of adaptive behavior.

First, individuals may, within certain prescribed limits, control their environmental transactions by selection. For example, if they lack the appropriate social skills, they may avoid social transactions that demand dancing and choose those in which existing abilities will gain the acceptance of the social group. Second, individuals may be able to modify their environment to meet their needs and certain external demands. For example, students who find sharing a room with a younger brother or sister disruptive to studying may be able to modify this situation by arranging to study elsewhere.

Adjustive behavior refers to the ability and flexibility of individuals to modify their behavior to meet environmental demands and to solve problems. Such behavior modification may include the development of new abilities or skills, a change of attitudes, or a change in method of operation or approach to the demand situation. In the examples of adaptive behavior just mentioned, individuals might use adjustive behavior by learning to dance rather than avoiding dancing, and they might develop new study skills so they are able to study while sharing a room.

The basic competencies in this area involve an individual's ability to demonstrate adaptive and adjustive behavior in dealing with school and social demands and in solving problems that restrict the ability to meet such demands. The competencies may be achieved by applying existing abilities or by learning new ways of meeting demands.

Generalization level. Competencies at the generalization level imply a high level of functioning that enables individuals to (a) accommodate environmental and cultural demands, (b) achieve personal satisfaction from environmental transactions, and (c) demonstrate competence through mastery of specific tasks and through the generalization of learned behavior, attitudes, and values to new situations. Behavior that characterizes the achievement of generalization-level competencies may be described as purposeful and effective by one's own or intrinsic standards and by societal or extrinsic criteria. Individuals should be able to demonstrate behavioral consistency, commitment to purpose, and autonomy in meeting educational, occupational, and social demands. Individuals exhibiting such behavior therefore are relatively independent and predictable. Guidance competencies at this level are classified as *accommodation, satisfaction,* and *mastery.*

The concept of sequential and positive progress implies a continuous process of internalization, including applicational transfer of behavior and a dynamic, rather than a static, condition in the achievement of goals. The achievement of generalization competencies may be interpreted as positive movement (at each level of development) toward the ideal model of an effective person (self and socially derived) without assuming that individuals will ever fully achieve the ideal.

Accommodation competencies relate to the consistent and enduring ability to solve problems and to cope with environmental demands with minimum conflict. Accommodation of cultural and environmental demands requires that individuals make decisions and take action within established behavioral tolerances. The applicational transfer of adaptive and adjustive behavior, learned in other situations and under other circumstances, to new demand situations is inferred by the nature of the competencies classified in this category. The achievement of accommodation competencies can probably best be evaluated by the absence, or the reduction, of unsatisfactory coping behavior. The wide range of acceptable behavior in many situations suggests that individuals who perform within that range have achieved the accommodation competencies for a particular demand situation, whereas those outside that range have not achieved these competencies. For example, a student is expected to attend class, to turn in class assignments, and to respect the property rights of others. If there is no record of excessive absences, failure to meet teacher assignment schedules, or violation of property rights, it may be assumed that the student is accommodating these demands with normative tolerances. In a sense, the objectives in this category represent the goal that individual behavior conform to certain limits of societal expectancy, whereas the other categories of generalization competencies tend to be more self-oriented. The achievement of accommodation competencies may imply congruence of individual values with the values of one's culture. Caution should be exercised in drawing such inferences, however, because the individual may demonstrate relative harmony externally but have serious value conflicts that do not emerge in observable behavior.

Satisfaction competencies reflect the internal interpretation that individuals give to their environmental transactions. Individual interests and values serve as criteria for evaluating the decisions made and the actions taken within the guidance domains. Although the evaluations of parents, peers, and authority figures may influence individuals' interpretations (satisfactions), these competencies become genuine only as they are achieved in congruence with the motivations and feelings of individuals. The description of satisfaction competencies consistent with guidance programming should include individuals' evaluation of affiliations, transactions, and adjustments in terms of personal adequacy, expectations, and congruency with a perceived ideal lifestyle. Expressed satisfaction, as well as behavioral manifestations from which satisfaction may be inferred (such as persistence), seem to be appropriate criterion measures. Congruency between measured interests and voluntarily chosen career activities also should be considered.

Mastery competencies include the more global aspects of achievement and generalization of attitudinal and behavioral modes. Long-range goals, encompassing large areas of achievement, are emphasized here rather than the numerous short-range achievements that may be required to reach a larger goal. For example, a young child becomes aware of task demands and different ways to meet them (perceptualization). At the conceptualization level, task-oriented behaviors are developed and made meaningful. Generalization (mastery) competencies reflect the internalization of these behaviors so that tasks are approached and achieved to the satisfaction of self and social expectations.

In the social area, mastery competencies relate to social responsibility and individuals' contributions with respect to social affiliations and interactions appropriate to their developmental level. All of the competencies in this category are framed in the context of self and social estimates of potential for achievement. Therefore, criteria for the estimation of achievement of mastery competencies should be in terms of congruency between independent behavioral action and expectations for action as derived from self and social sources. For example, a mastery competency in the educational area might be achieved by high school graduation by one individual, whereas graduate work at the university level might be the expected achievement level for another individual.

Individual Student Planning

The Need For and Importance of Individual Student Planning. Concern for student development in a complex society has been a cornerstone of the guidance movement since the days of Frank Parsons. In recent years the concern for student development has intensified as society has become even more complex. This concern is manifested in many ways, but perhaps it is expressed most succinctly in a frequently used goal for guidance and counseling: helping students become the people they are capable of becoming.

Casting guidance and counseling in a personal development, personal advocacy role is not new. Years ago Lortie (1965) suggested that one grouping of tasks school counselors might accept as part of their role could be that of advocate. Building on this same theme, Cook (1971) urged that school guidance and counseling claim the role of student advocate, with the end result being the enhancement of students' development. Similarly, Howard Miller, president of the Los Angeles Board of Education, supported the need for guidance and counseling programs to attend to the individual development of students.

Writing in the *Los Angeles Times* about needed next steps for the Los Angeles schools, he described the kind of school programs that were needed. Among the critically important programs he described were "extensive counseling resources insuring personal direction and monitoring for each student" (Miller, 1977, p. 5).

The goal of helping students plan for the future continues to be important now and in the future. In a study of the youths of Indiana titled *High Hopes Long Odds,*

> the difference in the high school experiences of students with plans for 4 years of high school courses and career plans versus students without such counselor-assisted plans was so great that providing help with these plans must be offered at every school. (Orfield & Paul, 1994, p. 11)

In 1996, the state of Utah (*Student Education Plan,* 1996) translated the idea of individual plans for students into state law and state board of education policy requiring that all elementary students develop and implement personalized student education plans and that all secondary students develop and implement personalized student education/ occupation plans. In the same year, the National Association of Secondary School Principals (1996) published a report titled *Breaking Ranks.* In it they recommended that each student in high school develop and use a personal plan for progress. In addition, the state of Missouri required that an individual student planning system be in place in school no later than eighth grade and that it include the necessary planning forms and procedures (Missouri Department of Elementary and Secondary Education, 1997).

The importance of individual student planning was emphasized again with the publication of *Breaking Ranks II* (National Association of Secondary School Principals, 2004). Recommendation 12 stated:

> Each student will have a Personal Plan for Progress that will be reviewed often to ensure that the high school takes individual needs into consideration and to allow students, within reasonable parameters, to design their own methods for learning in an effort to meet high standards. (p. 84)

The idea behind personalized learning is that it "allows the student to understand who he or she is, what adult roles seem most desirable, and how to get from here to there in the most productive way" (p. 169). The American College Testing Program (2004) also stressed the importance of individual student planning in *Crisis at the Core: Preparing All Students for College and Work.* They recommended that career and educational planning services be provided to all students. In addition, they stated that parents must be involved in key educational and postsecondary planning.

The Purpose of Individual Student Planning. The purpose of the individual student planning component of the guidance and counseling program is to provide all students with guidance and counseling activities to assist them to plan for and then monitor and manage their personal/social, academic, and career development. The focus of the activities in this component is on students developing life career plans consistent with their personal/ social, academic, and career goals. Through the activities of this component, school counselors and others with guidance responsibilities serve students and their parents or guardians as facilitators of students' personal/social, academic, and career development.

The life career plans that students develop and use are both processes and instruments. As processes, students' plans evolve throughout the school years responding to successions of the learning activities in the overall school program as well as the guidance and counseling activities provided through the guidance curriculum and individual student planning components of the guidance and counseling program. As instruments, plans provide structured ways for students to gather, analyze, synthesize, and organize self, academic, and career information. As processes, plans are vehicles through which this information is incorporated into short- and long-range goal-setting, decision-making, and planning activities. As instruments, plans are not tracks to be plotted and followed routinely; they are, instead, blueprints for life quests. According to Orfield and Paul (1994),

> The purpose of a plan is not to force students to make career decisions early in their experiences, but rather to ensure that they make no academic decisions that might close doors to opportunities that they later wish were open. (pp. 11–12)

The Foundation for and Scope of Individual Student Planning. The foundation for individual student planning is established during the elementary school years through guidance curriculum activities. Self-concept development, the acquisition of learning-to-learn skills, interpersonal relationship skill development, decision-making skill building, and awareness and beginning exploration of educational and occupational possibilities are sample subjects that are covered during these years. Subjects such as these continue to be covered through the guidance curriculum during middle school and high school, providing new information and experiences to enable students to regularly update, monitor, and manage their plans effectively.

Building on the foundation provided in elementary school, beginning planning for the future is undertaken during the middle school years through the individual student planning component. During this period, students' plans focus on high school course selection, taking into account graduation requirements and the requirements of their postsecondary academic and career goals. Guidance curriculum activities continue to support and guide the planning process.

During the high school years, plans developed in the middle school are reviewed and updated periodically in accordance with students' postsecondary personal, academic, and career goals. The individual student planning component provides time for regular individual work with students as well as group sessions focusing on individual student planning. Guidance curriculum activities continue to support student planning by giving emphasis to the development and use of decision-making, goal-setting, and planning skills. The importance and relevance of basic academic and career and technical education preparation skills are stressed. The goal is for students' plans to become pathways or guides through which students can use the past and present to anticipate and prepare for the future.

Implementation Strategies. Individual student planning is implemented through the following strategies:

- *Individual appraisal:* School counselors assist students to assess and interpret their abilities, interests, skills, and achievement.
- *Individual advisement:* School counselors assist students to use self-appraisal information along with personal/social, academic, career, and labor market information to help them plan for and realize their personal, social, academic, and career goals.
- *Transition planning:* School counselors and other education personnel assist students to make the transition from school to work or to additional education and training.
- *Follow-up:* School counselors and other education personnel provide follow-up assistance to students as well as gather follow-up data for evaluation and program improvement.

Planning Formats. Student plans that are developed as a result of individual student planning activities come in a variety of formats. One format is the traditional 4-year high school plan. It focuses on high school course selection consistent with meeting high school graduation and postsecondary education goal requirements. Another format that is being used increasingly is the student portfolio either in a paper or electronic form (Davis, 1997). The portfolio is much more comprehensive than a 4-year plan. It is designed to help students record and document their work, their education and training, as well as the personal experiences they have had and the skills they have acquired. It may have a job performance part with sections presenting personal, educational, and work-record information and primary job skills. Another part often presents work interests, traits, and attitudes; special training or skills; favorite classes, training programs, subjects, and educational activities; and social/leisure activities. Still another format is the career passport. It contains some of the same information found in the portfolio but is less detailed and concentrates more on information needed for job interviews and job applications.

When students leave school, they take their life career plan folders with them. Whether they go to work or continue their education, the folder and the accompanying competency lists are available for additional goal-setting, decision-making, and planning activities. Information in the folder can assist them in a variety of job-seeking and job-keeping activities, including filling out application forms, writing resumes, developing curriculum vitae, or preparing for job advancement. As new experiences are acquired, they can be analyzed and added to the appropriate sections of the folder. Thus the individual life career plan folder with accompanying competency lists can become an ongoing goal-setting and planning vehicle for individuals as long as they wish to use it.

Educational and career decision making, planning, and goal setting are primarily the responsibility of students and their parents or guardians. Parent and guardian involvement in the activities of the individual student planning component is essential to students' successful development and implementation of education and career plans. For student planning to be effective, parents or guardians need accurate information in a timely manner as guidance and counseling activities are implemented.

Student Advisory Systems: A Way to Implement Individual Student Planning. One of the recommendations in *Breaking Ranks II* (National Association of Secondary School Principals, 2004) stated that schools should implement "a comprehensive advisory program that ensures that each student has frequent and meaningful opportunities to plan and assess his or her academic and social progress with a faculty member" (p. 10). The faculty member was called a "Personal Adult Advocate" (p. 10). We concur with this recommendation and provide the following example of a way to develop and manage a student advisory system. Northside Independent School District,[1] San Antonio, Texas found that such a system is an effective and efficient way to assist students individually to develop personal, social, educational, and career goals and to monitor their progress toward those goals. Northside Independent School District has implemented an advisory system in which advisers guide individual advisees in partnerships with their parents. It is through involving large numbers of professional staff that all students receive a meaningful amount of personalized, individual planning assistance. In the traditional guidance and counseling program, this assistance was systematically provided only by school counselors. Once the comprehensive guidance program had clarified the distinctions among the four program delivery components, augmentation of the individual planning component through implementation of a student advisory system was conceptually and operationally seen as desirable and feasible.

Structure. The student advisory system works within Northside's comprehensive guidance and counseling program structure. Students in prekindergarten through 12th grade

---

[1]This example was prepared by Debbie Krueger, district student advisory coordinator, and RoseMary Martinez, middle school counselor in Northside Independent School District (www.northside.isd.tenet.edu; departments; guidance).

are provided, on a regularly scheduled basis, time to meet with their advisers for guidance, goal setting, and self-evaluation. The essence of the student advisory system consists of a small group of students and an adviser who guides each student in such activities as setting personal goals, addressing social skills and academics, solving problems, and exploring career options.

The basic content of Northside's advisory system consists of the goal-setting process and developmentally appropriate applications. For example, the elementary school content includes learning how to write and plan to accomplish a group goal; middle school applications include organizational skills; and high school targets helping students transition into the larger high school setting and out to the work world and postsecondary education/training. Schools and districts across the United States have had varying degrees of success in maintaining student advisement systems over the years, but along the way much has been learned about what does and does not work for students—the primary "client" of the system. Operating such a system entails answering several logistical questions, such as who, how, and when.

Who questions include how many students make a viable advisory group. Current recommendations are that 6 to 8 students work well at the elementary level, 10 to 12 students at the middle school level, and 12 to 15 students at the high school level (Carnegie Council on Adolescent Development, 1989; Vars, 1997; Whitmer, 1992). Most concur that advisers and advisees should remain together throughout students' tenure in a school, and that advisory groups represent all of the grade levels in a school. If there is an adviser–advisee combination that is not effective, a student is reassigned through a school counselor or a campus student advisory system facilitator. How students and advisers are matched in the first place must be decided, for example, by dividing class lists in random order or by having students select their advisers.

When advisory groups meet affects their effectiveness. Research and experience indicate that elementary children are best served by meeting with their adviser at the end of the day because this allows them to get organized to go home. Middle school students are best served by meeting first period of the day because this allows them to focus on their short-term goals and plans for the day. High school students are best served by meeting second period because first period typically involves specialty classes for students who begin their day before school (Carnegie Council on Adolescent Development, 1989; Myrick, 1990).

Adviser competencies. Prior to becoming advisers, teachers, administrators, other educational specialists, and school counselors must have acquired the competencies needed to carry out the adviser role. As it is not a separately certifiable role, implementation of the student advisory system entailed identifying the competencies needed. All advisers in Northside are professional educators who have, in addition, been trained to demonstrate the following competencies:

- a knowledge base of the goal-setting and implementation process—and how that process supports the curriculum and enhances learning, effective teaching, and applications of learning styles and multiple intelligences—and of the developmental level of the students they advise
- applications of specific skills, such as how to build trust, listen, solve problems, communicate, and guide
- familiarity with the materials available and needed to implement the system.

Personnel roles. The roles in Northside's advisory system are clearly defined: adviser, counselor, administrator, parent. Advisers guide students and collaborate with their parents in providing students accurate information and appropriate processes through which students can set and monitor their progress toward their goals. Guiding students involves connecting with students within appropriate boundaries, providing a link to school counselors for personal problem solving, and mentoring.

In the student advisory system, school counselors fulfill three roles: (a) They provide career and educational information addressing the needs of individuals and groups of students. (b) They train advisers, counsel students who have been referred by their advisers, consult with advisers and parents, and serve as resources for advisory session content. (c) They ensure accurate interpretation of tests and other information, assist in material development and acquisition, and participate as members of the campus advisory leadership teams.

Administrators support the development and implementation of the advisory system in their buildings, construct schedules that provide time for advisory groups to meet, participate in adviser training, and serve as advisers. Parents collaborate with their children and their children's advisers in setting goals and making plans for implementing them. They stay informed of their children's goals and participate in advisory system events.

Initial development. The implementation of Northside's advisory system originated with the district's initial and subsequent strategic plans (Northside Independent School District, 1995, 1998). It had support from the community and the school district board of trustees—that is, from the top down.

Certain elements were put in place at the district level before the advisory system concept was introduced to building administrators and staff members. A district-level coordinator of the system was funded and selected. A steering committee was formed to design the basic content to be addressed through the system—student goal setting—and to outline the basic structure for the system. The scope and sequence of the Northside goal-setting curriculum was laid out, as were initial lessons for teaching the process and sessions for guiding students' application of it. Support materials and resources were identified and acquired.

A multitiered implementation process for buildings to follow in initiating and enhancing the student advisory system was developed. This process included developing a training plan to ensure that the district was prepared to provide the training known to be essential to successful advisory system implementation (Ayers, 1994; Cole, 1994; George & Oldaker, 1995; James, 1986) and then preparing the initial training, which was provided by the district advisory system coordinator and guest presenters.

To initiate development of a building-appropriate student advisory system, the district coordinator invites principals to apply to participate. Only a few schools from each level may begin to participate each year so that the district coordinator can be fully involved and provide a full measure of support from startup through implementation.

In accord with the site-based decision-making process in place in Northside, a school advisory leadership team is formed and oversees the incorporation of the advisory system into its school improvement plan. These teams consist of a building administrator, a counselor, and a core of teachers (6 to 8 from the elementary schools, 8 to 10 from the middle and high schools). The building-level leadership teams participate in the initial training provided at the district level and begin planning initial implementation and training of other members of their schools' staffs. One campus advisory facilitator is designated to coordinate continuous campus planning and training, materials acquisition and distribution, and promotion for parent and community support.

The first step in building-level implementation is for teachers and other educators to incorporate teaching and application of the goal-setting process into their regular curriculum and work with students. The district coordinator provides supervision and supportive consultation.

Ongoing implementation. As the original set of schools worked its way through the initiation and implementation process, the district anticipated the next steps by designing needed training and materials resources. A handbook has been written that describes the system.

Once the building-level advisory system leadership team is successfully implementing the goal-setting materials in their own classrooms, they provide the series of trainings to their peers as well as supervision and supportive consultation. They continue to participate in the district-level leadership training.

The actual implementation process that a building goes through consists of the following:

- planning
- infusion of goal setting into leadership team members' regular curriculum
- infusion of goal setting by educators schoolwide
- guiding students through setting of goals that are broader than the teachers' immediate curriculum
- designing and implementing the building-specific advisory system

Evaluation. Each building is asked to evaluate the increments of the student advisory system as they are put in place. These evaluations have focused on self-studies regarding the implementation of the advisory process and on student outcomes, particularly as they relate to goal setting. Advisers' performance is evaluated through observations and other supervision activities carried out by the district advisory system coordinator, by the campus facilitator, and by building administrators and counselors.

Questions and concerns. A student advisory system has often been greeted with skepticism because of a history of attempts and failures. In Northside as well as elsewhere, two concerns have been voiced most frequently by staff members: concern about not having enough time to "do one more thing" and concern about "doing the job of the counselor." The Northside model attended to both from the outset.

In anticipation of the first concern, it was the teachers, administrators, counselors, and other district staff members—all cognizant of and sensitive to the many demands already placed upon the staff—who created the system and its resources. Other built-in safety nets, rewards in themselves, were the systematic networking, training, resource personnel, and administrative support. Because the system was implemented gradually by an ever-widening cadre of building staff members, other staff members were able to see the success of others in incorporating the strategies. Keeping the advisory system activities focused on students' individual planning rather than on system needs and convenience was a must. The purpose of every advisory activity must have an objective that directly results in students' learning or doing something meaningful to their goals and plans.

In addressing the second concern—doing the job of the counselor—the answer in part was what most staff members already knew: It takes everyone working together to truly educate a child. The adviser training reinforced that concept and distinguished between the roles of an adviser and the roles of a school counselor. The boundaries were made very clear. Thus all staff involved could see that they were not doing the counselor's job but were providing support in helping all students set and monitor their own individual plans. In so doing, students gained a sense of connectedness with school and their education. Staff involved also saw that students who were better connected became more confident and improved their grades, attendance, and behavior.

No student arrives at a Northside school planning to fail. Often students do not plan at all. Guiding them to set, plan, implement, and evaluate goals is essential for their success in school and in the community. Northside's student advisory system now not only provides for the guidance needed for students to succeed but also nurtures their sense of connectedness.

Responsive Services

The Purpose of Responsive Services. The purpose of this component of the organizational framework is to work with students whose personal circumstances, concerns, or problems are threatening to interfere with or are interfering with their healthy personal, social, career, and educational development. Specific issues facing some students include academic success, career choice, child abuse, cross-cultural effectiveness, dropping out of school, educational choices, family loss, relationships, school attendance, stress, substance abuse, and suicide. As a result, there is a continuing need for individual counseling, small-group counseling, diagnostic and remediation activities, and consultation and referral to be an on-going part of a comprehensive guidance and counseling program. In addition, there is a continuing need for the guidance program to respond to the immediate information-seeking needs of students, parents, and teachers. The responsive services component organizes guidance and counseling techniques and methods to respond to these concerns and needs as they occur. In addition, the responsive services component is supportive of the guidance curriculum and individual student planning components.

Responsive Services Activities. Responsive services consist of activities to meet the immediate needs and concerns of students whether these needs or concerns require counseling, consultation, referral, or information. Although counselors have special training and possess skills to respond to immediate needs and concerns, the cooperation and support of the entire faculty and staff are necessary for the component's successful implementation. Parent or guardian involvement with and participation in activities of this component are critical in helping students overcome barriers to their educational progress and academic achievement. Parent involvement may include referring their children for assistance, working with school counselors and other school staff to identify issues of concern, giving permission for needed special services, and providing help in resolving the issues.

Implementation Strategies. Responsive services are implemented through the following:

- *Individual counseling:* School counselors provide individual counseling for students who are experiencing educational difficulties, personal concerns, or normal development tasks. Individual counseling assists students in identifying problems, causes, alternatives, and possible consequences so that appropriate action can be taken.
- *Small-group counseling:* School counselors provide small-group counseling to students who need and will benefit from a small-group setting to address their needs and concerns. Interventions may take the form of short-term issue groups or crisis intervention groups that deal with such topics as social skills, anger management, relationship issues, grief issues, and study skills.
- *Consultation:* Consultation is an interactive process that school counselors provide to help parents or guardians, teachers, and administrators address the academic, personal/social, and career needs of students.
- *Referral:* School counselors are familiar with school and community referral sources that deal with crises such as suicide, violence, abuse, and terminal illness. These referral sources may include mental health agencies, employment and training programs, vocational rehabilitation, juvenile services, and/or social services.

Adjunct guidance staff—peers, paraprofessionals, and volunteers—can aid school counselors in carrying out responsive services. Peers can be involved in tutorial programs, orientation activities, ombudsman functions, and—with special training—cross-age counseling and leadership in informal dialog. Paraprofessionals and volunteers can provide assistance in such areas as placement, follow-up, and community–school–home liaison activities.

System Support

The Purpose of System Support. The administration and management of a comprehensive guidance and counseling program require an ongoing support system. That is why system support is a major program component. Unfortunately, it is an aspect of a comprehensive program that is often overlooked or only minimally appreciated. And yet the system support component is as important as the other three components. Why? Because without continuing support, the other three components of the guidance and counseling program will be ineffective. Activities included in this program component are by definition those that support and enhance activities in the other three program components. That is not to say that these activities do not stand alone. They can and often do. But for the most part, they undergird activities in the other three components.

Implementation Strategies. The system support component consists of management activities that establish, maintain, and enhance the total guidance program. This component is implemented and carried out through activities in the following areas:

- *Research and development:* Guidance and counseling program evaluation, follow-up studies, and the continued development and updating of guidance learning activities and the guidance and counseling program for enhancement purposes are examples of the research and development work of school counselors.
- *Professional development:* School counselors need to be involved regularly in updating their professional knowledge and skills. Examples are participating in regular school in-service training, attending professional meetings, completing postgraduate coursework, and contributing to the professional literature.
- *Staff/community public relations:* This involves orienting staff and the community to the comprehensive guidance and counseling program through newsletters, local media, and school and community presentations.
- *Committee/advisory boards:* Serving on departmental curriculum committees and community committees or advisory boards is an example of activities in this area.
- *Community outreach:* Included in this area are activities designed to help school counselors become knowledgeable about community resources, employment opportunities, and the local labor market. This may involve school counselors visiting local businesses and industries and social services agencies on a periodic basis.
- *Program management:* This area includes the planning and management tasks needed to support the activities of a comprehensive guidance and counseling program. It also includes responsibilities that members of the school staff may need to fulfill.
- *Fair-share responsibilities:* These are the routine "running of the school" responsibilities that all members of the school staff take equal turns doing to assure the smooth operation of the school.

Also included in the system support component are those activities in the school that support programs other than guidance and counseling. These activities could include helping interpret test results to teachers, parents, and administrators; serving on departmental curriculum committees (helping interpret student needs data for curriculum revision); and working with school administrators (helping interpret student needs and behaviors). Care must be taken, however, to watch the time given to system support duties because the prime focus for school counselors' time is the direct service components of the comprehensive guidance and counseling program. It is important to realize that if the guidance and counseling program is well run, it will provide substantial support for other programs and personnel in the school and community.

Element 2: Organizational Framework: Time Allocations

Figure 3.2 presents some suggested time allocations for school counselors by program component. These time allocations are not *the* time allocations for all school counselors at all levels in all school districts. They are not prescriptive! School counselors at each level in a school district must decide on how to spend their time because the appropriate use of school counselors' professional time is crucial in developing and implementing a comprehensive guidance and counseling program. How should professionally certified school counselors allocate their time? What criteria should be used to guide the time allocation process? We recommend three criteria for your consideration: program balance, grade-level differentiation and need, and a 100% program.

Program Balance

The four program components provide the structure for making judgments about allocations of school counselors' time. One criterion to be used in making such judgments is program balance. The guidance curriculum, individual student planning, and responsive services program components represent the direct services school counselors and other guidance personnel provide to students, parents, teachers, and the community; the system support component organizes the indirect services of the program. The assumption is that counselors' time should be spread across all of the program components, but particularly the first three, perhaps in an 80:20 ratio, with 80% direct services to students, parents, teachers, and the community and 20% indirect services to these groups.

Grade-Level Differentiation and Need

Another criterion is that different grade levels require different allocations of school counselor time across the program components. For example, at the elementary level, more school counselor time may be spent working in the guidance curriculum with less time spent on individual student planning. In the high school, those time allocations probably will be reversed. How personnel in a school district or school building allocate their time depends on the needs of their students, parents or guardians, teachers, and their community as well as the resources that are available. Further, once chosen, the time allocations are not fixed forever. The purpose for making them is to provide direction to the program, to the administration, and to the school counselors involved.

A 100% Program

Because the program is a "100% program," 100% of school counselors' time must be spread across the four program components. Time allocations can be changed on the basis of newly arising needs, but nothing new can be added unless something is removed. The assumption is that school counselors should spend 100% of their time on task, on implementing the guidance and counseling program. Remember that this 100% includes the fair-share responsibilities found in the system support component.

The determination of school counselor time is a critical decision made in the designing phase (see chapter 5). The time allocations presented in Figure 3.2 are those suggested by the state of Missouri as points of departure for local school district guidance and counseling program planning (Gysbers et al., 2002). These percentages were suggested by Missouri school counselors and administrators who had participated in the early field testing of the Missouri comprehensive guidance program model in the 1980s. Remember, the word is *suggested,* not required or mandated. School counselors working closely with administration establish their own time allocations according to grade level, building, need, and resources.

Element 3: Program Resources

While local school district resources vary, sufficient resources are required to fully implement a district comprehensive guidance and counseling program. The resources that are required include personnel resources, financial resources, and political resources.

Personnel Resources

The personnel resources of a comprehensive guidance and counseling program—school counselors, guidance and counseling program staff leaders, teachers, other educational specialists, administrators, parents or guardians, students, community members, and business and labor personnel—all have roles to play in the guidance and counseling program. Although school counselors are the main providers of guidance and counseling services and coordinate the program, the involvement, cooperation, and support of teachers and administrators are necessary for a successful program that offers a full array of guidance and counseling activities. The involvement, cooperation, and support of parents or guardians, community members, and business and labor personnel also are critical for full student participation in the guidance and counseling program.

Financial Resources

Appropriate and adequate financial resources are crucial to the success of a comprehensive guidance and counseling program. The financial resource categories required for a program include budget, materials, equipment, and facilities. A budget for the guidance and counseling program is needed to fund and then allocate those funds across the buildings and grade levels of the district. Materials and equipment are needed so that guidance and counseling activities across the four program components can be implemented fully. Well-designed facilities in each building, organized to meet the needs of the guidance and counseling program, are required.

Political Resources

The political resources of a comprehensive guidance and counseling program include district policy statements, pertinent state and federal laws, state and local board of education rules and regulations, and professional association statements and standards. Clear and concise board of education policies are mandatory for the successful operation of guidance and counseling programs in school districts. They represent statements of support and courses of action, or guiding principles designed to influence and determine decisions in school districts; those that pertain to guidance and counseling programs must take into account pertinent laws, rules and regulations, and standards as they are being written, adopted, and implemented.

Element 4: Development, Management, and Accountability

The development, management, and accountability element of a comprehensive guidance and counseling program (see Figure 3.2) describes the five transition phases required to fully operationalize a comprehensive guidance and counseling program: planning, designing, implementing, evaluating, and enhancing. This element also includes the various management tasks that need to be completed in each transition phase to enable the change process to unfold smoothly and efficiently. Finally, this element describes how a comprehensive guidance and counseling program is accountable through program, personnel, and results evaluation all leading to program enhancement to make a district's comprehensive guidance and counseling program even more effective.

The Development Process

As noted in chapter 2, the development of a fully functioning comprehensive guidance and counseling program proceeds through the five phases of planning, designing, implementing, evaluating, and enhancing. There is an example timeline for these phases in chapter 2. Also the layout of this book is organized around these five phases, enabling you to first grasp the overall change processes involved and then to see how these processes can be subdivided into a logical sequence of transition phases, one building on the other. Chapters 2 and 3 describe the first two points of the planning phases, and Chapter 4 completes the description of this phase. Chapters 5 and 6 focus on the design phase, and chapters 7, 8, and 9 describe implementation issues. Finally, chapter 10 looks at evaluation, and chapter 11 describes the enhancement phase.

Management Tasks

Each phase of the change process contains a number of management tasks that must be addressed. These tasks are described in detail in each of the chapters of the book beginning with chapter 2. It is important that the guidance and counseling program leader and members of the steering committee know what the tasks are for each transition phase and have a plan to use work groups when appropriate to complete the tasks.

Accountability

A major set of management tasks focus on the need for accountability: on the impact of guidance and counseling program activities and services on students' academic, career, and personal/social development. There are three types of evaluation that lead to being accountable. The first type is program evaluation, the second type is personnel evaluation, and the final type is results evaluation. The details of each of these types of evaluation and their relationships are presented in chapter 10. Chapter 11 follows, focusing on how to use data from the above types of evaluation to improve a district's comprehensive guidance and counseling program—the program enhancement phase.

Understand the Power of Common Language

To be effective, guidance and counseling programs require consistency, logical coherence, and functional continuity in their organizational frameworks. The program presented in this chapter was designed to meet these requirements. With this program, a common language for guidance and counseling is established. The language is marked by the orderly and logical relation of the four elements of a comprehensive guidance and counseling program and affords easy comprehension and recognition by lay persons and professionals alike.

Why is common language important for the framework of guidance and counseling programs? Common language enables school counselors, administrators, teachers, and parents or guardians to "coordinate their work and multiply the power of their intellects" (American College Testing Program, 1998, p. 9). Common language for the framework of guidance and counseling programs also allows these "individuals to communicate and replicate" guidance and counseling program activities (American College Testing Program, 1998, p. 9). In addition, common language for the framework of guidance and counseling programs provides the basis for program, personnel, and results evaluation across a school district, Grades K–12.

Appreciate the Flexibility and Adaptability of a Program

Does the use of common language for the framework of guidance and counseling programs restrict all school counselors in the district to carrying out the same tasks, in the same way with the same timeline, for the entire school year? The answer is no. School buildings, grade levels, and students in districts differ in their needs. School counselors' expertise differ. School resources also differ. Although the common language of the framework of the guidance and counseling program is a constant and must remain so, school counselors' time allocations, the tasks they do, and the activities and interventions they use within the program structure to work with students, parents, and teachers will vary by school building and grade level and are often adjusted on the basis of evaluation data. Differentiated staffing using the professional expertise of the personnel involved often is a necessity (Henderson & Gysbers, 1998).

Learn About Six Program Imperatives

A comprehensive guidance and counseling program by definition leads to guidance and counseling activities for all students. It removes administrative and clerical tasks not related to the operation of the guidance and counseling program (remember that fair-share responsibilities of all staff members are part of the system support component), one-on-one counseling only, and limited accountability. It is proactive rather than reactive. School counselors are busy and unavailable for unrelated administrative and clerical duties because they have a planned comprehensive guidance and counseling program to implement. School counselors are expected to do individual and small-group counseling as well as provide structured developmental activities for all students.

To reach these outcomes, it is imperative to

1. understand that a comprehensive guidance and counseling program is student development oriented, not school management oriented or school administration oriented;
2. operate a comprehensive guidance and counseling program as a 100% program in which the four program components constitute the total program with no add-ons;
3. begin the comprehensive guidance and counseling program the first day of school (not in the middle of October) and end it the last day of school (not at the end of April);
4. understand that a comprehensive guidance and counseling program is program focused, not position focused;
5. understand that a comprehensive guidance and counseling program is education based, not agency or clinic based; and
6. understand that while a comprehensive guidance and counseling program uses a common organizational framework, the contents, activities, and school counselor time allocations are tailored to meet local student, school, and community needs and resources.

References

American College Testing Program. (1998, Spring). The power of a common language in workplace development. *Work Keys, USA, 3,* 9.

American College Testing Program. (2004). *Crisis at the core: Preparing all students for college and work.* Iowa City, IA: Author.

American School Counselor Association. (1984). *The school counselor and developmental guidance: Position statement.* Alexandria, VA: Author.

American School Counselor Association. (2005). *The ASCA national model: A framework for school counseling programs* (2nd ed.). Alexandria, VA: Author.

Ayers, L. R. (1994). Middle school advisory programs: Findings from the field. *Middle School Journal, 25*(3), 8–14.

Borders, L. D., & Drury, S. M. (1992). Comprehensive school counseling programs: A review for policy makers and practitioners. *Journal of Counseling & Development, 70,* 487–498.

Carnegie Council on Adolescent Development. (1989). *Turning points: Preparing American youth for the 21st century.* New York: Carnegie Corporation.

Cole, C. G. (1994). Teachers attitudes before beginning a teacher advisory. *Middle School Journal, 25*(5), 3–7.

Commission on Precollege Guidance and Counseling. (1986). *Keeping the options open: Recommendations.* New York: College Entrance Examination Board.

Cook, D. R. (Ed.). (1971). *Guidance for education in revolution.* Boston: Allyn & Bacon.

Davis, D. (1997). The comprehensive guidance program in Davis County schools. In N. C. Gysbers & P. Henderson (Eds.), *Comprehensive guidance programs that work—II* (pp. 107–123). Greensboro, NC: ERIC Counseling and Student Services Clearinghouse.

ERIC Counseling and Personnel Services Clearinghouse. (1983). *Comprehensive guidance program design* [Fact sheet]. Ann Arbor, MI: Author.

George, P., & Oldaker, L. (1995). *Evidence of the middle school.* Columbus, OH: National Middle School Association.

Gysbers, N. C., & Henderson, P. (1988). *Developing and managing your school guidance program.* Alexandria, VA: American Counseling Association.

Gysbers, N. C., & Henderson, P. (1994). *Developing and managing your school guidance program* (2nd ed.). Alexandria, VA: American Counseling Association.

Gysbers, N. C., & Henderson, P. (2000). *Developing and managing your school guidance program* (3rd ed.). Alexandria, VA: American Counseling Association.

Gysbers, N. C., Heppner, M. J., & Johnston, J. A. (2003). *Career counseling: Process, issues, and techniques* (2nd ed.). Needham Heights, MA: Allyn & Bacon.

Gysbers, N. C., Kosteck-Bunch, L., Magnuson, C. S., & Starr, M. F. (2002). *Missouri comprehensive guidance program: A manual for program development, implementation, evaluation, and enhancement.* Columbia, MO: Instructional Materials Laboratory.

Gysbers, N. C., & Moore, E. J. (1975). Beyond career development—life career development. *Personnel and Guidance Journal, 53,* 647–652.

Gysbers, N. C., & Moore, E. J. (1981). *Improving guidance programs.* Englewood Cliffs, NJ: Prentice-Hall.

Henderson, P. (2005). The theory behind the ASCA national model. In American School Counselor Association. *The ASCA national model: A framework for school counseling programs* (2nd ed.). (pp. 79–101). Alexandria, VA: Author.

Henderson, P., & Gysbers, N. C. (1998). *Leading and managing your school guidance program staff.* Alexandria, VA: American Counseling Association.

James, M. (1986). *Adviser–advisee programs: Why, what, and how.* Columbus, OH: National Middle School Association.

Jones, A. J., & Hand, H. C. (1938). Guidance and purposive living. In G. M. Whipple (Ed.), *Yearbook of the national society for the study of education: Part I* (pp. 3–29). Bloomington, IL: Public School.

Lortie, D. C. (1965). Administrator, advocate, or therapist? Alternatives for professionalization in school counseling. In R. L. Mosher, R. F. Carle, & C. C. Kehas (Eds.), *Guidance: An examination* (pp. 127–143). New York: Harcourt Brace Jovanovich.

Markus, H., & Nurius, P. (1986). Possible selves. *American Psychologist, 41,* 954–969.

McDaniels, C., & Gysbers, N. C. (1992). *Counseling for career development: Theories, resources, and practice.* San Francisco: Jossey-Bass.

Miller, H. (1977, July 17). Which way next for L.A. schools? *Los Angeles Times,* Section VIII, p. 5.

Missouri Department of Elementary and Secondary Education. (1997). *Missouri school improvement program standards and indicators manual.* Jefferson, City, MO: Author.

Myers, G. E. (1923). A critical review of present developments in vocational guidance with special reference to future prospects. *The Vocational Guidance Magazine, 3,* 139–140.

Myrick, R. D. (1990). *The teacher advisory program.* Ann Arbor, MI: ERIC Counseling and Personnel Services Clearinghouse.

National Association of Secondary School Principals. (1996). *Breaking ranks: Changing an American institution.* Reston, VA: Author.

National Association of Secondary School Principals. (2004). *Breaking ranks II: Strategies for leading high school reform.* Reston, VA. Author.

Northside Independent School District. (1994). *Comprehensive guidance program framework.* San Antonio, TX: Author.

Northside Independent School District. (1995). *Strategic plan: 1994–99.* San Antonio, TX: Author.

Northside Independent School District. (1997). *Guide to counselor performance improvement through job definition, professionalism, assessment, supervision, performance evaluation, and professional development goal setting.* San Antonio, TX: Author.

Northside Independent School District. (1998). *Strategic plan: 1998–2003.* San Antonio, TX: Author.

Orfield, G., & Paul, F. G. (1994). *High hopes long odds: Next steps.* Indianapolis: Indiana Youth Institute.

Random House Webster's Unabridged Dictionary. (2001). New York: Random House.

Reich, C. A. (1971). *The greening of America.* New York: Bantam Books.

Richardson, H. D., & Baron, M. (1975). *Developmental counseling in education.* Boston: Houghton Mifflin.

Sink, C. (2002). Comprehensive guidance and counseling programs and the development of multicultural student-citizens. *Professional School Counseling, 6,* 130–137.

Student education plan/student education occupation plan amendments, Utah Stat. Ann. 53A-1a-106 (1996).

Texas Education Agency. (2004). *A model comprehensive developmental guidance and counseling program for Texas public schools* (4th ed.). Austin, TX: Author.

Vars, G. F. (1997, March/April). Creating options, getting closer to middle level students: Options for teacher–adviser guidance programs. *Schools in the Middle, 17.*

Wellman, F. E., & Moore, E. J. (1975). *Pupil personnel services: A handbook for program development and evaluation.* Washington, DC: U.S. Department of Health, Education, and Welfare.

Whitmer, J. (1992, May). Teachers as advisers. *Executive Educator,* 41.

Wolfe, D. M., & Kolb, D. A. (1980). Career development, personal growth, and experimental learning. In J. W. Springer (Ed.), *Issues in career and human resource development* (pp. 1–56). Madison, WI: American Society for Training and Development.

⌐ Chapter 4 *⌐*

Assessing Your Current Guidance
and Counseling Program

Planning—Conducting a Thorough Assessment of the Current Program

- Gather student and community status information.
- Identify current resource availability and use.
- Study current guidance and counseling program delivery.
- Gather perceptions about the program.
- Present a report describing the current program.

⌐ The next phase of the program improvement process involves assessing your current program. Current program assessment is a process for obtaining a concrete, detailed description of your school or school district's guidance and counseling program as it currently exists. The program is viewed from as many angles as possible to discern its design. Current program assessment is not a way of measuring students' needs; it is rather a way of determining what the current guidance and counseling program is.

The current program assessment tells you what resources are already available to the guidance and counseling program and how those resources are being used for students and the school community. It is prerequisite to suggesting how to use the resources differently (Adelman & Taylor, 2003, p. 7). The assessment is done by describing the program using the framework of the four elements of the comprehensive guidance and counseling program model described in chapter 3: (a) content; (b) organizational framework, structure, activities, and time; (c) resources; and (d) development, management, and accountability. The assessment process reveals the current program's accomplishments, shape, and priorities. You are enabled to answer questions such as the following: What competencies do students acquire as a result of their involvement in the program's activities and, ultimately, in the program as a whole? What are the theoretical and policy supports for the program? What is the structure of the program? How are the competencies of the professional school counselor(s) applied in the program? What are the other personnel and financial resources that are used? and How is the program developed, managed, and accountable? The program assessment provides the basis for identifying what is good about the program that needs to be retained, for recognizing critical gaps in service delivery, and for planning needed program changes.

Knowing the "design" of the program is knowing its various parts and how they are arranged to form its shape. The design has two facets: qualitative and quantitative. The qualitative design describes the program's substance, the "what/who" of the program. Specifically: What activities are conducted within each component? What use is made of the professional school counselors' specialized competence, their talent? Who is served through the program activities—students, parents, teachers, administrators, and other adults who work with the students? What are the results for students who experience these activities? The possibilities within the qualitative design are many, perhaps infinite, and so the qualitative design is shaped by priorities. Often the current priorities of schools' guidance and counseling programs have not been consciously set, but that does not make them any the less real.

The quantitative design describes the program's amounts, the measurable and countable parts, the "how much" of the program. Specifically: How much of the professional schools counselors' time is spent in each component, that is, what is the balance of the program? How many students are served through each of the program components? How many students are served in each of the levels of need category? How many students (what proportion) are served by population subgroup compared with the makeup of the total student population? The quantitative design is shaped by finite numbers that establish the parameters of its dimensions, and it consequently sets the parameters for the qualitative design. The priorities of the qualitative design establish the substance of the program.

This chapter first discusses preparing for the assessment of your current program. Second, we suggest you study your students and school community to best understand the makeup of your program's client population. Different communities have different needs that have influenced and will continue to influence the guidance and counseling program. Third, we describe ways to assess what personnel, financial, and political resources are available to the current program as well as how these resources are used. Fourth, we outline ways to study your current program delivery, the qualitative and quantitative facets of its design. Fifth, we suggest ways for you to gather perceptions about the program from students, teachers, administrators, parents, community members, and school counselors themselves. Sixth, we emphasize the importance of pulling together all of the data gathered in the assessment of your current program and preparing and presenting a report to the people concerned with improvement of the guidance and counseling program. Seventh, we encourage you to pay special attention to the realities of and the issues posed by the diversity of today's school populations. The chapter concludes with an exploration of the leadership roles and responsibilities required to accomplish your current program assessment.

Getting Ready

Assessing the current program provides information that is the foundation of your future guidance and counseling program. It is important to take the time needed to ensure gathering accurate data because these data help the guidance and counseling staff understand the current program design. The data are also useful in helping others understand the current status of the program. The data become the baseline from which your decisions for change are made and against which your changes will be evaluated. Having accomplished such a study, Taylor (2002) found,

> First, school counselors were able to document the amount of time they spent in guidance and
> non-guidance tasks and compare this with the state model. Second, school administrators and

counselors obtained critical information regarding how others perceived guidance services and how they might be improved. Finally, administrators received information about state-of-the-art developmental guidance and counseling programs. . . . Until this time, the counselors' supervisor had been unaware of the developmental guidance model. (p. 26)

Assessing the current program takes time. You need to be realistic in establishing the time frame. Specific suggestions for accomplishing each of the tasks that will help save you some time are offered in the following sections, but it still could take from 6 months to a year to complete a thorough assessment.

To accomplish current program assessment, several work groups need to be formed. Identifying current program activities, their applications of school counselors' competence, their clients, and their outcomes are interrelated tasks; thus gathering this information should be either the work of one group or of groups working closely together. Concurrently, other work groups can begin identifying current program resource use and collecting perceptions about the current program. To make the data you gather useful in future planning, one basic rule must apply to all work groups and other data collection efforts: Always organize your current assessment according to the program components— guidance curriculum, individual student planning, responsive services, and system support.

Because assessing your current program is a substantial undertaking, guidance program leaders have important roles to play. If you are the leader of the guidance and counseling program, you have the primary responsibility for data collection and for ensuring the full and appropriate summary, analysis, and dissemination of the results. We recommend, however, that all school counselors in the building or district affected by the potential changes be involved in the current program assessment. Involvement in accomplishing the assessment tasks helps the staff become familiar with the program model selected and feel not only that most of what they are currently doing fits into the components of the model but also that the "new" program will not be completely different from the current program.

Involvement of administrators in work groups is also needed. This way, administrators learn about the program model and are in a better position to support the changes called for in the future. Some administrators have been school counselors in the past and have strong experience based opinions on how the program can and should be changed. Administrators help students, staff, and others understand where the guidance and counseling program is going. By helping craft the needed program changes, they provide support for the implementation of changes in their schools or districts. The work of some groups, however, is at times truly laborious. Staff who are not directly concerned with each minute detail may find it somewhat tedious, for example, to analyze the time study data for similarities and differences for each school or grade level. It is important to use administrators in areas where they can make a solid contribution to the deliberations and not let them get bogged down in data that are in fact the internal concern of the guidance department.

We recommend that steering committee members chair the various work groups. Steering committee meetings can then provide the opportunity to monitor and coordinate the work of the various groups. In any case, some vehicle for coordinating the work groups' efforts needs to be established; a committee of committee chairs also would work.

In planning your current program assessment, you should use current program description materials. Many states have led schools and districts in the development of guidance and counseling program "handbooks" or "plans." Much useful information can be extracted from these existing documents, such as listings of current program activities, to facilitate current assessment efforts. A word of caution: It has been our experience that these plans are often outdated or include activities that are not actually performed.

Gather Student and Community Status Information

What Information Is Useful

Students

An important part of assessing the current program is gathering information about the current status of students: what they know, learn, and need. Data regarding students' achievement and conduct are useful. Sources of achievement information include standardized and criterion-referenced tests, portfolio assessments, and patterns of students' grades; attitude surveys and career development surveys; follow-up and dropout studies; and failure and promotion/retention rates. Student conduct data include discipline reports, attendance and absence rates, and rates of participation in extra- and cocurricular activities.

School Community Context

Information about the context in which students live also suggests values and priorities for the guidance and counseling program. Useful demographic data include ethnic makeup, languages spoken and preferred, socioeconomic status, economic base and labor market pool and placement, mobility rate, special program enrollments, parental level of education, family configuration, neighborhood makeup and issues, political climate, immigration patterns, and homelessness numbers. As Lee (2001) pointed out,

> More than three-quarters [of the growth in the numbers of students in public elementary and secondary schools in the United States] can be attributed to an increase in the number of Hispanic and Asian students. Data further indicate that the overall proportion of minority public school students increased from 1987–1988 to 1990–1991 while the proportion of White non-Hispanic students declined (National Center for Education Statistics, 1996). In concrete terms, these demographic estimates mean that, as never before, U.S. schools are becoming a social arena where children who represent truly diverse behavioral styles, attitudinal orientations, and value systems have been brought together with one goal—to prepare them for academic, career, and social success in the 21st Century. (p. 257)

In addition to student data, other relevant data about the community context are useful in understanding the students' worlds. These data include community demographics, economics, and social, cultural, and political orientations. As public schools are state governed, the political context includes the prevailing legislative climate.

The context of the school and school district environment also must be considered. Such information as the size of the school; the prevailing professional values, beliefs, mission, and goals of the institution; and the cost per student of the education provided by the school district have impact on the guidance and counseling program. It is also important to learn about the available special programs and technology.

Ideas About How to Conduct an Assessment of Student and Community Status

If this information has not been gathered already in developing the rationale for your program, a work group or groups should take on the task of identifying and collecting as much of these data as are readily available. Initial collection of this information is not the responsibility of the guidance department and should probably not be taken on in this effort, but much is available through other sources. Schools' and districts' Web pages are a rich source of information. On the Northside Independent School District Web site (http://www.nisd.net), a reader is able to learn about the numbers of various categories of staff members (professional, support, administrative, auxiliary), the range of teachers' salaries, administrative ratios, student–teacher ratios, and student–computer ratios. A reader can learn about the bus fleet, including the salient detail that 50% of all Northside students ride the bus (Northside Independent School District, 2004). Information is also provided about student ethnicity, academic achievements, enrollment numbers, dropout numbers, and numbers of students in special education, career and technology education, and who are college bound. There is also information about the community: the number of residents, households, and businesses.

In this era of accountability, many of these data are gathered and reported to the public. In Texas, for example, the Academic Excellence Indicator System (AEIS) pulls together a wide range of information on the performance of students in each school and district each year and includes academic information: state-administered assessment performance, attendance rates, dropout and completion rates, participation in advanced courses, and participation in the SAT and ACT college entrance examinations (Texas Education Agency, n.d.). Data about the number of students per grade level, their sex, and their ethnic distribution (African American, Hispanic, White, Asian/Pacific Islander, and Native American) are also provided. Mobility rates and percentages of students who are economically disadvantaged, who have limited English proficiency, and with disciplinary placements are given. Demographic information is reported about the professional and paraprofessional staff. Information is provided about student enrollment in special programs and about amounts and distribution of budget.

When compiled, such information can provide insight into how well the current program is meeting student needs. In light of the school's and/or district's mission, such information also suggests what the student needs are for your program. These needs data should be related as much as possible to the list of student results you identify.

In addition to providing insight into how well the current program is meeting student needs, student data play another role in program improvement. They provide a baseline against which to compare students in future years. They provide opportunities to look at trends concerning student growth and development.

Identify Current Resource Availability and Use

The efficiency of a program is measured in terms of the ratio of resources applied to the benefits accrued. Thus, gathering concrete information about the resources currently available to the guidance and counseling program is essential to any program improvement decisions to be made. In addition, not only is having complete information about what is available useful, but also most guidance and counseling program administrators will be encouraged by learning the actual quantity of resources available to them. The more complete your knowledge of the resources currently available, the more room you have for creativity as you decide to redirect them for program improvements (Adelman & Taylor, 2003), and the more specific you can be in your requests for additional resources. At this point you are studying what is or is not currently in place. It is premature to make recommendations about what you want to have in place. That comes later and is described in chapter 5.

As described in chapter 3, we categorize resources as personnel, financial, and political. Personnel resources include staff members' time and talents. Financial resources are those applied through the budget to provide materials, equipment, and facilities for the guidance and counseling program. Political resources are represented by policy statements and supporters of the current program and staff. Because of the variety of resources used in a comprehensive guidance and counseling program, this is a giant step that requires time and staff commitment to accomplish. Some of the ways that districts have accomplished this task and assessed resource availability are described by category in the following discussions. How these resources are used is described in the section of the chapter, "Study Current Guidance and Counseling Program Delivery."

Personnel Resources

Personnel resources that need to be assessed include school counselors and guidance department paraprofessionals. Teachers and administrators often conduct guidance activities, so they also need to be included. Related mental health professionals, such as school social workers and school psychologists, may participate in guidance program activities. If your school or district uses community volunteers, such as business community representatives as career speakers or PTA volunteers as coleaders of parent involvement efforts or as clerical support, you will need to list them as well. Of course, it is imperative that all personnel are fulfilling roles for which they have training and competence. Assessing these human resources involves identifying their talents and the time they spend on the program.

Professional School Counselors

Data are needed on the professional school counselors' training and experience, counselor–student ratio, counselor–student assignment patterns, and counselor time available.

School Counselor Training and Experience. The school counseling staff is the basic resource of the guidance and counseling program. Clarification of school counselors' unique talents provides qualitative data about the contribution they are able to make to students' growth and development. It is the school counselors' unique training and experiences that allow us to seek accountability for helping students learn to make decisions, solve problems, and perform other personal and social developmental tasks. Indeed, more often than not, when principals are asked to describe their guidance and counseling programs, they will say, "I have five counselors" or "I have six counselors and a registrar." They focus on their staffing units—the positions—rather than the program components or results.

There is, however, a widespread lack of information as to what school counselors' unique talents are. As a result, it is useful to specify the requirements for school counselors' background and training. Ways to do this include ensuring that everyone concerned is aware of the certification requirements for professional school counselors, publicizing the training requirements for the master's degree in counseling, publicizing appropriately written job descriptions of school counselors, and disseminating the American School Counselor Association (ASCA, 2004b) role statement, *The Role of the Professional School Counselor.*

A review of the literature (ASCA, 2005) describing the specialized training professional school counselors are expected to have in the 21st century suggests that they are equipped to provide individual counseling, small-group counseling, and large-group guidance; teaching for student competency development in academic, career, and personal/social content domains; consultation with other adults who work with students; case management; coordination of resources on behalf of students; advocacy on behalf of individual and groups of students; and management and evaluation of school guidance and counseling programs.

Traditionally, school counselors have read and talked much about the unique roles and functions they fulfill in schools. Thus another way to make school counselors' skills known is to ask the school counselors themselves to identify their performance roles and relate them to the four program components. In Texas, professional school counselors have identified eight performance domains and their related standards to describe their competencies:

guidance, counseling, consultation, coordination, assessment, program management, adhering to professional standards, and professional behavioral expectations (Texas Counseling Association, 2004). Competencies are subsets of performance domains; for example, within the counseling performance domains, individual counseling is one area of competence and small-group counseling is another. Within the consultation domains, consulting with parents is one area of competence, consulting with teachers is another, and consulting with school administrators is a third.

Although all of these domains come into play in more than one of the program components, each component draws more heavily on some of the roles. Table 4.1 displays which domains are used primarily in each of the comprehensive guidance and counseling program components. Relating the familiar performance roles to the program components also helps school counselors distinguish between the components and build a common terminology base. If some of the professional school counselors are used in specialized roles, identifying the performance domains that are emphasized in their responsibilities allows for using common language to describe their expertise, and at the same time clarifying differences in their applications of it.

School Counselor–Student Ratio. An essential piece of quantitative data is the current school counselor–student ratio. During the discussions of the model program, everyone involved may be starry-eyed about the possibilities, but the realities of caseload must be ever present. The range of school counselor–student ratios by state for 2001–2002 is from 1:225 in Alabama to 1:971 in California. The national average ratio is 1:448 (ASCA, 2004c). Ultimately your program design will have to acknowledge what each school counselor can be expected to do for his or her 200, 500, or 1,000 students. Further, knowing whether the ratio is the same from school level to school level allows you to tailor your expectations accordingly. For example, in some districts, the recognition of disproportionately heavy loads at the elementary and middle school levels when contrasted with the high school level has led to immediate efforts to employ more elementary and middle school counselors.

School Counselor–Student Assignment Patterns. In addition to ratios, typical patterns of school counselor–student assignment need to be reviewed. Are school counselors assigned to a grade level or to an alphabetical group? How are specialized school

Table 4.1
School Counselor's Performance Domains and Program Components

Performance Domain	Primary Component Application
Program management	System support
Guidance	Guidance curriculum
	Individual student planning
Counseling	Responsive services
Consultation	Guidance curriculum
	Individual student planning
	Responsive services
	System support
Coordination	Guidance curriculum
	Individual student planning
	Responsive services
	System support
Student assessment	Individual student planning
	Responsive services
	System support
Professional standards	System support
Professional behavior	System support

counselors—career and technology, special education, substance abuse, multicultural—assigned their students? The rationale behind these assignments implies the philosophy of the guidance and counseling program. For example, caseload assignment by grade level reflects a developmental philosophy, whereas assignment by alphabet (i.e., surname) often reflects an emphasis on responding to students within knowledge of their family context.

School Counselor Time. The primary resource of the guidance and counseling program is the time of professional school counselors. How their time is used defines the program. At this point it is important to identify how much time is available to the guidance and counseling program so that a realistic baseline can be established. It is also important to specify the students' time that is available for guidance and counseling activities. Specific answers are needed to such questions as how many hours constitute a school counselor's workday? How many hours are in a student's school day? For example, a counselor's workday may be 8 hours, whereas the student's school day is $7\frac{1}{2}$ hours. Students may be available for services before or after school; some of that quantity depends on whether students walk to school, are bused, and so on. How many days are in a student's school week? Some schools build schedules for specialists over 6- or 7-day spans. How many weeks or days are in a school counselor's school year? Lengths of school counselors' contracts vary from district to district, and from level to level. A school counselor on a 202-day contract might accomplish a lot more program planning and staff development on nonstudent time than a school counselor on a 180-day contract. How many weeks or days are in a student's school year? Lengths of the school year vary from state to state—from 173 days in North Dakota to 187 days in Texas (National Center for Education Statistics, 2002). Ultimately, the expectations for the program must fit within the parameters of actual time that school counselors work and that students are available for direct services.

Other Personnel

School staff members are important members of the guidance team, and as such their competencies and contributions to the program need to be identified. In some schools, school counselors share caseloads with campus administrators. Paraprofessionals and secretaries fulfill essential roles. Career center technicians, for example, provide many guidance activities for students. Teachers assist, particularly in the delivery of guidance curricula and in the referral of students for services. Other related school specialists, such as school nurses, psychologists, and social workers, fulfill roles as referral sources. Students also are important members of the guidance team when, for example, they work as peer counselors or aides in career centers or make alumni presentations to younger students. Data on such contributions need to be identified and collected. The same is true for contributions by business and community representatives and PTA volunteers.

Financial Resources

Financial resources that need to be assessed include all budget items that support the guidance and counseling program. In addition to salaries and other staff costs, budget categories consist of appropriations for materials, equipment, and facilities.

Budget

The place to begin the assessment of financial resources is identifying the specific district or building budget line items that relate to the current guidance and counseling program. Even if there is no official budget labeled "guidance," as is often the case at the both the district and building levels, funds are being spent for guidance, so begin there. Consider collecting data on such items as salaries for school counselors, secretaries, and aides; staff and program development appropriations; money spent for supplies such as paper, pencils, and record folders; money spent for guidance and counseling program materials such as books, videos, films, pamphlets, standardized tests, and scoring services; and capital outlay money available. All expenses for guidance activities in the district should be included as well as any special funding from federal, state, or private groups—like the PTA—or foundations. This information will give you a perspective on the guidance department's share of the total school district budget. It is often much larger than the guidance staff thinks.

Materials

If you do not already have one, it is important to take an inventory of the materials you have available. You will want to categorize your inventory by program model components and by student outcomes as well as by grade level. The listing should include title, copyright date, a brief description of the content, and the use for which the resource was developed. Assuming that you will want to disseminate this list to the guidance staff, it also is helpful to include information about how to obtain the resource and about any restrictions on borrowing it.

Equipment

A study of your equipment inventory will reveal the quantity and kinds of audiovisual and computer equipment available as well as how the equipment is distributed. How accessible is it to all staff? You may want to consider an equipment use study to determine if you are using the equipment to its maximum potential or to evaluate if your current distribution system is the best for you. Depending on the size of your program and the quantity of audiovisual equipment, you need to consider whether the equipment is best used if housed centrally and shared on a checkout basis or permanently housed on each of the campuses. You need to carefully consider how the computer equipment is used and by whom and to what purposes, for example, legitimate guidance activities or nonguidance tasks.

Facilities

Baseline information as to the facilities available to the current guidance and counseling program is needed on a building-by-building basis. This, again, will show you the evenness of facility availability. As you begin to implement desired new program activities, your baseline data will provide realistic planning information about the space available currently. Any necessary remodeling takes time and planning. If additional space is needed, such as a classroom for developmental guidance or a guidance information or career center, that information must be ready for submission to the district as the superintendent makes overall plans for the ensuing year.

Political Resources

Political here means the support that is rooted in district or building policies; in state and federal laws, rules, or regulations; or in the standards adopted by accreditation bodies or other professional associations to which your school or district subscribes. It also includes staff members' support for guidance and counseling program improvement. A political reality to consider is the staff members who are not supportive of the change efforts.

Policy Statements

Relevant policy statements are made at the local, state, and national levels. Knowing these philosophical tenets that undergird your program provides you the context within which to operate.

Local Policies. To build the program from its current base, it is important to identify statements that indicate the rationale for, the underlying assumptions of, and the mission of the current guidance and counseling program—the structural components of the comprehensive guidance and counseling program model. Some of these may be overtly stated; others may have to be inferred from what is written. Chapter 5 outlines more specifically the kinds of information that make up each of these components. One glaring gap in policy statements was pointed out by MacDonald and Sink (1999), who studied state program models to identify the "developmental constructs in the models and their integration within each state's published guidelines and curricula" (p. 419). They found that most models lacked identification of a developmental theory base and also lacked attention to students' developmental needs and the developmental needs of specific groups of students (e.g., gifted students). "The most significant gap across the models [they found] is in attention to culture and ethnic developmental issues" (p. 424).

Adelman and Taylor (2003) noted,

> Of particular importance is awareness of prevailing and pending policies, institutional priorities and their current status. . . . This involves, for example, amassing information that clarifies the school and community vision, mission statements, current policies, and major agenda priorities. (p. 7)

It is useful to identify the school district's vision for its students. The district may have an existing board policy about the guidance and counseling program, although it may be incomplete, focusing on activities provided, the needs of students, or the staff members with responsibility (Gysbers, Lapan, & Jones, 2000). It surely has a statement about the educational mission of the district that has implications for the guidance and counseling program. In all likelihood, there are procedural expectations for school counselors expressed in administrative handbooks. You need to review these official pronouncements and extract and synthesize from them the basic political platform supporting the current guidance and counseling program.

If you have followed our suggestions so far, you have already begun to develop policy statements about the guidance and counseling program by adopting a program model, and in using the comprehensive program model described in chapter 3, developing the three structural components. Writing your own program rationale, assumptions, and definition provides you with policy support that is most relevant to your efforts. Indeed, it is our opinion that unless you have these statements in hand, your reorganization effort may be ineffective because it will lack the needed focus that a theory-based belief system provides (ASCA, in press). A key point has been made by MacDonald and Sink (1999) after studying current guidance program models. They noted that the theoretical underpinnings for the programs were either not stated or not acknowledged or were only superficially apparent. This may be true of your current guidance and counseling program also. If so, identifying the underlying program assumptions will be an important exercise.

State and Federal Policies. Another useful survey is that of existing state and federal education laws, rules, and regulations that pertain to guidance. Federal education laws that allow money to be spent for guidance and counseling include those supporting bilingual, compensatory, migrant, special, and career and technology education; dropout prevention; and the Safe and Drug Free Schools and Communities Act. This money is appropriated to the states, which in turn develop rules and regulations for its distribution within the state.

Because guidance is still a relatively new part of the total educational program, there may be no specific state guidance and counseling program legislation with related rules and regulations. Some states are including guidance curriculum as part of the regular instructional curriculum, and many state legislatures and boards of education are making guidance and counseling issues a high priority. In addition, many states have expressed concerns through policies or laws regarding high rates of dropping out, school violence, adolescent suicide, substance abuse, teen parenting, and child abuse and neglect. With concern about these issues and awareness of the all-too-typical underutilization of professional school counselors, some states have passed laws or established administrative regulations that would remedy the problem. For example, Texas passed a law that mandates an appropriate set of responsibilities for school counselors (i.e., counseling, comprehensive developmental guidance and counseling program development, consultation, coordination, standardized test interpretation to help students make educational and career plans, and classroom guidance) and delineates what the Texas developmental guidance and counseling program consists of (i.e., guidance curriculum, responsive services, individual planning, and system support; Texas Education Code, 2001).

Certification of educators is a state's right and responsibility. Thus, states have established certification laws and rules that stipulate the entry level and, often, the continuing education requirements prerequisite to earning and maintaining school counselor certification. A work-group visit with the state education department guidance staff may reveal much about state goals and the larger perspective. If you have not availed yourself of the statewide viewpoint, join the members of the work group on their visit to the state capitol.

Professional Standards. Standards relevant to guidance and counseling have been established by State Departments of Education guidance departments, regional accreditation, and professional associations. Some of these standards include school counselor–student ratios; for example, the ASCA (2004b) has identified 1:250 as an appropriate ratio. Standards for comprehensive guidance and counseling programs have been established by more than 30 states (Sink & MacDonald, 1998) and in the ASCA National Model (ASCA, 2005). In its National Standards, ASCA (1997) established standards for the content of school guidance and counseling programs. The National Career Development Association (NCDA, 2003) has also expressed standards relative to career development for school-age children and youths. ASCA has published role descriptions for the three school levels: *Why Elementary School Counselors* (ASCA, 2004d), *Why Middle School Counselors* (ASCA, 2004e), and *Why Secondary School Counselors* (ASCA, 2004f). These describe students' developmental needs at each level and how school counselors respond. Both ASCA and NCDA are divisions of the American Counseling Association.

Staff Support/Nonsupport

Political also means the level of constituent support that is behind the momentum for change. Some school counselors are eager for changes and will accept them; others will resist. Guidance and counseling program leaders need to consider the feelings of the staff and make preparations for working with both supportive and nonsupportive individuals. Nurturing the positive attitudes of the school counselors who are supportive and building on their strengths allows the program to be improved.

As discussed in chapter 2, perhaps the majority of school counselors are, at first, resistant. Change is frightening to many people. Assessing the causes of their resistance will help you and your leadership team to address those concerns as much as feasible. Many of the resisters do not understand the program concept at first. Many are fearful that the new program will cause them to change their entire set of work-related behaviors. Many are fearful that they do not or will not have the competencies they will need in the new program. And some will resist until they retire or are moved to other positions. We advise you to keep focused on the positive, manage the negative as best you can, and wait out the rest.

The support of administrators and teachers—the representatives of the primary clients of the program, the students—is needed to make changes effectively. As with the school counselors, they, too, will fall onto a continuum of support and nonsupport. By and large, they want what is best for the students. They also, by and large, will look to the school counselors' expertise to tell them how professional school counselors can best help students. As mentioned previously, their representation on the steering, advisory, and other working committees as appropriate is essential to hearing and responding to their perspectives and needs. Political support from the school board and the senior administration also promotes support from other administrators and school staff members. Indeed, without board and senior administrative support, changes take longer or may not get done at all (Taylor, 2002).

Study Current Guidance and Counseling Program Delivery

This step in assessing your current program entails gathering and analyzing data that will tell you the design of the current program. By studying actual program implementation, you identify the actual priorities of the current qualitative design and the actual parameters of the quantitative design.

Understanding the current qualitative design consists primarily of the study of the current, actually done guidance and counseling program activities. From studying the activities, you see how your current program aligns with the comprehensive guidance and counseling program components: guidance curriculum, individual student planning, responsive services, and system support. From studying the actual activities, you can determine the priorities for the use of the professional school counselors' competencies—the roles they perform in conducting the activities. You learn about the priorities of the clients within the program—by category, who is actually being helped. You identify the anticipated results for the program participants—the actual content addressed in the program. Thus carefully and thoroughly identifying the program activities is essential to the overall program improvement process.

Understanding the quantitative design consists primarily of the study of how school counselors' time is currently allocated, again using the framework of the program delivery components. Through this information about the time spent on the components and from the analysis of what activities are done within that time, the numbers of students and other clients actually served can be inferred, as can the categories of clients actually served.

In the sections that follow, each part of the design is described, that is, what is to be assessed. Some example results are displayed. Finally, ideas about how you can gather the data need are also provided. We firmly believe that the more thoroughly you gather these data, the more solid your foundation for program change will be. However, in some instances school counselors or their administrators are under pressure to get recommendations made. Thus, we first describe legitimate ways to gather the data, and then we offer some "shortcuts" that have been used with some degree of success in other schools or districts.

Qualitative Design

Identify Current Guidance and Counseling Activities

What Is Assessed. In this part of the study, you identify the specific activities that are conducted at each school level within each of the four comprehensive guidance and counseling program components. Identification of specific nonguidance tasks is also recommended. Studying the program activities provides information about many of the facets of the current program design. As described in chapter 3, the program components are made up of activities that serve different purposes. You are identifying what the activities are that make up your current program and how they fit within the program model. Additionally, an activity includes all aspects of the design: one or more school counselors' competencies are being applied; one or more categories of students or other program clients are being served; an intentional activity targets an objective for student competency development or learning—what the anticipated student results are. Quantitatively, you are able to identify how much time school counselors spend on the activity and how many students or other clients are actually served. When you aggregate this information by component, you learn a lot about your current program's priorities and shape (i.e., about which components are emphasized, which are not).

Although identifying and recording the activities in which the guidance department and other staff members are involved yields worthwhile information about your program, it is a major task. There are several reasons for conducting it. One reason is that recording the actual activities accomplished ensures preciseness in program details. Another is that recording these activities renders them visible and thus more understandable to others. This is important because so much of what we do is invisible to others. Visibility helps school counselors see the commonalities among their programs. In some districts it has provided a bridge between the elementary and secondary counselors and enabled them to focus on the similarities rather than on the differences of their programs. Yet another reason is that recording encourages school counselors as they learn more about the new program model and how what are currently doing fits into the model. In our experience, recording has helped the school counselors who are not in the mainstream of program remodeling and revitalization better understand the four program components by providing operational definitions for them.

In getting started, it is important that the school counselors involved in the data submission, collection, and recording understand the kinds of activities that make up each component. Table 4.2 provides some examples of activities (by program component). These are activities that groups of school counselors and school counselors-in-training (teachers) typically identify. These include guidance curriculum lessons that school counselors or their colleagues have taught to classrooms of students, traditional individual student planning activities such as test results interpretations and applications or helping students decide on

Table 4.2
Examples of Traditional Guidance Activities by Program Component

Guidance Curriculum	Individual Student Planning	Responsive Services	System Support	Nonguidance Tasks
Classroom guidance lessons re: program content	Career pathways	Individual counseling: school behavior, family problems, friendship problems	Faculty in-service training re: standardized testing	Lunch duty
Career Day	Assessment results interpretation		Counselor staff development	Writing schedule changes
Character education	Progress on personal plans	Small-group counseling	Guidance program annual planning	Coordinating standardized testing programs
Red Ribbon Week	Course selection	Child study teams	PTA meetings	Tracking special education paperwork
College nights	4-year high school plans	Crisis intervention	Counseling department meetings	Acting as administrative designee
	Graduation plans	Teacher consultation re: individual students		
	College searches and visits	Parent consultation		

their courses for the next year, counseling individuals with issues or problems, and conferencing with parents and teachers. Nonguidance tasks vary from school/district to school/district, but some recurrent themes are evident in these assignments as well.

Ideas About How to Conduct the Assessment of Current Program Activities. We suggest that one or more work groups be used to accomplish this part of the assessment. Groups can be organized by school level (elementary, middle/junior high, and high) or represent all school levels and be organized by the new program components. Every staff member should respond to the survey so that a complete picture is developed. However, if the staff is large, groups of staff members may complete the surveys together. Buildings with multiple staff members are an obvious grouping. Clusters of elementary counselors, or other clusters of single staff members, can be arranged.

The work groups—the group or groups processing this information—need to devise the forms they need to gather the information they want. It is important to anticipate that the data regarding the activities will be analyzed to learn how school counselors' competencies are used, what content is targeted, and what student results are anticipated. Often these analyses are done by different groups, so the data collection forms need to be developed with the subsequent process plan in mind.

Each group should then distribute the forms to the staff for whom they are responsible and ask them to list the guidance and counseling activities by program components. The forms could contain a few examples by grade level to assist staff in knowing what to list; the work group members could generate their own examples. Some districts have found it useful to use the activities described in their original district handbooks. Make sure that the activities listed are actual activities, however, not those that the staff would like to do. The next step is to aggregate the data from individual staff members into a level-by-level, component-by-component composite.

Sometimes schools or districts need to speed up the program assessment process—for example, the school board or senior administration wants to begin "now." Some shortcuts to substitute for the more thorough process described above include school counselors spontaneously generating lists of activities or using prepared models of program activities, or the district or building guidance and counseling program leader gathering information in light of a rubric.

All the school counselors in small districts or counselors representing each level in larger districts have in the context of an all-day meeting generated lists of the activities that they could think of on the spot—or have thought about as homework for the meeting—using the program components as the organizer. These are generated by each level group (elementary, middle, high school) separately and then brought to the whole group to review and supplement. Again these need to be recorded for presentation and further use, but it is a way to begin.

Table 4.3 displays what we have learned are the hallmark activities of established, high-functioning comprehensive guidance and counseling programs. Assessing the status of your school/district in light of these gives you a general impression about what you have in place currently and what you are missing. Another option is suggested in the ASCA National Model, which mentions using "the ASCA program audit to identify components and elements in place and to be developed." (ASCA, 2005, p. 69)

Another approach to this qualitative assessment of what actually occurs in the guidance and counseling program has been used by district-level guidance and counseling program leaders as they meet with each building-level staff group. Building-level staff are interviewed regarding a predetermined set of criteria that allows leaders to gather the data to compare their programs with the program model adopted by the district. The same approach is being used in a self-study format wherein leaders provide the questions to build-

Table 4.3
Hallmark Activities of Comprehensive Guidance Programs

Guidance curriculum	*Individual student planning*
Regular pattern of guidance lessons provided to every student in each grade level	Individual-focused educational and career guidance activities provided as students anticipate and make transitions from one educational level to another
	Individual student advisement system supported by individual student portfolios
	Delineated, articulated career development program for all students
Responsive services	*System support*
Small-group counseling	Staff education provided re: guidance program priorities and activity plan
Systematic, planned individual counseling	
Regular and systematic consultations with teachers and administrators re: unsuccessful students	Guidance provided by teachers, administrators, and counselors are coordinated
Effective system for student referrals	Parents are partners in program design and delivery (as needed)
Regular parent consultation	
Systematic procedure for helping students manage personal crises	Guidance advisory committee
Preplanned, team approach to crisis management	Meaningful and fair evaluation of guidance program and counseling staff

ing staff, who then complete the responses in writing for the comparison process that ensues. Neither of these approaches, however, provides the specific information about the range of activities that is so useful in understanding the complete texture of the current program; and neither approach is useful in determining specific student results.

Identify How Professional School Counselors' Competencies Are Used

What Is Assessed. To assess how professional school counselor specialized competencies are used in your current guidance and counseling program requires, first, that you identify the competencies relevant to your state's certification requirements and district's expectations. If you are following our suggested process, you have already done this in assessing the human resources available to the program.

Ideas About How to Conduct the Assessment of Current School Counselor Competence Application. In analyzing the activities provided in your current program, you are able to identify which school counselor competencies are used and with what level of priority. For example, a counselor-led classroom guidance lesson applies the school counselor's teaching skills; a school counselor developing a classroom guidance lesson with a teacher applies the school counselor's consultation skills. A school counselor assisting students to set educational, career, or personal goals applies the school counselor's guidance skills. A school counselor assisting parents to work with their students on their goals applies the school counselor's consultation skills. Individual and small-group counseling apply school counselor's counseling skills, and so on. The priority for each set of competencies (teaching, guiding, individual counseling, and so on) is inferred through the emphasis on the different kinds of activities—and ultimately is verified through the time study described later in this chapter.

Because by definition nonguidance tasks do not apply school counselors' specialized competencies that are the result of their advanced education and training, the competencies applied in those activities are not considered in this analysis. Some school counselor groups, however, have also considered what skills are used in nonguidance tasks at the same time as this assessment of professional competence use is being done. All too often, of course, nonguidance tasks apply quasi-administrative or clerical skills.

Table 4.4 provides an example of data similar to that found in several districts that we have worked with. It displays the school counselor performance domains described in the Texas Evaluation Model for Professional School Counselors (2nd ed.; Texas Counseling

Table 4.4
Current Priorities for Use of Counselor Competence/Performance Domain

Performance Domain	Elementary School	Middle School	High School
Program management	7	2	4
Guidance	6	6	6
Counseling	1	2	2
Consultation	2	5	1
Coordination	5	1	5
Student assessment	3	4	7
Professionalism	4	7	3

Association, 2004) and records the priorities inferred by school counselors after having analyzed the legitimate guidance and counseling activities they were currently doing: 1 is the highest priority; 7 is the lowest. It is an example of a shortcut approach to this assessment as it relates priorities to performance domains, not to the longer list of school counselor competencies.

Identify Who Is Served by the Current Program

What Is Assessed. In assessing your current guidance and counseling program, it is important to identify who actually is served by your program—who the clients are—and the balance of services or the level of service that each subset of clients receives. The assessment of your current program activities suggests who your student clients are and helps you be aware that there are many clients in addition to students, including teachers, students' parents, administrators, other specialists who work with the students, and the system itself.

According to the *ASCA Ethical Standards for School Counselors* (2004a), included in Appendix B, "The professional school counselor has a primary obligation to the student who is to be treated with respect as a unique individual" (A.1.a.). The students are the school counselors' primary clients. The student population comprises myriad subgroups, each of which call for assistance from the guidance and counseling program. First, they are divided into grade levels that are essentially age groups. The National Board for Professional Teaching Standards (2002) identified these age groups as 3–8 years, 7–12 years, 11–15 years, and 14–18 years (p. viii). Second, they are at different developmental stages: early childhood, middle childhood, early adolescence, and adolescence and young adulthood (p. viii). While not all students experience these *developmental* stages at the same ages, each of those developmental stages brings with it developmental tasks for all students to accomplish. All students, then, can benefit from school counselors' interventions that facilitate their educational, career, personal, and social developmental progression (e.g., developmental guidance). Students present a full range of developmental issues for which they are seeking help and with which school counselors help. Examples of educational developmental tasks that students need help with are those related to thinking and problem solving and those related to their future educational opportunities. Examples of career developmental tasks that students need help with are those related to their development as workers, decision making, and anticipating the future. Examples of social developmental tasks that students need help with are those related to their learning to behave according to the school's standards; their relationships with their parents, friends, teachers, and others; and their ethnic/cultural identity. Examples of personal developmental tasks that students need help with relate to their physical, self-concept, emotional, identity, personality, and moral development.

Third, students present different degrees of need for help from school counselors. In addition to their developmental needs, some students struggle more than others with the tasks for their stage, and some students face problems, issues, or barriers that interrupt their attention to the accomplishment of these tasks. These students can benefit from responsive interventions that *prevent* them from getting farther off track (e.g., individual or small-group counseling). Some—it is hoped a relative few—students have already made choices or experienced situations that derail their healthy development and can benefit from responsive interventions that help them *remedy* their situation or *rehabilitate* themselves and get back on track (e.g., referral to relevant specialists or special programs). Every once in a while, students face *crisis* situations, ones that are life threatening or are severely disruptive to their continued development. These students require immediate responses from school counselors (e.g., assessment, referral, and follow-up).

Fourth, students come from different cultures. They are of different genders, sexual orientations, and preferences. They live with a variety of parents or guardians (e.g., biological, single, grandparent, gay, adoptive, foster, or residential facility) and related family configurations (e.g., two biological parents and siblings or none, extended, and blended). Their lifestyles vary (e.g., mobile, migrant, homeless). They differ ethnically (e.g., African American, Hispanic, White, Asian/Pacific Islander, Native American). They come from a range of different economic circumstances (e.g., lower, middle, upper economic status). Their family incomes may be steady or not; and they may come from public or private sector jobs, the military, welfare, or even illegal work. They come from parents with a range of educational levels. Their parents may be absent because of incarceration or abandonment. They come from homes and communities that speak a variety of languages other than English and affiliate with various religious beliefs.

The array of potential subgroups of students is daunting. In assessing whom your current program actually serves, it is imperative to identify which of these subgroups of students receive help. If your goal is to serve the students as best you can, then you must be clear about who the students are who can be served to determine who you can best help. That is discussed more fully in chapter 5.

Students are the primary clients, but the many states' laws and the *ASCA Ethical Standards* (2004a) make it clear that school counselors also have responsibilities to the students' parents/guardians. School counselors also have responsibilities to colleagues and professional associates (*ASCA Ethical Standards*, Section C; see Appendix B), including teachers, administrators and staff, other mental health professionals, and other school specialists. They have responsibilities to the school, to the community, to themselves, and to the profession. These adult clients are also composed of subgroups, two of which are of particular importance: those who relate directly to the school counselors' student population and those who do not.

Ideas About How to Conduct an Assessment of Students Served. The most complete means to learn who is currently being served in the guidance and counseling program is through a process of logging who is served and coding them according to their subgroups. This happens most readily through sign-in or counselor recording sheets maintained in guidance centers and in school counselors' offices. Data can also be accumulated by having students sign in at all activities. Coding them usually requires computerizing the data collection so that their subgroup codes may be entered and tallied as well. Given the large number of variables described above, most districts with whom we have worked have undertaken this assessment and have preselected the client variables they need to track at this point—whether it is students' numbers by grade level, numbers by intervention levels, or by demographics—and which categories of adults or other clients: teachers, parents, administrators, staff, other mental health professionals, other school specialists, the school system, community representatives or groups, themselves (e.g., pursuing professional development), or the profession (e.g., association work).

The system-as-client is important to acknowledge also because the system is often the client of nonguidance tasks. In the districts with which we have worked, the most accurate data about this come from log keeping, including amount of time spent. By ensuring that the system-serving functions are distinct from the student-serving functions, the data may then be so analyzed. The results of one such log keeping for a group of high school counselors are presented in Table 4.5.

Another method for collecting this information relates to the current activities assessment discussed earlier in this section. By analyzing the activities accomplished, one can readily discern who the participants are in the activities—perhaps not by individual student but certainly by some of the categories. As generalizations, guidance curriculum and individual student planning activities are interventions provided for students with developmental needs. Responsive services are interventions provided for students with preventive, remedial, and crisis needs. System support activities serve the legitimate nonstudent clients. These last two sets of activities, then, have to be analyzed in more depth for classification according to the three need levels. This lends itself better also to assessing the issues presented and responded to, and the demographics of the students served.

Another shortcut to gathering the information about the clients served is a survey. This is not as precise as the techniques just suggested but can yield useful information. For example, school counselors in one district were asked to "guesstimate" the percentage of their client-contact time spent with a listed set of clients. The original list was developed by a work group and distributed to all school counselors. The group collected and tallied the results and was encouraged by the consistency of the guesstimates. Although this is an imprecise way to get information, if enough individuals submit input, any real aberrations are modified by the uniformity of the majority. The results of one survey of this type are presented in Table 4.6.

An even quicker and less accurate but useful method is for the school counselors as a group to guesstimate in a group setting the priorities for their client service. The method we use is to have individual school counselors guesstimate their own priorities and then

Table 4.5
Personnel Support Versus System Support (Baseline Data)

% of Time	Personnel Support — Function	Rank	vs.	% of Time	System Support — Function	Rank
12.8	Individual counseling	2		19.9	Professional responsibilities	1
8.0	Individual guidance	4		8.3	Planning	3
6.3	Conferencing—staff	6		6.9	Record keeping	5
4.2	Enrollment/registration	8		5.2	Miscellaneous paperwork	7
3.9	Consulting staff	9		3.9	Special education	9
3.2	Conferencing—parent	12		3.8	Administrative assignments	11
2.5	Counseling parent	13				
2.3	Coordinate agencies	14				
2.0	Consulting other school specialists	15				
1.7	Guidance activities	16				
1.5	Consulting parents	17				
1.4	Career education	18				
1.3	Conferencing—student/parent	19				
.6	Group guidance	20				
.4	Small-group counseling	21				
.2	Testing individuals	22				
.1	Test district program	23				
52.4				47.5		

Table 4.6
Guesstimates of Percentages of Time Spent With Clients (Baseline Data)

	Average[a] Elementary	Average[a] Middle	Average[a] High
Student contacts			
Development guidance			
Group	23	13	10
Individual	11	12	25
Basic testing program	7	3	10
Preventive (counseling)	12	18	11
Remedial (counseling, referral)	4	8	3
Adult contacts			
District administration	5	8	3
School staff			
Principals	5	4	3
Teachers	9	9	7
Other counselors	3	3	5
Special education staff	8	6	5
Other specialists	3	3	3
Parents	7	10	8
Outside agency staff	2	2	1
Community representatives	1	1	2

Note. Data from Northside Independent School District, San Antonio, TX. Adapted with permission.
[a]Because of rounding, numbers do not add to 100%.

compare them with those of others who work at the same school level. Sometimes these groups come to consensus about the districtwide priorities. This was the case of the group whose data are reflected in Table 4.7. It was decided by this group that students who are truly in a crisis need immediate attention and are, therefore, at that time the Number 1 priority; hence the asterisks (*) in that row. The primary criteria for the prioritization of the others, however, were based on a mixture of other variables, for example, the numbers of clients who presented themselves in each category, the amount of school counselors' time spent with each category of client, and the importance of the category as perceived by the school counselors and, in some cases, by the administrators. Sometimes it becomes clear that the variations from building to building are so wide the only conclusion is that the clients served are those who are selected for service at the building level. Such was the case for the

Table 4.7
Guesstimates of Current Client Priorities

Clients	Elementary School	Middle School	High School
Students with developmental needs	3	4	3
Students with preventive needs	2	5	1
Students with remedial needs	1	3	2
Students with crisis needs	*	*	*
Teachers	4 (varies)	6	5
Parents	4 (varies)	7	4
Administrators	4 (varies)	1	6
Others	7	2	7

Note. Asterisks indicate "not ranked" because when a student has a crisis, it always is the top priority, but over the course of the year crisis needs are not the top priority.

group in Table 4.7. The elementary school counselors determined that the priorities were very different in each building; hence the tie for 4th place reflected in that column.

Identify the Current Results of the Program

What Is Assessed. Identifying the intended results students achieve by participating in each current program activity is the next task. If the activity results (objectives) were not identified in the activities study, identifying them entails taking one activity at a time and asking such questions as, Why do we do this? How are students different as a result of this activity? What do students know, what attitudes do they form, or what can students do that they could not do before this activity? For example:

If the activity is	*then the result is*
• assist students in planning their schedules	• all students can select classes consistent with their abilities and interests
• conduct a Career Day	• students who participate can identify an occupation consistent with their abilities and interests

Although it is obvious that our major purpose as school counselors is to serve students, not all of us have had experience in clearly stating the results of the work we do. For years the profession subscribed to the notion that what school counselors did was not observable or measurable, or that what school counselors did were processes and so the results were not visible.

Ideas About How to Conduct an Assessment of Current Program Results. If you have already defined the content domains and competencies that drive your guidance and counseling program as suggested in chapter 3, your task may be merely to synthesize available written statements. If in adopting the guidance and counseling program model, you adopted an outline of student competencies, then your task is one of relating specific activities to student competencies. If neither of these options is available and your staff as a whole is not comfortable with the emphasis on results, you are advised to use your steering committee counselors or a group of other counselor leaders or all the school counselors in small groups as a work group and guide them through the basic process of identifying student results for the activities they are currently doing. It is by demonstrating school counselors' contribution to students' growth and development that our position in the educational setting is assured. Thus this exercise allows you to test the validity of program activities; if an activity has no visible outcome or if the identifiable outcome is of little relevance, then continuing it may be inadvisable.

After the guidance staff have identified the activities they perform and the intended results of each activity, the next question is, Have all students for whom the activity was conducted reached these intended results? Although the guidance staff may feel that the activities accomplished the desired results, there may be little evidence to prove it. Suggestions for assessing student results are provided in chapter 10.

Having determined the intended or actual results of each activity and the clients served, you can generalize competencies developed through program participation. By grouping activities that are intended to deliver similar results under a component, you can make general statements about the intended results of each program component. For example, the results of the two activities just cited—schedule planning and Career Day—are related to students' development of educational and career plans. Aggregating the results from all such activities will describe the results of the individual student planning component. With all the results listed, you can draw larger generalizations about the intended results of your total current program. This list then is ready for use in comparing the program you currently have with the program your district/school desires.

As a short cut, but on a much more global level, the steering committee and/or the counseling staff can, again, spontaneously prioritize the domains and/or competencies identified as those that define the program content. For example, in Texas, seven major guidance content areas have been recommended for use by schools and districts (Texas Education Agency, 2005). An example of such a prioritizing that is somewhat typical of "current programs" is provided in Table 4.8.

Quantitative Design

Understanding the current quantitative design comes from studying how school counselors actually are spending their time in delivering the current guidance and counseling program activities and figuring how many students and other clients actually participate in the program activities and program components. And, finally, if you already conduct results evaluation (as described in chapter 10), data may be available about the numbers of students achieving the various results from participating in the program's activities.

Identify How School Counselors Currently Spend Their Time

What Is Assessed. Assessing how school counselors use their time in relation to the comprehensive guidance and counseling program model provides quantitative data about the current guidance and counseling program. Because school counselors are the basic program resource, recordings of their actual program-related behaviors are the most critical data you will gather. These data provide the most concrete information about the actual design of your current program. Gathering this information is essential as it is basic to the rest of the program improvement process.

The most useful and frequently done study is one designed to determine how school counselor time is appropriated to the four program components: guidance curriculum, individual student planning, responsive services, and system support. It is also important to collect data regarding the time spent on nonguidance tasks. By specifying how school counselors allocate their time to each of the program components, you are able to see how the program is balanced. By aggregating the time of all the counselors at a school level, you are able to see how the program is balanced at each school level. You answer such questions as, Which of the components takes up most of the resources? Which the least? What proportion of school counselor time is spent on nonguidance tasks and are therefore depleted from the guidance and counseling program?

As was true for the qualitative design, these quantitative data also suggest information about to what extent school counselors' competencies are used, how many students are

Table 4.8
Current Program Content Priorities

Content Domain	Elementary School	Middle School	High School
Self-confidence development	6	5	2
Motivation to achieve	5	3	6
Decision making, goal setting, problem solving, planning	2	2	4
Interpersonal effectiveness	4	6	3
Communication skills	3	4	5
Cross-cultural effectiveness	7	7	7
Responsible behavior	1	1	1

served and from what subgroups of the total student population, and the kinds of results that might be achieved by the program's clients. In gathering the time information vis-à-vis the program components, you might also gather information regarding how the resource of school counselor time is appropriated to the school counselor performance domains. Figure 4.1 is a format that has been use by school counselors to document how their time is being applied in both the program components and the performance domains. For actual minutes or increments of time, school counselors record the component their activity fits in and the performance domain they are applying.

A note of caution: A time study provides a golden opportunity to learn a great deal about what is actually happening in your program, but you need to resist the temptation to learn everything you always wanted to know but were afraid to ask. Studies need to be as simple as possible to implement, or your data will be meaningless. Because school counselors and other guidance staff are busy, consider carefully what you are asking them to record. Collect only data you know you will use. The simpler the time-recording system is, the more accurate your information will be.

Ideas About How to Conduct a School Counselor Time-Use Study. Planning your time-use study carefully so that the data are meaningful and useful is also essential. Decisions need to be made about why you are conducting the study, whose time will be studied, and what you want to learn about their time as well as when, where, and how the study will be conducted. We recommend that you write out the purpose of the time study to ensure clarity among all school counselors and administrators; for example, the purpose of this time study is to determine how the resource of school counselor time is appropriated to the four components of the model guidance and counseling program. Before school counselors

Figure 4.1
Time Log: Components and Performance Domains

Date: _____

TIME	NOTE	PROGRAM COMPONENT[a]	PERFORMANCE DOMAIN[b]
7:00–7:15 a.m.			
7:15–7:30			
7:30–7:45			
7:45–8:00			
8:00–8:15			
8:15–8:30			
8:30–8:45			
8:45–9:00			

Total no. of minutes for the day	Guidance curriculum _____ Individual student planning _____ Responsive services _____ System support _____ Nonguidance _____	Program management _____ Guidance _____ Counseling _____ Consultation _____ Coordination _____ Student assessment _____ Professional behavior _____ Professional standards _____

[a]Program component legend: GC = guidance curriculum; ISP = individual student planning; RS = responsive services; SS = system support; NG = nonguidance tasks.
[b]Performance domain legend: PM = program management; G = guidance; Cou = counseling; Con = consultation; Cor = coordination; SA = student assessment; PB = professional behavior; PS = professional standards.

begin to log their time, it is important to define the kinds of activities that make up each component. Consistency of definition by the school counselors yields data that are consistently useful. Align each currently identified guidance and counseling program activity with its proper component.

You will want to be able to identify the results for the counseling staff in broad categories; for example, distinguishing among the elementary, middle/junior high, and high school counselors is useful because guidance and counseling programs at the different school levels are usually balanced differently. There may be concern that the data will be used for personnel evaluation rather than program description purposes. You need to decide if you are willing to provide for anonymity or need to establish an appropriate level of trust with the school counselors.

Because this is a time-use study, you need to decide when you will do the study and for how long: all year? a certain month? a scattering of days throughout the year? The study should cover enough time so that some activities that may occur only occasionally are not given undue attention. The most thorough study is one that is conducted for an entire school year. In this kind of study, school counselors log their time 1 day per week for a full school year, varying the day each week. They begin by recording time on Monday the first week, Tuesday the second week, Wednesday the third week, and so on (Gysbers, Kosteck-Bunch, Magnuson, & Starr, 2002).

You must also determine the increments of time that school counselors will be recording: by minutes? by quarter hours? by half hours? by class periods? by the length of guidance activities? A rule of thumb is that the shorter the length of time the data are gathered, the smaller the logged time increments should be. If the study covers 1 month, school counselors' actual minutes should be used. If the study covers the entire year, 15- or 30-minute intervals are better. An advantage to recording actual minutes is that so many school counselor interventions are spontaneously conducted brief interventions of inconsistent time increments that using this more flexible approach may be a better match with reality. The advantage to recording a set block of time is consistency for each school counselor and across all school counselors.

Another decision to be made is when the school counselors should log their time: as they go? at the end of the morning and afternoon? at the end of the day? We recommend that they only record time spent during the 8-hour workday or the time spent during student access time. When school counselors log their time for extra hours worked by some, the variances in the study's parameters become difficult to manage.

The forms for data collection need to be as simple to use as possible, both for recording and for tallying. If it is readily available to all school counselors, using a computer-based spreadsheet program for ease of ongoing and cumulative tabulation can facilitate a time study. At a minimum, you will want to use a computer for aggregating the data and generating the reports you need. Be sure to consider the dictates of the computer before developing your forms.

Directions for implementing the study must be precise and clear. School counselors need to be schooled in the purpose of the study and how to keep their records. The terminology used in the categories of the study needs to be thoroughly understood by everyone to ensure consistency of data. A system for fielding questions and for monitoring implementation of the study needs to be put in place. If you are running this from a central office location, you must ensure that the campus guidance and counseling program leaders—the head or lead counselors—understand the study and its purpose and can monitor its implementation effectively. (See Appendix C for time and task analysis procedures and forms developed and used by school counselors in Missouri.)

School districts have conducted time studies for shorter periods of time that provide less data and lead to less valid generalizations but that are useful as long as the data users are aware of its limitations. Such studies have been conducted for at least 1 or 2 months and, as described earlier, entail logging how actual minutes are spent. Additionally, some provision must be made to ensure consideration of the special events that alter the balance of a program at different points in the year, for example, educational planning and student course selection that occur in the spring at the middle and high school levels.

When they are really in a time bind to respond to opportunities to study their programs provided by school boards or school administrators, school counselors have guesstimated how they spend their time. This, of course, is vulnerable to the school counselors' perceptions that may or may not be closely aligned with reality. Our experience, however, supports the relative accuracy of this technique. Again, aggregating the guesstimates of individual school counselors into one generalization for all school counselors for each level tempers the results. Table 4.9 displays an example of the accuracy of this method of data collection from a district that used two methods of data collection regarding school counselor time use: guesstimating and short-term logging. You can see the results have some variance, but in analysis might lead to similar conclusions. For example, nonguidance tasks take too much time away from the guidance and counseling program; the time spent in responsive services is more than in the other program components; and the program is currently more responsive than developmental in nature.

Several examples of the results of school counselor time studies are provided in Tables 4.10, 4.11, and 4.12. Table 4.10 presents data from a study of how school counselors spend their time conducted and reported by the Texas State Comptroller (Rylander, 2002, p. 18) in response to a legislative mandate. Table 4.11 presents data from a study of how primarily high school counselors in Arizona (Vandergrift, 1999, p. 4) spend their time. Table 4.12 presents data from a study conducted by the North Carolina Department of Public Instruction (n.d.) on *How North Carolina School Counselors Spend Their Time* in 2000–2001. This study is interesting because, in recognizing that not all school counselors at a specific school level spend the same percentage of time on a component's activities, the results generated are broken down by the percentages of school counselors spending a given percentage of time on each component. What is presented here are the data for all those surveyed (p. 6); the full report also presents the information by school levels and by different categories of student services personnel. These ranges suggest the lack of uniformity for students across the state in guidance and counseling experiences. The

Table 4.9
Current Program Design: "Guesstimated" and Logged Percentages of Counselor Time

Program Component	"Guesstimated"			Logged (Logs Kept April, 2004)		
	Elementary School	Middle School	High School	Elementary School	Middle School	High School
Guidance curriculum	5	5	0	4	1	6
Individual student planning	0	10	5	0	3	14
Responsive services	50	50	40	40	21	28
System support	15	15	20	5	7	21
Nonguidance tasks	30	20	35	52	69	32

Table 4.10
Texas Comptroller School Counselor Survey
January/February 2002
Counselor Timesheets Statewide by School Type

Category	Elementary %	Middle/Junior High %	High School %	Alternative %
Guidance curriculum	17.6	8.0	9.2	12.3
Individual planning	9.5	10.7	22.3	12.8
Responsive services	21.4	18.3	16.7	24.3
System support	16.0	11.6	11.6	12.0
Subtotal	64.5	48.6	59.8	61.4
Nonguidance activities	15.6	31.5	18.1	22.5
Staff development	3.3	2.3	2.9	1.9
Personal leave	3.8	3.5	3.7	3.5
Administration or clerical tasks	7.5	9.1	10.4	8.3
Other	5.2	5.1	5.1	2.4
Total	100	100	100	100

data reveal that different school counselors work differently—they have different jobs—and that perhaps there is a lot of discretion being exercised by individual school counselors as to what they do. The report also presents information about the percentages of time varying percentages of school counselors spent on nonguidance tasks.

From these examples, you can see that useful information is generated that could lead to significant program improvement efforts, and that state-level policymakers are interested in the actual contributions that school counselors are making to students' development. The results they are seeing includes similarities (e.g., significant portions of school counselors time is spent on nonguidance tasks) and differences (e.g., the portions of time spent on the other components). These data are used as the baseline from which progress is measured over time.

Some districts have conducted specific activity or task assessments on a particular part of the current program that is perceived to be out of balance. For example, to better understand the nature of its nonguidance activities, one district conducted a study of the quasi-administrative and clerical tasks school counselors perform. The process used was similar to that just described. A work group of school counselors identified the tasks they performed that "did not require a master's degree in guidance and counseling to do." Individual staff members then estimated the number of hours or days a year they spent on each of these tasks. These specifics were then totaled, and their percentage of the total time was determined. Other districts have gathered this information in their original baseline study, as in the Missouri time and task analysis (see Appendix C).

Table 4.11
Arizona Counselors' Time Use
1996–1998

Delivery Strategy	% of Time
Developing/facilitating guidance curriculum	24.4
Individual academic/career planning	15.3
Responsive services	37.6
System support	8.1
Nonguidance	14.6

Table 4.12
How North Carolina Counselors Spend Their Time:
Percentages of Personnel/Percentages of Time Spent
All Student Services Personnel

Activity	<10%	10–20%	20–30%	30–40%	>40%
Guidance curriculum	37.8	29.0	13.5	8.2	6.8
Individual student planning	33.9	24	14.7	10.6	12.4
Responsive services	21.2	23.4	20.8	15.2	14.3
System support	32.2	29.0	13.5	8.2	6.8

Identify the Numbers of Students and Other Clients Currently Served

What Is Assessed. Assessing how many students and other clients are currently served by the program is also important baseline information. Traditionally, counseling services have targeted individual students and their related adults (teachers, parents, administrators). Programs of today emphasize a developmental basis and therefore target all students served in medium-sized groups to large groups. School counselors need to be accountable for the proportion of their caseload that benefits from the program, and students, teachers, administrators, and parents benefit from knowing how many students are actually served through each of the program components. It is important for all to understand that within the parameters of the school day, there are only so many minutes. And, depending on the design of the program, there is a finite number of students who can be served during each day. It also needs to be understood that the larger a school counselor's caseload, the less time each individual student can spend with his or her assigned school counselor either alone or in groups. By gathering the data regarding the numbers of students affected through each of the component's activities, school counselors and others will know what proportion of the student population currently benefits from the program activities. Similarly, it is useful to gather data about the numbers of student-related adults served through program activities. In doing the analysis of their data, one district learned that the school counselors were spending more time with students' teachers than they were with the students. Another learned that 30% of their time was spent with parents in face-to-face conferences, on the phone, or through e-mail but that 30% of the parents represented fewer than 10% of their students.

Ideas About How to Conduct a Study of the Numbers of Clients Served. The primary way to collect the data is to record and tabulate them as the program is implemented, not unlike the time study. It may be done along with the time study but could prove to be a distraction. Many guidance and counseling departments already track the numbers of students who come into the counseling center by using sign-in sheets. Professional school counselors also keep notes about their clients for their personal, professional use. Reviewing these notes and tabulating the numbers of students and others served is also a legitimate method of gathering data. School counselors' systematic review of and tallying from their daily calendars also yields fairly accurate information. The report of these data may be as simple as "X number of students were served through current guidance curriculum activities. X number were served through individual students planning activities. X number were served through responsive services." For system support activities, the clients served directly—teachers, parents, administrators, school counselors in program management or professional development—are reported.

Through school counselors' individual calendars and through the annual calendar for the program, an estimation of the numbers of clients served can be developed that, although not very precise, does provide substantiated data. These data could also be gleaned from the study of program activities described earlier in this chapter. This review of the planned activities entails calculating based on the typical numbers of students involved in the various kinds of activities, for example, guidance lessons (average class size), small-counseling groups (8–10), parent–teacher–student–school counselor conferences, teacher in-services (number of faculty), numbers of parents at parent education offerings, and so on. This coupled with the center sign-in sheets records regarding individuals served can provide descriptive numbers.

Identify the Numbers of Students and Other Clients Served by Subgroup

What Is Assessed. Another important set of information is to determine how many students from each subgroup are served and to determine if the proportions of service reflect the school population as a whole. As described above, subgroups of students include those in different grade levels, those with varying levels of need: developmental, preventive, remedial, and crisis, as described earlier, and those within the various demographic groupings you have determined to be worthy of in-depth analysis, such as by family configurations, ethnicity, socioeconomic status, or languages spoken at home. Many districts and schools have learned, to their chagrin, that their minority students are underserved.

Ideas About How to Conduct a Study of the Numbers of Clients Served by Subgroup. These data are subsets of the data gathered during the study of the numbers of clients served. The more global the subgroup, the easier it is to identify this information; for example, the numbers of students served by grade levels should be evident. The various program activities and interventions are developed to meet different levels of student need. Numbers information can be divided on the basis of that premise; that is, classroom guidance serves those with developmental needs; small-group counseling typically serves those with prevention needs; individual counseling often serves those with remedial needs; and crisis counseling serves those in crisis. Assessing the numbers of clients served according to the demographic categories requires collecting data that includes students' names or other identifiers. This kind of assessment may require an additional study specifically designed to address these questions.

Identify the Numbers of Students Currently Achieving the Anticipated Results of Program Activities

What Is Assessed. In addition to knowing how many clients participate in the guidance and counseling program, it is highly useful to know how many of them actually learn or are able to do what the program's activities were designed to help them with. This stage of the program improvement process is not the time to begin results evaluation, but if the information is readily available, it certainly informs the next decisions to be made.

Ideas About How to Conduct a Study of the Numbers of Clients Achieving Results. Indicate the number and percentage of students who have achieved a particular outcome and how it was determined that this outcome has been achieved. In this way the guidance staff defines the results for specific subpopulations in the school. Follow this technique for each activity (or grouping of activities), and the result will be a listing of the results that the activity is achieving and its impact on students (see Table 4.13). It may be that only a small number of students attain many guidance objectives, or there may be little proof that any results are attained at all.

Table 4.13
Activity/Results/Impact

Activity	Result	Impact
Assist students in planning their schedules.	Students can select classes consistent with their abilities and interests.	1. Only 12% of the students change classes. 2. Follow-up study of graduates: 68% reported curriculum satisfaction.
Conduct Career Day.	Students can identify an occupation consistent with their abilities and interests.	1. Participation-attendance records at the Career Day: low (only 30%). 2. Counselor contacts: high-quality response, but only 12% of the student body.

Gather Perceptions About the Program

What Is Assessed

Gathering perceptions about the current program from students, teachers, school counselors, administrators, parents, and community members yields valuable insights about how the program is viewed. This task of the assessment focuses on what individuals from such groups think about the activities of the current program. The focus is not necessarily on the realities of the current program or on the perceived needs of individuals, the school, or society. Needs assessment comes later in the program improvement process.

The data gathered may help you identify supportive people and groups who may be used as resources and inform you about what is right with the current program in your users' perceptions and about what might need to be changed. You can also use the baseline data in subsequent public relations efforts.

Ideas About How to Conduct a Perception Survey

The most direct way to find out what people think about your current program is to ask them. However, as with any market research effort, selecting the population to be surveyed is very important. The sample must be representative of your program's consumers and reflective of the social and cultural demographics of your school community. Not all the perceptions will be flattering and not all will be negative; there may not be much uniformity between consumer groups. The more accurate your sample, the truer the picture of how people perceive your current program.

Gathering the perceptions of all your constituents at once is a one-time activity and should be done with proper care. (After you have made some program improvements, you may do some selective market research to gather opinions about the changes, with the current study results serving as baseline data.)

If your system is small enough to tabulate by hand, or if you have access to a computer, it is best to survey random samples of students and parents. However, surveying total samples of school counselors and administrators is advised. Whether you poll all your teachers or a random sample depends on the size of your school system. If it is small, poll them all. If it is large, identify a statistically sound random sample. Most districts' computerized databases can generate a sound random sample. You need to ensure the sample appropriately reflects the demographics of the school community and the student population.

We suggest that you ask the members of your advisory and steering committees—who are representatives from their groups—to help you in this process of gathering perceptions. The parents as well as administrators and teachers on your school–community advisory committee, for example, can help you word the questions to parents, administrators, and teachers, respectively, by suggesting proper terminology and effective ways to encourage parents to respond to your questions.

Guesstimates and Brainstorming

Because steering committee members have agreed to help undertake responsibility for guiding the change process and are now faced with doing additional work, you can provide extra motivation by taking a quick assessment of their general perceptions of the program. One way to do this is to ask them to write their impressions of the design of the current guidance and counseling program. For example, they can guesstimate what percentage of school counselors' time they think is spent in each of the four components, what percentage is spent with each of the subcategories of clients, or what are the top three or five priority results of the program. A simple worksheet for gathering this information is displayed in Figure 4.2.

Another way to take a quick assessment is to have the steering committee members and/or representatives from other groups identify, in brainstorming style, what activities they think of when they think of the guidance and counseling program. The guidance and counseling program leader records these spontaneous inputs according to the program components, including a column for nonguidance tasks. If the program is in much need of improvement, the priorities evidenced by either of these exercises will help steering committee members who want valid data from which to suggest changes and will forewarn them of the probable results of the current program assessment.

Interviews

One way to find out what people think of your program is to interview a representative sample of individuals from the various groups involved using a structured approach. Separate work groups with advisory and steering committee members as leaders can help accomplish this task. Consider having your advisory and steering committee members interview leaders of various subgroups because leaders are representatives of their groups. For example, the PTA representative to the advisory committee could interview the presidents of local unit PTAs. A danger here is that the leaders' opinions may not be representative of the mainstream of their groups.

The guidance and counseling program leader has a specific role to play in this process. Especially if there is widespread and generalized criticism of the current guidance and counseling program, there is merit to the leader in asking key individuals such as superintendents, principals, teachers, and parent leaders direct questions such as, What do you like about the current guidance and counseling program? What do you dislike about it? What would you change about the program? What would you add to the program?

Elementary, middle, and high school teacher leaders from one district with which we have worked responded as follows:

- *Program strengths:* classroom guidance, communication with parents and teachers regarding topics, parent communication, parenting skills information readily available, one-on-one and crisis counseling, planned small-group counseling, provision of resources for teachers.

Figure 4.2
Current Program Design Worksheet

PRIORITY STUDENT/COMMUNITY GUIDANCE-RELATED NEEDS
1.
2.
3.
4.
5.

COUNSELOR PERFORMANCE DOMAINS (SKILLS/COMPETENCIES)	PRIORITIES (1–7)
Program management Guidance Counseling Consultation Coordination Assessment Professionalism	

CLIENTS	PRIORITIES (1–8)

STUDENTS
  Development needs
  Preventive needs
  Remedial needs
  Crisis needs
TEACHERS
PARENTS
ADMINISTRATORS
OTHERS	

STUDENT COMPETENCIES	PRIORITIES (1–7)
Self-confidence development Motivation to achieve Decision making, goal setting, problem solving Interpersonal effectiveness Communication skills Cross-cultural effectiveness Responsible behavior	

COUNSELOR TIME/PROGRAM COMPONENT	PRIORITIES # % (1–5) (=100%)
Guidance curriculum Individual student planning Responsive services System support Nonguidance	

- *Program, student, and teacher needs:* less paperwork, more clerical help, more school counselors; assessment of student needs annually, bullying, violence, gang involvement, school crowding, inattentiveness, children of substance abusers, lack of connectedness or involvement with school, stress management, low sense of self-worth; more help with specific classroom problems and consultation regarding problematic students, improved teacher awareness of counseling program services, operation, and ethical standards.

- *Program improvement suggestions:* 75% of school counselor time spent counseling; more small-group counseling; more counseling with students about emotional problems, family concerns, making good decisions; collaborative delivery of guidance curriculum by teachers and school counselors; more career education.

All of these strengths, weaknesses, and suggestions for improvement were items that the school counselors had identified previously. They were pleased for the support generated from other groups.

The advantages of using an interview approach are the direct contacts with members of the various groups and the in-depth responses that can be gathered. The disadvantages include the time-consuming nature of the task, the small number of people who can be contacted, and the difficulty in tabulating the results.

Questionnaires

Another way to ask people for their perceptions is to use a questionnaire or a series of questionnaires. Questionnaires can be prepared and distributed to large numbers of people. Tabulating results is easy, especially if you have access to a computer.

We suggest the same cautions in the development of the questionnaires or questions as we did in the development of logs. Avoid the temptation to ask every question you ever wanted answered; keep the questions straightforward and simple. It is imperative that your questions be related to the components of your program model or to the results desired for students and other clients rather than to school counselors' functions. How you do your job is a professional decision.

The questionnaires should have wording suitable to the population being polled. Thus the questionnaire for elementary children will be different from the questionnaire for adults, but for correlation, the substance must be the same. The questions and answers must correspond from one survey form to another so that you can aggregate the results and analyze them together. Comparisons of perceptions held by different groups are often useful.

Three questionnaires used successfully to assess high school students', teachers', and school counselors' perceptions about the services they received and the results students achieved from participating in guidance activities are provided in Appendix D. In the first, high school students are asked to state the approximate number of times they met with school counselors in classroom presentations, small-group meetings, one-on-one meetings, student–parent–school counselor conferences, student–teacher–school counselor conferences, and meetings with a school counselor and someone from outside the school. From these, data inferences can be made about which components students have participated in. The questionnaire then asks the students two sets of questions: Was a topic discussed with them? (Did a service occur?), and Was it helpful? (Was it beneficial? Did results occur?) The questions cover the content strands of the guidance curriculum component, the major activities of the individual student planning system, and the primary school counselor responses in responsive services.

In the second questionnaire, school counselors are asked to provide similar information from their perspective. The questions again cover the content strands of guidance curriculum, the major activities of individual student planning, and the primary responses in responsive services. In the third questionnaire, teachers are asked to provide their perceptions regarding school counselor activities for both students and teachers. The questions cover system support efforts in addition to guidance curriculum, individual student planning, and responsive services efforts. The response ranges in the questionnaires include a 3-point scale for identifying occurrence of a service (*yes, unsure, no*), a 5-point scale for classifying helpfulness (*very much, quite a bit, somewhat, very little, not really*) for students and teachers, and a 4-point scale for classifying helpfulness (*11, 1, 2, —*) for teachers. Six additional questionnaires (students', teachers', and school counselors' for the elementary and middle school levels) have the same response ranges and address the same topics, but with the wording changed to suit the population. (These are not included in Appendix D.)

If the same forms are used at the start of the program improvement process and then several years later as measures of program effectiveness, powerful sets of information can be gathered about the value of the program approach to guidance and counseling! We recommend that questionnaires like these be prepared for the elementary, middle/junior, and senior high levels. Note that the range of responses concerning helpfulness could be modified to three (*agree, no opinion, disagree*) or even two (*yes* or *no*).

Present a Report Describing the Current Program

As mentioned earlier, the data gathered on current resource availability, including school counselor time use, will be used again and again as your improvement efforts proceed. A first use of the data collected is to aggregate them into a meaningful report.

At the completion of your current guidance and counseling program assessment, you will have gathered an enormous quantity of information, all of which is needed as you proceed with the program improvement effort. At this point a report that presents the gathered data must be written and disseminated. Then, once the report is prepared, various decision-making groups can analyze the information and draw conclusions from it, which in turn inform the program-designing process. Information about both the qualitative and quantitative designs of the guidance and counseling program has been gathered. The data that we have found useful, the methods possible to use to collect them, and those data that represent parts of the qualitative design and of the quantitative design are summarized in Table 4.14.

Attending to Diversity

As described in the sections of this chapter, the efforts to assess the current guidance and counseling program should attend to the diversity of the community and of the guidance and counseling program clients—students and others. Attention should be paid to the current activity topics and anticipated student results that address multicultural competency and other issues raised by diversity in the school community. The demographic diversity of the professional school counselors and their multicultural competence should also be assessed.

The demographics of the school community and, perhaps more importantly, the demographics of the student population as a whole set the standard for appropriate representation in the guidance and counseling program improvement process and for assessing the appropriateness of current guidance and counseling program participation. The makeup of the steering committee, advisory committee, and work groups that are leading, providing input, and analyzing the program data should reflect the diversity in the community and the school. Not only should the community representatives reflect the ethnic makeup of the community, but as much as possible they should also reflect the various family configurations, lifestyles, economic levels, and educational levels.

The demographics of the students and other clients who are served in the current program should reflect the demographics of the student body. If the makeup of the student body is 8% African American, 80% Hispanic, 11% White, and 1% Asian and Native American, then the makeup of the students participating in guidance and counseling activities should also be

Table 4.14
Reporting the Results of the Assessment of the Current Program
Data/Methods/Element

Data	Collection Method	Element/Design
Community context	Demographic studies	Context
Student status	Risky behavior indicators	
	Discipline reports	
	Achievement indicators	
Counselor talent	Certification requirements	Personnel resources
Responsibilities of other personnel	Job descriptions	Personnel resources
Budget	Budget review	Financial resources
Materials and equipment	Inventory	Financial resources
Facilities	Inventory	
Laws, rules, regulations	Guidance office, state department of education	Political resources
Policies and procedures	Board and district publications	Political resources
Activities conducted according to program component	Activity survey	Qualitative
	Self-study	
	Program handbooks	
Counselor talent use	Job descriptions	Qualitative
	Calendars	
Clients served	Activity review	Qualitative
	Survey	
Results attained	Activity review	Qualitative
Counselor time use	Time/task study	Quantitative
	Calendars	
Numbers of clients served	Sign-in sheets	Quantitative
	Records review	
Perceptions	Surveys, questionnaires	Political resources
	Interviews	

8% African American, 80% Hispanic, 11% White, and 1% Asian and Native American. The current program assessment should include gathering data that describe the program's clientele. In gathering the perceptions of the current guidance and counseling program, schools and districts are well advised by Dellana and Snyder (2004) "to devote more research to the customer service perceptions of their distinct customer groups and to more fully consider the obstacles to trust that might be created by these perceptions" (p. 39). Identification of groups that are overserved or underserved suggests many possibilities to consider in the next phases of guidance and counseling program improvement work. As Lee (2001) pointed out,

> School counselors are becoming increasingly aware that their practices are rooted firmly in the values of European-American middle class culture, whereas the cultural values of a significant portion of the students with whom they work represent worldviews whose origins are found in Africa, Asia, Mexico, Central America, the Caribbean, or the Middle East (Herring, 1997; Lee, 1995). (p. 258)

More diverse practices are needed to respond appropriately to students from non-European or non-American middle-class cultures. Data as to whether the program currently responds to students with developmental, preventive, remedial, and crisis needs in proportion to their percentage of the population would shed light on whether the school counselors' practices are or are not being well received by some groups.

If the school or district in which you work serves a diverse community, program activities that address relevant cultural and social topics and issues should be evident in the program. In addition, helping students develop multicultural competence should be evident. There is evidence that suggests that much of the violence and gang involvement prevalent in our schools often have roots in racial and ethnic differences. The review of the activities and anticipated student results should be done with this in mind.

In assessing the current guidance and counseling program and its attention to diversity, the demographic diversity of the professional school counselors and their multicultural competence need to be assessed. The makeup of the school counseling staff should reflect the makeup of the student and the school community. Minorities have historically been underrepresented as educators, including school counselors. Strides are being made in the recruitment and training of school counselors, but in school practice balancing a staff takes years. It often requires waiting for the retirement of currently in-place school counselors, expanding staff through student population growth, or decreasing the school counselor-to-student ratio.

School counselors' multicultural competence or lack thereof has significant bearing on their ability to work with students from cultures different from their own. Constantine and Gushue (2003) noted:

> A growing number of studies have begun to empirically examine aspects of multicultural competence in school counseling personnel. Multicultural counseling competence is referred to as counselors' attitudes/beliefs, knowledge, and skills in working with individuals representing various cultural groups (Sue, Arredondo, & McDavis, 1992; Sue et al., 1998). (p. 185)

One of their findings was that multicultural training has an impact on school counselors' multicultural competence. Therefore, it can be concluded that those who have not had such training—either in their preservice counselor education programs or in subsequent in-service training—are less competent in working across cultures than those that have.

In their study, Constantine and Gushue (2003) examined school counselors' case conceptualization competence—a highly important skill in effective counseling. Specifically, their study looked at school counselors' abilities to conceptualize immigrant students' issues. They found that

> school counselors who have higher ethnic tolerance attitudes may be better able to consider and integrate salient cultural information in the context of conceptualizing and addressing the presenting concerns of immigrant students. . . . [and] that school counselors with higher levels of racism may be less aware of cultural issues in conceptualizing the mental health concerns of immigrant students, and these attitudes may ultimately compromise the emotional and developmental well-being of these students. (p. 189)

The potential for helping school counselors increase their effectiveness with students from cultures different from their own is tremendous. Knowing if the school counselors on the current guidance and counseling program staff need to further develop their multicultural competence is an important set of information to have.

Leadership Roles and Responsibilities

If you are the guidance and counseling program leader—be it a district guidance and counseling program administrator or a school counselor in a building,—you are responsible for accomplishing the current program assessment and for ensuring that the results are communicated to all interested parties. In fact, throughout the program improvement process you should be communicating regularly and often with all the administrative and counseling staff members, but at each of the milestones of the process, communication is imperative. The scope of the undertaking will call upon all of your leadership, supervision, management, and administration skills. Dollarhide (2003, p. 305) described the leadership experience of a new school counselor in a building who successfully redefined the guidance and counseling program in her new school by working in four leadership contexts described by Bolman and Deal (1997):

1. Structural leadership, or leadership in the building of viable organizations.
2. Human resource leadership, or leadership via empowerment and inspiration of followers.
3. Political leadership, or leadership in the use of interpersonal and organizational power.
4. Symbolic leadership, or leadership via the interpretation and reinterpretation of the meaning of change. (p. 305)

As you read through the descriptions of the various tasks to be undertaken in this phase of program improvement, you will no doubt come to that conclusion. This summary is provided to clarify your roles. Essentially, you have specific responsibilities for the initiation, implementation, and closure of this phase of the program improvement project.

Initiation

As the program leader, you need to keep the adopted program model in front of everyone involved in the project, including the decision makers and every member of the counseling staff. At this point you may be the only person who truly understands the concept. You will find yourself continually clarifying and explaining the model.

Fullan, Bertani, and Quinn (2004) cautioned us: "Think of the vision as an iceberg, the vast majority of which is underwater. Many leaders take shortcuts by slicing off the visible part of the iceberg and then assuming that they have captured its full power" (p. 43). They suggested "10 crucial components" for effective leadership for change: a compelling conceptualization, collective moral purpose, the right structure for getting the job done, individual capacity building, lateral capacity building, ongoing learning, productive conflict, a demanding culture, external partners, and focused financial investments.

It is your responsibility to conceptualize the current program assessment process. As the guidance and counseling program leader, you need to identify the tasks to be performed and be able to explain them to the staff. We have described a multitude of tasks for accomplishing a complete assessment; you may not choose to do them all at this time or in the order we have set out. Ultimately, however, all the tasks need to be completed as the program improvement efforts continue. Once school administrators have a vision of what an improved program will look like, they are eager for changes to occur. As the guidance and counseling program leader, you need to respond to their needs, but you also need to ensure that the program change decisions are the right decisions. This is why a factual assessment of the current program is so essential: to ensure making the right changes, not just responding to some individuals' pet concerns. You need to determine how much time you have to complete your assessment and the data that are most critical to progress at a reasonable rate. Thorough planning is essential, and so is effective use of your time.

If you are in a multischool or multibuilding district, you need to share the leadership of the program with the school counselor staff leaders. These school counselors can become the leaders of the subparts of the project and lead their colleagues by influence and delegated authority. You continue to lead by influence coupled with the authority of your position. You need (a) to be sure that the school counselors selected are ready to be effective leaders and (b) to work out mechanisms for being able to continue to provide leadership to them. The whole process becomes a matter of balance. In this case, you must strike a balance among knowing where you are going, what you need and want in results, and letting the staff of the work groups determine how they are going to provide results.

Implementation

You are the overall leader of the data collection efforts. You must staff your work groups to get the tasks done, and you must delegate effectively. Effective delegation means being explicit and precise in the charges you give work groups and monitoring their progress as they proceed. We feel it is important, if possible, for you to meet with each work group and, indeed, to become a member of each group. Although you are the ultimate leader of these efforts, you do not have to have all the answers. We have found that thinking together with the work-group members is a useful strategy. Every district with which we have worked has implemented its current program assessment somewhat differently. The data needs are the same, but the process routes may be different.

In your district you may need to engineer the development of the assessment instruments and procedures to be used for a variety of reasons. You need to ensure the adequacy of instrument development and then ensure that the instruments are relevant to the selected program model. Your perspective is broader than that of your staff, and you are more aware of the resources available to you from other district or campus departments; you will know about reports generated by district departments, and you will know about district computer capabilities. Your involvement will allow you to coordinate the work of the various work groups. It is imperative that you not bombard the staff with a variety of similar surveys. It is also appropriate for you, as the guidance and counseling program administrator, to collect and present some of the data on your own. For example, you probably already have much of the budget and facilities information. You are also in a better position to survey other administrators.

There are a variety of ways in which you will be able to help the committees implement their processes. Your authority will facilitate data collection. You can ensure the involvement, understanding, and responsiveness of every staff member. You will need to not only educate the counseling staff as to what they are doing and why but also understand and manage the resistance of some staff members.

Senge and Kaeufer (2000) identified three phases of the change process and the forces within each that impede change and suggested ways to deal with each. They described challenges in initiating change, challenges in sustaining change, and challenges in building a new design. Challenges in initiating change are time (as discussed in chapter 2), needed help, perceived irrelevance, and leaders perceived as not walking the talk. The challenges in sustaining and spreading change are fear and anxiety, lack of immediate results, and conflicts between those who believe in the potential of the anticipated changes and those who do not. The challenges in building a new design are governance issues—of accountability and power, diffusion, and clarification of strategy and purpose.

Some example strategies Senge and Kaeufer (2000) offered to address the challenges associated with initiating the change—where we are at this point in our description of the change process—are to "enable people to regain control over their time," invest in help, "make information available to members," "build credibility by demonstration" (p. 4), and "develop patience under pressure" (p. 5).

If you have taken the steps in program improvement that we are suggesting, then you will be armed with the policy support you need to answer the concerns. It also is helpful to remind staff that the current assessment needs to be accomplished only once; after the program redesigning efforts are completed, you will evaluate what you have done, but your basic program description will be finished. You may find that you need to mandate some of the work, particularly the time-use study. The time-use study will involve more work on the part of each staff member than will other aspects of the assessment, and the importance of its results is such that completeness and accuracy are imperative. Further, there is a high correlation between your use of your supervisory skills of encouraging and praising and the success of this phase of the project. The more accessible you are to the counseling staff, both to the work groups and to the staff as a whole, the more comfortable everyone will be with the new model and its implementation.

Closure

Your final set of responsibilities in accomplishing the current program assessment will be to help the work groups summarize and disseminate the data they have collected and to help the steering committee and the staff analyze the results. Organizing the presentation of the data is not easy. You probably will want to present all of the data to the steering committee and to the counseling staff but only an executive summary to other interested staff such as building-based educators, campus administrators, and other guidance staff. It is useful to have leaders of the work groups present the information that their groups have gathered, but you must assume responsibility for ensuring that the information is understood. You will need to allow as much time to do this as is required. Some schools have used as much as an entire in-service education day for this purpose. This allows the staff time to process the information and to begin drawing their own conclusions. It also provides them the opportunity to raise questions and to learn more about the implied program changes. The data that have been gathered are tangible and impressive, and by presenting them all together, perspective is maintained. It will be rewarding to staff to see the fullness of their program. As already mentioned, this will probably be the first time that the entire program will seem visible, tangible, and concrete.

The data need to be analyzed by you, the steering committee, and, either together or separately, by the school counselor leadership team or all of the school counselors if they are not all a part of the steering committee. You must be clear about what the data say to you. You must draw conclusions about what the current program is and what it is accomplishing. Then you are in a position to state what the design of the current program is and what the current priorities are.

By design, we mean the balance that has been struck between the program components and among the school counselor functions. You can state that as of this time, for example, the largest component of the current guidance and counseling program is system support, the second is individual student planning, the third responsive services, and the fourth guidance curriculum. You now know, for example, that the primary mode of operating for the counseling staff is individual counseling, the second is completing administrative assignments, the third is doing special education administrative work, and so on. An example of presenting that information from the Northside Independent School District's (1986) program improvement project is presented in Table 4.15.

Program component priorities clearly emerged in Northside Independent School District as a result of aggregating the information gleaned in the study of how school counselors applied their time:

- *First priority*
  Individual student planning
  Middle school: System support

Table 4.15
Current Guidance Program Component Priorities (Baseline Data)

| | Priority/School Level | | |
Component	Elementary	Middle	High
Guidance curriculum	4	4	4
Individual student planning	1	3	3
Responsive services	3	2	2
System support	2	1	1

Note. Data from Northside Independent School District, San Antonio, TX. Adapted with permission.

  High school: System support
- *Fourth priority*
  Elementary school: Guidance curriculum
  Middle school: Guidance curriculum
  High school: Guidance curriculum

After determining program component priorities, you can state the priority order of the student results addressed and of the clients served by the current program. For example, you may have learned that at the elementary level 20% of your activities are aimed at helping students be safe at home and in the neighborhood. Those activities thus have a high priority. At the high school level, you may have learned that 60% of your activities relate to scheduling and schedule changes. You also now know the rank order that applies to the clients you serve. You may have learned that your first-priority clients are individual students who come to the counseling office, second are teachers, third are groups of students with remedial-level needs whom you call in for group counseling, and so on.

If you have not already done so, you need to write down these conclusions. This will help you bring this phase of the project to closure and provide you baseline information that will enable you to move on to subsequent steps without having to reanalyze the data every time you pick them up. The value of written statements, as mentioned earlier, forces you to be precise, provides a tangible focus for the steering committee and the school counselors to endorse, and provides a vehicle for communicating with others about the results of the work that has been accomplished.

Concluding Thoughts

In summary, your current program assessment has contributed much to your program improvement project. The staff have been involved and learned about the program as it exists. They have a vision of the model to be adopted or adapted. A full, concrete description of the current program has been made.

You have broadened the involvement of staff in the program improvement process. School counselor leaders have been identified and are beginning to fulfill their roles. All school counselors and other relevant guidance and counseling program and administrative staff have been working in groups. The steering committee members have been used in operational roles to lead the work groups as well as in their advisory capacity on the committee, and thus their investment in the overall project has increased.

In addition, a sense of the need for change has begun to emerge. The school counselors know that changes will come but feel reassured that the decisions to change are not being made hastily. This suggests that the leadership is seeking to make the right changes.

From a staff development perspective, the school counselors have learned more about the adopted program model and the components through record keeping, data gathering, and discussion. They have begun to understand the relationship between their current program and the new program model. They have come to know their current program in concrete detail. They have begun to learn about and practice the important program improvement skills of planning and data gathering.

You as the program leader, the steering committee, the guidance staff, and the administrators now know what resources you have available in the current program and how you use them. You know the activities that compose the current program, what your current program emphasizes, its variety, and the balance of your use of the components in the delivery system. You now know at least the probable student results of your program and the scope of your impact on the students you serve. You know the clients your current program serves and the proportion of services it provides to the various subsets of these populations. You know the perceptions of your primary program users. In short, you, the steering committee, and the guidance and administrative staff know the design and priorities of the current guidance and counseling program.

The scope of the current program assessment is such that, once done, there is a tendency to think that the program improvement project is completed. It is not. Although you can now relate your current program data to the program model, making judgments at this time is premature. Your next questions are, What do we desire our guidance and counseling program to be? (discussed in chapter 5) and How does what we are doing now compare and contrast with what is desired from our program? (discussed in chapter 6). The concreteness of your knowledge about what is and the vision you have about what could be will provide you the impetus to begin to navigate the difficult program improvement steps of planning the transition from where you are to where you want to be and then implementing changes.

References

Adelman, H. S., & Taylor, L. (2003). On sustainability of project innovations as systemic change. *Journal of Educational and Psychological Consultation, 14*(1), 1–25.

American School Counselor Association. (2004a). *Ethical standards for school counselors.* Retrieved from http://www.schoolcounselor.org/content.asp?contentid=173

American School Counselor Association. (2004b, June). *The role of the professional school counselor.* Retrieved from http://www.schoolcounselor.org/content.asp?contentid=240

American School Counselor Association. (2004c). *State-by-state student-to-counselor ratio*(2001–2001). Retrieved December 21, 2004, from http://www.schoolcounselor.org/files/ratios.pdf

American School Counselor Association. (2004d). *Why elementary school counselors.* Retrieved from http://www.schoolcounselor.org/content.asp?contentid=230

American School Counselor Association. (2004e). *Why middle school counselors.* Retrieved from http://www.schoolcounselor.org/content.asp?contentid=231

American School Counselor Association. (2004f). *Why secondary school counselors.* Retrieved from http://www.schoolcounselor.org/content.asp?contentid=233

American School Counselor Association. (2005). *The ASCA national model: A framework for school counseling programs* (2nd ed.). Alexandria, VA: Author.

American School Counselor Association. (1997). *National standards for school counseling.* Alexandria, VA: Author.

Bolman, L. G., & Deal, T. E. (1997). *Reframing organizations: Artistry, choice, and leadership* (2nd ed.). San Francisco, CA: Jossey-Bass.

Constantine, M. G., & Gushue, G. V. (2003). School counselors' ethnic tolerance attitudes and racism attitudes as predictors of their multicultural case conceptualization of an immigrant student. *Journal of Counseling & Development, 81*, 185–190.

Dellana, S. A., & Snyder, D. (2004). Student future outlook and counseling quality in a rural minority high school. *High School Journal, 88*(1), 27–42.

Dollarhide, C. T. (2003). School counselors as program leaders: Applying leadership contexts to school counseling. *Professional School Counseling, 6*, 304–308.

Fullan, M., Bertani, A., & Quinn, J. (2004, April). New lessons for districtwide reform. *Educational Leadership*, 42–46.

Gysbers, N. C., Kosteck-Bunch, L., Magnuson, C. S., & Starr, M. F. (2002). *Missouri comprehensive guidance program: A manual for program development, implementation, evaluation, and enhancement.* Columbia, MO: Instructional Materials Laboratory.

Gysbers, N. C., Lapan, R. T., & Jones, B. A. (2000). School board policies for guidance and counseling: A call to action. *Professional School Counseling, 3*, 349–353.

Lee, C. L. (2001). Culturally responsive school counselors and programs: Addressing the needs of all students. *Professional School Counseling, 4*, 257–261.

MacDonald, G., & Sink, C. A. (1999). A qualitative developmental analysis of comprehensive guidance programmes in schools in the United States. *British Journal of Guidance and Counselling, 27*, 415–430.

National Board for Professional Teaching Standards. (2002). *School counseling standards.* Retrieved April 10, 2004, from http://www.nbpts.org/pdf/schoolcounsel ing.pdf

National Career Development Association. (2003). *Career development: A policy statement of the National Career Development Association board of directors.* Retrieved December 21, 2004, from http://www.ncda.org/pdf/policy.pdf

National Center for Education Statistics. (2002). *Table 128, Digest of Education Statistics, 2002.* Retrieved from http://NCES.ed.gov/programs/digest/d02/tables/dt128.asp

North Carolina Department of Public Instruction. (n.d.) *How North Carolina school counselors spend their time.* Retrieved July, 30, 2003, from http://www.ncpublicschools. org/curriculum/guidance/time.htm

Northside Independent School District. (1986). *Comprehensive guidance program framework.* San Antonio, TX: Author.

Northside Independent School District. (2004). *Northside Independent School District - San Antonio, TX 78238: Facts and figures.* Retrieved December 29, 2004, from http:// www.nisd.net/general/figures

Rylander, C. K. (2002, August). *Guiding our children toward success: How Texas school counselors spend their time.* Austin, TX: Office of the Comptroller.

Senge, P. M., & Kaeufer, D. H. (2000). Creating change. *Executive Excellence, 17*(10), 4–5.

Sink, C. A., & MacDonald, G. (1998). The status of comprehensive guidance and counseling in the United States. *Professional School Counseling, 2*, 88–94.

Taylor, E. R. (2002). Evaluation of counseling services in a rural school district: Assessing current program status. In P. Henderson & N. Gysbers (Eds.), *Implementing comprehensive school guidance programs: Critical leadership issues and successful responses* (pp. 23–30). Greensboro, NC: CAPS.

Texas Counseling Association. (2004). *Texas evaluation model for professional school counselors* (2nd ed.). Austin, TX: Author.

Texas Education Agency. (n.d.). *About the AEIS: An overview of the academic excellence indicator system for the state of Texas.* Retrieved December 23, 2004, from http://www. tea.state.tx.us/perfreport/aeis/about.aeis.html

Texas Education Agency. (2005). *A model comprehensive, developmental guidance and counseling program for Texas public schools: A guide for program development pre-K–12th grade* (4th ed.). Austin, TX: Author.

Texas Education Code. (2001). *Chapter 33, Service programs and extra-curricular activities; Subchapter A, School counselors and counseling programs.* Retrieved from http://www.capitol.state.tx.us/statutes/ed/ed0003300.html

Vandergrift, J. A. (1999, April). *Are Arizona public schools making the best use of school counselors? Results of a 3-year study of counselors' time use* (Arizona School to Work Briefing Paper No. 16). Tempe: Arizona State University, Morrison Institute for Public Policy.

~ Part II ~

Designing

Chapter 5

Designing the Comprehensive Guidance and Counseling Program

Designing—Adapting the Guidance and Counseling Program Model

- Define the basic structure of your program.
- Identify and list student competencies by content areas and school levels or grade groupings.
- Reaffirm policy support.
- Establish priorities for program delivery (qualitative design).
- Establish parameters for resource allocation (quantitative design).
- Write down and distribute the description of the desired program.

☞ Once a comprehensive guidance and counseling program model has been selected and data have been gathered that describe the current guidance and counseling program in light of the model, the next phase of the program improvement process is to design the specific program that is desired for your school district or school building; that is, to tailor the model to suit your school or district. In the American School Counselor Association (ASCA) National Model, this is the "Designing the Delivery System" phase (ASCA, 2005, p. 70). Conceptualizing the desired program in concrete terms is essential because, as you will find, the program improvement process is somewhat analogous to remodeling your home while you are living in it. A specifically drawn blueprint of the renovations for your home is needed so that the renovations may be made in an orderly sequence without totally disrupting your lifestyle. The more precise the blueprint, the more efficient the renovation, the more likely it is that the ultimate product will reflect what you want. The same is true for a comprehensive guidance and counseling program. Further, you may have a somewhat idealistic picture of the guidance and counseling program you want, at this point, but you need to begin to temper this vision with reality. You need to be specific about the changes you want to make and feel confident that those changes are the right changes.

During the designing phase of the program improvement process, you will continue to use the steering and the school–community advisory committees already established. By this time, these committee members have become knowledgeable about the current program and have grasped the concept of the new program model. As representatives of the professionals who work in the program as well as the constituents who use the program, they can help in hammering out the hard decisions to be faced. Basic questions that need to be asked include the following:

- Which program component should have priority for the counselors?
- Of the competencies that students need to learn, which should be emphasized at each grade level or grade grouping?
- Who will be served and with what priority—all students in a developmental mode or some students in a preventive services mode? Or a few students in a remedial or crisis services mode? And what are the relationships between services to students and services to the adults in the students' lives?
- What content domains will describe the scope of the guidance and counseling program, and how will the competencies and results be sequenced?
- What skills will be utilized by the school counselors—teaching, guiding, counseling, consulting, testing, record keeping, coordinating, disseminating information—and with what priority?
- What school levels will benefit, and to what extent, from the resources appropriated to the program—elementary, middle/junior high, or high school?
- What is the relationship between the guidance and counseling program and staff members and the other educational programs and staff members? Is the sole purpose of guidance to support the instructional program? Or does guidance have an identity and responsibilities of its own? (Henderson, 1987, p. 26)

The answers to these questions are dictated by the values and priorities of the system in which the guidance and counseling program and school counselors find themselves and by the quantity and quality of resources supplied to the program. The steering and advisory committees can help ensure that the changes you will be recommending are responsive to the needs of the school district and the community, and they may help in generating the new resources you undoubtedly will need.

If you are the guidance and counseling program leader, you have primary responsibility for the decisions and their implementation, but we believe the broader your support base, the sounder your decisions. You will need to continue to clarify information and the impending decisions. You will need to move the decision process along. In all likelihood, you will have major responsibility for putting the vision of the model program in operation.

Establishing the design of your desired program entails describing in concrete and relevant terms the content; the organizational framework's structure, activities, and time; and the resources of your improved program. In other words, the elements of the comprehensive guidance and counseling program described in chapter 3 need to be tailored to fit the realities and priorities of your school buildings and district. The basic question at this point is, How do you want to use the resources available to the guidance and counseling program in your setting to have a comprehensive and well-balanced program?

It is essential to establish the design that you want to have for your program so that the implementation that follows can be realistic. If you are from a school district that has more than one building, clarifying the desired design at the district level will ensure consistency of the program from one building to another. The district design should be general enough, however, to allow buildings to tailor their programs to meet local building and neighborhood needs.

This chapter describes six major tasks that, when completed, will make up the established design for your program. The first task is to define the basic structure that will be the organizer for your program. This task includes crafting the structural components and defining the program components to suit your school/district program. The second task is to identify and list student competencies by content areas and school level or grade groupings. The third task is to reaffirm the policy support for the emerging guidance and counseling program. The fourth task is to establish priorities for program delivery—to complete the qualitative design. The fifth task is to establish parameters for program resource allocations—to complete the quantitative design. The chapter then discusses the guidance and counseling program leader's roles and responsibilities in carrying out the designing phase of the program development process. The sixth task, one of the tasks of the guidance and counseling program leader, is to put all of the decisions in writing and distribute the program description to all counselors and administrators. We then suggest ways for attending to diversity in your program.

Define the Basic Structure of Your Program

With the assistance of your steering and school–community advisory committees and your district policymakers, decide what the guidance and counseling program structure will be for your district/building. Currently, the structure in use may follow the guidance services model (orientation, assessment, information, counseling, placement, and follow-up activities), or it may be organized around the processes of counseling, consulting, and coordination, or it may be described by a list of duties. The comprehensive guidance and counseling program structure described in chapter 3 is more in keeping with a developmental guidance perspective. The structural components—definition, rationale, and assumptions—provide the ideological underpinnings for your program. The program components—guidance curriculum, individual student planning, responsive services, and system support—provide the organizational framework for your guidance and counseling program activities, pre-K through 12th grade.

Local community, district, and state needs will dictate the specific content to be included in each program component as well as the overall balance among the components. This section briefly summarizes the recommended structural and program components.

Structural Components

Definition

The program definition includes the mission statement of the program and its centrality within the school district's total educational program. To be complete, the definition statement should answer at least four questions:

- Who delivers the program—professional certified school counselors, teachers, social workers, psychologists, administrators and other staff, parents, other community members?
- What competencies will students or others possess as a result of their involvement in the program? Be responsible citizens, use problem-solving skills, seek to achieve excellence, communicate effectively (from the district's mission)? Respect others, respect themselves (from the school's mission)? Maintain self-esteem, relate effectively across cultures?
- Who are the clients of the program? Which students' development is assisted—all students; 12th-grade, 8th-grade, 5th-grade, pre-K students; college-bound students, work-bound students, disabled students, minority students, poor students, at-risk students, grieving students, drug-abusing students? And what about parents and teachers?
- How is the program organized? Through the comprehensive guidance and counseling program components of guidance curriculum, individual student planning, responsive services, and system support? Or through some other organizational grouping?

Rationale

The rationale discusses the importance of guidance as an equal partner in the educational system and provides reasons why individuals in our society need to acquire the competencies as a result of their involvement in a comprehensive guidance and counseling program (as exemplified in chapter 3). The rationale suggests that the guidance and counseling program is also engineered to help all students develop their potential through provision of developmental assistance for all students and of specialized assistance for individuals with unique needs. Although the purpose of the rationale is to express the needs for the program, it also guides program design decisions (e.g., subgroups of students to be served) and provides direction to implementation of the program. It includes the conclusions drawn from student and community needs assessments, as well as clarifications of goals of the local and state educational system and those of the nation as a whole. It references current professional theories, school/district mission and goals, and professional trends—both in education and in professional school counseling—that support the program and its design.

Student Needs and Realities. As detailed in chapter 4, specific student needs related to guidance and counseling program outcomes should be identified for students in each of the grade levels, including the needs suggested by their developmental levels. Needs may be assessed through surveys of the program's consumers or through opinions of the school and community experts (e.g., counselors, teachers, principal, and other educators; community leaders).

Examples of general guidance-related subjects are students' self-concept, identity, cultural identity, sexuality, personality, and moral, social, and career development. Another popular, research-based approach to identifying students' developmental needs is through assessing students' needs vis-à-vis the "40 Developmental Assets" described in the work of the Search Institute (n.d.). It is important to keep in mind that "developmental research has been emerging that focuses on strengths as a means to promote positive student development" (Akos & Galassi, 2004, p. 196).

In addition to their developmental needs, specific information should be identified regarding how many students have needs for preventive, remedial, and crisis interventions and the specific issues or situations that cause these needs. For example, today's societal problems facing all schools include underachievement, adolescent pregnancy, child and adolescent suicide, child abuse and neglect, substance abuse, racial tension and turmoil, bullying, violence, and shifts in family structures and the labor market. All of these issues differ from community to community and need to be assessed locally.

Community Context. In assessing your current program (chapter 4), you gathered community status information. Some of this information suggests some of the needs that students have in relation to their healthy development and to success in school and life. The specific needs of students for whom the school presents a second culture and who are striving to manage successfully the acquisition of that culture (Coleman, Casali, & Wampold, 2001), for example, should be specified. Students whose parents have not been fully educated by today's standards have different needs than those whose parents have benefited from college or some form of postsecondary education.

Professional Theories. A part of the reasoning behind the program—its rationale—is the belief system held by the guidance and counseling program leadership, including the steering and advisory committees and the professional counseling staff, about what is best for students. Developmental guidance and counseling programs should be based on developmental theory and principles (MacDonald & Sink, 1999). The theories used to explain what having mental health entails and those that explain how to help students regain lost mental health should be clarified. Henderson (ASCA, 2005) reminds us that professional school counseling practice rests on psychological theories (from Sigmund Freud to William Glasser) that seek to explain why people act, think, and feel the way that they do, what counselors can do to help them attain whatever goals they are striving for, and how they can best do that. Theories regarding the stages and facets of human growth and development (e.g., those described by John Dewey, Jean Piaget, Erik Erikson, and Lawrence Kohlberg) also support the work of professional school counselors and guidance and counseling programs. Additionally, there are theories about how learning occurs and what promotes learning. In chapter 3, we offer a learning theory for sequencing activities that lead to student competency development. Appendix A provides an application of this theory—a scope and sequence to facilitate students' life career development.

School Mission, Goals, Educational Trends. In addition to the federal, state, and local policy statements identified in chapter 4 as political supports for your improving guidance and counseling program, the current trends—the "state of the art"—of the education profession should also be considered. While most educators agree that challenging all students, regardless of their background or circumstances, to strive for high levels of achievement is paramount, at this time the education profession is caught in a dilemma of wanting to respond to the continuing demands for accountability, as set out in the federal mandates of the No Child Left Behind Act (2002) and related state mandates, and of increasing recognition that children are diverse individuals with multiple facets and needs that must be addressed in order for optimal learning to occur. Many of the needs of students—feeling unsafe, unable to concentrate on schoolwork, and the like—cause barriers to student academic success.

Professional School Counseling Trends. As the state of the art of teaching and learning are important, so are the current trends in professional school counseling. Trends can be determined that suggest program priorities and some of its practices. *The ASCA National Model: A Framework for School Counseling Programs* (2nd ed., ASCA, 2005) and its companion, *Sharing the Vision: The National Standards for School Counseling Programs* (Campbell & Dahir, 1997), provide standards to guide the rationale for establishing your basic program structure and the student competencies you aim to help students achieve. In their position statements, *Why Elementary School Counselors* (ASCA, 2004c), *Why Middle School Counselors* (ASCA, 2004d), and *Why Secondary School Counselors* (ASCA, 2004e), ASCA delineated some of the needs of students at each school level, what school counselors are qualified to do for the students, and how they implement the guidance and counseling program at that level. The papers close with an answer to the title questions, Why . . . ? These succinct pieces are useful to support local rationale and to guide the development of local rationale statements.

Counseling journals, such as American Counseling Association's *Journal of Counseling & Development,* and school counseling journals, such as the American School Counselor Association's *Professional School Counseling,* consistently provide updated information about practices that have worked for counselors in addressing issues faced by students today. One noteworthy example is the 2004 issue of the *Journal of Counseling & Development* that includes a special section on school violence ("School Violence," 2004). These journals also present articles describing current research and evaluation. One of the major trends in the school counseling profession is the measurement of the effectiveness of school counselors, of guidance and counseling programs, and of specific practices. While much of this research is documented elsewhere (National Center for School Counseling Outcome Research at the University of Massachusetts, Amherst), ASCA summarizes a broad scope of research in its paper on the "Effectiveness of School Counseling" (2002–2003). One study of interest was conducted by the California Department of Education (2003). The study was mandated by the California Assembly and led to findings that suggested the need for more pupil support—including counseling—services, particularly "school-wide prevention and intervention strategies and counseling services, psychological counseling for individuals, groups, and families, and targeted intervention strategies for children and families such as counseling, case management, and crisis intervention" (p. 2).

Studies of effectiveness of school guidance and counseling often focus on its primary outcomes, those related to students' personal/social, educational, and career development. Because the accountability measures currently applied to the educational system focus primarily on reading and math achievement and on school safety, there are an increasing number of studies that focus on school counselors' impact on these factors. For example, Brigman and Campbell (2003) conducted a research project that provides a good model for other researchers in this area: "The goal of the project was to examine the impact of school-counselor-led interventions on student academic achievement and school success behavior" (p. 96). The interventions focused on specific skills related to cognitive, social, and self-management skill development, three areas directly connected to school success. "The results reveal that the combined school counselor interventions of group counseling and classroom guidance were associated with a positive impact on student achievement and behavior" (p. 97). They also concluded that "the facts that the interventions were targeted on specific skills associated with school success and that school counselors used research-based techniques to teach these critical skills were seen as central to the positive outcome of the study" (p. 97).

Assumptions

Assumptions are premises that shape and guide the program and its design. Many times assumptions are not expressed; they are things that individuals take for granted but that others may not have thought about or agree with. Assumptions are made about students and other clients, the program, and the program staff. In designing the program, it is very important for individuals' assumptions to be brought to the table and discussed. We offer some examples below to help trigger your thinking, but the assumptions on which your program is based must be your assumptions.

Assumptions About Students/Other Clients. Some assumptions about students and other clients include the following:

- All children and adolescents can and want to learn.
- Guidance and counseling programs assist students in developing their individuality, functioning effectively with others, and managing their own destiny (Borders & Drury, 1992).
- All students deserve assistance with their personal, social, educational, and career development.
- "Cultural differences are real and cannot be ignored" (Lee, 2001, p. 259).
- All students, parents, teachers and other program users have equal access to the program regardless of their levels of need (developmental, preventive, remedial, or crisis) or of personal characteristics (e.g., gender, race, ethnicity, cultural background, sexual orientation, disability, socioeconomic status, learning ability level, or language) (Texas Education Agency, 2004, p. 12).
- Parents are invited to be full partners with educators in the education of their children.

Assumptions About the Program. Some assumptions about the program include the following:

- Accountable guidance and counseling programs provide an appropriate balance of activities and services, are an integral part and an independent component of the total educational program, and are systematically planned, designed, implemented, and evaluated.

- The minimum-level program provides for each of the four delivery system components.
- The conditions required for effective program implementation include being in a positive work environment: one with favorable interpersonal relations among the school staff; one with administrative commitment to and support of the guidance and counseling program; and one that provides an adequate budget and guidance materials.
- For guidance and counseling programs to be effective, the educational system must be characterized by a healthy interpersonal climate and must be supportive of the program in terms of its policies and provision of resources.
- The services provided to all our students are equitable.
- Guidance is a schoolwide responsibility.
- The essential goal of a school guidance and counseling program is to help students succeed academically.
- Time and opportunity are provided for guidance and counseling program planning, designing, and evaluation.
- The counselor-to-student ratio is adequate to implement the designed program; or the program is designed within the parameters of the ratio.
- Facilities are readily accessible to students, allow for implementation of the comprehensive, developmental guidance and counseling program, and assure privacy and confidentiality for the program's clients.

Assumptions About Program Staff. Some assumptions about the program staff include the following:

- Professional school counselors are essential in today's public schools.
- School counselors spend the majority of their time working directly with students.
- Counselors are fully certified by their state's certification office and have the special training needed to carry out specialized job assignments.
- All school counselors are highly proficient in guidance and counseling competencies.
- School counselors adhere to the ethical standards of the profession.
- Time and opportunity are provided for in-service training for school counselors and other guidance and counseling program staff members.
- All staff members accept responsibility for guidance and counseling program goals and objectives.
- The roles of each of the staff members and their organizational relations are clearly defined.
- Professional and interprofessional relationships are characterized by respect, collaboration, and cooperation.
- School administrators protect the professional integrity of the guidance and counseling program and the school counselors.
- The school/district employs professionally certified school counselors in sufficient ratio to carry out the intended design of the program.
- School administrators understand the program's priorities and demands and make decisions and establish procedures in light of this understanding.

Program Components

Guidance Curriculum

The guidance curriculum is the center of the developmental part of the comprehensive guidance and counseling program. It contains statements as to the goals for guidance instruction and the competencies to be developed by students. The curriculum is organized by grade level; that is, a scope and sequence of learnings for Grades K–12 is established. It is designed to serve all students and is often implemented through classroom or group guidance.

Individual Student Planning

The activities of the individual student planning component are provided for all students and are intended to guide students in the development and implementation of their personal, social, educational, and career plans. They help students to understand and monitor their growth and development and to take action on their next steps educationally or vocationally. The activities in this component are delivered either on a group or an individual basis with students and parents. Teachers are often involved as advisers.

Responsive Services

The purpose of this component is to provide special help to students who are facing problems that interfere with their healthy personal, social, career, or educational development. It includes the provision of preventive responses to students who are on the brink of choosing an unhealthy or inappropriate solution to their problems or of being unable to cope with a situation. Remedial interventions also are provided for students who have already made unwise choices or have not coped well with problem situations. This component includes such activities as individual and small-group counseling, consulting with staff and parents, and referring students and families to other specialists or programs.

System Support

In implementation it helps to divide the system support component into two parts: (a) guidance and counseling program management and (b) support services. Guidance and counseling program management includes the activities necessary to support the other three program components. It includes designated program and staff leadership; program and staff development; actions that result in budget, facilities, and appropriate policies, procedures, and guidelines; research; community relations; and resource development. Support services includes the activities implemented by guidance staff that support schoolwide or other specific educational programs. These activities include consultation with teachers; efforts to enhance parent involvement in school, school improvement planning, and input to policymakers and curriculum developers on behalf of students; and efforts to ensure school counselors' fair share, neither too much nor too little, of schoolwide responsibilities.

Identify and List Student Competencies by Content Areas and School Levels or Grade Groupings

Once you have selected your overall program structure, you next decide on the competencies that the guidance and counseling program will take responsibility for helping students acquire. What knowledge will students gain, what skills will students develop, and what attitudes will students form as a result of their participation in the guidance and counseling program? For help in answering these questions, go to the results section of the current program assessment you have already completed. In that process you identified the intended student outcomes resulting from guidance activities K–12 in the current guidance and counseling program. As we suggested earlier, compare these with lists generated from the goals of your school district, your state department of education, or your local community. Some school districts and some state departments of education have developed competency lists to be used as part of their graduation requirements. Use such lists in the comparison process. Also review the lists of competencies presented in chapter 3 and Appendix A. Then decide on the list to be used in your program.

The just-mentioned sources will give you a plethora of ideas, but we recommend that you build your own list, one that fits your school district's and community's stated mission, goals, and priorities. One of your ultimate goals is to ensure the centrality of the guidance and counseling program within the school district's total educational program. The more direct the link between the school district's goals and your program, the more clearly related the guidance and counseling program will be to the basic mission of the school district. For example, if the district's educational philosophy includes such items as helping students to become good citizens, be responsible for their actions, and make wise choices, then these words should be incorporated in the student competencies addressed by the guidance and counseling program.

You need to proceed through the list-building process in as systematic a way as possible. Thus you first need to identify the broad areas of human growth and development that you established as the scope of the guidance and counseling program (in chapter 3 we called these *domains*). Then specify competencies for each domain and for each grade grouping or end point of a school level, such as at the end of the 6th grade for the elementary guidance and counseling program, at the end of the 9th grade for the junior high school program, or at the end of the 12th grade for the high school program.

The preliminary work of assembling this list can be done by a work group. Reviewing lists of competencies generated by others may be confusing at first, but once the work group gets involved it is an exciting task. It allows professional counselors to focus on the contributions they can make to students' growth and development. At each stage of the development of the list—after establishing the domains and stating the competencies—the list should be reviewed and approved by the total guidance staff as well as by other key members of the school staff, administration, students, and the community. Use your school–community advisory committee to assist you in the process.

Be parsimonious when it comes to the number of domains, goals, and competencies used as the basis for your improved program. The models presented in chapter 3 exemplify how the content domains, goals, and competencies expand when the specifics are addressed. The life career development model identifies three domains and has 5 goals per domain, resulting in 15 goals for the overall program model. The ASCA model identifies three domains and 3 goals per domain, resulting in 9 goals overall. The Texas model identifies seven domains that incorporate 28 skill goals. The Northside Independent School District model identifies seven domains and 24 skill goals for the overall program model. We suggest that you not exceed these numbers because longer lists become difficult to manage effectively, especially given the resources typically available to the guidance and counseling program. This list of competencies is the heart of the comprehensive guidance and counseling program. Every activity conducted in each component of the program should aim toward mastery of one or more of these competencies.

Reaffirm Policy Support

If you have followed the process of program change outlined so far and are using a steering committee or a school–community advisory committee, you already have a group of guidance-educated and supportive others that includes administrators, parents, teachers, community representatives, and business and industry personnel. At this point in the process, however, it is a good idea to reaffirm the support of the school system's policymakers and administrators for the structural components, competencies, and delivery system model of the program. Remember that they need to know what is envisioned for the guidance and counseling program and be willing to support the improvement efforts not only with the public but also with the guidance staff and other school staff members who may be anxious about the proposed changes.

To learn if you have the support of the administrators in your school or district, begin with your immediate supervisor. If you are at the district level, this means your assistant or associate superintendent; if you are at the building level, it means your principal. Remember that to ensure that the changes you envision are consistent with the district's vision, you need at least one of the administrators to help you keep in touch with the district's basic mission. You also need the administrator to help you gain the support of the school district's board of education, and you need the administrator's assistance in enlisting the support of the other administrators, at the campus or district level, who supervise or have expectations for counselors. In addition, you need the reaffirmation of the upper-level administrators to convince counselors who resist the impending changes that the changes are, indeed, what the district wants and that they need to be responsive to those changes.

Because school districts operate within a delicate political balance, recognized leaders or a majority of constituents—including parents, principals, counselors, teachers, students, superintendents, other administrators, and board members—have to be willing to sign on to the new program vision. The more you prepare them at this stage of the process, the stronger your support will be in the challenging times of actual implementation.

Now that the program structure has been selected and student competencies have been listed, it is time to seek a guidance and counseling program policy statement. The fact that the advisory or steering committee has already endorsed the program helps because its members can take the program structure and student competency list to their constituent groups, educate them, and solicit feedback. However, it also is highly desirable to have your board of education adopt a guidance and counseling program policy that affirms the structure of the desired program. Some districts adopt the program definition as the basic policy. Some policymakers state the priorities for the program, such as serving students with needs for developmental, preventive, remedial, or crisis help, and the relative priority of each of the four program components as well as the priorities for student skill development. You may find some of the data gathered in your study of the perceptions of the current guidance and counseling program useful in presenting the policy to the school board. You may also find useful the Resolution on Guidance and Counseling adopted by the Delegate Assembly of the National School Boards Association in April 1986 (cited in chapter 2). An example of a state board of education policy is provided in Appendix E.

Establish Priorities for Program Delivery (Qualitative Design)

With your program broadly outlined, basic policy support established, and the rationale for the program in place, you are now ready to define in specific terms the desired design for the district's/building's comprehensive guidance and counseling program. The following are the basic questions that you are answering now:

- How do you want to use the resources available to the guidance and counseling program to ensure attainment of the program mission?
- What are the priorities within each component of the program?
- How much of the available resources should be expended within each component?

As described in chapter 4, the priorities express the qualitative design of the program; the parameters for resource allocation express the quantitative design.

In developing the rationale, assumptions, and definition for the program, you began the values clarification exercise that must be completed now as you establish the qualitative and quantitative designs for program delivery. Once the program improvement leadership has completed assessment of the current program design, they will be able to see that choices are made, sometimes unconsciously, in program implementation. It is also no doubt clear that the students' needs for and within the program seem endless, but the resources available to the program are quite finite. Purposeful development of the desired program design allows these choices to be made consciously and conscientiously. The design decisions provide the guidelines so that your guidance and counseling program can be organized for effective and efficient use of the resources currently and potentially available.

Designing the qualitative dimension of the program entails making decisions regarding the specific definitions of and the priorities for program delivery. Priorities are established for the use of counselors' and others' competencies, for the clients to be served, for the student competencies to be targeted, and for the activities to be provided. Which student groups should have what priority? Which student competencies should be emphasized? What activities make up each of the comprehensive guidance and counseling program components and their priorities? Your answers should be based on the rationale that you have offered for the program, and your answers should suggest the priorities for staff roles, clients to be served, topics to be addressed, and activities to be undertaken within each component.

Priorities for School Counselors' Competencies

Before making specific recommendations concerning the school counselors' role, it is important to remember the unique contributions that school counselors can and do make to students' growth and development. Although states vary in their requirements for certification of school counselors, some consensus is seen at the national level. The primary content suggested by national certification and accreditation agencies (e.g., Council for Accreditation of Counseling and Related Educational Programs, 2001; National Board of Certified Counselors, 2004; National Board for Professional Teaching Standards, 2004) include human growth and development, fundamentals of school counseling, student competencies, social and cultural contexts, counseling theories and techniques, consultation with other adults in students' lives, student assessment, program development, professional orientation, information resources and technology, and practicum/internship.

Counselor role expectations and job descriptions need to be written. This process requires knowledge about what school counselors are educated to do and what competencies they have acquired in gaining certification. At this stage of the evolution of school counselor education, consensus is being approached as to this set of competencies. For example, the *Texas Evaluation Model for Professional School Counselors* (2nd ed.; Texas Counseling Association, 2004) delineates eight domains that describe school counselors' responsibilities: program management, guidance, counseling, consultation, coordination, student assessment, professional behavior, and professional standards. These are further described in 33 standards of competence and 230 descriptors.

Because standard job descriptions have not served well in the past, we recommend that you consider drafting position guides first. These provide a general guide for all staff members holding the specific position title, and they also offer more detail than the standard list of 9 or 10 duties found in most traditional job descriptions (with the last duty always being "and other duties as assigned by the administrator"). Subsequently, job descriptions that specify each individual counselor's responsibilities can be written (Henderson & Gysbers, 1998).

Position guides include sections that describe the primary function of the position holder within the program, the major responsibilities involved, illustrative key duties, organizational relationships, and performance standards (Castetter, 1981). Sample position guides are included in Appendix F.

Having defined clearly what counselors are educated to do and what their generic responsibilities are within the program, priorities for the use of their competencies can now be established. Using rank order by roles is one method, but establishing priorities by competency provides more direction. For example, should the counselor spend more energy and time teaching the guidance curriculum or conducting small groups, more energy and time counseling individuals or coordinating resources? What is being determined at this point is the relative value of each of the counselors' specialized skills in the context of the program. Table 5.1 displays the priorities for use of school counselors' competencies as determined by the Northside Guidance Steering Committee (Northside Independent School District, 1994).

In the interest of time and simplicity, some districts have chosen to use broader categories to represent counselor competence than actual delineations of specific competencies (as seen in Table 5.1). Texas school districts have used the performance domains described in the *Texas Evaluation Model for Professional School Counselors* (2nd ed.; Texas Counseling Association, 2004). As previously described, a "performance domain" includes multiple standards of competence; for example, the guidance performance domain includes seven standards, and the counseling domain, three. Each standard is further described through multiple descriptors. An example of a district's priorities for the desired use of counselors' competence categorized by performance domain is provided in Table 5.2. As you can conclude from this, the district had already determined it wants to have a developmental guidance and counseling program.

Priorities for Other Guidance and Counseling Program Staff

Now is also an appropriate time to consider the roles of the other guidance department personnel such as registrars, career center technicians, counselors' secretaries, office aides, and peer facilitators. Ultimately, all personnel who work in the guidance and counseling program must have their roles defined, including teachers who act as advisers or who teach guidance or psychology classes and community volunteers who augment the guidance staff in specific guidance activities. The guidance and counseling program roles of related mental health specialists, such as licensed counselors, school social workers, and school psychologists, also should be delineated. We recommend that you write the job descriptions for each of the positions so that differentiation of the various roles and multiple responsibilities is clear to all concerned.

Table 5.1
Priorities for Use of Counselor Competencies

Priority	Competency
1	Plan, implement, and evaluate a comprehensive program of guidance, including counseling services.
2	Counsel individual students with presenting needs/concerns.
3	Counsel small groups of students with presenting needs/concerns.
4	Consult with parents, teachers, administrators, and other relevant individuals to enhance their work with students.
5	Use accepted theories and techniques appropriate in school counseling.
6	Assist teachers in teaching guidance-related curriculum.
7	Guide individuals and groups of students through the development of education and career plans.
8	Coordinate with school and community personnel to bring together resources for students.
9	Teach the school developmental guidance curriculum.
10	Use an effective referral process for assisting students and others to use special programs and services.
11	Interpret test and other appraisal results appropriately.
12	Use other sources of student data appropriately for assessment purposes.
13	Participate in the planning and evaluation of the district/school group standardized testing program.
14	Supervise activities of guidance-program-related clerical, paraprofessional, and volunteer personnel.

Note. From *Comprehensive Guidance Program Framework*, by Northside Independent School District, 1994, San Antonio, TX: Author. Adapted with permission.

Table 5.2
Desired Priorities for Use of Counselor Competence/Performance Domain

Performance Domain	Elementary School	Middle School	High School
Program management	6	5	1
Guidance	1	1	4
Counseling	2	2	3
Consultation	3	3	5
Coordination	5	4	6
Student assessment	7	6	7
Professionalism	4	7	2

Because human resources are basic to the guidance and counseling program, you may find it useful to consider who else in addition to the school staff is available to help deliver the guidance and counseling program. Community members, for example, are some of education's chronically untapped resources. Thus an inventory of community members who may be willing to serve is an important part of a community resource list. Historically, the most dramatic examples of community-assisted guidance and counseling programs have been provided in career education programs. Business, industry, and labor groups, service club members, and the like are often willing to speak on occupation-specific or employment realities. They may also become mentors to unmotivated students. Further, parent and grandparent groups have been used to provide role models of caring adults for elementary school children. PTA leaders can be used to lead parent education groups, using the national PTA resources (http://www.pta.org).

Priorities for Parents

Ideally and importantly, school staff and parents are partners in providing guidance to students. The ASCA (2004a) Ethical Standards state that professional school counselors "respect the rights and responsibilities of parents/guardians for their children and endeavor to establish as appropriate, a collaborative relationship with parents/guardians to facilitate the student's maximum development" (B.1.a.). From the parents' perspective, what school guidance and counseling programs accomplish with their children is supplemental to their efforts. From the guidance and counseling program perspective, parents are extensions of the guidance and counseling program staff. Some parents at some times benefit from program activities or use program services and are therefore clients of the program. It is the responsibility of the school-based guidance and counseling program staff members and leaders to include parents in the delivery of the program as well as to provide them appropriate services as needed.

Parents as Program Staff

As partners with the school-based guidance and counseling program staff, parents assist in planning and designing the program by providing input as to students' needs and the desired outcomes. From the parents' perspectives, they have ideas about what their children need and what they, as parents, would appreciate help with. They also have a voice in establishing program priorities. They provide data as to the apparent effectiveness of the activities of which they are a part. After data have been gathered as to the program's effectiveness and efficiency, parents assist in evaluation of the implemented program.

As extensions of the guidance and counseling program staff, parents are aware of what students are taught in guidance curriculum and reinforce the skills at home. Specific educational and career goal setting, planning, and decision making are the primary responsibilities of students and their parents. Parents fulfill these roles best when they participate fully in the activities of the individual student planning component. School guidance staff and the parents ensure that parents have the information they need to fulfill these roles and know when to participate.

In school counseling, the primary goal of responsive services is to help students overcome barriers to their successful educational progress. For students whose problems require non-school-based resources and solutions, parents are the primary resource providers. They arrange for and pay for therapy, for example. For students whose parents do not fulfill this responsibility or who are part of the cause of the problem, school counselors may have to extend themselves further into identifying resources or advocating for students, but they must be careful not to assume the parental role. (See Appendix G for an example of procedures for helping students manage personal crises.)

Parents who are partners with school counselors on behalf of their children refer their children to the counselors for help and allow counselors to apply their skills within the ethical standards of the profession. They work with counselors and other school staff members to clarify the issues affecting students' success in school and participate in implementing the solution plan.

Further, parent partners fulfill several roles in activities of the system support component. They assist in community relations, education, and outreach efforts of guidance and counseling program staff. They participate on guidance and counseling program steering and advisory committees. Some assist school counselors in providing education and training to other parents.

Parents as Clients

As benefactors or recipients of guidance and counseling program activities and services, parents are helped in implementing their home-based guidance and counseling by professional school counselors. Guidance curriculum activities assist parents teach their children such basic life skills as self-acceptance, setting meaningful goals, making sound decisions, getting along well with others, and behaving responsibly. Through school-based individual student planning activities, parents are provided information that helps them help their children make and implement plans for their next steps in life. For example, as counselors anticipate what students will do after high school, they provide students and parents information about and guide them in the use of information about careers as well as about colleges and other pathways to adult career lives.

As their children experience learning or social problems at school, parents benefit from consultations with school counselors. Through responsive services consultations, school counselors help parents to better understand their children, the typical learning and behavior patterns of children their age, the operations of the school, and other special programs and services the school offers. When parents select additional program or service options for their children, often it is the school counselor who coordinates the transition with the parent and child.

It is not appropriate for school counselors to provide counseling services for parents. The students in their schools are the school counselors' primary counseling clients. The mission of most schools is to assist young people to learn; therefore, school counselors' counseling work (the application of counseling skills and techniques) targets the students and the barriers to their learning. When parents' issues get in the way, school counselors consult with them about problems and solutions, advocate with them on behalf of their children, provide them information, and refer them to appropriate sources for help.

In addition to consultations provided through responsive services, professional school counselors offer opportunities for parents to further develop their parenting skills. These parent education classes or workshops are offered under the umbrella of system support as they always have as one of their anticipated outcomes that parents will feel more closely connected to their children's school and to their children's learning.

Priorities for Clients to Be Served

During the assessment of your program, you identified the current program clients. Either by building on that list or by creating a new one, you need to consider all of the possible populations that could benefit from the comprehensive guidance and counseling program and to answer the question, What priority-for-service should be assigned to each of the various subsets of these populations?

Globally, there are two basic populations with whom school counselors work: students and the adults who relate to the students. Within the student population, there are students with needs for developmental interventions, preventive interventions, remedial interventions, or crisis interventions. In the building, each grade level represents a subpopulation developmentally and includes students with needs for preventive, remedial, or crisis interventions. Within the adult population, there are parents, school-related adults, and community-based adults who work with students. The parent population reflects the subsets of the students. School staffs include regular and special education teachers, other specialists, other counselors, and administrators. Community-based adults are those related to the direct delivery of the program, community-based specialists, and representatives from community resources—providers of mental health as well as educational services.

Using a process similar to that described later in this chapter in the section "Establish Parameters for Resource Allocation (Quantitative Design)," under Set Priorities for Counselors' Time, the Northside Independent School District's steering committee established the client priorities presented in Table 5.3. The numbers suggest guidelines for percentages of time counselors should spend with the various population categories. Students clearly hold the highest priority, but other adults in students' lives are seen as important clients as well. There are differences in priorities for elementary, middle, and high school. Each campus and, indeed, each counselor specify even more discretely which subsets within those categories are served. For example, do all students in all grade levels benefit from equal developmental assistance, or do some grade levels of students benefit more? In assessing the students' needs, priorities for the more specialized responsive services are evidenced. For example, questions that are answered here include, Which subgroups of

Table 5.3
Desired Priorities for Clients Served (in Percentages)

Client Category	Elementary School	Middle School	High School
Students			
Developmental	29	24	17
Preventive	21	19	26
Remedial	15	15	23
Subtotal	65	58	66
Adults			
District administration	2.5	3.0	2.0
School staff	—	—	—
Principals	4.5	4.0	4.0
Regular ed teachers	8.5	9.0	5.0
Counselors	3.5	5.0	6.0
Special ed teachers	3.5	4.0	3.0
Other specialists	2.0	2.0	2.0
Parents	9.0	12.0	9.0
Community representatives	1.5	3.0	3.0
Subtotal	35.0	42.0	34.0

those students, as delineated in chapter 4, should benefit from small groups? and thus, What topic-focused small-group counseling should be offered?

Priorities for Student Competencies

Basic Guidance Skills/Domains

It is important to have both the counselors and the consumers of the guidance and counseling program establish priorities for the competencies that students will acquire as a result of their participation in the guidance and counseling program. Helping all students in a school building or a system make progress toward acquiring competencies contained in the 15 goals—or 12 goals, or however many you have agreed on in your model—presents an overwhelming challenge if you are just beginning to implement a competency-based comprehensive guidance and counseling program. This challenge is compounded because you also are accepting accountability for helping students with developmental, preventive, and remedial needs. Thus priorities as to which competencies are to be included at any given time in the program need to be established.

The goals for student competency development can and should be ranked according to their overall importance for all students. You also may wish to suggest the importance of various goals (and the competencies involved) by different grade or grade-grouping levels. The sequence for helping students reach these goals needs to be agreed on as well. For example, many groups have agreed that helping students know and understand themselves is prerequisite to their learning to know and understand others.

This process of setting priorities becomes complicated, but the various approaches usually produce some consensus in terms of overall top priorities for attention, and as you move to more specific implementation plans, you will have a sense of where to begin and where to end. Figure 5.1 presents the goal priorities established in its initial qualitative program design by Northside Independent School District (1986). These skills are still stated in very broad terms; they are comparable with content element domains as defined in chapter 3. If you are in a smaller setting and can manage the attendant tasks, this is an appropriate time to conduct a student and community needs assessment to ascertain priorities for student competency development. In a larger district setting or a multibuilding setting, however, the competency statements are still too broad to be used as an assessment of students' needs. (Ideas on assessing needs are presented in chapter 6.)

Again, some Texas districts have set their desired program priorities using the more global student content domains (7) rather than the related list of skill goals (28). This leaves more specific prioritization to be done by staff for the three school levels and ultimately for each grade level. Table 5.4 displays an example.

Anticipated Student Results

In previous work you have established the domains, goals, and competencies for student development for which the guidance and counseling program and counseling staff are willing to be held accountable. And you have developed competency statements to describe the goals. At this point, you need to specify relevant results the program will aim for at each grade level, grade grouping, or school level. This simply means breaking the competencies into their subparts and establishing results appropriate to the age levels of the students served by the program activities. The outcome lists for the life career development model presented in chapter 3 (in "Program Content," the first element) result in specific statements. These expand quickly from the basic list of 15 goals. For each grade level there are 15 competencies, or 225 competencies for Grades K–12 (listed in Appendix A).

Figure 5.1
Priorities for Student Skill Development

Recommended Program Design

In order to have a comprehensive and appropriately balanced program, the following priorities for allocation of resources need to be considered as goals for campus programs.

Priority Rankings Assigned to Skills

Students will	Importance	Sequence	Level of Emphasis
1. understand and respect themselves	1	1	E
2. understand and respect others	2	2	E
3. behave responsibly in school	3	3	E
4. behave responsibly in the family	9	6	E
5. behave responsibly in the community	9	10	M
6. make wise choices	3	3	M
7. manage change successfully	7	8	M
8. solve problems	5	5	M
9. use educational opportunities well	8	9	M
10. communicate effectively	6	6	M
11. plan for personally satisfying and socially useful lives	11	11	H
12. prepare for personally satisfying and socially useful lives	12	12	H

Note. From *Comprehensive Guidance Program Framework,* by Northside Independent School District, 1986, San Antonio, TX: Author. Adapted with permission.
E = elementary; M = middle; H = high school.

Again, we stress the need to be parsimonious in identifying results for which you will be held accountable. Base the actual number you use on the assessment of your student needs and the priorities that are set. Seeking too many outcomes makes the program unworkable. The allocation of counselor time to the different program components has a direct bearing on what results you are able to assist students reach developmentally. As the program development efforts proceed, every one of these results can become an aim of some lesson, unit, or counseling session. In the comprehensive guidance and counseling program, every activity has a student objective, and every activity's objective must relate to a grade-level-specific result that is on this list. An example of this conceptual flow is as follows:

Domain 1: Self-Knowledge and Interpersonal Skills
Goal A: Students will develop and incorporate an understanding of the unique personal characteristics and abilities of themselves and others.

Table 5.4
Desired Program Content Priorities

Content	Elementary School	Middle School	High School
Self-confidence development	2	6	2
Motivation to achieve	3	1	3
Decision making, goal setting, planning, problem solving	4	3	1
Interpersonal effectiveness	6	5	4
Communication skills	1	4	6
Cross-cultural effectiveness	7	7	7
Responsible behavior	5	2	5

- *Competency:* Students will specify those personal characteristics and abilities that they may value.
- *Student result:* Fifth-grade students will identify a variety of things that they value.
- *Activity objective:* Through this lesson, each student will identify six things he or she values.

The task of specifying competencies by grade level, grade grouping, or school level is one that counselors need to do. The work group that defined the broader list of goals and competencies should either continue with this task or provide leadership to an expanded group of counselors working on the results or outcomes list. It is instructive for all the counselors to have some experience in developing at least a portion of the list. It helps them think in terms of student outcome so that when the shift is made to the activity development phase of the project, they are used to thinking in terms of specific student behaviors.

When it is near completion, the list of outcomes should be reviewed and ratified by the total counseling staff and by all others—the steering committee or the administrative staff—who are providing leadership to the program change efforts. The total list of outcomes will be a bit much for noncounselors to review, but the counselors need the opportunity to think through every piece of the outline. Further, the review by administrators and others allows people with different frames of reference to consider the specifics of the guidance and counseling program. In this way, outcomes that are potentially unpalatable to some community members or outcomes that have been overlooked and are seen as important can be identified and addressed from the beginning.

Priorities for Guidance Activities for Each Component

The program components now need to be defined in finer detail by describing the primary emphases and the major activities included in each. Each component of the desired program should list activities that are performed effectively in the current program and identify and envision new activities that can better meet the program goals.

Guidance Curriculum

To further describe the guidance curriculum component, identify the curriculum strands, the basic student competencies that were established for the comprehensive program (see Figure 5.1). These describe the scope of the guidance curriculum. Next, priorities for guidance instruction are established. This process serves to help counselors know the topics to be taught at particular school levels and, because there are time limitations for teaching students, the competencies that have top priority. The sequence for assisting students to learn the competencies is also established. This may entail merely restating the student outcomes specified for each grade level in the previous effort. However, if in specifying student results you expressed outcomes by grade spans or school levels, you now need to clarify what is to be taught at each grade level. Again, an example from the life career development model (provided in Appendix A) helps portray this. The scope and a sequence for the kindergarten guidance curriculum in this model is depicted in Table 5.5.

Having done that, the next step is to group the outcomes into units for instruction. The domains have been the organizer for your development of student competencies so far. Now, as you identify specific outcomes for each grade level and sequence them, some natural groupings for learnings from the different goal areas probably will emerge. For instructional purposes, you will probably want to teach these by logical units rather than in the order specified in your outline of competencies. The units that emerge from the kindergarten outcomes in our example might be as follows:

Table 5.5
Kindergarten Guidance Curriculum Scope and Sequence

Kindergarten students will
 1. describe their appearance
 2. describe ways they care for themselves
 3. describe areas in which they are self-sufficient
 4. describe growing capabilities
 5. describe choices they make
 6. realize the difficulty of making choices between two desirable alternatives
 7. recognize that they listen to and speak with a variety of people
 8. describe people and activities they enjoy
 9. describe their work and play relationships with others and their favorite activities
10. describe those things they learn at school
11. describe their daily activities at school
12. recognize the town, state, and country in which they reside
13. describe the work activities of family members
14. mentally project adults into work activities other than those they do presently
15. describe situations that are going to happen in the future

Unit	Competencies Addressed (from Table 5.5)
Self	1–4
Decision Making	5 & 6
Others	7–9
School	10 & 11
Community and Work	12–14
Future	15

Individual Student Planning

To further describe the individual student planning component, identify the major activities that assist students to make their personalized plans. For elementary, middle/junior high, and high school, this component includes activities that help students orient themselves to new school settings; set goals, make plans, and take their next steps toward these goals; and factor in their own aptitudes and disabilities that are relevant to their planning. In the schools and districts with which we have worked, these activities focus on students' educational and career plans. If your program is so directed, you also might have activities that help students make plans that relate to their personal and social lives. These major activities must be related to the broad goals of the guidance and counseling program. An example of the activities and the skills they relate to as delineated by Northside Independent School District is provided in Table 5.6.

As you can see, these are activities traditionally found in guidance and counseling programs. Decisions need to be made as to the priorities for the time spent within this component. Assisting students to complete their elementary and secondary education successfully is usually a priority for school counselors, with the transition grades receiving the highest priority. However, college, postsecondary vocational/technical, and career planning fall in this component as well. At the elementary level, orienting primary-grade children to school and helping upper-grade children adjust to the increasing demands of the academic curriculum by developing effective, personalized approaches to studying and time management may have priority. Where counselor caseloads are larger than the 100:1 ratio suggested by those who would have school counselors work with individuals in one-on-one relationships, this component needs to be built around group activities. The group activities need to be designed to assist individuals to develop personally relevant plans and should provide for one-on-one assistance as follow-up.

Table 5.6
Individual Student Planning: Activities and Student Skills

Activity	Student Skills
Orientation	Use well their educational opportunities in school
Educational planning	Plan/prepare for personally satisfying lives
Preregistration[a]	Make wise choices
Registration[a]	Manage change successfully
Dissemination and interpretation of standardized test results	Understand/respect themselves
Career/vocational planning	Plan/prepare for personally satisfying/socially useful lives
Application of other skills taught in guidance curriculum	(As identified through local needs assessment)

Note. From *Comprehensive Guidance Program Framework*, by Northside Independent School District, 1986, San Antonio, TX: Author. Adapted with permission.
[a]Overlaps with system support.

Responsive Services

To further describe the responsive services component, identify the topics that students, their teachers, and parents present most frequently, as well as those identified in any completed needs assessments. This will enable the establishment of a systematic means for attending to the high-priority topics or problems faced by the high-priority student clients. What problems interfere most often with the students' personal, social, career, or educational development? How many students need counseling, consulting, or referral, and for what reason? What percentage needs preventive help, small-group counseling, or brief family interventions? What percentage needs remedial help, one-on-one counseling, or referral? What percentage is apt to need crisis intervention? Which parents, teachers, and administrators need consulting help? The more specific you are, the more focused and accountable implementation can be.

In the initial Northside Independent School District project, a subcommittee of the guidance steering committee asked the school counselors to list the topics they found themselves responding to over the course of the year. The steering committee established priorities for the counselors' attention to these topics from the school district's point of view. Again, each of these topics was related to the competencies the counselors strive to help students master. Clarifying this relationship from the outset assisted counselors to specify appropriate student objectives for their counseling activities. The list of topics, the grade levels at which they were identified, and their priorities are presented in Table 5.7 (Henderson, 1987).

The information was surprising in two ways: First, there were not that many topics (12 in all), and second, there was much similarity between the lists submitted by the elementary and the secondary counselors. These two factors made the job of becoming better at helping students handle their problems more manageable. In-service training could be focused on these issues. Exemplary practices could be developed and shared. Northside Independent School District counselors feel that one side benefit of this massive redesigning effort has been learning that there is not as much difference among the programs at the three levels (elementary, middle, and high) as they had believed. The programs are shaped differently, but students' needs are similar, and counselors' skills and interests are similar.

Because society changes, neighborhoods and schools change, and students change; thus the needs for these specialized counselor services should be assessed each year and responded to accordingly. Although the major categories of problems are constant, the specific topics within these categories change. For example, counseling students with "discipline/behavior problems" usually are a high priority for school counselors, but unfortunately, such topics as gang involvement have surfaced as well.

Table 5.7
Responsive Services: Topics, Skills, and Priorities

Grade Level	Recurrent Topic	Skill
K–12	1. Academic failure	Use well their educational opportunities in school
K–12	2. Child abuse	Behave responsibly in the family
K–12	3. Divorced/single parents	Behave responsibly in the family
K–12	4. Grief/death and dying/loss	Manage change successfully
MS/HS	5. Suicide threats	Understand and respect themselves; solve problems
MS/HS	6. Sexuality issues such as appropriate dating behavior and wise date selection; pregnancy; sexually transmitted diseases	Understand and respect themselves; solve problems
K–12	7. Tardiness/absences/ truancy/school phobia/ dropping out	Use well their educational opportunities; plan and prepare for personally satisfying and socially useful lives
K–12	8. Discipline/behavior problems	School-related: behave responsibly in school
K–12	9. Peer problems	Understand respect themselves/others
K–12	10. Alcohol/drug/inhalant abuse	Understand and respect themselves
K–12	11. Family situations	Behave responsibly in the family
K–12	12. Information seekers	(Varies with different information needs)
K–12	13. Application of other skills taught in guidance • academic problems • behavior problems • social problems	Solve problems

Note. From "A Comprehensive School Guidance Program at Work," by P. H. Henderson, 1987, *TACD Journal, 15,* 25–37. Adapted with permission.

If you are just beginning a program, we offer the following list of categories and some recurrent topics to spur your thinking:

- *Personal development issues:* cultural/ethnic identity; emotional disturbances; grief/loss; health (AIDS, serious/terminal illnesses, eating disorders); managing disabilities or disorders; misbehavior; self-esteem; sexuality, pregnancy, gender; spirituality, morality; stress; substance use/abuse; suicide (prevention, intervention, postvention).
- *Social development issues:* adult relationships; athletic involvement; delinquency; family problems, divorce; bullying, violence; isolates; mobility; multicultural problems (ethnicity, racial tension, bigotry); physical/sexual abuse; peer relationships; sociopathology.
- *Educational development issues:* attendance, school phobia, dropping out; attention deficit disorders; attitudes; behavior or conduct problems or disorders; being gifted/talented; being new; lack of academic success; making educational choices (courses, high school, college); managing learning disabilities; study skills and habits; test anxiety.
- *Career development issues:* applying interests and aptitudes; balancing dreams with reality; developmentally "stuck"; lack of goals; hopelessness; indecision.

The length of the list reinforces our point about the need to establish priorities relevant to the guidance and counseling program's mission, the goals of the school, and the needs of the students and community.

The responsive services component includes a continuum of school counselor activities from identification through appraisal, intervention, and follow-up. Counselors are competent to identify students with special needs and/or school-related issues. These needs may be those of one individual student or groups of students. They may relate to school, home, or community situations. They may be affected by ethnic, racial, or other demographic variables. School counselors are competent to lead, coordinate, or participate in the specification of these students' problems through appraisal efforts. They gather and analyze personal and social data regarding the student and the situation. When students' issues are clarified, counselors are competent to intervene by providing individual, small-group, or crisis counseling; by consulting with parents, teachers, or others; and by coordinating or referring them to other service providers. School counselors are also trained to follow up with students in a planned, consistent, and evaluative manner and to determine if in fact the planned problem solution is being carried out and is effective.

The qualitative program design should provide guidelines for school counselors as to the priorities for the use of these competencies (identification, appraisal, intervention, and follow-up) within the school. Where others also are competent, their talents should be drawn on as well. Typically, teachers, relevant paraprofessionals, and administrators can identify and specify students with special needs. Teachers and school psychologists can appraise students. School counselors' unique competencies support counseling and consultation interventions. Follow-up may be divided among the adults on the campus involved with a student in the specific situation.

System Support

Providing the detail to describe and define system support divides this component in two parts. One part defines the support that the guidance and counseling program needs from the system, that is, the management activities. The other part defines the activities and support that the guidance and counseling program provides to other programs, such as elementary and secondary education; special, gifted, vocational, and compensatory education; and the testing program.

Guidance and Counseling Program Management. The level of support needed for the guidance and counseling program from the system needs clarification. In order for the program to function optimally and accountably, some counselors must be designated as leaders of program implementation and of the program staff (Henderson & Gysbers, 1998). Designation of leaders and clarification of their responsibilities at the building and district levels are necessary. Generally, their responsibilities are to ensure accountable program delivery in accordance with established standards and to promote continuous improvement of the guidance and counseling program. The staff leadership responsibilities include holding school counselors and other guidance and counseling program staff members accountable for carrying out their professional responsibilities and providing support for their continuous professional development. They are also responsible for advocating for the guidance and counseling program and the staff and for the personal, social, career, and educational needs of students. They act as liaisons between the guidance department and administration and other departments.

Recommendations should be made as to the appropriate placement for guidance within the organization. Should guidance be aligned with administration? With instruction? With student services? Or stand alone? These questions have been asked throughout our history, and this model does not include a recommendation because in our experience the right placement varies from district to district depending on the size and the philosophy of the district. Program-based rationale needs to be established: for example, aligned with administration as it is a program that is central to the whole school; aligned with instruction as it is a developmental curriculum-based program; aligned with student services as it includes a special set of services; or stand alone as it is uniquely multifaceted.

The various activities counselors participate in require policies and administrative procedures, staff and program development opportunities, reasonable levels of budget provisions, adequate facilities and equipment, appropriate staff allocations to implement the desired program, and public relations support. At this stage these requirements may be more of a wish list than a statement of realistic choices, but constraints can wait until later when specific implementation plans are made. These items are discussed more fully in chapter 6 because many are keys to the actual implementation of the newly conceptualized program.

Support Services. The first step in establishing the desired or needed support from the guidance and counseling program to schoolwide activities of the other specific programs is to develop the list of major activities that the guidance staff is called on to participate in—if this has not already been accomplished in the assessment of your current program. The second step is to prioritize the list and to determine which of these tasks are appropriate for counselors to do and which are nonguidance tasks by asking the question, Is a master's degree in guidance and counseling needed to accomplish this task? If the answer is no, then it becomes the responsibility of the counselors and the steering committee or the school–community advisory committee to make recommendations as to what other departments are served by—and thus responsible for—the tasks. Decisions are made about what the school counselors' fair share is of schoolwide activities and in relationship to other programs; that is, how much of the guidance and counseling program resources should be spent on programs other than guidance? Considering these factors at this time will help later as you consider ways to handle activities that need to be displaced. This concept and the issues involved are discussed more fully in chapter 8. Priorities for possible displacements, however, can be suggested at this point. Table 5.8 displays the order of priority established by the Northside Independent School District for counselor support to other programs. It is based on the lists originally generated in the assessment of the current program; that is, it ranks what the counselors were then doing and is not a statement of what they should do. In theory, displacements should start with the activities listed at the bottom and continue until the lowest priority tasks are displaced completely, shared equitably, or streamlined (see chapter 8).

Table 5.8
Support Services

Elementary	Middle	High
1. Consult with staff and parents	1. Consult with staff and parents	1. Consult with staff and parents
2. Student referrals	2. Preregistration	2. Preregistration
3. Test administration and interpretation to staff	3. Test interpretation to staff	3. Test interpretation to staff
4. School climate	4. Student referrals	4. Staff development
5. Staff development	5. School climate	5. School climate
6. Special education	6. New student registration	6. Curriculum planning
7. Gifted education	7. Record keeping	7. New student registration
8. Preregistration	8. Referrals to special education	8. Record keeping
9. Discipline management	9. Curriculum planning	9. Schedule changes
10. Curriculum planning	10. Schedule changes	10. Student referrals
11. Compensatory programs	11. Master schedule development	11. Admission, review, dismissal, committee meetings
12. Accreditation	12. Vocational education	12. Vocational education
	13. Attendance/discipline	13. Other special programs
	14. Other special programs	14. Test administration
	15. Test administration	15. Discipline management

Note. From *Comprehensive Guidance Program Framework*, by Northside Independent School District, 1986, San Antonio, TX: Author. Adapted with permission.

Qualitative Design Summary

Once the questions have been answered regarding what is most important to be delivered by the comprehensive guidance and counseling program, the answers should be summarized and presented to all the participants in the decision-making process: the steering committee, the advisory committee, relevant district and building administrators, and the school counselors. This review helps bring key players along as well as makes clear the decisions made to date. An example of such a summary is provided in Table 5.9.

Establish Parameters for Resource Allocation (Quantitative Design)

Having established the priorities for the substance of the program, the next set of decisions result in setting parameters for allocating the program resources, that is, in establishing the quantitative design for your program. The two factors that affect the quantitative program design are the program balance and the counselor–student ratio.

Deciding how much can be done by school counselors is expressed in the recommended balance among the program components—how counselors' time is best divided in providing the various kinds of program activities. Anticipating how many program clients will

Table 5.9
Comprehensive Guidance Program Qualitative Design: Executive Summary

	Guidance Curriculum	Individual Student Planning	Responsive Services	System Support
Student clients	Developmental	Developmental	Preventative Remedial	Significant adults
Content priorities	Communicative skills Cross-cultural effectiveness Decision making and problem solving Interpersonal effectiveness Motivation to achieve Responsible behavior Self-esteem development	Educational and career goal setting and action planning	Academic success Career choice Child abuse Cross-cultural effectiveness Dropping out of school Educational choices Family issues Loss and grief Relationships with adults Relationships with peers Responsible behavior School attendance Self-esteem Sexuality Stress Substance abuse Suicide	Guidance program management Schoolwide activities Services to other programs
Priority activities	Lessons and units	Portfolio development Advisement Testing Transition Preregistration	Individual counseling Small-group counseling Referral Parent conferences Teacher conferences	Program development Staff development Resource development Public relations Other program support
Counselor role priorities	Guidance Consultation	Guidance Consultation Coordination Assessment	Counseling Consultation Coordination Assessment	Program management Professionalism

benefit from program activities is determined by the counselor–student ratio. Thus, a new recommendation emerges and is supported by program design rationale.

At this point, a "Which came first, the chicken or the egg?" issue arises: Should the desired outcomes and program design dictate the allocation of resources, or should the allocation of resources dictate the shape of the program? In an ideal setting, the identified student and community needs will justify the allocation of sufficient resources to provide a complete, comprehensive program for meeting those needs. In a real setting, however, there are no doubt more needs and desired outcomes than the school or district is able to attend to, given feasible resource allocations. This is part of the challenge of "remodeling your house while you are living in it." You are probably not creating a program from scratch nor one with the realistic potential for unlimited resources. In the last analysis, a guidance and counseling program must be designed to use resources that are available, or the campus or district must make available resources that are needed to implement the program as designed.

You must make recommendations based on current resource allocations with some projections or requests for expanded resources. In our experience, school counseling staffs first have to redirect their current resources and have to be prepared to use augmented resources appropriately. At this point, then, you need to make resource allocation decisions based on the priorities and realities of your schools. For example, you have identified what a fully implemented guidance curriculum would contain; however, if there is time in the students' or counselors' schedules for only one guidance lesson per week (or month, or grading period), then the full guidance curriculum cannot be implemented at first.

In terms of both specialized skills and salary dollars, the most valuable resource applied to the guidance and counseling program is the time of the professional school counselor. Thus priorities for the use of counselors' time must be decided to ensure that the program that is delivered makes the best use of these resources as defined by the steering committee and the counselor leadership. The two basic questions that are answered by the quantitative design are

- What constitutes a well-balanced program for your building or district?
- What counselor-to-student ratio is needed to best ensure attainment of the priorities established in the qualitative design?

Set Priorities for School Counselors' Time

An important consideration in designing your program is to assign time to be spent implementing the activities within each program component. This is a critical issue because of the traditional add-on nature of guidance. In the past, as new issues or concerns were addressed in the school, tasks were added to school counselors' job responsibilities without much thought as to the time these tasks might take to complete. A comprehensive guidance and counseling program is not an add-on program. The program structure is established and the time available to staff is allocated so that, accounting for all school counselors, the time allocated to the program components equals 100%. Allocations of time for individual staff members may be different because of differences across grade or grade-grouping levels; and the allocation of time may vary from school building to building and district to district, depending on the needs of the students and communities.

To help establish the desired time allocations for the program components of the comprehensive guidance and counseling program, we have found that the steering committee and school–community advisory committee can provide direction. We also have worked with separate groups of counselors, principals and other administrators, and parents, but this is cumbersome. Consensus among the groups is hard to achieve when each group cannot hear the deliberations of the other groups.

As the preceding discussion implies, you need to implement a process that will lead the group(s) to consensus because most likely you will not find unanimity among the decision makers. The Northside Independent School District project used its steering committee and applied a modified Delphi process to reach a decision about the allocation of time across the program components. The committee first was asked to establish priorities for component resource allocation. Its decision is reflected in Table 5.10 (compare it with Table 4.15). Then committee members, who had become educated about the program model, were asked to write down individually the percentage of counselor time that they thought ought to be appropriated for each of the four program components. Each member then posted his or her percentage allocations on blank sheets of easel paper that had been hung on the walls of the meeting room. These postings are displayed in Table 5.11. Note the ranges of time. The steering committee as a whole considered the ranges and apparent "median" ratings, and deliberated and debated. Consensus on the percentages for each category was then reached. At a subsequent meeting—after some percolating time—the final balance in terms of percentages was considered and agreed on. The balance that was established as desired by the district is presented in Table 5.12 (Northside Independent School District, 1986). These figures were used to suggest allocations of staff time for Northside's desired program, and they became the template against which the current program assessment data were compared and contrasted. The St. Joseph School District (Hargens & Fuston, 1997) also established desired percentages, displayed in Table 5.13, for the allocation of time for the program components.

States using the comprehensive guidance and counseling program model, such as Missouri (Gysbers, Kosteck-Bunch, Magnuson, & Starr, 2002) and Texas (Texas Education Agency, 2004), as well as some districts suggest ranges of percentages of time to be spent in each component so that appropriate balances can be set for each district or building. This approach provides guidelines for program consistency and at the same time encourages local school staffs to make decisions appropriate for their students and school community. (An example of suggested ranges for an appropriately balanced guidance and counseling program is displayed in chapter 3, Figure 3.2.)

Although each district or building within the district should decide on the program balance that best fits local needs and priorities, the developmental ages of students permit some generalizations supporting different program balance recommendations for different school levels. The balance among the developmental guidance components shifts as students mature and accept more responsibility for their own growth and development. That is, the guidance curriculum component takes a larger share of the program pie at the elementary level than at the secondary level. In turn, the individual student planning system is larger at the secondary level than at the elementary level. Junior high school students are devel-

Table 5.10
Desired Guidance Program Priorities

Component	Priority/School Level		
	Elementary	Middle	High
Guidance curriculum	1	1	2
Individual student planning	2	1	1
Responsive services	2	3	1
System support	4	4	4

Note. Data from Northside Independent School District, San Antonio, TX. Adapted with permission.

Table 5.11
Individual Committee Members' Counselor Time Appropriations

Component	% Counselor Time		
	Elementary	Middle	High
Guidance curriculum	40 40 40 35 40 50 40 40 40 30 60 45 65	40 35 30 30 30 30 30 40 30 15 30 50 50 50	25 10 20 15 35 40 35 25 20 10 30 20 30 40 50
Consensus:	40	30	25
Individual student planning	20 25 35 30 30 20 20 20 10 10 20 10 10	20 25 30 25 30 40 30 25 20 30 15 25 15 15	30 35 40 40 25 20 20 30 40 40 30 35 30 20 20
Consensus:	25	30	30
Responsive services	20 20 25 15 15 20 20 20 40 40 20 25 15	30 25 30 25 30 15 25 25 30 40 25 30 15 15	30 40 25 20 20 20 30 30 20 40 30 35 30 20 15
Consensus.	25	25	30
System support	10 10 10 15 15 10 10 10 20 30 10 10 10	10 15 10 10 10 15 15 30 20 15 30 15 20 20	20 10 10 30 20 20 20 15 10 10 10 10 10 20 15
Consensus:	10	15	15

Note. Data from Northside Independent School District, San Antonio, TX. Adapted with permission.

opmentally ready to begin to formulate tentative career plans and make related educational decisions. It is developmentally necessary for high school students to make sound educational and other career-related choices to best ensure their readiness to enter postsecondary education or training and the work world.

The needs for responsive services and system support stay fairly constant, regardless of the students' ages; thus these components maintain a similar share of the program throughout. The nature of responsive services may change from an emphasis on preventive counseling and consultation with parents and teachers at the elementary level to one of counseling directly with students at the high school level.

The system support component, representing indirect services to students, is consistently the smallest of the four components. Note that in the models presented, the fifth "component," nonguidance activities, is not included as this is the desired design. Because they are included as part of the data describing your current program design, however, you may want to include here a zero percentage for this collection of tasks. In so doing, you provide a vehicle for the steering and advisory committees to make the very important statement that extraneous tasks should not take up the guidance and counseling program's time.

Helping counselors and others envision what the program balance means for program implementation is better understood by translating the balance to number of hours per student school day, and the student school days per year, rather than by the percentages above. Table 5.14 displays this for Northside Independent School District's desired program balance. The

Table 5.12
Desired Guidance Program Balance: Northside Independent School District

Component	% Counselor Time/School Level		
	Elementary	Middle	High
Guidance curriculum	40	30	25
Individual student planning	25	30	30
Responsive services	25	25	25
System support	10	15	15

Note. Data from Northside Independent School, San Antonio, TX. Adapted with permission.

Table 5.13
Desired Guidance Program Balance: St. Joseph School District

| Component | % Counselor Time/School Level | | |
	Elementary	Middle	High
Guidance curriculum	25	20	15
Individual student planning	5	15	30
Responsive services	60	50	35
System support	10	15	20

Note. From "Comprehensive Guidance Program of the St. Joseph School District in Buchanan County, Missouri," by M. Hargens and J. K. Fuston, 1997, in N. C. Gysbers and P. Henderson, Eds., *Comprehensive Guidance Programs That Work—II* (pp. 61–74), Greensboro, NC: ERIC Counseling and Student Services Clearinghouse. Adapted with permission.

information regarding the days per year and hours per day per component has provided guidelines for counselors as they plan their weeks, months, and year and has helped program monitors understand in a tangible way what is desired for the program to be considered effective. Further, the statements of priorities are used heavily in the next stage of program improvement, planning the transition to the comprehensive guidance and counseling program, and subsequently to guide program scheduling to ensure appropriate balance in actual program implementation. (Scheduling is discussed in some detail in chapter 8.)

Recommend Design-Related Counselor–Student Ratios

With the program's basic structure and the desired levels of service to students and other clients outlined, it is now possible to use this information to suggest the ratios needed to conduct the program as desired qualitatively and quantitatively. For example, using the Northside Independent School District's desired program figures, the mathematical process displayed in Figure 5.2 can be used to recommend appropriate ratios at the elementary, middle, and high school levels. (See chapter 8 and Appendix H for examples of how different ratios affect the numbers of program clients that can be served in the various program activities.)

Other districts have relied on other methods of establishing a recommended counselor–student ratio. Many use the 1:250 recommendation of the American School Counselor Association (n.d.) or those of their state. The Texas Comprehensive, Developmental Guidance and Counseling Program model (Texas Education Agency, 2004, p. 47) includes a recommended counselor–student ratio of 1:350, based on recommendations of the Texas School Counselor Association, Texas Association of Secondary School Principals, and the Texas Elementary Principals and Supervisors Association. In the context of their published statewide

Table 5.14
Desired Percentages for Allocation of Counselors' Time During Student School Days[a]

| | Elementary School | | | Middle School | | | High School | | |
	%	Hours/ Day	Days/ Year	%	Hours/ Day	Days/ Year	%	Hours/ Day	Days/ Year
Guidance curriculum	40	$2\frac{1}{2}$	73	30	4	51	25	$1\frac{1}{2}$	44
Individual student planning	25	$1\frac{1}{2}$	44	30	4	51	30	$1\frac{3}{4}$	51
Responsive services	25	$1\frac{1}{2}$	44	25	$1\frac{1}{2}$	44	30	$1\frac{3}{4}$	51
System support	10	$\frac{1}{2}$	14	15	1	29	15	1	29

Note. Data from Northside Independent School District, San Antonio, TX. Adapted with permission.
[a]Based on a 6-hour student day, 175-day student year. Figures are per counselor.

Figure 5.2
Counselor–Student Ratio Recommendations

Elementary Ratio Recommendations

- Desired program design:

Curriculum	$40\% \times 70 = 28$ slots	
Individual student planning	$25\% \times 70 = 17$ slots	
Responsive services	$25\% \times 70 = 18$ slots	
System support	$10\% \times 70 = 7$ slots	

Program activity slots = 30 minutes each (average)
Student school day = 7 hours
7 hours yield 14 activities per day
14 activities × 5 days/week = 70 activity slots/week

- To implement *guidance curriculum* as desired:

$$\begin{array}{r} 28 \text{ slots} \\ \underline{-12} \text{ for planning}^a \\ 16 \text{ classes}^b \\ \underline{\times\ 25} \text{ (average number students per class)} \\ 400 \end{array}$$

400 students per counselor is the ratio needed to implement the guidance curriculum.

- To implement *responsive services* as desired: 18 slots
  60% for preventive level, small group counseling
  40% for remedial level, individual counseling

$$\begin{array}{rr} 18 & \qquad 18 \\ \underline{\times\ .6} & \underline{\times\ .4} \\ 11 \text{ groups} & 7 \text{ students} \\ \underline{\times\ 5} \text{ students} & \\ 55 \text{ students} & \end{array}$$

55 students + 7 students = *62 students* in responsive services caseload
  Responsive services attends to 15% of population on the average
  62 is 15% of *413 students per counselor*

- *Thus 400:1 is the recommended ratio for elementary counselors to implement the program as designed.*

Middle School Ratio Recommendations

- Desired program design:

Curriculum	$30\% \times 35 = 10.5 = 11$ slots	
Individual student planning	$30\% \times 35 = 10.5 = 10$ slots	
Responsive services	$25\% \times 35 = 8.75 = 9$ slots	
System support	$15\% \times 35 = 5.25 = 5$ slots	

Program activity slots = 1 hour each (average)
Student school day = 7 hours
7 hours yield 7 activities per day
7 activities × 5 days/week = 35 activity slots/week

- To implement *guidance curriculum* as desired:

$$\begin{array}{r} 11 \text{ slots} \\ \underline{-2} \text{ for planning}^c \\ 9 \text{ classes per week per counselor}^d \end{array}$$

$$\begin{array}{r} 18 \text{ classes} = \text{curriculum caseload} \\ \underline{\times\ 27} \text{ (average number students per class)} \\ 486 \end{array}$$

486 students per counselor is the ratio needed to implement the guidance curriculum.

- To implement responsive services as desired: 9 slots
  50% for preventive level, small group counseling
  50% for remedial level, individual counseling

$$\begin{array}{rr} 9 & \qquad 9 \\ \underline{\times\ .5} & \underline{\times\ .5} \\ 4.5 \text{ groups} & 4.5 \text{ students} \\ \underline{\times\ 9} \text{ students} & (8\text{--}10 = \text{average size group}) \\ 40.5 \text{ students} & \end{array}$$

40.5 students + 4.5 students = 45 students in responsive services caseload
  Responsive services attends to 15% of population on the average
  45 is 15% of 300 students per counselor

- *Thus 393:1 is the recommended ratio for middle school counselors to implement the program as designed.*

(*continued on next page*)

Figure 5.2 (*Continued*)
Counselor–Student Ratio Recommendations

High School Ratio Recommendations

- Desired program design:

Curriculum	25% × 35 = 8.75 = 9 slots
Individual planning	30% × 35 = 10.5 = 10 slots
Responsive services	30% × 35 = 10.5 = 11 slots
System support	15% × 35 = 5.25 = 5 slots

Program activity slots = 1 hour each (average)
Student school day = 7 hours
7 hours yield 7 activities per day
7 activities × 5 days/week = 35 activity slots/week

- To implement guidance curriculum as desired:

$$\begin{array}{r} 9 \text{ slots} \\ - \ 2 \text{ for planning}^c \\ \hline 7 \text{ classes per week per counselor}^d \end{array}$$

$$\begin{array}{r} 14 \text{ classes 5 curriculum caseload} \\ \times \ 27 \text{ (average number students per class)} \\ \hline 378 \end{array}$$

   378 students per counselor is the ratio needed to implement the guidance curriculum.

- To implement responsive services as desired: 11 slots
   50% for preventive level, small group counseling
   50% for remedial level, individual counseling

11	11
× .5	× .5
5.5 groups	5.5 students
× 9 students	(8–10 = average size group)
49.5 students	

   49.5 students + 5.5 students = 55 students in responsive services caseload
   Responsive services attends to 15% of population on the average
   55 is 15% of 366 students per counselor

- *Thus 375:1 is the recommended ratio for high school counselors to implement the program as designed.*

[a]Two slots per week at six grade levels.   [b]Each class is to be guided one time per week.
[c]Planning: teachers, 1:6, counselors, 2:9.   [d]Each class is to be guided every other week.

ratio of 1:954, the California Department of Education (2003) study found that surveyed respondents wanted "more" school counselors. They perceived "adequate ratios" to be 1:834 for elementary schools, 1:461 for middle and junior high schools, and 1:364 for high schools.

Determine Minimum Numbers of Students to Be Served

With the recommended program balance percentages determined, it is then possible to establish standards for minimum numbers of students and other clients to be served through each program component and ultimately for the program as a whole. The mathematical process for doing this is explained in detail in chapter 8 in the section "Enhance the Role of the Professional School Counselor." In summary, to determine the *minimum* number of students to be served entails determining the minimum number of students/clients served by a typical activity in the component and multiplying that number by the minimum number of that kind of activity that can be provided by counselors in the time appropriated through the program balance. For example, following Figure 8.1, it is determined that with the balance recommended for Henderson Public Schools' elementary counselors, 28 guidance curriculum activities should be provided per week. If the minimum number of students in a guidance classroom is 25, then in 1 week, multiplying 28 × 25, 700 students a week would benefit from guidance curriculum activities. This provides opportunities for professional school counselors to be accountable for the numbers of students they serve and to be able to publicize that number so that the program's consumers can know what level of service it is realistic to expect. The latter is particularly important with responsive services activities that are often a balance of individual and small-group work. Not nearly as many students can benefit from these 28 time slots, only 98 students a week (as displayed in Figure 8.2).

Leadership Roles and Responsibilities

As the guidance and counseling program leader during the designing phase of the program development process, you must pay special attention to your responsibilities regarding the decision-making process used in determining the desired program design, in the writing of the agreed-on program description, and in continuing to empower the professional school counselors.

The Decision-Making Process

As you have surmised in reading the sections on qualitative and quantitative designs and on establishing priorities and parameters for resource allocation, providing the detail to describe your desired program design is no small task. Again, the resources you use in this task will vary depending on the program redesign mechanism you are using. We recommend that you use the counselors from the steering committee to do or lead the bulk of this work. The same principle applies here as earlier: The more involved more counselors are, the smoother the needed transitions will be. In any case, counselor leaders need to ensure that the recommendations made are supported by the steering committee. The committee needs to assist in making the hard decisions, such as the priorities for displacing unwanted nonguidance tasks; but in many cases they need only to be educated as to what the priorities are that will become internal operating rules for the guidance department, such as determining who else on a campus can count the test booklets after administering standardized tests. The preliminary activities and design decisions to be made in establishing priorities and parameters are summarized as displayed in Table 5.15.

You need to be aware of topics that are of particular importance to the noncounselors on the steering committee and attend to these appropriately. For example, your high school principals might be attached to the traditional conferences held with individual 12th graders as to their post high-school plans. You need to make the effort to ensure that they understand the time these conferences take relative to the benefit in terms of student outcomes achieved. Any decision that will result in changing the shape of a major activity needs to be carefully considered by the committee. A helpful rule of thumb might be that if one committee member wants to discuss an issue, you better give it fair hearing. Even if none of the other committee members are particularly interested in the discussion, there will be others outside the committee who hold that position as well, and ultimately that discussion will recur.

In guiding the agenda of the decision-making process, remember that you need to discuss each topic—from defining the basic program structure to making recommendations regarding the levels of support needed by the guidance and counseling program—in separate meetings. The group will still be struggling to understand the basic concepts, thus making the necessary decisions is not easy. Allowing them to focus on one topic at a time helps you in the long run, although it may extend the time you take on this step. It is your job, as the guidance and counseling program leader, to frame the questions for the group to answer. As it can take up to a year to assess your current program, it can take a year to

Table 5.15
Establishing Program Priorities and Parameters: Preliminary Activities and Design Decisions

Preliminary Activity	Design Decision
	Qualitative design
Student competency development List needed student competencies.	Establish priorities for content domains and student goals, competencies by grade span, results by grade level.
Clients to be served Define the student and adult populations served.	Establish priorities for subpopulations served through each component.

Program activities
  Specify minimum expectations for activities done within each component.
	Establish priorities within each component:
	  • Guidance curriculum: most needed outcomes by grade level
	  • Individual student planning: most timely outcomes/activities at priority grade level
	  • Responsive services: most relevant, recurrent topics
	  • System support: most needed activities and programs making best use of counselors' time and professional skills

Counselors' roles
  Redefine/reaffirm counselor's job descriptions.
	Establish priorities for use of the counselors' skills and service expectations.
	  • Comprehensive counselors
	  • Specialist counselors

Redefine/reaffirm job descriptions of other guidance program personnel.	Establish priorities for others' skills.
	Quantitative design
Program balance Define the priorities among program components.	Establish parameters for balanced program delivery in terms of percentages of resource allocation. Establish priorities for use of the counselors' time.
Number of clients served Establish numbers of students to be served in program components.	Establish priorities for others' time. Establish recommended counselor-to-student ratio.

select your desired program design. That design, however, as stated earlier, becomes the goal statement for everything that follows, so it must be done thoroughly and with sufficient deliberation (argument) to ensure support as you move into implementation.

Write Down and Distribute the Description of the Desired Program

With the design of the desired program established, your last task is to put in writing all of the decisions made. If you are the leader of the program improvement efforts, this task is yours alone. As with any written publication, the document must portray a cohesive whole, have a logical sequence, and be written in a consistent and concise style; thus one writer is mandatory. As stated earlier, the written description depicts the basic structure that you have decided on and becomes the working document for you and your staff henceforth. It replaces the former guidance and counseling program handbook or plan. The Northside Independent School District called this document the *Comprehensive Guidance Program Framework*.

We recommend the write-up contain at least five sections: the structural components, the recommended design/resource allocations for the program, the position guides, the program components, and appendixes.

- *Structural components.* This first section should include the statements that express the philosophical basis of your program: the final versions of the rationale, the assumptions, and the program definition. In addition, the list of student competencies that are to be developed through the guidance and counseling program should be presented. Listing the specific grade-level outcomes is probably too lengthy for this section of the document, but these may be listed fully in an appendix (or in a separate document).

- *Recommended design/resource allocations.* The second section of the write-up should contain statements that describe the appropriate balance among the four components, the priorities for the clients to be served, the competencies to be sought, and the school counselors' skills to be used. This section presents numerically what the program should look like to be considered comprehensive and well balanced.

- *Position guides.* The third section should describe the various jobs guidance and counseling program staff perform. This section should contain guides not only for the elementary, middle/junior, and senior high school counselors but also for any counselor specialists you have in your school/district, such as career and technology, special, or compensatory-education-funded counselors, and for head counselors. Job descriptions also should be included for other staff members who have been identified as having roles integral to the delivery of the guidance and counseling program, such as career center technicians, registrars, and related professionals (such as social workers, community-based licensed counselors, school psychologists). If you are using or plan to use community volunteers, their positions also should be described here.

- *Program components.* The fourth section should include more detailed descriptions of each component as tailored by your local decisions. Each component description should begin with the definition of the component and contain the design decisions made regarding each. The priorities for students by subgroup, the priorities for other clients, and the minimum expectations for numbers of students to be served in component activities come next. The strands in the guidance curriculum, the major activities that make up the individual student planning component, the recurrent topics that are the focus of the responsive services, and the specific activities identified in system support should be listed. The content priorities and anticipated results within each component should be identified. The roles fulfilled by counselors, teachers, administrators, and parents in component implementation should be defined. The guidelines established for component activity implementation should be detailed and include the minimum number of component activities to be provided. The recommended mode of delivery for each component (i.e., small-group counseling as the preferred mode for responsive services, classroom-sized groups as the preferred mode for guidance curriculum, and so on) as well as the recommended allocation of resources to the component—especially that of the school counselors' time—should be written down. Each component description should end with statements of expectations regarding evaluation of the overall impact on students of the component's activities, each activity's effectiveness, and the quality of the competencies used by the professional staff. All of the decisions made by the program developers that relate to a component should be reflected in the write-up so as not to be lost over time.

After you have written the program description and have it typed and printed, you need to have the steering committee and the school–community advisory committee, the upper-echelon administrators, and the counselors review it in detail. We suggest that you view this as the last chance for input before complete, final adoption. For this final review, you need to use strategies that will assure you that everyone has read and considered the document. With the steering committee, this might mean one meeting spent discussing the overall product of its labors section by section. Framing basic questions for them to respond to may help focus their attention on the salient points.

Each counseling staff member must be held accountable for reading the document and must be provided an opportunity to discuss it. A strategy used successfully with counselors has been to schedule an in-service education day during which the counselors from the steering committee explain each of the sections, particularly those describing the four program components. If you then prepare an agenda for discussion and train the head secondary and elementary counselors in its use, you provide a means for counselors to consider the full scope and depth of the program design. With the discussion agenda in everyone's hands, small groups of counselors can be asked to consider the major tenets of each section of the document and to voice support or disagreement with each concept. Specific items of confusion or concern can be identified at this time.

The final revision of the document needs to be completed and presented to the school district board of education for adoption. In some districts, board members read these documents *in toto* and then ratify them. In others, members are presented an overview of the program and priorities and are then provided copies for review at their discretion. In yet other districts, board members are satisfied with a presentation and the knowledge that the documents are available should they choose to review them. The document becomes the basic administrative regulation of the guidance and counseling program.

Complete distribution to relevant parties then needs to be made. At a minimum, every counselor needs to have a copy of the document, as does every school principal. Other administrators need copies on a need-to-know basis. For example, if you are using vocational funds to support part of your guidance and counseling program, then your district's vocational director needs a copy. You also may wish to consider publishing sections of the document for those who need only portions of it. For example, the personnel department must have copies of the position guides; the instructional staff will want copies of the curriculum-related sections, and so forth.

Empowering School Counselors

Professional school counselors are empowered through the designing process if the guidance leadership communicates openly with them. They feel empowered when they have input into their own professional destiny and when their opinions, ideas, and concerns are heard and responded to (Henderson & Gysbers, 1998). Fulfilling meaningful roles in designing the program is in and of itself empowering. Designing a program that envisions making the best use of their talents for the students perceived as having the highest need for those talents is also empowering. Just as empowering is having their unique expertise appreciated not only by other counselors but also by the noncounselors involved in the process—the steering and advisory committees, the principals, and other school and district administrators. As their leader, you want to ensure that all the counselors are aware of the process that is occurring, have input into the decisions, and understand the results of the decision-making work.

The new program design reflects a vision of how the program will better serve students. It is important that this vision be shared by all counselors—or as many as possible—and, as much as possible, by their principals. As Senge (2004) wrote, "New leadership roles require new leadership disciplines. Three of the most critical disciplines are building the shared vision, surfacing and challenging mental models, and engaging in systems thinking" (p. 16). As the leader, you must allow counselors to share their personal visions and help them blend them into a common vision for the program and for their work. You need to help them bring their personal models to the surface and to challenge them to consider ways the emerging schoolwide or districtwide vision will help them accomplish their goals. Many counselors have, unfortunately, lost the idealism that they had when they first entered the profession. Helping them refind those ideals is a useful exercise.

Finally, the comprehensive guidance and counseling program requires a team approach to program implementation. Counselors may be used to operating independently, even in isolation, from other counselors and other school staff members. The team approach brings with it collegiality, cooperation, and collaboration. "A team is a group of people working together to achieve mutual goals" (Henderson & Gysbers, 1998, p. 62). But teams do not just result from bringing a group of people together. Leadership is required to help them work through the form, storm, norm, and perform process. Blanchard, Carew, and Parisi-Carew (2000) described the essentials of high-performing teams: shared purpose and values, empowerment, open relationships and communication, flexibility of members and the team itself, optimal performance as the goal, recognition and appreciation of the individuals, and high morale. Your responsibility is to lead them when leadership is required and to be a contributing member of the team.

Attending to Diversity

Lee (2001) identified 12 characteristics of a culturally responsive school. The school

1. has adopted a "salad bowl" as opposed to a "melting pot" philosophy of education.
2. has forged a sense of community out of cultural diversity.
3. has the same high academic expectations for all students.
4. has a curriculum that fairly and accurately reflects the contributions of many cultures.
5. infuses multiculturalism and diversity in a nonstereotypical manner throughout the curriculum and the school year.
6. provides students with forums outside of the classroom to communicate with and learn about their peers from diverse cultural backgrounds.
7. has mechanisms in place to deal with racial/cultural tensions.
8. has committed educators who engage in ongoing staff development and are not afraid to take risks or improvise when necessary.
9. actively recruits a diverse staff of educators.
10. has educators who consider language and cultural customs in their interactions with parents.
11. has high levels of parental involvement representing the diverse cultures found in the school community.
12. defines cultural diversity to include people with disabilities, diverse sexual orientations, diverse religious traditions, and a range of ages—including older people. (p. 258)

To be culturally responsive, comprehensive guidance and counseling programs need to have the same characteristics. Much can be done during the designing phase of program development to attend to the diversity in the school/district. Principles regarding awareness, acceptance, and celebration of the diversity in the community and the school should be reflected in each of the structural components. The definition should assure that *all* students are served through the program.

The rationale should include assessment of the special needs of diverse students. "Compelling data underscore the need for school counselors to work effectively to improve academic results for low-income students and students of color" are words in the mission statement of the "Transforming School Counseling" project of The Education Trust (2003). Schools, including guidance and counseling programs, must accept the reality that is continuously documented in dropout and graduation rates. For example, results of a study conducted by the Manhattan Institute for Policy Research and reviewed by Stanard (2003) in the *Journal of Counseling & Development* (2003) showed that "The nationwide graduation rate for the class of 1998 was 74%. By subgroup the rates were White students 78%, African American students 56%, and Latino students 54%" (p. 217). Stanard recognized that "school counselors are in a prime position to have a positive impact on the problem of high school dropouts" (p. 219). She cited the nonacademic problems that dropouts have and suggested systemic and programmatic interventions.

The assumptions should include beliefs about diverse individuals and groups, about diversity itself, and about what contributions the guidance and counseling program makes in enriching the campus climate by valuing its diversity. The content competencies should address multicultural competence. The percentages of subgroups of students and other clients served in the program should reflect the percentages of the subgroups of the total school population

The program itself should attend to topics that address differences among people. Cross-cultural effectiveness is a curriculum strand in the Texas program model (Texas Education Agency, 2004). Rayle and Myers (2004) reported a research study that indicated that "ethnic identity was a significant predictor of wellness for minority adolescents" (p. 87) but not for nonminority students. Perhaps this indicates a need to address ethnic identity for part of the student population. If the program design did not include that as an important topic for all students, attention could be paid to that by providing differentiated guidance curriculum offerings or by providing it through a responsive service, such as small-group counseling.

The professional school counselors should continually be developing their cultural competencies as described in the American Counseling Association's Multicultural Competencies and Objectives and included in Appendix I. ASCA's (2004b) basic position statement on cultural diversity is that "Professional school counselors advocate for appropriate opportunities and services that promote maximum development for all students regardless of cultural backgrounds and strive to remove barriers that impede student success." The ethical standards established by both ACA (2005) and ASCA (2004a) make clear the expectation that professional counselors be multiculturally competent and advocates for embracing diversity.

Concluding Thoughts

Through the designing process, schools and school districts answer the fundamental questions (ASCA, 2005) that must be answered to deliver meaningful, effective, and efficient guidance and counseling programs:

1. What do students need that school counselors with their special body of knowledge can best address?
2. Which students benefit the most from the activities designed to meet these needs?
3. What are school counselors best qualified to do to help them?
4. How does the guidance and counseling program relate to the total educational program?
5. How can guidance and counseling be provided most effectively and efficiently?
6. How is a good school guidance and counseling program developed and maintained by a school?
7. How are the results of school counselors' work measured?

At this point, you have addressed these questions. The blueprint for your new program is completed; the vision of what you want is clearly delineated. The steering committee members and the counselors are apt to think—again—that the work is done. However, in terms of the improvement process of the guidance and counseling program, you have established only the objectives to be accomplished. What remains is planning the transition to the desired program and its actual implementation. Thus as you distribute the program description, you must be prepared at the same time to outline the next steps in the program development efforts. The momentum that has been generated for change now must be channeled toward making plans and implementing changes systematically. The details of how to accomplish these phases of the program improvement process are provided in chapters 6, 7, and 8.

References

Akos, P., & Galassi, J. P. (2004). Training school counselors as developmental advocates. *Counselor Education and Supervision, 43,* 192–206.

American Counseling Association. (2005). *Code of ethics.* Alexandria, VA: Author.

American Counseling Association. (n.d.) *Cross-cultural competencies and objectives.* Retrieved January 17, 2005, from http://www.counseling.org/Content/NavigationMenu/RESOURCES/MULTICULTURALANDDIVERSITYISSUES/Competencies/Competencies.htm

American School Counselor Association. (2002–2003). *Effectiveness of school counseling.* Retrieved May 4, 2004, from http://www.schoolcounselor.org/content.asp?contentid=241

American School Counselor Association. (2004a). *Ethical standards for school counselors.* Retrieved from http://www.schoolcounselor.org/content.asp?contentid=173

American School Counselor Association. (2004b). *Position statement: Cultural diversity.* Retrieved January 11, 2005, from http://www.schoolcounselor.org/content.asp?contentid=249

American School Counselor Association. (2004c). *Why elementary school counselors.* Retrieved from http://www.schoolcounselor.org/content.asp?contentid=230

American School Counselor Association. (2004d). *Why middle school counselors.* Retrieved from http://www.schoolcounselor.org/content.asp?contentid=231

American School Counselor Association. (2004e). *Why secondary school counselors.* Retrieved from http://www.schoolcounselor.org/content.asp?contentid=233

American School Counselor Association. (2005). *The ASCA national model: A framework for school counseling programs* (2nd ed.) Alexandria, VA: Author.

American School Counselor Association. (n.d.) *Student-to-counselor ratios.* Retrieved December 21, 2004, from http://www.schoolcounselor.org/content.asp?contentid=133

Blanchard, K., Carew, D., & Parisi-Carew, E. (2000). *The 1-minute manager builds high performing teams.* New York: William Morrow.

Borders, L. D., & Drury, S. M. (1992). Comprehensive school counseling programs: A review for policy makers and practitioners. *Journal of Counseling & Development, 70,* 487–498.

Brigman, G., & Campbell, C. (2003). Helping students improve academic achievement and school success behavior. *Professional School Counseling, 7*(2), 91–98.

California Department of Education, Counseling and Student Support Office. (2003). *Study of pupil personnel ratios, services, and programs* (School Counseling Research Brief 2.4, September 13, 2004). Amherst: University of Massachusetts, National Center for School Counseling Outcome Research. Retrieved from http://www.umass.edu/schoolcounseling.

Campbell, C. A., & Dahir, C. A. (1997). *Sharing the vision: The national standards for school counseling programs.* Alexandria, VA: American School Counselor Association.

Castetter, W. B. (1981). *The personnel function in educational administration.* New York: Macmillan.

Coleman, H. L. K., Casali, S. B., & Wampold, B. E. (2001). Adolescent strategies for coping with cultural diversity. *Journal of Counseling & Development, 79,* 356–364.

Council for Accreditation of Counseling and Related Educational Programs. (2001). *Standards for school counseling programs.* Retrieved April 8, 2004, from http://www.cacrep.org/2001Standards.html

The Education Trust. (2003). *Mission statement: Transforming school counseling.* Retrieved January 13, 2005, from http://www2.edtrust.org/edtrust/TransformingSchool Counseling/missionstatement

Gysbers, N. C., Kosteck-Bunch, L., Magnuson, C. S., & Starr, M. (2002). *Missouri comprehensive guidance program: A manual for program development, implementation, evaluation, and enhancement.* Columbia, MO: Instructional Materials Laboratory.

Hargens, M., & Fuston, J. K. (1997). Comprehensive guidance program of the St. Joseph School District in Buchanan County, Missouri. In N. C. Gysbers & P. Henderson (Eds.), *Comprehensive guidance programs that work—II* (pp. 61–74). Greensboro, NC: ERIC Counseling and Student Services Clearinghouse.

Henderson, P. H. (1987). A comprehensive school guidance program at work. *TACD Journal, 15,* 25–37.

Henderson, P., & Gysbers, N. C. (1998). *Leading and managing your school guidance program staff.* Alexandria, VA: American Counseling Association.

Lee, C. C. (2001). Culturally responsive school counselors and programs: Addressing the needs of all students. *Professional School Counseling, 4,* 257–261.

MacDonald, G., & Sink, C. A. (1999). A qualitative developmental analysis of comprehensive guidance programmes in schools in the United States. *British Journal of Guidance and Counselling, 27,* 415–430.

National Board for Certified Counselors. (2004). *The National Certified School Counselor (NCSC) credential.* Retrieved April 8, 2004, from http://www.nbcc.org/cert/ncsc.htm

National Board for Professional Teaching Standards (2002). *School counseling standards.* Retrieved April 10, 2004, from http://www.nbpts.org/pdf/schoolcounseling.pdf

National School Boards Association. (1986). *Resolution on guidance and counseling.* Alexandria, VA: Author.

No Child Left Behind Act of 2001, Pub. L. No. 107–110 (1992). Retrieved from http://www.ed.gov/policy/elsec/leg/esea02/index.html

Northside Independent School District. (1986). *Comprehensive guidance program framework.* San Antonio, TX: Author.

Northside Independent School District. (1994). *Comprehensive guidance program framework.* San Antonio, TX: Author.

Rayle, A. D., & Myers, J. E. (2004). Counseling adolescents toward wellness: The roles of ethnic identity, acculturation, and mattering. *Professional School Counseling, 8*(1), 81–90.

School Violence. (2004). [Special section]. *Journal of Counseling & Development, 82,* 259–312.

Search Institute. (n.d.). *Introduction to assets.* Retrieved from http://www.search-institute.org/assets/

Senge, P. (July 2004). Building vision. *Executive Excellence, 21*(7), 16.

Stanard, R. P. (2003). High school graduation rates in the United States: Implications for the counseling profession. *Journal of Counseling & Development, 81,* 217–221.

Texas Counseling Association. (2004). *Texas evaluation model for professional school counselors* (2nd ed.). Austin, TX: Author.

Texas Education Agency. (2004). *A model comprehensive, developmental guidance and counseling program for Texas public schools: A guide for program development pre-K–12th grade* (4th ed.). Austin, TX: Author.

Chapter 6

Planning the Transition to a Comprehensive Guidance and Counseling Program

Designing—Planning the Transition

- Specify changes needed to implement a comprehensive guidance and counseling program districtwide.
- Develop a plan for accomplishing districtwide program improvement.
- Begin building-level program improvement efforts.
- Expand the leadership base.

☞ Chapter 5 has described the tasks and issues involved in delineating the design for a comprehensive guidance and counseling program. Delineating the design is an important phase of the change process because it describes and specifies the directions for change that will be required to install a comprehensive guidance and counseling program. Unfortunately, some administrators who wish to make program changes stop after the designing phase. They conclude, wrongly, that if directions for the desired changes are clear, the desired changes will occur. We believe, however, that for the desired changes to occur, those changes need to be planned. Remodeling the guidance and counseling program entails building on some of the original structure, removing some of the parts that do not belong in the new structure, and adding some new ones. Making such renovations takes time, energy, and other resources. Thus planning how you will make the transition to a comprehensive guidance and counseling program is vital.

Careful planning is also required because of the complexity of actually implementing the program. Implementation is accomplished in increments. Although some implementation tasks are completed at the district level, much of the actual program implementation occurs at the building level. Thus two levels of planning are required: districtwide and buildingwide. Remember that these two levels of planning interact. Some building changes cannot be made without district changes occurring first, and some district changes cannot be made without building initiatives preceding them. The district initiates changes in policy, regulations, or support that facilitate building program implementation. Building trials of new activities and procedures often are needed before district changes can be made.

This chapter describes in detail the tasks involved in planning the transition to a comprehensive guidance and counseling program. First, changes that are indicated must be stated specifically. The desired program description (see chapter 5) serves as a template to lay over your current program so that similarities and differences can be seen. What should be adopted directly from the comprehensive program model? What current activities should be maintained? What components of the program model not presently complete need to be created to fill gaps in the current program? Your answers to these questions will provide the information you need to establish goals for change and identify ways to effect change. Second, if you are working in a large school system, you need to make plans to accomplish program improvement at the building as well as the district level; thus improved designs for the building programs and plans for implementing them must be developed. Third, you need to begin the building-level program improvement efforts. Fourth, as you move into implementation, multiple opportunities will become available to you to better attend to the diversity found in your students and in your communities. Fifth, if you are the program's director, we encourage you to expand your leadership base to include all the school counselors in a small school district or more of the school counselor leaders in a larger district. As you prepare for implementation, the more grassroots leaders you have available, the more effective your transition will be. You also will have the benefit of their advice and counsel in making the transition workable in this phase of remodeling and revitalizing your guidance and counseling program. To conclude the chapter, we summarize your roles and responsibilities as the guidance and counseling program leader during this transition period.

Specify Changes Needed to Implement a Comprehensive Guidance and Counseling Program Districtwide

Planning the transition to a comprehensive program entails specifying the needed changes. To do this, you will need to compare and contrast your current program with the program you desire, establish goals for change, and identify ways to bring the changes about. When you have completed this, you will have specified the changes that are wanted and be ready to begin the process of making or helping others make the required changes.

Comparing and Contrasting Your Current Program With Your Desired Program

Having studied your current program and having established a design for the program you want, you now have the information you need to compare and contrast the two. The goal is to identify places where the programs overlap, but even more important, where there are gaps that may need to be filled. You also will identify some places where the design of the current program goes beyond the design that is desired. You will be asking and answering the question, Is there a discrepancy between what you want your guidance and counseling program to accomplish and what your guidance and counseling program is accomplishing currently?

We advise you to conduct this discrepancy analysis from your data for both the current program and the desired program. If you have followed our suggestions in chapter 4, you have information about student outcomes/results, the appropriation of school counselors' time and competence to the program components, the makeup of the program components, and the clients served. Careful analysis of this information provides you the data you need to specify needed changes.

Northside Independent School District studied the discrepancies in each of the aspects of the program design. The most useful data for redirecting the program were the data about the allocation of school counselor time to each program component and to nonguidance activities. As explained earlier, the program components consist of activities. An activity incorporates all the aspects of the design: Students or other clients participate in the activities; content objectives to yield specific student results are targeted; and school counselors' competence is utilized.

Some of the Northside Independent School District (1986) data gathered in assessing its then-current program design were displayed in chapter 4 (see Table 4.15). Similar information was presented from the design for the desired program in chapter 5 (see Table 5.10). When both sets of data were presented to the steering committee, the administrators, and the school counselors, they led to the obvious conclusion that change had to occur and sparked creative thinking as to how these changes could occur.

Others have found the data as to how school counselors allocate their time useful as well. In Table 6.1 the data generated in the Texas study, *Guiding Our Children Toward Success: How Texas School Counselors Spend Their Time* (Rylander, 2002), are presented side by side with the percentages of how their time should be spent according to the Texas program model (Texas Education Agency, 2004). The information is presented in terms of percentages of school counselors' time that are and should be spent in delivery of the four program components and in nonguidance activities.

The discrepancy analysis of the quantitative design between what is and what should be yielded the following information concerning program components:

- Compares favorably (appropriate amount of time spent):
  Individual student planning: elementary, high
  System support: elementary, middle/junior high, high
- Gaps (too little time spent):
  Guidance curriculum: elementary, middle/junior high, high
  Responsive services: elementary, middle/junior high, high
  Individual student planning: middle/junior high
- Spillovers (too much time spent):
  Nonguidance activities: elementary, middle/junior high, high

In addition to analyzing the hard data collected in the current program assessment, analyzing more subjective data is also useful. Some themes have probably emerged as you gathered perceptions of the current program. Now that you have agreed on what is wanted from your desired program, other people's opinions about what has been good and what has been missing from the current program will give you more information on which to base your decisions for change. The subjective information regarding results sought, clients served, school counselors' and other staff members' roles, and resources thus needs to be

Table 6.1
Texas School Counselors Actual Time Use and Texas Education Agency (TEA) Suggested Time Allocations (in Percentages)

Category	Elementary School		Middle School/Junior High		High School	
	Survey Results	TEA Suggested	Survey Results	TEA Suggested	Survey Results	TEA Suggested
Guidance curriculum	17.6	35–45	8.0	35–40	9.2	15–25
Responsive services	21.4	30–40	18.3	30–40	16.7	25–35
Individual student planning	9.5	5–10	10.7	15–25	22.3	25–35
System support	16.0	10–15	11.6	10–15	11.6	15–20
Subtotal	64.5	80–100	48.6	90–100	59.8	80–100
Nonguidance	35.5	0	51.4	0	40.2	0
Total	100	100	100	100	100	100

Note. Survey results are from Rylander (2002, p. 19); TEA suggested time allocations are from Texas Education Agency (1998).

analyzed as to how your current program compares and contrasts with the desired program. Categorize your analysis in the same manner as you did your analysis of hard data (compares favorably, gaps, and spillovers). For example, equal access by all subpopulations of students to the program is desired. The results of a survey might show that most people felt that the high school guidance and counseling program served the college-bound students adequately, did not serve the work-bound or minority students sufficiently, and invested too much time in serving individual students with difficult personal problems. The first is a subjectively stated favorable comparison, the second identifies a gap, and the third indicates a spillover from the desired design.

The degree of congruence between your objective and subjective data in relationship to the improved program you envision also needs to be studied. The ideal is for the hard data and subjective data to be as congruent as possible, and for your current and desired programs to match for each component of the program, the clients served, school counselors' functions, and so on. If your objective and subjective data are congruent but the two designs do not match, you have descriptive information from the subjective data on which to base your recommendations for change. For example, if your objective data tell you that school counselors spend too much time in system support or on nonguidance tasks, and the program's users feel that the school counselors function too much like clerks, you have a rationale to support the recommendation to decrease the time in the system support component or on nonguidance tasks. If your objective data and subjective data are not congruent, but the two program designs match, you have identified a need for public relations efforts. For example, if your school counselors are spending an appropriate amount of time responding to students with personal problems but your consumers do not perceive this, you know you need to educate all your consumers. At the same time, the subjective data might alert you to the reality that the school counselors are, for example, responding to students with personal problems on a one-to-one basis but that more group work is desirable so that more students with problems could be served.

If your objective data and subjective data are not congruent in an area where the current and desired programs do not match, then the decisions you make depend on whether the subjective data represent a favorable or unfavorable opinion and on whether the mismatch in program design is a gap or a spillover. If the subjective data about the current program are favorable, our advice is to leave well enough alone until you have begun to implement your desired program. If the subjective data represent the opinion that you are not doing something that in fact takes a disproportionate amount of time, you need to educate the opinion holders before you can implement needed changes. For example, if high school principals think high school counselors are not spending enough time changing schedules and your current assessment data tell you they are, you need to help principals know about the disproportionate investment of valuable talent in an activity that does not use school counselors' education and talents to effect appropriate changes. That is, the principals need assistance to see the problem. School counselors should present these data to their principals because they have examples and anecdotes to share that will put life and meaning into the data.

Identifying, quantitatively or subjectively, the places where your current program compares favorably with the desired program tells you and the staff what is right with the current program. That provides a morale booster for the staff, who by now are probably quite anxious about ongoing or proposed changes. It also provides you with a good foundation on which to build.

Identifying gaps in the design of your current program vis-à-vis the desired program points to two kinds of changes that may need to be made. The gaps mean either you are simply not doing enough of what is desired or you are not doing it at all. For example, in the Texas study (Rylander, 2002), the analysis of the discrepancies displayed in Table 6.1 (i.e., the difference between the Texas Education Agency's suggested time allocation and the actual time use) shows there was a 6%–16% gap in the use of the guidance curriculum component at the high school level, a 27%–32% gap at the middle school/junior high level, and a 17%–27% gap at the elementary school level. Thus a change recommendation is to augment the current guidance curriculum efforts. In comparing and contrasting their current content emphasis with their desired content, through Northside's study of school counselors' use of their special knowledge and skills, it was learned that no time was spent by middle school counselors at most schools in career guidance activities. Thus career guidance activities must be a new dimension to be added to the program at those middle schools.

Identifying where the design of your current program goes beyond that of the desired program also points to two kinds of potential changes. You may be doing too much of what is desirable, or you may be doing something that is seen as inappropriate for the guidance and counseling program or a waste of school counselors' time and talent. One conclusion drawn in the Texas study (Rylander, 2002) was that the data indicated

> that counselor time in specific guidance areas during the survey period was far below the recommended level due to the impact of non-counseling duties. . . . In particular, the category "guidance curriculum," the area of guidance where counselors help students develop basic life skills such as problem-solving and goal-setting strategies, seemed especially low during the survey period among counselors in middle school/junior high and high schools. Guidance curriculum involves a significant amount of student contact, so the statistics seem to indicate that counselor time with students may be lost due to a counselor's need to perform other duties. (p. 19)

This echoes one of the conclusions from the Arizona study (Vandergrift, 1999), that "time spent on non-guidance activities clearly is time *not* spent working with students, faculty and staff" (p. 5).

In the North Carolina Department of Public Instruction (n.d.) study of how North Carolina school counselors spend their time,

> the results revealed that school counselors in North Carolina are not dividing their time according to the suggested national standards and that a significant amount of time is spent on non-counseling activities, such as testing, covering classes, and registrar activities. (p. 17)

In the Arizona study (Vandergrift, 1999), it was learned that an average of 15% of Arizona school counselors' time is being spent on nonguidance activities. "Of course, using counselors in more proactive capacity suggests redirecting their time. The most obvious place to start is to *not* use counselors for 'non-guidance' activities" (p. 5). The report also identified that 40% of Arizona counselors' total time use was devoted to responsive services, raising the question, "Is it sound practice for counseling to be reactive or should it be more proactive?" (p. 5). The report concluded, "There will always be circumstances that warrant responsive services. However, the question is whether schools could, in fact, reduce the need for behavioral counseling by improving the quality and nature of educational services" (p. 5).

Establishing Goals for Change

Having clearly identified discrepancies between the current program and the desired program, you are ready to draw conclusions. This entails studying each set of discrepancy data and identifying the gaps and spillovers. As discussed above, the following conclusions from the Texas study (Rylander, 2002) were drawn from contrasting current and desired program designs:

- Too little time is spent in curriculum at all three levels.
- Too little time is spent in responsive services at all three levels.
- Too much time is spent in nonguidance activities.

The guidance and counseling program leader develops the list of conclusions. This list needs to be presented to the steering and the school–community advisory committees, the school counselors, and other administrators to enable them to see the specific problems that need to be addressed. It is from this list of conclusions that recommendations for change are drawn. Recommendations for change are restatements of the data-based conclusions into "should" statements. Recommendations for change from the Texas study in relation to the conclusions just listed are presented in Table 6.2.

Another step in the process is to assign priorities to the recommendations. For example, in a "Study of Pupil Personnel Ratios, Services, and Programs" conducted by the California Department of Education (as cited in Gray, Elsner, & Poynton, 2004), it was learned that

> The top priority identified by districts was the need for more school-wide prevention and intervention strategies. This calls for the development of a comprehensive pupil support program that serves all students proactively through prevention programs, and reactively through intervention strategies. (p. 4)

Some school districts with which we have worked have chosen to establish priorities by identifying changes that *need* to be made and those that they *want* to make. In a national survey of guidance program and staff leaders (Henderson & Gysbers, 2002), 10 recurrent issues were identified as critical—"recurrent" in that they occurred in multiple schools, districts, and states; "critical" in that their resolution makes for a strengthened guidance program, and if not resolved, the program is weakened. The 10 issues are listed below in priority order. The priority was established on the basis of the issues' frequency of occurrence and rated importance:

Table 6.2
Guidance Program Change Goals

To attain the desired comprehensive, balanced guidance program for Texas Public Schools, it is recommended that counselors and administrators work together

At the elementary school level:
- To increase the time spent by counselors in guidance curriculum
- To increase the time spent by counselors in responsive services
- To decrease the time spent by counselors in nonguidance activities

At the middle school/junior high level:
- To increase the time spent by counselors in guidance curriculum
- To increase the time spent by counselors in responsive services
- To decrease the time spent by counselors in nonguidance activities

At the high school level:
- To increase the time spent by counselors in guidance curriculum
- To increase the time spent by counselors in responsive services
- To decrease the time spent by counselors in nonguidance activities

1. Displacement of non-guidance tasks, including school counselors' appropriate role in standardized testing programs
2. Program accountability
3. Accountability for the quality of school counselor performance
4. Program advocacy
5. Leader empowerment
6. Enhancement of an existing comprehensive guidance program
7. Appropriate use of technology
8. Parent involvement, including responding to parents who are critical of the program
9. Program development process
10. Enhancement of the cross-cultural competence of school counselors. (Henderson & Gysbers, 2002, p. 8)

(You may be interested to know that examples of successful responses to these issues are also provided in the referenced book.)

Whether you choose to state the recommendations as needs and wants or you list all of them in order of priority is up to you. Because the process we have outlined generates rather lengthy lists of recommendations for change, listing changes in priority order makes accomplishing the changes more manageable.

Identifying Ways to Effect the Changes

Now that the issues have been identified through discrepancy analysis and explicit recommendations for changes have been made, all staff and others involved in the program development effort need to identify ways to attain the recommendations and to make the changes. Adelman and Taylor (2003) referred to this as "clarifying feasibility" and described two steps in this phase: "clarifying whether changes can be made through existing, modified or new activities; and clarifying how these changes can be accomplished" (p. 8).

We recommend that those involved—the steering committee, the school–community advisory committee, the school counselors, the administrators, and other staff—brainstorm ways to make the changes. It is best to involve everyone who will be affected by the changes; this process allows them to sense the feasibility of the changes and sets their thoughts in motion as to how recommendations might be carried out.

The steering committee should be the first to do this, preferably at the same meeting during which the recommendations for the changes are developed, as a reality check. Brainstorming allows committee members to consider whether the recommendations they are making are feasible. The steering committee also ought to help design the process for presenting the change recommendations and soliciting ideas about how to make the changes from the appropriate staff. If your building/system is large enough, it is advisable to use the steering committee members to conduct the brainstorming meetings with the rest of the staff. These meetings ought to include enough people so that true brainstorming can occur, that is, so that many ideas can be thrown onto the table for further consideration.

In Northside Independent School District, the school counselors and principals from the steering committee conducted meetings with each of the three different principal groups: elementary, middle, and high school. The school counselors conducted the meetings with the other school counselors. Each group was presented with the discrepancy information relevant to its own level and was guided through the brainstorming process for each discrepancy and resultant recommendations. The groups responded to the question, How could this be done? For example, How could school counselors spend more time in the guidance curriculum component? How could they spend less time on nonguidance tasks? The ideas generated for increasing high school guidance staff time spent in guidance curriculum are provided in Figure 6.1.

The data from separate meetings such as these can then be aggregated and presented to the steering and school–community advisory committees to do the second half of the brainstorming process: applying judgments to the myriad suggestions. The committee next draws from these ideas to develop the list of what needs to be done to bring about

Figure 6.1
Results of Brainstorming Ways to Reduce Discrepancies
Between the Current and the Desired Guidance Program

Steering Committee Ideas

High School Level
To increase time spent in curriculum
- work with groups (vs. individuals) to disseminate information, e.g., junior and senior credit checks, test score interpretation
- become involved with clubs, organizations, and other extracurricular activities, through assignment if necessary
- increase time spent in group activities
- set yearly calendar that will facilitate counselors' keeping on task for group activities
- get into the classroom—be a visible part of the educational team

All Levels
To increase time spent in curriculum
- define program expectations, monitor implementation
- develop curriculum resources
- provide staff development for counselors
- communicate program to and enlist support of administration and faculty
- design systematic delivery system (calendar, time line, individual vs. group)

High School Principals' Ideas

To increase time spent in curriculum
- use the following times that are available to conduct curriculum activities:
  — advisories
  — fourth-period study hall
  — on-campus suspension class
- institute a club schedule
- identify and work with classes that have needs, e.g., lower-functioning academic classes
- use different methods of assigning counselors to caseload job responsibilities
- prioritize for students on campus now, not for their future
- provide in-service for teachers on such topics as behavior management, listening skills
- plan for the year
- set a consistent calendar

High School Counselors' Ideas

To increase time spent in curriculum
- provide group guidance to teach decision-making skills, self-esteem
- plan more in-service with teachers, e.g., with teachers of freshmen to help freshmen become successfully involved in school
- increase time in ninth-grade advisories
- plan freshmen advisory guidance in the first month of school to include orientation to high school, study skills, attendance, 4-year plan revision, involvement
- provide ninth graders' orientation to Career Center
- increase time interpreting vocational interest surveys
- provide facilities to do group guidance
- increase use of advisory to have small groups with all students
- hold "brown bag" sessions
- make "official time" for counselors to go into classrooms through, e.g., restructuring school day periodically; increase faculty involvement with credits, clubs, etc.; increase principals' verbal support; sell ideas to key teachers or department heads
- provide counselors needed planning time
- set as priorities: feeling good about themselves, decision-making and study skills

---

Note. Data from Northside Independent School District, San Antonio, TX: Author. Adapted with permission.

the desired changes. The groups that brainstormed the suggestions need to see the notes from the various meetings so that they know their ideas were heard and are being considered. These lists also are useful in the future when specific changes are being implemented, both at the district and at the local levels.

You should now have a clear and concrete picture of what changes need to be made in your current program. You have formulated recommendations for the changes you are getting ready to implement, so that you will know you have achieved what you want when you get there. And you have begun to identify how to effect the desired changes. You are now ready to plan your program improvements.

Develop a Plan for Accomplishing Districtwide Program Improvement

At the district level, the steering committee and the school–community advisory committee and the guidance and counseling program leader should devise a master plan of action for accomplishing the districtwide tasks. A list of tasks to do can be developed from the suggestions resulting from the brainstorming sessions described in the preceding section. Then an action plan for accomplishing these recommendations needs to be written.

Listing What Needs to Be Done to Implement Changes

From the various lists of ideas generated in the discrepancy analysis of the current and desired programs, the guidance and counseling program leader and the steering and school–community advisory committees need to develop a list of things to do to facilitate implementation of the comprehensive guidance and counseling program. The list should be an action-oriented list, not a list of vague wishes, and the actions should be feasible.

The list may be rather long. Districts we have worked with have generated a range of 25 to 40 items that needed to be done before complete implementation could become a reality. This does not mean that all tasks have to be accomplished before some changes can be made, but it does mean that policy makers have to be realistic about their expectations for the new program implementation. To help you envision what it might take, we include a partial list of such actions from Northside Independent School District in Table 6.3.

As you can see, these are major tasks to accomplish. By scanning the list, you also can see that there are categories of items, for example, those that relate to staff development, to budget development, and to product development. As an interesting staff development recommendation and to help displace nonguidance duties, one of the recommendations from the Arizona time study was "The Arizona Department of Education and/or State Board of Community Colleges should consider developing a career path/credential for counseling paraprofessionals" (Vandergrift, 1999, p. 6).

Other categories of recommendations might be those that relate to policy development and program development. In the Arizona study (Vandergrift, 1999), a primary concern was about school counselors' student caseloads. Given the national recommendations of a maximum of 300 students per school counselor, "Three years of data on Arizona school counselors' caseloads shows that nearly three out of every four school counselors in 1997–98 (up from two-thirds in 1996) are responsible for more than 300 students" (p. 5). In response to this concern, the Arizona study recommended that "the Arizona Department of Education should consider introducing a policy recommendation and/or legislation to reduce the caseloads of Arizona counselors" (p. 7). As a result of her analysis of the Texas school counselor time study, Rylander (2002) made three recommendations: (a) each district develop a local policy on the use of school counselors' time; (b) the

Table 6.3

Recommended "To Do's" to Accomplish the Comprehensive Guidance Program

Develop guidance program component guides
Develop a system for assisting local campuses to design their guidance programs
Establish communication mechanisms
Design a relevant counselor staff development program
Design a relevant counselor evaluation system
Provide program development time for counselors
Establish campus departmental budgets for guidance department
Assess costs associated with implementation of program and develop an appropriate
    budget (district)
Review and make recommendations to ensure adequacy of guidance facilities
Modify counselor staffing formulas as recommended
Hire technical assistants at secondary schools
Review and recommend extended contracts for counselors
Establish parameters for counselor access to students
Develop a public relations plan
Explore use of other-than-local funding sources
Develop job descriptions for guidance department clerical staff.

Note. From *Comprehensive Guidance Program Framework*, by Northside Independent School District, 1986, San Antonio, TX: Author. Adapted with permission.

Texas Education Agency monitor local policies through the agency's compliance reviews; and (c) the Texas Education Agency automate the information it collects from school counselors for better use in holding school districts accountable for their guidance programs. And, as a final example, recommendations made for reducing the gaps between how school counselors should spend their time as described in a model by the National Consortium for State Guidance Leadership and how the 2000 North Carolina school counselors were spending the time included the following:

- Staff development activities to help principals and school counselors schedule their time appropriately and to increase understanding of the major function areas.
- A study on how support personnel can be used to eliminate non-counseling duties.
- Resources to eliminate non-counseling functions are needed.
- A revised guidance curriculum for the school counseling program is needed. (North Carolina Department of Public Instruction, n.d., p. 12)

To ensure the completeness of your list, you may want to group the list by the categories of resources used in the original program assessment: personnel resources (talent, time, ratio, assignments), financial resources (budget, materials, equipment, facilities), and political resources (policy, identification of program supporters). Grouping by categories will help you and the committees make the next set of decisions: What to do first.

Outlining Your Master Plan for Resource Development

Needless to say, all of these tasks cannot begin at once. Adelman and Taylor (2003) described this in their clarifying feasibility stage as "formulating a longer range strategic plan for maintaining momentum, progress, quality improvement, and creative renewal" (p. 8). Some tasks to be done depend on the accomplishment of others. Thus the next step is to list the tasks to do in the chronological order in which they are to be done. Chronology is guided by consideration of whether certain tasks are prerequisite to the other tasks. Consider whether tasks are developmental or experimental and whether they are feasible to do at this time or if they might be difficult to accomplish. If they are tied to other, larger processes—such as district budget development—they must be done at times relevant to those processes. A part of the Northside Independent School District master plan is displayed in Table 6.4. The first four items were related to the development of the district's budget for the next fiscal year and were also of top priority. The budget is submitted for consideration by the superintendent by May l; thus the research work needed to be done in March and April. The written program description obviously needed to be finished before it could be presented to the board of education, and the board needed to approve the program description before it could be presented to the school counselors with authority.

The master plan specifies what needs to be done in what order and by whom. If you are the guidance and counseling program leader, the master plan gives you your job-related mandates for continuing the project you have been working on. You also have to identify the areas where the members of the steering committee can help you and where you and the school counselors are on your own.

Begin Building-Level Program Improvement Efforts

At this point the guidance and counseling program improvement project becomes two tiered. Up to now we have been working primarily from the frame of reference of the school system. Building school counselors and administrators have been involved more or less on a voluntary basis, except for responding to the project's data-gathering needs. If you have followed our advice, many of the school counselors and some administrators have been involved in the work groups. Those school counselors who envision the new program as the wave of the future or the answer to their dreams have probably already experimented with new activities.

When the statement of the district's minimum expectations for the guidance and counseling program is adopted, responsibility shifts to the local school buildings in the district; their programs must be changed to meet these minimum expectations or go beyond them. They are now challenged to identify changes that are needed in their building programs and to make those changes successfully. What you should have been saying to the building school counselors and administrators all along, as they raised the usual concerns regarding district mandates, is that there will be room for tailoring the desired program to

Table 6.4
Master Plan for Implementation of a Comprehensive Guidance Program

Task	Deadline
Make recommendations regarding extended contracts	2/25
Make recommendations regarding counselors' preference (lowered caseload vs. technical assistant)	3/28
Make recommendations regarding priorities for implementing lowered caseloads; elementary, middle, high	3/28
Send memos to principals regarding campus guidance department budgets	4/5
Develop counselors' position guides for inclusion in framework	5/1
Complete framework; prepare for board presentation	6/1
Plan guide development process	5/1
Seek approval/funding	5/15
Conduct leadership training	6/30
Develop recommendations for minimum standards for facilities/ equipment for principals	8/1
Plan/implement in-service sessions for counselors on minimum expectations (framework)	8/30

Note. Data from Northside Independent School District, San Antonio, TX. Adapted with permission.

local community needs. It is at this time that the statement becomes the challenge. To make the right changes, school counselors and administrators in each building must redesign their programs to better align them with the district program and also to ensure meeting their students' and local communities' highest priority needs. It must be remembered that school counselors and principals need to share a common vision about the guidance program.

> The mission of the school guidance program is a subset of the school's mission. The primary mission in any building is to help students learn. Thus, the guidance program supports the learning environment; at the same time, guidance programs make unique contributions in meeting students' needs and nurturing their progress. (Henderson & Gysbers, 1998, p. 58)

To ensure that program changes are made successfully, school counselors and administrators must use processes that support change and meaningful program planning.

Assisting Building Staff to Prepare for Change

If you are the guidance and counseling program leader, you will need to assist the counseling staff as they face this challenge and empower them to make the needed changes. Often-cited obstacles to change include school counselors' needing to change their philosophies about what they do and why they do it, to overcome their fears of failure in fulfilling new or different roles, to seek support from faculty and administration, and to learn to work together as a team (American School Counselor Association [ASCA], 2005). Guidance program leaders nurture school counselors' professional empowerment by establishing respectful interpersonal climates, by ensuring their understanding of the envisioned program and the expectations for their performance within it, by developing and maintaining a team approach to program development and implementation, and by holding school counselors accountable for their work in the program (Henderson & Gysbers, 1998).

Ultimately, the school counselors need help to internalize the desired comprehensive guidance and counseling program as described. They need to be familiar with the program development model they will be asked to follow. They need to assess their current program in relation to the district model and to identify local needs and establish priorities for meeting those needs. Further, they need to design the desired program for the building on the basis of the desired district model. Sound familiar? It is the same process you have just been through at the district level. The basic difference is in the level of specificity, and of course, that difference depends on the size of the district. In the buildings, each school counselor needs to begin to think in personal terms, saying "I spend X hours a week in counseling," "I spend X hours a week in clerical tasks," and so on, as well as "At the building level, the 20 students who are contemplating suicide and need responsive services are somewhere in these hallways" and "At the building level, if a guidance activity is selected for third graders, I am the one who will or will not implement it." There is no longer room for "that's a good idea for someone else" kind of thinking. Each school counselor needs to become an instrument of change.

Understanding the Districtwide Desired Program Design and Description

It has probably taken you some time to reach this point—up to a year or more—so the school counselors have had time to understand the concept of the comprehensive program and to know about the major impending changes, such as developmental guidance, small-group counseling, and more emphasis on career development. The proper balance for the district program has been decided. Now each school counselor needs to understand fully the new program structure.

We recommend that after a formal presentation and the distribution of the written comprehensive program description, small-group discussions be held with the school counselors to clarify any misconceptions, correct any misinformation, and ensure as much as possible not only that they have read it but also that they understood it. The most logical small groups should be used—a building staff, a cluster of elementary school counselors, and so on. By small groups, we mean 5 to 10. Although the discussions are led by the school counselor leaders, the guidance and counseling program administrator needs to be present at as many of these discussions as feasible because the shifting of focus to the buildings in anticipation of moving from planning to implementation represents a milestone in the project.

The strategy mentioned in chapter 5 and used in Northside Independent School District involved the use of a discussion agenda. The director of guidance developed a form that identified key topics and issues addressed in the comprehensive guidance and counseling program guide. Head counselors were assigned to discuss the agenda with their staffs. The director explained the issue points and the rationale behind the choices made. The school counselors were given 2 weeks to read the guide, write responses to the discussion agenda, and discuss these items in building staff meetings. Each head counselor wrote a summary of the building discussion; when the director came to the next staff meeting, those items became the focal point of the discussion. The director also collected the completed forms because several topics surfaced that needed to be addressed further. The summary information was discussed with all head counselors at one of their meetings. By the end of this process, the school counselors could legitimately be expected to know the district guidelines for the comprehensive guidance and counseling program.

As a final step, the school counselors were asked to conduct a meeting with their building administrators to summarize the program description and to suggest what it might mean to the building program. Because the principals already had been made aware of the document by the director, this was the opportunity to enlist the building administrators' support for the development of the building plan

Understanding the Program Development Process

The responsibility for developing the building plan belongs to the building staff. It is therefore important to ensure that building school counselors understand the program development process and establish mechanisms to facilitate it. At this point, we suggest that the school counselors be educated about the steps in the process that you want them to use. Following the process suggested in this book entails assessing their current program, assessing student and community needs, designing the desired program, establishing goals for change, and planning how those changes will be made. Again, depending on the size of the district, the process model may not need much elucidation if most school counselors have been involved in the development of the district program. But if the district is large, at least one round of in-service education about the program development process may be required.

In addition to benefiting from the experiences of the district as a whole, the building staffs have the benefit of the district's theoretical base as written in the rationale, assumptions, and definition. The district program description also portrays the model for the program structure and lists student competencies to be addressed in the program. Thus one challenge to the building staff is to study how their current program compares and contrasts with the district's desired program and make plans to improve. Another is to assess the needs of their students and the local community in terms of the broad parameters established for the district program and implement a program targeting these needs.

We also recommend that the building counseling staff lead the guidance and counseling program development effort but that they involve others as well. Representatives from the faculty, the student body, parents, the administration, and any other group of significant others should be involved. If a school has a building improvement committee or a community advisory committee, use it—or form one for the specific purpose of designing the local guidance and counseling program. We recommend that you continue to consult with the committee even after you have achieved the changes you are working for to give you continued advice and counsel. In fact, the Texas statute directing "school counselors and school counseling programs" (Texas Education Code, 2001) mandates that "A school counselor shall work with the school faculty and staff, students, parents, and the community to plan, implement, and evaluate a developmental guidance and counseling program"(§33.005). We, too, believe that a program always benefits from advice and counsel from its constituents or collaborators, but remember that the guidance staff and appropriate administrators need to remain the decision makers of the implementation and management of the guidance and counseling program.

Assessing Current Building-Level Program Status

The current-status study of the building program consists of the same steps needed in the district study. These were fully described in chapter 4. Most likely, the building data are available from the original assessment, so at this time the task is not to collect the data but to study them in light of the now-established desired program design. Building guidance staff members should be cognizant of their currently available resources and how they are used. You will recall that we discussed three kinds of resources: human, financial, and political. Personnel resources include not only the guidance and counseling program staff but also the specialized talents of each, their caseloads, assignments, and time available as well as the appropriation of that time to the various functions and activities of the program. Financial resources include budget, materials, equipment, and facilities. Political resources include policy support as well as support by individuals within the building and the community.

At this point, the guidance activities conducted in the current building program need to be arranged according to the comprehensive guidance and counseling program components, and the competencies that they assist students to attain need to be specified. A listing of clients the building program serves needs to be made, not by names of specific individuals but by categories and by numbers. For example, it is important to know how many or what percentage of students in the building receive preventive, remedial, or crisis assistance; how many or what percentage of faculty receive consultation services; how many parents have sought consultation or referral services; and so on. Other data that districts and schools have found enlightening are the data regarding the mix of students and other clients served. It is important to know if the demographic mix of the clients actually served by the guidance and counseling program matches the demographic mix of the school. If it does not, that generates another set of goals. In fact, every bit of concrete data that can be gathered regarding the current program needs to be assembled, so that as the building staff develops its plan for change, it is grounded solidly in reality. A premise here is that the design of the current guidance and counseling program has emerged in response to the most immediate and most visible student, teacher, administrator, and parent needs. Thus the current program provides an informal assessment of these needs from these perspectives.

Assessing Building-Level Student and School Community Needs

Perceived Student Needs. Some program planners do this task before any other step in the planning process. The ASCA National Model (ASCA, 2005) stresses the value of gathering data and its use in focusing program planning, subsequent monitoring of student progress, and allowing for program accountability. Although this assessment can be done first, we do not believe the results will be as useful as those of one done during this phase of the program improvement process. A major reason we recommend waiting until this phase is that it is not until now that you have identified the student competencies for your program.

> A counseling needs assessment item which reveals a counseling need must be specific enough to indicate clearly that school counselor intervention is implicit and necessary for that particular student, even if that intervention is in terms of referral to a more appropriate source of assistance. The focus of a specific item, therefore, must be in an area in which [a school counselor] can take appropriate action on behalf of the child in question. (Thompson, Loesch, & Seraphine, 2003, p. 36)

In the type of assessment we are proposing, student competency statements become, in effect, the needs assessment items. In fact, this part of the designing process could just as well be called an inventory of student competencies—an inventory of where students are in competency development and where they should be in their competency acquisition. To illustrate how the competencies you have chosen can be converted to needs assessment items, we have provided examples in Table 6.5. From the competencies presented in chapter 3, we have selected one competency from Grade 1, one from Grade 8, and one from Grade 11. To show you what a needs assessment questionnaire using converted competencies looks like, a section of a questionnaire on life career planning competencies used for Grades 10, 11, and 12 is presented in Figure 6.2. (See Appendix A for a full list of competencies.)

Thompson et al. (2003) cautioned school counselors that "a results-based school counseling program necessitates the collection of data, but the data collected are meaningful and useful only to the extent that the means used to obtain them are psychometrically sound" (p. 38). They developed the Intermediate Elementary School Students Counseling Needs

Table 6.5
Competencies as Needs Assessment Items

1st grade	
Competency:	Students will describe how exercise and nutrition affect their mental health.
Needs assessment:	I can tell how exercise and eating habits make a difference in how I think, act, and feel.
8th grade	
Competency:	Students will analyze effective family relations, their importance, and how they are formed.
Needs assessment:	I can tell why good family relations are important and how they are formed.
11th grade	
Competency:	Students will evaluate the need for flexibility in their roles and in their choices.
Needs assessment:	I can explain the need for flexibility in my roles and in my choices.

Figure 6.2
Life Career Planning

To fill out this questionnaire, students are asked to complete the following steps.

Step 1: *Read each sentence carefully.* Each one describes things students are able to do in order to demonstrate learning in that particular area.

Now make a decision. Are you able to do what the sentence describes? Are you not able to do what the sentence describes?

Fill in the circle that shows what you think.

If you think you are able to do what the sentence describes . . . fill in circle A   (A) (B) | (C)

If you think you are not able to do what the sentence describes . . . fill in circle B   (A) (B) | (C)

Step 2: *Choose the five sentences on each page that describe what you would really be interested in learning to do.* Some of the statements will really interest you and some will not. *In the second column (circles are lettered C), fill in the circle for each of the five statements that you feel/ you need to learn how to accomplish.*

For example, if you feel you would really be interested in learning to analyze how characteristics and abilities develop, you would mark as follows:

I can

1. describe and analyze how an individual's characteristics and abilities develop.   (A) (B) | (C)

The statements that follow are about things you can do to show you are preparing yourself for the future and are able to make decisions about what you want to do in your life. Review your instruction sheet carefully. Then fill in the circle that shows what you think about that statement.

I can

1. evaluate the importance of having laws and contracts to protect producers.   (A) (B) | (C)
2. provide examples of decisions I have made based on my attitudes and values.   (A) (B) | (C)
3. analyze the decision-making process used by others.   (A) (B) | (C)
4. distinguish between alternatives that involve varying degrees of risk.   (A) (B) | (C)
5. evaluate the importance of setting realistic goals and working toward them.   (A) (B) | (C)
6. describe my rights and responsibilities as a producer.   (A) (B) | (C)
7. explain and analyze how values affect my decisions, actions, and lifestyles.   (A) (B) | (C)
8. identify decisions I have made and analyze how they will affect my future decisions.   (A) (B) | (C)
9. analyze the consequences of decisions others make.   (A) (B) | (C)
10. explain how my values, interests, and capabilities have changed and are changing.   (A) (B) | (C)
11. speculate what my rights and obligations might be as a producer in the future.   (A) (B) | (C)
12. summarize the importance of understanding my attitudes and values and how they affect my life.   (A) (B) | (C)
13. use the decision-making process when making a decision.   (A) (B) | (C)
14. provide examples and evaluate my current ability to generate alternatives, gather information, and assess the consequences in the decisions I make.   (A) (B) | (C)
15. assess my ability to achieve past goals and integrate this knowledge for the future.   (A) (B) | (C)

Survey based on *The National Standards for School Counseling Programs* (Campbell & Dahir, 1997). It is "a psychometrically sound needs assessment instrument appropriate for use with students in the upper three grades of an elementary school" (p. 36).

Needs assessment is commonly described as a way of determining the discrepancy between what exists and what is desired. If this practice is observed rigidly, only contemporary needs will be recognized, and the needs of the past, or those that already have been met, may be overlooked. When asked to respond to a needs statement, individuals are justified in asking whether it makes a difference if the statement represents a need they feel is important but is being satisfied or if the statement represents an unmet need. For program planning, it is important to know the needs that are being met as well as the needs that deserve additional attention.

An additional means for considering met needs is to review the needs being met in the current program. It is likely that current program activities grew out of a prior informal or formal needs assessment. If students' evaluations of their activities indicate that they are valuable, then it is a good assumption that the activities are meeting a relatively important need. The opportunity to respond to a relevant sampling of needs is another important point. Simply stated, How can a need be identified if no one presents the statement? Limited coverage, insignificant choices, or redundancy may distort a needs survey. We recommend that you develop your own needs assessment survey from the list of competencies you have established as essential in your program.

If your district is similar to those with which we have worked, more needs (competencies) will be identified than the program resources can provide for; thus one purpose of a needs assessment is to determine priorities for needs (competencies). Further, although there will be common needs (competencies) across a school district, there also may be differences as dictated by the needs of particular buildings in a district. If you are uneasy about or inexperienced in developing such surveys, you may find it advantageous to use an adopt–adapt strategy, that is, to select and modify needs statements from existing instruments rather than construct new ones. Be sure, however, to include a needs statement for each competency for which your program is accepting responsibility.

A final point to keep in mind is whose perceptions of students' needs should be assessed. The answer is those of anyone involved in the educational process, including those receiving education. This includes the following groups:

- *Students:* This group should receive top priority in any needs assessment. Who knows more about students than students? Students can tell you what they need as a group and as individuals. They will also let you know whether the current program is meeting their needs.
- *Educators:* Assessing members of this group will give you their perceptions of students' needs as well as perceptions of their own needs.
- *Parents:* Members of this group will help you identify what they feel their children should learn from school experiences. Including parents in the needs assessment process offers them an opportunity for involvement in planning the guidance and counseling program. As a result of their personal involvement, they may be more willing to offer their support.
- *Community members:* Included in this group are individuals who are not employers yet support the school financially. Information from this group may give a somewhat different perspective on the information gained from an assessment of parents.
- *Employers:* Those who are responsible for hiring graduates of your school system or for hiring students still in school have definite ideas about the outcomes of education they expect. Including employers in the needs assessment process will give the

school an opportunity to know what employers expect as well as offer the employers a chance to know more about the guidance and counseling program.

- *Graduates:* An assessment of members of this group can provide information about the effectiveness of the guidance and counseling program for those who are applying their skills in post-high-school pursuits. They can help identify areas that are of the most benefit as well as areas that need strengthening.

Because of time and resource limitations, you may not be able to assess all of these groups about student needs. If you must restrict the number of groups to be assessed, students and educators should receive attention first by virtue of being the most immediately involved. It may be that you could assess students and educators the first year and members of the other groups during following years, or it may be that you could use a formalized, paper-and-pencil assessment with students and educators and a less exacting strategy with parents and employers, such as a discussion format with a representative group. Each of these groups should, however, be assessed at some point in the periodic needs assessment process.

School Community Needs. Although students are the primary clients of the guidance and counseling program, it is important to remember that there are other clients whose actual and perceived needs must be surveyed and addressed as well. The school as a whole, individual teachers and administrators, other school specialists, and parents are all clients in one way or another. Some student needs are best identified by a thorough understanding of the community in which the students live. It is imperative that in helping students' personal, social, career, and educational development, you are knowledgeable about what those developmental areas and stages mean within the community and cultural contexts.

As we begin the 21st century—which marks only the beginning of the second century of education for everyone regardless of economic or social class—individual schools are challenged to assess and respond to the needs of their students in relation to specifically defined academic standards. Schools are encouraged to respond at each site as they determine the best uses of resources to achieve their goals for raising students' achievement levels. Progress toward these standards by individual students and by a school as a whole is often measured by standardized tests (criterion referenced to a state's standards).

This accountability and site-based decision-making system provides both challenges and opportunities for guidance and counseling program planners. School counselors are challenged to relate their programs and outcomes to the overall improvement and success of the school. In other words, they must be part of the site-based decision-making process and be clear as to which school goals their programs contribute most meaningfully. In most buildings, the students who are most challenging academically are those whose personal and social needs are greatest. School counselors' work with these students in helping them remove or overcome their barriers to successful learning is a key part of a building's school improvement plan. School counselors and their expertise are valuable assets to most of the schoolwide improvement efforts that we are aware of (such as goal setting, character development, social responsibility).

In addition, individual and specialized groups of teachers, parents, other school specialists, and administrators can identify ways in which the guidance and counseling program can assist them in addressing specific students' or sets of students' needs. A survey of these needs should be related to the student competencies you are seeking to develop or enhance. For example, ask teachers to respond to items in terms of their needs for assisting students attain the desired competency. Using the same examples as we did for the student needs assessment (see Table 6.5), we present a sample of teacher items in Table 6.6.

Assessing staff needs for system support activities is also important. This needs assessment can be focused in two ways. You can assess your clients' needs for system support ac-

Table 6.6
Teacher Needs Assessment

1st grade

Student competency:	Students will describe how exercise and nutrition affect their mental health.
Teacher need:	I need assistance in helping students learn to tell how exercise and eating habits make a difference in how they think, act, and feel.

8th grade

Student competency:	Students will analyze effective family relations, their importance, and how they are formed.
Teacher need:	I need assistance in helping students learn why good family relations are important and how they are formed.

11th grade

Student competency:	Students will evaluate the need for flexibility in their roles and in their choices.
Teacher need:	I need assistance in helping students learn to explain the need for flexibility in their roles and in their choices.

tivities performed in the current program, or you can assess their perceived needs for the proposed activities of the desired program. If the latter is your aim, this assessment cannot be done in a building until after the desired program has been established. At this time, however, it may be relevant to assess perceived needs for current activities or those you are thinking of doing, using the district's suggested activities. If conducted in the appropriate context—for example, in conjunction with the assessment of student needs—you will probably build a powerful case for reassigning some of the typical quasi-administrative and clerical tasks to other personnel. Staff assessment will identify their perceptions of the need for school counselors to do such tasks as senior credit checks or bus duty supervision. You also will identify tasks to be displaced or streamlined, such as recommending students for above- or below-average-level course offerings or coordinating the testing program.

The context data gathered in clarifying the current program design suggest some needs inherent in the community served by the school. Different communities send their children to school with variations in such things as school readiness, parent involvement in and support of schooling, feelings of personal safety, optimism about the future, and cultural congruence with the culture of the school.

Such variations must be factored into program planning. In addition to addressing these needs with the students, you can identify topics that you need to address in faculty and parent workshops and consultation sessions.

Designing the Desired Building-Level Program

Armed with the district's model for a properly balanced and comprehensive guidance and counseling program, with data regarding their students' and other clients' needs, and with concrete information about the design of their current guidance and counseling program, the building guidance staff, with the assistance of the school–community advisory committee, must now design their desired building guidance and counseling program. The vision of the comprehensive guidance and counseling program is made realistic in the buildings through a clearly stated operational definition. The operational definition includes both the qualitative and quantitative designs and must reflect what is desired tempered by the reality of available resources. It must be written rather than oral, for all the reasons explained heretofore.

The building description of its desired program should include the same parts as does the district program description. There should be a statement of the rationale for the building program, using local needs and demographic data, as described in chapter 4, that support its unique design. The assumptions should mirror the district's philosophical statement but, in addition, be localized to incorporate the philosophy of the building and its surrounding community. The program definition should likewise mirror the district's definition but provide specific detail for the desired structure and balance of the program. The competencies students are to attain as a result of participating in the school's guidance and counseling program need to be listed. Following the district-established minimum expectations, the building design needs to spell out the following for each component of the delivery system:

- *definition:* purpose and characteristics
- *clients served:* identified and prioritized
- *content:* topics and priorities, materials used
- *staff roles:* school counselors and other staff
- *modes of delivery:* basic activities and how they are done
- *scheduling:* such items as how often students benefit and when during the school day/year
- *resources available:* relevant building-established policies and procedures, budget, facilities, equipment; school counselors' time
- *evaluation strategies:* specific to the results students are expected to achieve, the activities of each component that are conducted, and the roles fulfilled by school counselors

As you can see, this basic design is quite lengthy, but its development forces the local planning/designing group to make the operational decisions essential to program implementation. Once this document is developed, it stays in place until a revision is needed. Although 8 to 10 years is the suggested length of time before complete redesign is undertaken, the actual length should be based on such factors as changes in the school's priorities, community, administration, or guidance staff. Annual program plans are also made to incorporate newly identified needs and goals, as is discussed further in chapter 8.

An important consideration in writing the description of the program that is desired for your building is the format you will use to present the program. As you no doubt have gleaned from the preceding discussion, the write-up must be as specific as you can make it, complete with the listing of materials and other resources you will use in program delivery. A committee of school counselors from the various school levels of your district needs to be formed to establish the format to be used by all buildings. Whatever format is chosen (and districts we have worked with have chosen different formats), the format must make sense to the school counselors and to others who will be reading and using the program design. Further, the same format must be used by all buildings so that the quality of programs can be judged across the district and consistency ensured across the district. A format that has been used to summarize program activities is presented in Figure 6.3. This format serves as a vehicle for identifying all activities provided for a certain competency (skill), a specific set of student clients (grade level; developmental, preventive, remedial), or a particular program component. The school counselors have found it a relatively easy and understandable vehicle for displaying their repertoire of activities. These provide the detail behind the yearly program calendar.

Once the program for a building has been written, building school counselors can work with their administration and faculty to show them what the guidance and counseling pro-

Figure 6.3
Sample Format to Summarize Building-Level Program Activities

Building Name: _____

COMPREHENSIVE GUIDANCE PROGRAM
Identification of Activities

STUDENT SKILL: _____ GRADE LEVEL: _____

| Student Need Level:
(Circle One) | Developmental | Preventive | Remedial |

| Program Component:
(Circle One) | Guidance Curriculum | Individual Student Planning |
| | Responsive Service | System Support |

INTENDED OUTCOMES: _____

_____

_____

_____

PROGRAM ACTIVITIES AND RESOURCES:

Activity Title	Resource Materials	Calendar Notations (Date/Length of Activity)

gram for their building is. The appropriate roles for the school counselors can be clarified. Current activities can be judged as appropriate or inappropriate for the use of school counselors' time. The school counselor–student ratio can be evaluated, and if it is not appropriate, the principal, teachers, parents, and students can be enlisted in the struggle to improve it. Where better procedures are needed for delivering activities, a building team can be charged to develop them. Having established what is desirable, building staff can develop guidance and counseling program budget requests and renovate facilities. With a concretely drawn vision in hand, the building staff, in collaboration with the district staff, can work together to specify and implement the changes needed to attain the desired building programs.

With development of the design for each building's desired program, the designing phase of the program development efforts is finished. You are ready to make the transition to program implementation. Before we move on to suggestions for making the transition to the new program, however, it is time to consider expanding the leadership base for the program implementation efforts.

Attending to Diversity

As it was important in the previous phases of program development, attending to diversity is important in this phase in which you move from design to implementation. A plan for capitalizing on the rich diversity of the schools and district should be a component of every plan for program improvement.

Many schools and districts with which we have worked have identified discrepancies in their levels of service to minority students or to students who were from cultural, ethnic, and/or economic backgrounds different from those of the school counselors. Gaps in school counselors' multicultural competence were discussed in chapter 5. While included in the ASCA's National Standards (Campbell & Dahir, 1997) as "recognize, accept, and appreciate ethnic and cultural diversity" and "individual differences" and "recognize and respect differences in various family configurations" (p. 29), content targeted at helping students improve their cross-cultural effectiveness is often overlooked or avoided, no matter the demographics of the school community. Goals for filling in these program gaps must be included in the strategic plan for guidance and counseling program change. It is, however, our experience that every community is culturally different from every other community; thus at the district level diversity might be recognized globally, but each building and school community should be very specific about how its guidance and counseling program will be culturally responsive.

It is the guidance and counseling program district- and building-level leaders' responsibility to scrutinize the district's guidance program framework and building guidance program designs as well as the program improvement plans to ensure attention to the challenges and opportunities afforded by the diversity present in the district's and school's populations. The counseling field may be ahead of other disciplines in recognizing the importance of attending to the diversity of students and helping them to capitalize on the riches that diversity brings, not suffer from others' ignorance or prejudice—overt or covert. For others, discussions of diversity-related topics and issues may be uncomfortable; it is imperative that school counselors advocate for creating a climate that is culturally inclusive.

Expand the Leadership Base

If you are the district guidance and counseling program leader and are approaching implementation of a redesigned districtwide program, you will benefit from expanding your leadership base at this point. To date, leadership has been provided by the school counselors on the steering and school–community advisory committees. In addition, there are other designated leaders of school counselors—the building guidance and counseling program staff leaders (Henderson & Gysbers, 1998)—who have had some responsibility for the program improvement efforts and who will have much more responsibility as you move into building program redesign and implementation.

The leadership base should be expanded in two ways at this juncture:

- increase the number of school counselors developing appropriate program activities
- enhance the leadership role of the building guidance and counseling program and staff leaders

In some cases, the program development leaders are building guidance and counseling program and staff leaders, but by establishing two different categories of leaders, some options are provided in selecting leaders for program development. Thus the program development leaders are those who assist in districtwide implementation of the new program and new program activities; they are the program innovators. The building guidance and counseling program and staff leaders are the managers of the program as implemented in the buildings; they are the program maintainers. They are accountable for program implementation.

The guidance and counseling program and staff leader for the district needs to be cognizant of the strengths and weakness of the designated, formal school counselor leaders in the buildings—the building guidance and counseling program and staff leaders—and needs to identify potentially successful program development peer leaders to build a strong leadership team for program implementation. In fact, one of the issues critical to effective comprehensive guidance program implementation identified in the national survey of school guidance and counseling program leaders and practitioners was that of empowering guidance leaders in schools and districts (Henderson & Gysbers, 2002). Clarifications of their roles and of their delegated authority are essential; that is, what are they supposed to do, and how are they connected to the organizational structure of the building and of the district? With both sets of leaders in hand, the tasks each group will do then need to be specified, and the leaders have to be trained to do the tasks and must have opportunities to use their designated roles. The efforts they make need to be recognized and reinforced.

Building-Level Guidance and Counseling Program and Staff Leaders

For comprehensive guidance programs to be implemented successfully, leaders must be designated for each building (Henderson & Gysbers, 1998). In anticipation of the positive leadership that will be needed from them, they need to have their roles enhanced and supported. As just mentioned, the building guidance and counseling program and staff leaders in each building may already be in place, so identifying them is not a challenge, but becoming familiar with their operational style may be. Further, because the district guidance and counseling program and staff leader (Henderson & Gysbers, 1998) has the chance to participate in the selection of new building guidance and counseling program and staff leaders, he or she needs to work diligently and skillfully with principals to ensure the selection of individuals who are aligned with the new program. In our experience, building principals want someone who will be loyal to them and to their school, but they will leave the assessment of the individual candidates' guidance and counseling expertise to the district guidance and counseling program and staff leader. Principals also want someone who will provide good leadership to the building program and who will work to make their building program the "best in the district."

If you are the district guidance and counseling program and staff leader and if you have not already begun to assist the building guidance and counseling program and staff leaders to fulfill their roles more fully, you should begin at this time. Many districts with which we have worked have not spelled out their responsibilities. If your district does not have a specific job description for building guidance and counseling program and staff leaders, one needs to be developed. If you are starting from scratch, you may want to consider the position guide originally developed in Northside Independent School District, expanded in *Leading and Managing Your School Guidance Program Staff* (Henderson & Gysbers, 1998) and provided in Figure 6.4. We suggest, however, that you begin the development of their job description with the building guidance and counseling program and staff leaders themselves. By being asked what they do that is unique to their role, they not only develop an investment in the job description but also begin thinking of themselves as different from and leaders of the campus staff. They need to be identified as the on-campus program managers and supervisors of the guidance staff.

Once responsibilities are specified, you need to assist guidance and counseling program and staff leaders to develop the skills they need to carry them out. If they are not internalizing the new program concept, you need to help them do that. You can help them through programmatic discussions in regularly scheduled meetings and by modeling for them during building school counselor staff meetings. They, too, want to do the best job they can, and they can benefit from a role model.

Because of the lack of specialized training for building guidance and counseling program and staff leaders and the dearth of literature on the subject, they probably need inservice education and training on the staff leadership aspects of their jobs, including supervision. This is detailed in *Leading and Managing Your School Guidance Program*

Figure 6.4
Building Guidance Program and Staff Leader Position Guide

Title:	*Building Guidance Program and Staff Leader*
Primary Functions:	As a member of guidance department staff, fulfill the role of school counselor as described in the position guides; as the leader of the guidance department, effect the continuous improvement of the guidance program and personnel performance.
Major Job Responsibilities:	1. Implement the campus comprehensive guidance and counseling program and specifically provide services to meet the special needs of his/her caseload. 2. Administer the campus guidance program. 3. Lead the guidance department staff. 4. Contribute to the development of the district's guidance program, policies, and procedures. 5. Provide leadership to buildingwide goals and practices in cooperation with building administrators.
Key Duties:	1. *Implement the campus comprehensive guidance and counseling program and specifically provide services to meet the special needs of his/her caseload:* please refer to the appropriate level position guide. 2. *Administer the campus guidance program:* lead the development and implementation of the campus guidance program consistent with the district and school goals and objectives; prepare request for and use allocation of department budget; conduct campus guidance department meetings; represent the guidance department to the administration and to other department coordinators; supervise the maintenance of student records and other guidance department procedures. 3. *Lead the guidance department staff:* supervise the department staff; assist the principal and director of guidance in observations and evaluations of staff; assist the principal in selection of new counselors; assist the principal and director of guidance in providing staff development programs. 4. *Contribute to the development of the district guidance program, policies, and procedures:* represent the campus staff at the district building guidance program and staff leader meetings; communicate and promote implementation of district policies and procedures. 5. *Provide leadership to buildingwide goals and practices in cooperation with building administrators:* participate as a member of building leadership teams; assist in the development of schoolwide policies and workable procedures; provide input to and from the guidance department and the administration; cooperate with administration in mutually relevant program efforts and student cases.
Organizational Relationships:	Is supervised by the principal and the director of guidance; supervises and coordinates the work of department staff, professional and paraprofessional; collaborates with administration; cooperates with district and campus instructional staff leaders.
Performance Standards:	A building guidance program and staff leader's performance is considered satisfactory when 1. the principal and director of guidance concur and the building guidance program and staff leader's level of competence is reflected as such on the Northside Independent School District Building Guidance Program and Staff Leader Evaluation Form; and 2. evaluation of the Annual Guidance Program Plan indicates overall effectiveness of the program.

Staff (Henderson & Gysbers, 1998) and is discussed in more depth in chapter 9. Eleven essential leadership skills were identified in the examples of leaders who successfully resolved critical issues (Henderson & Gysbers, 2002):

1. Be sensitive and responsive to others' needs.
2. Accept reality.
3. Be open to and accepting of others.
4. Build rapport with others.
5. Communicate and collaborate with others.
6. Maintain the integrity of your professional value/belief system.
7. Accept responsibility for what is yours.
8. Accept the consequences of your actions.
9. Develop and make good use of support systems and the resources available to you.

10. Recognize that we are all works-in-progress.
11. Set improvement goals and plan how to achieve them. (p. 256)

Particularly critical to making optimum use of the program's resources is a team approach to program implementation: "A team is a group of people working together to achieve mutual goals" (Henderson & Gysbers, 1998, p. 62). Teams do not just happen; they have to be created and nurtured. Guidance program staff leaders should be trained in this important leadership dimension. Regularly held staff meetings are essential, because they provide opportunities for empowering individuals and the group as a whole, and for team maintenance as well as for accomplishing program-related tasks, communicating information, and carrying out departmental business. In addition, most building guidance and counseling program and staff leaders we have worked with have sought help in learning such basic skills as how to conduct effective meetings, provide constructive criticism, build a team, and help staff set appropriate goals.

If the district is large enough, or if there are neighboring districts/schools with which to cooperate, the building guidance and counseling program and staff leaders enjoy providing a support system for each other, that is, being a team of their own. This provides them a support group that serves to enhance their growth as building leaders. They need to be supported as they try out new strategies and as they carry out the guidance and counseling program leaders' assignments. As discussed previously, they should be held accountable for the on-campus discussions of the district program framework and other topics related to the new program. As districtwide mandates are given for implementing new program activities, building guidance and counseling program and staff leaders should be held accountable for seeing that they are performed.

The building guidance and counseling program and staff leaders will need to have their authority supported in their newly defined roles. As they supervise and monitor their staff members, their leadership must be recognized, and the central office guidance and counseling program leader should model this recognition for the school counselors. Building guidance and counseling program and staff leaders' effectiveness will mirror the amount of authority that is delegated to them. In this area, the principal's role is also key. The principals want their department heads to be effective; it makes the principals' job easier. The more work that is done through the building guidance and counseling program and staff leaders and with the principals, the clearer the building guidance and counseling program and staff leaders' responsibilities for campus program operation.

Districtwide Program Development Leaders

What we are calling program development leaders, Adelman and Taylor (2003) labeled as the "change team" (p. 13). This team "has responsibility for coalition building, implementing the strategic plan, and maintaining . . . oversight, problem solving, conflict resolution and so forth" (p. 13). Depending on the size of the district and the representation on the steering committee, it is probable that the number of program development leaders will need to be expanded by involving more school counselors as improved program implementation approaches. Program development leaders should be chosen from school counselors who are visibly supportive of the new program directions, have enough vision to be able to anticipate the benefits of the improved program, are either informal or formal leaders of other school counselors, and are creative innovators.

To identify these individuals, the steering committee school counselors should be consulted. They need to feel comfortable with the new additions to their group as they have responsibility for bringing these new leaders on board and working with them. Their recommendations do not have to be binding, but their thoughts and concerns need to be attended to. Again, it depends on the size of the district, but even in reasonably small districts school counselors may not know each other from one building to the next. The person with primary responsibility for the program development efforts is the one with the broader perspective.

After identifying the school counselors who are going to be brought onto the program development leadership team, you must take time to ensure that they feel comfortable in their understanding of the comprehensive program concept. That they were selected because of their initial understanding and support of the new concepts helps; and although initiation does not take a great amount of time, it does need to be done. At the same time, the expanded group needs to be built into a cohesive team of workers. This is accomplished by clarifying the roles and tasks that they need to help accomplish. The model that worked effectively in Northside Independent School District was to develop subgroups of experts for each component; that is, subcommittees were formed for each component—a guidance curriculum committee, an individual student planning committee, a responsive services committee, and a system support committee. Each committee had representation from each of the school levels—elementary, middle, and high school. Thus the total group also could be divided by level grouping, which was later useful for certain activities. A major responsibility of each committee was being the voice of its particular component to its colleagues.

A task for the committees to accomplish that is a good place to start is coordinating the collection of current practices that are examples of implementation of the various components. For instance, the curriculum committee collects sample guidance lessons and units that assist students at various grade levels to reach the priority competencies; the individual student planning committee collects samples of activities that help students develop personalized educational or career plans; the responsive services committee collects samples of exemplary counseling, consulting, and referral practices. When compiled, these collections become resource guides for all school counselors to use as they add to their programs.

The program development leadership team then has the data it needs to become truly expert in the implementation of the components at the relevant school levels. After being trained in the component definitions and after reviewing and selecting the multiple exemplary practices, the team is equipped to disseminate these ideas to its colleagues. We also have found that they too benefit from training in leadership skills so that they can present themselves as peer leaders.

The more the team members are used as leaders, the more depth their role takes on. If they are collecting materials for resource guides, let them plan the guide formats and their own processes for collecting the materials and for acknowledging other school counselors who are taking strides in the new direction. Provide them the opportunities they need to communicate with their colleagues; that is, call meetings as they need them, support their efforts with the rest of the school counselors, and so on. They operate from the power that is delegated to them; this delegation must be clear to the total group of school counselors.

Resource guide development is not the only task that a program leadership team can take on. As you approach implementation of the new program, many innovative or pilot efforts will need to be tried. Such efforts might be curriculum writing, experimenting with new activities (including the use of teacher advisory systems like the one described in chapter 3), or developing a recommended protocol for a campus response to a student suicide. Program leaders might take on the responsibility for designing the district's staff development plan. Whatever the project, the same principles apply. The team leaders' task needs to be given distinctly, their expertise developed carefully, and their authority recognized clearly.

If motivated and professionally committed individuals have been selected, and if they have been given meaningful tasks to do, they will be working hard at something that their colleagues may still be dubious about. It is imperative that their work and their worth be reinforced. Rewards for professionals, according to Hurst (1984, p. 84), may come from any of six motivators: "Achievement (what you believe you did), Recognition (what others think you did), Work itself (what you really do), Responsibility (what you help others do), Advancement (what you think you can do), Growth (what you believe you might do)." Program leaders feel a sense of achievement in completing each task that is part of their charge, for example, when the position statements or resource guides are published. They receive recognition by their very selection to be a program leader, and this is maintained as they present new concepts and ideas to their peers. We have found that encouraging them to make presentations at local, state, and national professional growth conferences not only is good for the emerging leaders but also helps others learn from what they are doing. If the new program leaders have been selected as we suggested from the ranks of those who believe in the new program concept, the work they do to better understand the new program and to help implement it is rewarding to them. If part of their charge is to help their colleagues learn about and implement new program strategies, the leaders are vitally responsible for the successful implementation of the program and for the effective performance of the rest of the counseling staff. Program leaders can be helped to feel like leaders and to envision themselves as the building guidance and counseling program and staff leaders and guidance supervisors/administrators of the future. Program innovators with whom we have worked consistently talk about how much they are learning from their experiences; they are eager to grow and find new opportunities, such as program improvement, as fuel for their own professional development.

District-Level Guidance and Counseling Program Leader Roles and Responsibilities

This phase of the guidance and counseling program improvement project results in a shift in overt leadership from the steering committee and the school–community advisory committee to the guidance and counseling program leaders. If you are the district guidance and counseling program and staff leader, the district master plan for program improvement becomes the responsibility of your office. You also are responsible for helping building staffs plan their improved programs. You have program management and administrative tasks as well as staff leadership and supervision tasks to accomplish. You also need to be clear about how much of the new design can be implemented with the currently available resources. Expectations for immediate change must be realistic.

As in the prior phases, you must as the guidance and counseling program leader continue to be the prime mover. Although we describe the process as though tasks are done one at a time, in reality many activities go on simultaneously. For example, while you are developing the master plan, you also are helping buildings assess their current program, and you will be training your new leaders and providing supervisory in-service to building guidance and counseling program and staff leaders. Again, it is up to you to keep each part of the project moving along a constructive course. You must use every opportunity to reinforce positively the individual change efforts the school counselors make. You are probably the only individual in the district who sees the whole picture, although by this time the expanded program leadership team and the building guidance and counseling program and staff leaders are beginning to see a lot of it, too, provided you keep them informed.

In all likelihood, there are some tasks in this project phase that only you can do. You need to compile and present the discrepancy data, that is, display the data and note the conclusions. You need to maintain an open discussion climate as staff members brainstorm ideas for discrepancy reduction. You need to write the district master plan and select and train the coleaders. You need to be prepared to use the expanded or redirected resources that begin to flow to the guidance department as soon as the steering committee makes its recommendations for changes. If ratios improve, you will be hiring more school counselors, and your selection criteria must be tailored to identify those who will fit into the new program. If your department receives a higher budget allocation, you need to be prepared to spend it. If you are allowed facility improvements, you need to have your blueprints ready. If school counselors' contracts are extended, you need to have your in-service training or program development activities ready to implement. This is the part of the project that is most fun, but it also represents challenges for you.

By now many of those with whom you work, including fellow administrators as well as school counselors, are beginning to get the program concept. This, too, is exciting; but you may find the school counselors frustrated that they have not been freed yet of all the undesirable system support activities and the administrators frustrated that school counselors are not yet seeing all their students more often. You need to transform these frustrations into the energies that will cause the needed changes. The will to overcome the inertia simply to maintain the current program as it is comes from being dissatisfied with the current status, having a vision of how the situation could be better, and believing that the benefits you will reap when the vision becomes reality outweigh the anticipated costs of changing.

Concluding Thoughts

The school counselors and principals will use their energy as they begin to feel empowered to make the needed changes. Empowerment comes from having knowledge and information, the support of others, and leadership. In the process we are recommending, the vision of the desired program and the data gathered in assessing your current program provide the knowledge and information. According to the principles of total quality leadership and the professional school counselor (Burgess & Dedmond, 1994; Schmoker & Wilson, 1993), in the system of interrelated parts that make up the school, the support of other stakeholders in the school community comes through soliciting others' input and advice, such as surveys and advisory committees. The leadership is provided by the district model and by the committed leaders you are nurturing. Ultimately, all school counselors become leaders of change because they have the guidance expertise and they are the biggest stakeholders in the program. Helping them find the courage they need to use their assertion skills appropriately is your responsibility.

You probably will—and possibly should—feel at this point that you are constantly swimming upstream, explaining rationale, defending recommendations; but each constructive change begets another. Ultimately, the momentum for change takes over. At this time you are moving into the implementation phase of the program improvement project.

References

Adelman, H. S., & Taylor, L. (2003). On sustainability of project innovations as systemic change. *Journal of Educational and Psychological Consultations, 14*(1), 1–25.

American School Counselor Association. (2005). *The ASCA national model: A framework for school counseling programs* (2nd ed.). Alexandria, VA: Author.

Burgess, D., & Dedmond, R. (1994). *Quality leadership and the professional school counselor.* Alexandria, VA: American Counseling Association.

Campbell, C. A., & Dahir, C. A. (1997). *Sharing the vision: The national standards for school counseling programs.* Alexandria, VA: American School Counselor Association.

Gray, K., Elsner, D., & Poynton, T. (2004, September 13). *Study of pupil personnel ratios, services, and programs in California* (School Counseling Research Brief 2.4). Amherst: University of Massachusetts, Center for School Counseling Outcome Research. Retrieved from http://www.umass.edu/schoolcounseling

Henderson, P., & Gysbers, N. C. (1998). *Leading and managing your school guidance program staff.* Alexandria, VA: American Counseling Association.

Henderson, P., & Gysbers, N. (Eds.). (2002). *Implementing comprehensive school guidance programs: Critical leadership issues and successful responses.* Greensboro, NC: CAPS.

Hurst, D. K. (1984). Of boxes, bubbles, and effective management. *Harvard Business Review, 62,* 78–88.

North Carolina Department of Public Instruction. (n.d.). *How North Carolina school counselors spend their time.* Retrieved July, 30, 2003, from http://www.ncpublicschools.org/curriculum/guidance/time.htm

Northside Independent School District. (1986). *Comprehensive guidance program framework.* San Antonio, TX: Author.

Rylander, C. K. (2002, August). *Guiding our children toward success: How Texas school counselors spend their time.* Austin, TX: Office of the Comptroller.

Schmoker, M., & Wilson, R. B. (1993). Transforming schools through total quality education. *Phi Delta Kappan, 74,* 389–395.

Texas Education Agency. (1998). *A model developmental guidance and counseling program for Texas public schools: A guide for program development, pre-K–12th grades* (3rd ed.). Austin, TX: Author.

Texas Education Agency. (2004). *A model comprehensive, developmental guidance and counseling program for Texas public schools: A guide for program development, pre-K–12th grade* (4th ed.). Austin, TX: Author.

Texas Education Code. (2001). *Chapter 33, Service programs and extra-curricular activities; Subchapter A, School counselors and counseling programs.* Retrieved from http://www.capitol.state.tx.us/statutes/ed/ed0003300.html

Thompson, D. W., Loesch, L. C., & Seraphine, A. E. (2003). Development of an instrument to assess the counseling needs of elementary school students. *Professional School Counseling, 7*(1), 35–39.

Vandergrift, J. A. (1999, April). *Are Arizona public schools making the best use of school counselors? Results of a 3-year study of counselors' time use* (Arizona School to Work Briefing Paper No. 16). Tempe: Arizona State University, Morrison Institute for Public Policy.

Part III

Implementing

Chapter 7

Making the Transition to a Comprehensive Guidance and Counseling Program

Implementing—Making the Transition

- Develop the personnel, financial, and political resources needed for full program implementation.
- Focus on special projects.
- Facilitate building-level changes.
- Implement public relations activities.

☞ Having organized for change, adopted a comprehensive guidance and counseling program model, assessed the current program, established the design for the desired program, and planned the transition, you, as the guidance and counseling program leader, are now ready to make the transition to an improved program. You also are ready to develop mechanisms to maintain the program once it is in operation. This is one of the most critical phases of the entire program improvement process. The questions to be answered include, How is the transition to a comprehensive guidance and counseling program to be made? What new resources are needed to enhance the effectiveness and efficiency of the program? Are there special projects that will provide impetus to the needed changes in direction? How can we assist each building to improve its program?

This chapter first discusses the tasks involved in implementing the master plan for change and presents recommendations concerning the staffing patterns and the financial and political resources required to operate a comprehensive guidance and counseling program. The change strategy of focusing on special projects is then introduced. Attaching the guidance and counseling program improvement process to federal, state, and local priorities can provide the energy, motivation, and support to carry the overall improvement process to completion. Next, the chapter describes how to facilitate the building-level changes required to implement the district comprehensive guidance and counseling program fully in each building, as well as how to institute a districtwide system for monitoring program changes and overall program implementation at the building level to ensure that the program does not revert to its original, traditional operation. We also present ideas about planning and implementing, with district leadership, public relations activities to make sure that students, teachers, parents, administrators, and the public at large are aware of the remodeled and revitalized comprehensive guidance and counseling program. Next, we focus on methods for attending to the diversity in the district and buildings. Finally, the chapter delineates the roles and responsibilities of guidance and counseling program leaders in the transition process.

Develop the Personnel, Financial, and Political Resources Needed for Full Program Implementation

In developing the master plan for system-level resource development, the guidance and counseling program leader with the help of the guidance steering committee identified the major tasks that needed to be done, developed an order for doing them, and identified people who would be involved in accomplishing them. Plans of action to accomplish the major tasks also might need to be developed to facilitate the efficiency of those responsible. A plan of action includes several parts: identification of the tasks to be done, the order in which they must be done, the person(s) doing them, the time for accomplishing them, and a statement of how you will know they have been done, that is, identification of the end product or result. Table 7.1 presents a sample plan of action from the Northside Independent School District master plan.

The tasks that need to be done, their degree of feasibility, and the specific time frame for each building or district may be different. For example, if the school system is currently into curriculum writing, then resource/curriculum guide development fits right into already established district priorities. Or if the system's thrust is staff development, then the recommendations for in-service training, job description development or supervision, and performance evaluation improvement might be the most feasible to accomplish. Of course, any systemic improvement of resources requires the support and collaboration of the district administration. The guidance and counseling program leader must continue to work closely with the superintendent and other senior-level administrators to effect needed changes.

There are, however, some recurrent recommendations that need attention for the program actually to change. Ideas that the guidance and counseling program leader might want to consider for the improved use of personnel, financial, and political guidance and counseling program resources as the master plan for change is implemented are included in the following list and explained in detail in this section.

Personnel Resources
1. Implementing recommended counselor–student ratios
2. Developing school counselors' job descriptions
3. Establishing roles and responsibilities for building-level guidance and counseling program leaders
4. Developing job descriptions for other staff members working in the guidance and counseling program
5. Clarifying organizational relationships within the guidance and counseling program

Financial Resources
6. Establishing budgets for guidance departments at the district and building levels
7. Exploring use of other-than-local funding sources
8. Developing guidance and counseling program component resource guides
9. Establishing guidance facilities standards and making recommendations for their application

Table 7.1
Plan of Action

Major Task	Enabling Tasks	Person Responsible	Date to Be Completed	Resources Needed	Comment
Make recommendations regarding extended contracts	1. Develop questionnaire	1. Director of guidance	1. March 1	None additional	
	2. "Train" steering committee counselors and principals to conduct survey with counselors/principals using questionnaire	2. Director of guidance	2. March 5		
	3. Place on meeting agendas	3. Steering committee, principals, and counselors	3. March 5		
	4. Make presentation, conduct surveys	4. Steering committee, principals, and counselors	4. March 6–13		
	5. Tally results by school level (elementary, middle school, high school)	5. Director of guidance	5. March 20		
	6. Prepare report and make recommendations	6. Director of guidance	6. March 25		

Political Resources
10. Updating policies and procedures
11. Engendering support from building staff
12. Working with resistant staff members
13. Working with critical constituents: concerned parents

Personnel Resources

As the preceding list indicates, to improve use of personnel resources, you need to consider implementing recommended counselor–student ratios, developing counselors' job descriptions, establishing roles and responsibilities for building guidance and counseling program leaders, developing job descriptions for other staff members working in the guidance and counseling program, and clarifying organizational relationships within the guidance and counseling program.

Implementing Recommended Counselor–Student Ratios

Based on the rationale of the design for the desired program, recommendations have been established for appropriate counselor–student ratios. Ratio improvement, however, is one of the more difficult resource improvements to make for two reasons: It is extremely costly, and there must be some evidence that the counselors already in the system are willing to extend their services to all students. Once that intent has been established and some effort has been applied in that direction, justification for improved ratios is more credible.

As districts with which we have worked have implemented the comprehensive guidance and counseling program more fully, lower ratios have been put in place. Elementary counselors have been added in rather dramatic numbers in these program development projects. Further, many elementary guidance and counseling programs are developmentally based and thus are already closer to the desired program as defined by these districts than are secondary programs, which are traditionally entrenched in reactive services and system support or quasi-administrative/clerical tasks (Peer, 1985). No district with which we have worked has stated that counselors as supporters of the system should have top priority in the program; all of the districts have assigned high priority for all school levels to the guidance curriculum and to individual student planning assistance for *all* students at the middle and high school levels.

It should be clear that the effectiveness of the program is tied directly to the ratio. The number of counselors needed to staff the program depends on the students' and school community's needs and the program goals and design. Thus the ratio must be sufficient to implement the designed program; or conversely, the program has to be designed within the parameters of the ratio. The larger the counselor's caseload, the less individual attention students receive; the smaller the load, the more individual attention is allowed for. The larger the number of students in a caseload who have high-priority needs for responsive services, the lower the ratios must be. A mechanism for ensuring a match between the design and the ratio and for communicating the impact of the ratio on the realities of service delivery is discussed in more detail in chapter 8.

In school districts, salary costs often make up more than 80% of the budget. The salary costs associated with dramatic ratio improvement are high, tying this resource improvement to the district's overall financial situation and budget development procedures. The guidance and counseling program leader must present not only the rationale for the improvement but also the data that substantiate or project its value to students.

You also need to be prepared to implement the improvement incrementally. Stages of implementation might include extended counselor contracts so that there is more non-student time for them to accomplish some of the indirect services vital to success, such as planning and developing the program, benefiting from staff development activities, or accomplishing some of their system support responsibilities. Some districts have found it more feasible economically to raise existing counselors' salaries, because of increased recognition of their professionalism, than to lower their caseloads. Interim ratio improvements might occur. For example, instead of moving directly from a ratio of one elementary counselor per building to a ratio of 1:350, a 1:450 ratio might be affordable first.

A lowered caseload is one of the primary goals of program improvement, but it is one of the most difficult to attain. Thus we advise you to continue to implement other, more feasible changes while you are working toward that goal rather than waiting until ratios are improved to begin.

Developing School Counselors' Job Descriptions

Identifying the various personnel resources available to the guidance and counseling program brings with it the need to define the roles and functions of the various personnel to ensure appropriate use of their education and talents. The position guide format was discussed in chapter 5 as a means for outlining the school counselors' primary job responsibilities. In chapter 8 we suggest a process for specifying each counselor's job description each year by detailing the specific ways each applies their competencies within the yearly program plan (Henderson & Gysbers, 1998). The professional school counselor is trained to fulfill the roles required to deliver the comprehensive guidance and counseling program. (For a summary of their application within the program components, see chapter 4.)

Most school counselors fulfill comprehensive roles with their students; that is, they provide or are the links to the services needed by the students in their caseloads. Some school counselors may be assigned to carry out special program assignments or to serve special student groups. These special assignments often require additional training and may be tied to special funding sources, as described later in this chapter. Examples of special program assignments include guidance department leadership and crisis team membership. Examples of special student groups that may benefit from additional program services include students in compensatory education, special education, violence and substance abuse prevention programs, or career and technology education. It is essential to efficient implementation of the comprehensive guidance and counseling program that the services provided by such specialist counselors be integrated into the program delivery design. We recommend that position guides for these and other full-time, professional members of the guidance staff be developed and that they delineate clearly the organizational relationships among counseling professionals. Often these counseling positions are funded or partially funded by the other-than-guidance programs; so there are specific expectations agreed to in appropriating the money. Thus, specially funded counselors have some prescribed responsibilities to the program that funds them. Their responsibilities to both programs and their placement in the organizational structure need to be clear: They are, first and foremost, school counselors and a part of the comprehensive guidance and counseling program. Their special assignments may also link them with other programs and departments, in which they must also continue to develop their specialty in the specific area; for example, counselors funded from special education funds provide guidance and counseling to students in special education; they need to continue to develop their competence in working with special needs students. Additionally, they need to understand the special education program rules and priorities and be able to interpret those rules to their colleague counselors.

Establishing Roles and Responsibilities for
Building-Level Guidance and Counseling Program Leaders

Key to implementing quality comprehensive guidance and counseling programs in the buildings is appropriate delegation of responsibility and authority to leaders of guidance departments throughout a district. Their authority can be delegated from both the building principal and the district guidance and counseling program leader. Such delegation must be clearly spelled out and be such that their responsibilities are clearly supported. On a day-to-day basis, they lead and manage the details of program planning and implementation as well as the quality of school counselors' use of their time and applications of their talent.

The roles that guidance and counseling program leaders fulfill are those of administration, management, supervision, and professional leadership (Henderson & Gysbers, 1998). In their administration role, they apply their authority and responsibility over the guidance and counseling program and its staff. They are ultimately accountable for the quality of program delivery and staff performance. In their management role, guidance and counseling program leaders acquire the personnel, material, and political resources needed to implement the program. In their supervision role, they strive for efficient and effective use of these resources. In their professional leadership role, they assist school counselors to enhance their professionalism through adherence to the standards and the advancement of the school counseling profession.

The responsibilities of guidance and counseling program leaders include carrying out the tasks required in program planning, designing, implementation, and evaluation. Program planning includes projecting and managing such things as the department budget, acquiring and using appropriate program materials, and using the school's facilities. Designing the building guidance and counseling program includes developing the program calendar and assisting the school counselors in developing and adhering to regular schedules. Program implementation entails monitoring and participating in program delivery. Evaluation of the program, its results, and the performance of the school counselors and other program staff members require their leadership. Building guidance and counseling program leaders also advocate for the guidance and counseling program, its clients, and staff with such groups as the building and district administrators, local site-based decision-making groups, teachers, parents, and other community representatives.

By far the largest resource provided to guidance and counseling programs in schools is that of the school counselor staff. Helping them to carry out their roles and responsibilities with highest levels of professionalism is imperative to excellent program implementation (Gysbers & Henderson, 1997). Leadership of school counselors as staff members entails establishing and maintaining healthy and productive work climates. Leaders carry out the tasks required in implementation of the district's system for enhancing school counselors' performance. They help each school counselor define his or her job for the year, assess his or her levels of professionalism, and set goals and implement plans for enhancing his or her professional maturity. Building guidance and counseling program leaders provide professionally appropriate supervision to school counselors and evaluate their performance (Henderson & Gysbers, 1998).

Developing Job Descriptions for Other Staff Members
Working in the Guidance and Counseling Program

More concise guidance and counseling program-related role statements and job descriptions need to be in place for others working in the guidance and counseling program. Some of these staff members might be full time, such as licensed professional counselors, social workers, parent involvement/education specialists, guidance department clerical help, or paraprofessionals. In many of the districts with which we have worked, insufficient use has been made of support staff, because of either understaffing or underuse of existing staff. Underuse is often the result of incomplete statements of job responsibilities. (Sample job descriptions/position guides for career center technicians and high school registrars are included in Appendix F.) Clear job descriptions allow others to recognize the importance or complexity of guidance department paraprofessionals' responsibilities, particularly as they assume the nonguidance tasks previously done by counselors. Such descriptions have led to upgraded pay classifications and extended contracts.

Some staff members only augment the guidance and counseling program as part of their responsibilities, such as teachers, administrators, and related specialists, including school psychologists or diagnosticians, community volunteers, and peer counselors. Although these job descriptions will not be as extensive as those for full-time staff members, they are just as important because they are the vehicle for ensuring that program delivery is coordinated and carried out by a cohesive staff team.

Not only do the roles and responsibilities of others need to be spelled out, but they also need to be appropriate to their training and competence. Personnel without school counselor certification should be trained to carry out their roles in the comprehensive guidance and counseling program. For example, teachers should be trained to be advisers, community representatives to be mentors, and parent volunteers to be parent liaisons.

Individuals without school counselor certification should not be used in place of certified professional school counselors but rather should augment the services provided by school counselors (American School Counselor Association [ASCA], 2000). All staff members assisting in the delivery of the guidance and counseling program should adhere to the ethical and legal standards of the counseling profession. Key standards are those regarding students' and parents' rights and confidentiality.

Remember that job definition is prerequisite to any staff expansion, particularly if staff members with new job titles are to be added. It is through job task analysis and the development of related job descriptions that the functions of proposed new staff members can be delineated from those of existing staff. Such delineation supports the rationale for the new positions.

Clarifying Organizational Relationships Within the Guidance and Counseling Program

After clarifying the roles and expectations of each category of staff members in the delivery of the comprehensive guidance and counseling program, your next step is clarifying the organizational relationships between the counselors and the other professionals who augment the program or whose services dovetail with the program, and among the guidance department staff in a building.

Caseload Assignments: Team Approach. In implementing the guidance and counseling program, it is important to recognize that counselors are members of four teams. They are an integral part of the instructional team, along with teachers, administrators, and other education specialists, in implementing the developmental components of the program. Counselors are an integral part of the school and district special services team, along with school psychologists, social workers, nurses, and administrators, in responding to the special needs of some students and parents. Counselors also form teams with community representatives who collaborate with the schools, specifically the business and the mental health communities, to augment the program. Perhaps most important, counselors from each school level and each building are part of the guidance team, working together to articulate and improve programs systemwide.

Clarifying who the team members are and respecting the roles that each member plays and the systems that each operates within are prerequisites to effective teamwork. Mutual design of the way teams operate contributes to efficient operation. For example, there is renewed interest in using the schools to integrate public health and human services provided to children, youths, and families. Coalitions of related professionals must meet and have open dialogue to determine how such integration will work. At the national level, the American Counseling Association (ACA) represents counselors in the National Alliance of Pupil Services Organizations (NAPSO, 1993). This coalition endorses a collaborative approach among its members. In addition to ACA, members of NAPSO include organizations representing school nurses, teachers, occupational therapists, physical therapists, school psychologists, school social workers, special educators, speech-language pathologists, audiologists, and therapeutic recreation specialists as well as art, music, and dance therapists, and administrators of pupil services programs. Although defining how collaboration occurs is a local challenge, a commitment to work together is a major step.

Implementation of the comprehensive guidance and counseling program as it is defined and designed is the guidance department's responsibility. It is our opinion that personnel without school counselor certification who are active participants in program delivery should do so under the supervision of professional school counselors.

Caseload Assignment: Staffing Patterns. Within a guidance department staff, the organizational patterns for operation need to be clearly established. Across the United States there is wide variation in size of guidance department staffs. On the one hand, a large, urban high school might have 10 to 15 counselors, including comprehensive school counselors and specialist counselors, and 6 or more support staff, such as registrar, career center technician, counselors' secretary, data-processing clerk, and a scheduling assistant. On the other hand, it is not unusual for one counselor to serve the elementary, middle/junior high, and high schools in a small, rural community. In this case, the definition of guidance staff must include the administrators, teachers, and support staff at each of the schools. Regardless of the size of the staff involved, some organizational keys apply universally to enhancing healthy interprofessional and interpersonal relationships, which, in turn, affect program quality.

Caseload assignments for staff members need to be supported by rationale relevant to the program design that is appropriate to each person's program responsibilities, training, and specialization. The question still arises, What is the "best" way for comprehensive school counselors to divvy up students into their caseloads? Some of the options in use are dividing students by grade levels, alphabetically by surnames, by their teachers, or, for specialists, by their participation in special programs. Not much research has been done to help school counselors answer this question. As discussed in chapter 4, the decision about how to divide students among the comprehensive counselors should match the philosophy behind the guidance and counseling program.

1. *Caseload assignments by grade level.* Caseload assignments by grade levels is consistent with a developmental philosophy, with thinking of the program in terms of how to best prepare to help the students of different ages. This assignment pattern supports a counselor's guidance curriculum or individual student planning services and is often found at the elementary and middle school levels. It also effectively divides regular consultation with teaching and instructional staff among the counselors. This method also entails counselors' consulting with each other about children from the same homes and families who are in different grade levels. Consistency of services for students suggests that a student benefits most from having the same counselor during his or her tenure in the school, making it clear that counselors should move up a school's grade levels as his or her students move. Quality and amount of time available for services also suggest that each comprehensive counselor serve a similar number of students as other comprehensive counselors. One problem with this method of assignment is if the grade levels in a school vary widely in size;

for example, in many high schools there are many more 9th graders than 12th graders. Another issue is that if a district or school adds one additional counselor, how, then, do the grade levels of children become evenly divided; for example, if a middle school serves three grades of similar size (e.g., 6th, 7th, and 8th grade) and has four counselors, what is a logical caseload assignment for the fourth counselor? Typically more than one of the grade levels is split up among the counselors. It then can be awkward for students, parents, and others to decipher who the counselor is for a particular student.

2. *Caseload assignment by surname.* Assigning students to counselors on the basis of the students' last name often reflects an emphasis on responding to students' needs and issues within knowledge of their family context. This often enhances the quality of a counselor's responsive services. While not all children from the same home bear the same last names, many do. Working with siblings and parents over time provides counselors with increased information about the issues and assets of the child's home environment. It also supports the team approach to guidance and counseling program delivery, as developmental activities provided for each grade level are a shared responsibility among all counselors. It also dictates that all counselors consult consistently with all of the teachers and other instructional staff.

3. *Caseload assignment by teachers.* Caseload assignment for counselors according to groups of teachers focuses on the system support component. It emphasizes the counselors' role of helping teachers improve their work with individual and groups of students, and within their classrooms. It may facilitate implementation of counselors' classroom-based, developmental guidance activities. A large disadvantage is that students change counselors each year as their teachers change, minimizing consistency of counselors' services and demanding even more time in counselor-to-counselor consultation. It is also difficult for parents—and students, for that matter—to know who their children's counselors are each year.

4. *Special responsibilities.* Any special responsibilities need to be clearly stated and understood by other staff members. The department leader should be designated with the authority to manage the program and staff (Henderson & Gysbers, 1998), including the capability to mediate between staff members when necessary. Intradepartmental rules need to be established to facilitate coordination and cooperation. For example, if two or more counselors provide services to the same student, the responsibilities, methods, and standards need to be spelled out to ensure that such services are conducted with the best interests of the student in mind. If teachers have the responsibility for contacting parents regarding their child's school-related problems and recommended solutions, the responsibilities and methods for ensuring that all staff members working with a student has the information they need must to be spelled out. Staff meetings need to be held regularly to ensure open communication among staff members, coordinate program planning, and do the necessary problem solving (Henderson & Gysbers, 1998).

Financial Resources

To improve use of financial resources, consider establishing budgets for guidance departments at the district and building levels, exploring use of other-than-local funding sources, developing guidance and counseling program component resource guides, and establishing guidance facilities standards and making recommendations for their application.

Establishing Budgets for Guidance Departments at the District and Building Levels

In the assessment of the current program, one of the tasks was to review the financial resources available. In the review, you may have found that the financial resources were described in terms of a well-defined budget in which all of the money spent on guidance, including salaries, was part of the budget. Or you may have found that only money for such items as testing materials and a few other guidance resources was included. Or perhaps there was no budget at all. Within the budget policy guidelines for the school/district, the task is to establish a budget. To do that, consider such major categories as those displayed in Table 7.2.

Prerequisite to any resource expansion is ascertaining the cost of implementing the recommendations. The guidance and counseling program leader needs to develop a cost analysis for each of the items for inclusion in the district department budget or in other budget categories if that is where an item fits. The total amount, presented all at once, could be overwhelming, so our advice is to prepare these cost analyses on an item-by-item basis. Thus as each recommendation is brought forward for consideration, the guidance and counseling program leader can present the dollar figures associated with it. For example, if implementing the improved ratios recommended entails adding counselors to the staff, it is the guidance and counseling program leader's responsibility to know how much those additional staff positions will cost. Having specific cost information available allows the guidance and counseling program leader to anticipate others' concerns about the increased expenditures and to be prepared to defend the allocation of additional dollars.

Table 7.2
Budget Categories

I. *Personnel salaries and benefits*
   A. Counselors
   B. Secretarial/clerical
   C. Guidance administrators
II. *Program development*
   A. Curriculum development
   B. Local materials development
   C. Pilot projects
III. *Materials acquisition*
   A. Student materials
      1. Texts and workbooks
      2. Audiovisual materials
      3. Testing materials
      4. Reference materials
      5. Career/guidance center materials
      6. Assessment materials
   B. Professional resource materials
      1. Professional library books
      2. Journal subscriptions
      3. Training materials
   C. Supplies
      1. Office supplies
      2. Computer-assisted guidance equipment supplies
      3. Instructional supplies
IV. *Capital outlay*
   A. Furniture
   B. Equipment and maintenance
V. *Professional development*
   A. Meetings and conferences
      1. Registration
      2. Expenses
   B. Consultants
VI. *Office expenses*
   A. Telephone
   B. Postage
   C. Fax
VII. *Research and evaluation*

Exploring Use of Other-Than-Local Funding Sources

A majority of the funds for the program probably comes from local and state regular education sources. There are, however, funds from other sources. Federal legislation is one source. Federal funds available to augment the comprehensive guidance and counseling program include those that support career and technology education, special education, compensatory education, bilingual and migrant education, and special topics of national priority such as drug abuse prevention education and safety in schools. Federal employment and training legislation also may have guidance funds available for schools.

Most federal funds are distributed by the state department of education. If the guidance and counseling program leader is not already familiar with these sources, a visit with the state's guidance consultants should be a rewarding experience. They will be able to tell you about federal and state moneys that may be available for guidance and counseling programs. Although many states still have not solved the problem of adequate school financing, many states have established guidance-relevant priorities. For example, renewed interest in support for elementary guidance is being expressed by state legislatures.

Keep in mind that most federal or state sources do not usually fund an entire program. Rather, they provide supplemental or additional support for target populations or facilitate achievement of their program objectives, such as counseling disadvantaged or substance-abusing students, augmenting a career center, or implementing a vocational assessment program. Most of the time access to these funds is through a proposal or the development of a written plan. With the comprehensive program already designed, such a proposal or plan is readily developed because the program context and student needs already have been established. The proposal writer has to extract only the portions of the total program that are of interest to the funding source to present the plan.

Developing Guidance and Counseling Program Component Resource Guides

A major task in making the transition to a comprehensive guidance and counseling program is to choose the guidance activities and materials that will assist students to develop the competencies that have been decided on. Basing the work on sound ideas and research-based concepts and materials is one key to having good quality activities through which the program is implemented and the identified desired results are achieved. Galassi and Akos (2004) identified examples of some bases on which to build your program's specifics, including resiliency and the development of competence in youths.

Describing the specific activities that make up the program and having adequate program materials is prerequisite to successful implementation of the program. Counselors must have tools to assist them in their changed roles. Whether such guides are written for use in a building's program, for use in a small school district, or for use in an entire large district makes a difference in the approach to this task, but the end products will be similar. In the first two situations, the product may be one binder with four sections. In the case of the large district, the products are usually four binders, one for each component. The resource guides describe activities used in the implementation of the comprehensive guidance and counseling program components. In developing the guides, new activities may be created, or activities may be collected that have been used successfully in a building.

The scope of resource guide development should vary with the size of the district guidance and counseling program. No matter how large or how small the program is, however, the guidance and counseling program leader should attend to the details of the guide writing. In Northside Independent School District, the compilation of ideas into guides took 3 years to accomplish. Once guides are published, they have a permanency that provides part of the foundation on which the new program can rest. It is important that this foundation be solid.

A work committee comprised of the program development leaders was used in Northside Independent School District to develop the formats to be used in the guides, such as lesson plans, activity plans, and counseling session outlines. In turn, the work committee trained the rest of the counselors in how to complete the forms. When counselors submitted their "promising practices" in the prescribed format, their suggestions were ready to be typed for inclusion in the guide. The work committee screened the inputs and selected the best practices. The difference between these guides and those developed in a single building or a small district is that these become illustrative examples that a building program can use as a pattern, as contrasted with those that represent actual descriptions of a particular building's guidance activities. Suggestions for developing guides for the four comprehensive program components follow.

Guidance Curriculum Guide. A curriculum guide provides the description of curriculum units and specific lessons. We suggest that the guidance and counseling program leader use the curriculum-writing expertise that is available, such as instructional supervisors if the district has them, the administrator in charge of curriculum development or instruction, or regional consultants in curriculum writing. The leader must also keep in mind that there will probably not be a one-on-one match between a specific activity or resource and a specific competency. Often a single guidance activity may result in the achievement of a number of student objectives.

To illustrate how an activity may be written and to show its relationship to the goals and competencies of the guidance curriculum suggested in previous chapters, an example is displayed in Figure 7.1. The example is from the Self-Knowledge and Interpersonal Skills domain of the life career development model and relates to Goal A for the fifth grade. You may wish to consider this format for your own activity descriptions. Note that the activity is described on one page and follows a straightforward outline that defines the

Figure 7.1
Sample Activity and Format

Domain I Goal A Grade 5 Performance Indicator 2	
	COAT OF ARMS
Domain I:	Self-Knowledge and Interpersonal Skills
Goal A:	Students will develop and incorporate an understanding of the unique personal characteristics and abilities of themselves and others.
Competency:	Students will specify those personal characteristics and abilities that they value.
Performance Indicator 2:	Students will identify a variety of things that they value.
	Activity Objective:
	The student will identify six things he or she values.
Materials:	Coat of arms, pencil
Time:	One session of approximately 30 minutes
Directions:	Have each student fill in an outline of a shield with the following for a personal coat of arms:
	Box 1: Draw a symbol to represent your greatest success. Box 2: Draw a symbol to represent your family's greatest success. Box 3: Draw a symbol to show a place you dream about. Box 4: Draw symbols to show two things at which you are good. Box 5: Draw a picture to show what you would do if you had 1 year to live and could be a success at anything you do. Box 6: On one-half of the box write two words you would like used to describe you; on the other half write two words you would not like used to describe you.

basic activity. Counselors are encouraged to develop the lesson plan according to their teaching style.

Individual Student Planning Guide. An individual student planning guide describes in detail activities and procedures to help students apply information and develop their personalized plans. These write-ups exemplify the refocusing of some current activities from system support activities to student result-focused activities that help them make their educational plans. For example, the objective for preregistration of secondary-level students can be changed from "students will circle course numbers on course selection cards" to student learning objectives, such as "10th graders will select an 11th-grade course of study that is an appropriate next step toward their educational/career goals." The activities that might be envisioned as a unit include interpretation of career interest and aptitude assessments, information exploration in the guidance center, review of the high school graduation and college entrance requirements, revision of the students' high school 4-year plans, and, finally, preregistration for the 11th-grade year. Or the objective for an elementary school Career Day can be changed from "the school staff will provide X number of career speakers" to "3rd-, 4th-, and 5th-grade students will list the educational requirements for five careers that relate to their identified career interests." The guidance and counseling program activities provided to assist students attain the objective might include a career interest inventory, a guidance lesson on the relationship between levels of education and levels of occupations available in various job clusters, and Career Day speakers who describe their educational histories as they relate to their occupations. Parent involvement activities related to individual student planning should be described as well.

Responsive Services Guide. A responsive services guide can provide a description of the topics and modes—such as counseling, consultation, or referral—the counselor uses in response to student, student–parent, or student–teacher problems. Counseling session plans and the overview of a planned series of counseling activities can help other staff members as well as less-experienced counselors benefit from the ideas used in activities. Many sound commercial materials are available to support this component. In addition to helping new counselors get started, identifying the materials used in the current program supports consistency in program delivery across schools and consultation among counselors. Including a list of the community referral sources counselors use in the building or across the district also enhances the implementation of this component. Developing this list not only provides the names of outside source people who have cooperated effectively with school counselors in the past but also can provide a vehicle for gathering consistent information about these sources' areas of expertise.

System Support Guide. The system support component guide needs to be written specifically to clarify what the guidance department staff does to support other programs and to itemize the support they need to ensure appropriate delivery of their own program. Support to other programs should be listed by program (state the activity and briefly describe the counselor role or roles and responsibilities). Support needed from the administration and staff should include such items as policy and procedural assistance; budget, equipment, and facilities needs; support for specific staff development opportunities; and public relations activities. Outlines of successful teacher in-service presentations should be included.

Describing Exemplary Activities. To begin the task of guide development, we suggest using the results of the current program assessment already completed. Take those current activities and materials you feel are in keeping with the improved program that has been designed—those that have the potential of helping students to develop the chosen competencies—and place them in the appropriate component and grade-level grouping.

If, as guidance and counseling program leader, you are working in a single school or in a small district setting, this may be accomplished easily; however, if the setting is larger, you may need to implement a process similar to that done in Northside Independent School District. This approach was developed after a group of 12 counselors from the district—4 counselors from each school level—spent a week (the district's typical allotment for curriculum writing) to develop the units and lessons to teach decision making to Grades 4 through 12. The work was aligned more closely with textbook writing than with typical curriculum guide development efforts. In addition, that district had identified 15 guidance curriculum strands; the counselors as well as the director concluded that they could not wait 14 more years to have the curriculum guide completed, to say nothing of the guides for the other components. It also was not realistic to expect the district to hire the counselors as a curriculum-writing team for a year or whatever it took to accomplish the tasks. The counselors decided to collect exemplary practices that were currently performed in district buildings, write them up in consistent formats, and categorize them by program component. They found this to be an excellent vehicle for cross-fertilization of ideas. Working with counselors from different school levels to pool ideas helped everyone learn about each other's programs and was a major step toward an articulated K–12 program. It had the additional benefit of helping all participating counselors see how what they were currently doing fit into the new program concept.

Establishing Guidance Facilities Standards and Making Recommendations for Their Application

Ensuring adequate guidance facilities and equipment may be difficult, considering the costs that may be involved. However, physical facilities are so important because they often provide students with their first and sometimes permanent impression of the guidance and counseling program. Now that you have identified the desired program design and have chosen guidance activities for the program components, you also are aware of the facilities required. For example, if classroom guidance is to be an essential part of the developmental program, a guidance classroom may be deemed essential; if counselors are expected to conduct small-group counseling, an adequately sized room is needed; if a guidance center is to be the hub of the program, a large classroom and offices are needed; and so on. Space in growing districts may be at a premium, but in schools and districts where enrollment is declining, the facilities development challenge may not be as great.

Improving the facilities and equipment available to the guidance and counseling program, as with other program improvements, entails knowing what you want, being able to communicate that knowledge to others, and inserting guidance and counseling program needs into relevant district processes. In planning for building new facilities or remodeling existing ones, and in upgrading the furniture and equipment, you will be communicating with architects, facilities planners, engineers, and purchasing agents. These professionals and technicians may or may not understand the guidance and counseling program, as you may or may not understand construction and purchasing. Your program is best served if you work with them to develop standards for the design of the guidance facilities and for provision of the basic equipment needed. You also need to work with them to incorporate into the overall system the plan to bring the guidance department's facilities up to the standards.

Facilities Standards. These standards detail the type of facilities needed, their size and most suitable locations, and other basics that should be incorporated when schools are built or remodeled. Specific items often included in facilities standards are outlined in Table 7.3, with examples for a guidance and counseling program. When approved by the district administration and the school board, these standards become the specifications from which architects draw their plans and others contract to build or fulfill.

Table 7.3

Facilities Design Standards Categories and Examples

A. *Room type:* counselor's office; secretary and reception area; records, storage, and workroom area; group counseling room; conference room; registrar's office; data processing and scheduling assistant's area; career center area

B. *Location:* centered in the building; location of each of the offices and areas relative to one another

C. *Square footage:* in addition to activities done in the particular space, size depends on level (size of student body), size of school (typical numbers using facility at one time), furniture and equipment needed

D. *Functions performed in room type:* specific to each area and personnel working in the area

E. *Walls:* covering, tackable, soundproof, concrete blocks, fireproof

F. *Floor:* carpeting or vinyl

G. *Cabinets:* location, floor-to-ceiling, waist-high with countertop, depth, lockable, open

H. *Storage requirements:* specific equipment, types of materials, amount

I. *Lighting:* number, separate controls for fixtures

J. *Electrical outlets:* number and placement, computer hook-ups

K. *Plumbing:* not applicable

L. *Communications:* private telephone lines; intercoms with lights to ensure privacy; not hooked up to school public address system

M. *Unusual electrical requirements:* e.g., air conditioning separate from classrooms for counselors on contracts that extend into the summer; dedicated copier circuit

N. *Unusual equipment requirements:* marker boards, bulletin boards

O. *Other:* such as lockable doors, small windows; acoustic considerations (privacy in counseling offices and rooms); noise in the area that contains the audiovisual equipment used in the center.

Furniture and Equipment. The guidance facilities should be furnished in as comfortable a way as possible for all users. Remember that students as well as staff and parents gain impressions about the program from your facilities.

A basic furniture and equipment list also must be developed. Such furniture items, and their types and sizes, might include a professional desk and chair, guest chairs, bookshelves, credenza, file cabinets, and student tables and chairs. Equipment might include bulletin boards, videocassette recorders or DVD players, TVs, and computers.

Equipment needs are identified by a process similar to that used for facilities. In the current program assessment, you surveyed the equipment available. Having identified the major material resources, you can now specify related equipment needs. Again, this information allows you to analyze the costs involved and to develop your budget request. The request is substantiated by the clearly stated relationship between equipment and facilities and the program design.

Guidance Center: A Way of Organizing Guidance Facilities. Attention to the type and use of physical space and equipment of a comprehensive guidance and counseling program often is neglected in the change process. Unfortunately, what attention is given remains fixed to the traditional ways of organizing guidance. To make the guidance curriculum, individual student planning, and responsive services function effectively, and to provide appropriate support to other programs, a new way of organizing guidance facilities is needed.

Traditionally, guidance facilities have consisted of an office or suite of offices designed primarily to provide one-on-one counseling. Such an arrangement frequently has included a reception or waiting area that serves as a browsing room where students have limited access to displays or files of educational and occupational information. This space typically has been placed in the administrative wing of the school so that the counseling staff can be close to the records and the administration. The need for individual offices is obvious because of the continuing need to carry on individual counseling sessions. However, there is also a need to open up guidance facilities, to make them more accessible to students, teachers, parents, and community representatives. One approach to making guidance facilities more usable and accessible is to reorganize traditional space into a guidance center.

A comprehensive guidance center can bring together available guidance information and exploration resources and make them easily accessible to students. The center can be used for such activities as group sessions, self-exploration, and personalized research and planning. At the high school level, students can gain assistance in such areas as occupational planning, job entry and placement, financial aid information, and postsecondary educational opportunities. At the middle school/junior high school level, students can gain assistance in such areas as career planning, high school educational opportunities, community involvement, and recreational opportunities. At the elementary school level, students and their parents can gain information about the school, the community, and parenting skills as well as read books about personal growth and development. An area for play therapy can be provided.

Although the center is available for use by school staff and community members, it should be student centered, and many of the center activities should be both student planned and student directed. At the same time, the center is a valuable resource for teachers in their program planning and implementation. Employers, too, will find the center useful when seeking part- or full-time workers. Viewed in this way, the impact of the center on school and community can be substantial.

If community members and parents are involved in the planning and implementation of the center and its activities, their interest could provide an impetus for the involvement of other community members. When parents and other community members become involved in programs housed in the center, they gain firsthand experience of the educational process. Through these experiences, new support for education may grow.

The guidance center should be furnished in as comfortable a way as possible for all users. Provision should be made for group as well as individual activities. Coordinating the operation of the guidance center should be the responsibility of the guidance staff. All school staff should be involved, however. We recommend that at least one paid paraprofessional be employed to ensure that clerical tasks are carried out in a consistent manner. Volunteers also may be used.

Political Resources

To improve use of political resources, consider updating policies and procedures, engendering support from building staff, and working with resistant staff members and critical constituents (i.e., concerned parents).

Updating Policies and Procedures

Another task to be completed to implement the new program is updating the policies and procedures that govern guidance as they appear in the district policy and procedural handbooks (those you identified in assessing the current program). If you have not already done so, you must—as a prerequisite to procedural changes—update the board policy that defines the purpose and design of the comprehensive guidance and counseling program. A model policy statement developed by the Missouri School Board Association (1996) is provided in Appendix E. Some of these procedural and regulatory changes may be merely editorial or cosmetic; others will be major changes in procedure and will not be easy to bring about. The former changes are those that merely translate board policy to administrators;

the latter are those that will need to be negotiated, particularly those that describe how the guidance department interacts with and supports the programs of other departments. All of these statements should be built on the premise that the guidance and counseling program is an integral part of the total educational program with an integrity of its own.

In analyzing how the current program compares and contrasts with the desired program, you have documented something you already knew: A number of activities for which you are responsible are not guidance activities at all or are, at best, only tangentially related to guidance. They have become a part of the guidance and counseling program over the years, perhaps by design, but more likely by default. As you also know, no matter how these activities became part of the program, once established, they are difficult to remove. And what is worse, these responsibilities consume the valuable time and resources needed to conduct the actual guidance and counseling program. Ways to manage the improvement of program activities, including displacing nonguidance activities, are discussed in chapter 8.

Making optimum use of school counselors' professional skills is a goal of program remodeling. An issue related to recommending lower ratios, which increase student access to their counselors, is ensuring opportunities for the counselors to access their students. Time for guidance and counseling must be seen as legitimate and valuable, and policies and procedures must be established to ensure that there is time to deliver the program appropriately.

Engendering Support From Building Staff

Recognizing that the new program design causes many operational-level changes in a building's guidance and counseling program, the district guidance and counseling program leader and all school counselors need to expend some energy reeducating the building staff members about the rationale and goals for the changes. Reeducation and engendering support call for communicating clearly what these changes are, providing guidelines for support from building administrators, and collaborating with building personnel to design and implement the local changes.

Armed with the district plan for guidance and counseling program improvement, you need to ensure that every staff member has the working knowledge he or she needs to respond to the changes. This entails formal presentations regarding the program conducted at the district level for the principals and at the building level for the faculty.

Because principals are accountable for the successful operation of every program in their buildings, they should have available a copy of the program framework written at the end of the designing phase. It is also useful to provide a written set of guidelines that suggest to building administrators appropriate levels of support for their guidance and counseling programs. These might entail statements about adequate facilities for counselors as well as adequate budget appropriations for guidance department supplies. Statements also might be made about work schedules for counselors concerning, for example, their expected work hours and including recognition of lunch hours and preparation periods. Some tasks identified for displacement may be handled in this manner, especially those that have become common practice at the building level but are not rooted in district policy. Examples include stating that elementary counselors should benefit from the secretarial services available at the school and should not be required to do their own typing; recommending that new middle school students begin the registration process in the administrative office and be referred to the guidance department after such items as verification of address and immunizations are taken care of; and recognizing that the standardized testing program provides useful information to faculty and administration as well as counselors and thus test administration is a shared responsibility of all building staff members.

Another way to encourage building principals' support is for the senior district staff member who evaluates the principals to ask each one, "What have you done this year/evaluation period to support improvement of the guidance and counseling program in your building?"

We believe that it is essential to involve the others who will be affected by the changes in the guidance and counseling program in designing what those changes will be and how they will be made (Henderson, 1989, pp. 37–38). We recommend that you use the existing building program improvement committee to assist you in planning, designing, implementing, and evaluating the building guidance and counseling programs. A process for doing this is suggested later on in this chapter. Other formal mechanisms for collaborating with building staff colleagues are staff meetings. Counselors should meet periodically with the teachers they work with through grade-level, department, and faculty leadership meetings. Seeking their input, hearing and responding to their concerns, and informing them of your plans are essential to the success of the guidance and counseling program change process.

Working With Resistant Staff Members

By now it will be clear that there are school counselors and other guidance staff who understand the new program and are eager for its implementation. And by now it will also be clear that there are school counselors and other staff members who resist the changes that are called for. The resisters probably fall into several categories: those who have not yet quite grasped the program concept; those who disagree with the educational-developmental basis of the program, preferring the psychological-crisis-oriented services approach; those who are skeptical as to the validity of the changes; those who do not believe the changes will ever occur; those who are worried about their own competence for meeting the new mandates; and those who do not want change, period.

We recommend that the guidance and counseling program leader continue open dialogue with the counselors and other guidance staff about their concerns. As the change process continues to unfold, however, more and more of their concerns, anxieties, and fears will be addressed. Changes do not happen overnight, and the concept does become clearer with time. The superintendent is in support of the program; in-service training is provided. We also recommend that the district guidance and counseling program leader identify ways to acknowledge those who do support the changes and the efforts that lead in the right directions. We discuss this point more extensively in chapter 8.

Working With Critical Constituents: Concerned Parents

All parents want to know, understand, or have some input into what happens to their children at school. Some parents want to control what happens and are highly critical of things that do happen to their children at school. Often these parents are driven by anger or fear for what might happen to their children, making them emotional, irrational, or defensive and difficult to deal with. Many of these difficult and defensive parents are acting as individuals concerned about their own children. However, some of them come forward to try to censor school guidance and counseling. They are overtly or covertly representatives of local, state, or national groups that do not believe counseling belongs in the schools. Different ways that school counselors can address those who are parents of students in their schools, and whose concerns are similar to those that are heard with some frequency around the country, need to be considered. (Note that interacting with the parents of children in their schools is for counselors very different from lobbying a group of parents at the school board or legislature or some place beyond the school.)

It is important for school counselors to respond to concerned parents appropriately (White, Mullis, Earley, & Brigman, 1995). These parents often initiate the dialogue with their children's school counselors unexpectedly, catching the counselor off guard and unprepared. However, school counselors are usually ready to advocate for—to share their perspectives about—their program and their students' needs (Henderson & Gysbers, 1998). One principle that school counselors endorse is that children's personal and educational well-being is best served when school counselors (and other educators) and parents are partners working together on behalf of the children and youths. By responding to these difficult parents, school counselors strive to better align the parents' agendas with their own, to work together on behalf of children. Additionally, school counselors have skills that allow most of their parent contacts to be of the highest professional quality—that is, open, positive, and collaborative; based on professional analysis and reflection; and carried out with professional detachment.

Every parent who comes forward should be treated as an individual first, and, after sufficient indicative data have been accrued, as a possible antischool counseling group member. Most parents come forward on behalf of their own children and with concerns about one or two topics, and most of the time, the school counselor can address the parents' concerns for their children. As in effective counseling, the first step in working with concerned parents is to address their presenting concerns and to keep the discussion focused on them.

Never assume that every parent who comes in and uses a conservative group buzzword is a card-carrying member of the Eagle Forum. Just be aware that some of them might be. Even with parents who are affiliated with or representing a group, and who appear to have broader agendas than those related to their own children, school counselors are advised to address the topics they present.

To prepare themselves for these interactions, school counselors should learn about the concerned parents early on in the relationship. Do they in fact represent groups of parents? What are their specific issues? In striving to work successfully in interactions with such parents, school counselors, then, must rise to two challenges: first, identifying the specific topic of concern to the parents and the motivation for their concern; second, selecting the response(s) to the parents that is(are) appropriate to the parents' topics and motives as well as to the counselors' own agendas.

Because these adversarial parent–counselor interactions are usually initiated by parents, the parents are initially in the driver's seat. But by definition, interactions go back and forth: parent to counselor, counselor to parent. As these relationships unfold, counselors assume the management of the relationships, taking control once the objectives are clear(er) and appropriate responses to the situation are planned and implemented. Although school counselors have no control over parents' responses, each parent response provides new data that augment the counselors' original assessment of the situation and inform the counselors' next set of choices.

When it appears that parents are not going to be easily pleased, when their concerns are emotionally driven, counselors strive to maintain their professional detachment and implement a systematic process, as illustrated in Figure 7.2, for managing the interactions, the relationships, and the situation. Responding appropriately and managing the interactions most effectively entail assessing the situation and selecting responses.

Situation Assessment. Assessing the situation entails identifying who the parents represent and their specific topics and motives. It includes school counselors' understanding their own topics and motives and clarifying the objectives both of the confronting parents and their own.

Figure 7.2
Strategy Selection Logic Flow Used by School Counselors in Response to Concerned Parents

	PARENT		SCHOOL COUNSELOR
1	Initiates conversation		
		2	Determines who parent represents
3	Expresses topic(s) of concern	4	Specifies parent's topic; identifies own topic
	Evidences motive for interaction	5	Identifies parent's motive(s); clarifies own motive(s)
6	States objective(s)	7	Understands parent's objective; determines own objective
		8	Chooses advocacy response: skills, resources, response level
		9	Implements advocacy strategy through an activity
10	Participates in counselor-selected activity and responds		
		11 and 12 and 13 . . .	Implements response activities through to problem resolution

1. *Who do the parents represent?* Identifying who the parents represent involves learning about who they are as individuals and if they are affiliated with a group of parents who are averse to schools or school counselors. Parents who present themselves to school counselors and have questions or concerns about the guidance and counseling program or the roles fulfilled by counselors in the school come from an array of perspectives. Not only does each parent have an individual perspective on life and school (e.g., history, background, culture, education, school experiences, beliefs), but each parent may also be part of a group that has a specific, expressed platform.

Concerned individual parents may be concerned only for their own children, or they may personally be resistant to counseling or to counselors' recommendations for a variety of reasons. Group representatives may be interested in the operations of the specific school or may have political interests covering a larger span (e.g., the policies of the school district, the state, the nation). They may be basically supportive of the schools and only curious or concerned about specific guidance-related items. They may be basically nonsupportive of the public schools or of school guidance and counseling programs and school counselors.

Some nationally visible, conservative, and typically religious groups of parents believe that counseling is an invasion of privacy, is an attempt to undermine family values, and is antispiritual, and that counseling does not belong in the schools. Groups of such parents voice their concerns at local and state school board meetings as well as in the media. Individuals challenge teachers, counselors, and principals. They are often hostile and aggressive in expressing their criticism of the public schools and often see the schools' goal as teaching only reading, writing, and mathematics or teaching a particular set of religious beliefs or censorship.

2. *What are the parents' topics and motivation?* Identifying what the parents' topics are entails hearing what their presenting concerns are and how much of their concern is generated by or on behalf of any larger group they are affiliated with. It is important to recognize clearly and specifically the presenting concerns, topics, and issues of parents who come forward.

Nationally visible, conservative groups express some recurrent topics. Although most parents who represent a group do not come forward on behalf of all of the issues, the scope of the agendas of organized groups that are against public schools or against guidance and counseling activities is broad. Thus parents may confront school counselors with concerns about the purposes of school or the purposes of the guidance and counseling program, about guidance topics or methods, or about specific activities they have heard about or experienced. A standard form letter has been distributed widely that provides a summary of their concerns. The letter is based on an overinterpretation of the Hatch Amendment (and is included in Appendix J).

In questioning the broader purposes of public schools, parents may question career and technology education and creative activities by children as well as courses in which controversial issues are addressed. In questioning the guidance and counseling program mission, they may express their fear that it represents the secular humanistic arm of the school. They do not believe that therapy belongs in school and assume that counseling is therapy.

Guidance topics that parents may find objectionable include self-esteem, decision making, attending to children's feelings, affective education, or exploring family values and practices. Parents may want their religious beliefs to be taught and upheld in schools. They may believe firmly in parents' rights to complete authority over their offspring, including knowing and controlling what their children experience in school and choosing disciplinary methods.

They may express concern about an array of guidance methods. They may be wary of psychological or career assessments, surveys that include any questions regarding the home and family, role-playing, guided imagery, group counseling, and confidentiality. They may want their children to have fewer guidance services than are part of the comprehensive guidance and counseling program (i.e., no responsive services). Some guidance activities may be of specific concern, such as traditional values clarification activities (e.g., lifeboat exercises) or behavior modification practices.

Not all of these sometimes fearful or angry parents have the same motivation, however, although nearly all are also motivated by concern for their own children. In working effectively in the often difficult interactions with these parents, determining motivation is important. The motivations tend to fall into five categories. Some parents are *misinformed*, some are concerned about *materials*, some *mistrust* certain practices, some have experienced *mistakes*, and some are *misusing* an issue. Identifying which category describes a parent's motivation helps to suggest an appropriate response.

Most of the parents who question guidance and counseling programs either individually or at the building level fit into the first category. They are misinformed about a program or practice, or about public schools in general. These parents often hear concerns from other, more politically active patrons, and in some cases, they fear for their children's psychological or spiritual safety. When they receive accurate information about the program and become acquainted with the professionalism of the school counseling staff, their concerns are usually addressed.

In the second category are the concerned parents who hear about commercially produced materials that have been targeted by national groups as undermining the development of wholesome, family values.

A third category of critical parents consists of those who mistrust certain practices of the public schools in general. This category includes parents who worry that counseling is brainwashing or instilling a specific set of values that are contrary to their own. Most often they see the public schools in general as an arm of an atheistic state.

The fourth category is the smallest by far and comprises those who, in fact, have experienced mistakes made by staff members. Sometimes school counselors have the right intentions but choose the wrong strategy. In other cases, it is sad but true that some educators are not ethically or professionally sound.

The fifth category are those parents/constituents who are acting in bad faith, those who are misusing an issue for their own purposes. Such purposes may be political; they may want to engender support for a school board candidate. Such purposes may be economic; they may be trying to nurture a clientele for a private or parochial school. Such purposes may be immoral or illegal; they may be hiding something going on in their homes. Some of the parents who use this critical posture are child abusers who do not want to be found out. It is fortunate that the number of critics in this category is very small because they are the most difficult to deal with.

3. *What are the school counselors' topics and motivations?* School counselors in these situations are well served by being clear as to their own topics and motivations. The ASCA (2002) position statement on censorship states a belief of the professional as follows:

> In order for students to develop in a healthy manner and obtain the skills necessary for citizenship, they need to exist in a climate that fosters the ability to make informed decisions based upon independent inquiry and sound scholarship. Professional school counselors have a personal and professional obligation to support the basic tenets of democracy to help ensure information about—and access to—a range of developmentally appropriate school counseling programs for every student.

Their topics fit into three categories. Counselors want to (a) improve the services provided to the specific parents' individual children or to all students, (b) maintain the program benefits for individual or all students, and (c) allow the program to continue for students other than those of the critical parent(s). While keeping the conversation focused on manageable problems, school counselors usually identify which of these represents the best-case scenario for the outcomes of these interactions.

In some cases—perhaps many—school counselors want the children of the adversarial parents to be able to benefit from more extensive services than they are participating in. Specifically, many of the children evidence themselves as being in need of individual or small-group counseling services. Some of the parents are fearful of what counseling will do to the minds of their children. Others fear what counseling will reveal about the family dynamics, abuses, or other practices. In advocating for the students, school counselors strive to convince parents to let their children participate fully in guidance and counseling activities.

Adversarial parents often do not want their own children to participate in some or all of the activities and services in the comprehensive guidance and counseling program. Typically they do not want their children to participate in counseling. Many request that they not participate in guidance curriculum activities as well. Those who are truly fearful of government intervention in their lives do not want their students participating in career development activities, including career assessments, or other individual student planning system activities. Some parents are not content with protecting only their own children; they want these activities dropped from the school program all together. Having carefully designed their programs to meet students' needs, school counselors believe in and advocate for the program to stay intact for all students.

Further, some parents threaten the very existence of the program in schools. School counselors' agendas then are aimed at maintaining the program for students other than those of parents who do not want the program, at making the program optional. Many counselors find it difficult to give up this ground—they have worked hard for the programs to be in place. However, some battles cannot be won, and rather than lose the war, it is better that some children not participate than for the program to be eliminated all together.

School counselors also are well served by clarifying their own motivations in these situations. They, too, have a wide array, from altruistic to self-serving. On the altruistic end of the continuum, school counselors are motivated to maintain the integrity of the program. A previous example was to strive to maintain the design of the program by providing activities and services that meet the identified needs of the children and youths served. School counselors are best served in the face of adversaries when they are secure in the basis of their program, when they know what the content and rationale are. They are secure when the basic mission of the program is tied to the mission of the school and school district. They are secure when they are well grounded in their own professional integrity, in their competent work with and on behalf of children and youths in school.

Most districts have policies and procedures regarding censorship and the curriculum. If you or the counselors are not aware of these, they should be included in the department's operational handbook. Especially when districts have designed their guidance and counseling programs as carefully as we are suggesting and have defined so clearly the integral nature of their program, defense of program participation is soundly supported. Program modifications must not be made without due consideration of whether the modification violates the integrity of the program.

Sometimes school counselors become fearful or angry and are motivated not on behalf of children but on their own behalf. There are times when groups of parents threaten the very existence of the program, and school counselors fear that their jobs are not secure. Such times, however, are not that frequent. Not all parents who disagree with the program want it and the counselor eliminated from the school.

Sometimes concerned parents want to change the shape of the program—by, for example, eliminating group counseling—and thereby change the job description of the school counselors. Some school counselors get angry and defensive about being told what to do. Guarding against overreacting in these circumstances is essential for school counselors. Fear for job security or anger at differences of opinion are not strong positions, and they may add grounds for other confrontations.

School counselors may also be fearful of parents' concerns because they do not fully understand them and may be threatened by the lack of clarity of the parents' goals. They may resent having others suggest that what they do is inappropriate when they believe it is appropriate (and the right thing to do). They may be hurt by the appearance of someone not liking them. If they are insecure in their role or unsure about the value of their programs, this insecurity may undermine their professional demeanor.

4. *What are the parents' and school counselors' objectives?* School counselors are best served when they can state for themselves and for the parents, after analysis and reflection on the opening parts of the dialogue, what each "side" has as objectives for the interactions and the relationships. It is to be hoped that these are in the best interest of the children in question. Parents' objectives relate to their topics of concern and their motivations. Counselors' objectives are specific to each child–parent situation and to their motivations on behalf of the specific children involved or all children whose access to services are threatened. For example:

- Misinformed parents may ask to have their children removed from classroom guidance because of fear of the humanistic nature of the content. A counselor's objective would be to allow the child to reap the benefits of the guidance curriculum.

- Parents who have heard negative things about particular material may want that material's use censored from the program (Brigman & Moore, 1994). A counselor's objective would be to maintain its use in relevant aspects of the program.
- Mistrusting parents may not want their children to participate in small-group counseling. A counselor's objective would be for the students to participate in groups that serve their needs.
- Parents who have experienced a mistake made by counselors may want to have different counselors assigned to their students. A counselor's objective would be for parents to recognize the counselor's awareness of the error and assurance that it was a momentary lapse, not a permanent condition of incompetence.
- Parents who want visibility in the community may want the guidance and counseling program eliminated from the school. A counselor's objective would be to provide means for those parents' children to opt out of the program, leaving it intact for the children of parents who want the program to continue.

Appropriate Response Selection. Supported by the clarity of their own objectives, school counselors choose from one of nine advocacy response levels. In choosing their responses, they identify the skills and resources that best apply in the particular situation. They identify potentially successful response strategies and implement strategically relevant activities. For themselves and for the parents, they clarify the status of the situation at the conclusion of their interactions.

1. *What advocacy response level is appropriate?* As described in more detail in *Leading and Managing Your School Guidance Program Staff* (Henderson & Gysbers, 1998), and as defined and exemplified in counseling/school counseling literature (e.g., journals of the American School Counselors Association, Association for Counselor Education and Supervision, and American Counseling Association), there are nine advocacy responses, each varying in involvement and intensity on the part of the advocating counselor. These responses fall on a continuum of involvement by school counselors (e.g., degree of participation, energy expended, level of commitment, as evidenced by the resources they expend). The responses range from being physically present to acting assertively on someone's behalf, from giving time to giving time plus ideas, initiative, power, professionalism, and so on.

Having chosen how limited or how expanded the advocacy role that is appropriate to contribute, the counselors consider whether they will simply represent the program/profession, inform the parents, welcome them, reach out to them, support their objectives, cooperate or collaborate with them as they work toward their objectives, or consult or advocate with them on behalf of their children. Activities that school counselors do at each advocacy response level include the following:

- representing their program at parent functions
- informing parents about their program in conferences
- welcoming parents who come into the guidance center and reaching out to those who seem reluctant
- supporting parents who have concerns about the school and are seeking ways to communicate these to the right people
- cooperating with parents, even those who are critical of the program, and seeking collaborative opportunities to work with parents on mutual agendas
- consulting with parents about ways they can help their children be successful in school
- advocating for parents with other school staff members, when the parents are fearful or for some reason cannot find their own voices

School counselors consider the skills and resources they can best apply to bring the situation to successful conclusion. To advocate effectively, counselors consciously decide how best to apply their skills in response to the parents' agendas and to advance the agendas of the school counselors. Their skills include their communication, consultation, and political skills (Henderson & Gysbers, 1998). Influence over others stems from their wanting something that another individual can offer them. The resources school counselors have to share include competence, ideas, time, power, involvement, and energy that stems from commitment. If counselors determine the parents they are currently working with can be influenced, they need to determine which resource will be most influential. Parents might be influenced by knowing what the counselors understand about schooling, about children, and about the teachers their children are working with. They may be appreciative of being treated humanely and having the counselors give them time for the conversation. They may be influenced by the counselors' professionalism.

2. *What strategies are potentially successful?* When managing such relationships, school counselors consciously select strategies that incorporate their and the parents' objectives, allow them to apply their skills and resources effectively, and are within the identified level of advocacy response they have decided is most efficient. They select strategies and related activities that appear to have the best chance of responding to the parents' agenda and to best move their own agenda on behalf of students. The goal is, of course, resolution of the issues to the satisfaction of both sides of the dialogue and in the best interest of the students involved.

3. *What response activities are strategically appropriate?* Advocacy strategies are carried out through activities. Having selected the strategy (objective, advocacy response level, skills and resources), school counselors carefully select appropriate activities, plan how they will conduct them, and carry them out. With parents who are misinformed, some proactive efforts that school counselors can undertake are to present overviews of their programs at open houses, PTA meetings, and parent workshops, and to publish newsletters or articles regarding the topics included in guidance curriculum.

With those who complain about specific materials, if such materials are used in the program, it is important that people be allowed to study them to become familiar with their actual content. Again, most often what they think is there is not, and their concerns are alleviated. Encouraging parents to preview materials before they become concerned is proactive, and with a planned program this is feasible.

Even though the district has established the needs for and the values of a comprehensive guidance and counseling program, to help keep confrontations from escalating it may be useful to have procedures for opting out of nonmandatory aspects of the program or for benefiting from alternative assignments. For example, Northside Independent School District developed a procedure for parents to follow that requires their learning the information they need to make good decisions about their children's participation in the developmental guidance and counseling program, and that requires them to be very specific about what content they do not want their child exposed to (see Appendix J). Counseling is provided only with parental permission. These procedures help counteract parents' feelings of having no control over what happens to their children at school.

The distrust of the parents who question the purposes of the guidance and counseling program usually goes beyond that of the program and the individual counselor. Their concerns should be attended to by the principal. Schools cannot and probably should not change to attend to the concerns of these parents, and administrators are able to express best what is legally required and done in the best professional judgment of those responsible for the school program.

For the parents who have experienced mistakes of bad practice by school counselors, the first step is to hear and investigate the parents' complaints. Again, these occasions are best handled by the building administrators involved. They, in turn, need to follow due process as spelled out in policy or regulations to determine the facts and consequences. Those parents who misuse the guidance and counseling program by making it an issue for their own purposes are also best handled by administrators or other authorities. Political candidates may be listened to and then turned over to administrators to handle. Entrepreneurs are best exposed for what they are. Those involved in illegal activities, including child neglect, need to be reported to the proper authorities. (A sample response to the standard letter described earlier is provided in Appendix J.)

It is clear that proactive strategies are preferable to reactive ones. Parents feel attended to and appreciate the openness of the guidance department. Counselors feel comfortable as they initiate the involvements and manage the relationships from the outset. Thus at the beginning of the second year, proactive counselors reach out to inform parents of their program plans for the year, hiding nothing. They invite parents to preview materials. They collaborate with school administrators and PTAs to help all parents value the gifts of the school. They are especially vigilant about not making or appearing to make mistakes. They are prepared to work politically to address those who would misuse their guidance platform for other agendas.

4. *How is the conclusion clarified?* As with any counselor–client problem-solving interaction, the counselor ends the conference or meeting by summarizing the original problem and the status of that problem at the time, and the plan for the future regarding the problem and any related issues. The summary statement may include such items as restating the original problem, how the differences have been resolved so far, and what measures are planned to continue resolution of the problem. One resolution of the problem is to agree to disagree. Hopefully, there will also be next steps planned that relate to working together for mutual goals regarding the children involved in the situation. Such summarizing provides clarity for the counselors and for the parents.

Being confronted or challenged by individuals presents an uncomfortable situation. For their own peace of mind, school counselors continue to keep in touch with parents who are supporters of their work. They develop strategies for adding to or using their support base. They do this formally through the school–community advisory committee, and informally by hearing from the multitude of appreciative clients who have been well served by the program. In times of conflict, many supporters are willing and eager to present their side of the story. Do not be shy about using them.

Focus on Special Projects

Once the design for the guidance and counseling program has been established, guidance and counseling program leaders are encouraged to focus on special projects that help incorporate current trends in education, to keep pace with their educator colleagues. The energy provided by an educational reform or other professionwide movements can facilitate some of the changes that need to be accomplished. New directions from the federal, state, local community, district, and building level could be mirrored by special emphases within the guidance department. Such changes keep counselors abreast of changes in the total educational system and help maintain their position on the educational team. That is, other staff who have to change see that counselors have to change also.

Such changes also have the side benefit of helping counselors avoid having change forced on them that may be inappropriate to the directions of the new program. For example, many of the current reforms have increased the paperwork/accountability burden of the school staff, such as noting students' mastery of required instructional outcomes. If the counselors have to attend to changes of their own, they can better avoid being assigned to some of the paperwork tasks that belong to teachers or administrators; if the counselors are visibly augmenting the guidance curriculum component, for example, fellow staff members will see more readily that the counselors do not have time to make such notations and instead make them themselves.

Recurrent issues that were deemed as critical to successful development and implementation of comprehensive school guidance and counseling programs were identified in a national survey (Henderson & Gysbers, 2002). These issues, in priority order, are

1. Displacement of non-guidance tasks, including school counselors' appropriate role in standardized testing programs
2. Program accountability
3. Accountability for the quality of school counselor performance
4. Program advocacy
5. Leader empowerment
6. Enhancement of an existing comprehensive guidance program
7. Appropriate use of technology
8. Parent involvement, including responding to parents who are critical of the program
9. Program development process
10. Enhancement of the cross-cultural competence of school counselors. (p. 8)

Examples of leadership responses that led to successful resolution of these issues are offered in Henderson and Gysbers (2002).

Federal and State Priorities

The review of the history of guidance and counseling provided in chapter 1 demonstrates the impact of *federal priorities* on the development of our profession. In addition, contemporary guidance and counseling program changes can and should relate to the current federal emphasis on at-risk populations. Surely, children and youths who are at risk because of violence, drug and other substance abuse, lack of academic success, disabilities (hidden or otherwise) that interfere with their learning, premature sexual activity, or adolescent depression are priority clients for school counselors implementing the responsive services component of a comprehensive guidance and counseling program. That these clients have federal priority (Office of Public Policy and Legislation, 2004) provides rationale for their needing counseling services. That the effectiveness of counseling has been established (ASCA, 2002–2003; Office of Public Policy and Legislation, 2004) provides rationale for the guidance department to receive some of the funds appropriated for the special programs designed to meet these needs. In addition, some priority has been given for character education at the federal level (Office of Public Policy and Legislation, 2004). Fittingly, ASCA (1998) has taken a position that "endorses and supports character education in the schools."

State-level reforms at the beginning of the 21st century emphasize excellence in education as defined in tighter standards for instructional methodology, improved curriculum, improved student achievement, and improved student discipline. These emphases have caused the development of new teacher appraisal/evaluation systems, new requirements for lesson planning, efforts to better facilitate the achievement of academic excellence, and increased emphasis in career and technology education on preparation for a highly technological work world. There has been a renewed interest in accountability as demonstrated through achievement of minimum competencies on tests and other standardized achievement measures. Mandates for improved student discipline include systems that provide consistent and logical consequences for student misbehavior and require more parental involvement for students who act out.

Reforms have focused on the science of education and on the human dimensions of education. Politicians and businesspeople have had a big say in educational reforms. Legislators and businesspeople have stated what they think students should know and be able to do as a result of schooling (Secretary's Commission on Achieving Necessary Skills, 1991). Thus the results-based education movement suggests to educators what our product should be but—because the movement is coupled with an interest in the principles of total quality management—leaves the methodology decisions to the "workers," the professional educators. Standards are high, accountability is measured by such hard data as test results, but increasing autonomy is given to local districts and schools to plan their own methods for achieving the standards. The focus is on excellence in the education system and on recognition of the diversity of students served, and it is balanced with calls for equity and for attending to the unique needs of individual students. The continued fiscal conservatism of state governments has helped public servants recognize that getting more money for services is very difficult. Thus efforts to integrate educational, health, and human services as well as to coordinate provision of vocational education and training continue.

Each of these efforts can be used to enhance and support needed changes in the guidance and counseling program. The actual specifics of reforms vary from state to state and according to local priorities and needs; nonetheless, some common themes point to directions for counselors. New systems for assisting teachers to use current teaching methodology include clinical supervision strategies of observation and feedback, refined appraisal/evaluation models, and professional development plans. The same strategies can be used for counselors and are discussed more extensively in chapters 9 and 10 and more fully in *Leading and Managing Your School Guidance Program Staff* (Henderson & Gysbers, 1998). Asking counselors to write their plans for counseling sessions and guidance lessons is a companion piece to asking teachers to develop better lesson plans. Districts across the United States are using school improvement planning techniques and developing multiyear strategic plans. Counselors and guidance departments, too, should be asked to clarify their plans for the year by submitting calendars and using a goal-based improvement approach. This fits nicely into the comprehensive program concept.

Curriculum development in other disciplines provides counselors with the opportunity to write the guidance curriculum and to provide for infusion of guidance curriculum in the academic curricula. For example, in addition to the guidance dimension within the mental health curriculum strand in the health and science curricula, the social skills outcomes that are part of the guidance curriculum can easily be infused into the social studies curricula; communication skills can be infused into language arts; and problem solving can be infused into science and math. Perhaps because the concept of a guidance curriculum has grown, much of what we see as students' needs already has been stated in outcome terms, making us prepared to work within the outcomes-based approach. Another relevant aspect of this approach, and one that already is a part of the guidance curriculum, is the emphasis on helping students learn processes, such as decision making, planning, and relating to others, including those from cultures different from their own.

The continued emphasis on testing calls for counselors to help students with their test-taking skills and to help teachers use test results responsibly. This provides counselors the opportunity to shift their role from being test administrators to being consultants in appropriate test use. Adding the dimension of attending to each individual student's needs renews the interest in one of counselors' basic services: identification of individual student's strengths, weaknesses, and needs. Although counselors are already recognized for this expertise, the magnitude of the challenge of providing such insights for every student means ensuring that counselors' own methods are up-to-date (e.g., recognizing the limits of tests and being comfortable with using multiple sources of data) and entrusting some of this responsibility to other educators, under the counselors' supervision.

Similarly, improved discipline-management programs rest heavily on guidance content—the content of psychology. Counselors can seize this area of high priority to administrators and work collaboratively with them in helping students learn new ways to behave responsibly and to make decisions through activities in the guidance curriculum. Both of these emphases give counselors clear priorities for providing students with special services; students who fail to meet minimum academic standards and students who consistently misbehave often can benefit from effective small-group or individual counseling.

Further, the effort to bring community services into the schools draws on counselors' expertise in coordination and augments the mental health services provided to children, youths, and families. How this is accomplished will be different in each locale, but school counselors must be in on the planning of integrated delivery systems to ensure that students' needs are well articulated and to ensure that the role envisioned for them is professionally appropriate. The emphasis on coordinating the resources for helping children, youths, and adults enter and succeed in the workforce also provides opportunities for school counselors to enhance the career development dimension of their programs, providing that they (and you) are involved in the development of the new systems.

District Priorities

With or without impetus from federal or state sources, school districts typically have priorities of high interest to their school boards or to their superintendents. School board members are often interested in academic excellence reflected in the number of scholarship winners, or in the "back to the basics" of the schools' mission that can include the basic of responsible behavior. District administrators are challenged by declining or expanding enrollment; both have implications for teachers' morale. Counselors can be visible in their role of helping others as well as themselves cope with change in a healthy manner. Wellness programs bring with them a potential interest in mental health. These activities that apply the expertise of the guidance and counseling field are system support of the best kind. For example, districts around the country are responding to the challenge to help students connect with the adults in the schools, minimizing alienation and making the interpersonal climate more inviting. One mechanism for doing this is having effective classroom meetings at all school levels (Edwards & Mullis, 2003). Several roles for professional school counselors in instituting successful classroom meetings are to advocate for the practice, explaining the benefits for students; to train teachers in how to conduct effective meetings; and to consult with teachers as they implement them.

Community Priorities

Influential community groups, such as the PTA, chamber of commerce, and service clubs (e.g., Lions and Kiwanis), have priority projects that can bring positive visibility to improving the guidance and counseling program. The PTA is interested in youth problem topics such as suicide prevention. Lions clubs are actively working to combat drug abuse and to help children care for their personal safety. In some areas, locally elected public officials are concerned about violence and gangs. Economic development groups are interested in career development programs. As education opens up to the communities it serves, guidance and counseling program reformers are advised to listen to the priorities of these groups; areas in which their interests dovetail with guidance goals suggest priority areas for guidance efforts as well.

Building Priorities

In addition to the expanded opportunities for program improvement provided to counselors in the localization of school improvement efforts, major events in school buildings can highlight the need for specific changes in the guidance and counseling program. Accreditation self-studies and visits provide opportunities to make recommendations for improving the guidance and counseling program. Visible student problems—teen suicides, drug busts, gang-related uprisings—demand counselors' attention. Principals have goals for their schools.

Counselors should collaborate with their administrators by showing them how the comprehensive guidance and counseling program supports the development of strategies to help attain the school goals. Principals' goals quite often include such items as holding high expectations for students, working to enhance the self-esteem of students, and improving interpersonal relationships among the staff. Counselors can and should share parts of these goals. Needless to say, the more counselors' and principals' goals have in common, the more support counselors will have from key decision makers. The more school counselors are viable members of schoolwide teams, the more support they have in their buildings.

Further, individual counselors or counseling staffs have special talents, interests, and areas of expertise. Some high school counselors are expert in helping teenagers deal with grief and loss; some elementary counselors are creative in using popular toys as materials in developmental guidance and counseling programs. By capitalizing on these, the guidance and counseling program leader not only can give appropriate recognition to those counselors but also can provide for the development of special projects that, when successful, can be shared with other buildings.

Facilitate Building-Level Changes

The district-level guidance and counseling program leader assists the building-level leaders and counselors by establishing systems that help make the operational-level changes needed to effect implementation of the comprehensive guidance and counseling program. This entails, as Adelman and Taylor (2003) phrased it, "Establishing an infrastructure and action plan[s] for carrying out the changes" (p. 9). Two such mechanisms are as follows:

- Have building staffs commit to goals for program improvement and develop the plans for achieving those goals. This is a way to repair discrepancies identified between the current and desired program designs and a means for changing the activities done within the program.
- Have building staffs develop transition and implementation plans similar to those developed at the district level. This is a way to change the resources appropriated to the guidance and counseling program at the building level.

At the building level, school counselors, their department heads, and principals use the strategies described here: a goal-based program improvement system, a master plan for change, and action plans for implementation.

Using a Goal-Based Program Improvement System

Goals are tools for turning visions into realities. They help individuals focus their energies on changes counselors and others perceive as important, and they make change manageable. In the circumstance we are describing—remodeling and revitalizing your program while you are living in it—the thought of striving to implement all the changes at once can be overwhelming. Focusing on a handful of goals is conceivable to most people; being allowed to develop their own strategies for attaining those goals allows counselors a sense of autonomy and comfort in making the needed changes. In the Northside Independent School District, the goal areas are established at the district level. The district initiates the goal-setting and action-planning processes, but each building has latitude in choosing specific implementation strategies that fit its needs or specialties. Establishing the goals for high-priority skill development, clients, or activities as well as the process of goal setting, action planning, monitoring, and evaluating progress toward the goals provides a consistency of focus across the district. These efforts serve to affect the continuity of newly implemented programs, allow for the continuation of dialogue between counselors from different buildings about change efforts, and give direction for in-service training and staff development activities.

Goal Setting

In reviewing the current guidance and counseling program and the desired guidance and counseling program, you discovered some discrepancies, as we discussed in chapter 6. These discrepancies are the targets for program improvements districtwide. Likewise, each building's guidance and counseling program design team should compare and contrast their existing program with their articulated desired program. These identified discrepancies become additional targets for program improvement goals.

The number of goals people are asked to consider depends on the number of discrepancies found, the size of the discrepancies, and the priorities the district or building has set. Goals should be delineated for program improvements and for performance improvements. A sample of a memo used in Northside Independent School District to assist counselors to attend to meaningful goals is presented in Figure 7.3. The goals are presented to individual staff members as challenges to each to do something to help repair the identified discrepancies.

Figure 7.3
Goals Memo

To:	Counselors
From:	Director of Guidance
Re:	Program and Performance Goals

Below are listed general goals that have been identified for *program* and *performance* improvements. Please pick two from each category to focus on for this school year, and specify the improvement you envision on the action planning form that is attached.

Program Goals
- to increase time spent in *curriculum*/developmental guidance
- to decrease time spent in *responsive services*/to improve quality of time spent in responsive services
- to decrease time spent in *system support*
- to decrease time/to improve quality of time spent with school *staff*
- to increase time spent with *parents*

Performance Goals
- to improve group guidance skills
- to improve counseling skills
- to improve consulting skills
- to improve program planning/evaluation skills
- to improve referral skills

Note. Data from Northside Independent School District, San Antonio, TX. Adapted with permission.

These goals are broad and leave each counselor or building staff with choices. What they do "to improve the quality of time spent in responsive services" and how they do it are left to them. For example, counselors may strive to decrease individual counseling time by initiating small-group counseling or systematically consulting with teachers. A sample of more specific goal targets is presented in Figure 7.4. These goals establish more specific activities for counselors to implement at the building level but leave the implementation plan to them. For example, they are asked to conduct group counseling for targeted populations, but the actual design of the counseling series is left to them. In both cases the counselors specify the student outcomes and objectives for their new activities; they plan their own strategies and methods of evaluation on the basis of local needs and their own resources.

Counselors are asked to set their own goals to be reviewed by their immediate supervisor. Where there is more than one counselor in a building, the guidance department as a whole should have goals also, such as "The department will develop an annual plan for expanded implementation of the guidance curriculum."

The individuals' goals within the department should be related to each other's, and all counselors on a staff should be cognizant of their colleagues' goals. This helps to develop a support system that is useful in assisting the counselors meet success in striving for their goals. We also recommend that building principals sign off on the goals to indicate not only their awareness of the counselors' endeavors but also their approval. The head counselor or, in buildings where there is no such designated department leader, all of the counselors should meet and discuss the goals with the principal. This ensures that the guidance goals are consistent with the general building goals and provides a vehicle for enlisting the prin-

Figure 7.4
Counselors' Goals Memo

To:	Elementary School Counselors
From:	Director of Guidance
Re:	Counselors' Goals

The goal-setting process implemented for the past several years worked well to help focus the guidance program improvement efforts. The districtwide goals are listed below. Please discuss these goals with your principals and add others that are in response to the needs of your campus community.

1. To continue to contribute to students' education by effectively teaching guidance curricula outlined in the *Comprehensive Guidance Program Framework*.

2. To respond to campus-identified high-priority student-clients through effective group counseling. "High-priority student-clients" may include students who are underachieving or who are behaving irresponsibly.

3. To respond to campus-identified high-priority parent-clients through systematically implemented parent consultation or parent education.

4. To decrease student-contact time spent in clerical/quasi-administrative tasks by identifying personal "time-eaters" and minimizing the time spent on these.

5. To provide a better balanced guidance program by systematically planning the year's activities to adhere as much as feasible to the district-outlined and campus-specified comprehensive program design. (Planning assistance will be provided by the Director of Guidance.)

6. To increase the effectiveness of counseling and guidance activities by clear articulation of the counselor's theoretical base.

As in previous years, we will be discussing the strategies you identify as appropriate for striving to attain your goals. A copy of the revised Planning Form is attached. Please submit a copy of your "Guidance Program Improvement Planning" forms to me by September 15.

Approved: _____
              Associate Superintendent

cc: Elementary School Principals

Note. Data from Northside Independent School District, San Antonio, TX. Adapted with permission.

cipal's support in goal attainment. The goals ultimately should be submitted to the district office for review by the administrator responsible for guidance.

Guidance and Counseling Program Improvement Planning

Once specific goals have been established, each counselor and each department should develop plans for meeting these goals. As mentioned previously, such planning encourages forward and realistic thinking. It sets in motion a series of decisions and actions that actually help implement the strategies. A sample planning form is provided in Figure 7.5.

Once counselors' goals have been identified and counselors have committed themselves to implementation strategies, the guidance and counseling program leader has a means of monitoring counselors' progress toward these goals. This process is discussed in more depth in chapter 8.

Developing and Implementing the Building Master Plan for Change

As at the district level, a master plan for change should guide the transition efforts at the building level. In addition to making changes in the activities done in the guidance and counseling program through the previously described goal-setting process, the building staff needs to consider the need for improvement in the resources that support the program at their level. The counselor(s), principal, guidance and counseling program development team, school–community advisory committee—all of the players with an interest in the program—should consider the status of the personnel, financial, and political resources available to the program. At this point in the improvement process, there are probably systemwide standards or guidelines established for resource allocation in the buildings; however, if there are not, then the local team(s) can develop its (their) own "realistic ideals" to shoot for by asking the questions outlined here and others that come to mind as they consider the questions.

- *Personnel resources.* Have all school staff members accepted responsibility for the guidance program? Are the guidance-program-related jobs being done in accord with the system's job descriptions? Are the organizational relationships among the guidance and counseling program staff clear and working well? Are the organizational relationships between the guidance staff and the administrative staff, the instructional staff, and the other subsets of campus staff members working well? Do counselors have access to students to provide the program fully? Is time and money allocated to support program and professional development activities by the counselors and other guidance staff?
- *Financial resources.* Is there a guidance department budget for supplies and materials? Is it adequate? Are there other funding sources that could augment the budget, for example, PTA for parent workshops; federal, state, district, or other grants for pilot projects; local businesses for career development or mentoring programs? Are adequate materials available to support the program? Is time available to the staff to develop needed materials? Do the facilities meet established standards? Are the facilities welcoming and attractive? Is the necessary equipment available and working?
- *Political resources.* Are campus policies and procedures supportive of implementation of the desired guidance and counseling program design; for example, are counselors' nonguidance tasks decreasing and student-centered activities increasing? Is the principal supportive of the newly defined and designed program and the staff? Are the teachers? How are resisters being handled? Is the guidance and counseling program

Figure 7.5
Guidance Program Improvement Planning Form

GUIDANCE PROGRAM IMPROVEMENT PLANNING

School: _____

Name: _____

Principal/Head Counselor Signature: _____

Date: _____

USE A SEPARATE FORM FOR EACH GOAL

	PLANNING (To Be Completed by September 1)		EVALUATION (To Be Completed by Contract End-June)	
Program Objective/Strategy	Tasks to Accomplish	Time Frame	Level of (1–5) Accomplishment	Students'/Others' Outcomes

Goal: _____

Overall Assessment of Level
of Accomplishment:

1   2   3   4   5
(Not Achieved)   (Fully Achieved)

Counselor's Signature: _____

Principal/Head Counselor: _____

Date: _____

an integral part of schoolwide programs? Are school counselors active members of schoolwide planning teams? Are there guidance and counseling program objectives in the school improvement plan? Are there systematic mechanisms such as weekly or monthly meetings that facilitate communication between the counselor(s) and the administrator(s), between the counselor(s) and the teachers? Are the relationships between the guidance and counseling program staff and the community good? Is there an effective advisory committee? Are the guidance and counseling program public relations objectives a part of the school public relations efforts? Is there an active/almost active group of critical constituents who need to be/are being worked with in a concerted manner?

After asking and answering these and other questions, the next step is to identify the goals/targets and relative priorities for change and then to lay out the master plan, listing what needs to be done, in what order, within what time frame, and who the person is with primary responsibility (see Table 6.4).

Developing the Building Action Plans for Implementation

As the time approaches to accomplish each of the goals/targets, a relevant plan of action should be developed (see Table 7.1). For example, if in order to access students in a junior high school, guidance curriculum time must be negotiated with the academic teachers, several tasks need to be accomplished before the counselor can infuse the guidance learning activities into the various curricula: (a) The counselor must have lesson objectives planned, (b) the principal's support must be enlisted, (c) a meeting with the academic department chairs needs to be established, and so on. Plans must be made to accomplish each of these tasks successfully.

A point needs to be made here: The changes must begin with reallocation of the resources currently available and in anticipation of new resources that probably will be allocated. Counselors must resist the mentality of waiting until everything at the system level has been done. This is where the top-down/bottom-up dynamic (Fullen, 2001) is most evident. Only so much change can occur at the building level within the current resource allocation, but those changes need to be made. For example, if a principal wants counselors teaching or developing guidance lessons for use in a homeroom-type situation and perceives counselors as sitting in their offices spending undue amounts of time with individual students, the counselors should devise ways to attend to the principal's goal. It is conceivable that if they manage their time with the consideration that the principal has an important priority for them, the lessons could be developed. The principal, then, will be more likely to believe that the counselors use their time efficiently when they ask for other considerations.

Often the success of district resource expansion depends on the evidence of maximum resource use at the school level. Spending all the money appropriated for buying program materials is an obvious example. Further, once buildings have established their local plans, the district can identify and target problems and solutions identified in several buildings. For example, if several building guidance and counseling program plans seek to augment the guidance curriculum through use of homeroom periods, a districtwide group might be formed to work together to develop appropriate guidance learning activities.

Implement Public Relations Activities

Now that you have a grasp of the new program and have clarified the language used to describe it, you are ready to plan and implement public relations activities. Because the best generator of good public relations is a good program, counselors need to feel that they are conducting the best program feasible. They need to feel secure in the priorities that have been set and feel that they can explain them to the many publics served such as students, teachers, administrators, parents, the business community, and community members at large. They need to make every consumer contact a high-quality, customer-friendly experience (even at those impossibly busy times of the year).

Planning public relations begins with study of the data that were gathered in the assessment of the current program on how others perceive the guidance and counseling program. Because one purpose of public relations is for people to know more about the program so they can access and appreciate its services, the goal at this time is to help people move from what they thought the program was to what the new program structure is. To accomplish this task, we recommend that a work group be formed to assist in planning and implementing the public relations program. The work group should include not only counselors but also representatives—preferably leaders—of the publics to whom you plan to relate. It could be an ad hoc group, and it could include representatives from the steering or school–community advisory committees. Ultimately, the group that will continue public relations activities, once they are undertaken, is the school–community advisory committee.

Planning Your Public Relations Program

Public relations program planning is no different from the planning used in the rest of the guidance and counseling program improvement process. You need to know where you are by performing a current assessment—in this case, the perception survey. You need to know where you want to go—the desired end—in this case, the established goals for the public relations program. And you need to know how you are going to get there. Establish a plan of action that includes the public relations objectives and strategies to be accomplished and the time frame involved.

Public relations should be systematically installed as an ongoing part of the program's overall improvement and management procedures. Public relations activities that are not related in this integrated fashion to the total program may be superficial and, as a result, may not have sufficient impact. Thus careful attention to the planning is important.

To develop your plan for public relations, consider these steps:

1. Establish goals for your public relations efforts. Examples include program consumers being informed about, understanding, and being supportive of and able to use the comprehensive guidance and counseling program.
2. Identify the target populations for your public relations efforts. Examples include students, teachers, parents, administrators, school board members, referral agency personnel, and community representatives/leaders.
3. Find out what these publics think about what you are doing and what they think you should be doing. The specific data gathered in the current program perception survey should tell you this.
4. Establish specific objectives for each subgroup. Examples include informing all parents about the program and gaining support from some parents for the program.
5. Identify the resources available to assist in your efforts. Examples include Meet Your Counselor pamphlets, PTA newsletters and programs, daytime radio talk shows, and school official communiqués.
6. Consider the relative impact each resource may have on the target population. Examples include inviting PTA leaders to serve on the advisory committee to pro-

vide them an opportunity to fulfill their leadership/representative role and, if advice is taken, to enlist their support for the program.

7. Translate these resources into strategies to be used. Where possible, use the already existing resources that have demonstrated effectiveness for reaching the target population, such as the administrator's association newsletter to communicate with administrators. Where none exists, consider creating unique resources such as guidance department newsletters or Counselor Corner columns in the local newspaper.
8. Outline the steps that will be taken in the development of these strategies and relate them to the overall plan.
9. Assign a person to be responsible for the activities.
10. Establish your time frame.

Well planned public relations activities are an integral part of the guidance and counseling program improvement process. Remember that an effective public relations program is sincere in purpose and execution in keeping with the total guidance and counseling program's purpose and characteristics, positive in approach and appeal, continuous in application, comprehensive in scope, clear and with simple messages, and beneficial to both sender and receiver.

Public relations activities have two purposes: (a) to let consumers know how good the program is and how to access it and (b) to change any negative perceptions they may have to more positive ones. To do this, it is important to listen for and understand the negative perceptions that some consumers may have. For example, some teachers do not know about our program and are often dissatisfied that they do not get instant service when they think they need it. They are not aware that we, too, take work home at night. They do not think that we, too, are tied to a set schedule that someone else has determined. Many are not familiar with our role as student advocates; they see us in problem situations as adversaries. For another example, administrators may think that counselors do not work very hard. Administrators work evenings supervising activities, and they do not think that counselors do, too. Further, some counselors are perceived as not being loyal to the school because they do not attend extracurricular activities. For yet another example, some parents do not feel that they get the response they want, or perceive counselors as having made recommendations about their children that have damaged their educational careers. Many are not aware of our specialized training.

Some in the population at large still—unfortunately—have negative bias against people with psychological problems and are skeptical about the value of mental health services. In addition, some students do not recognize or acknowledge the help they receive from counselors. They perceive us as paper pushers who were not helpful when they perceived they were having a problem. In general, because our programs have not been well defined, people have had unrealistic expectations about counselors and the services counselors can and should provide.

We might consider some food for thought gleaned from the corporate reputation literature. Corporations and companies have learned that their reputations are important in achieving not only employee but also customer satisfaction. One delineation (Davies, Chun, Da Silva, & Roper, 2004) of the dimensions that make up a corporation's image identifies them as "Agreeableness," "Competence," "Enterprise," "Ruthlessness," and "Chic." Davies et al. found positive customer satisfaction to be most highly correlated with Agreeableness. The second highest correlation is with Competence. A reputation for Enterprise and Chic correlated with customer satisfaction, but not as highly as the first two. Agreeableness, as defined by Davies et al., entails honesty and social responsibility and not being aggressive or arrogant. Competence is defined as being reliable and ambitious. Enterprise is defined as being innovative, exciting, and daring and is likened to extroversion in human personalities. Chic is defined as stylish and prestigious. The one dimension that correlates negatively with customer satisfaction is Ruthlessness, defined as arrogant and controlling. Professional school counselors can learn from these corporate reputation makers and consider ways to project their program (the corporation) and themselves (the employees) positively to their customers.

Implementing Your Public Relations Program

There are two essential factors to consider in implementing your public relations program: timing and quality. Public relations activities should be planned to capitalize on times when you have your audience's attention. The quality of any activity ought to be high; you need to put your best foot forward. Having handout materials prepared in advance helps you be ready at a moment's notice. An example is a flier developed and used by Missouri school counselors to explain their programs and services in Appendix K.

We suggest that you consider conducting your public relations activities with your various target populations at those times when you are changing or working on improved activities that affect particular consumer groups. When you are asking teachers for classroom time to conduct the guidance curriculum activities, some may be reluctant to cooperate. This can be balanced by conducting effective lessons when an opportunity is provided. Teachers may be quite upset when they look for a counselor to assist them with a problem and learn that the counselor is scheduled into classrooms for guidance for a certain amount of time. This can be the ideal time to explain to them the benefits gained from developmental guidance. Administrators also may be resistant when counselors try to divest themselves of the quasi-administrative/clerical tasks that take up so much time and talent. They get weary of counselors saying, "That's not my job." If, however, they become convinced that the time saved is focused directly on helping students through guidance curriculum, individual student planning, or responsive services, this negative feeling may be dissipated. Parents who are used to the notion that counselors work one-on-one with students may be put off by group guidance activities. If group guidance is unexplained, it may further parents' feelings of not getting adequate service from this specialist for their own child. At such times, careful explanation of how many more students and parents are receiving service offsets this concern.

Shepherd (2000) offered 29 proven strategies for "informing" and "engaging" the multiple publics of professional school counselors: students, parents, teachers, administrators, community, and school board members. She indicated that implementing them is the third phase of a process. "Once program goals have been set in motion and an action plan prepared, the third, nitty-gritty phase of a professional advocacy initiative can begin." They include a variety of ideas about making presentations; participating on site-based teams; publishing newsletters and columns, brochures, calendars, and annual reports; attending school functions; sharing resources with staff members; and having ongoing communications within the building.

Attending to Diversity

In making the transition to a comprehensive guidance program, professional school counselors and guidance and counseling program leaders need to keep their eyes open for opportunities to attend to diversity realities and issues. As human, material, facilities, and political resources are developed, special projects are implemented, goals are set, and public relations efforts are designed and made, many opportunities arise to enhance the multicultural dimensions of the guidance and counseling program. Some of them are mentioned in this section. As discussed in previous chapters, a basic awareness is that schools tend to represent and professional school staff members are members of the middle socioeconomic class. Therefore gaps occur between the values and experiences held by "the school" and those of individual students and individual families.

In developing human resources, attention can be paid to ensuring the cultural and ethnic representativeness of the counseling and guidance program staff. Every staff member must acknowledge the cultural backgrounds of the individuals with whom they come in contact. They need to develop respect for and their capacity to work with people from the diverse cultures in their community. Virtually every school and school counselor we have worked with can grow in this area. In the first place, multicultural competence development is a life-long process. We are just now coming out of a long period of denial about differences among people—color-blindness that only focused on similarities. Similarities are good; but so are differences. The American Counseling Association's (n.d.) Multicultural Competencies and Objectives (see Appendix I) provide guidelines for counselors targeting this area of their professional development. Some counseling staffs have designated one of the counselors to be the Multicultural Competence specialist, whose responsibilities are to have internalized the competencies and objectives and to help the entire staff keep their work and the program cognizant of the impact that diversity might be having.

All guidance and counseling program staff members need to work constantly to establish a welcoming and respectful climate in the guidance office (and the school). The office receptionist staff is particularly critical in this endeavor. The attitudes, thoughts, words, and deeds of professionals and paraprofessionals must be respectful and inclusive. Many school paraprofessionals come from the local school community. It is wise, however, to remember the local community is probably not all of one mind, even though they may be primarily from one ethnic/racial group. Many of the school paraprofessional staff, although local, have worked hard to raise their standards of living and are relatively new arrivals in the middle class. Some are not as tolerant as they should be for those who are more content with their economic status and are not struggling to improve their condition.

Developing the component resource guides provides many opportunities to enhance the multicultural nature of the guidance and counseling program. Each guide can include examples of techniques that are effective across various cultures and include information for counselor-users about keeping students' cultural identities in mind and being responsive to them. The guidance curriculum guide should include lessons aimed at enhancing students' multicultural competence. Also, lessons should be included that address intercultural issues in the buildings. The individual student planning guide should include activities based on the same expectations, hopes, and dreams for all students and not be ratcheted up for some groups of students and "dumbed down" for others because of stereotypes. Test-results interpretation activities that help students establish educational and career plans must be done with awareness of biases found in most standardized assessments. The responsive services guide should include activities that portray a range of counseling and consultation modalities, helping counselors be ever-mindful that the development of our profession is deeply rooted in European American, middle-class culture (Lee, 2001). The highest level of multicultural competence development is that counselors use "culturally appropriate intervention strategies" (American Counseling Association, n.d.). Advocacy is defined in the ASCA National Model as

actively supporting causes, ideas or policies that promote and assist student academic, career, personal/social needs. One form of advocacy is the process of actively identifying underrepresented students and supporting them in their efforts to perform at their highest level of academic achievement. (ASCA, 2003, p. 129)

Responsive services need to be implemented that help students whose culture is different from that of the school or the dominant society as they wrestle with their racial/cultural identity development and with finding their place in the larger society. The system support guide should provide strategies that demonstrate how school counselors can help their schools become "culturally responsive" (Lee, 2001), including but not limited to reaching *out* to their communities and inviting the community *in*—to lower its protective walls, both literal and figurative, that are effectively keeping out the community.

In recreating the facilities of the guidance program—the guidance center, offices, reception area, career center, conference room—counselors should ensure that the presentation of information reflects diversity, from the reading materials available for center users to the posters on the walls. ("A picture is worth a thousand words!")

In developing and using the political resources inclusion, the conscious engagement of all of your constituent groups must be a rule. In dealing with the program's critics, in particular seemingly hostile parents, counselors learn much by being sensitive to their personal histories with school: Many non-middle-class, minority, and poor people have had school experiences that have led to mistrust of school systems. Listen carefully and probe sensitively and without prejudice.

In considering special projects, there are also multiple opportunities for attending to the diversity of students and of the school community. One expressed intent of the current accountability movement is to strive to ensure that schools hold all students to the same standards—the standards for achievement being academic tests. The requirements to disaggregate the data generated regarding the test scores force schools and local, state, and federal policymakers to recognize those who are not being well served by the current system. Federal funds are targeted toward helping underachievers, unsuccessful learners, and dropouts; those who are neglected, latchkey, delinquent, or at risk; racial/ethnic minorities; children from lower economic classes; children who are or have been violent; children who use/abuse drugs; children who are truant, suspended, or expelled; and children in correctional facilities or who are homeless. These groups of students have needs that counselors can and should be responding to. Many of them come to school from cultures that are very different from that represented in the school. Counselors can be the bridge. Finally, schools across the United States are experiencing racial/ethnic tension among faculty or between faculty and students. In the national survey of critical issues facing comprehensive guidance programs (Henderson & Gysbers, 2002), the example successful responses to the issue of enhancing school counselors' multicultural competence were by counselors who facilitated strategies for enhancing all staff members in a school (Locke, 2002) and in a school district (Zambrano, 2002). They provide excellent models of counselors advocating for improved situations for students.

The goals set for guidance program improvement in a school building must relate to the realities of the school's demographics, not be based on the population the school "used to have" or that people perceive is there but on the population that the *data* tell you is there. Goals should target discrepancies in services to various groups of students or issues with the faculty projecting stereotypes. On the positive side, goals can be established that celebrate diversity—that help counselors, students, faculty, and parents acknowledge, learn to work with, respect, and value all of the differences that individuals and groups bring to the community.

Any public relations or communications program or plan should consider the strategies that are most apt to reach all of the publics of the service provider. Therefore, nontraditional means of communication and working with the public must be considered. For example, in communities in which parents are intimidated or otherwise made uncomfortable by the school and school staff, providing services on their turf can be effective. Our ethical standards suggest we communicate with our clients in language that they understand; so too should we communicate in situations in which the clients are comfortable and, thereby, more apt to understand our messages.

Guidance and Counseling Program Leader's Roles and Responsibilities

The role of the guidance and counseling program leader shifts during this phase to that of staff leader and program manager for ongoing successful program implementation, and to that of advocate for the changing program and the guidance program staff. While the transition to the new program is being made, the roles that the leader will play in continuing leadership and supervision of the improved program begin.

The guidance and counseling program leader keeps the momentum for change focused and alive during the transition, and in implementation maintains the focus on continuing improvement and fine-tuning of the improved program (Henderson & Gysbers, 1998). The person responsible for program development leads the district changes and is the chief implementer of the district master plan for change. The leader brings in appropriate consultants to assist with the implementation of special projects. The central office guidance staff members are in position to know what is going on at the district, state, and federal levels and have the responsibility to communicate and interpret that information to the rest of the guidance staff. The guidance and counseling program leader manages the ongoing public relations efforts.

The guidance and counseling program leader develops building planning and improvement systems to be used when the program has settled into ongoing planning–evaluating–adjusting. The ultimate accountability for program success and for performance improvement is up to the designated guidance and counseling program leader. The guidance and counseling program leader works not only to ensure that guidance department staff continue to strive for program improvements but also to encourage and reinforce their efforts. One of the methods for empowering the staff is allowing them to select and plan their own improvements (Henderson & Gysbers, 1998). At the same time, it is conventional wisdom among personnel specialists that employees do what is "inspected" not what is "expected"; thus an inspector is needed.

Some of this authority is delegated to the other designated leaders such as building guidance and counseling program staff leaders. Those leaders need assistance in carrying out their roles effectively. As is discussed more fully in chapter 9 and in *Leading and Managing Your School Guidance Program Staff* (Henderson & Gysbers, 1998), this will probably entail direct modeling of appropriate conduct as administrator, supervisor, manager, and professional leader. It will also entail encouraging these leaders as they try leadership strategies. To ensure full implementation, we encourage the continued use of other staff leaders—informal or otherwise—to ensure healthy communication between the district guidance and counseling program leader and the entire guidance staff. Informal leaders are often the best vehicles for honest feedback.

Senge and Kaeufer (2000) delineated several forces that might impede change during this developmental phase, which they labeled "Challenges of Initiating"(p. 4). These challenges occur "often after groups have achieved certain goals, only to encounter new problems, [and] as the project draws in more people" (p. 5). One is based on the fear and anxiety of the staff. They are anxious because they are afraid to make mistakes, show ignorance, or hurt others. The anxiety needs to be acknowledged or individuals withdraw and become defensive. A second challenge that often arises at this phase is captured in the sentiment, "'This stuff is not working'" (p. 5). This is a result of expecting immediate results from implemented changes. Senge and Kaeufer offered two suggestions to leaders of change: "to appreciate the time delays involved in profound change" (p. 5) and develop clear mechanisms for assessing progress toward the desired goals. The third challenge they discussed is the tendency for staff members to "split into believers and non-believers" (p. 5). They explained,

> Because innovative groups create sub-cultures, a clash between insiders and outsiders is inevitable, but it need not escalate if leaders: 1) operate effectively within new sub-cultures and the mainstream culture; 2) seek mentoring from other leaders with high credibility in the mainstream culture; 3) build the group's ability to engage the larger system; 4) cultivate openness; 5) respect people's inhibitions about change; and 6) develop common language and values. (p. 5)

Central office guidance and counseling program leaders need to establish their roles with the principals and other administrators. Because administrative responsibilities probably are shared with them, they must be educated as to the guidance department's goals and priorities, and their support must be enlisted for the changes and the ongoing efforts as well. Their concerns and goals need to be attended to and supported by the counselors.

A goal we have not discussed fully is that of striving for open and clear communication between the building counselors and their administrators; this is sometimes problematic and deserves conscious attention. For guidance and counseling program change efforts to be successful, collaboration must occur between the counselors and the administrators (ASCA, 2005). Often this puts counselors in the role of advocating for their program. The interactive nature of educational program decision making presents challenges to both building and district administrators; successful program implementation depends on taking correlated steps toward program improvement. The more these actions are orchestrated, the more effective the guidance and counseling program will be in achieving its goals of helping students learn what the program can offer. The better training support building-level counselors have for their advocacy role, the better implementation will be.

During implementation of the newly conceived guidance and counseling program, it is time to focus on efforts to ensure that the guidance department staff members—professional and paraprofessional, leaders and followers—have the competencies they need to conduct the well-balanced and comprehensive guidance and counseling program that is envisioned. Chapter 9 discusses in more detail how the staff leader can work to ensure that each staff member is striving to reach full professional potential, that each staff member is operating competently.

Concluding Thoughts

To make the transition to the comprehensive guidance and counseling program at the building level, we have drawn up several sets of plans: a plan for change, action plans, guidance and counseling program improvement plans, and guidance and counseling program implementation plans. The building plan for change is similar to the district's master plan for program improvement. It includes a list of resources that must be accrued and tasks that must be accomplished to implement the desired program fully. Action plans outline the actions to be taken to accomplish targeted changes. Guidance and counseling program improvement plans focus on improved program strategies and are the means for systematizing the improvement process. The guidance and counseling program implementation plan is a description of the actual activities that need to be accomplished to deliver the comprehensive program components. This is discussed in more detail in chapter 8. Henceforth, the emphasis is on managing a continuously improving program.

References

Adelman, H. S., & Taylor, L. (2003). On sustainability of project innovations as systemic change. *Journal of Educational and Psychological Consultation, 14*(1), 1–25.

American Counseling Association. (n.d.). *Multicultural competencies and objectives.* Retrieved from http://www.counseling.org/Content/NavigationMenu/RESOURCES/MULTICULTURALANDDIVERSITYISSUES/Competencies/Competencies.htm

American School Counselor Association. (1998). *Position statement: Character education.* Alexandria, VA: Author. Retrieved February 12, 2005, from http://www. schoolcounselor. org/content.asp?contentid=193

American School Counselor Association. (2000). *Position statement: Use of noncredentialed personnel.* Alexandria, VA: Author. Retrieved February 12, 2005, from http://www. schoolcounselor.org/content.asp?contentid=222

American School Counselor Association. (2002). *Position statement: Censorship.* Alexandria, VA: Author. Retrieved February 12, 2005, from http://www.schoolcounselor.org/content.asp?contentid=192

American School Counselor Association. (2002–2003). *Effectiveness of school counseling.* Retrieved May 4, 2004, from http://www.schoolcounselor.org/content.asp? contentid=241

American School Counselor Association. (2005). *The ASCA national model: A framework for school counseling programs* (2nd ed.). Alexandria, VA: Author.

Brigman, G., & Moore, P. (1994). *School counselors and censorship: Facing the challenge.* Alexandria, VA: American School Counselor Association.

Davies, G., Chun, R., Da Silva, R. V., & Roper, S. (2004). A corporate character scale to assess employee and customer views of organization reputation. *Corporate Reputation Review, 7,* 125–147.

Edwards, D., & Mullis, F. (2003). Classroom meetings: Encouraging a climate of cooperation. *Professional School Counseling, 7*(1), 20–28.

Fullen, M. (2001). *Leading in a culture of change.* San Francisco: Jossey-Bass.

Galassi, J. P., & Akos, P. (2004). Developmental advocacy: Twenty-first century school counseling. *Journal of Counseling & Development, 82,* 146–157.

Gysbers, N., & Henderson, P. (1997). *Comprehensive guidance and counseling programs that work—II.* Greensboro, NC: ERIC Counseling and Student Services Clearinghouse.

Henderson, P. (1989). How one district changed its guidance and counseling program. *The School Counselor, 37,* 31–40.

Henderson, P., & Gysbers, N. C. (1998). *Leading and managing your school guidance program staff.* Alexandria, VA: American Counseling Association.

Henderson, P., & Gysbers, N. (Eds.). (2002). *Implementing comprehensive school guidance programs: Critical leadership issues and successful responses.* Greensboro, NC: CAPS.

Lee, C. C. (2001). Culturally responsive school counselors and programs: Addressing the needs of all students. *Professional School Counseling, 4,* 257–261.

Locke, D. (2002). Applying multiculturalism in a problem(matic) situation. In P. Henderson & N. Gysbers (Eds.), *Implementing comprehensive school guidance programs: Critical leadership issues and successful responses* (pp. 233–240). Greensboro, NC: CAPS.

Missouri School Board Association. (1996). *Sample policy: Student guidance and counseling program.* Columbia, MO: Author.

National Alliance of Pupil Services Organizations. (1993, January). *Policy statement on school-linked integrated services.* (Available from the American Counseling Association and other member organizations)

Office of Public Policy and Legislation. (2004, August). *No Child Left Behind: Sources of funding that support school counseling and mental health services.* Alexandria, VA: American Counseling Association. Retrieved January 12, 2005, from http://www.counseling.org/Content/NavigationMenu/PUBLICPOLICY/NOCHILDLEFT BEHIND/NCLB_Programs_August_2004.pdf

Peer, G. G. (1985). The status of secondary school guidance: A national survey. *The School Counselor, 32,* 181–189.

Secretary's Commission on Achieving Necessary Skills. (1991). *Report.* Washington, DC: U.S. Department of Labor.

Senge, P. M., & Kaeufer, D. H. (2000). Creating change. *Executive Excellence, 17*(10), 4–5.

Shepherd, L. J. (2000). Promoting professional identity in an era of educational reform. *Professional School Counseling, 4*(1), 31–41.

White, J., Mullis, F., Earley, B., & Brigman, G. (1995). *Consultation in schools: The counselor's role.* Portland, ME: J. Weston Walch.

Zambrano, E. (2002). Opening the dialogue. In P. Henderson & N. Gysbers (Eds.), *Implementing comprehensive school guidance programs: Critical leadership issues and successful responses* (pp. 241–249). Greensboro, NC: CAPS.

Chapter 8

Managing the New Program

Implementing—Managing the New Program

- Improve program activities.
- Enhance the role of the professional school counselor.
- Develop the building program plan.
- Monitor program implementation.

⌐ At this point in the program improvement process, you are ready to focus on implementation. You know what changes your students need and what the professional and parent community want from your program. The plans and systems are in place to facilitate ongoing improvement as well as implementation. Challenges continue in the buildings and the district, however. In this chapter, we discuss some concrete ways to help make program changes in the buildings successful and suggest ideas for maintaining the momentum for change in the years to come. Questions answered in this chapter include the following: How can the counselors do new student-centered activities when they are still faced with so many nonguidance tasks? What is the new role for the school counselor? What does the new program look like in a building? What is the role of the guidance and counseling program leader in ongoing implementation?

First, ideas for improving program activities are discussed. These include displacing some activities from the guidance and counseling program and streamlining the involvement of the school counselors in others as well as adding activities to your program and augmenting existing activities. Next we present ideas for enhancing the role of the school counselors through a job description process, through explicit program planning and accountability, and through time management skills. Ways for you to monitor and encourage continuous program improvement and ways to attend to diversity are then discussed. Finally, guidance and counseling program leader roles and responsibilities are again considered.

Improve Program Activities

In comparing and contrasting their current programs with those desired, building personnel have identified places where the designs match and where there are discrepancies. In a building these point to specific program activities. As we discussed in chapter 5, where the qualitative and quantitative designs match—that is, where the activities are effective in helping the right number of students achieve important outcomes and do not take an undue amount of school counselors' time—changes are not called for. It is our recommendation that in your program improvement process you take time to consider what you are doing that is right. Be careful not to throw the baby out with the bathwater. In addition, identifying effective, efficient, high-quality activities in the program is good for the staff's morale; it assures them that a lot of what they have been doing is worthwhile.

Where there are discrepancies between the designs—either spillovers or gaps—changes in program activities need to be made. Spillovers in design include activities that take more program resources (e.g., more school counselors' time) than is desirable. Gaps indicate that too few resources are appropriated (e.g., not enough school counselors' time). To eliminate the design spillovers, activities need to be eliminated—or displaced—from the program, or the appropriation of resources needs to be streamlined. To fill in the design gaps, desirable activities need to be added, or existing activities need to be augmented to allow more fully for program goal achievement. Using the goal-based program improvement system described in chapter 7, school staffs systematically set about repairing the discrepancies by developing specific program improvement plans for ways to displace, streamline, add, or augment activities.

As goals are set and changes made, guidance and counseling program leaders in the buildings need to ensure that the right changes are made. Right changes are those that have been identified by the guidance and counseling program improvement planning team as having high priority for the students and for the best use of the professional school counselor's time. For example, if adding parent education activities is the first priority, and adding an afterschool small group for latchkey children is the second priority, those should be the first and second activities added to the newly arranged program. If removing the clerical work associated with referrals for special education is the first priority for displacement, and shifting the counseling of students who are returning from school suspension back to the administrators is the third priority, these need to be accomplished in the order set. This order may differ from the counselor's preferences, but such is the collaborative process.

In addition to ensuring that only important changes are made, the counseling staff should strive to make the changes successful, to do them well, or to help others do them well. In general, this means having the skills needed to do the activity well, planning the activity carefully, and including those affected by the change in the planning process.

Displacing Nonguidance Activities

Activities from the current program that do not fit into the desired program become targets for displacement. The displacement strategy entails replacing undesired or inappropriate activities or duties with desired guidance and counseling program activities. Even more than the other strategies, displacing extraneous tasks from the guidance department is accomplished in increments.

In describing the current program (see chapter 4), you identified ways the guidance department provides support to the overall educational program. Many activities to be displaced are those performed in support of other programs; others are administratively based activities. If you have followed our suggestions, you have identified these by specific program.

Guidance departments often provide support for regular educational programs by, for example, referring students to special programs, implementing orientation and articulation activities, participating in curriculum planning, assisting in the development of accreditation reports, preregistering students for next year's courses, consulting in the development of the master schedule, and making the student schedule changes. Guidance departments also sometimes provide support for other programs such as testing, discipline management, gifted education, special education, and vocational education. In the Northside Independent School District study, the activities performed in support of these various programs were time consuming, accounted for 30% to 40% of the school counselors' time districtwide, and left far less than 100% for the delivery of the guidance and counseling program. Similar results were found in the statewide time studies discussed in chapter 4. In the study conducted by the North Carolina Department of Public Instruction (n.d.), specific noncounseling activities were identified, and counselors recorded the range of the percentages of their time spent on those five tasks and on "other." What is displayed in Table 8.1 is the percentage of counselors who spent more than 10% of their time on each task. A study was conducted in Missouri (Gysbers, Lapan, & Roof, 2004) to determine what nonguidance tasks were being done by their school counselors. Table 8.2 displays the percentages of counselors in Missouri at each level who reported spending more than their fair share of time (i.e., more than 10%) on the identified nonguidance activities. It is clear that in neither case are students benefiting from a "100% guidance and counseling program." In both cases, the differences and similarities across the school levels are interesting.

Nonguidance tasks performed by counselors fit into four categories: student supervision, instruction, clerical, and administrative. Supervisory duties include developing and monitoring assemblies and hall, cafeteria, bus, or restroom duty. Instructional duties include tutoring or substitute teaching. Clerical duties include selling lunch or bus tickets, collecting and mailing progress reports, maintaining permanent records and handling transcripts, counting the credits that high school students accumulate toward graduation, monitoring attendance, calculating grade point averages, developing student handbooks and course guides, and scheduling admission, review, and dismissal committee meetings. Administrative duties include coordinating a schoolwide testing program, developing the master schedule, covering for the absent principal, assigning disciplinary consequences, writing principals' annual reports, making schedule changes, or even supervising teachers. Such tasks are targets for displacement.

Solid data provide strong rationale for the displacements. They suggest which activities that, when removed, would return the most to the guidance program. Additional data that help support displacements include identification of the number of tasks involved, the amount of time spent, and the dollar cost of having counselors or others do them. But time is the essential quantity. Others often do not understand how much time is consumed by the activities that inhibit counselors and students working together for legitimate guidance purposes. Sometimes school counselors' perceptions as to how much time different nonguidance tasks take are colored by their feelings about having to do them. The data help the counselors as well as the other decision makers in the process (Madden, 2002).

Table 8.1
Percentage of North Carolina School Counselors
Spending More Than 10% of Time in Specific
Noncounseling Activities, by School Levels

Non-counseling Activity	Elementary School	Middle School	High School
Duty (e.g., bus, lunch)	13.1	16.9	8.5
Registrar responsibilities	17	47.9	54.5
Schedule changes	2	24.6	53.6
Test coordination	48.9	51.8	50
Substitute teaching (covering class)	2.2	1.8	2.6
Other noncounseling	11.3	11.7	10.8

Table 8.2
Percentage of Missouri School Counselors Performing Nonguidance Duties,
by School Levels

Task	Elementary School	Middle School	High School	K–12 Schools
Coordinating testing program	71	83	64	81
Individual testing for special/ gifted education	67	65	37	56
Coordinator/manager "504" files	45	58	36	10
Supervision: cafeteria	42	37	15	37
Supervision: bus loading/unloading	40	26	9	10
Coordinating/monitoring school assemblies	33	28	20	32
Supervision: hallway	32	35	26	24
Principal of the day	32	9	7	22
Maintaining permanent records	31	51	46	66
Coordinating/managing Individualized Education Plan process	29	33	12	
Administering discipline	24	17	6	10
Handling transcripts	22	41	65	73
Copy/mailing new student enrollment records	21	40	31	46
Monitoring attendance	21	27	27	27
Substitute teaching	18	23	19	32
Balancing class loads	17	69	70	56
Calculating GPAs, class ranks, honor rolls	6	36	46	56
Developing/updating student handbook/course guides	6	25	57	34
Building the master schedule	4	51	44	54
Supervision: restroom	3	9	4	0
Collecting/mailing progress reports	3	30	29	24
Managing schedule changes	3	74	86	71
Selling lunch tickets	1	2	0	0

Note. From "Non-Guidance Duties Performed by School Counselors," by N. C. Gysbers, R. T. Lapan, and C. Roof, 2004, *The Counseling Interviewer, 36,* Tables 1–4, pp. 28–31. Copyright 2004 by the Missouri School Counselor Association. Adapted with permission.

In addition, negotiating to displace activities requires solidarity among counselors. That is, they all must agree that the tasks are not appropriate guidance tasks and should be given up. As Anderson (2002) put it,

> I may be extreme, but I believe counselors must realize their role in the school building is as important as any other professional. Counselors are not in the building to "serve" others; they are in the school to implement a program and apply the distinct skills and knowledge that only they possess. . . . It requires a belief that what counselors and counseling programs do in the school is so important that, without them, the school could not meet its mission and the needs of all students. (p. 320)

Displacement entails a process of specifying the tasks that are done and either eliminating them or shifting the responsibility for doing them to someone else. It is easiest to manage if the big nonguidance responsibilities are broken down into a collection of small tasks. Then decisions can be made regarding each task rather than the whole project.

A special time study was conducted in Northside Independent School District whereby counselors identified the amount of time they spent in specific school management tasks, that is, quasi-administrative and clerical tasks that did not require a master's degree in guidance and counseling to accomplish. The first step in conducting the survey was to develop the list of tasks. Of such tasks, 41 were identified by the elementary counselors, 47 by the middle school counselors, and 34 by the high school counselors. The counselors then determined how much time each of these tasks took in an average year. If part of the task required counselors' expertise, it was recommended for streamlining—for keeping the subtasks that made good use of counselors' professional skills and displacing the others. The next steps were to identify the nature of each task (Was it clerical or professional?) and answer the question, Who else could do this task? Table 8.3 presents data excerpted from the Northside study and displays the level of specificity that was found to be useful.

Although none of the tasks took an overwhelming amount of time, the total of all of the "nickel and dimed" time was 39 days per counselor per year at the elementary level, 54 days at the middle school level, and 66 at the high school level! If all of the desired displacements were accomplished, 27 days of elementary counselor time could be recaptured, 35 days of middle school counselor time, and 45 days of high school counselor time. Having the data regarding the specific tasks and the amount of time made it possible to set priorities for displacing or eliminating the worst time eaters, and knowing the nature of the task suggested which other staff members could accomplish the task most efficiently.

Table 8.3
Quasi-Administrative and Clerical Tasks Study
(School Management Tasks)

Program/Tasks	Average Time/ Counselor/Year	Recommen- dation[a]	Nature of Task	Who Else?
Elementary School				
Special education				
Initial referral paperwork collection	7 days	D	Clerical	Principal's secretary
Test individuals	4 days	S	Prof	Teachers
Attend admission, review, dismissal conferences	5 days	S	Prof	Teachers
Total of all	39 days (21%)			
Middle School				
Regular education				
Register new student	8 days	S	Clerical	Administrative secretary
Change schedules	9 days	D/S	Clerical	Scheduling secretary
Special education				
Initial referral paperwork collection	4–5 days	D	Clerical	Secretary
Attend admission review, dismissal conferences	5 days	S	Prof	Teachers
Total of all	54 days (29%)			
High School				
Regular education				
Check numbers of courses chosen	6 days	D	Clerical	Secretaries
Change schedules	11 days	D/S	Clerical	Scheduling secretary
Check graduation status	7 days	D	Clerical	Registrar
Total of all	66 days (34%)			

Note. Data from Northside Independent School District, San Antonio, TX. Adapted with permission.
[a]D = displace; S = streamline.

Identification of the tasks leads to another question to be answered before displacement is considered: Does this task need to be done at all? The Northside study, which involved several buildings, found that counselors were doing tasks on some campuses that were not done at all on other campuses. Different buildings have different procedures and habits in place that need to be scrutinized.

If you decide that the task does need to be done, then the question is, How can it be done most efficiently? Efficiently means least expensively in labor costs or in time. Identifying who should spend time on these activities or how else the activity might be accomplished is the responsibility of the counselors seeking to divest themselves of the tasks. If the counselors suggest a reasonable plan, their chances of effecting the displacements are increased substantially. They need to answer such questions as, Who is the primary beneficiary of the activity? Who has the knowledge or skills to conduct the activity? How can the task be delegated to as many people as possible so as to take as little time as possible from each individual's time?

At the district level, agreements can be made between the guidance and counseling program leader and the leaders of other programs to facilitate the shift in responsibility for these activities to the related department staff. If you have other department administrators on the steering committee, you will benefit from their understanding of the comprehensive guidance and counseling program's primary mission and the new expectations for counselors. It is not easy to figure out who else will add these usually tedious or burdensome tasks to their calendars because other staff will not volunteer for them eagerly. If, however, the administrators know that counselors are not just saying, "It's not my job," but rather, "But my job is to guide and counsel students," these transitions can be supported. Again, these changes are not made overnight or magically. Some fit into the hard-to-do category and require clarity of direction and joint planning by those involved (Petersen, 2002). The guidance and counseling program leaders and the counselors must work with others to develop the new procedures for implementing the changes. An example of such a plan is included in Appendix L.

The additions to the guidance and counseling program that result from the additional time recaptured from displaced tasks should be made highly visible. An example of what we often hear principals say is, "If I assign the testing administration to the assistant principal, what will I get from the counselors?" In addition to being prepared for such negotiation, counselors are advised to follow up by presenting the information about the additional student activities they are now able to do. To illustrate, consider another example from the Northside Independent School District project. Middle school counselors were spending 7.1% of their time on special-education-related administrative tasks and 2.15% in group guidance. Further data showed that counselors were attending the annual review meetings during which the individualized educational plans (IEPs) were developed for students already enrolled in special education. Because special education staff members were already familiar with the students, the primary purpose for counselors' attendance was to ensure that the proposed schedule could be accommodated rather than to provide professional input regarding the students' needs. It was agreed that in lieu of counselors attending these meetings, special education staff would consult with them before and after the meetings. The counselors translated the hours of meeting time saved directly into a schedule for conducting classroom guidance, which benefited all of the students.

As counselors must plan with others how the nonguidance tasks will be displaced from the guidance and counseling program, so must they train those newly assigned to these responsibilities. Training people to do new assignments helps ensure that they will be done correctly. If you truly want to be free of these assignments, the first few experiments in accomplishment by others must be successful. This is easy to see if new personnel are hired, but not as clear if the task is given to someone who has worked around the district for a while. If, for example, you are asking teachers to make the schedule changes associated with their decisions to change individual students or groups of students to better match individual teachers' curriculum, training the teachers in the steps involved in making the changes is essential. Unless the teachers are naturally gifted at jigsaw puzzles, they will need to be taught about the delicate balances reflected in the school master schedule, about checking the impact that their change will have on the students' other subjects and other teachers, about completing the necessary forms precisely to communicate clearly with the data-processing system, and so on. In other words, moving students from one class to another is not as easy as it sounds!

Some displacements will entail hiring additional staff. Often the case can be made for hiring less-expensive staff to free the counselors for activities that their guidance and counseling education has prepared them to do. For example, counselors often are asked to maintain cumulative student records, to become the school registrar. Those of you who have this responsibility know that it is time consuming. The answer to this problem is to work toward hiring a registrar or at least sufficient clerical personnel to do the job. A secretary or paraprofessional can handle the clerical aspects of scheduling. The sample nonguidance activities reassignment plan in Appendix L also identifies costs associated with needed new personnel.

Streamlining Counselor Involvement in Nonguidance Activities

The displacement strategy for reducing what we have labeled design spillover is to give up the task altogether. The second strategy is to reduce the amount of time that professional school counselors spend on an activity, that is, to streamline their involvement. In the activities targeted for streamlining, there is often an appropriate role for counselors to play, but over time counselors' involvement has become counselors' overinvolvement. Useful resources in streamlining efforts are the position statements adopted by the American School Counselor Association (ASCA) that articulate the appropriate role for school counselors in relation to a variety of issues.

Which activities are targeted is, again, a decision best made by the committee recommending ways to improve the guidance and counseling program based on the time study's data. The hard questions are, again, the following: If this task needs to be done, who can best do it? How can it be done more efficiently? Taking time to answer them is worth your while. The Northside Independent School District, for example, learned from its time study that by spending half as much time on the tasks recommended for streamlining, on average an elementary counselor could spend 6 more days a year on guidance and counseling activities, a middle school counselor 7.5 more days, and a high school counselor 11 more days.

Streamlining the counselors' involvement in an activity, like displacing, usually means increasing someone else's. By carefully analyzing the tasks that make up an activity, we can answer the questions, Who else can do it? Who best can do it? We have learned that there are others in a building who are better equipped or who want to do some of the tasks. In some cases, clear procedures or definitions need to be established and committed to paper to help someone else accept his or her responsibilities. In other cases, technology can help, or the best answer is to spread the responsibility across a larger number of staff members. In still other cases, counselors can handle activities that do belong in the guidance department more efficiently than they are currently.

Some of the tasks that counselors do in support of other programs are, in fact, tasks that others are better equipped to do, but because of their systemic link to counselor-appropriate tasks, they have become the counselors' responsibilities. For example, assisting students to make and implement their educational plans, including selection of their courses for the following year, is an appropriate counselor responsibility. However, linked to that are activities such as making recommendations regarding the next math class the student might be best suited for or developing course description catalogues. But the math teacher who has the students in class has more complete information on which to base recommendations: He or she knows the student's math skills and apparent abilities and knows the math curriculum more fully than the counselor. And the staff members who are closest to the information for describing every course available in a comprehensive high school or middle/ junior high are the teachers who teach those courses; thus the instructional leaders of a district or building are the best producers of course guides.

Other tasks that counselors do are those that rightfully belong to someone else but that have been delegated inappropriately to the guidance department. Examples include developing the master schedule, the vehicle for putting students and teachers together. (The curriculum guide example may fit here as well.) Building the master schedule reflects the educational philosophy and priorities of the school, and it is the principal's responsibility. The graduate school program in which master schedule building is taught is educational administration, not counselor education. Delegation skills are critical for the counselors to develop as they implement an improving program; delegating up is a particularly sensitive but viable undertaking. Petersen (2002) described an example of a school district that completed a process that ended with building administrators being in charge of the standardized testing program, and with all school staff being part of its coordination and implementation. If the school is large, remember that a vice principal or assistant principal could develop the master schedule. These individuals often want to become principals and are eager to have the experience of doing the task.

Hidden resources for streamlining counselors' involvement in tasks often are individuals on campus, such as the administrators just mentioned, who want to do the identified tasks because they are related to their program responsibilities or professional goals. In the Northside Independent School District, for example, classroom teachers, who feel great responsibility for helping each student in their classrooms to learn the subject matter, wanted to be involved more intimately in the process of identifying their students' special needs. They wanted to learn from being part of the process that occurs prior to and when referring a student for special education services; thus they were willing to coordinate the initial referral paperwork and have a voice in the admission, review, and dismissal committee meetings. Subsequently, the federal regulations guiding special education have clarified that the representative of the school on the "IEP team" must be someone who

1. Is qualified to provide, or supervise the provision of, specially designed instruction to meet the unique needs of children with disabilities
2. Is knowledgeable about the general curriculum
3. Is knowledgeable about the availability of resources of the public agency
4. Has the authority to commit agency resources and be able to ensure that whatever services are set out in the IEP will actually be provided

(Department of Education, Rehabilitative Services rule, July 1, 2004)

Related to counselors fulfilling more appropriate roles in this committee that is charged with developing a disabled child's IEP, the regulation states, "(6) At the discretion of the parent or the agency, other individuals who have knowledge or special expertise regarding the child, including related services personnel as appropriate" (Department of Education, Rehabilitative Services Rule, 2004). School counselors are considered "related services personnel."

Other examples of "who else can and may want to have" responsibilities currently assigned to school counselors include program specialists, such as reading teachers and teachers of gifted and talented students, who we have found often want to do the individual assessments needed for students to benefit from their program. Yet other examples are staff members who are willing to carry out tasks because they consider the experience to be beneficial, teachers who benefit from covering the office in the absence of the principal because they want to be administrators, and teachers who enjoy helping to plan and implement such activities as assemblies and student recognition programs because they believe that education is larger than what goes on in classrooms.

To make some larger activities more efficient, clear procedures often help streamline the work involved. As operational policies are set, procedural guidelines for conducting a series of activities or activities that involve many staff members need to be written. Such guidelines ensure that each staff member involved has the needed information and that there is consistency of implementation. In the Northside Independent School District effort, guidelines for making schedule changes brought order to what was formerly beginning-of-the-semester chaos in the middle and high schools. Guidelines for times when testing individuals was encouraged—which implied when it was discouraged—helped save large amounts of elementary counselor time.

The secretarial and paraprofessional staff may also be used more effectively to streamline the amount of counselor time spent on nonguidance tasks. Tasks that are primarily clerical should be assigned to appropriate personnel; for example, routine dissemination of information and paperwork associated with such activities as registration for school and applying for scholarships can be distributed by clerks.

In many instances modern technology can be more guidance department friendly. We often hear the complaint that the computer runs the staff rather than vice versa. Thus each computer-related decision and deadline should be analyzed with the same detail that other tasks are by asking such questions as, Does this need to be done? Is this the best time to do this task? Is there a simpler way to handle this? If there is a computer-assisted system for storing and processing student information, routine tasks related to this information, such as compiling lists of retainees or potential graduates, monitoring student attendance, and computing grade point averages, should be done by computer rather than by hand by a staff member.

As discussed in considering the design of the desired program, some activities are necessary for the operation of the school program and benefit all or large numbers of students. These can be massive, labor-intensive jobs. Most often these tasks could be done with less cost borne by any one program by spreading the responsibilities to all or a large number of staff members and by allowing students to take some of the burden. Examples of these schoolwide labor-intensive tasks include supervision of students during their nonclass time on campus, providing extracurricular activities for students, preregistering students for classes, and assisting students to monitor their educational progress. Helping the entire staff to understand that the activities benefit them and thus are their responsibilities, and designing systems for accomplishing them efficiently, are ways to effect these shifts.

In a teacher–student advisory system, such tasks as checking students' progress toward successful completion of the school year or high school graduation become staffwide responsibilities rather than time-consuming tasks for one relatively small group of staff members. Further, by giving some of the responsibility to the students, counselors enable them to monitor their own progress toward graduation and thus be more in control of their own status. Advanced technology can assist this greatly, as exemplified in Provo, Utah, and described by Evans and Ward (2002). In addition, scheduling does not have to be done one student at a time by guidance staff over a period of 3 to 4 months—and then, in our experience, done again in the next school semester through massive numbers of schedule changes. If the entire staff and the various departments work together, a university-type scheduling or Internet/telephone registration system can allow the vast majority of scheduling to be accomplished in 1 day.

Some streamlining can be done within the guidance department itself. As schools have grown and times have changed, many activities have "grown like Topsy," with innovations—and time—added on to the activities already in place. An example of an activity that needs streamlining is beginning the preregistration process in high schools in December, continuing it throughout the spring, and giving students a week to consider their course selections. An example of streamlining is using the information stored in permanent record files rather than regathering similar information, such as using group-standardized test results generated in another district in lieu of conducting new individual assessments. Another example of streamlining is using a subgroup of two or three to develop the details of an activity and present them to the staff instead of having the larger counseling staff plan every activity as a whole group. Another example of an activity that needs streamlining is maintaining systems of checking and double-checking work in reaction to previous errors, even though such systems take even more time and provide additional opportunities to make mistakes. We are aware of one high school in which each counselor checked the senior students' credit accrual three times! Streamlining in this case could be establishing a system in which the registrar maintains the report of each student's progress and counselors review the exceptions or complicated cases.

More about helping counselors manage their time is discussed later in this chapter, but at this point it is important to recognize that individual counselors fall into habits that eat up valuable student-contact time. Some counselors keep copious notes regarding their sessions with students, teachers, or parents; keeping records is important, but systems used should be efficient. Some counselors take extended coffee or lunch breaks, often without realizing it, because student-centered conversations occur with other staff members who are also in the staff lounge; the relative priority of these conversations needs to be considered. Some counselors do their paperwork on student time, but teachers do much of their paperwork outside of the school day.

As guidance staff members strive to streamline the amount of time spent in nonguidance tasks, communicating and collaborating with those affected by the changes are critical to the successful implementation of changes. Through communication, others can be helped to understand the original problem, the rationale for the change that is to be made, and the ideas behind the change. As activities are eliminated or moved from the guidance and counseling program to others' programs, counselors must collaborate with the others to ensure that the plans are complete and that those responsible have the knowledge and skills they need to accomplish them.

Adding New Activities

The third strategy to improve program activities is adding new activities. As mentioned earlier, new activities must be developed to address high-priority but underaccomplished guidance and counseling program outcomes and objectives. It is imperative that the new activities be recognized as important and that they be done well so that their success is reasonably assured. In adding new activities, you most likely have displaced some traditional ones; thus others will be observing the merit of the new activities very closely. Counselors who conduct the new activities, therefore, must have the skills needed to ensure that the activities are of high quality. As with everything else, careful planning ensures more successful implementation.

One set of new activities that is consistently identified as needed is small-group counseling in high schools. Ripley and Goodnough (2001) "offer strategies [they] found to be successful in planning and implementing group counseling" (p. 62) when they were high school counselors. They learned that successfully "implementing group counseling in a high school was contingent upon supportive school policies and personnel, thorough planning, and advocating for programmatic initiatives" (p. 65). It did not just happen because they wanted it to. They implemented a plan for improvement, gathered the necessary support, and added a set of new activities that benefited students highly.

Just as counselors help others who pick up new responsibilities to develop the competencies they need to accomplish them successfully, so do counselors need to strive to be highly competent as they undertake new challenges. If middle and high school counselors are just beginning to conduct classroom guidance sessions, for example, they should update their instructional skills. In the Northside Independent School District program, high school students only benefit from an average of six counselor-led guidance lessons a year and middle school students an average of eight. Even in the elementary schools, where there is a regulation that every classroom of children receives a guidance lesson once a week, there are only 36 weeks in the school year. It is clear that those few lessons need to be delivered skillfully not only to best ensure achieving the objectives for the students' sake but also to model student-centered instruction (guidance) for the teachers. Ways to assist school counselors develop the competencies they need to implement the comprehensive guidance and counseling program are discussed in chapter 9.

New activities need to be planned thoroughly so that students accomplish the desired objectives and outcomes. Thorough planning entails stating the objective(s) clearly, designing an effective and efficient procedure for helping students achieve the objectives(s), using relevant materials to support the procedure, collaborating with others involved, and managing the logistics of implementing the activity.

In chapter 5 we described the conceptual flow for defining the domains, goals, competencies, outcomes, and objectives of guidance and counseling program activities. In designing your program, you have identified the outcomes appropriate for each grade level. In planning each activity, you need to specify the objective(s) that students will attain as a result of the session. Here is an example:

Domain: Make Wise Choices

Goal: Students will use a systematic decision-making process.

Competency: Sixth graders will apply the eight-step decision-making process with emphasis on generating alternatives and understanding decision strategies.

Student Outcome: Sixth graders will describe the advantages and disadvantages of using the three decision strategies they use most often.

Activity Objective: At the end of the guidance lesson introducing decision-making strategies, each student in the class will describe accurately 10 of the 13 decision strategies. (Gelatt, 1972)

At each level of increased specificity, more potential subitems exist. For example, in the Make Wise Choices domain, more goals are possible than the one cited, such as "Students will use an emotionally based decision-making process." Within the goal "Students will use a systematic decision-making process," there are more competencies than the one given, such as "Sixth graders will apply the eight-step decision-making process with emphasis on the role their values play in making a decision" or "Seventh graders will apply the eight-step decision-making process with emphasis on gathering facts." Within the one competency cited, there are more outcomes for sixth graders, such as "Generate at least three alternatives in a variety of decision-making situations" or "Apply the eight-step decision-making process to the selection of their eighth-grade elective." Further, within the outcome given, there are more objectives than "describing accurately 10 of 13 strategies," such as "Identify the three strategies they use most often" or "Describe the advantages and disadvantages of using the 'wish' strategy." The objectives for a whole content unit of activities should be outlined from the beginning.

As described in chapter 3, activities within the different delivery system components of the guidance and counseling program typically have different kinds of objectives. In the guidance curriculum component, groups of students make developmentally appropriate cognitive progress. In the individual student planning component, individual students make implementation plans to progress toward identified goals. Through responsive services, students with problems or special needs strive to work out those problems or meet those needs. Activities in the system support component are focused on helping the students indirectly by consulting with others regarding them. An example of a series of activity objectives related to the same outcome is as follows.

> Outcome: Seventh graders will manage their moods to be optimally receptive to learning.
> Sample Activity Objectives:

> - *Guidance curriculum.* All seventh graders will compare/contrast the appearance of different moods in seventh graders.
> - *Individual student planning.* Each seventh grader will analyze the causes of his or her most prevalent, negative mood(s) and plan ways to cope with those causes.
> - *Responsive services.* Eight to 10 seventh-grade boys identified as being emotionally withdrawn by their teachers will express their feelings in the counseling group.
> - *System support.* All seventh-grade teachers will evaluate the moods displayed by their students for the purpose of identifying those students who are unable to manage their moods to be optimally receptive to learning.

In addition to demonstrating the interrelationship between the four program components, the differently stated objectives clearly lead to different kinds of activities.

An activity also may help students or others achieve more than one objective. For example, in the group counseling session implied in the responsive services activity objective just given for seventh-grade boys, a companion objective might be that the boys will identify words to label their feelings.

After stating your objectives, the next step in planning a new activity is to determine the best procedure for attaining the objective(s), including identifying useful and relevant materials. Gelatt (1975, p. 26) identified some things to consider in developing a new activity:

- *Magnitude*: How much of the total school population or program will be affected?
- *Complexity*: How many other changes will it incur?
- *Convenience*: Can it be developed and operated locally, or will it require outside consultants?
- *Flexibility*: How rigidly must the method be followed to be successful?
- *Distinctiveness*: Is it new and different?
- *Interaction with other programs*: Does it stand alone or require other programs to be involved for success?
- *Readiness*: Can it be applied immediately?

- *Cost*: What are the initial costs and future funding needs?
- *Content*: Is the content innovative or a redo of an old method?

The selected procedure needs to be written down, again not only to ensure precision in planning but also to allow all counselors involved with the activity to be operating somewhat literally from the same page. With the procedure written down, reusing or revising the activity is easier.

If you are operating on a multischool basis, using the same format systemwide facilitates sharing of successful ideas and strategies. It is our opinion that all proactive guidance and counseling program activities—that is, guidance lessons, individual student planning sessions, counseling, and consultation sessions—can and should be planned. Activity plans are different from the guidance and counseling program improvement plans described in chapter 7. The improvement plans outline how the counselors will accomplish changing their activities. The activity plans discussed here describe what counselors (or others carrying out the activity) will do in implementing an activity. Items to be included in the written plan are as follows:

- Program component
- Title (which relates it to other program activities, e.g., the unit title and session number)
- Grade level(s)
- Group size (e.g., individual, small, class-size, or large group)
- Time (of year; activity takes)
- Domain, goal, competency, and outcome(s)
- Objective(s)
- Key concept(s)
- Procedures outlined
- Suggested methods
- Resources needed
- Evaluation strategy

Some schools and districts have found different formats useful for the different program components; others use similar ones. In addition to the plans for specific sessions, the Northside Independent School District counselors found it useful to have an overview sheet to summarize the lessons in a unit, the sessions in an individual student planning series, the various strategies for intervening in recurrent student issues, and the various activities or tasks done by other personnel and counselors in the major system support activities.

Who develops new activities depends on whether you are changing a district program or the program of one school. In the Northside Independent School District project, activities to be implemented districtwide were developed by the program development leaders and reviewed by all of the counselors who were to be conducting the activities. Flexibility in methodology can be left up to the individual, but suggestions as to what works are helpful. Some activities were developed on individual campuses and shared with staff in other buildings. Activities that involve other staff members, such as teachers or administrators, should be developed collaboratively.

Relevant materials should be selected after the objectives have been determined; the program should dictate the materials, the materials should not dictate the program. Quality materials, however, not only assist the students but also can augment counselors' understanding of the topics. At the elementary level, various commercial materials are available to support the guidance curriculum and even, to some extent, the individual student planning and responsive services components. At the secondary level, not as many commercial materials are available, although the supply is increasing. It may be that materials will need to be developed locally to implement the activities properly for your community context. In any case, the guidance and counseling program leader and the counselors need to be realistic about how far the budget resources will go and should plan their expenditures in accordance with the program priorities. The new materials need to be ordered in ample time.

Whether a districtwide or single-building effort, new activities are best designed prior to the beginning of school (as much as possible). Once the school year has begun, it is difficult to take the necessary time to plan a new activity thoroughly to ensure its being done with quality. However, finishing touches to the activity itself and the logistics plan may have to be accomplished after the realities of the school year are known. Logistics to be determined include what facilities will be used, how the students will be accessed, and the time frame for the activity and securing the necessary equipment as well as the materials. Again, the decisions that affect other staff members, such as how to access the students and the best time frame, should be made jointly with those staff members or their representatives. Your steering, planning, and advisory committees can be helpful here.

Augmenting Existing Activities

Many activities currently being done are consistent with your program goals and fit in the desired design. The fourth strategy to improve the program is augmenting or adding to these activities. In addition to extending the resources appropriated to existing practices, activities can be augmented by improving their quality, by adding objectives, and by linking related activities.

With a clearly stated developmental emphasis to the comprehensive guidance and counseling program, many schools have extended the amount of time counselors at all levels spend in classroom guidance activities. In elementary school programs, the small-group counseling service has been extended, in contrast to the secondary school programs, where this service has been added. Extending activities may be easier to accomplish than adding activities because the rest of the staff and the students are already familiar with the counselors' fulfilling this role.

In this context, enhancing the quality of existing activities means ensuring that the activity objectives are student focused, not system focused. An example is shifting the emphasis in preregistration from submitting the information to helping students make their choices. Enhancements also might be related to activities being displaced or streamlined. For example, if counselor involvement in test administration is being streamlined, it might be politically astute for counselors to expand their efforts in assisting others to use the test results appropriately. If counselors are displacing the task of developing the lists of students who might be retained, in its place they could provide specialized counseling for students who have been held back. If counselors are being taken out of the role of disciplining students, they could substitute parenting skills workshops for those students' parents.

Another way to expand on existing activities is adding objectives to a set of activities. In other words, making an activity more efficient by having it help students take several steps at one time. Counselors need to examine what they do to ensure that the level of difficulty of their activities is developmentally appropriate and sufficiently challenging. If your program has not been well articulated from one school level to the next, there may be overlap (or gaps) in what counselors have as objectives for students. We have seen instances in which counselors from all levels of a system have attended an impressive workshop and returned to incorporate the ideas or materials into their programs. The net result of this was—and could be—for students to be exposed to the same material in elementary, middle, and high school. This exposure to the same material may be all right, but only as long as the applications increase in difficulty to match the developmental levels of the students.

Another way to add program objectives is to add to the number of staff members who help students attain outcomes. For example, if the teachers at a grade level help by doing preliminary activities before or follow-up activities after a counselor-led session, the students' progress will be enriched. For another example, teachers can infuse guidance content into their regular curriculum. Initiating this augmentation of the teachers' role in implementing the guidance and counseling program often entails the counselor assisting in the development of activities with the teachers.

Many guidance and counseling programs have grown like untended gardens. One result of this is that some activities have a relationship but that relationship is not formally established. The students will be better helped by connecting them. For example, activities that assist students' career development were developed more recently than the more traditional activities that assist students' educational development. We have seen guidance and counseling programs in which these activities were not viewed by the counselors, and thus not by the students, as related; yet it is clear that the more a person's career and educational development are intertwined, the richer that development. Linking career interest and aptitude assessments or visits to the career center with educational planning helps students learn the connection between education and work. Helping students as ninth graders redevelop the 4-year high school plan they did as eighth graders takes coordination by the junior high and high school counselors. By planning the sequence of the two activities jointly and overcoming the logistics hurdle of passing the 4-year plan forms on from one school to the next, the impact of the activities is enhanced.

Enhance the Role of the Professional School Counselor

Implicit in changing the activities done by counselors in the newly designed program is changing the role of those counselors. The first explicit way to ensure that counselors are used in ways appropriate to their training and expertise is to establish appropriate job descriptions for counselors within each building. A second is to help counselors recognize the potential numbers of students who will benefit from their activities. A third is to use methods for helping counselors manage their time. A fourth is to help counselors manage their caseloads.

Clarifying Job Descriptions

Earlier in the program improvement process, we recommended that you develop position guides to outline the professional school counselors' roles (chapter 5). It is now advisable to specify each counselor's job description within the program. The job description, rooted in the position guide based on the roles fulfilled by all school counselors carrying the same job title, clarifies the expectations for individual counselors, given their caseloads, work setting, special assignments, specific goals for the year, and any other relevant specifics (Henderson & Gysbers, 1998). For example, the sixth-grade counselors' job descriptions might have them accountable for weekly guidance curriculum lessons during the first grading period to facilitate the students' transition into middle school; the eighth-grade counselor's curriculum responsibility may be heaviest in the spring in anticipation of the transition to high school. The seventh-grade counselor's annual job description might include the expectation of more small-group counseling because it is not a transition year.

We recommend that each counselor's job description be defined collaboratively at the beginning of each year by the counselor and his or her evaluator. This process provides a way to use the different skills that individual staff members bring to the comprehensive program and helps them to know what each is accountable for. It allows the school administrator and the counseling department head to ensure that all the desired facets of the comprehensive guidance and counseling program are assigned to someone to carry out and that those responsibilities will be integrated through the program implementation process (Henderson & Gysbers, 1998).

Recognizing Potential

Role statements and job descriptions clarify what counselors do on their jobs. It is also important for counselors and their supervisors to be cognizant of how much they can do for how many of their clients (including students, teachers, parents). The quantity of services provided is a function of the quantitative design of the program, that is, the parameters set for the program by the desired program balance and the counselor–student ratio.

The desired program balance establishes the amount of counselor time available for the various kinds of program activities in a month or a week. The desired percentages of time to be spent in the four program components suggested in the Missouri Comprehensive Guidance and Counseling Program (Gysbers, Starr, & Magnuson, 1998, pp. 99–103) are displayed in Table 8.4.

We suggest that each local system (district or building) adopt its own desired percentage within the given range. Within the suggested ranges, a school might, for example, choose the balance displayed in Table 8.5. This is the range we use in the rest of our examples.

To translate these percentages into actual times available for guidance and counseling program activities, determine the average time allotted for an activity and divide the school day by that number to determine the number of activity slots per day, using 100% of the student school day. (It is realistic to deduct one or one-half an activity slot per day for the counselors' lunch.) Multiply that number by 5 to determine the number of activity slots per 5-day week. To determine the number of activity slots per week that, according to the desired design balance, ought to be allotted to a component, multiply the total number of activity slots by the component percentage. Figure 8.1 displays an example and includes some rounding for practicality.

Your translation computations tell you, from a counselor's frame of reference, how many of what kind of activities a counselor can provide in 5 school days (100% of student access time) if all the assumptions are true. Not all of the activities take one class period or

Table 8.4
Desired Program Balance—Missouri Comprehensive Guidance Program

	Elementary School	Middle School	High School
Guidance curriculum	35–40	35–40	15–25
Individual student planning	5–10	15–25	25–35
Responsive services	30–40	30–40	25–35
System support	10–15	10–15	15–20
Nonguidance	0	0	0

Note. From *Missouri Comprehensive Guidance: A Model for Program Development, Implementation, and Evaluation* (pp. 99–103), by N. C. Gysbers, M. Starr, and C. S. Magnuson, 1998, Jefferson City: Missouri Department of Elementary and Secondary Education. Adapted with permission.

Table 8.5
Desired Program Balance—Henderson Public Schools

	Elementary School	Middle School	High School
Guidance curriculum	40	35	20
Individual student planning	10	20	30
Responsive services	40	35	35
System support	10	10	15
Nonguidance	0	0	0

activity slot. If a counselor serves more than one building, the design desired for each building needs to be applied to the time (number of days per week) assigned to that building. Doing this somewhat oversimplifies the real complexities of a guidance and counseling program but nevertheless gives you a sense of what the balanced program would be like if all of the variables were in your control. Remember also that any change in the recommended program balance changes the projected time available to any kind of activity. Within a program, different counselors' job descriptions might call for their parts of the program to have different designs. For example, crisis counselors might spend a larger percentage of their time in responsive services than comprehensive program counselors. (The impact of a different program balance is included in Appendix H.)

To find out how many students can benefit from the activities, apply the counselor–student ratio. To figure the number of students affected, several assumptions again need to be established, such as the average number of students in a class for guidance activities and the average teacher–student ratio for teacher consultations. Some assumptions regarding the configurations of students in the activities also need to be applied. In the

Figure 8.1
Desired Program Balance—Henderson Public Schools:
Activity Slots/Program Component/Week

Elementary School
Activity slot = 30 minutes
School day = 7 hours
Activity slots/day = 14
Activity slots/week = 70
  Guidance curriculum   40% (70) = 28
  Individual student planning   10% (70) = 7
  Responsive services   40% (70) = 28
  System support   10% (70) = 7

Middle School
Activity slot = 45 minutes
School day = 7 hours
Activity slots/day = 9
Activity slots/week = 45
  Guidance curriculum   35% (45) = 16
  Individual student planning   20% (45) = 9
  Responsive services   35% (45) = 16
  System support   10% (45) = 4

High School
Activity slot = 55 minutes
School day = 7 hours
Activity slots/day = 7
Activity slots/week = 35
  Guidance curriculum   20% (35) = 7
  Individual student planning   30% (35) = 11
  Responsive services   35% (35) = 12
  System support   15% (35) = 5

examples in Figures 8.2, 8.3, and 8.4, it is assumed that guidance curriculum is conducted with class-size groups, that individual student planning activities are done one-on-one, that responsive services are equally balanced between one-on-one and small groups, and that system support is spent primarily in counselor–teacher consultation. The impact of the component balance and the ratio on the level of services that elementary students can receive is displayed in Figure 8.2, that middle school students receive in Figure 8.3, and that high school students receive in Figure 8.4. The ratio used is a not-atypical 1:300. To demonstrate the impact of different ratios on the potential levels of service, examples of the minimum recommendation (1:100) and an unfortunately typical ratio (1:500) are used in Appendix H. A blank worksheet is also provided in Appendix H for you to figure your own potential. Although the math is somewhat arduous, we strongly recommend that you do this exercise because it is essential to understanding the finite realities for your program. It helps you and others have realistic expectations for your work.

Potential for the Elementary School Program

In the Henderson Public School example, each elementary school class will benefit from at least two guidance lessons per week (see Figure 8.2). If seen individually, each child could receive individual student planning assistance from a counselor for 25 minutes a year. Of course, if children were grouped for guidance, each child would benefit from more time. At any one time, 32% of the children would benefit from responsive services, if the assumption is accurate that half the slots are spent on group counseling and half on individual counseling, parent consultation, or referral. An additional assumption about how many slots the average case or group uses could give an estimate of the total percentage of students in the caseload who could be served in this component in a year. A counselor could spend, on average, 15 minutes consulting with each teacher individually each week, or could take a little over 2 weeks to consult with each teacher for a full 30 minutes. Looked at another way, 42 minutes a day are available for other indirect services to students, such as program planning, public relations work, or professional development activities.

Figure 8.2
Elementary School Service Levels: Impact of Program Balance and
Counselor-Student Ratio of 1:300

Average class size: 1:25   *Average teacher–student ratio:* 1:20
36 weeks per school year

Guidance curriculum   40% (70) = 28 activity slots/week
   300 counselees/25 students per class = 12 classes
   28 activity slots/12 classes = 2.3 + activities/class/week
   83+ guidance lessons per year per class

Individual student planning   10% (70) = 7 activity slots/week
   7 activity slots × 36 weeks = 252 slots per year
   252 slots × 30 minutes per slot = 7,560 minutes per year
   7,560 minutes/300 counselees = 25+ minutes per student per year

Responsive services   40% (70) = 28 activity slots/week
   14 slots for groups (average 6)   = 84 students
   14 slots for individuals   = <u>14</u> students
   Total students served at one time   = 98
                                (98 is 32+% of the caseload)

System support   10% (70) = 7 activity slots/week
   300 students/20 students per teacher = 15 teachers
   7 slots/15 teachers = 1/2 slot per week per teacher
   7 slots per week × 30 minutes per slot = 210 minutes per week
   210 minutes/5 days = 42 minutes per day

Potential for the Middle School Program

Each class of middle school students in a counselor's caseload could experience one guidance lesson a week (see Figure 8.3). The students could be seen one-on-one for individual student planning for 48 minutes each year; but again, if grouped for these guidance activities, each child could have more counselor contact time. With the assumptions stated earlier, 27% of the counselees could receive responsive services at one time. It is not atypical for middle school small-group counseling offerings to last a grading period (6 weeks in Henderson Public Schools). Thus, in our example, 432 students (72 × six 6-week grading periods) could benefit from small groups over the course of a year. In other words, all children could be in at least one group and 132 could be in two groups. Each teacher served by a counselor could consult for 11 minutes a week; or it could take nearly 3 weeks to consult with all of them for a full 45-minute period. Because the system support component entails activities in addition to teacher consultation, a different way to consider how to use this time is to recognize that 36 minutes a day are available.

Potential for the High School Program

Given the length of the high school class periods (activity slots) and the shifted balance of the program, the students benefit from fewer guidance lessons: less than 1 per week or only 20 in a year (see Figure 8.4). High school counselors could take approximately 2 weeks to conduct an activity with each class in their caseload. However, 72 minutes per student per year are available to conduct individual student planning activities. Ideally, this is a mix of one-on-one and group guidance. At any one time, 22% of the students are receiving counseling, based on the assumption that half the slots are spent in group counseling and half in individual counseling or other responsive services work. As in the middle school program, small-group counseling series for high school students are usually planned for 6 weeks. Thus over the course of the year, 360 students could have this experience. Eighteen minutes are available to consult with each assigned teacher, or to consult with each for a full period could consume nearly 3 weeks of system support time. Grouping teachers by department or by shared students makes use of this time more efficient. From the other perspective, 55 minutes a day are available for other indirect services to students.

Figure 8.3
Middle School Service Levels: Impact of Program Balance and Counselor-Student Ratio of 1:300

Average class size: 1:25   *Average teacher–student ratio*: 1:20
36 weeks per school year

Guidance curriculum   35% (45) = 16 activity slots/week
  300 counselees/25 students per class = 12 classes
  16 activity slots/12 classes = 1.3 + activities/class/week
  42+ guidance lessons per year per class

Individual student planning   20% (45) = 9 activity slots/week
  9 activity slots × 36 weeks = 324 slots per year
  324 slots × 45 minutes per slot = 14,580 minutes per year
  14,580 minutes/300 counselees = 48+ minutes per student per year

Responsive services   35% (45) = 16 activity slots/week
  8 slots for groups (average 9)   = 72 students
  8 slots for individuals   = _8 students
  Total students served at one time   = 80
                    (80 is 27% of the caseload)

System support   10% (45) = 4 activity slots/week
  300 students/20 students per teacher = 15 teachers
  4 slots/15 teachers = 1/4+ slot per week per teacher
  4 slots per week × 45 minutes per slot = 180 minutes per week
  180 minutes/5 days = 36 minutes per day

Figure 8.4

High School Service Levels: Impact of Program Balance and Counselor-Student Ratio of 1:300

Average class size: 1:25   *Average teacher–student ratio:* 1:20
36 weeks per school year

Guidance curriculum   20% (35) = 7 activity slots/week
  300 counselees/25 students per class = 12 classes
  7 activity slots/12 classes = .58 activities/class/week
  20+ guidance lessons per year per class

Individual student planning   30% (35) = 11 activity slots/week
  11 activity slots × 36 weeks = 396 slots per year
  396 slots × 55 minutes per slot = 21,780 minutes per year
  21,780 minutes/300 counselees = 72+ minutes per student per year

Responsive services   35% (35) = 12 activity slots/week
  6 slots for groups (average 10)   = 60 students
  6 slots for individuals   =   6 students
  Total students served at one time   = 66
                                    (66 is 22% of the caseload)

System support   15% (35) = 5 activity slots/week
  300 students/20 students per teacher = 15 teachers
  5 slots/15 teachers = 1/3 slot per week per teacher
  5 slots per week × 55 minutes per slot = 275 minutes per week
  275 minutes/5 days = 55 minutes per day

Managing Time

Because the counselors' time is the most valuable resource in the guidance and counseling program, it is imperative that counselors and everyone else interested in the guidance and counseling program understand the possibilities and limitations of time. Developing the quantitative design (chapter 5) was the first step in striving to ensure that the program that is delivered is the one that is wanted. Through combining that design in terms of real time with the realistic parameters placed on counselors by their student ratios, we are able to recognize what levels of services to students are possible. A primary way to realize that potential is through time management. Indeed, time management strategies must be used to ensure making optimum use of the counselor's resources. As we believe that if something—especially something new—is not planned, it does not get done, so too do we believe that if an activity is not specifically scheduled, it does not get implemented.

Having established priorities for who is to be served, the content areas, and types of activities, and having committed to goals for program improvement, counselors have the basis on which to plan how to use their time most efficiently. This planning is reflected on a series of calendars: yearly, quarterly or monthly, weekly, and daily.

The yearly calendar is developed before school starts and is guidance staff members' means for projecting how the program will unfold over the months available. It requires discipline to be realistic about how much time the major activities identified in the building program plan (discussed in the next section of this chapter) will take. A format for a calendar portraying the yearly program plan is displayed in Figure 8.5. The format obviously provides only an overview of the activities and the time, both of which need to be spelled out in more detail in other formats. However, in addition to being an effective time management tool, the calendar is a simple and graphic way to make the guidance and counseling program visible to others. It allows others to see the totality of the program at a glance, including the time required to carry out the activities. Traditionally, others are only able to see the small pieces of the program that they experience.

Figure 8.5
Program Activities/Component/Month

Guidance Department CALENDAR for _____

Campus: _____

	Guidance Curriculum	Individual Student Planning	Responsive Services	System Support
Aug.				
Sept.				
Oct.				
Nov.				
Dec.				
Jan.				
Feb.				
Mar.				
Apr.				
May				
June				
July				

Things never go quite as planned in the school business. Activities take more or less time than anticipated; other priorities surface. The calendar should be restudied, adjusted, and filled out as needed regularly during the school year. Regularly might mean monthly, quarterly, or at the beginning of each grading period, whatever best fits your situation. At these intervals, measures of the progress being made are taken, and complete plans for activities for the upcoming time period are made.

To manage their own time and to ensure that they are adhering to the guidelines of the comprehensive guidance and counseling program and their individual job descriptions, counselors also establish a weekly schedule that details the major activities for the week and leaves sufficient space for responding to the unexpected. Depending on the consistency of the program and the students served, a weekly schedule may be set and used for a longer block of time. Elementary school counselors often are able to establish patterns, which (barring unforeseen events) are maintained for a year. Middle and high school counselors often are able to establish patterns for a month or for a grading period. To work compatibly with teachers, or in a school with a guidance schedule, a classroom guidance schedule is usually set and provides the basis for the weekly schedule. Small groups meet at set times, whether fixed or rotating, and are plotted on the schedule. Appointments for individual students who are regular clients for a time period also are set. Staffings and other regular or major activities are noted. Weekly schedule formats for elementary, middle, and high school are displayed in Figures 8.6, 8.7, 8.8, respectively.

To ensure achieving the desired program balance, the weekly schedule is developed to reflect that balance. In the Henderson Public Schools example (in Figure 8.1), the desired program balance yielded a specific number of activity slots per week for each component for each school level, as follows:

Elementary School

Guidance curriculum	28	30-minute slots
Individual student planning	7	30-minute slots
Responsive services	28	30-minute slots
System support	7	30-minute slots

Middle School

Guidance curriculum	16	45-minute slots
Individual student planning	9	45-minute slots
Responsive services	16	45-minute slots
System support	4	45-minute slots

High School

Guidance curriculum	7	55-minute slots
Individual student planning	11	55-minute slots
Responsive services	12	55-minute slots
System support	5	55-minute slots

Figures 8.6, 8.7, and 8.8 contain weekly schedules for each school level developed to reflect these balances. The projected program balance and thus the weekly schedule project the use of school counselors' time during the student school day. Schedules may be set for activities that are planned for before and after school hours as well; however, a majority of counselors leave those times unscheduled so as to be available for spontaneous responsive services ("reactive services") or for unanticipated system support activities such as teacher conferences.

Weekly schedules are built based on experience of such things as when responsive services typically occur in a week (Monday mornings, Friday afternoons) and when it is "quiet" enough to have a staff meeting (Thursday afternoons). Guidance curriculum schedules are worked out in collaboration with the teachers whose classes will be taught by the counselor and are typically arranged first before the schedule can truly be set. Although the schedule is planned using the class-period increments of a school, those time increments may be divided differently by counselors in their actual work. For example, high school counselors may not use a full hour for one responsive services activity but rather conduct two 30-minute activities or three 20-minute activities in the time available.

Because the weekly schedule reflects the desired program balance, that balance must be maintained to end the year with a balanced program. If something occurs that interrupts the weekly schedule, counselors know that subsequently—and, ideally, very soon—they need to make up the time lost. For example, if a true crisis comes up with a student, and the counselor cancels a classroom guidance appointment that day, the class that was missed should be made up the following week. It is through planning and calendaring that school counselors and their administrators are accountable for the use of the resource of school counselors' talent.

Each day should begin and end with the counselor planning and reviewing the details of the day and anticipating what comes next. Specific appointments are noted. Many counselors list the topic of the guidance lessons or group counseling sessions on their schedules and calendars for planning and for record-keeping purposes. The daily schedule should end up reflecting what really happened during the day, so that both counselors and their guidance and counseling program staff leaders, if need be, can analyze where their time is going. The schedules and calendars are tools used for both planning and tracking/monitoring the

Figure 8.6
Elementary School Counselor Weekly Schedule Format

MONDAY		
7:00 am	_____	11:20 am Individual Student Planning–3
7:15 am	_____	11:50 am Guidance Curriculum–3
7:30 am	_____	12:20 pm Guidance Curriculum–4
7:50 am Responsive Services–1		12:50 pm Guidance Curriculum–5
8:20 am Responsive Services–2		1:20 pm Responsive Services–4
8:50 am Responsive Services–3		1:50 pm Responsive Services–5
9:20 am Guidance Curriculum–1		2:20 pm Responsive Services–6
9:50 am Guidance Curriculum–2		2:50 pm _____
10:20 am Individual Student Planning–1		
10:50 am Individual Student Planning–2		

TUESDAY		
7:00 am	_____	11:20 am Guidance Curriculum–8
7:15 am	_____	11:50 am System Support–2
7:30 am	_____	12:20 pm Responsive Services–10
7:50 am Responsive Services–7		12:50 pm Guidance Curriculum–9
8:20 am System Support–1		1:20 pm Guidance Curriculum–10
8:50 am Individual Student Planning–4		1:50 pm Guidance Curriculum–11
9:20 am Responsive Services–8		2:20 pm Responsive Services–11
9:50 am Responsive Services–9		2:50 pm _____
10:20 am Guidance Curriculum–6		
10:50 am Guidance Curriculum–7		

WEDNESDAY		
7:00 am	_____	11:20 am Responsive Services–15
7:15 am	_____	11:50 am Individual Student Planning–5
7:30 am	_____	12:20 pm System Support–4
7:50 am Responsive Services–12		12:50 pm Guidance Curriculum–15
8:20 am Guidance Curriculum–12		1:20 pm Guidance Curriculum–16
8:50 am Guidance Curriculum–13		1:50 pm Guidance Curriculum–17
9:20 am Guidance Curriculum–14		2:20 pm Responsive Services–16
9:50 am System Support–3		2:50 pm _____
10:20 am Responsive Services–13		
10:50 am Responsive Services–14		

THURSDAY		
7:00 am	_____	11:20 am Guidance Curriculum–20
7:15 am	_____	11:50 am Responsive Services–19
7:30 am	_____	12:20 pm Responsive Services–20
7:50 am Responsive Services–17		12:50 pm Guidance Curriculum–21
8:20 am Guidance Curriculum–18		1:20 pm Guidance Curriculum–22
8:50 am System Support–5		1:50 pm Guidance Curriculum–23
9:20 am System Support–6		2:20 pm Responsive Services–21
9:50 am Responsive Services–18		2:50 pm _____
10:20 am Individual Student Planning–6		
10:50 am Guidance Curriculum–19		

FRIDAY		
7:00 am	_____	11:20 am Responsive Services–25
7:15 am	_____	11:50 am Guidance Curriculum–26
7:30 am	_____	12:20 pm Guidance Curriculum–27
7:50 am Responsive Services–22		12:50 pm Guidance Curriculum–28
8:20 am Responsive Services–23		1:20 pm Responsive Services–26
8:50 am Responsive Services–24		1:50 pm Responsive Services–27
9:20 am Guidance Curriculum–24		2:20 pm Responsive Services–28
9:50 am Guidance Curriculum–25		2:50 pm _____
10:20 am System Support–7		
10:50 am Individual Student Planning–7		

Note: Guidance Curriculum = 40%; Individual Student Planning = 10%; Responsive Services = 40%; System Support = 10%.

Figure 8.7
Middle School Counselor Weekly Schedule Format

MONDAY

8:00 am _____	2:20 pm Guidance Curriculum–3
8:15 am _____	2:45 pm System Support–1
8:30 am _____	3:30 pm _____
8:45 am Responsive Services–1	3:45 pm _____
9:30 am Responsive Services–2	4:00 pm _____
10:15 am Guidance Curriculum–1	4:15 pm _____
11:00 am Guidance Curriculum–2	
11:45 am Individual Student Planning–1	
12:30 pm Responsive Services–3	
1:15 pm Individual Student Planning–2	

TUESDAY

8:00 am _____	2:20 pm Individual Student Planning–4
8:15 am _____	2:45 pm Guidance Curriculum–6
8:30 am _____	3:30 pm _____
8:45 am Responsive Services–4	3:45 pm _____
9:30 am Guidance Curriculum–4	4:00 pm _____
10:15 am Individual Student Planning–3	4:15 pm _____
11:00 am Responsive Services–5	
11:45 am Guidance Curriculum–5	
12:30 pm System Support–2	
1:15 pm Responsive Services–6	

WEDNESDAY

8:00 am _____	2:20 pm Responsive Services–8
8:15 am _____	2:45 pm Responsive Services–9
8:30 am _____	3:30 pm _____
8:45 am Guidance Curriculum–7	3:45 pm _____
9:30 am Responsive Services–7	4:00 pm _____
10:15 am Guidance Curriculum–8	4:15 pm _____
11:00 am System Support–3	
11:45 am System Support–4	
12:30 pm Guidance Curriculum–9	
1:15 pm Guidance Curriculum–10	

THURSDAY

8:00 am _____	2:20 pm Individual Student Planning–7
8:15 am _____	2:45 pm Guidance Curriculum–13
8:30 am _____	3:30 pm _____
8:45 am Responsive Services–10	3:45 pm _____
9:30 am Guidance Curriculum–11	4:00 pm _____
10:15 am Individual Student Planning–5	4:15 pm _____
11:00 am Guidance Curriculum–12	
11:45 am Responsive Services–11	
12:30 pm Responsive Services–12	
1:15 pm Individual Student Planning–6	

FRIDAY

8:00 am _____	2:20 pm Guidance Curriculum–16
8:15 am _____	2:45 pm Responsive Services–16
8:30 am _____	3:30 pm _____
8:45 am Guidance Curriculum–14	3:45 pm _____
9:30 am Responsive Services–13	4:00 pm _____
10:15 am Individual Student Planning–8	4:15 pm _____
11:00 am Responsive Services–14	
11:45 am Guidance Curriculum–15	
12:30 pm Individual Student Planning–9	
1:15 pm Responsive Services–15	

Note: Guidance Curriculum = 35%; Individual Student Planning = 20%; Responsive Services = 35%; System Support = 15%.

Figure 8.8
High School Counselor Weekly Schedule Format

MONDAY

8:00 am	_____	3:45 pm _____
8:15 am	_____	4:00 pm _____
8:30 am	_____	4:15 pm _____
8:45 am	Responsive Services–1	
9:45 am	Responsive Services–2	
10:45 am	Guidance Curriculum–1	
11:45 am	Individual Student Planning–1	
12:45 am	Responsive Services–3	
1:45 pm	Individual Student Planning–2	
2:45 pm	Individual Student Planning–3	

TUESDAY

8:00 am	_____	3:45 pm _____
8:15 am	_____	4:00 pm _____
8:30 am	_____	4:15 pm _____
8:45 am	Responsive Services–4	
9:45 am	Individual Student Planning–4	
10:45 am	System Support–1	
11:45 am	Guidance Curriculum–2	
12:45 am	Individual Student Planning–5	
1:45 pm	System Support–2	
2:45 pm	Responsive Services–5	

WEDNESDAY

8:00 am	_____	3:45 pm _____
8:15 am	_____	4:00 pm _____
8:30 am	_____	4:15 pm _____
8:45 am	Individual Student Planning–6	
9:45 am	Guidance Curriculum–3	
10:45 am	Responsive Services–6	
11:45 am	Responsive Services–7	
12:45 am	Guidance Curriculum–4	
1:45 pm	Individual Student Planning–7	
2:45 pm	System Support–3	

THURSDAY

8:00 am	_____	3:45 pm _____
8:15 am	_____	4:00 pm _____
8:30 am	_____	4:15 pm _____
8:45 am	Guidance Curriculum–5	
9:45 am	Individual Student Planning–8	
10:45 am	Individual Student Planning–9	
11:45 am	Responsive Services–8	
12:45 am	System Support–4	
1:45 pm	System Support–5	
2:45 pm	Guidance Curriculum–6	

FRIDAY

8:00 am	_____	3:45 pm _____
8:15 am	_____	4:00 pm _____
8:30 am	_____	4:15 pm _____
8:45 am	Individual Student Planning–10	
9:45 am	Individual Student Planning–11	
10:45 am	Responsive Services–9	
11:45 am	Responsive Services–10	
12:45 am	Responsive Services–11	
1:45 pm	Guidance Curriculum–7	
2:45 pm	Responsive Services–12	

Note: Guidance Curriculum = 20%; Individual Student Planning = 30%; Responsive Services = 35%; System Support = 15%.

use of time. This not only helps counselors evaluate what they are doing now and this year but also allows for realistic planning in the future.

By definition, counseling is a responsive service, so unplanned-for events do occur. Some of these unexpected events affect counselors' daily plans, as when the parent of a troubled student finally chooses to visit. The effects of major crises, like students' or staff members' deaths or school fires, can last weeks or even months. The traditional response to a crisis has been to drop everything and respond to it until some resolution has been reached. Depending on the nature of the crisis and its school relevance, this still may need to happen; however, through intensive program planning, it is clear that there are other important priorities as well. The definition of a crisis needs to be clear; strategies for handling the drop-in visitor need to be developed; a balance needs to be struck. At the same time, schedules must be flexible enough to be adjusted while maintaining focus on the basic program.

An unfortunate by-product of the traditional, crisis-oriented, reactive approach to guidance and counseling is the perception that counselors and guidance and counseling programs are not accountable for what they do or do not do. Counselors may feel frustrated and are easily burned out when they feel impotent, when they feel that they do not manage their own professional destiny. Planning allows individuals to manage their own jobs and fulfill their promises to students, to the school system, and to themselves. Planning helps counselors know that the decisions they make about how they spend their time are in concert with those of other decision makers. Counselors can be and are accountable.

Managing Student Caseloads

In the local design of the comprehensive guidance and counseling program, priorities and parameters have been established for providing services to students. Not only are these priorities set for the provision of program activities and the results for students to achieve through participation in them, but they also identify priorities among the categories of students for the various levels of service provided. Thus, counselors are not only accountable for their time and for students' achievement of specified results but are also accountable for the provision of services to high-priority student clients. Managing their caseloads means that counselors intentionally provide for students according to these established priorities. Managing their caseloads also means that counselors operate in compliance with professional, legal, and ethical standards.

Professional school counselors' caseloads consist of the students assigned to them within the system. According to the *Ethical Standards for School Counselors* (ASCA, 2004), "The professional school counselor has a primary obligation to the student" (Standard A.1.a.). As described in earlier chapters, other clients with whom school counselors work include the students' parents, teachers, administrators, other specialists, and community representatives. The ethical standard guides school counselors to know that the students have the highest priority. Within the student population there are a range of subgroups, and it is within this range of subgroups that the next level of priorities are set and to which counselors adhere. In a developmental guidance and counseling program, the first priority for student clients is to address all of the students and focus on their developmental needs. By definition, this means to help 100% of the students in their caseloads to achieve their developmental tasks and to progress on to their next developmental level.

In addition, priorities have been set to guide counselors in responding to students with needs for preventive, remedial, or crisis interventions. It is the responsibility of each counselor to know the priorities and to allocate their resources (competence and time) accordingly. In managing their caseloads, counselors need to spend what has been designated as the right proportion of their time with students according to their priority for service.

Typically, students with needs for preventive interventions are school counselors' second highest priority; they benefit well from school-based counseling. Typically, the service provided to students with needs for remedial or crisis interventions is consultation with parents for the purposes of referral to community-based services.

In addition to adhering to the standards established for the program, caseload management entails adhering to relevant legal standards on behalf of the students. Legal standards are set for school counselors' competence in certification standards, job responsibilities in state statutes or in district policy, and record keeping and maintenance of personal notes in federal law (Department of Education, Family Educational Rights and Privacy Act, 1997). Other legal standards that must be adhered to have to do with such topics as parents' rights, the limited rights of minors, child-abuse reporting, duty to warn, and the rights of clients who are HIV positive. Although minors' rights may be limited, the exceptions are important to know. For example, in Texas, it is legal for minors to consent to counseling without parental permission for suicide prevention; sexual, physical, or emotional abuse; or chemical dependency or addiction.

To manage their caseloads properly, the ethical standards of both the ASCA (2004) and American Counseling Association (2005) provide guidelines. Both sets of standards address clients, relationships, services, and professional competence. They address issues related to working with other professionals, conducting group counseling, and developing and following treatment plans, as well as records and notes.

Professional school counselors must manage their student caseloads to provide the right services to the right numbers of students with the designated needs. They must also manage adherence to the professional, legal, and ethical standards related to the students and to the services school counselors provide.

Develop the Building Program Plan

If you have been following the process we are recommending, at this point each building in the system has studied its current program design and established the design desired for the building program. The available and needed human, financial, and political resources have been identified. A plan for the transition of the traditional program to a comprehensive one has been developed and implementation is under way. Program improvement goals for changing the program activities have been set: That is, new activities are envisioned, ways to augment previously done activities are being worked on, and there is a plan for displacing nonguidance tasks and for streamlining the counselors' involvement in marginal activities. Position guides are written to ensure that appropriate roles are played by guidance and counseling program staff members, including the counselors and others such as clerks, aides, teachers, and principals.

The building program plan reflects realistic application of the existing program resources to the new design for the program. Decisions are made about the student competencies that have priority for achievement, the activities that will be done through each program component, and how the program resources will be applied. The plan includes the annual job description(s) for guidance staff members. The activities are spelled out in enough detail so that it is clear what the program is accomplishing and how—that is, who does what, how long they take, what materials are used, which rooms activities are held in, and so on. Somewhere one or several large notebooks or file drawers contain plans for each activity session, so that a new counselor can walk into the program and carry it on without missing a beat.

Thus the building program plan is a very specific description of what is planned to happen in a school's comprehensive guidance and counseling program: how many guidance lessons are taught at each grade level, by whom, and what the topics are; what individual student planning activities are done for each grade level, how they are organized, what the outcomes are, and how they relate to the past and future planning activities; what the small-group counseling service offers, to how many children at which grade levels, and on what topics. Parent education and staff consultation plans are included. Further, the time frames for conducting the planned activities are established and laid out for the upcoming school year. The summary of this plan is displayed on the yearly calendar (see Figure 8.5).

The plan also contains relevant district and building definitions, rules, and regulations. Such clarifications as what constitutes a crisis and how counselors and other staff members should respond to a crisis are helpful. The principal's rules related to guidance and counseling are made visible and state, for example, that all advisories must meet for a minimum of 45 minutes a week, that procedures for consulting about students having difficulty should be lined out, and so on.

Monitor Program Implementation

By now, all involved are well into the implementation of a comprehensive guidance and counseling program. As difficult as planning and designing the program was, it is even more difficult to maintain the momentum for change and the improvements so that the program does not revert to its original traditional form. Systems for monitoring progress toward the established goals and for monitoring overall improved program implementation are developed and used. Staff continue to be encouraged to try the new activities and be reinforced in their efforts. Finally, program adjustments are made as a result of monitoring the changes.

Monitoring Improvement Plans

If you have used the guidance and counseling program improvement planning process and the format we have recommended, the guidance and counseling program leader, building principals, and counselors have vehicles for monitoring progress toward the goals that have been set. In planning the process to attain their goals, counselors have listed the activities they need to do and established a time frame for doing them. Depending on the size of the district, the guidance and counseling program leader can monitor counselors' efforts according to their time frames—a "tickler file" system will help—or reports of counselors' progress can be elicited on an announced schedule: monthly, quarterly, or once per semester. If there are head counselors, it is appropriate for them to monitor the progress of the counselors, and for the guidance and counseling program leader to monitor their progress.

Monitoring does not need to be heavy-handed; most staff will have worked hard to succeed and will be proud of their accomplishments. Indeed, monitoring provides the guidance and counseling program leader with the opportunity to support and reinforce their work. Further, if staff need resources that the guidance and counseling program leader can provide, the leader will be aware of their needs. If for some reason insurmountable obstacles get in the staff's way or a well-planned activity does not yield the anticipated results, the guidance and counseling program leader will be aware of their hurt and will be able to encourage them to continue to strive for improvement. Changing involves risk taking.

Monitoring Overall Program Implementation

The district has established guidelines or rules for the desired program and ways to accomplish it. Methods for monitoring the content and shape of the buildings' changing programs (and of the district's) must be used. These provide the guidance and counseling program leader with information about who is and is not working toward the desired improvements, and about what is and is not possible in the given circumstances—that is, about what else outside the guidance department needs to change for the guidance and counseling program to be as comprehensive, balanced, and student-directed as the newly established policy states.

To monitor the changing content of the program, the guidance and counseling program leader can use some of the methods described in chapter 10, such as aggregating student outcome data or using unobtrusive measures such as cataloging the new program materials that counselors order for their programs. To monitor the changing shape of the program, the guidance and counseling program leaders can continue to ask the counselors to account for their use of time through calendars or logs. We recommend that the guidance and counseling program leader use the same time accounting measures because over time they will provide graphic evidence of the shift in the program. This evidence proves to be a reward in itself for the counselors. Remember that success breeds success!

Providing Encouragement and Reinforcement

Part of the difficulty of maintaining a program stems from problems associated with trying to change staff work behavior patterns. It is relatively easy to do something new once, particularly if it is highly visible. Further, some staff members may sabotage the improvement process by going along with a new activity once but withdrawing their support when it is over. As a result, it is important to build into the program ways of assessing the need for reinforcement and ways to provide such reinforcement.

Because the need for reinforcement occurs over time, at least part of the staff development program should be designed to provide such reinforcement. Skill-building and discussion sessions that take place on a regular basis are vital. Skill-building opportunities can be provided by encouraging counselors in the system to share their successful new activities with others in a miniconvention-type format, if the system is large enough to do this, or at local, state, or national professional growth conferences.

Staff meetings provide the vehicle for ensuring that the school counselors on a campus provide a unified guidance and counseling program (Henderson & Gysbers, 1998). Through regular weekly meetings, counselors discuss the activities they have just completed and suggest any improvements that seem feasible for the next year. They finalize plans for the activities coming up in the next week and begin or continue planning for large events that are in the near future. They monitor the implementation of the program in line with the plans they have for the year, ensuring progress toward their improvement goals as well.

Staff meetings also provide the vehicle for school counselors on a campus to build a department team, and working as a team not only enhances integration of the program activities but also empowers counselors by providing them opportunities for professional "reassurance and collegiality" (Henderson & Gysbers, 1998, p. 74). Staff meetings also provide counselors opportunities to talk with their colleagues about guidance and counseling issues. Professional dialogues, noted Glickman and Jones (1986), are one of the critical factors in creating a successful school, and "essentially a dialogue occurs when supervisors provide the elements of time, focus, and structure for individuals to meet and talk" (p. 90). Thus counselors' staff meetings are an essential vehicle for continuing to encourage needed changes as well as for ensuring basic communication of information.

More informally, birthday parties, potluck dinners, and other socials are helpful ways to provide reinforcement and form interbuilding teams. When such events are planned, consider the downtime that occurs in any academic year. For example, the last part of January and the first part of February need special events to brighten the season. Midyear conferences can be held on a regional basis and are usually well attended.

Making Program Adjustments

As the program unfolds, there will be times when it is necessary to make program adjustments. Keep in mind that such adjustments are fine-tuning adjustments; they are not major adjustments made as part of the initial program improvement. Those come after more thorough evaluation, as discussed in chapter 10. Any changes made in the program now should be made only after careful thought. Some needed changes will be obvious, as in activities that simply do not work. Others will not be obvious on the surface but will become visible after systematic evaluation. As a rule, count to 10 before making any substantial changes. Some activities need time to take hold and as a result may not show up too well at first. For example, a shift from individual guidance to group guidance may not be appreciated at first by students who are used to individual attention, but as more students receive group guidance, its positive effects will influence the evaluation.

Monitoring and adjusting the program are the results of formative evaluation. For now, the kinds of changes you can expect to be making most often as you fine-tune the program may include modification of timetables, modification of activity schedules, substitution or modification of activities, substitution of resources, and changes in priorities for student competency development at various grade levels. Major adjustments are the result of summative evaluation and lead to program revision. The example of Northside Independent School District's revision process and product is discussed in chapter 11.

Attending to Diversity

This phase of the program development process—implementing the desired program design—presents opportunities to attend to the needs and wants as well as the topics and issues presented by the diversity found in the district's and building's students and communities. The recaptured time from displacing and streamlining counselor involvement in nonguidance activities can be directed toward adding or augmenting activities that fill in gaps in services that target students' cross-cultural competence and cultural identity development, and the like. As resources expand, professional school counselors who are hired can help balance the staff to reflect the demographics of the student population.

Program improvements can be designed that target enhancement of the buildings' cultural responsiveness. Within the goal-setting process, each building's guidance program staff can be encouraged to advocate for strategies that attend to the unique culture of its community. As each building identifies its demographics and related issues, each staff can better strive for equity of and equal access to services for all their students. Specific targets can be set for better serving underserved student clients, often the school's minority students.

Guidance and Counseling Program Leader's Roles and Responsibilities

During the program implementation phase, the guidance and counseling program leader's responsibility shifts to helping counselors to achieve the right program balance and to manage their time for efficiency and accountability. Monitoring their programs and performance is accomplished through ongoing use of goal-setting and planning processes. It is imperative that someone reviews the plans and encourages their implementation, and that someone assists the counselors to assess their level of goal attainment. Accountability is a key to successful ongoing implementation. Hersey, Blanchard, and Johnson (2001) echoed, "two basic tenets of management—measure and monitor your expectations. . . . Briefly, inspect what you expect" (p. 411).

Accomplishing the desired changes in a district takes continuing work also, both programmatically and in resource development. Hersey et al. (2001) made some relevant points about helping people change their work behaviors. One is to identify "areas where immediate successes can be achieved as a means of reinforcing implementation" (p. 408). Another "is to find a change that is not only easy to implement in terms of necessary skills, but that also will only minimally disrupt the usual roles in the organization" (p. 408). And then, "A related idea is to find a change that will have a high probability of acceptance" (p. 409) among leaders, counselors, and the clients.

It may be helpful to have a new emphasis each year for helping counselors focus on the program design discrepancies. As mentioned earlier, you work through the addition and subtraction of activities in priority order. The guidance and counseling program leader keeps track of that order. As activities are displaced, it is helpful for the district to issue some mandates for new or improved guidance and counseling activities. This helps make it clear that counselors are not just giving up some tasks but that they are being held accountable for other, more appropriate guidance activities. In several districts with which we have worked, the counselors had given up on parent education efforts, often because parents do not come to school functions readily. Guidance and counseling program leaders have restated the responsibility of counselors to help parents learn parenting skills and have encouraged the elementary, middle, and high school counselors in their community to work together to meet that responsibility in light of the community's needs. This has improved the parenting efforts as well as the collegiality within local communities.

Items in the district master plan for change that require money (such as ratio improvements) take time to accomplish. Not only does the program leader continue to seek these resource improvements, but also the designers and decision makers often have to be reminded that they cannot have more than the resources will cover. Remember: The counselor-to-student ratio has to be adequate to implement the designed program, or the program has to be designed within the parameters of the ratio; and until the desired ratio is established, the desired program cannot be implemented fully.

New and improved activities often call for new operational policies or administrative regulations. Broadly shared activities may need written definitions for tasks, responsibilities, and timelines that were formerly handled by one department. For example, with the entire school staff involved in preregistration tasks because of streamlining, the series of events needs to be planned carefully. However, an additional benefit has been that the overall job can be done in a shorter time frame because the labor is shared more broadly.

Clarifying responsibilities for the entire caseload and providing special services for identified high-priority caseload members dictate that leaders provide training and develop systems to help school counselors manage their caseload-related responsibilities. Renewed sensitivity to student issues and problems results in counselors (and other specialists) managing more complicated cases. It is important to define rather specifically what constitutes a student's crisis that is worthy of interrupting a counselor's planned schedule. Procedures for intervening appropriately should also be spelled out. Included in Appendix G is a regulation developed in Northside Independent School District to clarify the district's position about what various staff members should do to help students manage personal crises. The procedure outlined provides guidelines for balancing the responsibilities to the student and the parent with those of various staff members and suggests a procedure for collaboration. In Texas and other states, school districts and buildings are required to have crisis management plans that spell out what is to be done in case of a student suicide or other major catastrophe that affects the total—or a large portion of the total—school population.

An additional challenge for the guidance and counseling program leader in implementation is to build support continually for the program and the agreed-on design. There will always be a minority of staff members—counselors, administrators, teachers, and others—who do not understand or appreciate the changed program. In many districts there are new principals, counselors, and other key staff members who need to be educated about the program and its priorities. At the district level, this demands direct work by the district guidance and counseling program leader, and at the building level by the building program leaders and the counselors, with support from the district. Finally, the staff leadership continues to help all staff members be aware of and responsive to the full range of diversity presented by individual students and families, and to the issues posed and opportunities provided by the diversity in the United States and locally.

Concluding Thoughts

After 30 years of experience with developing and managing comprehensive guidance programs, we have identified several keys to successful implementation of a program. Having systems in place to support these strategies facilitates continuing improvement and maintenance of ground already gained in the program. Many of these have been described in this chapter; others are described in subsequent chapters. They are

1. Developing a yearly program plan each year.
2. Developing weekly schedules.
3. Planning, implementing, and assessing guidance program improvement goals.
4. Providing leadership and supervision for the guidance program and its staff.
5. Defining each individual professional school counselor's job for the year.
6. Helping school counselors plan, implement, and assess professional development goals for each year.
7. Holding weekly building guidance program staff meetings.
8. Holding regular district guidance program staff meetings.
9. Holding professional school counselors and their administrators accountable for achieving student results through the guidance program, adhering to guidance program implementation standards, evaluating the quality of school counselor performance, and striving to implement program improvements.

After 5 years or so of program implementation, the program design and framework ought to be reconsidered and revised as necessary. As discussed in chapters 10 and 11, evaluation results will have much to tell the redesigners. Experience with the program balance will have told you whether it is appropriate. Ongoing assessments of students', parents', and school staff members' needs will better guide prioritizing delivery of the program components. An enhanced role for school counselors allows for a focused staff development program, but priorities will change over time. As mentioned throughout, helping counselors have the competencies they need is essential to successful implementation of the comprehensive guidance and counseling program; ways to do this are discussed in the next chapter.

References

American Counseling Association. (2005). *Code of ethics.* Retrieved from http://www. counseling.org/resources/ethics.htm

American School Counselor Association. (2004). *Ethical standards for school counselors.* Retrieved from http://www.schoolcounselor.org/content.asp?contentid=173

Anderson, K. (2002). A response to common themes in school counseling. *Professional School Counseling, 5,* 315–321.

Department of Education, Family Educational Rights and Privacy Act, 34CFR99 (1997, July 1).

Department of Education, Rehabilitative Services rule, 34CFR300.344 (2004, July 1).

Evans, B., & Ward, S. (2002). Solving the "time and information" dilemma through technology. In P. Henderson & N. Gysbers (Eds.), *Implementing comprehensive guidance programs: Critical leadership issues and successful responses* (pp. 55–64). Greensboro, NC: CAPS.

Gelatt, H. B. (1972). *Deciding.* New York: College Entrance Examination Board.

Gelatt, H. B. (1975). *Selecting alternative program strategies: Module 7.* Palo Alto, CA: American Institutes for Research.

Glickman, C. D., & Jones, J. W. (1986). Supervision: Creating the dialogue. *Educational Leadership, 44,* 90–91.

Gysbers, N. C., Lapan, R. T., & Roof, C. (2004). Nonguidance duties performed by school counselors: What are they? Why are they a problem? What can be done about them? *The Counseling Interviewer, 36,* 23–32.

Gysbers, N. C., Starr, M., & Magnuson, C. S. (1998). *Missouri comprehensive guidance: A model for program development, implementation, and evaluation* (Rev. ed.). Jefferson City: Missouri Department of Elementary and Secondary Education.

Henderson, P., & Gysbers, N. C. (1998). *Leading and managing your school guidance and counseling program staff.* Alexandria, VA: American Counseling Association.

Hersey, P., Blanchard, K. H., & Johnson, D. E. (2001). *Management of organizational behavior: Leading human resources* (8th ed.). Upper Saddle River, NJ: Prentice-Hall.

Madden, J. (2002). Displacing nonguidance tasks and initiating program improvement. In P. Henderson & N. Gysbers (Eds.), *Implementing comprehensive guidance programs: Critical leadership issues and successful responses* (pp. 55–64). Greensboro, NC: CAPS.

North Carolina Department of Public Instruction. (n.d.) *How North Carolina school counselors spend their time.* Retrieved July 30, 2003, from http://www.ncpublicschools.org/curriculum/guidance/time.htm

Petersen, J. (2002). Sharing responsibility for schoolwide testing programs. In P. Henderson & N. Gysbers (Eds.), *Implementing comprehensive guidance programs: Critical leadership issues and successful responses* (pp. 65–74). Greensboro, NC: CAPS.

Ripley, V. V., & Goodnough, G. E. (2001). Planning and implementing group counseling in a high school. *Professional School Counseling, 5,* 62–65.

Chapter 9

Ensuring School Counselor Competency

Implementing—Ensuring School Counselor Competency

- Implement a counselor performance improvement system.
- Support professional development.
- Address incompetence.
- Bring new counselors into the program and to the proper roles.
- Clarify roles of building guidance and counseling program/staff leaders.

☞ In the past, the school counseling profession has emphasized the process (skills and techniques) of guidance, such as counseling, consultation, and coordination. Emphasis on the content of guidance, such as decision making, problem solving, and communicating, has been of secondary importance until recently. Currently, the National Standards for School Counseling Programs (Campbell & Dahir, 1997) established by the American School Counseling Association (ASCA) recommend content related to students' academic, career, and personal/social development. In addition, the comprehensive, developmental approach is relatively new to guidance and counseling program conceptualization and implementation. School counselors have been defining roles for themselves and have had their roles defined for them since the birth of the profession. Mirroring both history and the marketplace, school counselor training has been (and may continue to be) inconsistent across the United States. Essential, then, to successful improvement of today's guidance and counseling programs is ensuring not only that counselors' roles and responsibilities are defined clearly (as discussed in earlier chapters) but also that a system is in place for ensuring that school counselors have the competencies needed to carry out these expected roles.

This chapter discusses the facets of a performance improvement system. To achieve their optimum competence, professional school counselors should benefit from appropriate supervision and should be evaluated meaningfully. Their professional growth and development should be encouraged. The contextual resources supporting staff development are discussed, including consideration of counselors' preservice education experiences, the definition of the guidance and counseling program, and the availability of resources to support education and training. Although it is not pleasant to think about, guidance staff leaders must be prepared to address incompetent performance. Inducting new counselors into the field offers critical opportunities to start them off on the right foot. The section on "Attending to Diversity" highlights ways to ensure improved multicultural competence of school counselors. This chapter includes discussions about the changing role of building and district guidance and counseling program and staff leaders.

Implement a Counselor Performance Improvement System

School districts, historically and by law in many states, require job descriptions associated with credentialing requirements for professional staff. They assign someone to provide administration, supervision, and other leadership functions to school counselors and others. They evaluate their performance and provide or provide for staff development activities. When these activities are connected or brought together in one system, they become more meaningful to school counselors than if they are isolated events. As described in some detail in *Leading and Managing Your School Guidance and Counseling Program Staff* (Henderson & Gysbers, 1998), a complete performance improvement system is based on professionally appropriate standards for performance and has four groups of activities that assist school counselors' focus on meeting these standards. Table 9.1 provides a graphic overview of the grouped activities of a school counselor performance improvement system (Henderson & Gysbers, 1998). The responsibility for the quality and quantity of work an individual does belongs to the individual. The designated administrators/supervisors, whom we have elected to call *guidance and counseling program staff leaders* (Henderson & Gysbers, 1998, p. 21), assist by providing objectively collected data-based feedback to their subordinates comparing and contrasting the individual's performance with the performance standards. They also nurture the professionalism of their supervisees through feedback provision and assistance in goal attainment.

These groups of activities are tied together not only because they rely on the same set of performance standards but also because each group is an evolution from previous group activities. The job definition establishes the expectations for application of the standards by individual school counselors. Supervision is provided to assist school counselors improve their performance continuously. Performance evaluation is tied directly to individuals' job descriptions, and evaluative judgments are based on data gathered in supervision activities. Professional development goals are established as a result of feedback received by school

Table 9.1
Counselor Performance Improvement System

Job Definition	Supervision	Performance Evaluation	Professional Development
Components			
Position assignment	Clinical	Self-evaluation	Professionalism assessment
Job description	Developmental	Administrative evaluation	Goal setting and action planning
	Administrative	Assessment of goal attainment	In-service education and training
Forms			
Position guides	Observation	Self-evaluation	Professional development plan
Pre-evaluation conference worksheet	Action plans	Performance evaluation	Goal statement/ action plans
	Office management (e.g., calendars, sign-in sheets, phone logs)	Program and performance goals	District counselor staff development plan

counselors in supervision and evaluation activities. Each of the four groups of activities is described briefly in this section.

Standards

Accepted professional standards provide the basis for a counselor performance improvement system. They provide the specifics that clarify the expectations for and guide school counselors' work. We identify four categories of standards: performance, ethical, legal, and other professional standards. Legal standards must be adhered to. Ethical standards are expectations to which school counselors' clients, administrators, and colleagues have rights. Other professional standards inform school counselors of guidelines to follow in working in special areas of their practice.

Performance Standards

Performance standards describe the domains in which school counselors perform. As explained in chapter 5, domains are clarified by competency statements and further specified through performance indicators or descriptors. These are expressly stated by school districts in the criteria for evaluation that are adopted for school counselors by the local or state school board. The application of performance standards in performance evaluation is discussed later on in this chapter.

In the ASCA National Model (ASCA, 2005, p. 63), 13 performance standards for school counselor are delineated:

Standard 1: Program organization
Standard 2: School guidance curriculum delivered to all students
Standard 3: Individual student planning
Standard 4: Responsive services
Standard 5: Systems support
Standard 6: School counselor and administrator agreement
Standard 7: Advisory council
Standard 8: Use of data
Standard 9: Student monitoring
Standard 10: Use of time and calendar
Standard 11: Results evaluation
Standard 12: Program audit
Standard 13: Infusing themes (i.e., leadership, advocacy, collaboration and teaming, systemic change)

The National Board for Professional Teaching Standards (NBPTS, 2004) identified the following performance standards for school counselors. In their work, "teachers" includes all educators. They identify five core propositions that apply to all educators and 11 areas of standards for school counselors. The five core propositions are the following (pp. vi–vii):

1. Teachers are committed to students and their learning.
2. Teachers know the subjects they teach and how to teach those subjects to students.
3. Teachers are responsible for managing and monitoring student learning.
4. Teachers think systematically about their practice and learn from experience.
5. Teachers are members of learning communities.

The 11 areas of standards for accomplished school counselors include the following (pp. 5–6):

1. School counseling program
2. School counseling and student competencies
3. Human growth and development
4. Counseling theories and techniques
5. Equity, fairness, and diversity
6. School climate
7. Collaboration with family and community
8. Informational resources and technology
9. Student assessment
10. Leadership, advocacy, and professional identity
11. Reflective practice

Ethical Standards

Ethical standards are developed by professional associations and provide professional value statements and offer guidelines for professionals' actions. School counselors follow the *Ethical Standards for School Counselors* published by the ASCA (2004a) and the *Code of Ethics* published by the American Counseling Association (ACA, 2005). The former are provided in Appendix B. Additionally, the National Education Association (2003) published the *Code of Ethics of the Education Profession* that describes standards for all educators, including school counselors.

Legal Standards

Legal standards are expressed in the laws passed by federal, state, and local governing bodies with legal jurisdiction over the school district and related regulations developed by administrative bodies to implement those laws. Examples of legal standards that are relevant to school counselors include those regarding school counselor certification and certification renewal, job roles and responsibilities, parental rights, when minors may consent to counseling regardless of parent rights, child abuse and neglect responses, referrals to community-based services, rules regarding records and notes, and special considerations for special student populations (e.g., those affected by substance abuse, special education students, students from migrant families, and at-risk students).

Other Professional Standards

Other professional standards are statements published by professional organizations; for example, counseling associations that consist of specialists offer standards for others who practice within that specialty. School counselors need to know and apply the professional standards published by specialty groups that are relevant to their job assignments. Some particularly relevant standards are those related to group work, online communications, and assessment. Also essential in the 21st century are the standards for working across cultures.

The latter are discussed in the "Attending to Diversity" section of this chapter. The Association for Specialists in Group Work (ASGW) has established *Professional Standards for the Training of Group Workers* (ASGW, 2000) and *Best Practices* (ASGW, 1998a) to guide effective implementation of counseling groups. The National Board for Certified Counselors (NBCC, 2001) has published guidelines on *Ethics: The Practice of Internet Counseling,* and ACA (1999) on the *Ethical Standards for Internet Online Counseling.*

The Association for Assessment in Counseling (AAC) and the ASCA collaborated on a statement of *Competencies in Assessment and Evaluation for School Counselors* (AAC, 2001). It describes nine competencies that, in this era of high-stakes testing, all school counselors should possess. School counselors:

1. Are skilled in choosing assessment strategies.
2. Can identify, access, and evaluate the most commonly used assessment instruments.
3. Are skilled in the techniques of administration and methods of scoring assessment instruments.
4. Are skilled in interpreting and reporting assessment results.
5. Are skilled in using assessment results in decision making.
6. Are skilled in producing, interpreting, and presenting statistical information about assessment results.
7. Are skilled in conducting and interpreting evaluations of school counseling programs and counseling-related interventions.
8. Are skilled in adapting and using questionnaires, surveys, and other assessments to meet local needs.
9. Know how to engage in professionally responsive assessment and evaluation practices.

AAC (2001b) also has an informative policy statement on the *Responsibilities of Users of Standardized Tests.*

The American Psychological Association (2005) published the *Code of Fair Testing Practices in Education*, a guide for professionals for providing and using "tests that are fair to all test takers regardless of age, gender, disability, race, ethnicity, national origin, religious, sexual orientation, linguistic background or other personal characteristics." The guide described "four critical areas: Developing and Selecting Appropriate Tests, Administering and Scoring Tests, Reporting and Interpreting Test Results, Informing Test Takers." The National Council on Measurement in Education (1995) also has a *Code of Professional Responsibilities in Educational Measurement* that

> applies to any type of assessment that occurs as part of the educational process, including formal and informal, traditional and alternative techniques for gathering information used in making educational decisions at all levels. These techniques include, but are not limited to, large-scale assessments at the school, district, state, national, and international levels; standardized tests; observational measures, teacher conducted assessments; assessment support materials; and other achievement, aptitude, interest, and personality measures used in and for education.

Defining School Counselors' Jobs

In chapter 5 we described the value of position guides in outlining the roles fulfilled and competencies demonstrated by school counselors as they carry out their jobs. These guides apply to all individuals holding positions with the same title. In chapter 8 we described job descriptions as statements that distinguish each counselor's specific job responsibilities from every other school counselor's job responsibilities. Each individual's job description is unique within the context of the comprehensive guidance and counseling program and within the context of the individual schools in which he or she works.

The job definition is the basic statement of the expectations for counselors' performance for the year and becomes the basis for the rest of the performance improvement system activities for individuals. It clarifies how much is expected of the counselors in implementing each dimension (each role) of their job through the weighting process (Henderson & Gysbers, 1998). It describes how they will apply their competencies during the year. Based on their job definition, their guidance and counseling program staff leader reminds them of the relevant performance standards—the descriptions of the quality expectations.

The data gathered in preparing for an individual's performance evaluation are done in relationship to his or her job description. The staff leader's supervision activities are done to highlight the job priorities. At the beginning of the year, a conference is held between the guidance and counseling program staff leader and each school counselor. During this conference they agree on the specifics of each counselor's job description, agree on the weights assigned to each role, discuss how the evaluator will know what quality of performance is provided, discuss what constraints may get in school counselors' or their staff leaders' way of doing their jobs as defined, and reaffirm the school counselor's program improvement and professional development goals for the year.

Providing Appropriate Supervision

Professional supervision is the most effective means of assisting another's growth and development. Indeed, without it, there is some evidence that the skill level of counselors decreases (Wiley & Ray, 1986, cited in Borders, 1989). The basis of supervision is supervisors' firsthand observation of school counselors' performance. Through such direct observations, data are gathered and provided as feedback to the supervisee (Borders, 1991). The data are organized and analyzed according to professional and other work-related standards for performance. Another goal of supervision is to enhance counselors' thoughts and commitment to their professional responsibilities by creating meaningful dialogue between supervisors and counselors (Glickman, Gordon, & Ross-Gordon, 1995) and to influence the work of the supervisees (Bernard & Goodyear, 1992). In addressing challenges and opportunities for school counselors in the 21st century, Paisley and McMahon (2001) stated that school counselors will need to continue to update and upgrade their professional competence. They also noted, "Skill building alone will be inadequate, however. School counselors must also participate in continued clinical supervision in order to enhance their professional development" (p. 111).

As suggested by Barret and Schmidt (1986), we have found it useful in schools to use three types of supervision: clinical, developmental, and administrative. We believe that the effective use of these various modes of supervision is a primary vehicle for ensuring school counselor competency. Each mode entails targeting specific performance behaviors of counselors and provides mechanisms for assessment and feedback of the accomplishment of their desired objectives. Through these mechanisms, both supervisor and counselor are forced to be concrete about strengths and deficiencies. In our experience, when professional counselors have been assisted to see specifically what they can do to improve, they are eager to improve.

Each professional supervision type targets different dimensions of a school counselor's professionalism and uses different strategies in its implementation. These are fully detailed in *Leading and Managing Your School Guidance and Counseling Program Staff* (Henderson & Gysbers, 1998) and are only outlined briefly here. Staff leaders' use of each type and their approach within each type are based on the assessment of a school counselor's level of professionalism.

Clinical Supervision

Clinical supervision focuses on counselors' direct service delivery and on counselors' unique professional skills such as guidance, counseling, consultation, and referral. Observing counselors use of their skills and providing specific feedback regarding what was observed is the essence of clinical supervision. A five-step process model is suggested:

1. Preobservation conference
2. Observation
3. Analysis of data
4. Postobservation conference
5. Postconference analysis

Aubrey (in Boyd, 1978, p. 306) defined skills as "behaviors that are operational, ratable, and predictable within a delimited range of effects." The counselors' professional skills (we use the word *competencies*) can be delineated so as to lend themselves to this form of observation. Many counselor education programs and school districts have listed the competencies that they expect of school counselors they educate and employ. Competency lists provide the basis for observation. To illustrate, the descriptors used for this purpose by Northside Independent School District are provided in Appendix M.

Supervisors certified as school counselors (such as head counselors, central office guidance administrators or supervisors, or counselors assigned supervisory responsibility of their peers) should perform clinical supervision if it is to be effective. "Observation is actually the act of (1) noting and then (2) judging" (Glickman et al., 1995, p. 237). Forms can assist the supervisor to note the presence or absence of specific, important behaviors. They also provide vehicles for communication between the observer and the person being observed. Sample forms from Northside Independent School District are provided in Appendix N.

No matter how minutely competencies are described or how refined the observation forms are, training is required to provide supervisors with the background they need to make professionally appropriate judgments of the quality of an individual's performance and to provide meaningful feedback to the practitioners. The postobservation conference has two parts: "first describing what has been seen and then interpreting what it means" (Glickman et al., 1995, p. 238). This feedback should be given within 48 hours after an observation occurs so that both parties have a fairly accurate recollection of the events.

It is difficult to recommend an ideal number of contacts that the clinical supervisor and counselor should have. If counselors are not unduly threatened by such observations and the related feedback conferences, then the more the merrier because professionals do value feedback to help them improve their competencies. Clinical supervision is akin to tutorial assistance; it is one-on-one, direct, and competency focused. Counselors can benefit from clinical supervision in each of the functions required in their work: instruction, guidance, counseling, consultation, and referral. We recommend that observations occur at least twice a year. Remember that observation and feedback about counseling competencies will not necessarily provide counselors with ideas about how to improve their consultation competencies.

Developmental Supervision

Developmental supervision focuses on school counselors' knowledge base, including their theoretical and client understandings, their program and caseload management capabilities, and their commitment to their jobs, school, district, and profession. Its purpose is to direct counselors' professional cognitive and affective growth and development.

The traditional professional development activities of participating in in-service education, attending conferences, and professional association involvement support developmental supervision. Another strategy used in developmental supervision is assisting school counselors to implement their goal-related plans and to measure their levels of goal attainment. Monitoring their progress toward goals can be accomplished through individual conferences and sharing among the counselor team. Some goals lend themselves to written reports.

A third developmental supervision strategy is formal, planned case consultations. This strategy assists counselors to grow in their conceptualization of their clients (Biggs, 1988) and helps them learn not only to look objectively at their own experiences but also to learn from others' cases. The larger the supply of case examples a counselor has, the better he or she is able to recognize patterns in clients' behaviors and respond appropriately (Etringer, Hillerbrand, & Claiborn, 1995).

A fourth developmental supervision strategy is providing mentors to inexperienced or weak school counselors. Mentors share their experience and expertise with other counselors by, for example, teaching them, encouraging them, and befriending them (Tentoni, 1995). Being a mentor is also a developmental supervision strategy. Mentors learn as they articulate their learnings (VanZandt & Perry, 1992). The counseling literature also describes mentors' need for training to fulfill that role most effectively (Peace, 1995).

Administrative Supervision

As we have defined it, administrative supervision targets the traditional areas of the soundness of counselors' professional judgments, their mental health, their work habits, their adherence to rules and standards, and the effectiveness of their relationships with colleagues and clients (Henderson & Gysbers, 1998). Observing and assessing the adequacy of school counselors' professional judgments, their mental health, and their relationships with others require careful and complete data gathering and often ambiguous applications of standards. Observing and assessing work habits and compliance with professional, ethical, and legal standards are more concrete.

Administrative supervision relies on several strategies to address a wide range of topics. Administrative supervisors hold individual conferences with their supervisees; sometimes these conferences involve confrontation or counseling. Administrative supervisors also consult with supervisees spontaneously as difficult cases present themselves. Conducting staff meetings with the entire department team is another widely used administrative supervision strategy.

Assessing Professionalism

All of the efforts to assist school counselors continuously improve their performance are based on assessments of their levels of professionalism, a challenge mutually undertaken by school counselors and their staff leaders. These assessments are made by the individual school counselors for themselves and by their staff leaders. The former have subjective perspectives and large quantities of data. The latter have objective perspectives and selective data. Assessments are ever evolving: Every piece of data experienced by counselors, observed by supervisors, and received in feedback to school counselors, in turn, contributes to their professionalism assessments (Henderson & Gysbers, 1998).

Professionalism includes school counselors' competence to carry out the roles required in the fulfillment of their jobs. As defined in the model in this book, those roles and competencies are guidance, counseling, consultation, coordination, assessment, and program management. Professionalism also includes school counselors' commitment to their job, that is, their specific assignments within the program as well as their commitment to their place of employment (school and district) and to their profession. Each of these dimensions includes many facets. Individuals' professionalism levels vary from situation to situation; thus aggregating situational examples into patterns is one of the challenges for both school counselors and their staff leaders.

Evaluating Staff Fairly

Counselor evaluation is done most fairly when it is conducted as part of the total performance improvement system. The multiple activities of a complete counselor performance improvement system provide meaningful data on which to base the judgments relative to clearly stated performance standards. An approach to counselor evaluation is discussed extensively in chapter 10, but we include a brief discussion here to allow you to see how it is related to the other parts of an overall performance improvement system.

As with the other parts of an overall performance improvement system—job definition, supervision, and professional development—performance evaluation rests on the expectations held for the position of school counselor as clarified in the position guide, specific job description, and standards established for performance quality. Remember that the position guide was written on the basis of the desired comprehensive guidance and counseling program. There must, then, be congruence among the program, the position guide, and the procedures used for school counselor evaluation.

The purposes of the three groups of activities that build on job definition in the overall performance improvement system are related, but each has a separate goal. The goal of supervision is to use the resources (i.e., the supervisors) of the system to assist school counselors to reach their professional potential within the district. The goal of professional development is to encourage school counselors to continue to grow in their professional competency, using both school district and personal resources. The goal of evaluation is to rate the competency level of the school counselors from the school district's perspective, to judge how competently they are performing the job to which they are assigned.

In theory, supervision and professional development are conducted in a nonjudgmental manner, but in reality they also provide some of the data that support the judgments made in evaluation. If, for example, counselors are observed by their clinical supervisor as consistently giving misinformation to students or as consistently projecting their own values into students' decisions, the clinical supervisor is responsible for providing that information to the evaluator. The relationship can work the other way as well. If the evaluator perceives counselors not being authoritative enough with students, the clinical supervisor can explain to the evaluator the professional rationale for being nonjudgmental.

Supervision and professional growth also provide strategies for assisting counselors to repair deficiencies identified through evaluation. If the evaluator perceives that a counselor is not effective with groups of children, the clinical supervisor can observe the counselor in action with groups and provide technical assistance. In developmental supervision, the counselor and supervisor might agree that a professional development goal for the counselor is to improve the use of instructional methodology. Through strategies provided for professional development, the counselor might attend workshops on effective teaching techniques. Thus evaluation is the central part of an overall performance improvement system.

Support Professional Development

Although professional development is primarily the responsibility of the individual school counselor, district and building guidance and counseling program staff leaders also hold some accountability for the quality of individuals' performance. In addition to helping clarify job and performance expectations and providing data-based feedback, they nurture individuals' professional motivation and strive to empower them to attain optimum professional maturity (Henderson & Gysbers, 1998).

A school district can and should provide many resources, but the needs and wants of the district must be balanced with the needs and wants of the individuals on the staff.

From the district's perspective, the purpose of providing professional development opportunities is to provide cost-effective in-service education and training that meets the needs of the largest number of counselors in relation to priority needs of the district and building guidance and counseling programs. From the school counselors' perspective, the purpose of participating in professional development opportunities is to improve their professional and personal competencies in areas that they perceive as important. As stated earlier, the goal of professional development is to encourage staff members to continue to grow in their professional competency, using both district and personal resources.

The challenge is to provide mechanisms that help both the district and the district counselors target specific competencies—knowledge, skills, and attitudes—that need enhancement. We recommend developing a process for encouraging professional development that begins by having counselors, assisted by their guidance and counseling program staff leaders, identify their own competencies and compare them with the competencies required to implement the desired district comprehensive guidance and counseling program. From these two data sources, a master plan for counselor staff development for the district is developed that identifies the competencies to be addressed for the various subpopulations of school counselors and describes how these will be addressed.

Individual Responsibilities

Developing Individual Professional Development Plans

Paisley and McMahon (2001) identified ongoing professional development as essential to vital programs and professionalism in school counseling. As a result of clinical, developmental, and administrative supervision, and as a result of data-based performance evaluation, counselors and their staff leaders will have identified specific competencies that need to be targeted for improvement. Counselors' professional development plans are developed in the context of their long-range professional and personal goals as well as in the context of the comprehensive guidance and counseling program.

Some targets for professional development at the beginning of the 21st century relate to the currently defined *Role of the Professional School Counselor* (ASCA, 2004b). Today school counselors are expected to be competent to provide structured lessons, coordinated systemic activities, individual and group counseling, consultation with teachers and other educators, referrals to other school support services or community resources, peer helping, information dissemination, confidential relationships, program management and operations, professional development, use of data, planning, calendaring, and time management. In addition, in The Education Trust's (2003) Transforming School Counseling initiative, skills are called for in advocacy, leadership, teaming, collaboration, counseling, consultation, and use of data, and "to use these skills to effect systemic change that removes barriers that impede student achievement."

Modern technology also is affecting school counseling. Kenny and McEachern (2004) stated, "The field of counseling is certainly being affected by current technological advances. The use of the telephone and other telecommunications devices (i.e., faxes, electronic mail, Internet, cellular phones) are increasingly popular methods of providing counseling" (p. 200). These communications methods call for different competencies, or different applications of traditional competencies. They also pose some new ethical dilemmas.

Bowers (2002), Evans and Ward (2002), and Van Horn and Myrick (2001) identified different ways school counselors can utilize computer technology to work more efficiently and help students succeed. They mentioned retrieving and disseminating information through such tools as electronic mail, Web sites, electronic newsletters, online journals;

distance learning through video conferencing and online schools; helping students develop individual plans through computerized data storage and electronic (phone and Internet) registration; exploring colleges and careers through Web sites and guidance information systems; using the computer as a counseling tool; networking; and training and supervision.

In developing their professional development plans, counselors should be explicit about their long-range plans and be encouraged by their staff leaders to identify the intermediate and immediate goals that will help them reach their larger goals. Both sets of data—the specific job performance improvement targets and the professional–personal goals—provide information to counselors as they develop professional development plans. Counselors should be encouraged to develop such plans for a 5-, 2-, or even 1-year period. As a district, however, you will have more than enough data to work with if you know the counselors' immediate needs and wants for competency acquisition or improvement.

In a formally defined performance improvement system, school counselors write professional development plans in collaboration with their staff leaders and submit them to the guidance administrator. Methods and procedures for accomplishing this are described in *Leading and Managing Your School Guidance and Counseling Program Staff* (Henderson & Gysbers, 1998). A form used for this purpose is displayed in Figure 9.1. With a form such as this, counselors and their building guidance and counseling program staff leaders agree on a targeted competency area, such as the implementation of effective group counseling. They also discuss appropriate objective(s) that, if met, will increase counselors' effectiveness, such as the ability to (a) articulate a theoretical base for counselor behaviors, (b) use a variety of response techniques, and (c) facilitate students' development of behavioral plans. Counselors then identify tasks/activities that they plan to perform to meet the objectives. The plan includes a time frame and a statement to the guidance and counseling program staff leader about potential evidence of achievement. (The second half of the form relates to the evaluation of the counselors' accomplishment of the plan—when the tasks were completed, what documentation of accomplishment is available, and to what degree tasks were accomplished. These are reviewed at the end of the year by the counselors and the guidance and counseling program staff leaders as part of the evaluation system described in chapter 10.) Having received the counselors' plans, guidance and counseling program staff leaders and administrators know what their staff members want. They are then in a position to encourage counselors to seek educational opportunities.

Assessing Needs for Counselor Competency Development

Knowing what the counselors want is only one part of the needs assessment in a plan for staff development. Also necessary is assessing counselors' needs for performance improvement in terms of the competencies and commitments needed to implement the comprehensive program desired by the building or district. It is important to assess counselors' competencies to find out those they have as well as those they need to work on.

The same methodology that was used to assess the perceived needs of students can be used to assess counselor competencies; only the items are changed. The items to be used are generated from the standards for performance that have been identified as necessary to organize and implement the comprehensive guidance and counseling program. The competencies and their indicators and descriptors that you have identified to support the supervision and evaluation components of the performance improvement system provide these specifics. By using aggregated data from counselors' performance evaluations, questionnaires, or other assessment technique, data are gathered and tabulated. Many such assessments ask counselors not only how much they need to acquire the competency but also how important they feel acquiring the competency is.

Figure 9.1
Counselor Professional Growth Plan Form

COUNSELOR PROFESSIONAL GROWTH PLAN

School: _____

Name: _____

Principal/Head Counselor Signature: _____

Date: _____

USE A SEPARATE FORM FOR EACH COMPETENCY AREA

| PLANNING | | EVALUATION | | |
| (To Be Completed by _____) | | (To Be Completed by _____) | | |

Targeted Competency Area:
Objective(s):

Description of Tasks/ Activities	Time Frame	Evidence of Achievement	Actual Completion Date	Verification of Achievement	Level of (1–5) Accomplishment

Overall Assessment of Achievement:

1   2   3   4   5
(Not Achieved)   (Fully Achieved)

Counselor's Signature: _____

Principal/Head Counselor: _____

Date: _____

From the system's perspective, the guidance and counseling program staff leader also has a viewpoint as to the importance of each competency that should be considered as the plans for staff development are made. If in comparing and contrasting the current and the desired programs, discrepancies have been identified that seem to be related to competencies not used in the current program but wanted in the desired program, the district guidance and counseling program leader will know the importance of staff development in those competencies, whereas the counselors might not yet be aware. For example, if the desired program calls for more group counseling than is currently done, competency improvement in those skills will receive a high priority from the district's perspective.

Within the counseling staff, not only will different groups of counselors want to acquire different professional competencies, but also different groups of counselors will need to acquire different competencies. New counselors have different needs than do experienced counselors. Some experienced counselors are more competent than others and may need advanced training, whereas others may need remedial training. The program improvement process itself will dictate some staff development needs. The priority needs for training guidance and counseling program staff leaders may be different from those for staff counselors. If you have a cadre of peer leaders, they may have different professional development needs.

Relating Staff Development to the Program Improvement Process

As they proceed through the program improvement process, school counselors learn a variety of new concepts. They learn about the comprehensive guidance and counseling program, about their roles in it, and about some of the processes to implement it. The presentation of the information gathered in assessing the design of the current guidance and counseling program provides insights into the program and its facets, as does the recasting of the program that is presented in the expression of the district's basic structure. Whether you have chosen to select current examples of effective practices or ventured into innovative activities that fit the desired program, counselors learn about operational details of a comprehensive guidance and counseling program.

If as a first step in assessing the design of their building programs, counselors kept logs of their activities, they learned about their own piece of the program and watched as their data were aggregated with those of others. This helped them further internalize the program concept and provided them with insights into their own work habits. Such information, when compared with the expectations for their roles as stated in the position guides, provides counselors with ideas as to how they can add to their professional competencies. At the same time, study of the position guides of other staff in the guidance department helps all staff members understand the chain of command as well as the responsibilities of the guidance and counseling program staff leader and those of the various paraprofessionals.

One of the opportunities identified by Paisley and McMahon (2001) for school counselors in this century was "determining appropriate roles and areas of program focus" (p.110). Counselors need to learn processes related to planning such as goal setting, ranking for priority, and action planning. Counselors also need to learn about program planning and personal planning. By being involved in the program improvement process, they learn about program planning through such activities as conducting needs assessments, assessing the current program, and establishing the desired program structure. They learn about collaborating with other stakeholders to shape their programs appropriately and about setting appropriate boundaries to focus their roles to best assist students' development. By setting goals and developing action plans for attaining those goals, counselors learn personal planning.

One of the major benefits of establishing a comprehensive guidance and counseling program with clear-cut priorities is that the guidance and counseling program becomes manageable to the counselors. Instead of a series of days that just happen, the counselors' work year becomes a planned year. Not every minute of every day can be planned—that will never happen as long as the important responsibility of responding to students and others in crisis is present. The major events of the program can be planned, however, enabling counselors to feel a sense of accomplishment. Having control of the major parts of the program and their job empowers counselors and contributes to their professional pride and, consequently, helps revitalize their commitment to their profession.

Of interest here is a study that underscores the importance of program management: Fitch and Marshall (2004) found that "the area of program management, evaluation, and research showed the largest discrepancy" (p. 175) in how school counselors allocated their time between high- and low-achieving schools in Kentucky. Counselors in high-achieving schools also "spent more time on tasks relating to professional standards" (p. 176), and "coordination activities of school counselors were more prevalent in high-achieving schools" (p. 176). Their conclusions suggested that program management and evaluation leads to more systematic and continuously improving programs. Relating programs to professional standards helps programs to be focused on meaningful outcomes. And, through coordinating schoolwide activities and programs, counselors influence the total school.

Counselors, especially those who are not used to thinking of the program as having any resources, need to learn the processes for effective use of resources, such as budgeting, careful selection of materials, and time management. During the program improvement process, counselors need to learn to use assertion and political skills; they need to see themselves as being empowered.

Once the desired comprehensive program design has been established for the building and district, and the discrepancies between "what should be" and "what is" are clear, generating as many ideas as possible for repairing these discrepancies not only provides a plethora of ideas but also gets the counselors' creative juices flowing. Brainstorming sets in motion "How can I change?" thought processes.

If in the program improvement process special projects are used to enhance the program change process, some counselors may need competency development related to those special efforts. They need to learn to take risks comfortably, and they also need to learn the competencies associated with the specific projects they are participating in. If you are experimenting with curriculum writing, for example, in-service training in curriculum development is important, as is training in the specific content area to be developed. If some buildings are trying out large-group guidance activities, then competency in working with large groups is required. If you purchase materials for possible districtwide use, counselors need training in the effective use of these materials.

Once the analyses of the disparities between the current and the desired programs have been completed, and the basic directions for program change have been established, the training needs of counselors in the district can be anticipated. Much has been learned about the teaching–learning process in recent years, and counselors need updating in that process if they are to deliver the guidance curriculum effectively and maintain their credibility as consultants to teachers. They also can benefit from staff development activities that focus on instructional methodology such as task analysis, lesson design, and effective teaching practices. In addition, the new program design requires that counselors update their competencies in working competently across cultures; in guidance and counseling group work; in effective methods of parent and teacher consultation; in brief family intervention techniques; in addressing the needs of at-risk students (such as dropouts and potential dropouts, substance abusers and children of substance abusers, unmotivated learners and those who continually fail to succeed academically, depressed adolescents and those who threaten or attempt suicide); and in incorporating career development activities in the program such as decision making, planning, and problem solving. Another recurrent need, and one that administrators support wholeheartedly, is that of acquiring time management skills. Further, counselors need to fine-tune their advocacy and public communication skills.

As the guidance and counseling program shifts to require better use of counselors' educational talents, their sense of professionalism should be enhanced. Workshops or study sessions on ethical standards (ACA, 2005; ASCA, 2004a; NEA, 2003) and issues could be held to further this feeling. Counselors should also be encouraged to belong to professional associations and to become involved in association work. When available, attainment of licensure or registry should be encouraged, with such accomplishments being publicly acknowledged.

From the outset, guidance and counseling program staff leaders and other peer leaders can benefit from learning about leadership characteristics and leadership styles. A personal benefit from participating as leaders in the program is increased self-knowledge and actualization. Benefits also arise for leaders from learning about situational leadership, team building, the use of power, the needed balance of both task and relationship orientation, and the roles they play in groups and leader–follower situations (Hersey, Blanchard, & Johnson, 2001). As their program and staff leadership roles evolve, they acquire many new competencies (Henderson & Gysbers, 1998). If you are the guidance and counseling program leader, or if your role as program administrator does not require special administrative or supervisory certification, you too will benefit because most of this material is not included in guidance preservice education.

Staff Development Resources

Systematic efforts to ensure the competency of school counselors rest on knowledge and appropriate use of available resources. Relevant resources include preservice training experienced by certified school counselors, clear definition of the guidance and counseling program with specific expectations for school counselor positions, and the human, financial, and political support resources available to assist in professional development efforts.

Preservice Counselor Education

Certification of individuals' preparedness to counsel in the schools is a function of state departments of education. Requirements for certification vary from state to state, and within a state, institutions of higher education differ in how they prepare their students to meet requirements. National standards for school counselor preparation have been set by the Council for Accreditation of Counseling and Related Educational Programs (CACREP). These standards state that all counselors, regardless of specialty, should experience curriculum in areas of human growth and development, social and cultural foundations, helping relationships, group work, career and lifestyle development, appraisal, research and program evaluation, and professional orientation (CACREP, 2001, pp. 2–3). In addition, students preparing to practice school counseling should experience curriculum in foundations of school counseling; contextual dimensions of school counseling; and delineated knowledge and skill requirements for school counselors (pp. 28–30).

Knowing the competencies acquired through the counselor training programs in your area provides you with baseline information about the skills and knowledge competencies graduates of those programs bring to counseling jobs. Being familiar with the professors in the programs also gives you some idea about the attitudes and beliefs their students have been exposed to. The program for ensuring counselor competency builds from this baseline.

Guidance and Counseling Program Definition

In designing your comprehensive guidance and counseling program, you have written position guides that state the basic expectations of staff members in implementing the program. The example we used from Northside Independent School District delineates the expectations that school counselors should

- teach the guidance curriculum
- guide groups and individual students through the development of their educational and career plans
- counsel small groups and individual students with problems or concerns
- consult with teachers and parents
- refer students or their parents to other specialists or special programs
- coordinate the work of others (e.g., faculty doing tasks previously done by school counselors, and community volunteers participating in comprehensive guidance and counseling program activities)
- plan, manage, and evaluate the school's guidance and counseling program
- pursue continuous professional development.

Thus counselors in a system that uses this position guide are expected to have the competencies needed to teach, guide, counsel, consult, refer, and coordinate effectively. Further delineation of these competencies—the related skills, knowledge, attitudes, and beliefs—is not the subject of this book. What is important for our purposes here, however, is that you be aware that ensuring counselor competency can occur only if you and your district have identified the counselor competencies required to deliver a comprehensive guidance and counseling program successfully.

Support Resource Availability

As you work to ensure school counselor competency, you need to consider the resources available. Buildings, districts, and communities have human, financial, and political resources available to use in ensuring counselor competency. The question is, how can these resources be used most efficiently and effectively?

Personnel Resources. Effective performance in a position is a shared responsibility of the position holder and the school district. Counselor applicants have a responsibility to define themselves adequately so that prospective employers can evaluate whether they are right for the jobs available. Employers have the responsibility for clearly and specifically defining the positions available. Counselors have a professional responsibility to be competent in what the district has the right to expect, that is, the educational areas defined as minimum standards for certification by the state and the ethical and other relevant standards defined by the profession.

Every school and district employs administrators who are responsible for the performance of the guidance department staff. The titles of such administrators vary, as do levels of authority and responsibility. Administrators may have such titles as principal, superintendent, head counselor, guidance and counseling director, coordinator, or supervisor. The roles that each fulfills on behalf of ensuring school counselor competency need to be specifically defined. The number of these administrators who may be involved and the degree of their competency in guidance and counseling will vary by the size of the school district as well as by its commitment to the comprehensive guidance and counseling program concept. Chance may also enter the picture in terms of the career paths of the administrators involved. For example, a principal who was formerly an effective school counselor may provide a different type of administrative direction and supervision from one who has no counseling experience; and the quality of such direction and supervision may vary depending on the principal's experiences as a school counselor.

Certain communities and geographical regions have resources that counselors may be able to use. For example, there are over 600 counselor training institutions in the United States (Hollis, 1997). Many school districts are sufficiently close to these institutions to have access to counselor educators. Other school counselors, professional counseling association leaders, mental health counselors, counseling psychologists, psychiatrists, training consultants, business/industry human resources specialists, and other specialists also may be available. To make optimum use of these specialists for professional development, however, their expertise needs to be surveyed and cataloged. We suggest that you compile a list of such individuals and identify their areas of expertise, the topics on which they present workshops, their professional licenses and certificates, and their fees.

Financial Resources. The financial resources available to the guidance and counseling program should make provision for the professional development of the counseling staff. Districts provide money and opportunities for in-service training and attendance at professional conferences and conventions. Regional offices and state departments of education also provide education and training opportunities for school counselors. Larger school systems and intermediate school districts often provide professional journal subscriptions, books, and training tapes through professional libraries.

Political Resources. In this era of educational reform, there is increased support to enhance professional educators' competency and accountability. Many states' reform efforts include renewed emphasis on professional growth in the form of mandatory in-service education, professional renewal requirements for recertification, and career ladders. Even if counselors are not mentioned directly in these efforts, the movement to improve overall staff competency can be used specifically to assist counselors. For example, in 1995 Texas mandated a Professional Development and Appraisal System (Texas Education Code, 1995) that provided the training of the trainers, the training materials, and the hourly requirements for teachers and administrators to be trained in the supervision and evaluation model. Counselors and counseling supervisors were not included in the mandate; however, counseling administrators were. It then became the counseling administrators' responsibility to see that counselors were also provided opportunities to learn about effective teaching, counseling, and supervision.

Developing a District Master Plan for Staff Development

Knowing what the staffs' wants and needs are for competency development is a first step. The next step is to develop a plan to meet these needs efficiently and effectively. The plan includes identifying the strategies and resources available for staff development, developing a time frame for the staff development activities that the building or district will provide, and considering how to evaluate the effectiveness of the strategies used. Figure 9.2 displays a format that could be used for writing a building or district staff development plan.

Strategies

A variety of delivery methods are available for staff development, including lectures, reading materials, audiovisual materials, demonstrations, programmed learning, discussions, simulations, and direct experience. Each method has costs and benefits. Making decisions about which methods to use depends on the outcome intended for the staff. Lectures

Figure 9.2
Format for Staff Development Plan

| Staff Category | Staff Outcome | Strategy | Time Frame | Resources | | | Evaluation Method |
				Expertise	Facilities/Equipment	Cost	

typically help listeners to become aware of ideas or practices, whereas direct experiences such as internships or shadowing help participants internalize the content.

The lecture or activity-based learning formats are effective for in-service education. The lectures can be motivational or instructive. Consultants can be brought into the district, or staff can be encouraged to attend professional growth conferences held at the local, regional, state, and national levels. Skilled counselors should be encouraged to present at such conferences because organizing and presenting can help them refine their practices and ideas.

Reading materials include professional texts and journals. Individuals seeking growth in specific areas can use bibliographies. Some recent highly useful resources include an article, "Web-Based Resources for Legal and Ethical Issues in School Counseling," by Guillot-Miller and Partin (2003), and a Special Issue on "Professional School Counseling in Urban Settings" edited by Holcomb-McCoy and Lee (2005) that is a must-read for every school counselor in an urban setting.

If the goal is for a number of people to consider certain topics (as in the case of the Special Issue just mentioned), readings can be assigned and groups can be formed to discuss the content of the readings. The discussion can be focused by means of a discussion agenda such as that displayed in Figure 9.3 and used in the Northside Independent School District. Professional journal reading is a cost-effective, readily accessible, and professionally sound staff development vehicle that staff development planners typically underuse. Where such reading is encouraged, follow-up discussions to assist the readers to process the ideas they have read are not often held, but they should be.

Other vehicles for professional discussions include staff meetings and retreats. Case consultations, particularly those led by an expert consultant, provide meaningful learning opportunities as well. Feedback conferences held as a part of clinical supervision also can provide learning experiences for counselors. New counselors can learn much by observing master counselors as they demonstrate their skills in actual work settings.

Resources Available

Having identified the resources potentially available to help in staff development, it is important to be specific as to the expertise of the people available. Then the expertise available can be matched with the priority needs of the staff. Some consultants are available within the school system; others will cost money. Thus the guidance department budget must be considered. Once the priority needs of staff have been identified and the means

Figure 9.3
Group Counseling Project Discussion Agenda

High School Counselor Staff Meetings
Group Counseling Project Discussion Agenda
1. *Uses/values/limits of groups*
2. What *counseling* is/is not
3. Individual's *theoretical models*
4. Professional *processes and techniques* used in group counseling
5. *"Climate"* needed for group to succeed
6. Forming your groups
7. *Group process*
    Norms:
    Organization:
    Structure:
8. *Leader's role(s)/responsibilities*

Note. Data from Northside Independent School District, San Antonio, TX. Reprinted with permission.

by which they can pursue professional development have been decided, it is possible to project how much money is required to make optimum use of the resources. Ideally, every staff member has the opportunity to grow professionally in the course of a year. Thus the resources available should be distributed with this principle in mind. At the same time, means for having individuals share ideas and information they have gained is a way to spread the wealth. For example, if only one counselor from a district can attend a state or national professional conference, that counselor could give a report at the staff meeting.

A further important consideration in implementing the staff development plan is planning the use of the facilities and equipment available. Be sure to consider where the various activities will be held, what the seating capacity is, and whether the atmosphere is conducive to discussions. If plans include the use of equipment, make sure that the necessary equipment is present and that it is in working order. This may seem obvious, but all too often the excitement of the topic causes lapses in memory about meeting logistics.

Time Frame

Careful consideration should be given to when staff development activities will take place. Some writers suggest, with good reason, that late afternoon or evening sessions are to be avoided if possible. Sessions during school hours are recommended but are costly because they use staff student-contact time. Saturday and holiday sessions may work out well, particularly if you are in a state where certification or licensure requirements include accumulating continuing education hours.

We recommend that staff development activities be interspersed over the length of the program improvement process. Such activities often are enjoyable and serve as a means to increase morale. Staff development activities need to be planned well in advance so that all involved can participate. Further, staff development should not stop once the major program development efforts have ceased. Professional growth should continue as a means of maintaining continuous individual professional development and program improvement.

Evaluation

Each staff development activity should be evaluated so that its effectiveness can be judged. Ways to evaluate the impact of activities include questionnaires, achievement-type tests, observations, and demonstrations. Whatever approach is used, it should be appropriate to the outcomes sought for the staff development activity. For example, observation of new behaviors is a more appropriate evaluation device for experiential staff development activities than it might be for lectures.

The effectiveness of the overall staff development program also needs to be evaluated. Reassessment of the staffs' competencies through use of the original needs assessment instrument provides information as to the staffs' growth. Continued monitoring of the staffs' expressed needs through their professional development plans also provides evaluative data regarding the effectiveness of the professional growth activities provided.

Address Incompetence

As in all professions, there are some individuals in the counseling profession who have either made the wrong career choice or who do not develop their professional promise sufficiently. In short, there are those who are working as school counselors, as guidance and counseling program staff leaders, or as guidance administrators who are not competent to meet the position or job requirements. With performance standards outlined as concretely as we have recommended, and with a system in place to help staff improve their professional competence, it is possible to terminate those whose performance is detrimental to students' growth and development. Due process rules are in place in most states to protect individuals from arbitrary terminations or reassignments, yet most systems have procedures outlined for helping those who are not in the right career to move. It is important not only for the students we serve but also for the profession as a whole to help incompetent counselors find other jobs.

Termination involves legal procedures with important roles for administrators, personnel departments, and school system lawyers. Reassignment to different buildings sometimes helps employees regain their professional commitment. In many instances, the clarifying of expectations associated with the program and performance improvement processes causes individuals to see that they are in the wrong position. Such self-determination is—obviously—preferable, but it also entails work for the administrators.

In any of these circumstances, the guidance and counseling program staff leader's role is to base evaluative judgments on the concrete, behavioral criteria established in the writing of the comprehensive guidance and counseling program, the position guides, and related performance standards. If the less-than-competent staff members have been informed about the criteria and have been offered the staff development opportunities to acquire the competencies they need, it is professionally appropriate for them to be encouraged to leave the profession.

Bring New Counselors Into the Program and to the Proper Roles

Once position guides are written and available resources are identified, a systematic approach to staff development may begin. The primary task for ensuring competency of school counselors is to have the right people in the right roles. Finding the right people to hire requires the guidance and counseling program leader to collaborate with the colleges and universities in which most of the counselors are trained, to recruit the most highly skilled graduates to apply for available positions, and to select the most talented/skilled applicants to fill those positions. Helping school counselors fulfill the right roles requires the guidance and counseling program leader to place them properly and to orient them to their new assignments.

Collaboration

Most college and university counselor education departments seek to develop collaborative relationships with the school districts in their areas that are most apt to hire their graduates. Such relationships are built by the professors' seeking advice about various aspects of their training program. Many counselor education departments have formed formal advisory committees consisting of counselors and guidance and counseling program leaders from their neighboring districts. In addition, counselor educators seek advice through professional discussions and involvement in local or state professional associations for counselors. Often practitioners are invited to make presentations to counselor education classes, whereby both the students in preservice training and the professors themselves gain insight into the actual work of school counselors.

Field experiences provide a primary opportunity for meaningful collaboration between counselor educators and local school districts. Field experiences for counselors-in-training are an important aspect of their preservice education. In fact, the 2001 CACREP accreditation standards for counselor education programs require 100 hours of supervised practicum experiences and an additional 600 hours of supervised internship experience. Supervision is to be provided by a certified school counselor. Making these experiences effective is a shared responsibility of the college/university staff and the building/district staff. To ensure successful completion of coursework that includes fieldwork, professors need to be explicit about the experiences that counselors-in-training should have. Requiring them to counsel individuals and write up case studies, to conduct group counseling sessions with students with problems, and to teach developmental guidance lessons guarantees that counselors-in-training will have these experiences. At the same time, school counselors responsible for supervising counselors-in-training need to be explicit about the experiences they know to be valuable in relation to the design of their school guidance and counseling program. Figure 9.4 provides an example of guidelines for practicum students and interns used by Northside Independent School District to help counselors-in-training consider what experiences they would benefit from to learn to be effective school counselors within that district. Guidelines such as these and the related experiences that students have help the counselors-in-training to conceptualize the program and to understand the relationship between the skills and techniques they are learning and the program in which they will use these skills. For most counselors-in-training, it becomes their first opportunity to explore this relationship.

Recruitment

Interacting with counselors-in-training is one way to recruit applicants. The purpose of recruitment is to develop a quality pool of applicants. The better the applicant pool, the more potential there is for those selected to become outstanding counselors. The basis for recruitment is to have a quality program and to let people know about it. Explaining the guidance and counseling program clearly to district faculty provides teachers who are cer-

Figure 9.4
Guidelines for Practicum Students and Interns

To ensure that you have experience in each of the components that constitute the District's Comprehensive Guidance Program, please consider the following as activities to be included in your field experience.

Guidance Curriculum Component
• Developmental group guidance (guiding-teaching of guidance content using guidance techniques)

Individual Student Planning Component
• Helping groups of students apply
  1. skills learned through curriculum component
  2. test results information
  3. career information and experiences
• Helping groups or individuals develop educational plans

Responsive Services Component
• Individual counseling
• Small-group counseling
• Consultation with parents regarding students with issues
• Consultation with teachers regarding students with issues
• Referral of students for special services or programs

System Support Component
• Guidance program planning
• Interpreting group standardized test results
• Providing teacher in-service
• Participate in the CHILD process (interpreting information, participating in solution-focused staffings regarding students' individual learning and behavioral needs)

Please read the Texas Education Agency (2004) publication, *The Comprehensive, Developmental Guidance Program for Texas Public Schools* (4th ed.); the Northside Independent School District (2002a) publication, *Comprehensive Guidance Program Framework;* the Texas Counseling Association (2004) publication, *Texas Evaluation Model for Professional School Counselors* (2nd ed.); the Northside Independent School District (2002b) publication, *Guide to Counselor Performance Improvement.*

tified as counselors or those who are planning to seek advanced training an opportunity to consider the merits of being part of the school counseling staff. Providing teachers with quality feedback about students they refer and consulting effectively with them as they face problems with students or parents are often recruitment vehicles. If your school or district hires experienced counselors, presenting quality programs at professional conferences and workshops also is a useful recruitment activity. Further, the more active the school counselors in a district are in local, state, and national professional organizations, the more visible the program will be; if the quality of the school counselors' leadership and sense of responsibility is impressive, others will want to be part of the district's comprehensive guidance and counseling program.

Selection

After attracting quality applicants, the next challenge is selecting the best as candidates for school counseling positions. As we have said before, school counselor positions must be defined explicitly to match the applicants' qualifications with the expectations of the positions. The competencies required for the counselor positions already have been defined for the district, but each building may have specific demands that must be made explicit as well. These demands may include needing individuals with certain personality characteristics as well as certain preferences for various guidance and counseling program functions. The goal is to assemble a balance of characteristics and competencies across a building or district staff. For example, balanced staffs may have conceptualizers and logistics specialists, leaders and followers, those who enjoy group work and those who enjoy consultation, and so on. It may also include an ethnic/racial balance parallel to that of the student body, and a balance of men and women.

The process for staff selection includes interviewing applicants, considering the recommendations of people familiar with their work, and reviewing their experiences and achievements. Interviews of prospective counselors should be conducted not only by the personnel department staff but also by the supervisor or administrator who will oversee the work of the staff member. In the case of the school counselor, this means the building principal as well as the district guidance and counseling program leadership. Some systems also have effectively involved the current counseling staff in the interview process. Although effective interviewing by a large group is difficult to orchestrate, some schools have all the counselors participate in a group discussion with applicants. Others have had individual counselors conduct different parts of the interview, with, for example, one counselor taking the applicant on a tour of the school and another explaining the guidance center. The size of the current staff and the number of candidates to be interviewed directly influence the interview format to be used.

The interview should provide an atmosphere conducive to self-expression. Interview questions should lead the applicants to report as much about themselves in relation to the position as possible in a reasonable length of time. There should be a direct relationship between the questions asked in an interview and the job requirements. Much has been written about the value—or lack of value—of the interview as a selection tool, but it is one way of allowing candidates the opportunity to provide self-reports of their experiences and abilities to fill the position competently. It also allows the employer the opportunity to gain insight into the candidate's personality and professionalism.

In soliciting recommendations from other professionals who have worked with a candidate, the administrator or supervisor should ask specific questions about the quality of the applicant's experiences in relationship to the role of the school counselor in the district, such as, How effective a teacher has the applicant been? What has been the quality of the applicant's relationships with parents? People who give recommendations should be encouraged to provide concrete examples to support their opinions. In addition, a review of the applicants' strengths and weaknesses as noted in their past performance evaluations provides insight as to their probable success or failure as school counselors. We believe that it is imperative for a counselor to have been an effective teacher to begin to be an effective school counselor. School counselors should come from the ranks of the best teachers if they are to deliver a quality developmental guidance and counseling program that includes classroom guidance. Because the ability to be part of a team also is essential to delivering a comprehensive guidance and counseling program, indicators of individuals' past relationships in this regard are important. The guidance and counseling program and staff are on center stage in a school, thus potential counselors must have demonstrated that they are first and foremost good employees. Evidence of such traits as these is usually found in past performance ratings.

Proper Placement

A well-developed selection process provides needed information about candidates selected to fill available school counselor positions. It is imperative that staff members be placed in positions that will make maximum use of their strengths and in which their weaknesses will be minimized by the strengths of others. As already indicated, strengths and weaknesses in terms of competencies and personal characteristics need to be considered in placing individuals in specific assignments. The chemistry of a staff, although difficult to define, is as important to consider as are the competencies available and those required. For example, if a staff already has several highly assertive individuals, the addition of a follower will probably do more for staff balance than the addition of a person seeking a leadership position. With a clear definition in mind of the program that is desired for your building, you are better able to make judgments about who will best fit the job available.

Within a school system, it is often possible to redistribute staff members to make optimum use of their talents. The same clarity regarding the competencies and personality characteristics needed in a particular work setting is required if you have the opportunity to transfer individual staff members from one work setting to another. Transfer opportunities can occur naturally in districts in which growth provides new positions, or when counselors retire or move on.

Orientation

To help new counselors fulfill their roles properly, orientation to the requirements of the job itself and the context of the work setting is necessary. By orientation, we mean providing new counselors with as much information about the comprehensive guidance and counseling program policy and operations as possible. New counselors receive information about the counselor role in their training programs, and about the work setting in the job application and selection process. Once placed, however, they need more specific information about their role and the appropriate use of their competencies in the program. If the new counselor previously was a teacher, it is important to remember that counselors' roles and teachers' roles are different; the transition from one to the other is not automatic. New counselors need to know how the guidance and counseling program, perhaps only globally defined to them up to now, actually operates in the building to which they are assigned. The specific activities that define the four comprehensive program components need to be conveyed. New counselors also need to be informed about the structure of the building in which they will work, the principal's priorities, and the organizational relationships.

A member of the existing staff should be designated to help newcomers learn the facts they need and to ease their evolution into the new role. Helping new counselors use their unique competencies is a role for the building guidance department head. This may include helping new counselors to broaden their perspective from a classroom perspective to the school perspective, to act as a consultant to other staff members and as an advocate for students, to put the concept of the guidance and counseling program in operation, and to learn the informal power structure of a school.

Orientation should begin with formal meetings conducted by supervisors and administrators. Other topics are best handled through ongoing dialogue with the new counselor and a counselor colleague, who may or may not be the building supervisor. In some programs a designated mentor system has been used effectively. In any case, there is a lot of information for new counselors to learn, and the more systematic their induction into their new position is, the smoother the transition will be.

Attending to Diversity

The pluralism of our society, the students who come to our schools, and school counselors' professional and ethical standards dictate that school counselors be as cross-culturally competent as they can. Unique among the various counseling settings, school counselors work with all students and strive to do it without discrimination based on something other than the priorities established for the guidance program by the representative groups involved in the program design process. It is not sufficient in this era to be nonjudgmental; key to a school counselor's meeting the challenges of the 21st century is "becoming a culturally responsive counselor" (Paisley & McMahon, 2001, p. 112).

Working with all students poses some daunting challenges as the counselors themselves probably are not representative of or even knowledgeable about every facet of diversity present in their schools. School counselors must learn to respond in responsible and sensitive ways to individuals who present to them a wide range of differences. In addition, it is well recognized that "integrating multicultural factors into the counseling process is an extremely complex challenge" (Coleman, 2004, p. 62). But these are challenges school counselors must respond to.

Standards and Definitions

In their efforts to further develop their cultural responsiveness, school counselors must be guided by the ethical standards and by the established multicultural competencies. The structured ways to help school counselors continue to develop their professional competency are described in this chapter. In each of the ways described—job responsibilities, supervision, professional development, performance evaluation—both the counselors' and their leaders' awareness of and commitment to a counselor's enhanced cross-cultural effectiveness facilitate counselors' development.

Ethical Standards

The ethical standards that guide professional school counselors' practice that are relevant to this discussion are clear in their mandate. The ASCA (2004a) *Ethical Standards for School Counselors* state in the Preamble:

> Each person has the right to be respected, be treated with dignity, and have access to a comprehensive school counseling program that advocates for and affirms all students from diverse populations regardless of ethnic/racial status, age, economic status, special needs, English as a

second language or other language group, immigration status, sexual orientation, gender, gender identity/expression, family type, religious/spiritual identity, and appearance.

In the section on "Responsibilities to Students" (A.1.), it is stated that

> The professional school counselor:
> a. Has a primary obligation to the student, who is to be treated with respect as a unique individual.
> c. Respects the student's values and beliefs and does not impose the counselor's personal values.

The ACA (2005) *Code of Ethics* states in the Preamble that counselors "recognize diversity and embrace a cross-cultural approach in support of the worth, dignity, potential, and uniqueness of people within their social and cultural contexts." In Section A: The Counseling Relationship it is stated in the introduction: Counselors actively attempt to understand the diverse cultural backgrounds of the clients they serve. Counselors also explore their own cultural identities and how these affect their values and beliefs about the counseling process.

In Section A.4.b. Personal Needs and Values, it is stated:

> b. *Personal Values.* Counselors are aware of their own values, attitudes, beliefs, and behaviors . . . and respect the diversity of clients, trainees, and research participants.

In Section C: Professional Responsibility. C.5. Nondiscrimination, it is stated:

> a. Counselors do not condone or engage in discrimination based on age, culture, disability, ethnicity, race, religion/spirituality, gender identity, sexual orientation, marital status/partnership, language preference, socioeconomic status, or any basis proscribed by law.

Multicultural Counseling Standards

The profession's statement of standards for multicultural counseling competence were presented first in 1992 by Sue, Arredondo, and McDavis as the Multicultural Counseling Competencies and Standards, and currently by ACA (n.d.) as Multicultural Competencies and Objectives (see Appendix I). These standards outline the attitudes and beliefs, knowledge, and skills needed by multiculturally competent counselors. These standards address needed competency by counselors in

1. Counselor awareness of their own cultural values and biases
2. Counselor awareness of the client's worldview
3. Culturally appropriate intervention strategies

The Association for Multicultural Counseling and Development (AMCD) has continued refinement of the multicultural counseling competencies by supporting development of "explanatory statements" that are now published in the document titled *Operationalization of the Multicultural Counseling Competencies* (Arredondo et al., 1996). The explanatory statements offer criteria for counselors to meet in achieving each competence. These standards are increasingly well recognized in the counseling field and are being adapted by groups to fit their counseling specialty and membership; for example, the Association for Specialists in Group Work (ASGW, 1998b) has adapted them to guide group workers.

Definitions

The use of several labels—*diversity, multicultural,* and *cross-cultural*—describing similar or related concepts is confusing for some and calls for some clarification. Dialogue about these definitions is ongoing in our society. The terms *multiculturalism* and *diversity* are often used interchangeably, blurring the distinctions. Vontress and Jackson (2004) agreed that the concepts are used imprecisely:

> In the literature and society at large, these terms often convey the same meaning. We have resisted using them when we wish to refer to therapeutic encounters. Instead, we use cross-cultural counseling to communicate the idea of a helping dyad or group consisting of at least one person who perceives him- or herself to be culturally different. (p. 76)

Coleman (2004) pointed out that the purpose of the multicultural competencies is "to focus on those competencies that need to be integrated into a mental health professional's practice when working with racial, ethnic, or cultural minorities" (p. 58). The authors of the multicultural counseling competencies clearly stated that the competencies are aimed to assist counselors in working with clients from "the five major cultural groups in the United States and its territories: African/Black, Asian, Caucasian/European, Hispanic/Latino and Native American or indigenous groups who have historically resided in the Continental USA and its territories" (p. 1).

Some distinctions have been made between considering "multicultural factors (e.g., race, ethnicity, or culture) [and] diversity factors (e.g., physical or intellectual ability, sexual orientation, or age)" (Coleman, 2004, p. 57). By dictionary definition, *diverse* means different and has come to imply consideration of all of the variables that describe potential differences in individuals. Having defined their meaning for *multicultural,* AMCD suggested that the "dimensions of personal identity" (Arredondo & Glauner, 1992) describe facets of individuals that contribute to their uniqueness—to their similarities and differences from each other. The following variables are cited: age, culture, ethnicity, gender, language, physical/mental well-being, race, sexual orientation, social class, education background, geographic location, hobbies/recreational, health care practices/beliefs, religion/spirituality, military experience, relationship status, work experience, and historical context. These kinds of lists are ever growing. It is safe to say that each individual consists of myriad ingredients; and, in working with children, school counselors not only work with all of the facets presented by an individual child but also work with these facets in consulting with their parents and teachers.

We use the term *cross-cultural* to mean when one person from his or her personal cultural (Arredondo et al., 1996, p. 7) base reaches across to another's cultural base to collaborate on the work at hand. In this sense, *cultural* includes all of the variables cited. *Cross-cultural effectiveness,* then, is when that effort to reach across cultures results in successful work. The "work" for school counselors and their students includes all of the elements of school guidance and counseling work (e.g., relationship building, problem solving, continuing positive growth and development).

While the multicultural competencies may have been developed with the intent of guiding counselors' work with members of racial, ethnic, and cultural groups, they also are useful for work with students with other diversity factors. As mentioned earlier, the competencies themselves are about beliefs and attitudes, knowledge, and skills in working with people who are culturally different from the counselor. They guide a counselor to be self-aware, to be aware of the other member of the relationship, and to use intervention strategies and techniques that are appropriate to the client (Appendix I).

Similarities and Differences Between Counselors and Clients

Finding commonalities with their clients to build counseling relationships is basic to successful counseling. Awareness of differences is equally important and, again, is done for the purpose of being as effective a counselor as possible with each client. Building on commonalities and minimizing the impact of differences is most likely to lead to successful guidance and counseling interventions.

Similarities

Conventional wisdom based on experience and some research tells us that clients prefer counselors who they perceive have something in common with them. According to Vontress and Jackson (2004), "Perception is a significant relationship factor. Individuals generally establish better rapport with those they perceive to be like themselves than they do with those whom they perceive to be unlike themselves" (p. 76). Esters and Ledoux (2001) summarized, "The extant literature indicates that, if given the choice, most people prefer to enter into counseling with a counselor similar to them. It would appear that issues of similarity and difference are integral to understanding the nature of counseling relationships" (p. 168).

Today's research suggests that those preferences may go beyond "readily discernible physical characteristics" (Esters & Ledoux, 2001, p. 169). Esters and Ledoux (2001) summarized previous studies of clients' preferences among counselor characteristics and "the general conclusions derived from these studies support the hypothesis that participants of various races and ethnicities prefer counselors possessing characteristics similar to themselves, but that similarity is not necessarily defined by race or ethnicity alone" (p. 166). Their study was with at-risk high school students who were asked to rank order the importance of eight counselor characteristics. The rank-ordered preferences for counselor characteristics from highest to lowest were as follows: "same attitudes and values, same background and socioeconomic status, same sex, same race, opposite sex, different background and socioeconomic status, different race, different attitude and values" (p. 168). "The characteristics ranked highest were those indicating similarity and those ranked lowest were those indicating difference" (p. 169). They commented:

> After all, a school counselor who shares a student's attitudes and values and a similar background and socioeconomic status will, by most definitions of culture, share more of the culture and will thus be more similar than a school counselor who is simply a member of the same race. This finding should be encouraging to school counselors who find themselves attempting to build a counseling relationship with a student or a group of students with whom they differ in either race, sex, or both. (p. 169)

Differences

According to Constantine et al. (2001),

> Effective multicultural counseling is rooted in the premise that although people share common or universal experiences (e.g., basic biological functions or life processes), they also have important differences based on cultural group memberships such as race or sex (Fuertes, Miville, Mohr, Sedlacek, & Gretchen, 2000; Miville et al., 1999; Vontress, 1996). (pp. 13–14)

One premise is that

> counselors' ability to effectively communicate and interact with clients in therapeutic relationships involves the counselors' competence in focusing on both similarities and differences (Miville et

al., 1999). Thus, school counselors' awareness of how culturally diverse students may be alike and different from them may be vital to building successful alliances with these students (Fuertes et al., 2000). (Constantine et al., 2001, p. 14)

Some recurrent examples that school counselors come in contact with on a regular basis have been studied and have led to important clues about effective cross-cultural work for school counselors. The first example is from a study by Constantine and Yeh (2001) that addressed the differences in Eastern and Western cultures and the degree to which individuals are encouraged to define themselves as independent individuals, as in Western culture, or as interdependent on others, as in East Asian and African societies. Their results led them to caution:

> It is important to note that some behaviors of school counselors (e.g., offering specific opinions and advice, providing direction and structure, and being interpersonally assertive) are associated with having more independent self-construals (Lee, 1996; Leon, Wagner, & Tata, 1995). Thus, when such behaviors or values are displayed in counseling practice, they could be detrimental to the social, emotional, and academic development of culturally diverse, school-aged children with more interdependent self-construals. Consequently, school counselors with higher independent self-construals may incorrectly encourage interdependent students' (a) separation and individuation from the family, (b) emotional expressiveness without regard to important others' feelings, and (c) assertiveness in interpersonal relationships. (pp. 205–206)

Regarding cultural differences in expressing emotions, Constantine and Gainor (2001) reminded school counselors that

> it is crucial that [they] are cognizant of possible culturally based differences in students' expressions of emotional states. School counselors who are unaware of differences in how feelings may be expressed or regulated across cultures may erroneously interpret or even pathologize such behaviors in some students of color. As a result, these students may feel that their mental health issues are not being understood or addressed in culturally sensitive ways. (p. 135)

Professional Development Goals

Professional school counselors also recognize that, like every other aspect of counseling, growth in their multicultural competence is ongoing, and counselors working in a pluralistic society with an increasingly diverse population are always "works in progress." There are many strategies that professional school counselors use to continuously develop their competency. In our opinion, these strategies are most productively used when they are driven by professional development goals established by counselors, as described in this chapter. Potential goals for school counselors to enhance their multicultural competence relate to all 31 of the ACA multicultural competencies. Given the myriad goals potentially related to ensuring that they are works in progress in their effectiveness with the diverse populations they serve, professional school counselors probably ought to have a multicultural competence development goal every year of their professional lives.

It begins with self-awareness. Constantine et al. (2001) noted:

> The development of multicultural knowledge and awareness, particularly school counselors' own self-awareness in relation to various cultural issues, seems critical to their ability to (a) consider the potential salience of cultural variables in working with students, and (b) effectively meet the mental health needs of culturally diverse students. (p. 17)

Constantine et al. (2001) concluded, "it is feasible to consider that school counselors could have an interest in and appreciation for cultural diversity without necessarily experiencing comfort in interpersonal situations involving culturally diverse students" (p. 17). Constantine and Gainor (2001) conducted a study "to better understand the relationships among school counselors' emotional intelligence, empathy, and self-reported multicultural counseling awareness" (p. 132). They found that "School counselors with higher levels of emotional intelligence reported higher levels of multicultural counseling knowledge" (p. 135) and concluded that "emotionally intelligent school counselors appear to possess interpersonal strengths that may enable them to better comprehend or be attuned to the experiences of issues of culturally diverse others" (p. 135). They also made an interesting point about overempathizing. They found that school counselors who had higher personal distress scores (anxiety and discomfort) perceived themselves as having less multicultural counseling knowledge. They concluded:

> It is possible that school counselors who become unduly anxious or unsettled when empathizing with the difficulties of culturally diverse students may be somewhat less proficient in counseling situations because their anxiety may impede them from effectively applying their multicultural counseling knowledge. (p. 135)

They also wrote:

> A possible implication of these findings is that school counselors may wish to identify ways to increase their multicultural counseling awareness so that they may understand better how their own and others' cultural group memberships could affect counseling relationships. (p. 136)

Goals for developing appropriate cross-cultural interventions may cause changes in school counselors' techniques. Holcomb-McCoy (2004) noted:

> As school counselors work with larger numbers of ethnic minority students, they may need to alter their perceptions, learn to effectively counsel and consult with diverse populations, become knowledgeable of other cultures and the manifestations of racism, and assume the role of social change agent. (p. 182)

Holcomb-McCoy (2004) identified areas of multicultural competence that she "believes are essential for the practice of school counseling" and offered a "Multicultural Competence Checklist" to "guide professional school counselors' multicultural development and training" (p. 178). The checklist identifies nine categories of multicultural competence:

1. Multicultural counseling
2. Multicultural consultation
3. Understanding racism and student resistance
4. Understanding racial identity development
5. Multicultural assessment
6. Multicultural family counseling
7. Social advocacy
8. Developing school–family–community partnerships
9. Understanding interpersonal interactions

In addition to using the checklist "as a guide for professional development [goal-setting and] activities" (p. 181), she suggested "school counselors can enhance their multicultural counseling competence by soliciting feedback on their practice and understanding of multicultural issues from others who are culturally different" (p. 181).

Related to Esters and Ledoux's (2001) findings, one goal that when reached would help counselors be received more favorably by students would be to "present themselves as dispositionally more similar to the students, so long as the similarities are genuine" (p. 169). This is not to say that school counselors should falsely represent their attitudes and values or mislead the student to believe that the counselor is of a similar background and socioeconomic status.

> On the other hand, counselors who find themselves attempting to build a relationship with students who are different from them regarding attitudes and values and background and socioeconomic status should be aware that by consciously disclosing this difference, they might be alienating the student and endangering the formation of a solid, trusting counseling relationship. It would seem that school counselors who present themselves as dispositionally more similar to the student, so long as the similarities are genuine, may be received more favorably by that student. (Esters & Ledoux, 2001, p. 169)

Green and Keys (2001) challenged professional school counselors and comprehensive, developmental guidance programs to consider basing their programs on "development-in-context" (p. 86) models of development that demand consideration of the contexts in which students live. They stated, "Developing an awareness of self-in-context is both an important program focus and program outcome for all students" (p. 93). Certainly deeper understanding of the contexts in which students live, the impact that their community context has on their development, and its probable divergence from the school context are all areas for growth for school counselors. Specific strategies and references for enhancing your multicultural competence are provided in *Operationalization of the Multicultural Counseling Competencies* (Arredondo et al., 1996).

Clarify Roles of Building Guidance and Counseling Program/Staff Leaders

Strengthening the means by which we help counselors improve their job performance, as well as more clearly defining expectations for the guidance and counseling program, calls for recasting the role of the building guidance department head. Various titles are used to label this position, such as *head counselor, guidance department chair, guidance coordinator,* and *director of guidance.* We use *guidance and counseling program staff leader,* as explained in *Leading and Managing Your School Guidance and Counseling Program Staff* (Henderson & Gysbers, 1998). Traditionally, building guidance and counseling program staff leaders have served as liaisons between the guidance staff and the administration, and between the guidance department and the instructional departments. In some instances they have been expected to do the quasi-administrative tasks assigned to the guidance department, such as building the testing schedule or the master schedule.

In a building that is changing its guidance and counseling program to the comprehensive one that we are proposing, and that is striving to use all its available resources to enhance the effectiveness of the counselors, the guidance and counseling program staff leader's job description must change. First, it is imperative that some member of the staff be designated as the leader of the building guidance and counseling program. Second, a position guide appropriately tailored to address the additional responsibilities of that person must be written. A sample guidance and counseling program staff leader position guide is provided in Figure 6.4 (chapter 6). This guide states the expectations that guidance and counseling program staff leaders will provide leadership to the program development efforts on their campuses and that they will supervise the counseling staff in addition to the more traditional responsibilities of serving their own caseload and representing the department to others. The guide also clarifies that the authority for building guidance and counseling program staff leaders to fill the expectations is delegated to them by the principal and the district guidance and counseling program leader (those designated as their leaders in the building and in the central office). A full detailing of both building and district guidance and counseling program staff leaders' job descriptions and methods for carrying out these responsibilities are provided in *Leading and Managing Your School Guidance and Counseling Program* (Henderson & Gysbers, 1998).

The principals and the central office guidance and counseling program staff leaders must work with and for the building guidance and counseling program staff leaders to help them carry out their responsibilities. Lieberman (2004) systematically studied counseling literature and administration literature. He made the point "that effective schools are characterized by high agreement among staff as to the guidance goals and purposes" (p. 554) of the school and of their specific role in it. He described the concept of leadership density: "overall leadership available from different staff possessing various expertise and perspectives within their own areas, all on behalf of the school's work" (p. 554). In his research he found "statistically significant divergence in how principals and counselors each view the role of the counselor" (p. 556). Effective school leaders are "proactive in learning the appropriate roles and functions for school personnel so that they may direct and encourage more appropriate and productive functioning of each individual towards the overriding and shared school goals" (p. 555). He concluded that it is up to school leaders to learn the appropriate roles of their staff members. It is also a responsibility of the leaders of a staff group to educate the school leader about the expertise and perspectives their staff members bring to the school mission.

The newest challenge for building guidance and counseling program staff leaders is the responsibility of supervising the counseling staff in their buildings. The regular staff members need to be informed as to the authority of the building guidance and counseling program staff leader. The guidance and counseling program staff leaders should be provided the skill development they need to conduct their clinical, developmental, and administrative supervisory roles appropriately.

The performance improvement system model proposed in this chapter and the system for clearly defining individual guidance staff members' roles and responsibilities discussed in chapter 7 demand a partnership between professional school counselors and guidance and counseling program staff leaders. The latter's staff management responsibilities include negotiating the annual job description specification; team building to implement a coordinated, comprehensive program; orienting new counselors to the field of counseling as well as to the established guidance and counseling program; providing supervision; and performance evaluation. When these activities are to be accomplished should be spelled out; an example is provided in Figure 9.5.

The guidance and counseling program staff leaders benefit from specialized training that helps them to better implement their newly clarified roles. Where you begin their in-service training depends on the individuals involved and the roles identified for them. We recommend beginning with action planning because that is basic to their work with counselors and to their responsibilities for leading the building guidance and counseling program redesign and implementation. Guidance and counseling program staff leaders and peer leaders also may have needs for competencies in motivating staff members, conducting observations, providing constructive criticism, risk taking, delegating, asserting, and managing stress. They may need help in developing the skills and attitudes needed for effec-

Figure 9.5
Guidance Program Staff Leadership Activities: Suggested Time Frame

August
In-service training
Job description development
Yearly guidance program calendar development
Program and performance improvement goal setting/action planning
Administrative supervision

September
Clinical supervision
Administrative supervision

October
Clinical supervision
Administrative supervision

November
Clinical supervision
Administrative supervision

December
Formative performance evaluation
Clinical supervision
Administrative supervision

January
Goal accomplishment progress checks
Clinical supervision
Administrative supervision

February
Clinical supervision
Administrative supervision

March
Clinical supervision
Administrative supervision

April
Clinical supervision
Administrative supervision

May
Summative performance evaluation
Assessment of program and performance improvement goal attainment
Administrative supervision

June
Professional development goal setting/action planning
Administrative supervision
In-service training

tively encouraging others. They may need to learn the leadership roles associated with mutual goal setting as well as those associated with effective monitoring of plan implementation. If your district organizational structure involves a team approach with the principals sharing the guidance and counseling program staff leader responsibility for the counselors, principals need to be informed to ensure their understanding of the newly designed comprehensive guidance and counseling program. Thus the district staff development plan ought to include principals.

Not many universities offer training in school counselor supervision; thus the district or school system guidance and counseling program leaders may need to provide the skill development experiences needed by the building department heads. The Association for Counselor Education and Supervision (ACES) has adopted Standards for Counseling Supervisors (1989). These standards describe "eleven core areas of personal traits, knowledge and competencies that are characteristic of effective supervisors" (p. 8). These encompass

1. effective counselors
2. personal traits and characteristics
3. ethical, legal, and regulatory aspects
4. supervisory relationship
5. supervision methods and techniques
6. counselor development process
7. case conceptualization and management
8. assessment and evaluation
9. oral and written reporting and recording
10. evaluation of counseling performance
11. research in counseling and counselor supervision.

A companion piece to these standards is the *Ethical Guidelines for Counseling Supervisors* (ACES, 1993). These guidelines address

1. client welfare and rights
2. supervisory role
3. program administration role.

In addition to establishing these standards for counseling supervisors (Dye & Borders, 1990), ACES has supported the development of a curriculum guide for training counselor supervisors (Borders et al., 1991). An outline used to assist new Northside Independent School District guidance and counseling program staff leaders is available in *Leading and Managing Your School Guidance and Counseling Program Staff* (Henderson & Gysbers, 1998). Other resources to support such training include two handbooks developed through ACES, one on counseling supervision (Borders & Brown, 2005) and one on administrative supervision (Falvey, 1987; Henderson, in press).

Guidance and counseling program staff leaders in turn need to be supervised. Administrative supervision of the guidance and counseling program staff leaders is done by the building principal. Clinical and developmental supervision should be done by the central office guidance and counseling program leaders. Clinical supervision could entail observing a guidance and counseling program staff leader conducting a staff meeting and providing feedback in techniques for effective meetings. Developmental supervision could entail setting goals that are specific to guidance and counseling program staff leaders' program leadership responsibilities (e.g., instituting group guidance activities for 12th graders in which they learn their status relative to high school graduation, and initiating a post-high-school plan) and to staff supervision responsibilities (e.g., implementing a specific team-building strategy).

District Guidance and Counseling Program Staff Leaders' Roles and Responsibilities

Ensuring the competency of the school counselors is a primary responsibility of all of the guidance and counseling program leaders. The best-designed program is meaningless in the hands of insufficiently competent staff. We have said that an effective guidance and counseling program leader plays a range of roles to ensure against this. The leader collaborates with the preservice training institution staff as counselor educators develop their programs. Recruitment of qualified applicants provides a pool of talent available for filling jobs that become available. In addition to helping select the best people for the jobs, the program leader has a responsibility to strive to match new counselors' talent with the positions that will use their capabilities to the maximum advantage of the students and the program.

Once school counselors are selected, the leader orients them in the comprehensive guidance and counseling program design and goals and ensures their orientation to the buildings they will serve. The roles of the guidance and counseling program leaders and the campus administrators must be carefully outlined, and an efficient and effective performance improvement system should be designed. The district or system guidance and counseling program leader's role mirrors that of the building leaders and supports the systemwide program and performance improvement efforts. A primary role of the system leader is to train and supervise the building staff leaders. As we have said, the resources of supervision, evaluation, and professional development should be focused to assist the school counselors to attain their optimum level of professional competency. In the few cases of incompetence, the guidance administrator must be able to articulate the professional and program standards clearly so that such individuals can seek better use of their particular skills. Clarity of role expectations is critical to ensure the competency of school counselors.

A successful guidance and counseling program leader must maintain the vision needed to help the program succeed at its mission, must uphold the basic principles of the profession at large, must keep in touch with the staff and those whom the program serves, must be able to manage change, and must select good people as subordinates, trust them to carry out their roles appropriately, and help them when they do not. The program leader must develop appropriate and adequate performance indicators so that problems may be addressed in a timely fashion and opportunities for improvement are allowed to emerge. Further, with the program and performance standards in place, a district is ready to evaluate its guidance and counseling program and the school counseling staff. This is covered in detail in chapter 10.

Often it is not until the implementation phase of the program development process that school districts identify the need for expanded guidance program leadership at the district level. By this time, the need for a leader who has guidance expertise becomes quite apparent. Being a new district guidance program staff leader has its challenges (Krueger, 2002; Larivee, 2002). Learning new roles and responsibilities, meeting and engaging a larger staff more often than you are used to working with, developing your own leadership style, and implementing changes are only some of the challenges involved in these new positions. Larivee (2002) summarized some of her learnings in making the transition:

> My enthusiasm is not necessarily contagious. I have learned that no matter what kind of credentials I have, I still have to earn my stripes. I have been reminded that change is a slow . . . process. . . . I must be very passionate about my cause. . . . Making administrative decisions sometimes takes me out of my comfort zone. Professional peer groups are not as available in this position as in most others. (p. 40)

Concluding Thoughts

Ensuring that school counselors have the competencies and levels of commitment they need to fulfill their roles requires continuous attention. Not only can each individual continue to develop as a professional, but also the context in which he or she works is ever changing. Counselors mature professionally with each new client and with each new activity. Helping individuals process these new experiences and blend them into their existing competency system enhances their development and lessens the chances of burnout. The profession advances; resources change; new modalities for effective staff development are discovered. The program priorities shift as students present new challenges and as evalua-tion clarifies weaknesses and strengths of the program. Continuous program improvement depends on continued improvement of the staff members' competency.

References

American Counseling Association. (2005). *Code of ethics.* Alexandria, VA: Author.

American Counseling Association. (1999). *Ethical standards for Internet online counseling.* Retrieved February 28, 2005, from http://www.counseling.org/Content/Naviga tionMenu/RESOURCES/ETHICS/EthicalStandardsforInternetOnlineCounseling/ Ethical_Stand_Online.htm

American Counseling Association. (n.d.). *Multicultural competencies and objectives.* Retrieved October 21, 2004, from http://www.counseling.org/Content/Navigation Menu/RESOURCES/MULTICULTURALANDDIVERSITYISSUES/Competencies/ Competencies.htm

American Psychological Association. (2005). *Code of fair testing practices in education.* Washington, DC: Author.

American School Counselor Association. (2004a). *Ethical standards for school counselors.* Retrieved from http://www.schoolcounselor.org/content.asp?contentid=173

American School Counselor Association. (2004b). *The role of the professional school coun-selor.* Retrieved December 5, 2004, from http://www.schoolcounselor.org/con tent.asp?contentid=240

American School Counselor Association. (2005). *The ASCA national model: A framework for school counseling programs* (2nd ed.). Alexandria, VA: Author.

Arredondo, P., & Glauner, T. (1992). *Personal dimensions of identity model.* Boston: Empowerment Workshops.

Arredondo, P., Toporek, R., Brown, S., Jones, J., Locke, D. C., Sanchez, J., & Stadler, H. (1996). *Operationalization of the multicultural counseling competencies.* Alexandria, VA: Association for Multicultural Counseling and Development. Retrieved from http://www.counseling.org/Content/NavigationMenu/RESOURCES/MULTI CULTURALANDDIVERSITYISSUES/MCC96.pdf

Association for Assessment in Counseling. (2001a). *Competencies in assessment and eval-uation for school counselors.* Retrieved October 31, 2001, from http://aac.ncat.edu/ documents/atsc_cmptncy.htm

Association for Assessment in Counseling. (2001b). *Responsibilities of users of standardized tests.* Retrieved October 31, 2001, from http://aac.ncat.edu/documents/rust.html

Association for Counselor Education and Supervision. (1989, Spring). ACES adopts stan-dards for counseling supervisors. *ACES Spectrum,* 7–10.

Association for Counselor Education and Supervision. (1993). *Ethical guidelines for coun-seling supervisors.* Retrieved from http://www.acesonline.net/ethical guidelines.htm

Association for Specialists in Group Work. (1998a). *Best practices.* Retrieved from http://www.asgw.org/best.htm

Association for Specialists in Group Work. (1998b). *Principles for diversity-competent group workers.* Retrieved February 28, 2005, from http://www.asgw.org/diversity.htm

Association for Specialists in Group Work. (2000). *Professional standards for the training of group workers.* Retrieved February 28, 2005, from http://www.asgw.org/training_ standards.htm

Barret, R. L., & Schmidt, J. (1986). School counselor certification and supervision: Overlooked professional issues. *Counselor Education and Supervision, 26,* 50–55.

Bernard, J. M., & Goodyear, R. K. (1992). *Fundamentals of clinical supervision*. Boston: Allyn & Bacon.

Biggs, D. A. (1988). The case presentation approach in clinical supervision. *Counselor Education and Supervision, 27,* 240–248.

Borders, L. D. (1989). A pragmatic agenda for developmental supervision research. *Counselor Education and Supervision, 29,* 16–24.

Borders, L. D. (1991). Supervision is not equal to evaluation. *The School Counselor, 38,* 253–255.

Borders, L. D., Bernard, J. M., Dye, H. A., Fong, M. L., Henderson, P., & Nance, D. W. (1991). Curriculum guide for training counseling supervisors: Rationale, development, and implementation. *Counselor Education and Supervision, 31,* 58–80.

Borders, L. D., & Brown, L. (2005). *The new handbook of counseling supervision*. Alexandria, VA: American Counseling Association.

Bowers, J. (2002). Using technology to support comprehensive guidance program operations. In P. Henderson & N. Gysbers (Eds.), *Implementing comprehensive school guidance programs: Critical leadership issues and successful responses* (pp. 115–120). Greensboro, NC: CAPS Publications.

Boyd, J. (Ed.). (1978). *Counselor supervision: Approaches, preparation, and practices.* Muncie, IN: Accelerated Development.

Campbell, C. A., & Dahir, C. A. (1997). *Sharing the vision: The national standards for school counseling programs*. Alexandria, VA: American School Counselor Association.

Coleman, H. L. K. (2004). Multicultural counseling competencies in a pluralistic society. *Journal of Mental Health Counseling, 26*(1), 56–66.

Constantine, M. G., Arorash, T. J., Barakett, M. D., Blackmon, S. M., Donnelly, P. C., & Edles, P. A. (2001). School counselors' universal-diverse orientation and aspects of their multicultural counseling competence. *Professional School Counseling, 5,* 13–18.

Constantine, M. G., & Gainor, K. A. (2001). Emotional intelligence and empathy: Their relation to multicultural counseling knowledge and awareness. *Professional School Counseling, 5,* 131–137.

Constantine, M. G., & Yeh, C. J. (2001). Multicultural training, self-construals, and multicultural competence of school counselors. *Professional School Counseling, 4,* 202–207.

Council for Accreditation of Counseling and Related Educational Programs. (2001). *Accreditation standards and procedures manual*. Alexandria, VA: Author.

Dye, H. A., & Borders, L. D. (1990). Counseling supervisors: Standards for preparation and practice. *Journal of Counseling & Development, 69,* 27–32.

The Education Trust. (2003). *Transforming school counselor preparation*. Retrieved October 28, 2004, from http://www2.edtrust.org/EdTrust/Transforming+School+Counsel ing/rationale.htm

Esters, I., & Ledoux, C. (2001). At-risk high school students' preferences for counselor characteristics. *Professional School Counseling, 4,* 165–170.

Etringer, B. D., Hillerbrand, E., & Claiborn, C. D. (1995). The transition from novice to expert school counselor. *Counselor Education and Supervision, 35,* 4–17.

Evans, B., & Ward, S. (2002). Solving the "time and information" dilemma through technology. In P. Henderson & N. Gysbers (Eds.), *Implementing comprehensive school guidance programs: Critical leadership issues and successful responses* (pp. 121–135). Greensboro, NC: CAPS Publications.

Falvey, J. E. (1987). *Handbook of administrative supervision*. Alexandria, VA: American Counseling Association.

Fitch, T. J., & Marshall, J. L. (2004). What counselors do in high-achieving schools: A study on the role of the school counselor. *Professional School Counseling, 7,* 172–177.

Glickman, C. D., Gordon, S. P., & Ross-Gordon, J. M. (1995). *Supervision of instruction: A developmental approach* (3rd ed.). Boston: Allyn & Bacon.

Green, A., & Keys, S. G. (2001). Expanding the developmental school counseling paradigm: Meeting the needs of the 21st century student. *Professional School Counseling, 5,* 84–95.

Guillot-Miller, L., & Partin, P. W. (2003). Web-based resources for legal and ethical issues in school counseling. *Professional School Counseling, 7,* 52–57.

Henderson, P. (in press). *The new handbook for administrative supervision in counseling.* Alexandria, VA: Association for Counselor Education and Supervision.

Henderson, P., & Gysbers, N. C. (1998). *Leading and managing your school guidance and counseling program staff.* Alexandria, VA: American Counseling Association.

Hersey, P., Blanchard, K. L., & Johnson, D. E. (2001). *Management of organizational behavior: Leading human resources* (8th ed.). Upper Saddle River, NJ: Prentice-Hall.

Holcomb-McCoy, C. (2004). Assessing the multicultural competence of school counselors: A checklist. *Professional School Counseling, 7,* 178–186.

Holcomb-McCoy, C., & Lee, C. C. (Eds.). (2005). Professional school counseling in urban settings [Special issue]. *Professional School Counseling, 8*(3).

Hollis, J. W. (1997). *Counselor preparation, 1996–98: Programs, faculty, trends* (9th ed.). Washington, DC: Taylor & Francis and National Board for Certified Counselors.

Kenny, M. C., & McEachern, A. G. (2004). Telephone counseling: Are offices becoming obsolete? *Journal of Counseling & Development, 82,* 199–202.

Krueger, D. (2002). A leader's 3 r's: Reading, reflecting, and relationships. In P. Henderson & N. Gysbers (Eds.), *Implementing comprehensive school guidance* programs: *Critical leadership issues and successful responses* (pp. 43–49). Greensboro, NC: CAPS Publications.

Larivee, G. (2002). Establishing a new position: District director of guidance. In P. Henderson & N. Gysbers (Eds.), *Implementing comprehensive school guidance programs: Critical leadership issues and successful responses* (pp. 35–41). Greensboro, NC: CAPS.

Lieberman, A. (2004). Confusion regarding school counselor functions: School leadership impacts role clarity. *Education, 124,* 552–557.

National Board for Certified Counselors. (2001). *Ethics: The practice of Internet counseling.* Retrieved November 20, 2003, from http://www.nbcc.org/ethics/webethcis.htm

National Board for Professional Teaching Standards. (2004). *School counseling standards.* Retrieved April 10, 2004, from http://www.nbpts.org/pdf/schoolcounseling.pdf

National Council on Measurement in Education. (1995). *Code of professional responsibilities in educational measurement.* Retrieved February 28, 2005, from http://www.natd.org/Code_of_Professional_Responsibilities.html

National Education Association. (2003). *Code of ethics of the education profession.* Retrieved December 27, 2003, from http://www.nea.org/code.html

Northside Independent School District. (2002a). *Comprehensive guidance program framework.* San Antonio, TX: Author.

Northside Independent School District. (2002b). *Guide to counselor performance improvement through job definition, professionalism assessment, supervision, performance evaluation, and professional development goal-setting.* San Antonio, TX: Author.

Paisley, P. O., &, McMahon, G. (2001). School counseling for the 21st century: Challenges and opportunities. *Professional School Counseling, 5,* 106–115.

Peace, S. D. (1995). Addressing school counselor induction issues: A developmental counselor mentor model. *Elementary School Guidance and Counseling, 29,* 177–190.

Sue, D. W., Arredondo, P., & McDavis, R. J. (1992). Multicultural counseling competencies and standards: A call to the profession. *Journal of Counseling & Development, 70,* 477–483.

Tentoni, S. C. (1995). The mentoring of counseling students: A concept in search of a paradigm. *Counselor Education and Supervision, 35,* 32–42.

Texas Counseling Association. (2004). *Texas evaluation model for professional school counselors* (2nd ed.). Austin, TX: Author.

Texas Education Agency. (2004). *The comprehensive guidance and counseling program for Texas public schools: A guide for program development, pre-K through 12th grade* (4th ed.). Austin, TX: Author.

Texas Education Code. (1995). *Recommended appraisal process and performance criteria* (§21.351–353). Retrieved from http://www.tea.state.tx.us/rules/commissioner/adopted/0504/150-1003a-stat.html

Van Horn, S. M., & Myrick, R. D. (2001). Computer technology and the 21st century school counselor. *Professional School Counseling, 5,* 124–130.

VanZandt, C. E., & Perry, N. S. (1992). Helping the rookie school counselor: A mentoring project. *The School Counselor, 39,* 158–163.

Vontress, C. E., & Jackson, M. L. (2004). Reactions to the multicultural counseling competencies debate. *Journal of Mental Health Counseling, 26,* 74–80.

~ Part IV ~

Evaluating

Evaluating Your Comprehensive Guidance and Counseling Program, Its Personnel, and Its Results

Evaluating—Evaluating the Program, Its Personnel, and Its Results

- Evaluate school counselor performance.
- Conduct program evaluation.
- Conduct results evaluation.

☞ Now that the planning and designing phases of the program improvement process have been completed and the implementation phase is under way, we are ready to discuss the next phase of the process: evaluation. Three kinds of systematic evaluation are required to achieve accountability for your guidance and counseling program. *Personnel evaluation,* the first kind of evaluation, describes the procedures used by your district to evaluate school counselors and other personnel who may be assisting school counselors in implementing the district's guidance and counseling program. *Program evaluation* (program audit), the second kind, reviews the status of your district's guidance and counseling program against a set of established program standards. Sometimes the word *formative* is used to describe this type of evaluation because it looks at the degree to which your program is being implemented and on ways to improve program delivery based on the findings of the evaluation. *Results evaluation,* the third kind, focuses on the impact that guidance and counseling activities and services in your district's program is having on students, the school, and the community (Gysbers, Hughey, Starr, & Lapan, 1992). It is often called *summative evaluation* because it assesses program outcomes and impact. The data are also used to improve program effectiveness.

Each type of evaluation is important. Equally important, however, is how they relate to and interact with each other. To express this relationship, we use the formula:

Personnel Evaluation + Program Evaluation = Results Evaluation

The personnel of a program need to be doing the work of the program, and the program elements need to be fully in place and functioning the way they should to achieve the desired results.

This chapter presents detailed discussion of each of these kinds of evaluation. Attention is given to the procedures and instrumentation in personnel, program, and results evaluation as well as to the different kinds of data involved. In addition, data collection, data analysis, and writing and presenting results reports are discussed. Student and program advocacy using data are emphasized.

Before we focus on the three kinds of evaluation and the other issues involved, however, it is important to remember that evaluation is not something done only once at the end of a guidance and counseling activity to see how it came out. Evaluation procedures used initially are used again and again across the entire program as the program continues to unfold. Periodic monitoring of the program is required to provide information to make informed ongoing program refinements, adjustments, and enhancements. How this information is used for these purposes is discussed fully in chapter 11.

Why is evaluation an ongoing activity? Bleuer-Collet (1983) answered this question over 20 years ago and we believe that her answer is as valid today as it was then.

> No program is perfect when it is first implemented. Nor do students' needs remain the same over time. A self-monitoring evaluation system can provide information necessary to (a) prove program effectiveness thereby meeting external demands for accountability and (b) improve program effectiveness thereby maintaining a guidance program that is dynamically responsive to the changing needs of students and society. (p. 1)

Evaluate School Counselor Performance

As discussed in chapter 9, a key part of comprehensive guidance and counseling program implementation and management is a counselor performance improvement system. The basic purpose of such a system is to assist school counselors reach and maintain their professional potential. Such a system includes helping individuals define their jobs, providing professional supervision, conducting fair performance evaluation, and setting goals for professional development (Henderson & Gysbers, 1998). This section focuses on school counselor performance evaluation.

The purposes of evaluating school counselors' performance are to improve the delivery to and impact of the program on the students it serves and to provide for communication among school counselors, guidance program staff leaders, and school administrators. For school counselors, evaluation specifies contract status recommendations and provides summative evaluation as to their effectiveness. For the school district, evaluation defines expectations for counselors' performance and provides a systematic means of measuring their performance in relation to these expectations. Fair performance evaluations effectively done aims toward continuous improvement of professional school counselors' performance (Bunch, 2002).

The three facets to the performance evaluation component of a counselor performance improvement system are (a) self-evaluation, (b) administrative evaluation, and (c) assessment of goal attainment (Northside Independent School District, 1997). The self-evaluation and administrative evaluation focus on job performance competencies and represent data-supported professional judgments as to individuals' proficiency in using the skills and commitment levels required on their jobs. The assessment of goal attainment focuses on individuals' program and professionalism improvement efforts.

For performance evaluation to be done fairly, many data sources are used as each component of a performance improvement system is implemented. Specific examples of typical behaviors of individual school counselors are gathered throughout the year and documented. These patterns of behavior are then compared and contrasted with clearly, overtly stated professionalism standards. Standards are expressed professionwide for school counselors' performance and program delivery and regarding ethical judgments. Standards are expressed for educators in general through relevant laws and through district policies and procedures.

Self-Evaluation and Administrative Evaluation

We recommend that all counselors be evaluated annually. Often, counselors on probationary status, in the final year of their contract term, and whose term contracts have not been extended for performance reasons are evaluated more frequently. Appropriate dates are usually expressed in state law.

To carry out their evaluation responsibilities fairly, evaluators of school counselors' performance should be trained to understand school counselors' jobs and professional roles and in appropriate methods for gathering data to support evaluation (Synatschk, 2002). For elementary school counselors, the administrative evaluator is often the school principal. For counselors who serve more than one building, central-office-based guidance administrators may conduct the evaluations or designate one individual as the primary evaluator, with the other administrators providing relevant data to the primary evaluator. A primary evaluator conducts the evaluation conference or may coordinate a joint evaluation conference. A director of guidance is often a reviewing officer and, in this capacity, discusses the evaluation results with the primary evaluator before the results are presented to the staff member.

Central-office-based guidance administrators are also available to provide data or assist primary evaluators in making their evaluative judgments. District guidance program staff leaders usually are required to be involved in an individual counselor's evaluation when (a) the contract status recommendation will mean a decrease in contract status, (b) the overall rating of the counselor will be either *unsatisfactory* or *clearly outstanding*, or (c) there is disagreement among the evaluators, including the counselor, after his or her self-evaluation. District guidance leaders may also be involved at the request of any of the parties involved in the evaluation process—the counselor, the building guidance program staff leader, or principal—as a second evaluator.

The self- and performance evaluation process consists of six steps: data collection, data analysis, evaluation write-up/draft evaluation form completion, evaluation conference, postevaluation conference analysis, and evaluation form completion. In this process, the school counselor and the evaluator complete the first three steps separately. In the evaluation conference, the fourth step, they discuss their evaluations of the counselor's performance. The evaluator then effects the fifth and sixth steps, obtains the necessary signatures, and distributes the copies of the form as prescribed. The forms used in the process must support appropriate and fair performance evaluation of school counselors and be relevant to the expressed expectations for their performance within the context of the established guidance program as well as relevant to each school counselor's specific job description. Having a team of counselors or counselors and administrators develop the instrument and related process helps create a relevant and well-understood performance evaluation system (Bunch, 2002; Synatsck, 2002). A system for weighting a school counselor's various roles as well as rating them has been suggested by Northside Independent School District (2002) and the Texas Counseling Association (2004). In any case, appropriate performance evaluation forms must be designed to provide meaningful presentation of evaluative judgments. Figure 10.1 provides a form that has been used successfully for

Figure 10.1
Counselor Performance Evaluation Form

NAME _____

SCHOOL _____

REVIEW PERIOD: FROM _____ TO _____ DATE EVALUATION COMPLETED _____

RATINGS SUMMARY: POINTS   RATING

   1. Guidance curriculum implementation: _____   _____

   2. Individual student planning system implementation: _____   _____

   3. Responsive services implementation: _____   _____

   4. System support implementation: _____   _____

   5. Effectiveness of professional relationships: _____   _____

   6. Fulfillment of professional responsibilities: _____   _____

                                  Total Points   _____

CRITERIA FOR OVERALL   OVERALL
PERFORMANCE RATING   PERFORMANCE
SCORING RULES: The highest applicable rating applies.

                                               RATING

Clearly Outstanding is earned with at least 27 points and no rating   Clearly
   less than Satisfactory (3).   Outstanding   ☐

Exceeding Expectations is earned with at least 21 points points and   Exceeding
   no rating less than Satisfactory (3).   Expectations   ☐

Satisfactory is earned with a least 16 points, no more than two   Satisfactory   ☐
   scores less than Satisfactory (3), and no rating less than Below
   Expectations (2).

Below Expectations is earned with at least 14 points   Below
   and no more than one rating less than Below Expectations (2). Expectations   ☐

Unsatisfactory is earned in all other cases.   Unsatisfactory   ☐

EVALUATION: FALL _____SPRING _____

CONTRACT STATUS RECOMMENDATION: (Spring Only)

_____1-yr. term contract: Second

_____3-yr. term contract: First year of 3

_____Nonextension 3-yr. term contract: Second year of 3 years

_____Nonextension 3-yr. term contract: Third year of 3 years

_____Nonrenewal (term contract)

Signature of Evaluator: _____Title of Evaluator: _____

Signature of Reviewing Officer: _____

Title of Reviewing Officer: _____

Signature of Employee: _____Conference Date: _____

Original: Personnel

Copies: Yellow — Counselor   Pink — Principal   Gold — Director of Guidance

---

COUNSELOR PERFORMANCE EVALUATION FORM

1. Implement GUIDANCE CURRICULUM through the use of effective INSTRUCTIONAL SKILLS,
   including
     a. appropriate task analysis
     b. effective use of lesson design
     c. active involvement of students in learning
     d. selection of topics consistent with identified, high-priority student needs and district goals

Clearly Outstanding	Exceeding Expectations	Satisfactory	Below Expectations	Unsatisfactory
☐ (5)	☐ (4)	☐ (3)	☐ (2)	☐ (1)

COMMENTS: _____

_____

_____

(*continued on next page*)

Figure 10.1 *(Continued)*
Counselor Performance Evaluation Form

2. Implements the INDIVIDUAL STUDENT PLANNING SYSTEM through the effective use of GUIDANCE SKILLS, including
   a. careful planning of sessions
   b. presentation of accurate, unbiased information
   c. involvement of students in personalized educational and career planning
   d. accurate and appropriate test results interpretation
   e. selection of individual planning activities consistent with identified, high-priority student needs and district goals

Clearly Outstanding	Exceeding Expectations	Satisfactory	Below Expectations	Unsatisfactory
☐ (5)	☐ (4)	☐ (3)	☐ (2)	☐ (1)

COMMENTS: _____
_____

3. Implements RESPONSIVE SERVICES through effective use of COUNSELING, CONSULTATION, and REFERRAL SKILLS, including
   a. proper identification of problems/issues to be resolved
   b. selection of counseling, consulting, and/or referral interventions appropriate to students' problems and circumstances
   c. use of counseling, consulting, and/or referral skills appropriate to students' problems and circumstances
   d. conducting well-planned, goal-oriented sessions
   e. use of group and individual techniques that are appropriate to the topic and to students' needs and abilities
   f. active involvement of clients in the counseling, consulting, and/or referral process
   g. timely follow-up
   h. provision of services consistent with high-priority, identified student needs and district goals

Clearly Outstanding	Exceeding Expectations	Satisfactory	Below Expectations	Unsatisfactory
☐ (5)	☐ (4)	☐ (3)	☐ (2)	☐ (1)

COMMENTS: _____
_____

4. Implements SYSTEM SUPPORT through PROVIDING effective SUPPORT for other programs and by effectively ENLISTING SUPPORT for the guidance program, such as
   a. providing a comprehensive and balanced guidance program
   b. selecting program activities that meet identified, high-priority student needs and are consistent with campus and district goals
   c. collecting evidence that students achieve meaningful outcomes from program activities
   d. operating within established procedures, policies, and priorities
   e. contributing to organizational solutions outside of assigned responsibilities
   f. working cooperatively with school administrators to garner support for the guidance program
   g. implementing programs that explain the school guidance program
   h. attending to ideas/concerns expressed regarding the guidance program
   i. supporting campus administration policies and goals
   j. supporting district policies and goals

Clearly Outstanding	Exceeding Expectations	Satisfactory	Below Expectations	Unsatisfactory
☐ (5)	☐ (4)	☐ (3)	☐ (2)	☐ (1)

COMMENTS: _____
_____

5. Establishes effective PROFESSIONAL RELATIONSHIPS by building rapport with
   a. students
   b. staff
   c. parents
   d. other counselors
   e. administrators
   f. other in-school/district specialists
   g. community representatives

Clearly Outstanding	Exceeding Expectations	Satisfactory	Below Expectations	Unsatisfactory
☐ (5)	☐ (4)	☐ (3)	☐ (2)	☐ (1)

COMMENTS: _____
_____

(continued on next page)

Figure 10.1 *(Continued)*
Counselor Performance Evaluation Form

---

6. Fulfills PROFESSIONAL RESPONSIBILITIES by
  a. seeking professional development
  b. keeping records consistent with ethical and legal guidelines
  c. maintaining professional work habits
  d. practicing according to the profession 's ethical standards
  e. demonstrating appropriate personal characteristics
  f. demonstrating effective use of basic skills (e.g., communication, decision making, problem solving, educational)

Clearly Outstanding	Exceeding Expectations	Satisfactory	Below Expectations	Unsatisfactory
☐ (5)	☐ (4)	☐ (3)	☐ (2)	☐ (1)

COMMENTS: _____

7. Additional Comments:

Note. From *Guide to Counselor Performance Improvement Through Supervision, Evaluation, and Professional Development,* by Northside Independent School District, 1987, San Antonio, TX: Author. Reprinted with permission.

this process (Northside Independent School District, 1987). The Missouri Department of Elementary and Secondary Education (2000) has a similar model.

Details of how the self- and performance evaluation process works are as follows:

1. *Data collection.* Although the nature of evaluation is judgmental, fair and effective judgments concerning professional performance must be data supported. In drawing conclusions about performance, performance evaluators are asked to rely on data that have been gathered through the supervision system. In clinical supervision, observations and feedback conferences generate relevant data. In developmental supervision, program and performance improvement accomplishments generate data. In administrative supervision, data are gathered regarding daily adherence to standards for program implementation and professional standards, interprofessional relationships, work habits, commitment to the job and the profession, and sound professional judgment. Guidance program staff leaders keep notes and records of their supervisory and other leadership contacts with school counselors. Performance deficiencies are addressed in other leadership activities aimed at performance improvement before they are recorded in a formal, summative evaluation.

2. *Data analysis.* The school counselor and the administrative evaluator consider how the example data compare and contrast to the professionalism standards (Henderson & Gysbers, 1998). Where and how these data are to be collected are established at the beginning of the year in the job-defining conference.

3. *Completion of draft evaluation forms.* Draft evaluations are completed by both the school counselor, as a self-evaluation, and the evaluator. In completing the forms, the evaluators are drawing their preliminary conclusions—making their preliminary judgments—regarding the overall quality of a school counselor's professionalism. Primary evaluators are encouraged to consult with designated reviewing officers prior to completing the draft. The page that represents the summative judgment and overall rating of school counselors' performance is completed last.

On the sample form (Figure 10.1), the six areas for evaluation (instructional skills; guidance skills; counseling, consultation, and referral skills; system support implementation;

establishment of professional relationships; and fulfillment of professional responsibilities) are considered separately. Performance strengths and weaknesses are identified and are supported by specific, behavioral examples. (Example descriptors as well as example observation forms are provided in Appendixes M and N.) Suggestions for improvement are made for incorporation in the counselor's professional development plan.

We recommend holistic scoring. That is, the rating for an area reflects a summative judgment of the school counselor's performance of the various tasks that contribute to the delivery of the skills identified and produces a comment such as, "In most instances, the counselor performs most of these subskills in a(an) _____ manner." To be judged as *clearly outstanding,* performance of the listed indicators as well as many of the discretionary items is consistently outstanding, exemplary, excellent. To be judged as *exceeding expectations,* performance of the listed indicators as well as discretionary items is at an observably high level. In rating a counselor's performance as *clearly outstanding* or *exceeding expectations,* the evaluator considers how the school counselor handles not only required duties but also discretionary tasks.

Standards for professional school counselors should be high. To be judged *satisfactory,* performance of at least the listed indicators is judged as meeting standard expectations, that is, as being good most of the time. To be judged *below expectations,* performance on the listed indicators is in need of specifically identifiable improvement and judged as consistently poor most of the time. To be judged *unsatisfactory,* performance on the listed indicators is either not done or done in a clearly unacceptable manner. *Satisfactory* is the rating earned by counselors who perform their job skills with proficiency. Performance that is rated below or above that should be supported by documentation.

An overall performance rating is a reflection of the summary of ratings for each of the six skill areas plus consideration of the rating levels. To arrive at the overall performance rating, the ratings for each area and the related points are transferred to the cover page and the points totaled. The criteria for overall performance rating are studied, and the appropriate overall rating is applied and recorded.

The contract status recommendation is made in the summative evaluation, although an indication of probable/possible contract status recommendation may be discussed in the formative evaluation, especially for those counselors for whom a decrease in contract status is envisioned. State laws usually apply here.

4. *Evaluation conference.* The school counselor and the evaluator bring their drafts of the evaluation form to the conference to facilitate mutual discussion. The evaluation conferences are scheduled by the primary evaluator with sufficient advance notice provided so that the drafts and related data are available at the time of the conference. The school counselor's strengths as well as weaknesses are discussed. Discrepancies between the two evaluation drafts also are discussed. Because the purpose of evaluation is to help each counselor attain his or her professional potential, suggestions for performance improvement are offered for all counselors. The more collaborative this process is, the fairer the evaluation will be (Bunch, 2002).

5. *Postevaluation conference analysis.* The primary evaluator is responsible for developing the formal evaluation. The evaluator is encouraged to consider the school counselor's input in arriving at his or her final performance evaluation and may seek the advice of the director of guidance and other campus administrators, or may gather additional relevant data in resolving discrepancies between the two opinions.

6. *Evaluation form completion.* The primary evaluator completes the district-approved Counselor Performance Evaluation Form. It is typed by someone other than the counselor's secretary. The signature of the reviewing officer, indicating prior review, is obtained prior to obtaining the counselor's signature. The counselor's signature verifies that the eval-

uation has been discussed but does not necessarily indicate agreement with the information. In most states, the school counselor and the primary evaluator have the right to attach additional statements to the formal evaluation form, provided the statements are signed and dated by both parties and the reviewing officer; again, the signatures verify discussion, not agreement.

Assessment of Goal Attainment

The program improvement and professional development plans are a means for continuously improving the comprehensive guidance program as defined by the district. The purpose of this evaluation is to assess the level of the counselors' contribution to the improvement of the guidance program on the campus and in the district, as well as the level of their efforts to upgrade their professional skills knowledge and levels of commitment. The judgment assesses the counselors' efforts to reach goals they have set for themselves under the leadership of their guidance program staff leaders, directors of guidance, and principals. It also reflects, where appropriate, the effectiveness of an individual counselor's efforts as reflected in the guidance program evaluation.

The data for this evaluation grow out of the developmental supervision component. It is a summative judgment as to the counselors' level of effort in implementing the action plan directed toward the goal and in attaining the goals established at the beginning of the school year. Both are recorded on the Guidance Program Improvement Planning Form (see Figure 7.5) and on the Counselor Professional Growth Plan Form (see Figure 9.1). A performance report is submitted to the director of guidance at the end of the school year recording the primary evaluator's assessment of the levels of plan accomplishment and goal attainment (Henderson & Gysbers, 1998). Documentation includes student outcome data gathered in activity and program evaluation and skill improvement data gathered in clinical supervision.

Conduct Program Evaluation

As guidance and counseling emerged in the schools in the early 1900s, leaders were faced with the task of deciding what activities and services constituted a complete program. Proctor (1930) noted this when he stated:

> One of the great needs in the field of guidance is some fairly objective means of comparing the guidance activities of one secondary school system with that of another. It is only in this manner that we shall ever arrive at an estimate of what constitutes a standard set-up for the carrying out of a guidance program. (p. 58)

Today we know "what constitutes a standard set-up for the carrying out of a guidance program" (Proctor, 1930, p. 58). Owing to the work of Gysbers and Henderson (2000), Myrick (2003b), Johnson and Johnson (1991), and the American School Counselor Association (ASCA, 2005), we know what the guidance and counseling activities and services are that, when brought together, constitute a complete guidance and counseling program. This knowledge allows us to develop the program evaluation instrumentation and procedures necessary to conduct program evaluation. Examples of program evaluation instruments and procedures, as well as the types of data used in program evaluation, are discussed below.

Program Evaluation Instrumentation

Most program evaluation instruments consist of a number of standards that are derived from a model of a comprehensive guidance and counseling program. These standards are acknowledged measures of comparison used to make judgments about the size, nature, and structure of a program. How many program standards are required to establish whether a comprehensive guidance and counseling program is in place and functioning? The answer is enough standards to ensure that judgments can be made as to whether or not a complete comprehensive guidance and counseling program is actually in place and functioning to a high degree to benefit all students, parents, teachers, and the community fully.

Once a sufficient number of program standards are written to represent a comprehensive guidance and counseling program, the next step is to write criteria for each standard. Criteria are defined as statements that specify important aspects of the standards; thus enough criteria need to be written for each standard to provide evaluators with the confidence that each standard is in place and functioning. Then a 5- or 6-point scale is usually created for each criterion allowing for the quantification of data.

Adopt, Adapt, or Create an Instrument

Given the variety of program evaluation instruments available today, you can adopt an instrument as is from those available in your state comprehensive guidance and counseling program model or the ASCA National Model (ASCA, 2005). If adopting one does not work, then you can adapt an available instrument, tailoring it to fit your local circumstances. Finally, if none of the available instruments will work, you have the option of creating one specifically designed for your local situation. To help you in your search for a program evaluation instrument, several examples follow.

American School Counselor Association. The first example of a program evaluation instrument was developed by the ASCA (2003). It is called the Program Audit. It contains 17 standards under which criteria are listed that specify important aspects of the standards. It uses a 4-point scale to identify the degree to which a specific criterion is being met (*none, in progress, completed, implemented*). There also is a *not applicable* category available. The program audit is designed to be used primarily in a self-study of a program for program improvement purposes. See Figure 10.2 for a list of the standards and the criteria for one of the standards used in the ASCA Program Audit.

State of Utah. The state of Utah developed a program evaluation instrument that contains 12 standards derived from their state model (see Figure 10.3). The rating of each standard is done on a 5-point scale from 0 to 4. A scoring guide is provided for each point on the scale describing what an evaluator would look for, from 0 (*no evidence of development or implementation*) to 4 (*exemplary level of development and implementation*).

Missouri School Improvement Guidance Program Standards. As a part of the state of Missouri's accreditation process, five program standards were developed to assess the degree to which comprehensive guidance and counseling programs are in place and functioning the way they should. The standards (see Appendix O) were derived from the basic structure used to organize and implement the Missouri Comprehensive Guidance Program in local school districts.

Standards for a Guidance Program Audit. Appendix P contains eight standards against which a guidance and counseling program can be audited (reviewed). In this example, the standard is stated and then a description follows telling how a district would meet the standard. Next, the evidence an auditor would expect to find is presented along with the documentation required to show that the standard has been met.

Figure 10.2
American School Counselor Association Program Audit:
Standards and Example Criteria for One Standard

Foundation

1. Beliefs and Philosophy
2. Mission of School Counseling Programs

Example Criteria

2.1 A mission statement has been written for the school counseling program.
2.2 Written with the student as the primary client.
2.3 Written for every student.
2.4 Indicates the content or competencies to be learned.
2.5 Links with the vision, purpose, and mission of the state, district, and the school.
2.6 Indicates the long-range results desired for all students.
2.7 The mission statement has been presented to and accepted by administration, counselors, advisory council, and school board.

3. Domains and Goals
4. ASCA National Standards/Competencies

Delivery System

5. Guidance Curriculum
6. Individual Student Planning
7. Responsive Services
8. System Support

Management System

9. School Counselor/Administrator Agreements
10. Advisory Council
11. Use of Data and Student Monitoring
12. Use of Data and Closing the Gap
13. Action Plans
14. Use of Time/Calendar
15. Results Report
16. Counselor Performance Standards
17. Program Audit

Note: From *The ASCA National Model: A Framework for School Counseling Programs,* (2nd ed.) by the American School Counselor Association, 2005, Alexandria, VA: Author, pp. 131–141. Adapted with permission.

Program Evaluation Procedure

Self-Study Review

How frequently a district conducts program evaluation depends on the purposes to be achieved. If it is being done for self-study, the ASCA (2003) recommends that program evaluation be conducted when a program is being designed and then yearly thereafter. Whether it is done once a year, every other year, or periodically, the self-study process provides school counselors with the opportunity to determine if the written district program is the actual district implemented program. The results of program evaluation can reveal where progress has been made or where progress is lacking in program implementation. This allows school counselors, working closely with administration, to establish goals to ensure that the written district guidance and counseling program actually becomes the district's fully implemented program.

External Review

Sometimes program evaluation is conducted using personnel external to the school district. The board of education or the administration may want the program reviewed because of

Figure 10.3
Utah Comprehensive Guidance Program (CGP) Performance Review: Standards

---

STANDARD I: *Board Adoption and Approval.* Approval of the CGP by the local Board of Education and ongoing communication with the local Board regarding program goals and outcomes supported by data.

STANDARD II: *Comprehensive Counseling and Guidance Training.* Regular participation of Guidance Team members in USOE-sponsored Comprehensive Guidance Training.

STANDARD III: *Structural Components.* Structural components and policies support the CGP. This includes adequate resources and support for guidance facilities, materials, equipment, clerical staff, and school improvement processes.

STANDARD IV: *Time Allocation.* Evidence is provided that EIGHTY PERCENT of aggregate counselors time is devoted to DIRECT services to students through a balanced program of individual planning, guidance curriculum, and responsive services consistent with the results of school needs data.

STANDARD V: *Interschool Communication.* This includes communication, collaboration, and coordination with the feeder system regarding the CGP. The CGP is discussed and coordinated as a K–12 concept.

STANDARD VI: *Program Leadership and Management.* Structures and processes are in place to ensure effective program management, including an advisory and steering committee. Evidence is present that counselors are working as program leaders and the CGP is an integral part of the school improvement team

STANDARD VII: *Data and Program Effectiveness.* The program uses current school data including a formal student/parent/teacher needs assessment, which is completed and analyzed every 3 years, and annual data projects regarding program effectiveness as defined by USOE.

STANDARD VIII: *Responsive Services.* These services are available to address the immediate concerns and identified needs of all students through an education-oriented and programmatic approach, and in collaboration with existing school programs and coordination with family, school, and community resources.

STANDARD IX: *Guidance Curriculum.* The program delivers a developmental and sequential guidance curriculum in harmony with content standards identified in the Utah Model for CGP. The guidance curriculum is prioritized according to the results of the school needs assessment process.

STANDARD X: *Career Exploration and Development.* The program provides assistance for students in career development, including awareness and exploration, job seeking and finding skills, and post-high-school placement.

STANDARD XI: *SEOP Process.* Programs shall establish Student Education Occupation Planning (SEOP) for every student, both as a process and a product, consistent with local Board policy and the goals of the CGP, Secondary School Accreditation (R277-413) and Applied Technology Education (R277-911).

STANDARD XII: *Every Student.* All program elements are designed to recognize and address the diverse needs of every student.

Note: From *Comprehensive Guidance Program Performance Review: Connecting Program Improvement and Student Learning,* by the Utah State Office of Education (USOE), 2003, Salt Lake City, UT: Author. Reprinted with permission.

dissatisfaction with the program and they employ external evaluators. Or, the program may be seeking funding or accreditation, and external evaluators are often used for this purpose.

Curcio, Mathai, and Roberts (2003) reported on a situation in which a superintendent, prompted by the board of education because of criticism from parents, hired outside evaluators to review the district's guidance and counseling program. The evaluators developed surveys and interview protocols for school counselors, administrators, and parents, leaders, and students. On the basis of their work, they identified 27 findings, each of which was followed by a recommendation for program improvement.

In the state of Utah, program evaluation is conducted for the purposes of funding. The review process begins when district counselors use the Comprehensive Guidance Program Performance Review (Utah State Office of Education, 2003) to do a self-study of their program. The results of this review, along with other relevant information, are then presented to a review team composed of school counselors and administrators from other districts. To become an approved comprehensive guidance and counseling program and receive state funding, all standards in the Performance Review must be met. If all standards are not met, the school may be held harmless for 6 moths without losing funding, provided the program passes a reevaluation within that 6-month period.

Types of Data Used in Program Evaluation

One type of data used in program evaluation is the data generated from a program evaluation instrument. Using 5- or 6-point scales for the criteria under each standard, data can be quantified yielding means and standard deviations that can be used for yearly comparisons. Trends over time can be ascertained using these data.

Another type of data is called process data. Process data describe what guidance and counseling activities and services took place and for whom. For example, all 150 tenth graders were seen individually to review their individual plans. Process data provide an evaluator with documentation that guidance and counseling activities and services were actually provided to groups or individuals as specified in the program.

Still another type of data that can be useful in program evaluation is perception data. Perception data tell us what students, parents, teachers, and administrators think about or feel about guidance and counseling activities and services in the program and the work of school counselors. Surveys and interviews are typically used to collect perception data.

When combined, these three types of data can provide an overall picture of a district's existing guidance and counseling program. Areas of strengths as well as areas that need improvement become visible from three perspectives, allowing for the development of program improvement goals.

Conduct Results Evaluation

The Evolution of Results Evaluation in the Schools

Today, results evaluation is in the forefront of professional dialogue (Dahir & Stone, 2003; Gysbers & Henderson, 2000; Isaacs, 2003; S. K. Johnson & Johnson, 2003; Myrick, 2003a). School counselors, working within the framework of comprehensive guidance and counseling programs, increasingly are being asked to demonstrate that their work contributes to student success, particularly student academic achievement. Not only are school counselors being asked to tell what they do, but they also are being asked to demonstrate how what they do makes a difference in the lives of students.

Is the focus on results evaluation a new phenomenon, or has our profession always been concerned about assessing the effects of the work of school counselors? The answer is no, it is not a new phenomenon. Concern has been expressed about the need for results evaluation almost from the beginning of guidance and counseling in the schools in the early 1900s.[1]

For example, before the 1920s, the work of professionals focused on establishing guidance and counseling in the schools. However, by the 1920s, concern about the results of guidance and counseling was beginning to be expressed in the literature as indicated by this statement by Payne (1924):

> What method do we have of checking the results of our guidance? For particular groups was it
> guidance, misguidance, or merely a contributing experience? We simply must work out some def-
> inite method of testing and checking the results of our work. If we do not, some other group will,
> with possibly disastrous results for our work. (p. 63)

---

[1]For individuals interested in a detailed presentation of the evolution of accountability, see Gysbers, N. C. (2004). Comprehensive guidance and counseling programs: The evolution of accountability. *Professional School Counselor, 8*, 1–14.

Over the decades that followed, numerous statements were made in the literature about the need to focus on results evaluation. Already by 1930, desirable student outcomes of guidance and counseling programs were being identified. For example, Christy, Stewart, and Rosecrance (1930), Hinderman (1930), and Rosecrance (1930) identified the following student outcomes:

- fewer pupils dropping out of school
- increase in the standard of scholarship
- better morale in the student body
- better all-round school life
- fewer student failures and subject withdrawals
- young people better informed about the future
- satisfactory adjustment of graduates to community life and vocation and to a college or university
- fewer disciplinary cases
- fewer absences
- more intelligent selection of subjects
- better study habits

At the same time that student outcomes were being identified, discussion also was taking place about design issues. In a landmark document on evaluation that appeared in the 1940s, Froehlich (1949, p. 2) reviewed and classified 173 studies according to the following evaluation designs:

1. External criteria, the do-you-do-this? method.
2. Follow-up, the what-happened-then? method.
3. Client opinion, the what-do-you-think? method.
4. Expert opinion, the "Information Please" method.
5. Specific techniques, the little-little method.
6. Within-group changes, the before-and-after method.
7. Between-group changes, the what's-the-difference? method.

Thus, discussion concerning the need to use scientifically based research designs for results evaluation (Froehlich, 1949; Neidt, 1965; Travers, 1949) has appeared in the literature for many years. Not only did such discussion occur, but also a number of studies were actually conducted on the impact of guidance and counseling programs on student development using experimental and control group methodology. Kefauver and Hand (1941), Rothney and Roens (1950), Rothney (1958), and Wellman and Moore (1975) conducted such studies beginning in the 1930s on into the 1960s.

What Results Do We Have So Far?

Beginning in the 1930s onward, Kefauver and Hand (1941), Rothney and Roens (1950), Rothney (1958), and Wellman and Moore (1975) all described experimental control group studies that demonstrated that guidance and counseling programs positively affected the academic, career, and personal/social development of children and adolescents. More recently, in a major review of the literature in school counseling, Borders and Drury (1992) found that guidance program interventions have a substantial impact on students' educational and personal development and contribute to students' success in the classroom. Gerler (1985) analyzed a decade of research on the results of elementary school counseling and found that guidance program interventions in the affective, behavioral, and interpersonal domains of students' lives affected students' academic achievement positively. The results of a study by Lee (1993) showed that classroom guidance lessons in elementary school led by school counselors positively influenced students' academic achievement in mathematics. Similar results were found by St. Clair (1989) in her review of the impact of guidance program interventions at the middle school level. Further, Evans and Burck (1992) conducted a meta-analysis of 67 studies concerning the impact of career education interventions (career guidance) on students' academic achievement. The results supported the value of these interventions as contributors to the academic achievement of students.

In a study conducted in high schools in Missouri, Lapan, Gysbers, and Sun (1997) found that students in high schools with more fully implemented guidance programs were more likely to report that they had earned higher grades, their education was better preparing them for their future, their school made more career and college information available to them, and their school had a more positive climate. In Utah, Nelson and Gardner (1998) found that students in schools with more fully implemented guidance programs rated their overall education as better, took more advanced mathematics and science courses, and had higher scores on every scale of the ACT.

In their review of outcome research in school counseling, Sexton, Whiston, Bleuer, and Walz (1997, p. 125) made the following points:

- Reviews of outcome research in school counseling are generally positive about the effects of school counseling.
- Research results do indicate that individual planning interventions can have a positive impact on the development of students' career plans. There is some support for responsive services activities such as social skills training, family support programs, and peer counseling.
- Consultation activities are also found to be an effective school counseling activity.

In this first decade of the 21st century, student academic achievement has become a major concern in the schools since the passage of the No Child Left Behind Act (P.L. 107–110) in 2001 (McGannon, Carey, & Dimmitt, 2005). Studies conducted in this time period have demonstrated outcomes similar to studies conducted in the 1980s and 1990s. For example, Lapan, Gysbers, and Petroski (2001) found that when 4,868 middle school classroom teachers in Missouri in 184 small-, medium-, and large-size middle schools rated guidance programs in their schools as more fully implemented, 22,601 seventh graders in these schools reported that they earned higher grades, school was more relevant for them, they had positive relationships with teachers, they were more satisfied with their education, and they felt safer in school. Sink and Stroh (2003), in a comparison of elementary students (Grades 3 and 4) enrolled for several years in well-established comprehensive school counseling program schools with students enrolled in schools without such programs, found that students enrolled in schools with the well-established programs have significantly higher academic achievement test scores on the Iowa Tests of Basic Skills–Form M and the Washington Assessment of Student Learning. Brigman and Campbell (2003) tested a guidance curriculum titled student success skills that focuses on student cognitive, social, and self-management skills using a quasi-experimental, pre-post test design. School counselors conducted group sessions for students in Grades 5, 6, 8, and 9. The treatment group scored significantly higher than the control group on the reading and math scores of the Florida Comprehensive Assessment Test.

Developing a Results Evaluation Plan for Your School District

Do guidance and counseling programs produce measurable results? Because the answer is yes, does this mean that no further evaluation work is necessary since such evidence already exists in the literature? The answer is no because as Gerler (1992) pointed out, "although the cumulative evidence is clear, school superintendents and principals [and boards of education] will probably be convinced more by local data than by evidence gathered elsewhere" (p. 500). Following Gerler's admonition, our job is to establish a plan to conduct results evaluation at the local level. What are the tasks involved in developing and carrying out a results evaluation plan? The following sections describe those tasks.

Identify Student Outcomes

As you begin to develop a results evaluation plan for your school district, review the mission of your school district and your district's school improvement plan. Both of these documents, but particularly the school improvement plan, will help you identify student outcomes that are priorities for the district. To illustrate, these documents often focus on such goals as improving student academic achievement, creating safe building environments free from disruptive behavior, and ensuring that students are well prepared to go to work or on to further education upon graduation. Because comprehensive guidance and counseling programs have substantial contributions to make to the achievement of goals such as these, specific student outcomes within these goals can be identified that are believed to result from student participation in guidance and counseling activities and services. They become the outcomes you will focus on in your results evaluation plan.

Consider the Use of Different Types of Data

Four types of data need to be considered in developing your results evaluation plan: data available in your school district that identify student achievement, progress, and behavior; process data; perception data; and results data. (ASCA, 2005)

Student Achievement, Progress, and Behavior Data. These data identify possible outcomes of guidance and counseling programs and have been described in the literature since the 1930s. Types of these data include standardized test scores, grade point average, SAT and ACT test scores, course enrollment patterns, discipline referrals, suspension rates, attendance rates, and homework completion rates. Such data are already being collected in schools and are available to be used as outcome measures to establish the effectiveness of guidance and counseling programs.

Process Data. Process data are used in program evaluation but also can be used in results evaluation. Remember, process data describe what guidance and counseling activities and services took place and for whom. They provide evidence that guidance and counseling activities actually were provided.

Perception Data. Perception data can be used in program evaluation as we described earlier, but they also have a role to play in results evaluation as well. Perception data tell us what students, parents, teachers, administrators, or others think about or feel about guidance and counseling activities and services and the work of school counselors.

Results Data. What impact did guidance and counseling activities and services have on students? Results data consist of scores on knowledge tests or improvement on such variables as attendance rates, discipline referral rates, grade point averages, and achievement test scores. Something has changed in outcomes such as these as a result of students' participation in the guidance and counseling program.

Select an Evaluation Design

There are a number of different evaluation designs available for you to consider. Some of the more commonly used ones are listed below.

Evaluation Based on Predetermined Criterion Standard Comparisons. The process of specifying posttest performance expectations for students is one way to evaluate guidance and counseling program activities. This means that you need to establish minimally acceptable performance standards for an activity by indicating the percentage of students in the target population who must attain a particular result for the activity to be considered successful. For example, if it is expected that 95% of the students at a specific grade level will be able to select a course of study consistent with their measured interests and abilities after participating in a guidance and counseling activity, the minimum acceptable performance level has been established at 95%.

The specification of the minimally acceptable level should occur at the same time that the guidance and counseling activity is selected. There are no hard-and-fast rules for deriving performance standards. Rather, they are usually derived from professional judgment based on the experience of staff members. Student performance will vary by guidance and counseling activities rather than be uniform. Factors to consider in setting the minimal performance level anticipated include the judged importance of the activity, the place of the activity in the developmental sequence, and the probability of attaining the results expected from the activity.

The next step in the evaluation process consists of checking students' posttest performance to determine whether the stated acceptable percentage of students did, in fact, achieve the expected results. Summary data for making this determination consist of a tally of the number of students attaining the criterion level and the computation of the percentage of the target group achieving the expected results. When the sample is small, you can complete this process manually with a checkmark in a yes or no column for each student to indicate attainment or nonattainment of the expected result. With larger samples, or where more detailed information is desired, you may wish to use a distribution with means and standard deviations; percentiles can be used as summary data.

Evaluation Based on Pretest/Posttest Comparisons. Another method frequently used to evaluate guidance and counseling program activities is a pretest/posttest comparison. Before-and-after student data are collected prior to exposure to a guidance and counseling activity and upon completion of the activity. The observed differences in the two measures are interpreted in terms of (a) the statistical significance of the change, (b) the percentage of students attaining a predetermined change standard, or (c) the comparison of change among treatment and control groups.

Evaluation Based on Participation Versus Nonparticipant (Control) Comparisons. The criterion and pretest/posttest comparisons just discussed provide information that is particularly relevant for program development. The crucial questions regarding the cause of the observed performance or change, however, cannot be answered by these types of comparisons. The cause-and-effect questions are critical in program continuation or elimination decisions and necessitate comparisons of the performance or gains of participating students with those of nonparticipating students. These types of comparisons not only provide you with evidence of guidance results achievement of participating students but also support conclusions that guidance and counseling activities were the primary causative factors in the observed results (where significant group differences were observed).

Evaluation Based on Responsive Observations. Results evaluation provides information to determine whether specified student results have been attained because of their participation in the guidance and counseling program. Evaluation data that provide information about what was not predicted or what was unanticipated are also important. Data on unexpected side effects document unintended effects of process operations and dynamics. This type of evaluation not only looks at unanticipated results but also focuses on student and staff responses to their experiences in the program. Attitude surveys, structured reaction sheets, and case-study techniques can be used to collect these types of data.

Another reason for using a responsive type of evaluation is to provide for case studies that portray effects and impact in a natural and direct manner. Case studies can provide a feel for what has happened that may be difficult to determine from quantitative data. Reports of unusual impact on individual students as reported in case illustrations also can be used effectively in communicating more generalized group findings to the public. Take care, however, that this type of evaluation is not interpreted as the collecting of testimonies.

Example Ways to Conduct Results Evaluation

This section provides examples of ways to conduct results evaluation of selected guidance and counseling activities and services found in the four program components of a comprehensive guidance and counseling program: guidance curriculum, individual student planning, responsive services, and system support. For each program component, the activities to be evaluated are listed, followed by the anticipated results and the documentation required to provide evidence of results attainment. The documentation column can be subdivided into immediate, intermediate, and long-range results, if desired, to focus attention on the time period in which data will be collected. This recommended format is adapted from one developed by the school counselors of the Omaha Public Schools in Omaha, Nebraska (Maliszewski, 1997).

Examples of possible ways to do results evaluation for the four components using this format follow. Table 10.1 presents this format and lists expected results and documentation instrumentation examples for the guidance curriculum component. (See later in the chapter for individual student planning [Table 10.3], for responsive services [Table 10.4], and for system support [Table 10.5].)

Guidance Curriculum Results Evaluation

There are many ways to evaluate guidance curriculum activities. Here we use pre-post surveys, performance indicators, scoring guides, and office logs as examples of instrumentation.

Example: Pre-Post Survey. The Missouri Guidance Competency Evaluation Survey (Gysbers, Lapan, Multon, & Lukin, 1992), the first documentation instrument listed in Table 10.1, assesses the results of students participating in guidance curriculum activities.

Table 10.1
Program Component Evaluation: Guidance Curriculum

Program Component	Expected Results	Documentation
Guidance Curriculum		
Guidance activities K–12	Guidance competencies attained	Missouri Guidance Competency Evaluation Survey results pre-post
Guidance activities K–12	Guidance competencies attained	Performance indicators and levels
Guidance activities K–12	Guidance competencies attained	Scoring guides
Conflict resolution	Reduction in office referrals	Office logs

Two forms are available, one for Grades 6–9 and one for Grades 9–12. In the survey, students are asked to rate how confident they are that they have mastered guidance competencies using a 7-point scale, from *very low* to *very high* levels of confidence. Figure 10.4 illustrates the format in a brief sample from the Missouri survey.

Before beginning a guidance curriculum activity, school counselors ensure that all students complete a pretest survey. Group administration of the surveys takes approximately 20 to 25 minutes. Students not present for the pretest or the guidance curriculum activity do not take a posttest survey. Posttest surveys are given as soon as possible after the guidance curriculum activity is completed (usually within a week). The time between pretesting and posttesting should not be more than 3 months. The surveys, so administered, are designed to show change in students' confidence in their mastery of guidance competencies. They are not intended to be given at the beginning of the year and then at the end of the year to all students. Administration and interpretation of surveys are linked to specific guidance curriculum activities. Completed posttest surveys are mailed to the Assessment Resource Center (ARC) at the University of Missouri–Columbia. ARC scans the forms, an-

Figure 10.4
Format Sample From the Missouri Guidance Competency Evaluation Survey

Grades 6–9: Area I Career Planning and Exploration

Please rate how confident you are that you could successfully perform the following career planning and exploration tasks. **Blacken the circle** that indicates the level of your confidence for each item.

LEVEL OF CONFIDENCE

	Very Low	Low	Somewhat Low	Neither Low nor High	Somewhat High	High	Very High
I AM CONFIDENT							
1. that I understand my interests and abilities and how they help me make a career choice.	(VL)	(L)	(SL)	(N)	(SH)	(H)	(VH)
2. that I know how to handle adult disapproval if I have an interest in choosing a class usually taken or a job usually filled by the opposite sex.	(VL)	(L)	(SL)	(N)	(SH)	(H)	(VH)
3. that I know how to find out which leisure activities are best for me.	(VL)	(L)	(SL)	(N)	(SH)	(H)	(VH)
4. that I know how to explore careers in which I may be interested.	(VL)	(L)	(SL)	(N)	(SH)	(H)	(VH)
5. that I understand the importance of making plans for the future (jobs, vocational, technical education, employment and training programs, college, and military).	(VL)	(L)	(SL)	(N)	(SH)	(H)	(VH)
6. that I know about leisure activities I can do when I am older.	(VL)	(L)	(SL)	(N)	(SH)	(H)	(VH)
7. that all classes and jobs are acceptable for both females and males.	(VL)	(L)	(SL)	(N)	(SH)	(H)	(VH)
8. that I know about different hobbies, sports, and activities in which I could get involved.	(VL)	(L)	(SL)	(N)	(SH)	(H)	(VH)
9. that I understand how to prepare for careers in which I may be interested.	(VL)	(L)	(SL)	(N)	(SH)	(H)	(VH)
10. that I can handle "kidding" from other students if I have an interest in choosing a class usually taken, or a job usually filled, by the opposite sex.	(VL)	(L)	(SL)	(N)	(SH)	(H)	(VH)

Note. From *Missouri Guidance Competency Evaluation Survey — Grades 6–9, 9–12,* by N. C. Gysbers, R. T. Lapan, K. D. Multon, and L. E. Lukin, 1992, Columbia, MO: Center for Educational Assessment. Reprinted with permission.

alyzes the data, and returns a one-page data summary to the school counselors. The summary contains group scores only; it does not report individual student scores. ARC report forms are kept by school counselors as one type of documentation of the results of guidance curriculum activities in the guidance curriculum component of the overall school guidance and counseling program. (For more information about the development of the surveys, see *Developing Guidance Competency Self-Efficacy Scales for High School and Middle School Students* by Lapan, Gysbers, Multon, and Pike, 1997.)

Example: Performance Indicators and Levels. To establish whether students master guidance competencies as a result of their participation in guidance and counseling activities, performance indicators and performance levels can be specified to provide criteria as to what constitutes mastery. The establishment of criteria provides those who rate student mastery with the necessary benchmarks to make their judgments. To illustrate, we can use the list of student competencies in chapter 3 (the Life Career Development Model) in which 15 goals are grouped in three domains. For each goal there are 13 competencies, one for each grade level K–12. (See Appendix A for a complete list of all these goals and competencies.)

We can then, for example, select Goal A (from the Self-Knowledge and Interpersonal Skills Domain) and the competency for Grade 3 and the competency for Grade 12. The next step is to select performance indicators that will show whether students have acquired these competencies. We also need to suggest performance levels. Figure 10.5 presents this example and lists performance indicators and the suggested performance levels immediately after each competency.

With performance indicators and performance levels established, the next step is to answer the when, how, and who questions: When does something happen? How does it happen? Who is involved? The when question focuses on when the evaluation is done. In most situations it is done at the end of guidance and counseling activities. How the evaluation is completed pinpoints what has to be done by students to complete the activities so that they can be judged by counselors, teachers, or other appropriate personnel as having mastered the competencies. To indicate mastery, students can write something, talk about something, or demonstrate some specific behaviors. Who does the evaluation depends on the guidance and counseling activities. It could be counselors, teachers, career center technicians, or members of the community. To show how this approach to results evaluation works, we present in Figure 10.6 the when, how, and who answers for the competency for Grade 12 presented in Figure 10.5.

The competency in this example is one of several that may be included in a guidance and counseling activity focused on career and personal identity and team taught by English teachers and counselors. Because such activities from the guidance curriculum are being taught across grade levels, there is a need to bring together, in one place, the results of the individual evaluation efforts that take place at the close of each unit for each student. A variety of formats can be used to organize guidance competencies for reporting purposes. These include a report card format and a folder format. The report card format is similar to report card formats used in a number of instructional areas, such as reading and physical education. Specific competencies are listed on a report form with some indication as to whether students have mastered these competencies or are working on them. In this format the ratings are done by teachers or counselors in consultation with students. The report card is shared with parents as are report cards in instructional areas. Performance indicators and performance levels are used in the rating process. An example of a report card format for the 15 competencies for Grade 3 is presented in Figure 10.7.

Another format to consider is a student life career planning folder. This folder belongs to students and their parents; it is a vehicle for them to keep a record of such things as academic

Figure 10.5
Sample Performance Indicators and Levels

Goal A

Students will develop and incorporate an understanding of the unique personal characteristics and abilities of themselves and others.

Grade 3 competency: Students will describe themselves accurately to someone who does not know them.

Performance indicators	*Suggested performance levels*
Students are able to	Students are able
1. describe the physical and personality characteristics they would like others to know about them.	1. describe six (three physical and three personality) characteristics of themselves.
2. recognize any discrepancies in their descriptions and correct them.	2. correct any incorrect descriptions that they gave for #1.
3. describe themselves correctly to someone they are meeting for the first time.	3. describe themselves to one person they do not know well.

Grade 12 competency: Students will appreciate their uniqueness and encourage that uniqueness.

Performance indicators	*Suggested performance levels*
Students are able to	Students are able
1. describe their uniqueness and why they appreciate that uniqueness.	1. a) describe two ways they are unique. b) describe their appreciation of that uniqueness in respect to benefits for self and others, and the effects upon the feelings of self and others.
2. describe methods they currently use to encourage their uniqueness.	2. describe three methods currently used to encourage uniqueness (for example, time and effort in learning, practicing, evaluation responses, and so on).
3. predict methods they might use in the future to encourage their uniqueness.	3. predict two methods they might use in the future (for example, time and effort in further practice, further learning, further evaluation or responses, and so on.)

progress, extracurricular activities, important conferences, and future education and work plans. Using this format to help students keep track of the competencies they are mastering requires developing competency lists that can be made a part of the folder. We suggest that individual sheets of heavy stock paper be used to list the competencies for each grade level included in the folder. The folder checklist format for Grade 12 is illustrated in Figure 10.8.

Competency rating using this format could be done jointly by a student and a counselor or an adviser in an adviser–advisee system. The rating can be done by initialing a competency on the form when the counselor/adviser and the student feel it has been mastered. The performance indicators and performance levels for each competency are used as a basis for making a judgment.

Figure 10.6
An Example of Answers to When, How, and Who: Grade 12

Competency	Performance Indicator	Performance Level
Students will appreciate their uniqueness and encourage that uniqueness.	Students are able to describe their uniqueness and why they appreciate that uniqueness.	Students are able to describe two ways they are unique.
When	**How**	**Who**
At the end of a unit in a 12th-grade English class	Students complete an essay in English class on the concept of uniqueness using themselves as an illustration	English teacher and counselor

Figure 10.7
Report Card for Guidance Program Competencies: Grade 3

Your child can	Quarters			
	1	2	3	4
describe himself or herself accurately.				
describe personal mental health care.				
describe adult responsibilities.				
recognize that actions affect other's feelings.				
talk and listen to close friends and those who are not close friends.				
realize study skills are necessary for learning school subjects.				
define *consumer*; describe how he or she is a consumer.				
recognize that people have varying roles; describe personal roles.				
recognize why work activities are chosen and that choices may change.				
define what *future* means.				
realize that people obtain rewards for their work.				
recognize those accomplishments he or she is proud of.				
describe personal thought processes before making a decision.				
recognize the need to assess possible consequences before making a decision.				
realize that environment influences interests and capabilities.				

The Rating Key
✓ Student has accomplished this competency.
W Student is still working on this competency.
□ This competency does not apply at this time.
(Blank)

Figure 10.8
Folder Checklist for Guidance Program Competencies: Grade 12

Student's Initials	Counselor's Initials	*I can*
_____	_____	appreciate and encourage my uniqueness.
_____	_____	analyze my personal skills that have contributed to satisfactory physical and mental health.
_____	_____	assess how taking responsibility enhances my life.
_____	_____	understand the value of maintaining effective relationships in today's interdependent society.
_____	_____	evaluate my current communication skills; continually improve those skills.
_____	_____	evaluate ways I currently learn; predict how learning may change.
_____	_____	analyze how I as a citizen and consumer help support the economic system.
_____	_____	assess the interactive effects of life roles, settings, and events and how they lead to a personal lifestyle.
_____	_____	analyze the effects stereotypes have on career identity.
_____	_____	analyze how concerns change as situations and roles change.
_____	_____	speculate what my rights and obligations might be as a producer in the future.
_____	_____	summarize the importance of understanding attitudes and values and how they affect my life.
_____	_____	implement the decision-making process when making a decision.
_____	_____	provide examples and evaluate my current ability to generate alternatives, gather information, and assess consequences in the decisions I make.
_____	_____	assess my ability to achieve past goals; integrate this knowledge for my future.

Example: Scoring Guides. Scoring guides can provide clear expectations concerning what is required to be accomplished by students if they are to achieve mastery of specific guidance competencies. In using scoring guides for evaluation, the competencies to be mastered by students are identified for each guidance curriculum activity. Then "gradations of quality" (Goodrich, 1996, p. 14) are specified using a 3- or 4-point scale with one end of the scale marked, for example, *incomplete* and the other end marked *strong proficiency.* The guidance activity in Figure 10.9 illustrates the use of a scoring guide in making a judgment about the degree of achievement of a guidance competency. The activity is from *The Box: Secondary 9–12* (Missouri Department of Elementary and Secondary Education, 1998). *The Box* contains two or more guidance activities for each of the guidance competencies of the Missouri Comprehensive Guidance Program (Gysbers, Kosteck-Bunch, Mahnuson, & Starr, 2002). The activity in the figure is titled Understanding Credits and is used to assist students to achieve knowledge so that they can master the competency concerning requirements for high school graduation.

After students have participated in the activity, ask them to write a short paragraph explaining the requirements for high school graduation. A scoring guide for evaluating the level of proficiency of students' understanding based on their written paragraph is shown in Table 10.2.

Example: Office Logs. In the spring of 1989, the Ferguson-Florissant School District (Rain, Walker, & Jenkins, n.d.) initiated a program called Resolve All Problems Peacefully

Figure 10.9
Guidance Activity, Grades 9–10

I Know the Requirements for High School Graduation

AREA:	Career Planning and Exploration	
CATEGORY:	Planning High School Classes	
TIME:	30 minutes	
GROUP SIZE:	Class	GRADE LEVEL: 9–10
MATERIALS:	A list of diploma program requirements at your school, actual diplomas	

Understanding Credits

Introduction:

Students who are well informed of graduation requirements are typically better able to meet those requirements. They are also more apt to take courses that interest them or aid them in postsecondary plans. Informed students generally do not duplicate courses. This activity informs students of graduation requirements.

Procedure:

1. Define a *credit* using the following definition. A *credit* is a numerical weight awarded each class successfully completed. Each class is generally awarded one-half credit per semester. For example, when a student successfully completes 1 year of school, on a schedule of six classes per semester, he or she earns six credits for the year or three credits per semester.
2. Inform students of the credit requirements for each diploma program at your school.
3. Show the students an example of each diploma.
4. Check for understanding by asking the following:
   a) What are the differences in the diplomas?
   b) How many credits are needed for each?
   c) How many electives credits are needed?
5. Answer any questions and invite students to the guidance office for individual assistance.

Notes:

Be aware of students who appear to be confused during the presentation. They may need individual assistance.

Evaluation Suggestions:

Refer to Section VI of the manual.

Note. From *The Box: Secondary 9–12,* by Missouri Department of Elementary and Secondary Education, 1998, Jefferson City, MO: Author. Reprinted with permission.

Table 10.2
Scoring Guide

Competency	1 Incomplete	2 Minimal Proficiency	3 Basic Proficiency	4 Strong Proficiency
I know the requirements for high school graduation.	Cannot specify any specific graduation requirements. Paragraph written in very general terms.	Identifies number of credit hours needed for graduation.	Identifies number of credit hours needed for graduation. Knows meaning of word *credit* but unclear about types.	Identifies number of credit hours needed for graduation. Knows meaning of word *credit* (required and elective). Knows types of diplomas issued.

(RAPP) in Ferguson Middle School. It is a conflict-resolution program that involves counselors, teachers, administrators, parents, and students and that is an all-school program, part of the overall guidance and counseling program of that school. The program subsequently was initiated in other buildings and at other levels in the district. The primary goal of the program was to decrease fighting in the school. A second goal was to create in students positive attitudes toward others and toward school. When these two goals were achieved, the result was expected to be a more pleasant and positive classroom atmosphere.

The program was put into operation by counselors who visited classrooms and explained the program. In addition, intensive training was provided to all who were to participate in the program—students, teachers, counselors, and administrators—to immerse the school fully in the goals and activities of the program.

What were the results of the program? Here is what happened at Ferguson Middle School:

> The conflict resolution program at Ferguson Middle School has been successful beyond anyone's expectations. Mediators have helped their peers resolve their conflicts peacefully about 10% of the time. There has rarely, if ever, been a fight between students who have reached a resolution in a RAPP mediation. Office referrals for the first quarter of the 1989–90 school year were down 75% over the same time 1 year ago (before RAPP). Fights, which had been increasing every year, have dropped dramatically since the inception of RAPP. In the first semester of the 1986–87 school year, there were 66 fights; 1987–88, 73 fights; 1988–89, 88 fights; (RAPP began in the spring of '89) 1989–90, 36 fights.
>
> Many teachers have commented on the increased self-esteem of RAPPers. These students are proud to be selected by their teachers and responsible for maintaining a peaceful school environment. We are noticing a change in the attitude of our student body. There is great prestige connected with being a member of RAPP and associating with lawyers and administrators. Many students want to be a part of RAPP and therefore model that behavior, it is now considered the "in thing" to break up fights instead of starting them. (Ferguson Middle School, 1990)

Individual Student Planning Results Evaluation

Evaluation of the individual student planning program component focuses on students' education and career plans and includes the planning conferences that teachers or counselors hold with students and parents. Three kinds of evaluation are described here: scoring guides, conference evaluation by students, and conference evaluation by parents (see Table 10.3).

Example: Scoring Guides to Judge Plan Quality. To judge the quality of a student life career plan, it is first necessary to establish criteria to judge quality. We recommend four criteria. A plan, regardless of content and format, should be the following:

- *Comprehensive:* Life career plans should be guides to help students, working closely with parents, manage their lives. Plans should help them define their goals and identify and expand their aptitudes, abilities, interests, values, and skills. It should be a record—never completed—of their past, present, and future experiences and goals. Plans should provide a way, in written form, for students to identify and consider who they are, where they are going, and how they are going to get there in terms of their current and future life roles.

- *Developmental:* Life career plans should be designed to be used beginning in middle school and continuing through the adult years. They should be documents that are changeable. Although they can be used on a one-time basis, they should be flexible documents that can be filled out and modified from time to time as new experiences are anticipated or completed.

- *Student centered and student directed:* Life career plans should belong to the students using them, although counselors, teachers, and parents are directly involved in how plans are developed and used. Plans are not the property of the schools, although they are kept there for the convenience of students. Wilhelm (1983) made the point that plans are student centered when he stated:

    Our task is to teach people the skills they need to manage their own careers. That doesn't mean telling people what occupations they ought to pursue; nor does it mean we tell them what education they should get. What it does mean is that we give them data—data about demographic trends, data about employers—all the data we can gather that in any way impacts upon their vocational lives and choices—and we teach them how to use these data to manage their own careers. (p. 12)

- *Competency based:* Life career plans should feature student competencies. Competencies are skills, knowledge, and attitudes students acquire as they live, learn, and work in such settings as home, school, the workplace, and the community. Of particular importance are the guidance competencies students gain through their involvement in the guidance program. Life career plans should have sections in which students can record competencies that have been mastered.

Once the criteria for life career plans have been established, then degrees of quality for each criterion need to be chosen. In the scoring guide example in Figure 10.10, the criterion

Table 10.3
Program Component Evaluation: Individual Student Planning

Program Component	Expected Results	Documentation
Individual Student Planning		
Student life career plan development	Plan meets quality criteria	Scoring guide
Student conference life career plan	The conference was helpful	Individual planning conference evaluation student form
Parent conference	The conference was helpful	Individual planning conference evaluation parent form

Figure 10.10
Life Career Plan Scoring Guide

Criteria	Quality		
	Level 1	Level 2	Level 3
Comprehensive			
Developmental	Plan was for grade 12 only	Plan started with grade 10 through grade 12	Plan started at beginning of middle school
Student centered and student directed			
Competency based			

chosen is developmental. To reach Level 3, the highest level of quality, the plan needed to begin at the beginning of middle school.

Example: Life Career Plan Conferences With Students and Parents. A major feature of the individual planning process for students and parents are regular conferences to review students' life career plans. Asking students and parents to complete a short survey is one way to assess the impact of student and parent conferences. Most often students and parents meet together with school counselors or teachers to review students' life career plans. Upon completion of the conference, surveys can be given to students and parents to fill out. Two sample surveys, one for students and one for parents, are in Figures 10.11 and 10.12.

Responsive Services Results Evaluation

Ways to evaluate the responsive services component include satisfaction surveys, case studies, focus groups, and office logs (see Table 10.4). Two of these approaches—case studies and focus groups—are highlighted here.

Example: Case Studies. Case studies enable school counselors to evaluate the results of such responsive services as small-group counseling and individual counseling. The Des Moines Public Schools (1994), for example, evaluated aspects of their elementary guidance program called Smoother Sailing through a report that presented data from the analyses of 25 case studies. For each case study, the counselors described the problem and then presented information about the instruments or methods used to identify the nature and severity of the problem, the interventions used, and the results.

Figure 10.11
Individual Planning Conference Evaluation: Student Form

Please tell us how helpful the Individual Planning Conference was for you by circling the appropriate number for each item.					
	Not Helpful		Somewhat Helpful		Very Helpful
	1	2	3	4	5
My Individual Planning Conference helped me to					
1. know what courses I need to complete my high school requirements	1	2	3	4	5
2. understand my scores on the SAT/ACT	1	2	3	4	5
3. clarify my post–high-school options	1	2	3	4	5
4. consider my goals for the future	1	2	3	4	5
5. select courses for my next school year	1	2	3	4	5

Figure 10.12
Individual Planning Conference Evaluation: Parent Form

Please tell us how helpful the Individual Planning Conference was for you by circling the appropriate number for each item.					
	Not Helpful		Somewhat Helpful		Very Helpful
	1	2	3	4	5
The Individual Planning Conference helped me to					
1. know what courses my daughter or son needs to complete for high school graduation	1	2	3	4	5
2. understand my son or daughter's scores on the SAT/ACT	1	2	3	4	5
3. think more about my daughter or son's post–high-school options	1	2	3	4	5
4. talk about my son or daughter's goals for the future	1	2	3	4	5
5. talk about my daughter or son's courses for the next school year	1	2	3	4	5

Individual and small-group counseling in combination with classroom guidance activities, behavioral plans, or referral to community-based services formed the core of the array of interventions used. The majority of the case studies indicated that students made progress toward resolving the issues that led to their initial referral and that the children had learned skills that improved their relationships with peers and adults and developed strategies for improving their work in the classroom (Des Moines Public Schools, 1994, pp. 9–10).

Example: Focus Groups. One way to evaluate responsive services activities such as consultation and referral is to use a survey to uncover the effectiveness of these activities as perceived by parents and teachers. Using focus groups of parents and teachers can help you develop such a survey. According to Krueger (1994), a focus group is "a carefully planned discussion designed to obtain perceptions on a defined area of interest in a permissive, nonthreatening environment" (p. 6) and should consist of from 7 to 10 individuals who have something in common.

In applying the use of focus groups to the development of surveys to assess the effectiveness of the responsive services activities of consultation for parents, the first step is to assem-

Table 10.4
Program Component Evaluation: Responsive Services

Program Component	Expected Results	Documentation
Responsive Services		
Small-group counseling	Improved personal/ social skills	Case studies
Aggression replacement training	Reduction in number of office referrals and suspensions	Office logs
Counseling	Student goals achieved	Case studies
Referral	Satisfaction with referrals	Referral satisfaction survey results
Consultation	Satisfaction with consultation	Parent consultation evaluation survey results
		Teacher consultation evaluation survey results
		Focus groups

ble a group of 7 to 10 parents who have experienced consultation. Then ask them to tell you how they benefited from consultation. To obtain enough comments, you may need to repeat the process with several more focus groups. On the basis of their comments, possible survey items can be identified and piloted with other parents. Modifications can be made to these items based on pilot test results and a usable survey developed. The same process can be used to develop a survey for parents about referral or for teachers concerning consultation.

System Support Results Evaluation

Activities that typically are part of the system support component of a school guidance and counseling program and can be evaluated include faculty development, school counselor professional development, and guidance program use/satisfaction (see Table 10.5). Ways to evaluate these activities are presented in the following examples.

Example: Faculty Workshop Evaluation Form. If school counselors conduct faculty development workshops, the expected result is faculty satisfaction with the workshops. Documentation of the results can be accomplished through workshop evaluation forms completed by teachers, with the forms used being those the district uses for all of its faculty professional development workshops.

Example: Recertification. Work on school counselor recertification, including taking courses and attending workshops and conferences, is an important part of school counselors' time commitments in the system support component. Documentation can be the renewal certificates school counselors receive upon completion of the recertification process. Other documents signifying completion of workshops or attendance at professional conferences could also be used.

Example: Use/Satisfaction Surveys. Another example of results evaluation in the system support component is the use of guidance and counseling program use/satisfaction surveys. These surveys entail asking students and teachers about the extent to which they used the guidance and counseling program and how satisfied they were with it. A similar survey could also be completed by school counselors assessing their perceptions of the services they provided to students and how helpful the services were. The survey results serve as documentation. See Appendix D for copies of a set of use/satisfaction surveys used with high school students, teachers, and school counselors in Northside Independent School District.

Establishing a Plan to Collect Results Evaluation Data

As is now clear, there are a variety of places in the program and a number of ways to collect results evaluation data. The four program components are used as the format to identify guidance and counseling activities to be evaluated and to organize the results evaluation process. An important task in this process is to establish a plan to collect results evaluation

Table 10.5
Program Component Evaluation: System Support

Program Components	Expected Results	Documentation
System Support		
Faculty development	Satisfaction with faculty workshop	Faculty workshop evaluation form results
School counselor professional development	Recertification	Renewal certificate form
Guidance program use/ satisfaction	Student, teacher, and parent satisfaction with the program	Use/satisfaction survey results

data. Figure 10.13 presents an example of such a plan. Note that once again, the four program components are used as organizers. Grade-level groupings are identified; space is provided for identifying which guidance and counseling activities are to be evaluated in a given year, how the evaluation will take place, who will be responsible, and when it will occur.

Select or Develop Instruments

We recommend the use of the following guidelines to select existing instruments or develop new instruments for collecting student results evaluation data.

1. The expected results for each guidance activity should be measured as directly as possible.
2. The instruments for collecting results evaluation data should be appropriate in terms of content, understandability, opportunity to respond, and mechanical simplicity.
3. Directions for the administration, scoring, and reporting for all instruments should be clear, concise, and complete to ensure uniformity and accuracy in data collection.
4. The time required for administering, scoring, and reporting evaluation instruments should be kept at a minimum to obtain reliable information.
5. Evaluation instruments should meet the tests of validity, reliability, and reasonableness.

Schedule Data Collection

C. D. Johnson (1991) suggested there are long-range, intermediate, and immediate results that need to be considered. According to Johnson, long-range results focus on how programs affect students after they have left school. Intermediate results emphasize what impact the program has had on students some period of time after they have participated in guidance and counseling program activities. Immediate results are results that describe the impact of specific guidance and counseling activities soon after the activities have been completed.

The data collection schedule for results evaluation should be established prior to the initial date of the results evaluation period and should specify

- the guidance activity for which the data will be collected
- the instrument(s) to be used
- the group(s) or individuals from whom data will be collected
- the time when data will be collected (pretest, posttest, end of year, and so forth) in relation to the process schedule
- the person(s) to be responsible for data collection

The evaluation design chosen, including the types of comparisons to be made, will dictate most of the decisions relevant to the data collection schedule.

Evaluation data collected for groups to make pretest/posttest comparisons or experimental group/control group comparisons need to conform closely to the time required to complete the chosen guidance and counseling activity. Pretest or baseline data need to be collected prior to the initiation of the guidance and counseling activities, and posttest data need to be collected at a specified time after completion of the guidance and counseling activities being evaluated (immediate results). Some designs also may require the collection of data at specified periods during the guidance and counseling activity period or as follow-up sometime after the completion of the guidance and counseling activity (intermediate or long-range results). All such data need to be collected on a predetermined schedule so that all persons involved in the results evaluation process can make plans and carry out the data collection in accordance with the design.

Figure 10.13
Annual Results Evaluation Plan

Component	Level	What/How/Who/When
Guidance curriculum	K–6	
	6–9	
	9–12	
Individual student planning	6–9	
	9–12	
Responsive services	K–6	
	6–9	
	9–12	
System support	K–12	

Ensure Staffing for Data Collection and Processing

Adequate staffing to handle results evaluation, including data collection and data processing, is essential. Organize your work groups to

- plan and coordinate data collection and processing
- conduct in-service training of the individuals who will be responsible for the actual data collection
- administer the instruments
- handle the clerical details of preparing and distributing the instruments, collecting and organizing the completed instruments, scoring them, doing the data entry and data analysis, and preparing tables
- write the evaluation report

The absence of adequate staffing for results evaluation is frequently the underlying cause for the breakdown of the whole results evaluation process. Symptoms of inadequate staffing may appear in the form of unmet schedules, resistance from teachers, errors in data entry and analysis, and incomplete reports that are not communicated adequately to program and administrative personnel.

The staffing needed for the results evaluation cannot be standardized because of the differences in the nature and the size of results evaluation projects from school to school. Staffing to conduct full-scale results evaluation for all grades in a large school system will obviously require more leadership and more person-hours than will the results evaluation of one specific guidance activity in one grade. In any case, large or small, comprehensive or specific, the success of results evaluation depends on the assignment of specific time to staff for the planning, implementation, and interpretation of the results evaluation data.

Collect the Data

All results data must be collected in accordance with a collection schedule and with the proper administration of evaluation instruments. This process requires careful planning and the full cooperation of all persons responsible for collecting or providing the needed information. The following suggestions may be helpful in implementing efficient and accurate data collection.

1. The purposes and details of the results evaluation plan should be communicated to all staff members who will be involved in the evaluation process. The threat of evaluation and the added burden of another task can be eased by a full explanation and

discussion of all details for implementation before assignments are given to teachers, counselors, and others. Work sessions can be used to discuss the data collection schedule and the instruments to be used. A good technique to acquaint teachers and counselors with the evaluation instruments is to let them complete all the instruments they will administer. Emphasis should be given to instructions for the administration of all instruments and the necessity for their uniform administration to all respondents. Further, where observers are to be used, it is important that they have thorough training in making and recording their observations.

2. All instruments and evaluation instructions should be prepared and assembled well in advance of the date for implementing data collection. Careful planning of the logistics of collecting and processing results evaluation data will help avoid delays and ensure compliance with the data collection schedule.

3. All respondents (students, teachers, parents) should be informed of the purposes for collecting information, and confidentiality should be ensured where appropriate. Steps should be taken to motivate students to the task of completing tests or other instruments, as would be done in any other school testing situation. The assumption is made that the responses to evaluation instruments represent the respondents' best effort and are honest. Any steps, within defined limits, that can be taken to ensure the validity of this assumption will increase the reliability and validity of the data collected.

4. The data collected should be identified properly with respect to target groups, date, and the person(s) responsible for their collection. This simple precaution will help prevent lost and mislabeled data and will enable follow-up in case questions arise regarding the data.

5. Evaluation tests and other instruments should be scored and coded for processing as soon as possible after the data are collected. The prearranged coding plan should be followed and then rechecked to ensure accuracy. Many instruments can be scored and the data entered when appropriate answer sheets have been used and the scoring equipment is available. Planning for the use of machine-scored answer sheets and the related data entry will result in greater speed and accuracy in processing evaluation data for analysis. (School systems that do not have their own test-scoring equipment and personnel with expertise in data processing should seek assistance from colleges and universities or commercial agencies that serve their area.)

Analyze Results Evaluation Data

"School counselors do not have to be skilled statisticians to meaningfully analyze data" (ASCA, 2005, p. 51). True, but school counselors do need to master some basic statistical concepts to successfully analyze and interpret results data. In addition, school counselors need to know how to disaggregate data appropriately, enter data on spreadsheets such as Excel, do appropriate analyses, and develop graphs and charts displaying the data in understandable ways.

Disaggregate Data. Data disaggregation is an important step in data analysis because it allows us to see if there are any students who are not doing as well as others. The ASCA (2005, p. 50) suggested that the common fields for disaggregation are as follows:

- Gender
- Ethnicity
- Socioeconomic status (free and reduced lunch)
- Vocational (multiperiod vocational program trades)
- Language spoken at home
- Special education

- Grade level
- Teacher(s)

Use Spreadsheets. An important tool for results data analysis is a spreadsheet such as Excel. Spreadsheets allow us to enter results data and conduct various statistical procedures as appropriate. In addition, various charts and graphs can be created to show relationships of results data to possible outcomes such as state achievement test scores and external tests such as the SAT or ACT.

Some types of evaluation information are not easily adaptable to spreadsheet analyses, however, and may in fact be more meaningful when analyzed by you and your staff. For example, subjective counselor reports of guidance and counseling activities or certain types of student behaviors may lose meaning if quantified. These subjective analyses may be critical in the interpretation of other outcome data. In addition, small samples of activities or students may not warrant the use of computer analysis and thus will need to be handled manually. In such cases, precautions should be taken to reduce human error to a minimum by establishing checks and rechecks.

Write Results Evaluation Reports

The reports of results evaluation should be addressed to those who have an interest in the basic evaluation questions asked in the results evaluation plan. Such people include district and building administrators, the board of education, program directors, teachers, counselors, and the lay public. The variance in the interests and level of research understanding of these audiences dictates the preparation of separate reports that are appropriate for each group. These diverse interests can be satisfied by preparing a *technical report* that constitutes a full research report of the design, all statistical data, and evaluative conclusions or a *professional report* that focuses on the conclusions regarding the effectiveness of program activities and recommendations for program emphases and modifications. Still another type of report is called a *report card*. These three types of reports are described in the following sections.

Technical Reports. A technical report should be a complete description of the results evaluation that was conducted, the design used, the results, and conclusions and recommendations. The following outline can serve for the content of the technical report of a comprehensive guidance and counseling program results evaluation.

- *Program description.* This part of the report should describe in detail the guidance and counseling activities that were evaluated as well as the target groups, the specific guidance and counseling activities that were evaluated, and the personnel and facilities involved.
- *Evaluation design.* Include a description of procedures used to formulate the evaluation questions and detailed descriptions of the specific evaluation hypotheses, the comparisons made, the operational definitions or instrumentation, and the types of analyses. In addition, establish the case for the design as an appropriate approach to answering the evaluation questions.
- *Evaluation results.* Report the results of the evaluation in complete detail in this section. Present each guidance and counseling activity that was evaluated with the evidence that it was, or was not, effective. Summarize relevant descriptive statistics and the statistical analyses to test hypotheses in proper table form. When a large number of statistical tables are needed to report the results, it may be desirable to place some of these tables in an appendix to the report.
- *Conclusions, discussion, and recommendations.* Provide answers to the basic evaluation questions and discuss the implications of the findings in this section of the re-

port. The strengths and weaknesses of the program should be identified as indicated by the results. The discussion of the findings can include subjective explanations and additional hypotheses suggested by the study's data. Recommendations for program modifications, and the nature of such modifications, should be presented along with the justifications based on the observed outcomes. These recommendations, supported by data and relevant to administrative and program decisions, are one of the most important parts of the report. This section may also include a discussion of the relationship between costs involved and the results achieved. Were the results worth the cost?

- *Appendixes.* Include materials that illustrate, describe, and support the other sections of the technical report as information for the reader. Forms and unpublished instruments should be appended as a matter of record (and for readers who may not be acquainted with the details of the methods used). Further, detailed descriptions of activities may be included in an appendix if their presentation in the body of the report would distract from the clarity and readability of the report.

Professional Reports. Reports of results evaluation for the professional and administrative staff and the board of education of a school district should be short and concise. Those interested in the details that support the professional report should be referred to the technical report. The professional report should include a brief summary of the findings, conclusions, and recommendations. Often most of this report can be taken directly from the conclusions, discussion, and recommendations section of the technical report. Statistical tables should be used only if absolutely necessary to document the results summarized. However, summary charts that symbolically or graphically show the results may be helpful. Technical language and reference to specific instruments should be avoided whenever possible. For example, it is better to say "the students had increased career awareness" than to say "the posttest scores on the vocational knowledge inventory were significantly larger than the pretest scores." This report should communicate in straightforward language what happened to students who participated in specific guidance and counseling activities. Uncluttered graphs or charts can be used effectively.

Report Cards. An example of a report card is the Support Personnel Accountability Report Card (SPARC). It was developed by personnel from the California Department of Education and the Los Angeles County Office of Education (2004). SPARC is a two-page document that provides space to report on 10 important aspects of a program, including principals' comments, school climate and safety, student support personnel team, student results, major achievements, parent volunteer involvement, measurements, focus for improvement, community partnerships/resources, and keeping you informed. As stated in the SPARC Web site (http://www.lacoe.edu/sparc/), the report card can be thought of as a "resume" of the program providing the opportunity to show case-relevant data to a wide range of audiences, all in two pages. Results data are featured.

Possible Unanticipated Side Effects

As results evaluation unfold, be alert to possible unanticipated side effects (C. D. Johnson, 1991). Sometimes guidance and counseling activities will create effects that were unforeseen when they were conducted initially. The results evaluation process used should be sensitive enough to pick up these effects so that they can be handled immediately or can be explained when they appear in later evaluation results.

Unanticipated outcomes may be positive or negative. On the one hand, student results may be achieved through the guidance curriculum but at an unusually high expense of students' time. The same may be true for the time of some teachers. On the other hand, some of the most valued outcomes of a guidance and counseling program may not have been stated in the original design. For example, attendance may have improved or the dropout rate may have declined.

Concluding Thoughts

Remember, a comprehensive guidance and counseling program is a student-driven program guided by the effective use of data. This means that the program improvement process is based on evaluation data. Thus, as the planning, designing, and implementing phases get under way, and during the time they are taking place, the activities involved and the guidance and counseling program frameworks and content that evolve need to be constructed and implemented on the basis of sound evaluation principles and procedures so that they can be evaluated. Thus the work completed in the first three phases of the improvement process must be done well so that the work involved in the evaluation phase can be completed in a similar manner. Demonstrating accountability through the measured effectiveness of the delivery of the guidance and counseling program and the performance of the guidance and counseling staff helps ensure that students, parents, teachers, administrators, and the general public will continue to benefit from quality comprehensive guidance programs.

Remember, too, that a major goal of results evaluation is to improve the activities and services provided to students, parents, teachers, the school, and the community. The data collected as a part of results evaluation provide feedback for improving the activities and services of a district's guidance program. How evaluation data are used to ensure quality comprehensive guidance and counseling programs is the subject of the next phase of the program change process—the enhancement phase discussed in chapter 11.

References

American School Counselor Association. (2005). *The ASCA national model: A framework for school counseling programs* (2nd ed.). Alexandria, VA: Author.

Bleuer-Collet, J. (1983). *Comprehensive guidance program design* [Fact sheet]. Ann Arbor, MI: ERIC Counseling and Personnel Services Clearinghouse.

Borders, L. D., & Drury, S. M. (1992). Comprehensive school counseling programs: A review for policy makers and practitioners. *Journal of Counseling & Development, 70,* 487–498.

Brigman, G., & Campbell, C. (2003). Helping students improve academic achievement and school success behavior. *Professional School Counseling, 7,* 91–98.

Bunch, L. K. (2002). Ensuring professionally relevant supervision and professional development: A state-level experience. In P. Henderson & N. Gysbers (Eds.), *Implementing comprehensive guidance programs: Critical leadership issues and successful responses* (pp. 193–198). Greensboro, NC: CAPS.

California Department of Education and the Los Angeles County Office of Education. (2004). *Support personnel accountability report card*. Los Angeles: Authors.

Christy, E. B., Stewart, F. J., & Rosecrance, F. C. (1930). Guidance in the senior high school. *The Vocational Guidance Magazine, 9,* 51–57.

Curcio, C. C., Mathai, C., & Roberts, J. (2003). Evaluation of a school district's secondary counseling program. *Professional School Counseling, 6,* 296–303.

Dahir, C. A., & Stone, C. B. (2003). Accountability: A M.E.A.S.U.R.E. of the impact school counselors have on student achievement. *Professional School Counseling, 6,* 214–221.

Des Moines Public Schools. (1994). *Smoother Sailing case studies summary report: 1993–94.* Des Moines, IA: Author.

Evans, J. H., & Burck, H. D. (1992). The effects of career education interventions on academic achievement: A meta-analysis. *Journal of Counseling & Development, 71,* 63–68.

Ferguson Middle School. (1990). *RAPP: Resolve all problems peacefully.* Florissant, MO: Ferguson-Florissant School District.

Froehlich, C. D. (1949). *Evaluating guidance procedures: A review of the literature.* Washington, DC: Federal Security Agency, Office of Education.

Gerler, E. R. (1985). Elementary school counseling research and the classroom learning environment. *Elementary School Guidance and Counseling, 20,* 39–48.

Gerler, E. R. (1992). What we know about school counseling: A reaction to Borders and Drury. *Journal of Counseling & Development, 70,* 499–501.

Goodrich, H. (1996). Understanding rubrics. *Educational Leadership, 54,* 14–1.

Gysbers, N. C. (2004). Comprehensive guidance and counseling programs: The evolution of accountability. *Professional School Counseling, 8,* 1–14.

Gysbers, N. C., & Henderson, P. (2000). *Developing and managing your school guidance program* (3rd ed.). Alexandria, VA: American Counseling Association.

Gysbers, N. C., Hughey, K. F., Starr, M., & Lapan, R. T. (1992). Improving school guidance programs: A framework for program, personnel, and results evaluation. *Journal of Counseling & Development, 70,* 565–570.

Gysbers, N. C., Kosteck-Bunch, L., Magnuson, C. S., & Starr, M. F. (2002). *Missouri comprehensive guidance program.* Columbia, MO: Instructional Materials Laboratory.

Gysbers, N. C., Lapan, R. T., Multon, K. D., & Lukin, L. E. (1992). *Missouri guidance competency evaluation survey: Grades 6–9, 9–12.* Columbia, MO: Center for Educational Assessment.

Henderson, P., & Gysbers, N. C. (1998). *Leading and managing your school guidance program staff.* Alexandria, VA: American Counseling Association.

Hinderman, R. A. (1930). Evaluating and improving guidance services. *Nations' Schools, 5,* 47–52.

Isaacs, M. L. (2003). Data-driven decision making: The engine of accountability. *Professional School Counseling, 6,* 288–295.

Johnson, C. D. (1991). Assessing results. In S. K. Johnson & E. A. Whitfield (Eds.), *Evaluating guidance programs: A practitioners guide* (pp. 43–55). Iowa City, IA: American College Testing Program.

Johnson, S. K., & Johnson, C. D. (1991). The new guidance: A system approach to pupil personnel programs. *CACD Journal, II,* 5–14.

Johnson, S. K., & Johnson, C. D. (2003). Results-based guidance: A systems approach to student support programs. *Professional School Counseling, 6,* 180–184.

Kefauver, G. N., & Hand, H. C. (1941). *Appraising guidance in secondary schools.* New York: Macmillan.

Krueger, R. A. (1994). *Focus groups* (2nd ed.). Thousand Oaks, CA: Sage.

Lapan, R. T., Gysbers, N. C., Multon, K. D., & Pike, G. R. (1997). Developing guidance competency self-efficacy scales for high school and middle school students. *Measurement and Evaluation in Counseling and Development, 30,* 4–16.

Lapan, R. T., Gysbers, N. C., & Petroski, G. (2001). Helping 7th graders be safe and academically successful: A statewide study of the impact of comprehensive guidance programs. *Journal of Counseling & Development, 75,* 292–302.

Lapan, R. T., Gysbers, N. C., & Sun, Y. (1997). The impact of more fully implemented guidance programs on the school experiences of high school students: A statewide evaluation study. *Journal of Counseling & Development, 75,* 292–302.

Lee, R. S. (1993). Effects of classroom guidance on student achievement. *Elementary Guidance and Counseling, 27*, 163–171.

Maliszewski, S. J. (1997). Developing a comprehensive guidance system in Omaha public schools. In N. C. Gysbers & P. Henderson (Eds.), *Comprehensive guidance programs that work—II*. Greensboro, NC: ERIC Counseling and Student Services Clearinghouse.

McGannon, W., Carey, J., & Dimmitt, C. (2005). *The current status of school counseling outcome research* (Research Monograph No. 2). Amherst: University of Massachusetts, School of Education, Center for School Counseling Outcome Research.

Missouri Department of Elementary and Secondary Education. (1998). *The box: Secondary 9–12*. Jefferson City, MO: Author.

Missouri Department of Elementary and Secondary Education. (2000). *Guidelines for performance-based professional school counselor evaluation*. Jefferson City, MO: Author.

Myrick, R. D. (2003a). Accountability: Counselors count. *Professional School Counseling, 6*, 174–179.

Myrick, R. D. (2003b). *Developmental guidance and counseling: A practical approach* (4th ed.). Minneapolis, MN: Educational Media Corporation.

Neidt, C. O. (1965). *Relation of guidance practices to student behavioral outcomes* (OE–5–99–222). Washington, DC: U.S. Department of Health, Education, and Welfare. (Mimeographed)

Nelson, D. E., & Gardner, J. L. (1998). *An evaluation of the comprehensive guidance program in Utah public schools*. Salt Lake City: Utah State Office of Education.

No Child Left Behind Act of 2001, Pub. L. No. 107–110, 115, Stat. 1434 (2001).

Northside Independent School District. (1987). *Guide to counselor performance improvement through supervision, evaluation, and professional development*. San Antonio, TX: Author.

Northside Independent School District. (1998). *Northside's comprehensive guidance program: Student and staff perceptions, 1995–98*. San Antonio, TX: Author.

Northside Independent School District. (2002). *Guide to counselor performance improvement through job definition, professionalism assessment, supervision, performance evaluation, and goal setting for professional development*. San Antonio, TX: Author.

Payne, A. F. (1924). Problems in vocational guidance. *National Vocational Guidance Association Bulletin, 2*, 61–63.

Proctor, W. M. (1930). Evaluating guidance activities in high schools. *The Vocational Guidance Magazine, 9*, 58–66.

Rain, B., Walker, J., & Jenkins, S. (n.d.). *Procedural manual: Resolve all problems peacefully*. Florissant, MO: Ferguson–Florissant School District.

Rosecrance, F. C. (1930). Organizing guidance for the larger school system. *The Vocational Guidance Magazine, 9*, 243–249.

Rothney, J. W. M. (1958). *Guidance practices and results*. New York: Harper.

Rothney, J. W. M., & Roens, B. A. (1950). *Guidance of American youth: An experimental study*. Cambridge, MA: Harvard University Press.

Sink, C. A., & Stroh, H. R. (2003). Raising achievement test scores of early elementary school students through comprehensive school counseling programs. *Professional School Counseling, 6*, 350–364.

St. Clair, K. L. (1989). Middle school counseling research: A resource for school counselors. *Elementary School Guidance Counseling, 23*, 219–226.

Sexton, T. L., Whiston, S. C., Bleuer, J. C., & Walz, G. R. (1997). *Integrating outcome research into counseling practice and training*. Alexandria, VA: American Counseling Association.

Synatschk, K. O. (2002). Ensuring professionally relevant supervision and professional development: A district-level experience. In P. Henderson & N. Gysbers (Eds.), *Implementing comprehensive guidance programs: Critical leadership issues and successful responses* (pp. 199–206). Greensboro, NC: CAPS.

Texas Counseling Association. (2004). *Texas evaluation model for professional school counselors* (2nd ed.). Austin, TX: Author.

Travers, R. M. W. (1949). A critical review of techniques for evaluating guidance. *Educational and Psychological Measurement, 9,* 211–225.

Utah State Office of Education. (1998). *Model for Utah comprehensive counseling and guidance programs.* Salt Lake City, UT: Author.

Utah State Office of Education. (2003). *Comprehensive guidance program performance review: Connecting program improvement and student learning.* Salt Lake City, UT: Author.

Wellman, F. E., & Moore, E. J. (1975). *Pupil personnel services: A handbook for program development and evaluation.* Washington, DC: U.S. Department of Health, Education, and Welfare.

Wilhelm, W. (1983). Career development in changing times. *Career Planning and Adult Development Journal, 1*(1), 9–14.

~ Part V ~

Enhancing

⌐ Chapter 11 ⌐

Redesigning Your Comprehensive Guidance and Counseling Program Based on Evaluation Data

Enhancing—Redesigning Your Comprehensive Guidance and Counseling Program

- Commit to the redesign process.
- Begin the redesign process.
- Gather updated needs information.
- Make redesign decisions based on evaluation data and new information.
- Implement the new design.
- Understand that revitalization follows redesign.

⌐ In chapter 2, the sample timetable of tasks suggests that after gathering program, personnel, and results evaluation data for several years, it is necessary to step back and rethink your entire program. It is time to consider redesigning it to incorporate any smaller revisions you have been making on a regular basis over time. Also, enough time has probably elapsed from the time you gathered student, school, and community data to the time you designed your original program that student needs and school and community circumstances have changed. We call this redesign process *program enhancement.*

Redesigning is based not only on conclusions drawn through evaluation but also on learnings from the passage of time in implementing your guidance and counseling program as well as on new realities that are currently present in your district and community. Redesigning the program periodically is how you ensure its relevancy for your students and for your schools and communities. Redesigning may lead to new or shifted priorities for the program's content, clients, and activities. It may also lead to new or shifted priorities for the use of school counselors' time and talent.

It is important to remember that the redesign process does not change the basic framework of the program as identified in chapter 3. The framework of the program found in the structural components and program components remains the same. What will change is the content of the program, the descriptions and assumptions of the program, the activities and services provided in the program, and the use of school counselor time and talent. Program and personnel priorities also will change.

In this chapter we first discuss the program redesign process: how often it occurs, and how it begins. The redesign process parallels the process used in the initial design of your comprehensive guidance and counseling program, as detailed in chapters 4 through 7. The second major topic of this chapter focuses on the uses of evaluation data to redesign your program paralleling the uses of data described in chapter 4, Assessing Your Current Guidance and Counseling Program. Third, redesigning—making new design decisions—is described as parallel to chapter 5, Designing the Comprehensive Guidance and Counseling Program. This chapter uses in its examples actual data gathered in a full-scale evaluation of the guidance and counseling program in Northside Independent School District (San Antonio, Texas) and shows how those data were used for redesign. Finally, strategies for preparing to implement a redesigned program are discussed and are parallel to planning for, making the transition to, and implementing the new program (chapters 6 and 7).

Commit to the Redesign Process

In thinking about redesigning a comprehensive guidance and counseling program, you need to answer three questions: How often should a program be redesigned? Who should be involved? What steps should be taken in the redesign process?

How Often Should a Program Be Redesigned?

Maintaining the quality of a program requires ongoing evaluation of program activities and their results. Every guidance and counseling program activity ends with a measure of its effectiveness in helping students learn or apply the guidance and counseling content that was the focus of the activity. Additionally, after every guidance and counseling curriculum lesson or unit, every guidance and counseling session aimed at assisting students' individual planning, and every counseling or consulting session held in response to a student's needs or parent's concerns, school counselors need to evaluate the activity's impact on students and parents and the quality and efficiency of the activity itself. In other words, each activity is evaluated as it is implemented, as described in chapter 10.

Continuous evaluation of program activities allows for ongoing monitoring and adjusting of the activities as the program is being implemented. If a guidance and counseling activity was not as effective as was hoped, then additional activities may be needed to ensure students' achievement of the desired outcomes. If, during a guidance and counseling session, for example, students were unable to complete action plans related to their personal goals, additional time and assistance may need to be provided (i.e., another activity in the near future). Many guidance and counseling program activities are annual events—done once a year. Thus if the implementation of an activity was not as streamlined or crisp as it might have been, determining how it could be more efficiently done next year is best done immediately after its conclusion this year. (Many details are forgotten in a year!)

In addition, the program should be reviewed annually according to the standards established in the program design. How closely did the program this year match the program's priorities for use of counselors' talent and time, for the student needs to be attended to, and for the program content and activities? The program as a whole should also be evaluated yearly regarding the match between the annual program plan and its actual implementation. The results of these evaluations should lead to ongoing revisions in the content, activities, and services of the program. Also, the quality of school counselors' performance and the measure of how they are spending their time should be evaluated continuously by themselves and their staff leaders (Henderson & Gysbers, 1998). At least once a year, formal personnel performance evaluations need to be completed.

While the evaluation of your guidance and counseling program, its personnel, and its results is ongoing and leads to regular revisions, program redesign is periodic. We recommend that the redesign of your program should take place every 8 to 10 years or as frequently as your school district reviews and updates any of its programs. In some districts this is on a 5-year cycle. In addition, program redesign may occur more or less frequently depending on how fast the context in which a program occurs changes or on other indicators that suggest how the guidance and counseling program might better meet the needs of students. Schools and school districts change their priorities as new educational reforms come to their attention, as new academic or behavioral goals for students surface, and for myriad reasons. As integral parts of their school systems, guidance and counseling programs need to have their priorities assessed on a timely basis to ensure alignment with the bigger systems in which they operate and with the district's school improvement plan.

Who Should Be Involved?

Redesigning your guidance and counseling program requires the same attention and thoroughness as was required in creating the initial design. Major changes require major efforts. Quick fixes and simple solutions disrupt program designs. They often add activities or consume time without consideration being given as to what activities will be replaced or streamlined to make room in the design for them. Redesigning a program is best done using the same program development steps that were taken the first time.

As in creating the initial design for a comprehensive guidance and counseling program, three different groups are involved in the redesign process: the steering committee, the school–community advisory committee, and work groups. The steering committee consists of individuals who support and implement the program. It includes school counselors who make up or represent the guidance leadership team and district-level administrators who manage programs that use the guidance program and staff and that provide resources to the program. Building-level representatives include principals and teachers. The steering committee guides the process and makes recommendations about the program, its structure, and priorities. Their recommendations are forwarded to district policy and administrative decision makers.

The school–community advisory committee, as you will remember from chapter 2, consists of program consumers: students, parents, teachers, and community members. Committee members may be representatives from student councils, from PTAs, from building site-based management committees, and from the business and mental health communities. They make suggestions from the perspectives of the groups they represent regarding the rationale for the program, possible priorities to be addressed in the program, and new directions they see in the schools of the district and in the community at large.

The work groups involve as many school counselors as possible. (Remember our adage: Never use one when two will do!) These groups assist in analyzing the evaluation data that describe the status of the current program, show the results of the program, and point out trends in the larger context of the school and community. They identify new and continuing needs of groups of students. They do much of the legwork in presenting data and information to the steering committee.

What Steps Should be Taken?

The redesign process is a major undertaking, and its steps mirror those used in the initial development of your program: getting organized, planning, designing, planning the transition, and implementing the new program design. Table 11.1 provides an overview of this redesign process.

As the steering committee proceeds through the phases of the program redesign process, its members consider evaluation data in the context of the initial program design, current realities, and new design possibilities. These considerations lead to new design decisions, such as new program priorities and new parameters for resource allocations. Evaluation data are provided to the steering committee regarding the use of counselors' talent and time, the program balance and activities conducted, the students served (by subpopulations), and the content outcomes addressed and achieved. Information is also provided regarding the other elements of your comprehensive guidance and counseling program: the structural components (chapter 3) and the resources appropriated, including the funding sources for the various aspects of the program.

Current realities are identified by data from the three kinds of evaluation (program, personnel, and results) and from new school and community information as well. Given that school counselors are making every effort to adhere to the originally established program priorities and parameters, areas in which evaluation data suggest good and bad matches with the desired design indicate a force that we are calling reality. Good matches indicate that the original design fits the realities (needs, goals, time parameters) of the school. Bad matches indicate that the original design may not be feasible. The steering committee, for example, may have set priorities for the topics or areas to be addressed through planned

Table 11.1

Program Redesign Process

Getting Organized
- Review external sources regarding status of guidance and counseling and in district/school personnel, results, and program evaluation data
- Secure commitment to redesign
- Convene guidance and counseling leadership team
- Identify need for redesign
- Develop redesign plan
- Form guidance and counseling steering committee, school–community advisory committee
- Develop student needs assessment strategy
- Gather input re: program improvement needs

Planning
- Review recent history of program development and implementation
- Reconfirm commitment to program model
- Assess students' and other clients' needs
- Discuss new contextual information
- Revise structural components: rationale, assumptions, definition
- Analyze evaluation data as current status assessment

Redesigning
- Revise qualitative design: priorities for student results, balance for client services, operational standards for components (program delivery), priorities for counselor competency use
- Revise quantitative design: program balance, ratio

Planning Transition
- Gather input to final draft of the redesigned program
- Gather additional data regarding redesigned program dimensions
- Rewrite comprehensive guidance and counseling program framework
- List final recommendations for program improvement
- Recommend district/campus program development process

Implementing the Redesigned Program
- Return to the Designing—Planning the Transition (chapter 6) and Implementing—Making the Transition (chapter 7) sets of tasks and subsequent tasks in the initial installation plan

---

activities in the responsive services component, but program evaluation data may indicate that in the last several years school counselors spent a portion of their time working in an area that was not even on the list. In Northside Independent School District, for example, evaluation data uncovered such an area in problems stemming from racial/ethnic tension and from the lack of student and staff effectiveness in cross-cultural situations.

Redesign possibilities are suggested by external sources and by increased experience in comprehensive guidance and counseling program implementation. These sources suggest national, state, or local trends in school guidance and counseling, in education, in the school district, and in the community. For Northside Independent School District, in the 1990s for example, external stimuli were provided by the Texas Education Agency's (1991) publication of *The Comprehensive Guidance Program for Texas Public Schools* and by several national and state reports regarding reform of elementary and secondary schools (e.g., the National Association of Secondary School Principal's *Breaking Ranks,* 1996). The Texas publication represented a statewide perspective regarding student needs and expectations for school counselors' performance. The school reform reports suggested trends regarding the future mission, strategies, and organizational structures of schools. In addition, during that time period the Northside Independent School District had undergone a fairly rigorous strategic planning exercise and had outlined 10 strategies for advancing the district's mission. Three of the strategies had direct implications for priorities within the comprehensive guidance and counseling program: establishing a system for student goal setting, implementing a student advisory system, and assisting schools to be safe and drug free.

At the beginning of the 21st century, there are newer publications that could be used to spur schools' and districts' redesigning efforts. Some states have updated their comprehensive guidance and counseling program models, for example, Texas (Texas Education Agency, 2004). The American School Counselor Association (ASCA) has established national standards for guidance and counseling program content (Campbell & Dahir, 1997) and a framework for school counseling programs (ASCA, 2005). Other associations continue to recommend reforms that would cause the improvement of schools, for example, the National Association of Secondary School Principals' *Breaking Ranks II* (2004).

Begin the Redesign Process

As mentioned at the beginning of this chapter, redesigning the program parallels the Planning—Conducting a Thorough Assessment of the Current Program set of tasks in the initial program development process (chapter 4). In anticipating program redesign, the steering committee and other decision makers have the benefit of evaluation data. They also have new information regarding newly identified student and school–community needs, shifts in school building and district goals, and emerging professional trends.

This section first discusses analyzing program, personnel, and results evaluation data and then gathering the updated information on needs and trends, both qualitative and quantitative, that redesigners of comprehensive guidance and counseling programs require. Throughout this section, data gathered in evaluations of Northside Independent School District's comprehensive guidance and counseling program during the time period 1995 to 1998 illustrate the use of data to guide program redesign. (See Figure 11.1 for the data they collected in executive summary form.)

Studying the data drawn from the three kinds of evaluation arms you with information as to what is or is not happening, and what is or is not working as well as it should. In terms of the qualitative design for the program, evaluation data provide insights regarding the quality of performance levels of the school counselors, which clients (e.g., students, teachers, parents) are being served and in what priority by the current program, the

Figure 11.1
Comprehensive Guidance Program: Executive Summary

Background

Four years ago, the Superintendent requested an evaluation of Northside's Guidance Program. Over the past 4 years over 17,000 3rd–12th grade students, over 1,450 teachers, and all counselors were surveyed on impact and benefit of the district's Comprehensive Guidance Program.

Findings

Below are two graphs that summarize the overall results.

Conclusions

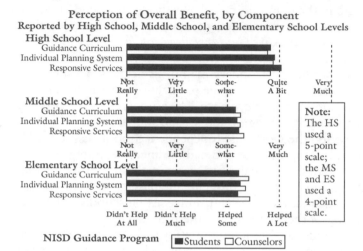

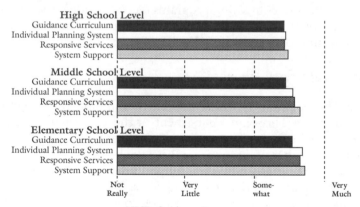

✓ **This is a comprehensive program.** The Guidance Program Framework is a model that is designed to provide a consistent, comprehensive program across the levels. It appears that is happening.

✓ **The overall benefit is substantial.** The differences between levels or components are relatively small.

✓ **The perceived level of benefit is very similar among the three most knowledgeable stakeholders:**
  • the client—the students;
  • the service provider—the counselors; and
  • the most aware third party—the teachers.

✓ **The program's benefit is stable over time.** Data were collected over a 4-year period at three distinct levels with nine different surveys. Yet the level of benefit remains consistent.

Note. From *Northside's Comprehensive Guidance Program: Student and Staff Perceptions 1995–98,* 1998, by Northside Independent School District, San Antonio, TX: Author. Reprinted with permission.

level of alignment with the program standards for activities, and the results attained by students. In terms of the quantitative design for the program, evaluation data provide information about the actual balance of the program (i.e., counselors' time spent in activities associated with the four program components), the actual counselor–student ratios and their impact on program implementation, and the actual (or approximate) numbers of students and other clients served through the currently desired/implemented design.

Qualitative Design Data

The qualitative data used in the redesign process include school counselor performance, clients served, program component standards, and student results.

School Counselor Performance

The strengths and weaknesses of the school guidance and counseling staff as a whole may be learned from aggregating the relative strengths and weaknesses of individual school counselors as reflected in the evaluations of their performance. The more closely aligned the school counselor performance evaluation form is with the program, the more relevant the conclusions will be. As discussed in chapter 10, analysis of performance evaluation data from a form that records evaluations according to program component tells you whether school counselors perform competently in the activities provided in guidance curriculum, individual student planning, responsive services, and system support. It tells you in which components the performance of school counselors is strongest or weakest. For example, school counselors may be most competent in providing responsive services and least competent in providing guidance curriculum. This tells you and your program decision makers that their performance is best when they are providing counseling and consultation services but not as effective when they are providing guidance instruction.

If the school guidance and counseling staff is large, there probably will be great variance in performance across the school levels. Elementary counselors may be evaluated as better at guidance curriculum work and high school counselors as better at individual student planning work. There may also be variances within levels. For example, some middle school counselors may be evaluated as better at small-group counseling than other middle school counselors.

Clients Served

Evaluations can be designed to tell you who is actually being served with which program activities. Not only can you determine the numbers of students, teachers, parents, and others involved, but you can also determine the balance of time spent among them. Subgroup information may be gathered as well, such as the level of participation in program activities by students in the various grade levels in a building, or across the district among buildings. This latter information tells you the implemented priorities for the current program. Tables 11.2 to 11.5 display data gathered for evaluation purposes and reported in *Northside's Comprehensive Guidance Program: Student and Staff Perceptions: 1995–98* (Northside Independent School District, 1998).

Table 11.2 presents data regarding the percentage of counselor time spent with each of three broad categories of clients: students, adults, and the system. The percentages depicted are the modal (most frequent) responses of the school counselors surveyed. They revealed that 50% of counselor time was spent with students, 20% with adults, and 10% in organizational duties. In the original program design, the desired balance between student and adult clients was 60% students to 40% adults. By comparing the desired balance with the data gathered on actual time spent, it is clear that adults were underserved.

Table 11.2
Client Category and Counselor Time

Client	% Counselor Time
With students	50
With adults	20
In organizational duties	10

Note. Data from *Northside's Comprehensive Guidance Program: Student and Staff Perceptions: 1995–98,* by Northside Independent School District, 1998, San Antonio, TX: Author. Adapted with permission.

Table 11.3 presents data regarding the percentage of elementary school students who reported meeting with their school counselors in activities according to the major school counselor–student configurations. In the original program design, all elementary children were to have participated in classroom guidance. Apparently 2% did not. This piece of data evokes the question, "Why not?" Breaking the data apart further, Table 11.4 displays the data by specific grade levels. The percentage of students participating in classroom guidance appeared to have declined as they moved up the grades. At the same time, the fifth graders' participation in small groups and one-on-one interactions with school counselors increased. These differences in services for each of the grade levels were not called for in the initial program design, suggesting the question, "Should this be the design or not?"

Table 11.5 presents similar data gathered from middle school students. Again, older students participated in fewer classroom guidance activities than did younger students. In this instance, however, a significantly larger percentage of eighth graders participated in individual student planning activities. If this matches the intent of the original design for the program, this balance of client services/component is appropriate.

Program Component Standards

As discussed in chapter 10, there are multiple ways to evaluate to what degree the implemented comprehensive guidance and counseling program meets the standards set out in the qualitative design for each program component. The design standards for each component state the priorities for guidance content addressed through program activities, the roles carried out by school counselors within component activities, and how the activities are conducted. School counselors should evaluate their entire program against the full set of standards on a regular basis. The aggregation of these data informs the redesign process.

Annual studies that ask school counselors to compare and contrast their yearly plan for activities with the activities actually conducted also keep everyone aware of emerging needs and new trends. Assessment of the attainment of program improvement goals provides two sets of information considered by the steering committee and other groups assisting in

Table 11.3
Elementary Student Participation

Configuration	% Students
As part of an entire class	98
As part of a small group	37
One-on-one	25
In a student/parent/counselor conference	5
In a student/teacher/counselor conference	5
In a student/counselor/social service conference	5

Note. Data from *Northside's Comprehensive Guidance Program: Student and Staff Perceptions: 1995–98,* by Northside Independent School District, 1998, San Antonio, TX: Author. Adapted with permission.

Table 11.4
Elementary Student Participation by Grade Level

Configuration	% 3rd Graders	% 4th Graders	% 5th Graders
As part of an entire class	99	98	97
As part of a small group	37	36	40
One-on-one	27	28	30
In a student/parent/counselor conference	5	4	5
In a student/teacher/counselor conference	3	5	6
In a student/counselor/social service conference	5	4	7

Note. Data from *Northside's Comprehensive Guidance Program: Student and Staff Perceptions: 1995–98,* by Northside Independent School District, 1998, San Antonio, TX: Author. Adapted with permission.

the redesign process. First, the choices for improvement themselves, when grouped, suggest improvement needs across school levels or within school buildings. Second, their aggregated levels of accomplishment can suggest the feasibility of adding/augmenting/streamlining/displacing activities districtwide. For example, expanding small-group counseling within responsive services is often a high priority in districts adapting a comprehensive guidance and counseling program. Annual reports that tell the number of small groups provided in each building, the topics they addressed, the numbers of students served through them, and the apparent quantity and level of attainment of the goals and objectives for the groups are useful pieces of information—especially when the groups are offered on the basis of assessments of students' and staff members' current needs.

When the district has set content priorities for the program, reports of activities completed to address these can (should) be submitted and totaled. For example, in Northside Independent School District, the districtwide strategic-plan-related guidance and counseling program content priorities were goal setting, conflict management, and substance abuse education and prevention. Annual reports by school counselors by building inform the district about such things as the numbers of school staff members who participated in goal-setting training and used goal-setting processes in their teaching and for themselves. The growth or decline in participation levels informs your district-level decision makers about adherence to their standards for student participation on the one hand, and the value placed on these priorities at the local level on the other hand.

One way to assess to what degree school counselors are fulfilling their assigned roles appropriately, as conceived by your original program designers, is to study the proportion of time they spend conducting activities in various configurations of meeting clients. Table 11.6 displays data gathered in Northside Independent School District's evaluation. Asking students if they met with their counselor as part of an entire class addressed school counselors' fulfillment of their developmental guidance role. Meeting as part of a small group addressed the group counseling role, meeting one-on-one addressed individual counseling, and so on.

Table 11.5
Middle School Student Participation by Grade Level

Component	% 6th Graders	% 7th Graders	% 8th Graders
Guidance curriculum	26	27	15
Individual student planning	21	25	37
Responsive services	15	9	19

Note. Data from *Northside's Comprehensive Guidance Program: Student and Staff Perceptions: 1995–98,* by Northside Independent School District, 1998, San Antonio, TX: Author. Adapted with permission.

Table 11.6
Program Delivery Modes by Counselor Time

Configuration	% Counselor Time
With an entire class	40
With a small group	20
One-on-one	20
In a student/parent/counselor conference	5
In a student/teacher/counselor conference	5
In a student/counselor/social service conference	5

Note. Data from *Northside's Comprehensive Guidance Program: Student and Staff Perceptions: 1995–98,* by Northside Independent School District, 1998, San Antonio, TX: Author. Adapted with permission.

Tables 11.3, 11.4, and 11.5 display the numbers of students served through guidance and counseling program activities. Table 11.6 displays the time spent by school counselors in each of the configurations, providing information as to how closely aligned their practice is to the original priorities established for the application of their talent. Clearly, the actual priorities displayed in Table 11.6 tell us that they applied their guidance and counseling skills with equal priority (40% each) and that their use of their counseling skills was split evenly between individuals and groups (20% each). The application of their consultation skills aggregated to the third priority (15%) and was evenly divided among parents, teachers, and social service agency personnel. In this example, the priorities matched those set out originally for the school counselors, which tells us that the school counselors were accomplishing their roles appropriately and informs the program redesigners that these priorities seem to be working.

Compliance with standards established for the guidance and counseling program components is important information, as is information that suggests how valuable this adherence is. For example, not only is it important to know that school counselors are conducting activities in all four program components, but it is also important to know how helpful these activities are to the students and other program clients. Table 11.7 displays information from one part of the Northside Independent School District evaluation study in which students were asked to rate the helpfulness of specific services/activities. These activities were grouped by program component and the ratings aggregated. The mean ratings are displayed in Table 11.7.

Table 11.7
Helpfulness of Component Activities

School Level and Program Component	Mean Rating
High school	(5-point scale)
Guidance curriculum	3.82
Individual student planning	3.90
Responsive services	4.03
Middle school	(4-point scale)
Guidance curriculum	3.15
Individual student planning	3.20
Responsive services	3.23
Elementary school	(4-point scale)
Guidance curriculum	3.24
Individual student planning	3.27
Responsive services	3.22

Note. Data from *Northside's Comprehensive Guidance Program: Student and Staff Perceptions: 1995–98,* by Northside Independent School District, 1998, San Antonio, TX: Author. Adapted with permission.

These data were gathered from 17,000 students from 3rd through 12th grade. The words attached to the numbers gave district decision makers a better sense of what the mean numbers meant. On the high school survey, the 3 meant *somewhat helpful,* the 4 meant *quite a bit.* On the middle and elementary school surveys, the 3 meant *helped some,* the 4 meant *a lot.* The finding by the district's program evaluation specialist was that "the overall benefit is substantial" (Northside Independent School District, 1998). Additionally, the district learned that activities in each of the three direct service delivery components were appreciated by students and that their levels of appreciation were equivalent at all three school levels.

Student Results

The content priorities of the program were also assessed in the Northside study. Tables 11.8, 11.9, and 11.10 display the percentages of students helped according to the content priorities within each program component. Table 11.8 displays the content taught through guidance curriculum activities; Table 11.9, the topics addressed through the guidance activities of the individual student planning; and Table 11.10, the topics for which responsive services were needed/provided. The numbers of students indicated the priorities as delivered by the school counselors (and remembered by the students).

Within the guidance curriculum component (see Table 11.8), helping students be responsible for their education, learn to make decisions, and set goals were the district's highest priorities for the middle and high school levels. At the elementary levels the substance abuse prevention curriculum was the number one priority, followed closely by getting along with others, goal setting, and decision making.

Within the individual student planning component (see Table 11.9), different priorities were evident at each of the three levels. There were more educational opportunities for high school students to consider than at the other two levels. Selecting courses was a new experience for middle school students; handling peer pressure was very important. Within this component, career exploration was developmentally appropriate for elementary children, while some of the other planning topics were not.

By their nature, responsive services address needs felt by students (see Table 11.10). As such, the actual content priority information from the Northside study assisted district decision makers to identify the problems and issues for which students sought help from their school counselors. Their degree of satisfaction regarding the results achieved indicated their value as well. Of the topics addressed, 85% to 95% of the high school students said they were helped *very much, quite a bit,* or *somewhat;* less than 5% on any one topic said *not really.* Of the topics addressed, 70% to 85% of the middle school students said they were helped *very much* or *somewhat* on all of the topics; less than 5% to 8% on any one topic said *not really.* On all of the topics addressed, elementary school students on the average were helped between *some* to *a lot.*

How many teachers benefit from activities in the system support component is valuable information for your program redesigners as well. Table 11.11 displays the percentage of teachers at each school level who benefited from the various guidance program management and support services provided through Northside's comprehensive guidance and counseling program.

Quantitative Design Data

Three sets of evaluation data are related to the quantitative design: the actual balance of the programs, the actual counselor–student ratio, and the actual numbers of students and other clients served through the program. How closely the building programs are aligned with the originally established design can be determined separately. And, if the alignments

Table 11.8
Actual Content Priorities by School Level: Guidance
Curriculum

School Level and Topics	% Students Participating
High school	
Responsibility for education	70
Decision making	58
Goal setting	51
Managing change	28
Accepting consequences	25
Managing feelings	19
Taking responsibility	15
Coping with peers	12
Understanding others' actions	11
Middle school	
Responsibility for education	51
Decision making	48
Goal setting	45
Accepting consequences	36
Coping with peers	36
Managing change	33
Taking responsibility	33
Understanding others' actions	32
Managing feelings	31
Elementary school	
What drugs can do to you	84
Getting along with others	83
Goal setting	82
Decision making	81
Getting along with others at school	79
Taking responsibility	65
Making friends	63
Identifying your feelings	55
Expressing your feelings	52
Respecting all cultural heritages	45

Note. Data from *Northside's Comprehensive Guidance Program: Student and Staff Perceptions: 1995–98,* by Northside Independent School District, 1998, San Antonio, TX: Author. Adapted with permission.

are fairly close, some inferences may be drawn about the overall impact of the balance of activities and the ratio on the numbers of clients served by interrelating the data.

Program Balance

Data had been gathered annually from the school counselors in each of Northside Independent School District's buildings regarding the percentage of time they spent in activities associated with the four program components. These data were used to compare and contrast the quality of program implementation across the various buildings of the district and, if there was consistency, to compare and contrast the districtwide aggregated data with the original design of the district's comprehensive guidance and counseling program goal.

If most of the buildings at a school level implement balanced programs but a few do not, the few that do not should be studied more closely to determine the reasons for their being out of alignment. If the differences are due to student needs, some consideration to these causes is in order. If the differences are due to lack of understanding of or adherence to the district program, attention should be given to the program leadership.

If most of the buildings at a school level are out of alignment with the originally established design, then the design should be reexamined. The original design maybe flawed.

Table 11.9

Actual Content Priorities by School Level: Individual Student Planning

School Level and Topics	% Students Participating
High school	
Providing information on educational opportunities	62
Selecting courses	61
Setting challenging educational goals	38
Setting short-/long-term goals	34
Establishing personal goals	29
Relating jobs to your traits	26
Career/vocational planning	24
Time management	17
Handling peer pressure	13
Middle school	
Selecting courses	51
Handling peer pressure	45
Providing information on educational opportunities	42
Setting challenging educational goals	39
Relating careers to your traits	38
Setting short-/long-term goals	38
Establishing personal goals	35
Time management	29
Career/vocational exploration	27
Elementary school	
Exploring career interests	61
Setting personal goals	52
Dealing with changes at school	41
Identifying your strengths/weaknesses	36

Note. Data from *Northside's Comprehensive Guidance Program: Student and Staff Perceptions: 1995–98,* by Northside Independent School District, 1998, San Antonio, TX: Author. Adapted with permission.

If the design is not flawed, then the obstacles to implementing the design need to be identified and considered as problems to be solved.

If most of the buildings at a school level implement programs that are balanced similarly, then evaluation of the degree of program alignment can be made, accompanied by analysis of why or why not the programs are in or out of alignment with the desired design. For example, in Northside Independent School District's redesign process, the steering committee considered the data presented in Table 11.12. The table displays the districtwide average for program balances as it was in 1983 before the implementation of a comprehensive guidance and counseling program and with the desired balance established in 1985 during the initial program design process. Much work was clearly needed to reach the desired percentages of time established when the original design was developed.

In addition, Table 11.12 displays the districtwide average program balance at the start of the redesign process in 1992 for comparison and contrast with the original current and desired program balances. Major changes in the shape of the programs at the three levels are evidenced by comparing and contrasting the initial status of the program with that of 1992. Analyzing the data in relationship to the initial desired design raised some questions. Guidance curriculum time had increased at all three levels, especially at the elementary level. The middle and high school levels were making progress but had a long way to go to align themselves with the initial design. With group work replacing individual work, individual student planning activity time had decreased significantly at the elementary and middle school levels; but with these shifts, they were farther out of alignment with what had been thought to be desirable. Responsive services time had increased significantly at the middle and high school levels, making them farther out of alignment than initially.

Table 11.10
Actual Content Priorities by School Level: Responsive Services

School Level and Topics	% Students Participating
High school	
Understanding test results	45
Listening	28
Dealing with academic problems	24
Dealing with a personal, private issue	18
Dealing with stress	15
Providing information on community services	15
Dealing with grief/loss	12
Conference with parents	9
Dealing with behavior problems	8
Dealing with health-related problems	6
Dealing with drug/alcohol problem	3
Middle school	
Understanding test results	39
Listening	35
Dealing with stress	26
Dealing with behavior problems	26
Dealing with grief/loss	25
Dealing with health-related problems	22
Dealing with academic problems	22
Dealing with a personal, private issue	21
Providing information on community services	21
Conference with parents	16
Dealing with drug/alcohol problem	11
Elementary school	
Getting along with others	35
Understanding feelings	28
Controlling anger	25
Making friends	25
Behaving correctly in school	24
Feeling better about yourself	23
Dealing with changes in your family	23
Dealing with sadness	22
Dealing with death of someone you knew/loved	19

Note. Data from *Northside's Comprehensive Guidance Program: Student and Staff Perceptions: 1995–98,* by Northside Independent School District, 1998, San Antonio, TX: Author. Adapted with permission.

System support time had changed significantly at the high school level but not at the elementary and middle school levels. None of the levels approximated the desired design time appropriation.

After analyzing the data and drawing conclusions, the steering committee made recommendations for what members should consider when they approached program redesign. These recommendations are summarized as follows.

- Considerations for elementary schools

  Guidance curriculum: Lower ratios to entail fewer classes resulting in reduced percentages.

  Individual student planning: Lower the desired percentage.

  Responsive services: Increase the desired percentage.

  System support: Assign other personnel some of the major activities that indirectly serve students.

- Considerations for middle schools

  Guidance curriculum: Lower the desired percentage (two lessons per grading period is 16%).

    Individual student planning: [None]
    Responsive services: Increase the desired percentage.
    System support: Realign the assignment of indirect services to other departments.

- Considerations for high schools
    Guidance curriculum: Lower the desired percentage.
    Individual student planning: [None]
    Responsive services   Increase the desired percentage.
    System support: Realign administrative tasks to administration or other departments.

- General consideration
Suggest a range of percentages for buildings to work within.

As a result of these discussions, the representatives of each of the levels at Northside drafted the tentative program design displayed in Table 11.13. It is interesting to compare and contrast these tentative thoughts prevalent at the time of this discussion with the final thoughts of the group after considering all of the evaluation data and updated information, and after finalizing the qualitative design for the program (see later, Table 11.20).

At this point, the desired balances presented by the middle and high school committees were in ranges of percentages they suggested, providing some flexibility to the buildings. In addition, nonguidance activities were included as a category of their own, distinct from system support. This distinction was made because staff members had (finally) learned to differentiate between support tasks that applied their professional competencies and those that did not. *System support* was used to describe the former, *nonguidance* the latter.

Counselor–Student Ratio

To evaluate the adequacy of the counselor–student ratios in effect at the time of redesigning your program, you may conduct comparison studies of the results and levels of service in

Table 11.11
Teachers Benefiting From Program Management and System Support by Topic and School Level

	% Elementary School Teachers	% Middle School Teachers	% High School Teachers
Guidance program management			
Standards	66	93	60
Professionalism		95	62
Techniques	65		
Program	64	79	50
Grade appropriate	62		
Facilities/equipment		62	
Student education and career planning			62
System support services			
Referral	63	70	45
Parent education	63		
Consultation	60	85	58
Parent consultation	56	80	50
Testing program		97	70
Collaboration		92	60
Schoolwide		90	
Test interpretation		86	65
Information sharing		63	35
Goal integration		48	30
Coordinated community services		45	30

Note. Data from *Northside's Comprehensive Guidance Program: Student and Staff Perceptions: 1995–98,* by Northside Independent School District, 1998, San Antonio, TX: Author. Adapted with permission.

Table 11.12
Appropriations of Counselors' Time

Program Component and School Level	Current Allocation (1983)	Desired Allocation (1985)	Current Allocation (1992)
Guidance curriculum			
Elementary school	7	40	40
Middle school	8	30	12
High school	5	25	10
Individual student planning			
Elementary school	37	25	5
Middle school	29	30	18
High school	27	30	25
Responsive services			
Elementary school	28	25	30
Middle school	31	25	40
High school	28	30	40
System support			
Elementary school	20	10	25
Middle school	32	15	30
High school	40	15	25

Note. Data from *Northside's Comprehensive Guidance Program Framework* by Northside Independent School District, 1994, San Antonio, TX: Author. Adapted with permission.

buildings with significantly different ratios. Using the mathematical model described in chapter 8 (see "Recognizing Potential" section) and applying the actual ratio information within the program balance actually implemented, you can estimate the differences in services resulting from different-sized student caseloads. Examples of Northside Independent School District's "realities" are given in Tables 11.14, 11.15, and 11.16 to illustrate the point.

The first ratio (350:1) represents the standard recommended by the ASCA (1993) at that time. The second (400:1) represents the average ratio used in counselor allocations for the district. The third ratio represents the actual caseload of the school counselor with

Table 11.13
Revised Desired Program Balance—Tentative

School Level and Program Component	%
Elementary school	
Guidance curriculum	35
Individual student planning	5
Responsive services	40
System support	20
Nonguidance	0
Middle school	
Guidance curriculum	10–15
Individual student planning	15–20
Responsive services	30–45
System support	25–35
Nonguidance	0
High school	
Guidance curriculum	10–15
Individual student planning	30–35
Responsive services	40–45
System support	0–15
Nonguidance	0

Note. Data from Northside Independent School District, San Antonio, TX: Author. Adapted with permission.

Table 11.14
Elementary School Service Levels: Impact of Student–Counselor Ratios

Program Component	Current Balance (Range Midpoint)	Service	Service Levels at:		
			Recommended Ratio 350:1	Current Average Ratio 400:1	Current Maximum Ratio 486:1
Guidance curriculum	32.5%	Guidance lessons per week[a]	1.6	1.4	1
Individual student planning	7.5%	Advisement minutes per student per year	15	13.5	11
Responsive services	42.5%	% caseload receiving services	36	31.5	26
System support	17.5%	Consultation minutes per teacher per week[a]	20	18	15

Note. Data from Northside Independent School District, San Antonio, TX: Author. Adapted with permission.
[a] 6 days per schedule week.

the highest number of students at that school level. The balance applied to the numbers is that tentatively set by the steering committee for use in the redesigned program. As explained in chapter 8, the amount of time estimated for each activity within that component varies by school levels. In our examples, we use 30 minutes for elementary activities, 45 minutes for middle school activities, and 55 for high school activities. The example levels of services do not, of course, cover all actual services provided in a program component but assume the primary service to the primary client of that component's activities.

These numbers make it clear that the levels of both student and teacher participation in the program are higher with smaller caseloads. At the elementary level, with the maximum actual caseload, 26% of the students could participate in responsive services, but that could increase by 10% with the recommended 350:1. Twenty minutes per teacher per week end up to be significantly more time per teacher per year than 15 minutes per week. At the middle school level, 22 counselor-led guidance lessons per year cover two thirds of the 36 weeks in the school year, but 18 cover only half. And, 5% more of the students could receive responsive services. At the high school level, in addition to these added benefits, each student could have 14 more minutes per year of assistance in individual student planning. When aggregated with groups of students, these 14 minutes result in several more activities per grade level per year.

Numbers of Students Served

A basic decision to wrestle with in the redesign process is the choice between a developmental guidance and counseling program and a program that is responsive to students' problems and concerns. Making this choice requires having a sense of what students need to make the best of their educational opportunities and knowing how school counselors can best be used to help them. In Northside Independent School District's original comprehensive guidance program design, the developmental guidance program components were assigned top priority at all three levels (guidance curriculum at elementary level and individual student planning at middle and high school levels).

Table 11.15
Middle School Service Levels: Impact of Student–Counselor Ratios

Program Component	Current Balance (Range Midpoint)	Service	Service Levels at:		
			Recommended Ratio 350:1	Current Average Ratio 400:1	Current Maximum Ratio 432:1
Guidance curriculum	20%	Guidance lessons per year	22	18	18
Individual student planning	20%	Advisement minutes per student per year	42	36	34
Responsive services	42.5%	% caseload receiving services	26	22.5	21
System support	20%	Consultation minutes per teacher per week	18	16	15

Note. Data from Northside Independent School District, San Antonio, TX: Author. Adapted with permission.

During program implementation, school counselors and administrators may feel pressured by those with needs that are not fully met through the program design. School counselors are particularly aware of the problems and issues that students face. In Northside Independent School District's evaluation efforts, data on the numbers of students served through responsive services component activities were gathered periodically. The guidance leadership team and the steering committee studied the actual percentage of students receiving the most common and manageable services in 1 year, as displayed in Table 11.17.

These data reflected total numbers of students served, not individual students. Thus, that 170% of the middle school students participated in individual counseling suggests that the majority of students participated more than once in either planned responsive or reactive individual counseling. Small-group counseling is planned and duplication of services avoided as much as possible; therefore to say that 24% of the elementary students, 19% of middle schoolers, and 14% of high schoolers participated may be an overestimate, but not by much. As you draw conclusions from your evaluation data and consider redesign possibilities, you will need to consider the variance in what constitutes responsive services at each of the school levels.

From the evaluation data gathered, the steering committee can identify where the program is working well and where it is not. Committee members have to determine whether where the program is working is still important and whether the program as originally designed should be maintained. Committee members also have to decide whether where the program is not working is still a priority and, therefore, should be targeted for improvement, or whether that program area should be replaced by something more appropriate.

Gather Updated Needs Information

For the redesign process to be effective, updated information is required regarding newly identified student needs as well as regarding the current community context of the program. Clear ideas about the current and future goals and school improvement plans of your school district and its buildings, and about trends in the school counseling profession that suggest new ways of accomplishing new goals, are needed. You will also use qualitative de-

Table 11.16
High School Service Levels: Impact of Student–Counselor Ratios

Program Component	Current Balance (Range Midpoint)	Service	Service Levels at:		
			Recommended Ratio 350:1	Current Average Ratio 400:1	Current Maximum Ratio 486:1
Guidance curriculum	10%	Guidance lessons per year	10	9	8
Individual student planning	32.5%	Advisement minutes per student per year	68	59	54
Responsive services	42.5%	% caseload receiving services	25	22	20
System support	12.5%	Consultation minutes per teacher per week	15	13	12

Note. Data from Northside Independent School District, San Antonio, TX: Author. Adapted with permission.

sign needs information concerning counselor performance, clients, standards, and results, as well as quantitative design needs information concerning program balance, counselor–student ratios, and number of students needing/receiving services.

Structural Components Needs Information

New information that informs the redesign of the guidance and counseling program's structural components comes from reassessing students needs, reexamining the community context, changed school goals, and new professional trends.

Table 11.17
Students Receiving Responsive Services by School Level

School Level and Responsive Service	Total Enrollment	% Served
Elementary school	23,300	
Individual counseling		24
Small-group counseling		24
Consultation		7
Referral		2.5
Middle school	10,500	
Individual counseling		170
Small-group counseling		19
Consultation		35
Referral		2
Schedule adjustment		7
High school	14,000	
Individual counseling		159
Small-group counseling		14
Consultation		146
Referral		49
Schedule adjustment		12
Information seeking		120
Information referral		16.5

Note. Data from Northside Independent School District, San Antonio, TX: Author. Adapted with permission.

Student Needs

Reassessments of students' needs for assistance from comprehensive guidance and counseling programs are done to identify new needs and to suggest new priorities among previously identified needs. From annual assessments for responsive services, student needs have emerged; for those topics that indicate widespread need, new guidance curriculum themes and activities emerge. An example of needs that appeared to be new in Northside Independent School District and elsewhere in the late 1990s included those associated with multicultural effectiveness, racism, and ethnocentrism. Prevention and intervention in situations involving violence in American schools and communities is not a new need, but its increase across the country has called for more work to help students cope with the violence around them in their communities as well as develop better anger and conflict management skills. Other student needs identified included increased numbers of students who felt alienated from school and school staff, and increased numbers of students who needed more assistance as they made educational and career development plans. Many students needed help in setting challenging goals for themselves.

Community Context

Communities change over time. They grow larger or smaller. The age of the population may shift, or the individuals who live there may change. People move in and out. Industries and businesses begin, grow, and decline. The labor market and workforce change. Houses gain and lose their value. All of these changes and nonchanges impact the school that serves that community. Guidance and counseling programs serve all the students in a school and provide special services to many of the students with personal, social, educational, and career needs.

At the time of redesigning a school or district's guidance and counseling program, you need to survey all of the relevant community variables to identify significant changes in demographics, socioeconomics, mobility rates, average levels of the parents' education, family configurations, immigration patterns, and so on. Growth and decline in the student population, changing ages of the faculty, and opening and closing of schools are also environmental events that have implications for the guidance and counseling program. As with the rest of these efforts, data are studied that, in turn, support conclusions about what these changes mean for the program in the current times and in the near future (i.e., for 10 years, if an original design can stay valid that long).

School Goals

As school boards, superintendents, principals, and other senior-level school administrators change, philosophies and policies change. As the community and school customers change, the priorities for education change as well. Even the mission of the school district may be altered by the political bent of the community. States' attempts to equalize funding have brought more money into some schools. Insufficient funds plague other school districts. District education goals and initiatives vary from year to year as legislatures change and as educators identify ideas for improvement. The standards movement brought increased emphasis on academic achievement. Districts' strategic-planning efforts such as their school improvement plans have enabled them to better understand their communities and to design their school system—building to building—to respond to the needs and goals of their communities.

The processes by which decisions are made in schools change, changing not only the climates of schools but also their priorities. Site-based decision making, whereby more people have input into the choices of what is most important for their schools and communities, is an example. Also, increasingly, districts and states are demanding that local decisions be based on hard data that present needs and solutions that are supported by research. These same data can support the priorities established for the guidance and counseling program because they include such things as clarity about what students know, learn, and need to learn. Schools are being held accountable for their retention and promotion rates. Students' adherence to conduct codes is reflected in discipline reports and in attendance and absence rates. Rates of participation in activities indicate how affiliated or how alienated students are from school.

Curriculum realignment has accompanied standards development and implementation. Ways to assist individual students succeed academically are being sought. The focus on individual students suggests they also need to become more responsible for their learning, which in turn emphasizes programs and processes that support student goal setting, self-evaluation, and self-tracking through such strategies as portfolios. As the society continues to become more pluralistic, conflict management, character development, and self-responsibility are being emphasized. Another trend that is seen currently is the increased involvement of parents and businesses in the schools. It is hoped that their involvement will help students learn the content they need to be successful in their adult lives, and at the same time bring more support for the education enterprise.

Professional School Counseling Trends

Trends in professional school counseling today include better understanding of new or additional groups of clients, different content and techniques addressing students' and society's needs, ways to organize and manage guidance and counseling programs to better serve students, and methods for assisting school counselors' professional development. New groups of clients include subgroups of students. Increasingly, it is recognized that elementary-school-age children benefit from guidance and counseling. In our increasingly pluralistic society, school counselors are working more with adolescents who are facing more openness regarding sexual preferences. The expansion of special education services has helped schools develop sensitivity to a diversity of disabilities that students manage and that affect their lives. Efforts are being made to help parents to be better partners with the schools and in their children's learning. Although school counselors have always provided bridges for parents to be part of the schools, recent parents' rights policies have opened the schoolhouse doors even wider.

As delineated in the ASCA National Standards (Campbell & Dahir, 1997), new guidance content includes helping students develop and maintain high expectations for their academic achievement. There is renewed interest in facilitating students' career development. Our diverse society has led us to understanding more fully what cross-cultural effectiveness entails. Helping students set goals, develop plans for achieving them, and monitor progress toward goal accomplishment requires culturally responsive approaches to this topic as well as a system for providing the help.

Organized guidance and counseling programs represent successes for the school counseling profession, even though many schools are still striving to implement comprehensive guidance and counseling programs. The ASCA National Model (ASCA, 2005) offers a professional consensus that comprehensive guidance and counseling programs are the most effective means for organizing the work of school counselors and assisting students to reach personal/social, educational, and career development results. The emphasis in schools on helping individual students achieve success requires more individualized guidance and counseling services. Systems are being set in place for schoolwide guidance and counseling approaches that involve teachers and volunteer community members. Site-based decision making is allowing for flexibility within buildings and for greater responsiveness to local needs.

Within the counseling field, professional supervision continues to develop as the standards for professionalism become clearer. Leadership for school counselors' professional development is emerging as a specialty of its own, as are specialties within school counseling (Henderson & Gysbers, 1998). External funds are supporting such specialists as substance abuse prevention counselors, special education counselors, and bilingual counselors. The use of paraprofessional guidance staff in appropriate roles, such as parent education coordinators, testing program specialists, data-processing clerks, registrars, and career center technicians, is helping guidance program delivery become systematic and efficient. Professionals from related specialties, such as school social work and school psychology, are increasingly being hired in schools and augment professional school counselors' work in the responsive services (Fuston & Hargens, 2002).

Qualitative Design Needs Information

Needs information relating to the guidance and counseling program's qualitative design emerges from analyzing data regarding the quality of school counselors' performance, identifying new subsets of clients needing services, reestablishing the standards for the program components, and identifying new results that are needed by students.

School Counselor Performance

Even with a program that is being well implemented, new or different needs for the application of school counselors' talents may be identified. In many districts, school counselors feel overwhelmed with the quantity of students who need their help, and at the same time, they still have too many nonguidance tasks and paperwork. Advisory committees suggest that more counselors are needed to serve fewer children. Appreciation is underscored for specialist counselors, and a need for additional specialties is often mentioned. Fuller use of support staff—educational and clerical assistants, other paraprofessionals, and expanded use of volunteers to help students within carefully defined roles (e.g., as mentors)—seems desirable.

School counselors themselves identify performance improvement needs. If you have followed our advice in chapter 9 and have school counselors set annual performance improvement goals, their needs are monitored regularly and, at this point, may be summarized for your program redesigners. Three kinds of decisions will be made by your program redesigners regarding school counselors' needs for professional development assistance:

1. Areas related to the ongoing expectations for their performance, as indicated by their performance evaluations
2. Areas where other staff members may be as competent or more competent to carry out responsibilities
3. New dimensions of the comprehensive guidance and counseling program design.

For example, aggregated school counselor performance evaluation data tell you and your program planners that school counselors' current needs for continued improvement may include such areas as enhanced group counseling competence, in both group process skills and specific information regarding recurrent topics addressed through small groups. Newer counselors may continue to need information and to hone their skills in working with referral sources. High school counselors may need more training in modern instructional technology, such as use of cooperative learning strategies in instruction. Although many school counselors perform well in teacher consultation, some do not. Many school counselors are still uncomfortable in advocating with and for parents.

You and your comprehensive guidance and counseling program redesigners need to discuss whether students are best served when teachers, who are competent in modern instructional methods, provide much of the guidance curriculum, with counselors helping teachers learn guidance content. Remember to consider identifying the in-service training needs of staff members whose roles will change as a result of the program redesign—as part of the transition process discussed at the end of this chapter. Further, you may learn that the school counselor performance evaluation process itself needs improvement to better assist school counselors' efforts to improve their performance. Northside Independent School District, for example, found that more specific standards for counselor performance, more distinct definitions among the basic performance roles of counselors, and more clarity regarding each individual's job description were needed (Henderson & Gysbers, 1998). The district also identified shortcomings in the performance evaluation form. Without a form that supports clarity and accuracy in drawing evaluative conclusions, aggregating data for improvement decisions is difficult.

Clients Served

Educators and concerned community members increasingly recognize the special needs of the majority of students who fall, educationally, in the center section of the bell curve. These students do not give evidence of needing highly specialized educational services nor intensified mental health treatment, but they nevertheless are students who may not feel self-worth, connected to school, or cared for at school, and they may not be getting help with the typical challenges of growing up. They may be inattentive in classes or have problems (as they define them) that make them unable to concentrate on academic learning. Many are stressed; and some (more than we admit) are abused. These students want/need to have opportunities to discuss their problems and to be taken seriously. At the same time, schools are formally identifying more special needs students, including those who are at risk, persistent misbehavers, homeless, or involved in gangs.

Teachers are seeking more help with specific classroom problems. They want even more consultation regarding individual students who are having problems. They want more consultation for themselves about student, school, and personal problems. They want fuller understanding of the guidance and counseling program, its practices, operations, and ethical standards. They want more help with understanding standardized testing and its appropriate uses. At the same time, parents seem to need and want more parenting skills, but new ways of providing them with these skills need to be developed. Their lack of involvement in schools may be indicative of their being busy or of their discomfort with school. The latter tells us we need to find more effective ways to reach out to them.

Program Component Standards

With the comprehensive guidance and counseling program in place, one of the side benefits is that school counselors not only are able to educate students, teachers, and parents regarding how they deliver the program but also have a common language to describe the program. The four program components are few enough and distinct enough in purpose and practice to be readily understood. Thus asking their opinions about the value of the activities in each of the components provides useful information to add to your redesign efforts.

Knowing the relative value assigned to each set of activities by your customers helps you establish priorities among the components. If, for example, program consumers value responsive services assistance significantly more than they value classroom guidance, that could support a significant rise in the priority of responsive services over guidance curriculum, or vice versa. If individual student planning activities are perceived as more valuable than responsive services, that could contribute to the priority setting. Table 11.18 provides an example of actual information gathered in the Northside Independent School District (1998) study. On a 4-point scale, the mean ratings are impressive.

Northside District's program decision makers learned several (exciting) things from these data. First, they learned that the program was, in fact, a comprehensive one, and that it was consistent and comprehensive across school levels. Second, they learned that the program's benefits are stable over time, as the data were collected over a 4-year period with consistency of results. Third, they learned that the overall level of benefit was substantial. The "grades" earned by each of the program components at each of the three levels were all well into the *helpful* range (3 or above). The differences between levels or program components were relatively small. Fourth, they learned that the perceived level of benefit was very similar between the primary clients (the students), the closest program observers (the teachers), and the program providers (the counselors).

If you have followed the model presented in this book for ongoing program improvement, you will have noted that guidance and counseling program improvement goals are set each year, based on the program's annual evaluation, across the buildings and districts. Aggregations of these building-specific goals also provide trend information regarding possible new program priorities. Annual program improvement goals, of course, reflect the improvements recommended in the initial program design process; but they also reflect new priorities at the district (all levels or across a specific level) and building levels. For example, in Northside Independent School District, new district priorities were established within the 1995–2000 strategic plan: goal setting, conflict management, career development, character development, and cross-cultural effectiveness. Traditionally, needed improvements that arise frequently from building needs include small-group counseling, parent involvement and education, and staff consultation. New topics arising from the buildings that need to be considered in program redesign include assisting teachers teach guidance curriculum, behavior management, educational motivation, making the best out of standardized testing, and responding to special needs students.

The school–community advisory committee or other parent and student advisory committees identify changes in the program they might like to see. These inputs provide ideas

Table 11.18
Perception of Overall Benefit by Students, Teachers, and Counselors (4-point scale)

School Level and Program Component	Students	Teachers	Counselors
Elementary school			
Guidance curriculum	3.24	3.55	3.44
Individual student planning	3.27	3.70	3.27
Responsive services	3.22	3.67	3.46
System support		3.74	
Middle school			
Guidance curriculum	3.15	3.45	3.27
Individual student planning	3.20	3.56	3.26
Responsive services	3.23	3.58	3.33
System support		3.65	
High school			
Guidance curriculum	3.06	3.42	3.04
Individual student planning	3.12	3.44	3.10
Responsive services	3.24	3.44	3.04
System support		3.48	

Note. Data from *Northside's Comprehensive Guidance Program: Student and Staff Perceptions: 1995–98,* by Northside Independent School District, 1998, San Antonio, TX: Author. Adapted with permission.

for the steering committee to consider. Advisory committee members often want more guidance curriculum, both more content and more frequent lessons. Sometimes they see the need for better presentation methodology. Advisory committee members also often want more individual student educational and career planning assistance than is currently done. Because a number of these activities are annual events, it is often hard for students, parents, and community people to identify what activities are provided in the individual student planning component. It is important to help students and parents make connections between elementary career days and middle school instruction regarding job families and clusters and high school career-center-based activities, between 8th- and 10th-grade career assessments and 11th- and 12th-grade college entrance examinations, and between middle school career-related goal setting and 4-year high school planning and high school career and educational planning.

Guidance and counseling program customers consistently want more counseling made available to students, both individual and group. Parents want more consultation opportunities and help with difficult moments with or for their children. Increasingly, crisis intervention is called for in our schools. Rethinking the priorities for the responsive services component and explaining them to students, parents, teachers, and others are essential. Finding ways to expand responsive services through referrals, collaborative relationships among service providers, and more efficient and effective strategies by school counselors is called for.

As education itself continues its efforts for reform, and as increasingly diverse students come to school, teachers' needs for training and support shift. In turn, school counselors are required to refresh their competence continuously in such topics as learning styles and motivation, classroom management and organization, teaching the hard-to-teach/reach students, and helping students develop social skills. Because standardized testing is a popular vehicle for holding school systems accountable, and because it is an area traditionally connected to guidance and counseling (albeit unfortunately so), school counselors continue to be challenged to help colleague educators maintain a balanced approach regarding the administration and use of test results. Balance in test administration means all staff members must fulfill their fair share of the responsibilities for this massive program. Balance in use of test results means helping staff members know the limitations of an individual test results and the value of using multiple sources of information to make judgments about students.

Student Results

Student needs assessment data provide important information regarding new or different needs that students have that should be considered by the steering committee as it approaches program redesign. As with the initial program design (chapter 6), identifying what students need is best accomplished by asking the students themselves as well as school counselors, teachers, parents, and others. Repetition suggests priorities. Student skill development needs identified in Northside Independent School District included the following:

- personal management skills
- career skills
- life skills
- goal-setting skills
- self-confidence development
- learning to give of oneself
- problem-solving skills
- valuing education as an investment in the future

In addition, teachers, parents, and administrators in Northside recognized that students in schools needed resources to help them as they faced the challenges of growing up and of being in school. Cited were needs for

- a sense of connection
- a sense of belonging in the school community
- someone to listen to them
- support systems
- advocacy

Each of these had implications for the redesign of the guidance and counseling program in Northside Independent School District.

Quantitative Design Needs Information

The needs information regarding each of the three dimensions of the quantitative design—program balance, counselor–student ratio, and numbers of students needing/ receiving services—result from your consideration of the qualitative needs as well as analyzing the reasons for lack of adherence to your previously set standards. For example, if for most of the years since the initial design, and in many of the buildings in which the program was implemented, actual program delivery has been out of balance, perhaps a new balance standard is called for. If the counselor–student ratio is such that the counselors and their clients are consistently frustrated because of insufficient time to connect, the ratio is probably not adequate for the needs. If the numbers and percentages of students who actually benefit from guidance services are unacceptably low in relation to their needs, then the quantitative design will need to be altered.

Make Redesign Decisions Based on Evaluation Data and New Information

At this point in the redesign process (program enhancement), evaluation data have been collected and updated needs information is available. The task now is to make the needed redesign decisions that will lead to a redesigned program, an enhanced program. As we stated in the Preface, the program enhancement process follows evaluation and connects back to the beginning as program redesign unfolds, but at a higher level. Thus the process is spiral, not circular. Each time the redesign process unfolds, a new and more effective guidance and counseling program emerges.

For the program redesign process to move forward, you will need to consider the conclusions drawn from the evaluation data about what and how well the program is doing and combine them with the information about new needs and trends. By combining the two, you can make decisions about the current program design (comparable with those described in chapter 5). You can decide whether or not the program is working as previously designed, whether it is still important, and whether it should be maintained. You can also decide where the design is not working, whether the priorities are still the same and, therefore, should be targeted for improvement, or whether they should be replaced by something more needed or feasible. These decisions lead to new standards for your redesigned guidance and counseling program.

Each of the comprehensive guidance and counseling program elements (as outlined in chapter 3) are considered in this task. New decisions are made or previous decisions are reaffirmed regarding the student domains and competencies developed through the program, the structural components (rationale, assumptions, and definition), the program delivery components (qualitative design), and the resource allocations (quantitative design).

Student Domains and Competencies Redesign

New ways of defining the basic content of the comprehensive guidance and counseling program have probably emerged since the initial program adoption. Thus the first set of recommendations for a redesigned program should be reaffirmation or readjustment of the basic student standards for the program. Changes may be made at the domain and competency levels.

A change in domains is evident in Northside Independent School District's redesigned program. At the start of the redesign process, the guidance steering committee accepted a recommendation from the school–community advisory committee to adopt the Texas Education Agency (1997) model's content goals. The state model was preferred because of the addition of cross-cultural effectiveness as a domain and the more contemporary and succinct wording of the other domains.

A change in competency statements is exemplified in the Texas model. In the original statement of student goals (Texas Education Agency, 1990), the first domain was self-esteem development. In the 1997 revision, the wording was changed to self-confidence development (Texas Education Agency, 1997). It was determined that the word *confidence* is a more results-oriented and therefore measurable word than *esteem*. Further, there was a constituency that did not support self-esteem as a legitimate outcome for schools to address.

Structural Components Redesign

After redesigning the basic content of the program, the next step involves revision of the structural components of the program: the statements of rationale for the program, the assumptions that undergird the program, and the definition of the program as well as the school district policy for guidance and counseling.

Rationale

Data from evaluation and from the updated needs information provide you with ideas to revise the rationale for your program. New information may, on the one hand, reveal seemingly larger numbers of students who are alienated from school: Increases in student violence and continued widespread substance abuse, the diversity of family configurations, and unstable economies result in students who come to school from situations that make it difficult for them to attend to their school work. New information may, on the other hand, also make clear that in the 21st century, schools will continue to be challenged to hold increasingly higher academic standards and expectations for students. Schools are charged to help every student, regardless of circumstances, to succeed in school. These somewhat conflicting aims for schools underscore the value of guidance and counseling for helping students manage their own destinies and solve their problems.

The new information may indicate that teachers, facing increasingly diverse student populations, need meaningful consultation to enhance their work with parents. The parents' rights movement has brought increasing numbers of parents to school in efforts to assist with or intervene in their children's education. The continuing shift of educational decision making to the building level requires counselors to have the knowledge, skills, and professional values to manage locally appropriate programs, with sufficient leadership available to nurture professional growth. Recognizing such community, school, and student needs is critical in redesigning your program in general and in reviewing and revising the rationale for the program in particular.

Assumptions

You will probably find you are more aware of the assumptions that undergird your program operation than you were during the original designing of your program. As mentioned earlier, because of their very nature, assumptions are somewhat hard to recognize until they are challenged. They also help staff members remember the basic values of the program. For example, Northside Independent School District's redesign work included reaffirming the following assumptions:

- Students are the primary clients of the program.
- All counselors are held to the profession's ethical standards.
- No matter what the presenting problem or issue, each student merits the same non-judgmental reception and assistance.
- The best program is one in which the resources are consciously allocated to the established priorities of the program.
- Differently credentialed staff members are used in job assignments that appropriately apply their training and competence.
- As much as possible, school counselors enlist parents as partners in assisting students' personal, social, educational, and career development.

Definition

Because by now you have had extensive experience with guidance and counseling program implementation, you may be more willing to debate and decide on the essential mission of the program than you were when everything was new. Members of the school–community advisory and steering committees have opinions based on their experiences as to who fulfills structured roles in the program, who the program's clients legitimately are in addition to the students, and the true meaning of the comprehensive guidance and counseling program's organizational structure. Further, because of the accountable nature of comprehensive guidance and counseling programs, you will probably be quite clear as to what the resources of the program will support. If all students in schools are to get more in-depth guidance and counseling assistance, more staff members will have to be involved. If additional individualized assistance is desired, then more individual advisers will have to be provided. If a broader range of troubled students is to have their specialized needs attended to, additional service providers will have to be identified. With changes such as these envisioned, the staff implementing the program might expand to include all teachers providing guidance curriculum, all professional staff providing individual student planning system assistance, and community-based mental health professionals and in-school related professionals providing responsive services. As a result, the definition of the program will need to be revised.

School District Guidance and Counseling Policy

If you followed our recommendations in the initial program development, your school district developed a policy that supports the guidance and counseling program. The initial policy statement was based on your previous identification of the content of the program, its rationale, assumptions, and definition. When the steering committee reaches consensus (remember that unanimity is often difficult to achieve if your committee is truly reflective of the diversity of your school community) regarding these basic statements, the new or newly reaffirmed content domains, rationale, assumptions, and definition of the program should be ratified by your school district's top-level administration and school board. An example of a new board policy statement, from the Missouri School Boards Association, is provided in Appendix E.

When that approval has been achieved, the new policy statement is distributed to the district's principals and counselors, and anyone else who is interested at this stage of the game. This is the perfect opportunity to help others begin to internalize the changes that may follow after the next step—program designing. It also provides a vehicle for eliciting even more people's input into the all-important priority setting that ensues.

Qualitative Redesign Decisions

Qualitative redesign decisions are those regarding priorities for the use of school counselors' competencies, for clients to be served, for program activities to be delivered, and for student results to be achieved. We suggest that you ask the qualitative design questions first. It is important for you to know what you want before you deal with the reality of how much of it you can have, given the resources available. Final recommendations nearly always include suggestions for additional resources.

School Counselor Performance

Based on the experience of working in a program after a number of years, the school–community advisory and steering committees need to establish at least two kinds of priorities regarding counselors' skills. These are priorities for the skills to be used within the program and for the skills that need strengthening through professional development. Table 11.19 displays the skills priorities set for school counselors in Northside Independent School District by the guidance steering committee charged with recommending redesigned program standards. It is clear that the members wanted the school counselors to manage their own program. They also valued both the individual and small-group counseling expertise that the school counselors bring to their buildings. Consulting with other adults on behalf of their students was the fourth priority. These priorities fit what the school counselors had envisioned as their appropriate roles.

Professional development needs are identified through a discrepancy analysis of priorities and evaluation information. Target areas are the high-priority competencies or commitments in which school counselors are not performing well. Some counselors may need further refinement of their program (including time) management skills. Some may need to attend to their small-group counseling skills, and so on.

With discussion focused on applications of school counselors' competence, new or refined ideas about ways to help school counselors improve their performance also come up. For example, the tool for evaluating the quality of school counselors' performance (the performance evaluation form) may need fine-tuning to provide better feedback to individuals. The activities that address job focus and improvement (job descriptions, professional supervision) may need clarification, strengthening, or more resources. In many districts, the professional leadership for school counselors is unclear or is provided by individuals without school counseling expertise, such as principals. Because of this, nationwide school counselors' leadership systems need substantial improvement (Henderson & Gysbers, 1998).

Clients Served

Evaluation data provide insights into who is actually being served in the current guidance program by revealing the balance among services provided to students, services provided

Table 11.19
Priorities for Use of Counselor Skills

Priorities			Counselor Skills/Roles
Elementary School	Middle School	High School	
			Program Management
1	2	1	1. Plan, implement, and evaluate comprehensive guidance program.
14	14	14	2. Supervise activities of clerical, paraprofessional, and volunteer personnel.
			Guidance
6	10	9	3. Teach the school developmental guidance curriculum.
8	6	7	4. Assist teachers in teaching guidance-related curriculum.
11	7	4	5. Guide individuals and groups of students through the development of educational and career plans.
			Counseling
2	1	1	6. Counsel individual students with presenting needs/concerns.
3	3	3	7. Counsel small groups of students with presenting needs/concerns.
5	5	8	8. Use accepted theories and techniques appropriate in school counseling.
			Consultation
4	4	4	9. Consult with parents, teachers, administrators, and other relevant individuals to enhance their work with students.
			Coordination
10	7	6	10. Coordinate with school and community personnel to bring together resources for students.
7	9	10	11. Use an effective referral process for assisting students and others to use special programs and services.
			Assessment
13	13	13	12. Participate in the planning and evaluation of the district/school group standardized testing program.
9	12	11	13. Interpret test and other appraisal results appropriately.
12	11	12	14. Use other sources of student data appropriately for assessment purposes.
			Professionalism
			15. Adhere to ethical, legal, professional, and district standards.

Note. Data from *Northside's Comprehensive Guidance Program Framework* (p. 109), by Northside Independent School District, 1994, San Antonio, TX: Author. Adapted with permission.

to adults, and system support tasks. The percentages of students served at each grade level and the percentages of students served through developmental, preventive, or remedial interventions as well as data regarding services provided to various subgroups of students, such as those experiencing divorce or grief, are also available. New information regarding students' needs and the needs suggested by the issues apparent in the school community may suggest different priorities for the clients to be served. Changed or refocused school and district goals may suggest different priorities.

In Northside Independent School District's redesign, the desired balance between serving elementary students and serving adults identified in the mid-1990s stayed the same as that desired in the mid-1980s: 65% of counselors' time with students, 35% with adults (see Table 5.3). Differences were seen, however, in the recommendations for the breakdown of times within these large categories. The time recommended to be spent providing students with developmental assistance was reduced about 10%, with that time reallocated to the students with needs for prevention or remediation. This was one of several recommendations that indicated an increased understanding of and respect for school counselors' specialized skills in working with students facing issues and problems.

Program Component Standards

The centerpieces of qualitative redesign are the minimum standards and operational definitions for each program component. The language used in defining the program components does not change. What is subject to change are the activities and the priorities for these activities within each component. For example, you may need to rearrange the priorities for each of the curriculum strands because of increased learning about what is most needed and appropriate at each grade level, or because of the changing needs of the population served by the school. Increasingly, the emphasis on career development as the purpose for educational planning may cause refinement of these activities within the individual student planning system. New needs identified for counseling services should be responded to. Specification of the school counselors' roles in relation to academic standards may be needed to enhance counselors' support for the total educational system.

A needed addition to many guidance and counseling program descriptions is clarification of parents' roles in each program component (see chapter 3). The reason for this is the increasing recognition of parents' rights with regard to their children's schooling and of the need for their involvement to enable their children's success in school. Spelling out parents' responsibilities and opportunities within guidance curriculum and individual student planning activities causes schools and counselors to better ensure that parents have the information they need to be active participants in the developmental guidance provided their children. Clarifying how parents' permission for counseling occurs in responsive services and how parents can access the services on behalf of their students is important, especially in light of those parents who do not want their children to benefit from these services at school. Expanding the parent involvement and education activities within the system support component, such as in advocacy activities and parent advisory roles, provides parents with vehicles for input into program development and delivery.

A change that had widespread impact in the Northside Independent School District's program was the expanded definition of teachers' roles in the delivery of developmental guidance and counseling activities. The expanded definition was based on the recognition that if we were truly going to help all students acquire all of the basic competencies in the major life skills represented by the guidance curriculum, every educator needs to contribute to these ends. If we were truly going to help each individual student establish educational and career goals and plans, as well as provide means for monitoring their progress, every educator must assist in providing accurate and unbiased information and meaningful advice to students in the individual student planning component.

Student Results

In assessing the needs of students, new priorities may emerge for the content of the guidance and counseling program. Evaluation data may clarify what students and others think is beneficial for the guidance and counseling program to address. Therefore, new strands, such as cross-cultural effectiveness, may be added to the content of the program and to the priority-setting process. Or evaluation data on effectiveness of the in-place content may raise or lower a strand's importance. For example, self-esteem development in children is increasingly recognized as not sufficient as an end in itself and is seen instead as a part of students' feelings of competence in other dimensions, such as making friends, acting responsibly, and being able to express themselves so others understand their thoughts and feelings.

Quantitative Redesign Decisions

Based on the qualitative design decisions, decisions on allocation of the program's resources need to be adjusted to match those revisions. The quantitative design is most influenced by the recommendations regarding the balance of resource allocation among the four program components, that is, by the guidelines regarding how school counselors spend their time. As described in chapter 8, the counselor–student ratio affects how many students can be served through the actual program balance.

Program Balance

Evaluation data concerning the initial program implementation provides a reality check for you. New priorities within the qualitative design also contribute to the deliberations regarding the new program balance. In the Northside Independent School District redesign process, the specialized skills of school counselors were better appreciated than they were during the initial program designing efforts. Therefore, ensuring effective use of these skills for as many students as possible became an overriding priority for the redesign decision makers. The time allocations for school counselors in Northside's redesigned program are presented in Table 11.20.

In comparing the redesign with the original Northside Independent School District's design (see Table 5.12), shifts in priorities can easily be seen. The amount of time projected for school counselors to spend in guidance curriculum was decreased at all three levels, most significantly at the high school level (by 15–20%), and was cut by half (from 30% to 15%–20%) for the middle school level. The amount of time allocated to individual student planning activities decreased significantly at the elementary level (from 25% to 5%–10%), decreased somewhat at the middle school level, and stayed about the same at the high school level. Responsive services time was increased at all three levels (from 25% to 40%–45%). System support time stayed fairly consistent. In addition, in the redesigned program, the steering committee chose to clearly express its opinion that school counselors' time should not be spent in nonguidance activities. They did this by appropriating zero time to these school management and clerical tasks.

Counselor–Student Ratio

Since the initial design of the comprehensive guidance and counseling program, the counselor–student ratio in the Northside Independent School District had been reduced sig-

Table 11.20
Revised Desired Program Balance—Final

Component	% Counselor Time/School Level		
	Elementary	Middle	High
Guidance curriculum	30–35	15–20	5–10
Individual student planning	5–10	15–20	30–35
Responsive services	40–45	40–45	40–45
System support	15–20	15–20	10–15
Nonguidance tasks	0	0	0

Note. Data from *Northside's Comprehensive Guidance Program Framework* (p. 110), by Northside Independent School District, 1994, San Antonio, TX. Adapted with permission.

nificantly, from 1:550 to an average of 1:400. The positive results of the evaluation study reinforced the value of lower ratios, and the lower ratios made some of the shifts in program balance possible. The district still wanted (and has) a developmentally based guidance and counseling program, but with each school counselor responsible for fewer students, all of a school counselor's caseload could be serviced in less time.

At Northside, the steering committee adopted a goal of one counselor for every 350 students (1:350), reflecting the statements of the professional associations (ASCA, 1993) and the Texas Education Agency (1991, 1997). Recommended ratios were altered for the school counselor specialists as follows:

- Guidance department heads: 1:250 in middle and magnet high schools
- High school head counselors: no assigned student caseload, considering the expanded expectations for their leadership roles (Henderson & Gysbers, 1998; Northside Independent School District, 1997)
- Substance abuse counselors: 1:100 in their active caseload
- Special education counselors: 1:250

Numbers of Students Served

With a new program balance and with lowered caseloads, coupled with a better understanding of what each component included, the potential numbers of students served at Northside Independent School District in the various component activities were projected. This allowed the steering committee to establish minimum standards for the provision of activities for students. For example, the steering committee in Northside determined that it was feasible, within the balance and with the caseload, for elementary school students to benefit from 12 counselor-led guidance lessons per semester, for middle school students to benefit from 8 counselor-led guidance lessons per year, and for high school students to benefit from 6 counselor-led guidance lessons per year. A legitimate expectation was that at any given time, approximately 25% of the students in a school counselor's caseload would benefit from responsive services.

Implement the New Design

Implementing a redesigned program entails specifying new directions for the redesigned program design and planning for and making the improvements that are called for. These steps are identical to those described in chapters 6 and 7 for implementing the initial comprehensive guidance and counseling program. The newly redesigned program must be approved by your district's policymakers, the senior administrators, and the school board. A new program handbook must be written and distributed to school counselors, building principals, and other program administrators. In-service education for these key players must be provided regarding the redesigned program and its implications.

Now that you have identified the discrepancies between the original design of your program and your redesigned program, you need to specify the changes required to implement the new design and to develop a plan for accomplishing the program improvements. Most likely, you will need new resources. Additional school counselors may be needed. New program improvement goals need to be set at the district and at the building levels. Using new staff members, such as teachers, in the program requires education and training for carefully defined roles. Targeted training and other professional development activities are needed by school counselors to assist them to make the needed changes in their job descriptions as well as to assure their competence in their changed roles. If new content areas are added, new materials must be developed or acquired. New advocacy efforts must be undertaken to inform staff members, parents, and other community members of the new priorities and resulting changes—especially the changes that will affect them.

During the redesign process, your school district's steering and school–community advisory committees may have also recommended some changes in the ongoing processes used to plan, implement, monitor, and evaluate the program, its staff, and its results. These need to be attended to. For example, a new performance improvement system was developed in Northside Independent School District (1997). New roles and responsibilities for guidance program leaders—the head and lead counselors—were also outlined (Henderson & Gysbers, 1998).

Understand That Revitalization Follows Redesign

Armed with data from the three types of evaluation described in chapter 10 and with the new information you gathered regarding changes in students and in the school and community, you have fuel to spark the redesign of your program. Redesigning results in new standards for the program, new priorities, and new parameters. The memo summarizing the changes made in Northside Independent School District's program is provided in Appendix Q. As can be seen, changes were made in every element of the program: content, use of counselors' skills, definition of the providers of the program, program shape and activities, and standards for accountability. In addition, the entire system for helping school counselors perform at their best was changed and is described in detail in *Leading and Managing Your School Guidance Program Staff* (Henderson & Gysbers, 1998).

An additional direct benefit in Northside Independent School District was that evaluation and the redesign sparked a revitalization of the program. The rethinking, replanning, and repreparing for implementation caused individual school counselors to recommit themselves as they pursue the growth it requires of them. Every building in the district took the opportunity to address the implications of the new design for their programs. At the district level, several initiatives were put in place to extend guidance program responsibilities across more staff members to provide more assistance for student development. The guidance curriculum component was extended by the addition of schoolwide character development programs. The individual student planning component was extended by implementing a student advisory program that focuses on helping students set and accomplish educational and career goals. The responsive services component was extended by more systematically coordinating the resources used to make schools safe and drug free with the guidance program and by establishing protocols for and clarifying staff roles in managing schoolwide crises.

In redesigning their programs after implementing them for some time, other school districts have enhanced their programs in other ways. In the School District of St. Joseph in St. Joseph, Missouri, they found a number of "ways to stretch the school day through collaborative strategies" (Fuston & Hargens, 2002, p. 211) that allow school counselors to do their work. They use retired counselors to substitute for absent counselors so that the work does not get omitted or backlogged. They have improved the ways that computers assist in guidance program implementation. Career education is done in collaboration with teachers and community members. The district hired social workers to respond to the social work-type needs of students and families and collaborate with community agencies that provide group counseling. In Davis School District in Farmington, Utah, they firmed up the relationship between the guidance program mission and that of the school district. Successful comprehensive guidance and counseling program implementation at the secondary level led to initiation of one at the elementary level and the hiring of elementary counselors (Davis, 2002).

In summary, redesigning your comprehensive guidance and counseling program after years of implementation leads to continued program enhancement and revitalization of the program, the school counseling staff, and the staff of the school as a whole. Revitalized commitment yields expanded services to students.

References

American School Counselor Association. (1993). *Position statements.* Alexandria, VA: Author.

American School Counselor Association. (2005). *The ASCA national model: A framework for school counseling programs* (2nd ed.). Alexandria, VA: Author.

Campbell, C. A., & Dahir, C. A. (1997). *Sharing the vision: The national standards for school counseling programs.* Alexandria, VA: American School Counselor Association.

Davis, D. (2002). Revising and enhancing Davis School District's comprehensive guidance program: Working together works. In P. Henderson & N. Gysbers (Eds.), *Implementing comprehensive school guidance programs: Critical leadership issues and successful responses* (pp. 219–228). Greensboro, NC: CAPS.

Fuston, J., & Hargens, M. (2002). Extending the program's resources. In P. Henderson & N. Gysbers (Eds.), *Implementing comprehensive school guidance programs: Critical leadership issues and successful responses* (pp. 211–217). Greensboro, NC: CAPS.

Henderson, P., & Gysbers, N. C. (1998). *Leading and managing your school guidance program staff.* Alexandria, VA: American Counseling Association.

National Association of Secondary School Principals. (1996). *Breaking ranks: Changing an American institution.* Reston, VA: Author.

National Association of Secondary School Principals. (2004). *Breaking ranks II: Strategies for leading high school reform.* Reston, CA: Author.

Northside Independent School District. (1994). *Northside's comprehensive guidance program framework.* San Antonio, TX: Author.

Northside Independent School District. (1997). *Guide to counselor performance improvement through job definition, professionalism assessment, supervision, performance evaluation, and professional development goal setting.* San Antonio, TX: Author.

Northside Independent School District. (1998). *Northside's comprehensive guidance program: Student and staff perceptions: 1995–98.* San Antonio, TX: Author.

Texas Education Agency. (1991). *The comprehensive guidance program for Texas public schools: A guide for program development, pre-K–12th grade.* Austin, TX: Author.

Texas Education Agency. (1997). *The comprehensive guidance program for Texas public schools: A guide for program development, pre-K through 12th grade* (Rev. ed.). Austin, TX: Author.

Texas Education Agency. (2004). *The comprehensive, developmental guidance and counseling program for Texas public schools: A guide for program development, pre-K through 12th grade* (4th ed.). Austin, TX: Author.

Appendixes

Life Career Development Model: Student Competencies by Domains and Goals

I. *Self-Knowledge and Interpersonal Skills*

A. *Students will develop and incorporate an understanding of the unique personal characteristics and abilities of themselves and others.*
   1. Students will be aware of the unique personal characteristics of themselves and others. Students will
      a. describe their appearance and their favorite activities (kindergarten)
      b. recognize special or unusual characteristics about themselves (first grade)
      c. recognize special or unusual characteristics about others (second grade)
      d. describe themselves accurately to someone who does not know them (third grade)
   2. Students will demonstrate an understanding of the importance of unique personal characteristics and abilities in themselves and others. Students will
      a. analyze how people are different and how they have different skills and abilities (fourth grade)
      b. specify personal characteristics and abilities that they value (fifth grade)
      c. analyze how characteristics and abilities change and how they can be expanded (sixth grade)
      d. compare their characteristics and abilities with those of others and accept the differences (seventh grade)
      e. describe their present skills and predict future skills (eighth grade)
      f. value their unique characteristics and abilities (ninth grade)
      g. analyze how characteristics and abilities develop (10th grade)
   3. Students will appreciate and encourage the unique personal characteristics and abilities of themselves and others. Students will
      a. specify characteristics and abilities they appreciate most in themselves and others (11th grade)
      b. appreciate their uniqueness and encourage that uniqueness (12th grade)

B. *Students will develop and incorporate personal skills that will lead to satisfactory physical and mental health.*
   1. Students will be aware of personal skills necessary for satisfactory physical and mental health. Students will
      a. describe ways they care for themselves (kindergarten)
      b. describe how exercise and nutrition affect their mental health (first grade)
      c. describe how they care for their physical health (second grade)
      d. describe how they care for their mental health (third grade)

    e. recognize that they are important to themselves and others (fourth grade)

    f. determine situations that produce unhappy or angry feelings and how they deal with those feelings (fifth grade)

    g. understand what stress means and describe methods of relaxation for handling stress (sixth grade)

2. Students will demonstrate personal skills that will lead to satisfactory physical and mental health. Students will

    a. distinguish between things helpful and harmful to physical health (seventh grade)

    b. distinguish between things helpful and harmful to mental health (eighth grade)

    c. predict methods they may use in caring for medical emergencies (ninth grade)

3. Students will demonstrate satisfactory physical and mental health. Students will

    a. effectively reduce their stress during tension-producing situations (10th grade)

    b. continually evaluate the effects their leisure-time activities have on their physical and mental health (11th grade)

    c. analyze their own personal skills that have contributed to satisfactory physical and mental health (12th grade)

C. *Students will develop and incorporate an ability to assume responsibility for themselves and to manage their environment.*

1. Students will be aware of their responsibilities in their environment. Students will

    a. describe areas where they are self-sufficient (kindergarten)

    b. describe responsibilities they have in their environment (first grade)

    c. give such examples of their environment as their address and the way from school to home (second grade)

    d. describe the responsibilities of adults they know (third grade)

2. Students will understand the importance of assuming responsibility for themselves and for managing their environment. Students will

    a. know their responsibilities and can be trusted to do them (fourth grade)

    b. analyze how growing up requires more self-control (fifth grade)

    c. know their responsibilities and evaluate their effect on others (sixth grade)

    d. compare and contrast the responsibilities of others in their environment (seventh grade)

    e. evaluate how responsibility helps manage their lives (eighth grade)

    f. analyze when they take responsibility for themselves and when they do not (ninth grade)

3. Students will assume responsibility for themselves and manage their environment. Students will

    a. show how they manage their environment (10th grade)

    b. assess how avoiding responsibility hinders their ability to manage their environment effectively (11th grade)

    c. assess how taking responsibility enhances their lives (12th grade)

D. *Students will develop and incorporate the ability to maintain effective relation-ships with peers and adults.*
 1. Students will be aware of their relationships with peers and adults. Students will
    a. describe their work and play relationships with others (kindergarten)
    b. describe the process of making a friend (first grade)
    c. describe the process of making and keeping a friend (second grade)
    d. recognize the actions they take that affect others' feelings (third grade)
    e. indicate methods that lead to effective cooperation with children and adults (fourth grade)
    f. describe their relationships with family members (fifth grade)
 2. Students will demonstrate a growing ability to create and maintain effec-tive relationships with peers and adults. Students will
    a. analyze the skills needed to make and keep friends (sixth grade)
    b. evaluate ways peers and adults interact (seventh grade)
    c. analyze effective family relationships, their importance, and how they have formed (eighth grade)
    d. evaluate the importance of having friendships with peers and adults (ninth grade)
    e. describe situations where their behaviors affect others' behaviors toward them (10th grade)
    f. assess their current social and family relationships and evaluate their ef-fectiveness (11th grade)
 3. Students will maintain effective relationships with peers and adults. Students will
    a. understand the value of maintaining effective relationships throughout life in today's interdependent society (12th grade)

E. *Students will develop and incorporate listening and expression skills that allow for involvement with others in problem-solving and helping relationships.*
 1. Students will be aware of listening and expression skills that allow for in-volvement with others. Students will
    a. recognize that they listen to and speak with a variety of people (kinder-garten)
    b. describe methods that enable them to speak so they can be understood by others (first grade)
    c. describe listening and expression skills that allow them to understand others and others to understand them (second grade)
 2. Students will use listening and expression skills that allow for involvement with others. Students will
    a. listen to and speak with friends and others who are not close friends (third grade)
    b. evaluate how what they say affects others' actions and how what others say affects their actions (fourth grade)
    c. evaluate ways others listen and express thoughts and feelings to them (fifth grade)
    d. use effective nonverbal communication (sixth grade)
    e. evaluate how listening and talking help to solve problems (seventh grade)
    f. analyze how communications skills improve their relationships with oth-ers (eighth grade)

g. analyze how communications skills contribute toward work within a group (ninth grade)

3. Students will use listening and expression skills that allow for involvement with others in problem-solving and helping relationships. Students will
   a. use communications skills to help others (10th grade)
   b. analyze how their communications skills encourage problem solving (11th grade)
   c. evaluate their current communication skills and continually improve those skills (12th grade)

II. *Life Roles, Settings, and Events*

A. *Students will develop and incorporate skills that lead to an effective role as a learner.*
   1. Students will be aware of themselves as learners. Students will
      a. describe things they learn at school (kindergarten)
      b. relate learning experiences at school to situations in the home (first grade)
      c. recognize some benefits of learning (second grade)
      d. realize that certain study skills are necessary for learning each school subject (third grade)
      e. describe the various methods they use to learn in school (fourth grade)
   2. Students will use skills that lead to an effective role as a learner. Students will
      a. analyze how their basic study skills relate to desired work skills (fifth grade)
      b. analyze how school learning experiences relate to their leisure activities (sixth grade)
      c. predict how they will use knowledge from certain subjects in future life and work experiences (seventh grade)
      d. learn both in and out of the school setting (eighth grade)
      e. describe personal learning and study skills and explain their importance (ninth grade)
      f. evaluate personal learning and study skills and explain how they can be improved (10th grade)
   3. Students will be effective in their roles as learners. Students will
      a. predict how their developed learning and study skills can contribute to work habits in the future (11th grade)
      b. evaluate ways they currently learn and predict how learning may change in their future (12th grade)

B. *Students will develop and incorporate an understanding of the legal and economic principles and practices that lead to responsible daily living.*
   1. Students will be aware of legal and economic principles and practices. Students will
      a. recognize the town, state, and country in which they reside (kindergarten)
      b. understand why people use money in our economic system (first grade)
      c. describe rules they follow in their environment and why those rules are necessary (second grade)

d. understand what a consumer is and how they are consumers (third grade)

e. describe how people depend on each other to fulfill their needs (fourth grade)

f. recognize that a wage earner is required to pay taxes (fifth grade)

g. describe how the government uses tax money (sixth grade)

2. Students will demonstrate a growing ability to use legal and economic principles and practices that lead to responsible daily living. Students will

a. describe the rights and responsibilities they have as citizens of their towns and states (seventh grade)

b. describe the rights and responsibilities they have as U.S. citizens (eighth grade)

c. evaluate the purposes of taxes and how taxes support the government (ninth grade)

d. evaluate their roles as consumers (10th grade)

e. analyze their legal rights and responsibilities as consumers (11th grade)

3. Students will use responsible legal and economic principles and practices in their daily lives. Students will

a. analyze how they, as citizens and consumers, help to support the economic system (12th grade)

C. *Students will develop and incorporate an understanding of the interactive effect of lifestyles, life roles, settings, and events.*

1. Students will be aware of lifestyles, life roles, settings, and events. Students will

a. describe their daily activities at school (kindergarten)

b. realize how they have changed during the past year (first grade)

c. describe necessary daily activities carried out by self and others (second grade)

d. recognize that people have varying roles and describe their own roles (third grade)

e. understand what important events affect the lives of self and others (fourth grade)

f. recognize what a lifestyle is and what influences their lifestyles (fifth grade)

2. Students will acknowledge the interactive effect of lifestyles, life roles, settings, and events in their lives. Students will

a. analyze ways they have control over themselves and their lifestyles (sixth grade)

b. evaluate their feelings in a variety of settings (seventh grade)

c. predict their feelings in a variety of potential settings (eighth grade)

d. analyze how life roles, settings, and events determine preferred lifestyles (ninth grade)

e. compare how lifestyles differ depending on life roles, settings, and events (10th grade)

3. Students will understand the interactive effects of lifestyles, life roles, settings, and events. Students will

a. determine how life roles, settings, and events have influenced their current lifestyles (11th grade)

b. assess the interactive effects of life roles, settings, and events and how these lead to a preferred lifestyle (12th grade)

D. *Students will develop and incorporate an understanding of stereotypes and how stereotypes affect career identity.*
   1. Students will be aware of stereotypes and some of their effects. Students will
      a. mentally project adults into work activities other than those they do currently (kindergarten)
      b. recognize how peers differ from themselves (first grade)
      c. distinguish which work activities in their environment are done by certain people (second grade)
      d. recognize why people choose certain work activities and that those choices may change (third grade)
      e. define the meaning of *stereotypes* and indicate how stereotypes affect them (fourth grade)
      f. describe stereotypes that correspond with certain jobs (fifth grade)
   2. Students will demonstrate a growing ability to understand stereotypes and how stereotypes affect career identity. Students will
      a. predict how stereotypes might affect them in work activities (sixth grade)
      b. describe occupations that have stereotypes and will analyze how those stereotypes are reinforced (seventh grade)
      c. evaluate the ways in which certain groups (men, women, minorities, and so on) are stereotyped (eighth grade)
      d. analyze stereotypes that exist for them and how those stereotypes limit their choices (ninth grade)
      e. analyze stereotypes others hold and how those stereotypes can limit choices (10th grade)
   3. Students will understand stereotypes in their lives and environment and how stereotypes affect career identity. Students will
      a. evaluate their stereotypes and explain those they have changed (11th grade)
      b. analyze the effect stereotypes have on career identity (12th grade)

E. *Students will develop and incorporate the ability to express futuristic concerns and the ability to imagine themselves in these situations.*
   1. Students will be aware of the future and what situations might occur in the future. Students will
      a. describe situations that are going to happen in the future (kindergarten)
      b. describe situations desired for the future and when they would like those situations to happen (first grade)
      c. recognize what they would like to accomplish when they are 3 years older (second grade)
      d. define what *future* means (third grade)
   2. Students will demonstrate a growing ability to express futuristic concerns and to imagine themselves in such situations. Students will
      a. imagine what their lives might be like in the future (fourth grade)
      b. imagine what the world will be like in 20 years (fifth grade)
      c. predict what they will be like in 20 years (sixth grade)
      d. predict ways in which some current careers may be different in the future (seventh grade)
      e. predict how they may have to change to fit into a career in the future (eighth grade)

f. analyze how choices they are making now will affect their lives in the future (ninth grade)

g. predict some of the concerns they will have as they get older (10th grade)

3. Students will express futuristic concerns and will imagine themselves in these situations. Students will

a. evaluate the need for flexibility in their roles and in their choices (11th grade)

b. analyze how concerns change as situations and roles change (12th grade)

III. *Life Career Planning*

A. *Students will develop and incorporate an understanding of producer rights and responsibilities.*

1. Students will be aware of what a producer is and that producers have rights and responsibilities. Students will

a. describe the work activities of family members (kindergarten)

b. describe different work activities and their importance (first grade)

c. define *work* and recognize that all people work (second grade)

d. realize that people obtain rewards for their work (third grade)

e. recognize that a producer can have many different roles (fourth grade)

f. recognize how they depend on different producers (fifth grade)

2. Students will demonstrate an understanding of what a producer is and producer rights and responsibilities. Students will

a. demonstrate steps they follow in producing a product or task they take pride in (sixth grade)

b. show appreciation when others successfully complete a difficult task (seventh grade)

c. analyze the relationship between interests and producer satisfaction (eighth grade)

d. analyze how producers may have to cooperate with each other to accomplish a large or difficult task (ninth grade)

e. evaluate the importance of having laws and contracts to protect producers (10th grade)

3. Students will understand and exemplify producer rights and responsibilities. Students will

a. specify their rights and responsibilities as producers (11th grade)

b. speculate what their rights and responsibilities might be as producers in the future (12th grade)

B. *Students will develop and incorporate an understanding of how attitudes and values affect decisions, actions, and lifestyles.*

1. Students will be aware of attitudes and values and their effects. Students will

a. describe people and activities they enjoy (kindergarten)

b. describe actions of others that they do not appreciate (first grade)

c. describe things they have learned that aid in making choices (second grade)

d. recognize accomplishments they are proud of (third grade)

      e. define *attitudes* and *beliefs* and describe the effects attitudes and beliefs have on decisions (fourth grade)

      f. define *values* and describe their own values (fifth grade)

2. Students will demonstrate a growing understanding of how attitudes and values affect decisions, actions, and lifestyles. Students will

      a. analyze how their attitudes and values influence what they do (sixth grade)

      b. compare and contrast others' values (seventh grade)

      c. predict how their values will influence their lifestyles (eighth grade)

      d. describe and set priorities for their values (ninth grade)

      e. describe decisions they have made that were based on their attitudes and values (10th grade)

3. Students will understand how attitudes and values affect decisions, actions, and lifestyles. Students will

      a. analyze how values affect their decisions, actions, and lifestyles (11th grade)

      b. summarize the importance of understanding their attitudes and values and how those attitudes and values affect their lives (12th grade)

C. *Students will develop and incorporate an understanding of the decision-making process and how the decisions they make are influenced by previous decisions made by themselves and others.*

1. Students will be aware of decisions and the decision-making process. Students will

      a. describe choices they make (kindergarten)

      b. describe decisions they make by themselves (first grade)

      c. recognize why some choices are made for them; they can accept those choices and make their own decisions when appropriate (second grade)

      d. describe their thought processes before a decision is made (third grade)

      e. describe why they might want to change a decision and recognize when it is or is not possible to make that change (fourth grade)

      f. describe the decision-making process (fifth grade)

      g. recognize how school decisions influence them (sixth grade)

2. Students will understand the decision-making process and factors that influence the decisions they make. Students will

      a. provide examples of how past decisions they have made influence their present actions (seventh grade)

      b. analyze how past decisions made by their families influence their current decisions (eighth grade)

      c. evaluate the influence that past legal decisions have on their current decisions (ninth grade)

      d. analyze the decision-making process used by others (10th grade)

3. Students will effectively use the decision-making process and understand how the decisions they make are influenced by previous decisions made by themselves and others. Students will

      a. identify decisions they have made and analyze how those decisions will affect their future decisions (11th grade)

      b. implement the decision-making process when making a decision (12th grade)

D. *Students will develop and incorporate the ability to generate decision-making alternatives, gather necessary information, and assess the risks and consequences of alternatives.*

   1. Students will be aware of methods of generating decision-making alternatives, gather necessary information, and assess the risks and consequences of alternatives. Students will

      a. realize the difficulty of making choices between two desirable alternatives (kindergarten)

      b. recognize those decisions that are difficult for them (first grade)

      c. realize that they go through a decision-making process each time they make a choice (second grade)

      d. recognize that they are able to assess possible consequences of a decision before actually making the choice (third grade)

   2. Students will demonstrate a growing ability to generate decision-making alternatives, gather necessary information, and assess the risks and consequences of alternatives. Students will

      a. generate alternatives to a specific decision (fourth grade)

      b. evaluate some of the risks involved in choosing one alternative over another (fifth grade)

      c. consider the results of various alternatives and then make their choice (sixth grade)

      d. provide examples of some consequences of a decision (seventh grade)

      e. demonstrate how gaining more information increases their alternatives (eighth grade)

      f. analyze the importance of generating alternatives and assessing the consequences of each before making a decision (ninth grade)

      g. distinguish between alternatives that involve varying degrees of risk (10th grade)

      h. analyze the consequences of decisions that others make (11th grade)

   3. Students will generate decision-making alternatives, gather necessary information, and assess the risks and consequences of alternatives. Students will

      a. provide examples and evaluate their current ability to generate alternatives, gather information, and assess the consequences in the decisions they make (12th grade)

E. *Students will develop and incorporate skill in clarifying values, expanding interests and capabilities, and evaluating progress toward goals.*

   1. Students will be aware of values, interests and capabilities, and methods of evaluation. Students will

      a. describe growing capabilities (kindergarten)

      b. identify capabilities they wish to develop (first grade)

      c. recognize activities that interest them and those that do not (second grade)

      d. realize that environment influences interests and capabilities (third grade)

      e. recognize different methods of evaluating task progress (fourth grade)

      f. describe the meaning of value and how values contribute toward goal decisions (fifth grade)

2. Students will gain skill in clarifying values, expanding interests and capabilities, and evaluating progress toward goals. Students will
   a. predict five goals (based on their interests and capabilities) they would like to achieve within 5 years (sixth grade)
   b. analyze various methods of evaluating their progress toward a goal (seventh grade)
   c. contrast goals they desire to complete with goals they expect to complete (eighth grade)
   d. define their unique values, interests, and capabilities (ninth grade)
   e. evaluate the importance of setting realistic goals and striving toward them (10th grade)
3. Students will clarify their values, expand their interests and capabilities, and evaluate their progress toward goals. Students will
   a. analyze how their values, interests, and capabilities have changed and are changing (11th grade)
   b. assess their ability to achieve past goals and integrate this knowledge for the future (12th grade)

American School Counselor Association Ethical Standards for School Counselors

The American School Counselor Association's (ASCA) *Ethical Standards for School Counselors* were adopted by the ASCA Delegate Assembly, March 19, 1984; revised March 27, 1992; June 25, 1998; and June 26, 2004.

Preamble

The American School Counselor Association (ASCA) is a professional organization whose members are certified/licensed in school counseling with unique qualifications and skills to address the academic, personal/social, and career development needs of all students. Professional school counselors are advocates, leaders, collaborators, and consultants who create opportunities for equity in access and success in educational opportunities by connecting their programs to the mission of schools and subscribing to the following tenets of professional responsibility:

- Each person has the right to be respected, be treated with dignity, and have access to a comprehensive school counseling program that advocates for and affirms all students from diverse populations regardless of ethnic/racial status, age, economic status, special needs, English as a second language or other language group, immigration status, sexual orientation, gender, gender identity/expression, family type, religious/spiritual identity, and appearance.
- Each person has the right to receive the information and support needed to move toward self-direction and self-development and affirmation within one's group identities, with special care being given to students who have historically not received adequate educational services: students of color, low socioeconomic students, students with disabilities, and students with nondominant language backgrounds.
- Each person has the right to understand the full magnitude and meaning of his/her educational choices and how those choices will affect future opportunities.
- Each person has the right to privacy and thereby the right to expect the counselor–student relationship to comply with all laws, policies, and ethical standards pertaining to confidentiality in the school setting.

In this document, ASCA specifies the principles of ethical behavior necessary to maintain the high standards of integrity, leadership, and professionalism among its members. The Ethical Standards for School Counselors were developed to clarify the nature of ethical responsibilities held in common by school counseling professionals. The purposes of this document are to:

- Serve as a guide for the ethical practices of all professional school counselors regardless of level, area, population served, or membership in this professional association;
- Provide self-appraisal and peer evaluations regarding counselor responsibilities to students, parents/guardians, colleagues and professional associates, schools, communities, and the counseling profession; and
- Inform those served by the school counselor of acceptable counselor practices and expected professional behavior.

A.1. *Responsibilities to Students*

The professional school counselor:
- a. Has a primary obligation to the student, who is to be treated with respect as a unique individual.
- b. Is concerned with the educational, academic, career, personal, and social needs and encourages the maximum development of every student.
- c. Respects the student's values and beliefs and does not impose the counselor's personal values.
- d. Is knowledgeable of laws, regulations, and policies relating to students and strives to protect and inform students regarding their rights.

A.2. *Confidentiality*

The professional school counselor:
- a. Informs students of the purposes, goals, techniques, and rules of procedure under which they may receive counseling at or before the time when the counseling relationship is entered. Disclosure notice includes the limits of confidentiality such as the possible necessity for consulting with other professionals, privileged communication, and legal or authoritative restraints. The meaning and limits of confidentiality are defined in developmentally appropriate terms to students.
- b. Keeps information confidential unless disclosure is required to prevent clear and imminent danger to the student or others or when legal requirements demand that confidential information be revealed. Counselors will consult with appropriate professionals when in doubt as to the validity of an exception.
- c. In absence of state legislation expressly forbidding disclosure, considers the ethical responsibility to provide information to an identified third party who, by his/her relationship with the student, is at a high risk of contracting a disease that is commonly known to be communicable and fatal. Disclosure requires satisfaction of all of the following conditions:
  - Student identifies partner or the partner is highly identifiable
  - Counselor recommends the student notify partner and refrain from further high-risk behavior
  - Student refuses
  - Counselor informs the student of the intent to notify the partner
  - Counselor seeks legal consultation as to the legalities of informing the partner
- d. Requests of the court that disclosure not be required when the release of confidential information may potentially harm a student or the counseling relationship.
- e. Protects the confidentiality of students' records and releases personal data in accordance with prescribed laws and school policies. Student information stored and transmitted electronically is treated with the same care as traditional student records.

f. Protects the confidentiality of information received in the counseling relationship as specified by federal and state laws, written policies, and applicable ethical standards. Such information is only to be revealed to others with the informed consent of the student, consistent with the counselor's ethical obligation.
g. Recognizes his/her primary obligation for confidentiality is to the student but balances that obligation with an understanding of the legal and inherent rights of parents/guardians to be the guiding voice in their children's lives.

A.3. *Counseling Plans*

The professional school counselor:
a. Provides students with a comprehensive school counseling program that includes a strong emphasis on working jointly with all students to develop academic and career goals.
b. Advocates for counseling plans supporting students right to choose from the wide array of options when they leave secondary education. Such plans will be regularly reviewed to update students regarding critical information they need to make informed decisions.

A.4. *Dual Relationships*

The professional school counselor:
a. Avoids dual relationships that might impair his/her objectivity and increase the risk of harm to the student (e.g., counseling one's family members, close friends, or associates). If a dual relationship is unavoidable, the counselor is responsible for taking action to eliminate or reduce the potential for harm. Such safeguards might include informed consent, consultation, supervision, and documentation.
b. Avoids dual relationships with school personnel that might infringe on the integrity of the counselor–student relationship.

A.5. *Appropriate Referrals*

The professional school counselor:
a. Makes referrals when necessary or appropriate to outside resources. Appropriate referrals may necessitate informing both parents/guardians and students of applicable resources and making proper plans for transitions with minimal interruption of services. Students retain the right to discontinue the counseling relationship at any time.

A.6. *Group Work*

The professional school counselor:
a. Screens prospective group members and maintains an awareness of participants' needs and goals in relation to the goals of the group. The counselor takes reasonable precautions to protect members from physical and psychological harm resulting from interaction within the group.
b. Notifies parents/guardians and staff of group participation if the counselor deems it appropriate and if consistent with school board policy or practice.
c. Establishes clear expectations in the group setting and clearly states that confidentiality in group counseling cannot be guaranteed. Given the developmental and

chronological ages of minors in schools, the counselor recognizes the tenuous nature of confidentiality for minors renders some topics inappropriate for group work in a school setting.

d. Follows up with group members and documents proceedings as appropriate.

A.7. *Danger to Self or Others*

The professional school counselor:

a. Informs parents/guardians or appropriate authorities when the student's condition indicates a clear and imminent danger to the student or others. This is to be done after careful deliberation and, where possible, after consultation with other counseling professionals.

b. Will attempt to minimize threat to a student and may choose to (1) inform the student of actions to be taken, (2) involve the student in a three-way communication with parents/guardians when breaching confidentiality, or (3) allow the student to have input as to how and to whom the breach will be made.

A.8. *Student Records*

The professional school counselor:

a. Maintains and secures records necessary for rendering professional services to the student as required by laws, regulations, institutional procedures, and confidentiality guidelines.

b. Keeps sole-possession records separate from students' educational records in keeping with state laws.

c. Recognizes the limits of sole-possession records and understands these records are a memory aid for the creator and in absence of privilege communication may be subpoenaed and may become educational records when they (1) are shared with others in verbal or written form, (2) include information other than professional opinion or personal observations, and/or (3) are made accessible to others.

d. Establishes a reasonable timeline for purging sole-possession records or case notes. Suggested guidelines include shredding sole possession records when the student transitions to the next level, transfers to another school, or graduates. Careful discretion and deliberation should be applied before destroying sole-possession records that may be needed by a court of law such as notes on child abuse, suicide, sexual harassment, or violence.

A.9. *Evaluation, Assessment, and Interpretation*

The professional school counselor:

a. Adheres to all professional standards regarding selecting, administering, and interpreting assessment measures and only utilizes assessment measures that are within the scope of practice for school counselors.

b. Seeks specialized training regarding the use of electronically based testing programs in administering, scoring, and interpreting that may differ from that required in more traditional assessments.

c. Considers confidentiality issues when utilizing evaluative or assessment instruments and electronically based programs.

d. Provides interpretation of the nature, purposes, results, and potential impact of assessment/evaluation measures in language the student(s) can understand.

e. Monitors the use of assessment results and interpretations, and takes reasonable steps to prevent others from misusing the information.

f. Uses caution when utilizing assessment techniques, making evaluations, and interpreting the performance of populations not represented in the norm group on which an instrument is standardized.

g. Assesses the effectiveness of his/her program in having an impact on students' academic, career, and personal/social development through accountability measures especially examining efforts to close achievement, opportunity, and attainment gaps.

A.10. *Technology*

The professional school counselor:

a. Promotes the benefits of and clarifies the limitations of various appropriate technological applications. The counselor promotes technological applications (1) that are appropriate for the student's individual needs, (2) that the student understands how to use, and (3) for which follow-up counseling assistance is provided.

b. Advocates for equal access to technology for all students, especially those historically underserved.

c. Takes appropriate and reasonable measures for maintaining confidentiality of student information and educational records stored or transmitted over electronic media including although not limited to fax, electronic mail, and instant messaging.

d. While working with students on a computer or similar technology, takes reasonable and appropriate measures to protect students from objectionable and/or harmful online material.

e. Who is engaged in the delivery of services involving technologies such as the telephone, videoconferencing, and the Internet takes responsible steps to protect students and others from harm.

A.11. *Student Peer Support Program*

The professional school counselor:

Has unique responsibilities when working with student-assistance programs. The school counselor is responsible for the welfare of students participating in peer-to-peer programs under his/her direction.

B. RESPONSIBILITIES TO PARENTS/GUARDIANS

B.1. *Parent Rights and Responsibilities*

The professional school counselor:

a. Respects the rights and responsibilities of parents/guardians for their children and endeavors to establish, as appropriate, a collaborative relationship with parents/guardians to facilitate the student's maximum development.

b. Adheres to laws, local guidelines, and ethical standards of practice when assisting parents/guardians experiencing family difficulties that interfere with the student's effectiveness and welfare.

c. Respects the confidentiality of parents/guardians.

d. Is sensitive to diversity among families and recognizes that all parents/guardians, custodial and noncustodial, are vested with certain rights and responsibilities for the welfare of their children by virtue of their role and according to law.

B.2. *Parents/Guardians and Confidentiality*

The professional school counselor:

    a. Informs parents/guardians of the counselor's role with emphasis on the confidential nature of the counseling relationship between the counselor and student.

    b. Recognizes that working with minors in a school setting may require counselors to collaborate with students' parents/guardians.

    c. Provides parents/guardians with accurate, comprehensive, and relevant information in an objective and caring manner, as is appropriate and consistent with ethical responsibilities to the student.

    d. Makes reasonable efforts to honor the wishes of parents/guardians concerning information regarding the student, and in cases of divorce or separation exercises a good-faith effort to keep both parents informed with regard to critical information with the exception of a court order.

C. RESPONSIBILITIES TO COLLEAGUES AND PROFESSIONAL ASSOCIATES

C.1. *Professional Relationships*

The professional school counselor:

    a. Establishes and maintains professional relationships with faculty, staff, and administration to facilitate an optimum counseling program.

    b. Treats colleagues with professional respect, courtesy, and fairness. The qualifications, views, and findings of colleagues are represented to accurately reflect the image of competent professionals.

    c. Is aware of and utilizes related professionals, organizations, and other resources to whom the student may be referred.

C.2. *Sharing Information With Other Professionals*

The professional school counselor:

    a. Promotes awareness and adherence to appropriate guidelines regarding confidentiality, the distinction between public and private information, and staff consultation.

    b. Provides professional personnel with accurate, objective, concise, and meaningful data necessary to adequately evaluate, counsel, and assist the student.

    c. If a student is receiving services from another counselor or other mental health professional, the counselor, with student and/or parent/guardian consent, will inform the other professional and develop clear agreements to avoid confusion and conflict for the student.

    d. Is knowledgeable about release of information and parental rights in sharing information.

D. RESPONSIBILITIES TO THE SCHOOL AND COMMUNITY

D.1. *Responsibilities to the School*

The professional school counselor:

    a. Supports and protects the educational program against any infringement not in students' best interest.

b. Informs appropriate officials in accordance with school policy of conditions that may be potentially disruptive or damaging to the school's mission, personnel, and property while honoring the confidentiality between the student and counselor.

c. Is knowledgeable and supportive of the school's mission and connects his/her program to the school's mission.

d. Delineates and promotes the counselor's role and function in meeting the needs of those served. Counselors will notify appropriate officials of conditions that may limit or curtail their effectiveness in providing programs and services.

e. Accepts employment only for positions for which he/she is qualified by education, training, supervised experience, state and national professional credentials, and appropriate professional experience.

f. Advocates that administrators hire only qualified and competent individuals for professional counseling positions.

g. Assists in developing (1) curricular and environmental conditions appropriate for the school and community, (2) educational procedures and programs to meet students' developmental needs, and (3) a systematic evaluation process for comprehensive, developmental, standards-based school counseling programs, services, and personnel. The counselor is guided by the findings of the evaluation data in planning programs and services.

D.2. *Responsibility to the Community*

The professional school counselor:

a. Collaborates with agencies, organizations, and individuals in the community in the best interest of students and without regard to personal reward or remuneration.

b. Extends his/her influence and opportunity to deliver a comprehensive school counseling program to all students by collaborating with community resources for student success.

E. RESPONSIBILITIES TO SELF

E.1. *Professional Competence*

The professional school counselor:

a. Functions within the boundaries of individual professional competence and accepts responsibility for the consequences of his/her actions.

b. Monitors personal well-being and effectiveness and does not participate in any activity that may lead to inadequate professional services or harm to a student.

c. Strives through personal initiative to maintain professional competence including technological literacy and to keep abreast of professional information. Professional and personal growth are ongoing throughout the counselor's career.

E.2. *Diversity*

The professional school counselor:

a. Affirms the diversity of students, staff, and families.

b. Expands and develops awareness of his/her own attitudes and beliefs affecting cultural values and biases and strives to attain cultural competence.

c. Possesses knowledge and understanding about how oppression, racism, discrimination, and stereotyping affects her/him personally and professionally.

d. Acquires educational, consultation, and training experiences to improve awareness, knowledge, skills, and effectiveness in working with diverse populations: ethnic/racial status, age, economic status, special needs, ESL or ELL, immigration status, sexual orientation, gender, gender identity/expression, family type, religious/spiritual identity, and appearance.

F. RESPONSIBILITIES TO THE PROFESSION

F.1. *Professionalism*

The professional school counselor:
  a. Accepts the policies and procedures for handling ethical violations as a result of maintaining membership in the American School Counselor Association.
  b. Conducts herself/himself in such a manner as to advance individual ethical practice and the profession.
  c. Conducts appropriate research and reports findings in a manner consistent with acceptable educational and psychological research practices. The counselor advocates for the protection of the individual student's identity when using data for research or program planning.
  d. Adheres to ethical standards of the profession, other official policy statements, such as ASCA's position statements, role statement, and the ASCA National Model, and relevant statutes established by federal, state, and local governments, and when these are in conflict works responsibly for change.
  e. Clearly distinguishes between statements and actions made as a private individual and those made as a representative of the school counseling profession.
  f. Does not use his/her professional position to recruit or gain clients, consultees for his/her private practice or to seek and receive unjustified personal gains, unfair advantage, inappropriate relationships, or unearned goods or services.

F.2. *Contribution to the Profession*

The professional school counselor:
  a. Actively participates in local, state, and national associations fostering the development and improvement of school counseling.
  b. Contributes to the development of the profession through the sharing of skills, ideas, and expertise with colleagues.
  c. Provides support and mentoring to novice professionals.

G. MAINTENANCE OF STANDARDS

Ethical behavior among professional school counselors, association members, and non-members is expected at all times. When there exists serious doubt as to the ethical behavior of colleagues or if counselors are forced to work in situations or abide by policies that do not reflect the standards as outlined in these Ethical Standards for School Counselors, the counselor is obligated to take appropriate action to rectify the condition. The following procedure may serve as a guide:

  1. The counselor should consult confidentially with a professional colleague to discuss the nature of a complaint to see if the professional colleague views the situation as an ethical violation.

2. When feasible, the counselor should directly approach the colleague whose behavior is in question to discuss the complaint and seek resolution.

3. If resolution is not forthcoming at the personal level, the counselor shall utilize the channels established within the school, school district, the state school counseling association, and ASCA's Ethics Committee.

4. If the matter still remains unresolved, referral for review and appropriate action should be made to the Ethics Committees in the following sequence:
   • state school counselor association
   • American School Counselor Association

5. The ASCA Ethics Committee is responsible for:
   • educating and consulting with the membership regarding ethical standards
   • periodically reviewing and recommending changes in code
   • receiving and processing questions to clarify the application of such standards; questions must be submitted in writing to the ASCA Ethics chair.
   • handling complaints of alleged violations of the ethical standards. At the national level, complaints should be submitted in writing to the ASCA Ethics Committee, c/o the Executive Director, American School Counselor Association, 1101 King St., Suite 625, Alexandria, VA 22314.

⌒ Appendix C ⌒

Time and Task Analysis
Procedures and Forms

A. *Conduct a Time and Task Analysis*

The time and task analysis is a survey of the time it takes for professional school counselors to perform the tasks they are assigned in the current program. The results of this analysis will provide a basis for comparing the time and tasks involved in the current program to the time and tasks chosen for the desired district's comprehensive guidance program. A district may conduct the time and task analysis using either 15- or 30-minute time intervals.

Before a time and task analysis is conducted, however, it is important for all of the professional school counselors in the district to meet by grade level (elementary, middle, and high school) to determine where their current tasks fit into the program components. (In small school districts, all professional school counselors in the district may work together to complete this task.) This can be accomplished by having each group divide large sheets of paper into five columns. The columns should be labeled (a) guidance curriculum, (b) individual planning, (c) responsive services; (d) system support, and (e) nonguidance activities. The task is for the professional school counselors at each level to list and categorize their current tasks. The result is a chart for each level that contains all of the tasks professional school counselors are currently responsible for, categorized by the four program components and nonguidance activities. This exercise will provide all professional school counselors in a district with the knowledge of what current tasks go where when they fill out the time and task analysis form so that everyone will interpret the form in the same way. It is important to remember that fair-share activities are included in system support.

The following steps are necessary to conduct the time and task analysis:

1. Identify the starting and ending time for the analysis based on the school schedule. The analysis can begin at any time as long as it is conducted for a full school year.
2. Use either the 15-minute or 30-minute time intervals and task analysis form. Begin collecting data on Monday, the first week. The next week collect data on Tuesday. On the third week, collect data on Wednesday. On the fourth week, collect data on Thursday, and on the fifth week, collect data on Friday. Beginning with the sixth week, repeat the process for a full school year.
3. Use the time and task analysis form selected to keep track of the actual time professional school counselors currently spend in activities in each program component plus nonguidance activities. Note that the form has a time block for before school, after school, and evening activities conducted as part of the program.
4. Determine the component into which the activity currently being conducted is placed. Place a check in the appropriate category for each 15- or 30-minute interval. For the nonguidance category, write in the actual nonguidance tasks.

5. Analyze the data by counting the total number of 15- or 30-minute daily blocks of time for each day. Do NOT count a block of time when not on duty. Next count the number of 15- or 30-minute intervals marked in each category. Record these figures in the appropriate blocks at the bottom of the survey. Calculate the percentages for the day in each category by dividing the total daily category blocks of time marked by the total daily blocks of time.

6. To get the grand total of the time and task analysis form, total the blocks of time for each category for all days. Calculate the percentages of time spent in each category by dividing each grand total category block by the grand total number of all blocks.

7. Chart these percentages for the current program using the time distribution forms.

Conducting an Internal Factors/Trends Analysis

This analysis examines factors/trends inside the schools of a district that may impact the development and management of the district's comprehensive guidance program. These factors/trends may include the following:

- Who the current program is actually serving
- Existing resources (personnel, equipment, materials, and facilities)
- Guidance activities presently in place, including those directed by professional school counselors and those directed by others
- Staff expertise that may be helpful in conducting a district's comprehensive guidance program activities
- Attitudes of faculty, staff, and students toward the district's current guidance activities
- The MSIP evaluation results

Conducting an External Factors/Trends Analysis

This analysis examines factors/trends outside the schools of the district that may impact on the district's comprehensive guidance program. These factors/trends may include the following:

- Postsecondary activities of graduates
- Economic conditions of the community
- Population changes
- Attitudes of community members
- Community resources

Time and Task Analysis Form
30-Minute Intervals

Time	Guidance Curriculum	Individual Planning	Responsive Services	System Support	Nonguidance Activities
7:00–7:30	❑	❑	❑	❑	❑ _____
7:30–8:00	❑	❑	❑	❑	❑ _____
8:00–8:30	❑	❑	❑	❑	❑ _____
8:30–9:00	❑	❑	❑	❑	❑ _____
9:00–9:30	❑	❑	❑	❑	❑ _____
9:30–10:00	❑	❑	❑	❑	❑ _____
10:00–10:30	❑	❑	❑	❑	❑ _____
10:30–11:00	❑	❑	❑	❑	❑ _____
11:00–11:30	❑	❑	❑	❑	❑ _____
11:30 12:00	❑	❑	❑	❑	❑ _____
12:00–12:30	❑	❑	❑	❑	❑ _____
12:30–1:00	❑	❑	❑	❑	❑ _____
1:00–1:30	❑	❑	❑	❑	❑ _____
1:30–2:00	❑	❑	❑	❑	❑ _____
2:00–2:30	❑	❑	❑	❑	❑ _____
2:30–3:00	❑	❑	❑	❑	❑ _____
3:00–3:30	❑	❑	❑	❑	❑ _____
3:30–4:00	❑	❑	❑	❑	❑ _____
4:00–4:30	❑	❑	❑	❑	❑ _____
4:30–5:00	❑	❑	❑	❑	❑ _____
5:00–5:30	❑	❑	❑	❑	❑ _____
5:30–6:00	❑	❑	❑	❑	❑ _____
6:00–6:30	❑	❑	❑	❑	❑ _____
6:30–7:00	❑	❑	❑	❑	❑ _____
7:00–7:30	❑	❑	❑	❑	❑ _____
7:30–8:00	❑	❑	❑	❑	❑ _____
8:00–8:30	❑	❑	❑	❑	❑ _____
8:30–9:00	❑	❑	❑	❑	❑ _____

	Guidance Curriculum	Individual Planning	Responsive Services	System Support	Nonguidance Activities
Number of Blocks:	▭	▭	▭	▭	▭
Daily Percentage:	▭	▭	▭	▭	▭

Grade Total Number of Blocks: ▭

Grade Total Percentages: ▭

Time Distribution Form
Elementary Level

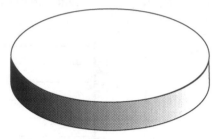

Current District Program Percentages

**Current District
Program Percentages:**

____ guidance curriculum
____ individual planning
____ responsive services
____ system support
____ nonguidance

**State-Suggested
Percentages:**

35%–45% guidance curriculum
5%–10% individual planning
30%–40% responsive services
10%–15% system support
0% nonguidance

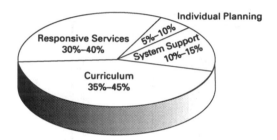

State Suggested Percentages

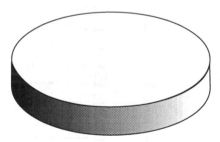

Desired District Program Percentages

**Desired District
Program Percentages:**

____ guidance curriculum
____ individual planning
____ responsive services
____ system support
____ nonguidance

Time Distribution Form
Middle School/Junior High Level

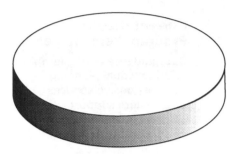

Current District Program Percentages

Current District Program Percentages:

____ guidance curriculum
____ individual planning
____ responsive services
____ system support
____ nonguidance

State-Suggested Percentages:

25%–35% guidance curriculum
15%–25% individual planning
30%–40% responsive services
10%–15% system support
0% nonguidance

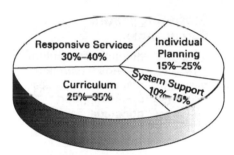

State Suggested Percentages

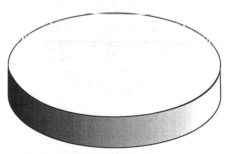

Desired District Program Percentages

Desired District Program Percentages:

____ guidance curriculum
____ individual planning
____ responsive services
____ system support
____ nonguidance

Time Distribution Form
High School Level

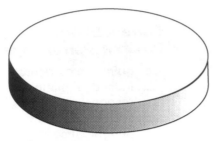

Current District Program Percentages

Current District Program Percentages:

____ guidance curriculum
____ individual planning
____ responsive services
____ system support
____ nonguidance

State-Suggested Percentages:

15%–25% guidance curriculum
25%–35% individual planning
25%–35% responsive services
15%–20% system support
0% nonguidance

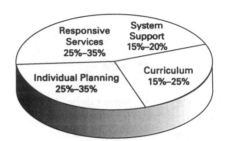

State Suggested Percentages

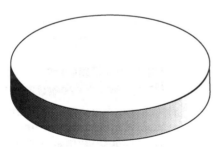

Desired District Program Percentages

Desired District Program Percentages:

____ guidance curriculum
____ individual planning
____ responsive services
____ system support
____ nonguidance

Appendix D

Guidance Program Evaluation Surveys

1. A LOOK AT THE COUNSELORS—FROM THE HIGH SCHOOL STUDENT'S POINT OF VIEW

INSTRUCTIONS: Circle one category in each of the three demographic areas in the box below.

GRADE: 9 10 11 12	GENDER: Female Male	ETHNICITY: Native American Asian Black Hispanic White

WAYS IN WHICH YOU MET WITH A COUNSELOR: About how many times has a counselor met with you in each of the following ways?

	Since Winter Vacation	For the Entire School Year
Classroom presentation by a counselor	_____	_____
Small group meetings with a counselor	_____	_____
One-on-one meetings with a counselor	_____	_____
Student/parent/counselor conferences	_____	_____
Student/teacher/counselor/conferences	_____	_____
Meetings with a counselor and someone from outside the school	_____	_____

SERVICES PROVIDED OR TOPICS DISCUSSED BY A COUNSELOR

	HAS A COUNSELOR MET WITH YOU TO . . .			IF IT HAPPENED, WAS IT HELPFUL?				
	Yes	Unsure	No	Very Much	Quite a Bit	Some-what	Very Little	Not Really
. . . help manage your feelings?								
. . . provide guidance so you can make good decisions?								
. . . guide you in taking responsibility for your educational planning?								
. . . assist in setting goals and making plans?								
. . . help you in accepting the consequences of your decisions?								
. . . help you manage changes?								
. . . aid in understanding others' behaviors?								
. . . help you take responsibility for your behavior?								
. . . help you cope with peer relationships?								
. . . set challenging educational goals?								

SERVICES PROVIDED OR TOPICS DISCUSSED BY A COUNSELOR (continued)

	HAS A COUNSELOR MET WITH YOU TO . . .			IF IT HAPPENED, WAS IT HELPFUL?				
	Yes	Unsure	No	Very Much	Quite a Bit	Some-what	Very Little	Not Really
. . . help establish personal goals?								
. . . make available information on educational opportunities?								
. . . help you select specific high school courses reflecting your educational goals?								
. . . assist in making plans for achieving short-, intermediate and long-term goals?								
. . . relate jobs to interests, skills, values, and education?								
. . . assist in career and/or vocational planning?								
. . . discuss the importance of time management?								
. . . talk about peer pressure?								
. . . address health-related problems?								
. . . help with behavior problems?								
. . . aid in explaining test results?								
. . . help you to deal with feelings of grief and/or loss?								
. . . give you information on community agencies and/or resources?								
. . . provide help when you were experiencing academic difficulty?								
. . . just listen?								
. . . help you deal with stress?								
. . . coordinate conferences between your parents and school staff?								
. . . help you deal with a drug and/or alcohol problem?								
. . . offer guidance on a personal, private issue?								

YOUR CLOSING THOUGHTS: What was the one service or topic of discussion that was *most beneficial* or *helpful* to you?

_____

_____

YOUR CLOSING THOUGHTS: Overall, is the high school guidance program meeting your needs?   YES   UNSURE   NO   Why?

_____

_____

2. A LOOK AT THE COUNSELORS—FROM THE HIGH SCHOOL COUNSELOR'S POINT OF VIEW

STUDENT CONTACT: Over the course of the 1994–95 school year, of the total student body, about what percent did you meet with in each of the following ways (to the nearest five percent)? To the nearest tenth (X.X times) about how many times did you meet with the average student in each of the following ways?

	Percent of Student Body	Number of Times per Student
Classroom presentations	___	___
Small group meetings	___	___
One-on-one meetings	___	___
Student/parent/counselor conferences	___	___
Student/teacher/counselor conferences	___	___
Meetings with a student and someone from outside the school	___	

SERVICES PROVIDED OR TOPICS DISCUSSED

	FOR THE STUDENTS FOR WHOM YOU WERE ASSIGNED, HOW MANY DID YOU MEET TO...							WAS IT HELPFUL TO THE STUDENTS?				
(see scale below)	6	5	4	3	2	1		Very Much	Quite a Bit	Some-what	Very Little	Not Really
...help manage their feelings?												
...provide guidance to help them make good decisions?												
...guide them in taking responsibility for their educational planning?												
...assist in setting goals and making plans?												
...help in accepting the consequences of their decisions?												
...help manage changes?												
...aid in understanding others' behaviors?												
...help take responsibility for their behavior?												
...help cope with peer relationships?												
...help set challenging educational goals?												
...help establish personal goals?												

6 = All, virtually all   5 = Most   4 = Quite a few   3 = Some; more than just a few   2 = Only a handful, or so   1 = None, virtually none

SERVICES PROVIDED OR TOPICS DISCUSSED
(continued)

	FOR THE STUDENTS FOR WHOM YOU WERE ASSIGNED, HOW MANY DID YOU MEET TO. . .						WAS IT HELPFUL TO THE STUDENTS?				
(see scale below)	6	5	4	3	2	1	Very Much	Quite a Bit	Some-what	Very Little	Not Really
. . . make available information on educational opportunities?											
. . . help select specific high school courses reflecting their educational goals?											
. . . assist in making plans for achieving short-, intermediate, and long-term goals?											
. . . relate jobs to interests, skills, values and education?											
. . . assist in career and/or vocational planning?											
. . . discuss the importance of time management?											
. . . talk about peer pressure?											
. . . address health-related problems?											
. . . help with behavior problems?											
. . . aid in explaining test results?											
. . . help in dealing with feelings of grief and/or loss?											
. . . give them information on community agencies and/or resources?											
. . . provide help when they were experiencing academic difficulty?											
. . . just listen?											
. . . help deal with stress?											
. . . coordinate conferences between parents and school staff?											
. . . help deal with a drug and/or alcohol problem?											
. . . offer guidance on a personal, private issue?											

6 = All, virtually all   5 = Most   4 = Quite a few   3 = Some; more than just a few   2 = Only a handful, or so   1 = None, virtually none

YOUR CLOSING THOUGHTS: What was the one service or discussion that was *most beneficial or helpful* to the students?

_____

_____

_____

YOUR CLOSING THOUGHTS: Overall, is the high school guidance program meeting your needs?   YES   UNSURE   NO   Why?

_____

_____

3. A LOOK AT THE COUNSELORS FROM THE HIGH SCHOOL TEACHER'S POINT OF VIEW

BACKGROUND INFORMATION:

Campus name: _____

Number of years on this campus (include this year): _____

All the grade levels with which you work: 9   10   11   12

Subject area(s) you teach (mark all that apply):

_____ English   _____ Mathematics   _____ Natural Sciences   _____ Social Sciences

_____ International Languages   _____ Career/Technology Education   _____ Fine Arts

_____ Special Education   _____ Other: _____

SPECIALIZED ROLES: Does your campus have a counselor clearly designated as a (circle one):

. . . Special Education Counselor?	YES	UNSURE	NO
. . . Substance Abuse and Prevention Education Counselor?	YES	UNSURE	NO

Using this coding scheme, circle your observations for each of the following statements.
Occurrence: Y = Yes, it occurred. U = Unsure if it occurred. N = No, it never occurred.
Helpfulness (If it occurred, did it help the students?):
+ + = Very helpful   + = Somewhat helpful   − = Not very helpful   − − = Not at all helpful

	Occurrence	Helpfulness
Counselors (using the Guidance Curriculum) . . .		
. . . assist students in their personal development.	Y U N	+ + + − − −
. . . assist students in their social development.	Y U N	+ + + − − −
. . . assist students in their career development.	Y U N	+ + + − − −
. . . assist students in their educational development.	Y U N	+ + + − − −
. . . help students function effectively with others in school.	Y U N	+ + + − − −
. . . are an integral part of the school community team.	Y U N	+ + + − − −
. . . have favorable interpersonal relations among the school staff.	Y U N	+ + + − − −
. . . have adequate physical facilities and equipment.	Y U N	+ + + − − −
. . . consult and coordinate with teachers in guidance curriculum delivery.	Y U N	+ + + − − −
. . . train teachers in guidance curriculum delivery.	Y U N	+ + + − − −
. . . directly teach the guidance curriculum.		
Counselors (using the Individual Planning System) . . .		
. . . conduct group guidance sessions.	Y U N	+ + + − − −
. . . ensure accurate and meaningful interpretation of tests and other appraisal results.	Y U N	+ + + − − −
. . . consult with those responsible for providing other career and educational information.	Y U N	+ + + − − −
. . . collaborate with teachers in the development of individual planning system activities and procedures such as preregistration and testing.	Y U N	+ + + − − −

(continued)

	Occurrence			Helpfulness				
. . . hold new-student orientation seminars.	Y	U	N	++	+	−	− −	
. . . disseminate information from special testing (e.g., PSAT, SAT, ASVAB).	Y	U	N	++	+	−	− −	
Counselors (using Responsive Services) . . .								
. . . conduct group counseling.	Y	U	N	++	+	−	− −	
. . . plan interventions to anticipate recurring problems/ situations faced by students due to their developmental stage.	Y	U	N	++	+	−	− −	
. . . collaboratively work with mental health specialists as needed.	Y	U	N	++	+	−	− −	
. . . maintain appropriate documentation and records as needed.	Y	U	N	++	+	−	− −	
. . . provide procedures whereby teachers can make referrals to the counseling office.	Y	U	N	++	+	−	− −	
. . . counsel individual students.	Y	U	N	++	+	−	− −	
Counselors (providing Support Services to other programs) . . .								
. . . maintain ongoing efforts for better integration of guidance program goals with district goals.	Y	U	N	++	+	−	− −	
. . . help in informing the school community of the program mission, purposes, and services available.	Y	U	N	++	+	−	− −	
. . . manage the guidance program competently and appropriately.	Y	U	N	++	+	−	− −	
. . . demonstrate professionalism.	Y	U	N	++	+	−	− −	
. . . guide individuals and groups of students through the development of educational and career plans.	Y	U	N	++	+	−	− −	
. . . consult with parents to enhance their relationship with their children.	Y	U	N	++	+	−	− −	
. . . consult with teachers to enhance their work with students.	Y	U	N	++	+	−	− −	
. . . coordinate with community personnel to bring together resources for students.	Y	U	N	++	+	−	− −	
. . . use an effective referral process for assisting students and others to use special programs and services.	Y	U	N	++	+	−	− −	
. . . participate in the standardized testing program.	Y	U	N	++	+	−	− −	
. . . interpret tests and other appraisal results to students.	Y	U	N	++	+	−	− −	
. . . adhere to ethical, legal, and professional standards.	Y	U	N	++	+	−	− −	
. . . work cooperatively with campus and district staff members.	Y	U	N	++	+	−	− −	

ONE FINAL THOUGHT: If you could make one change that would most improve the guidance program, what would it be? _____

_____

_____

⌒ Appendix E ⌒

Sample Board of Education Policy
on a Student Guidance Program

The district's guidance program provides important benefits to individual students by addressing their intellectual, emotional, social, and psychological needs. It is developmental and includes sequential activities designed to address the needs of all students by helping them to acquire competencies in career planning and exploration, knowledge of self and others, and educational and vocational development.

The program addresses the needs of students in our elementary, middle, and senior high schools as they encounter and deal directly with these and other important learning and life issues. The program is implemented in each attendance center and is considered an integral part of each school's education program. It is implemented by certified school counselors with the support of teachers, administrators, students, and parents.

Program Goals

At the elementary level, the guidance program promotes successful schooling by assisting students in learning the skills and attitudes necessary to be successful. It emphasizes decision-making skill development and awareness and beginning exploration of future educational and occupational possibilities. The program also stresses self-concept development and the acquisition of skills in developing interpersonal relationships.

The middle school guidance program focuses on the rapidly changing needs of pre- and young adolescents. It is especially sensitive to the struggles of middle school students for identity, for balancing the demands for academic, career, and social competence. The program begun at the elementary level is continued. However, they are adjusted to fit the special needs of the middle school students. In addition, counselors will work with the students to develop education/career plans that cover graduation requirements and beyond. The plan takes into account students' interests, abilities, and educational and occupation plans.

Building on the goals of the elementary and middle school, the guidance program in the high school assists students in becoming responsible adults who can develop realistic and fulfilling life plans based on clear understandings of themselves and their needs, interests, and skills. The education/career plans developed in the middle school are reviewed and updated periodically in accordance with students' postgraduation education and occupational goals. Continued attention is given to assisting students to develop competence in decision making, career planning, working with others, and taking responsibility for their own behavior.

Program Activities

To accomplish these goals, the guidance program is an integral part of the district's total educational program. The program is developmental and includes sequential activities in the elementary, middle, and high school.

Counselors work with all students, parents, teachers, administrators, and the community through a balanced program of direct and indirect services. Large and small group-structured learning units provide systematic instruction for all students in all grade levels. Counselors plan with teachers and then teach, team teach, or assist in teaching these coordinated units in classrooms or in other large group settings. Individual planning activities are provided to assist all students in planning activities. They are initiated in the upper elementary grades and continued and expanded in the middle and high school years. Individual, small group, personal, and crisis counseling are available to all students. Consultation services concerning student behavior and academic progress are provided for parents, teachers, and administrators. Referrals to other professionals in the school district or to agencies and institutions outside of the district are made as required or requested. Counselors support the overall district's educational program through general consultation activities and committee work. Counselors also support their own program through management and research activities, community outreach, business and industry visitation, and professional development.

Program Components

The guidance program components organize the work of counselors into direct and indirect activities and services. They include the direct counselor services of guidance curriculum, individual planning, and responsive services, and the indirect services of system support.

Guidance Curriculum includes structured developmental experiences presented systemically through classroom and group activities, kindergarten through Grade 12. The curriculum emphasizes decision making, self-understanding, career exploration and preparation, and the improvement of study skills.

Individual Planning includes guidance activities to assist all students to plan, monitor, and manage their own learning as well as their personal and career development. Individual student education/career plans are developed beginning no later than seventh grade in collaboration with parents/guardians. Individual planning emphasizes test interpretation, advisement, and the identification of short- and long-term goals.

Responsive Services include counseling, consultation, and referral activities to meet the immediate needs and concerns of students. Responsive services include personal counseling, crisis counseling, agency referral, consultation for parents, teachers, and other professionals, support groups, and problem solving.

System Support includes guidance management activities that maintain and enhance the total guidance program. Responsibilities in this component include staff and community relations, program evaluation, research projects, committee work, and professional development.

Within the areas of counseling and guidance responsibility, the counselor enters into professional relationships with three segments of the school community: students, school staff members, and parents/guardians. Consistent with the rights of the individual and the obligations of the counselor as a professional, the counseling relationship and resulting information are considered confidential. When appropriate, counselors will be responsible for explaining to students the ramifications of and exceptions to this confidentiality. All records and discussions of personal issues will be handled in a confidential manner. These records will be kept in the sole possession of the maker of the record and will not be accessible or revealed to any other person (except a temporary substitute for the maker of the record).

Referrals to Outside Agencies

The guidance counselor(s) and other professional staff members provide preliminary assessment of student problems and referrals to outside agencies, if necessary. The district will assist and cooperate with other agencies concerning the diagnosis and treatment of a referral student when applicable to his or her educational program in the school district. Except as otherwise required by law, costs for diagnostic and treatment services outside the district are the responsibility of parents or guardians.

⌒ Appendix F ⌒

Sample Position Guides

High School Counselor

Primary Function: to provide, as a member of the guidance department staff, a comprehensive guidance and counseling program for students in Grades 9–12 and specifically to provide services to meet the special needs of his/her assigned caseload (450); to consult with teachers, staff, and parents to enhance their effectiveness in helping students' educational, career, personal, and social development; and to provide support to other high school educational programs.

Major Job Responsibilities: (1) teach the high school guidance curriculum; (2) guide groups of students and individual students through the development of educational and career plans; (3) counsel small groups and individual students through the development of educational and career plans; (4) counsel small groups and individual students with problems; (5) consult with teachers, staff, and parents regarding meeting the developmental needs of adolescents and regarding specific information about the youths for whom they have responsibility; (6) refer students or their parents with problems to specialists or special programs; (7) participate in, coordinate, or conduct activities that contribute to the effective operation of the school; (8) plan and evaluate the campus guidance program; and (9) pursue continuous professional development.

Illustrative Key Duties:

(1) *teach the high school guidance curriculum:* conduct developmental guidance lessons in classroom settings as planned in conjunction with the instructional departments, or through the advisory system or study halls, or as otherwise devised in conjunction with the school administration; consult with or be a resource person to teachers to facilitate the infusion of guidance content into the regular education curriculum.

(2) *guide groups and individual students through the development of educational and career plans:* provide orientation activities for students new to the school such as brown bag lunch sessions; participate in orientation programs for incoming 9th graders; guide 9th and 10th graders in updating of their "High School 4-Year Plans"; guide 11th and 12th graders to evaluate their current status and plan their achievement of high school graduation; guide 12th graders to develop and take appropriate steps toward implementing their post-high-school educational or career plans; plan/coordinate/assist in preregistration of 9th, 10th, and 11th graders for 10th, 11th, and 12th grades, respectively; collaborate with middle school counselors to effect the preregistration of 8th graders for 9th grade; assist students new to the district with course selection at the time of registration; interpret standardized tests (TAAS [Texas Assessment of Academic Skills], PLAN [a career guidance and pre-ACT tool] results information to students, parents, and teachers; guide groups and individual students in applying the test results information to their educational and career plans; interpret results of college entrance tests or career assessments to groups of students; guide all students to develop tentative career/vocational plans through the conduct or supervision of career education activities such as career center orientations and use

of the DISCOVER system and other career center resources; provide a mechanism for the systematic and efficient dissemination of current, accurate information needed by individual students or parents as they develop their educational or career plans.

(3) *counsel small groups and individual students with problems:* conduct structured, goal-oriented counseling sessions in systematic response to identified needs of individuals or groups of students—recurrent topics at the high school level include academic failure, attendance and behavior problems, peer problems, family issues, child abuse, substance abuse, suicide threats and attempts, and sexuality issues.

(4) *consult with teachers, staff, and parents regarding meeting the developmental needs of adolescents and regarding specific information about the youths for whom they have responsibility:* participate in staffings; conduct in-service programs for faculty as a whole or by departments; conduct/facilitate conferences with teachers, students, or parents; conduct or provide opportunities for parent and education programs; write articles for parent newsletters; assist families with school-related problems.

(5) *refer students or their parents with problems to specialists or special programs:* consult and coordinate with in-district and community specialists such as school nurses, administrators, and psychologists and community-based psychologists, service agencies, and physicians.

(6) *participate in, coordinate, or conduct activities that contribute to the effective operation of the school:* cooperate with administration in planning and implementing preregistration and PREP days; interpret group test results to faculty and staff; contribute to the principal's goals for enhancing education on the campus; cooperate with instructional staff in implementing the "Placement Recommendation Guidelines"; establish effective liaisons with the various instructional departments; provide input to administration as the master schedule is built; act as an advocate for groups or individual students as system decisions are made; supervise the changing of student schedules in accordance with district policies; cooperate with other school staff in placing students with special needs in appropriate programs, including other regular education, special education, and career and technology education opportunities; cooperate with administration/coordinate campus-wide administration of the district testing program (TAAS, PLAN); supervise administration of special group testing (e.g., PSAT, SAT, ACT, AP; the Armed Services Vocational Aptitude Battery [ASVAB]); cooperate with administration/supervise the teacher advisory system.

(7) *plan and evaluate the campus guidance program:* annually design, with other members of the guidance department staff, the campus guidance program based on needs by clearly stating program goals and objectives, establishing the guidance department calendar, and completing the Annual Guidance Program Plan–High School; evaluate strategies as they are implemented; complete the annual Guidance Program Evaluation Report–High School.

(8) *pursue continuous professional growth:* attend district-sponsored staff development offerings; join associations (e.g., Northside Counseling Association, South Texas Counseling Association, Texas Counseling Association, American Counseling Association); read professional journals; attend relevant workshops and conferences sponsored by professionally appropriate organizations (e.g., Region 20, Texas Education Agency, and associations); take postgraduate courses.

Organizational Relationships: is supervised by the head counselor, the principal, and the director of guidance; works collaboratively with other counselors and guidance department staff; and works cooperatively with other campus or district staff.

Performance Standards: A high school counselor's performance is considered satisfactory when (1) the head counselor, principal, and director of guidance concur and the counselor's level of competence is reflected as such on the Northside Independent School District Counselor Evaluation Form; and (2) evaluation of the Annual Guidance Program Plan–High School indicates overall effectiveness of the program.

Director of Guidance

Reports to: Assistant Superintendent for Student Services

Educational and Certification Requirements:
Master's degree in School Counseling from an accredited program. Valid Administrators' certificate for elementary and secondary levels issued by the Texas Education Agency.
At least 5 years' successful experience in school counseling.

Supervises: 1. Comprehensive Guidance Program

Job Performance Statements

I. Instructional Management

1. Administers the efforts of the counselors to provide a guidance program that meets the needs of all students.
2. Plans, designs, implements, and evaluates the guidance program with counselors, principals, and other district administrators.
3. Works cooperatively with others in developing the mission and articulating a vision for the campus's and district's program.
4. Uses knowledge of guidance content and the program development process to facilitate counselor development of appropriate guidance and counseling experiences for students.
5. Works with building principals in creating more effective campus guidance programs.
6. Is aware of the district's curricula and instructional implementation strategies and the ways that the guidance department supports instruction.
7. Facilitates the use of existing technology in the guidance program.
8. Encourages and supports the development and implementation of innovative strategies to meet identified needs of students.
9. Is effective in involving guidance staff in evaluating and selecting materials to meet identified student needs and program goals.

II. School/Organizational Climate

10. Has high expectations and high regard for staff and communicates this perspective to them.
11. Effectively communicates with staff, community, media, and school board on the district's mission, policies, and programs, especially as they relate to the guidance program and the counseling staff.
12. Develops cooperatively with other district staff, long- and short-range plans related to department and division responsibilities.
13. Promotes collegiality, teamwork, and participatory decision making among guidance department staff members.
14. Demonstrates skill in conflict resolution with counselors, administrators, parents, and/or the community.
15. Responds appropriately to situations that could impair the educational environment or could threaten the safety and well-being of students and staff.

16. Adheres and promotes adherence to and interprets appropriately the Codes of Ethics related to school counseling.

III. School/Organizational Improvement

17. Focuses the guidance department's operations toward the accomplishment of the program and the district's mission and attainment of the program's and district's stated goals and objectives.
18. Plans and conducts needs assessments related to department's operations.
19. Applies the findings of research that relate effective guidance and counseling strategies to overall school district and campus program improvement.
20. Develops workable policies and procedures pertinent to the effectiveness of the department.
21. Systematically monitors guidance program implementation.
22. Uses relevant evaluative findings to determine the extent to which goals and objectives are met and to provide the basis for continuous program improvement.
23. Uses and helps others to use student assessment data appropriately in interpreting, reporting, and acting on results.
24. Actively supports the efforts of others to achieve district and campus goals and objectives.

IV. Personnel Management

25. Administers district program for recruitment, selection, orientation, and assignment of counselors.
26. Administers the district's program of counselor evaluation.
27. Administers the preparation and revision of guidance department job descriptions.
28. Maintains a viable application system for counselors that not only represents the district in a positive and professional manner but also facilitates the recruitment and selection process.
29. Administers the Northside Independent School District Counselor Performance Improvement System in collaboration with other responsible administrators.
30. Administers clinical supervision as a means to improve counselor effectiveness in the implementation of the guidance program.
31. Conferences regularly with counselors' supervisors to discuss performance quality.
32. Administers the system by which counselors develop performance improvement objectives and identify professional growth opportunities.
33. Provides guidance program resources and materials to counselors within the limits of available resources.
34. Secures consultants, specialists, and other resources to assist counselors in attaining guidance program objectives.
35. Uses the mission of the school district, program evaluation outcomes, and input from counselors and others to provide effective in-service activities for counselors.

V. Administration and Fiscal/Facilities Management

36. Prepares, recommends, and implements the budget for the guidance program.
37. Administers the process for selecting, evaluating, and purchasing varied materials and equipment to be used in the guidance program.

38. Offers constructive suggestions to ensure that policies and regulations support the educational environment.
39. Analyzes facility and equipment needs for optimum guidance program implementation.
40. Uses information to make necessary changes or adjustments in the guidance program.
41. Demonstrates responsible fiscal control over assigned program budgets.
42. Compiles and maintains written records and reports as required and/or as desirable for continued improvement of the guidance program.

VI. Student Management/Relations

43. Has sufficient understanding of the discipline management system to handle cases brought to his or her attention.
44. Ensures that the guidance program is effective in supporting the educational environment.
45. Supports district and campus rules for conduct.

VII. School/Organizational-Community Relations

46. Cooperates with nondistrict personnel to augment the resources available to students through the guidance program.
47. Articulates appropriately to the general public the school district's overall mission and goals and the ways in which the functions of the guidance department support these directives.
48. Communicates about the district guidance program to parents and the community; solicits their input on relevant issues.
49. Participates in activities of the Northside Council of PTAs to foster rapport and mutual respect between the district and the larger community.
50. Effectively communicates the district's philosophy and guidance program information to the media.
51. Demonstrates a commitment to the mission of the district as it is communicated to the public.

VIII. Professional Growth and Development

52. Actively seeks and uses evaluative feedback from subordinates, peers, and superordinates, using such information to improve performance.
53. Keeps abreast of the profession through participating in a variety of professional development activities.
54. Participation in professional development activities leads to improved job performance.
55. Performs duties in a professional, ethical, and responsible manner, as defined in the Texas Education Agency Code of Ethics for Educators and in the Code of Ethics of the American Counseling Association.

IX. Other

56. Performs other tasks and assumes other responsibilities as may be assigned.

Career Guidance Center Technician

Job Description

The Career Guidance Center Technician, under the supervision of the Head Counselor, operates the High School Career Center and implements portions of the Career Guidance Program.

Duties and Responsibilities

1. Collects and organizes occupational data to provide source materials for Career Center.
2. Teaches portions of the Career Guidance Program to all grade levels of students in class-size groups.
3. Assists teachers and counselors to locate and use career information and materials.
4. Orders, catalogues, maintains files on, and distributes materials relating to job opportunities, careers, vocational programs, schools, colleges, scholarships, grants and loans, armed forces, and other programs.
5. Operates and teaches students to operate audiovisual equipment, the computerized career information system, and personal computers.
6. Coordinates the career guidance speaker program.
7. Assists students to take and score self-administered career interest and other assessments.
8. Makes presentations to teachers and parents to encourage their and students' use of the center.
9. Maintains the Career Center facility and equipment, and schedules their use.
10. Performs some bookkeeping and other general secretarial functions.
11. Assists guidance department as assigned by the Head Counselor.

Minimum Qualifications

High school graduate and one of the following:

- business college certificate
- satisfactory completion of at least one semester of college work, including at least one business course
- enrollment in business college or has completed training in acceptable program leading to proficiency in job assignment
- successful completion of two courses in business college
- successful demonstration of several areas of technical competency, including typing, transcription, filing procedures, and office records management

High School Registrar

Job Description

Under the supervision of the Head Counselor, the High School Registrar maintains students' permanent records and generates related information from the records.

Duties and Responsibilities

1. Register/enroll students new to the district and transfer students within the district
2. Complete new student records
3. Input data via CRT
4. Maintain students' Academic Achievement Records
5. Maintain files for current and withdrawn students
6. Coordinate student withdrawals
7. Send transcripts for active/inactive students upon written request
8. Request transcripts for new/transfer students
9. Track graduation progress for all students, consulting with counselors on exceptional cases
10. Calculate sixth- and seventh-semester ranks and averages
11. Prepare inactive records for microfilming and destruction according to established schedule
12. Maintain office equipment and supplies
13. Do typing and correspondence required in the office
14. Provide information from the permanent records, in accordance with the Family Educational and Privacy Rights Act (FEPRA)
15. Train and supervise student office assistants
16. Communicate important information as pertains to counselors or administrators
17. Carry out other duties and responsibilities as assigned by the Head Counselor

Minimum Qualifications

High school graduate and one of the following:

- Business college certificate
- Appropriate clerical/secretarial skills
- Three years' experience as an educational secretary
- Satisfactory completion of at least one semester of college work, including at least one business course
- Successful demonstration of required technical competency and office records management

Note. From Northside Independent School District, San Antonio, TX. Reprinted with permission.

Procedures for Helping Students Manage Personal Crises

Subject: **Procedures for Helping Students Manage Personal Crises**

To: **All Personnel**

The following procedures have been developed over the past several years and are now being circulated to provide guidance to staff members in applying sound professional judgment when assisting students who are dealing with personal crises. Special reporting requirements, such as those relating to suspected child abuse, are not supplanted by these procedures.

Definition

Students in personal crises are defined as those who are in jeopardy of endangering their own or others' health safety and/or well-being. Students in such crises may be, for example:

- those who threaten to commit suicide, to run away from home, or to otherwise endanger themselves or others;
- those who are or who suspect themselves to be seriously ill, acutely or chronically depressed, grieving, or pregnant;
- those who are using illegal substances, and/or abusing drugs or other substances; or
- those who have engaged in, or are seriously contemplating engaging in, criminal activity (e.g., theft, arson, property damage).

Assumptions and Considerations

There are *constraints to confidentiality*. Students must be informed that some things cannot be kept confidential. School counselors, nurses, administrators, and others must balance their respect for the student's rights and their own responsibilities to the parent(s)/guardian and other authorities by adhering to the following ethical standard:

> Informs parents/guardians or appropriate authorities when the student's condition indicates a clear and imminent danger to the counselee or others. This is to be done after careful deliberation and, where possible, after consultation with other professionals. (ASCA Code of Ethics, 2004)

The school professionals must be careful not to assume the parental role. The student has a right to confidentiality within these limitations; when those limitations are crossed, the parent has the right to know so that appropriate responsibility can be taken to help the student resolve the problem that has precipitated the crisis.

The students must also be helped to feel that the school professionals care about their health, safety, and well-being and will help them resolve their problems within certain boundaries. They must also be helped to understand that their parents have primary responsibility for their health, safety, and well-being and, therefore, must be informed of the crisis and the students' intended plans.

Therefore, a goal of the student-professional interaction in managing a personal crisis situation is for the student's parent/guardian to be informed of the problem in a timely manner. It is preferable in most cases that the student inform the parent(s) and that the professional validate that the student has done so.

Parent/guardian is the person with the responsibility for the student in relationship to the school. For the purposes of this process, the student's having attained age 18 or being legally married does not remove the expectation that a responsible adult (e.g., parent, guardian, or spouse) be notified.

In a timely manner is relative to the situation; the time frame is dictated by the circumstance. The parent(s) or guardian must be informed in time to carry out parental responsibility to help the student. The time frame should also allow the professional(s) involved to provide appropriate consultation to the parent(s) or guardian.

Timeliness is not defined by an arbitrary time frame (e.g., 24 hours, 48 hours) but rather is relative to the situation. For example: the situation of a female student considering terminating a pregnancy within a day or two dictates a very short time frame; the situation of an elementary child planning in February to run away in the summer suggests a longer time frame may be available for resolving the problem.

Note: In some atypical situations, legal statutes, board policy, and/or sound professional judgment dictate that official agencies or other professionals responsible for the student (e.g., department of human services, local law enforcement agencies, probation officer, private therapist) be notified in addition to or instead of the parent/guardian. In making such a decision, it is always wise to consult with the principal.

Procedures

The staff members who typically are involved in helping students resolve personal crisis situations are counselors, nurses, and assistant/vice principals. Teachers and other staff members also need to be aware of those procedures and resources. The school principal is ultimately accountable for the professional management of such cases.

The procedures outlined below rest on the premise that the professionals involved make their decision based on the application of professional judgment to the presenting circumstances and given the information that is available to them.

1. Listen with care, compassion, and sensitivity to the student presenting a problem that may indicate a crisis or an impending crisis.
2. In responding, explain the limits of confidentiality, including clear and imminent danger, goal of informing parents, possibility of consultation and referral.
3. Gather data to make a professional determination about the case (e.g., actuality of the crisis situation, degree of danger, urgency).
4. Develop the plan of action. This step may entail:
   a. Consulting with other professionals, as appropriate, regarding the case and the plan of action.
   b. Referring the student to other professionals who have the expertise to help or who provide the link to community agencies with such expertise (i.e., the counselor

for psychological problems, the nurse for medical problems, the administration for legal problems).

    c. Making the principal aware of the situation.

5. Implement the plan.
6. Counsel the student and ensure that the parents are informed.
7. Monitor the student's progress through to resolution of the problem.
8. Follow up with the student, parent, and/or other professionals after apparent resolution of the problem.

Leadership/Responsibility

The professional who first receives the information from the troubled student must take the leadership in deciding how to handle the situation. This includes deciding which other professionals need to be involved, how, and to what extent. In conversation with the student, it is important to identify other individuals with whom the student has shared the information/problem in order to protect as much as possible the student's right to privacy and confidentiality. Others should be informed of the problem and the relevant details of the situation only on a need-to-know basis.

When more than one professional has received the information/is involved in working with the student to resolve the problem, a team approach is essential. The professionals should jointly decide on the best plan of action, including the time frame, parent notification, the actions to be taken, and the persons responsible. In establishing the plan for helping the student manage the crisis, consideration should be given to such things as the student's age, the family circumstance, the degree of danger, and the urgency of the situation. Relevant Central Office staff—e.g., the Director of Guidance, the Director of Psychological Services, the Coordinator of Health Services— are available for consultation.

If the professionals working with the case are unable to agree on a plan of action, the decision should be deferred to the principal.

Note. From Northside Independent School District, San Antonio, TX. Reprinted with permission.

Impact of Program Balance and Ratio on Program Implementation

Impact of Program Balance on Program Implementation

Alternate Desired Program Balance

	% ES	% MS	% HS
Guidance Curriculum	20	15	10
Individual Student Planning	20	30	40
Responsive Services	50	45	40
System Support	10	10	10
Nonguidance	0	0	0

Activity Slots/Program Component/Week

Elementary School
  Activity Slot = 30 minutes
  School Day = 7 hours
  Activity Slots/Day = 14
  Activity Slots/Week = 70

Guidance Curriculum	20% (70) = 14
Individual Student Planning	20% (70) = 14
Responsive Services	50% (70) = 35
System Support	10% (70) = 7

Middle School
  Activity Slot = 45 minutes
  School Day = 7 hours
  Activity Slots/Day = 9
  Activity Slots/Week = 45

Guidance Curriculum	15% (45) = 7
Individual Student Planning	30% (45) = 14
Responsive Services	45% (45) = 20
System Support	10% (45) = 4

High School
  Activity Slot = 55 minutes
  School Day = 7 hours
  Activity Slots/Day = 7
  Activity Slots/Week = 35

Guidance Curriculum	10% (35) = 4
Individual Student Planning	40% (35) = 14
Responsive Services	40% (35) = 14
System Support	10% (35) = 3

Impact of Ratio on Program Implementation Service Levels/ Program Balance and Counselor-Student Ratio, 1:100

Desired Program Balance

	% ES	% MS	% HS
Guidance Curriculum	40	35	20
Individual Student Planning	10	20	30
Responsive Services	40	35	35
System Support	10	10	15
Nonguidance	0	0	0

Elementary School

Average Class Size: 1:25   Average teacher–student ratio: 1:20
36 weeks per school year

Guidance Curriculum   40% (70) = 28 Activity Slots/Week
    100 counselees/25 students per class   = 4 classes
    28 activity slots/4 classes   = 7 activities/class/week
    252 guidance lessons per year per class

Individual Student Planning   10% (70) = 7 Activity Slots/Week
    7 activity slots $\times$ 36 weeks   = 252 slots per year
    252 slots 30 minutes per slot   = 7,560 minutes per year
    7,560 minutes/100 counselees   = 75 minutes per student per year

Responsive Services   40% (70) = 28 Activity Slots/Week
    14 slots for groups (average 6)   = 84 students
    14 slots for individuals   = <u>14</u> students
    Total students served at one time   = 98
        (98 is 98% of the caseload)

System Support   10% (70) = 7 Activity Slots/Week
    100 students/20 students per teacher   = 5 teachers
    7 slots/5 teachers   = 1.4 slots per week per teacher
    7 slots per week $\times$ 30 minutes per slot   = 210 minutes per week
    210 minutes/5 days   = 42 minutes per day

Elementary School Counselor Potential:
    7 guidance lessons per week
    75 minutes per student per year
    98% receiving responsive services in any one time period
    42 minutes per teacher per week
    42 minutes a day for indirect services to students

Middle School

Average Class Size: 1:25   Average teacher–student ratio: 1:20
36 weeks per school year

Guidance Curriculum   35% (45) = 16 Activity Slots/Week
    100 counselees/25 students per class   = 4 classes
    16 activity slots/4 classes   = 4 activities/class/week
    144 guidance lessons per year per class

Individual Student Planning   20% (45) = 9 Activity Slots/Week
    9 activity slots $\times$ 36 weeks   = 324 slots per year
    324 slots $\times$ 45 minutes per slot   = 14,580 minutes per year
    14,580 minutes/100 counselees   = 145 minutes per student per year

Responsive Services   35% (45) = 16 Activity Slots/Week
    8 slots for groups (average 9)   = 72 students
    8 slots for individuals   = <u>8</u> students
    Total students served at one time   = 80
        (80 is 80% of the caseload)

System Support   10% (45) = 4 Activity Slots/Week
  100 students/20 students per teacher   = 5 teachers
  4 slots/5 teachers   = 4/5 slot per week per teacher
  4 slots per week × 45 minutes per slot = 180 minutes per week
  180 minutes/5 days   = 36 minutes per day

Middle School Counselor Potential:
  4 guidance lessons per week
  145 minutes per student per year
  80% receiving responsive services at any one time
  36 minutes per teacher per week
  36 minutes a day for indirect services to students

High School

Average Class Size: 1:25   Average teacher–student ratio: 1:20
36 weeks per school year

Guidance Curriculum   20% (35) = 7 Activity Slots/Week
  100 counselees/25 students per class = 4 classes
  7 activity slots/4 classes   = 1.75 activities/class/week
  63 guidance lessons per year per class

Individual Student Planning 30% (35) = 11 Activity Slots/Week
  11 activity slots = 336 weeks   = 396 slots per year
  396 slots = 55 minutes per slot   = 21,780 minutes per year
  21,780 minutes/100 counselees   = 2,178 minutes per student per year

Responsive Services   35% (35) = 12 Activity Slots/Week
  6 slots for groups (average 10)   = 60 students
  6 slots for individuals   = _6 students
  Total students served at one time   = 66
                                         (66 is 66% of the caseload)

System Support   15% (35) = 5 Activity Slots/Week
  100 students/20 students per teacher   = 5 teachers
  5 slots/5 teachers   = 1 slot per week per teacher
  5 slots per week × 55 minutes per slot = 275 minutes per week
  275 minutes/5 days   = 55 minutes per day

High School Counselor Potential:
  > 1 guidance lesson
  2,178 minutes per student per year
  66% receiving responsive services at any one time
  55 minutes per teacher per week
  55 minutes a day for indirect services to students

Service Levels/Program Balance and Counselor-Student Ratio, 1:500

Desired Program Balance

	% ES	% MS	% HS
Guidance Curriculum	40	35	20
Individual Student Planning	10	20	30
Responsive Services	40	35	35
System Support	10	10	15
Nonguidance	0	0	0

Elementary School
Average Class Size: 1:25   Average teacher–student ratio: 1:20
36 weeks per school year

Guidance Curriculum   40% (70) = 7 Activity Slots/Week
　　500 counselees/25 students per class   = 20 classes
　　28 activity slots/20 classes   = 1.4 activities/class/week
　　50 + guidance lessons per year per class

Individual Student Planning   10% (70) = 7 Activity Slots/Week
　　7 activity slots × 36 weeks   = 252 slots per year
　　252 slots × 30 minutes per slot   = 7,560 minutes per year
　　7,560 minutes/500 counselees   = 15 minutes per student per year

Responsive Services   40% (70) = 28 Activity Slots/Week
　　14 slots for groups (average 6)   = 84 students
　　14 slots for individuals   = <u>14</u> students
　　Total students served at one time   = 98
　　　　　　　　　　　　　　　(98 is 19.6% of the caseload)

System Support   10% (70) = 7 Activity Slots/Week
　　500 students/20 students per teacher   = 25 teachers
　　7 slots/25 teachers   = 1/4 slot per week per teacher
　　7 slots per week × 30 minutes per slot   = 210 minutes per week
　　210 minutes/5 days   = 42 minutes per day

Elementary School Counselor Potential:
　　1+ guidance lessons per week
　　15 minutes per student per week
　　19.6% receiving responsive services at any one time
　　8 minutes per teacher per week, or nearly 4 weeks for all
　　42 minutes a day for indirect services to students

Middle School
Average Class Size: 1:25   Average teacher–student ratio: 1:20
36 weeks per school year

Guidance Curriculum   35% (45) = 16 Activity Slots/Week
　　500 counselees/25 students per class   = 20 classes
　　16 activity slots/20 classes   = 8 activities/class/week
　　28+ guidance lessons per year per class

Individual Student Planning   20% (45) = 9 Activity Slots/Week
　　9 activity slots × 36 weeks   = 324 slots per year
　　324 slots × 45 minutes per slot   = 14,580 minutes per year
　　14,580 minutes/500 counselees   = 29+ minutes per student per year

Responsive Services   35% (45) = 16 Activity Slots/Week
　　8 slots for groups (average 9)   = 72 students
　　8 slots for individuals   = <u>8</u> students
　　Total students served at one time   = 80
　　　　　　　　　　　　　　　(80 is 16% of the caseload)

System Support   10% (45) = 4 Activity Slots/Week
     500 students/20 students per teacher   = 25 teachers
     4 slots/25 teachers   = .16 slot per week per teacher
     4 slots per week × 45 minutes per slot   = 180 minutes per week
     180 minutes/5 days   = 36 minutes per day

Middle School Counselor Potential:
     > 1 guidance lesson per week
     29 minutes per student per year
     16% receiving responsive services at any time
     7 minutes per teacher per week, or 6weeks to consult with all
     36 minutes a day for indirect services to students

High School
Average Class Size: 1:25   Average teacher–student ratio: 1:20
36 weeks per school year

Guidance Curriculum   20% (35) = 7 Activity Slots/Week
     500 counselees/25 students per class   = 20 classes
     7 activity slots/20 classes   = .35 activities/class/week
     12+ guidance lessons per year per class

Individual Student Planning   30% (35) = 11 Activity Slots/Week
     11 activity slots × 36 weeks   = 396 slots per year
     396 slots × 55 minutes per slot   = 21,780 minutes per year
     21,780 minutes/500 counselees   = 43+ minutes per student per year

Responsive Services   35% (35) = 12 Activity Slots/Week
     6 slots for groups (average 10)   = 60 students
     6 slots for individuals   = <u> 6</u> students
     Total students served at one time   = 66
                              (66 is 13% of the caseload)

System Support   15% (35) = 5 Activity Slots/Week
     500 students/20 students per teacher   = 25 teachers
     5 slots/25 teachers   = .2 slot per week per teacher
     5 slots per week × 55 minutes per slot   = 275 minutes per week
     275 minutes/5 days   = 55 minutes per day

High School Counselor Potential:
     < 1 guidance lessons per week, or nearly 3 weeks to conduct an activity with each class
     43 minutes per student per year
     13% receiving responsive services at any one time
     11 minutes per teacher per week, or 5 weeks to consult with all
     55 minutes a day for indirect services to students

Service Levels/Program Balance and Counselor-Student Ratio, 1: (Yours)

Desired Program Balance

Level: _____

Guidance Curriculum	_____ %_____	Activity Slots
Individual Student Planning	_____ %_____	Activity Slots
Responsive Services	_____ %_____	Activity Slots
System Support	_____ %_____	Activity Slots
Nonguidance	_____ %_____	Activity Slots

Average Class Size: 1: _____

Average teacher–student ratio: 1: _____

_____ Weeks per School Year

_____ Minutes per Activity Slot _____ # Activity Slots per Week

Guidance Curriculum _____ % (_____) = _____ Activity Slots/Week
   _____ counselees/_____ students per class = _____ classes
   _____ activity slots/_____ classes = _____ activities/class/week
   _____ activities × _____ weeks per year = _____ guidance lessons per year per class

Individual Student Planning   _____ % (_____) = _____ Activity Slots/Week
   _____ activity slots × _____ weeks = _____ slots per year
   _____ slots × _____ minutes per slot = _____ minutes per year
   _____ minutes/_____ counselees = _____ minutes per student per year

Responsive Services _____ % (_____) = _____ Activity Slots/Week
   ———— slots for groups = _____ students (average #_____)
   ———— slots for individuals = _____ students
   Total students served at one time = _____
                                             (_____ is _____ % of the caseload)

System Support _____ % (_____) = _____ Activity Slots/Week
   _____ students/_____ students per teacher =_____ teachers
   _____ slots/_____ teachers = _____ slot per week per teacher
   _____ slots per week × _____ minutes per slot = _____ minutes per week
   _____ minutes/5 days = _____ minutes per day

Your School Counselor Potential:
   _____ guidance lessons per week
   _____ % receiving responsive services at any one time
   _____ minutes per teacher per week, or [#] _____ weeks for all
   _____ minutes a day for indirect services to students

Multicultural Competencies and Objectives

I. *Counselor Awareness of Own Cultural Values and Biases*

A. Attitudes and Beliefs
1. Culturally skilled counselors have moved from being culturally unaware to being aware and sensitive to their own cultural heritage and to valuing and respecting differences.
2. Culturally skilled counselors are aware of how their own cultural backgrounds and experiences and attitudes, values, and biases influence psychological processes.
3. Culturally skilled counselors are able to recognize the limits of their competencies and expertise.
4. Culturally skilled counselors are comfortable with differences that exist between themselves and clients in terms of race, ethnicity, culture, and beliefs.

B. Knowledge
1. Culturally skilled counselors have specific knowledge about their own racial and cultural heritage and how it personally and professionally affects their definitions of normality–abnormality and the process of counseling.
2. Culturally skilled counselors possess knowledge and understanding about how oppression, racism, discrimination, and stereotyping affects them personally and in their work. This allows them to acknowledge their own racist attitudes, beliefs, and feelings. Although this standard applies to all groups, for White counselors it may mean that they understand how they may have directly or indirectly benefited from individual, institutional, and cultural racism (White identity development models).
3. Culturally skilled counselors possess knowledge about their social impact on others. They are knowledgeable about communication style differences, how their style may clash or foster the counseling process with minority clients, and how to anticipate the impact it may have on others.

C. Skills
1. Culturally skilled counselors seek out educational, consultative, and training experience to improve their understanding and effectiveness in working with culturally different populations. Being able to recognize the limits of their competencies, they (a) seek consultation, (b) seek further training or education, (c) refer out to more qualified individuals or resources, or (d) engage in a combination of these.
2. Culturally skilled counselors are constantly seeking to understand themselves as racial and cultural beings and are actively seeking a nonracist identity.

II. *Counselor Awareness of Client's Worldview*

A. Attitudes and Beliefs
1. Culturally skilled counselors are aware of their negative emotional reactions toward other racial and ethnic groups that may prove detrimental to their clients in counseling. They are willing to contrast their own beliefs and attitudes with those of their culturally different clients in a nonjudgmental fashion.
2. Culturally skilled counselors are aware of their stereotypes and preconceived notions that they may hold toward other racial and ethnic minority groups.

B. Knowledge
1. Culturally skilled counselors possess specific knowledge and information about the particular group they are working with. They are aware of the life experiences, cultural heritage, and historical background of their culturally different clients. This particular competency is strongly linked to the "minority identity development models" available in the literature.
2. Culturally skilled counselors understand how race, culture, ethnicity, and so forth may affect personality formation, vocational choices, manifestation of psychological disorders, help-seeking behavior, and the appropriateness or inappropriateness of counseling approaches.
3. Culturally skilled counselors understand and have knowledge about sociopolitical influences that impinge upon the life of racial and ethnic minorities. Immigration issues, poverty, racism, stereotyping, and powerlessness all leave major scars that may influence the counseling process.

C. Skills
1. Culturally skilled counselors should familiarize themselves with relevant research and the latest findings regarding mental health and mental disorders of various ethnic and racial groups. They should actively seek out educational experiences that foster their knowledge, understanding, and cross-cultural skills.
2. Culturally skilled counselors become actively involved with minority individuals outside of the counseling setting (community events, social and political functions, celebrations, friendships, neighborhood groups, and so forth) so that their perspective of minorities is more than an academic or helping exercise.

III. *Culturally Appropriate Intervention Strategies*

A. Attitudes and Beliefs
1. Culturally skilled counselors respect clients' religious and/or spiritual beliefs and values, including attributions and taboos, because they affect worldview, psychosocial functioning, and expressions of distress.
2. Culturally skilled counselors respect indigenous helping practices and respect minority community intrinsic help-giving networks.
3. Culturally skilled counselors value bilingualism and do not view another language as an impediment to counseling (monolingualism may be the culprit).

B. Knowledge
1. Culturally skilled counselors have a clear and explicit knowledge and understanding of the generic characteristics of counseling and therapy (culture

bound, class bound, and monolingual) and how they may clash with the cultural values of various minority groups.

2. Culturally skilled counselors are aware of institutional barriers that prevent minorities from using mental health services.

3. Culturally skilled counselors have knowledge of the potential bias in assessment instruments and use procedures and interpret findings keeping in mind the cultural and linguistic characteristics of the clients.

4. Culturally skilled counselors have knowledge of minority family structures, hierarchies, values, and beliefs. They are knowledgeable about the community characteristics and the resources in the community as well as the family.

5. Culturally skilled counselors should be aware of relevant discriminatory practices at the social and community level that may be affecting the psychological welfare of the population being served.

C. Skills

1. Culturally skilled counselors are able to engage in a variety of verbal and nonverbal helping responses. They are able to *send* and *receive* both *verbal* and *nonverbal* messages *accurately* and *appropriately*. They are not tied down to only one method or approach to helping but recognize that helping styles and approaches may be culture bound. When they sense that their helping style is limited and potentially inappropriate, they can anticipate and ameliorate its negative impact.

2. Culturally skilled counselors are able to exercise institutional intervention skills on behalf of their clients. They can help clients determine whether a "problem" stems from racism or bias in others (the concept of health paranoia) so that clients do not inappropriately personalize problems.

3. Culturally skilled counselors are not averse to seeking consultation with traditional healers and religious and spiritual leaders and practitioners in the treatment of culturally different clients when appropriate.

4. Culturally skilled counselors take responsibility for interacting in the language requested by the client and, if not feasible, make appropriate referral. A serious problem arises when the linguistic skills of a counselor do not match the language of the client. This being the case, counselors should (a) seek a translator with cultural knowledge and appropriate professional background and (b) refer to a knowledgeable and competent bilingual counselor

5. Culturally skilled counselors have training and expertise in the use of traditional assessment and testing instruments. They not only understand the technical aspects of the instruments but are also aware of the cultural limitations. This allows them to use test instruments for the welfare of the diverse clients.

6. Culturally skilled counselors should attend to as well as work to eliminate biases, prejudices, and discriminatory practices. They should be cognizant of sociopolitical contexts in conducting evaluation and providing interventions and should develop sensitivity to issues of oppression, sexism, elitism, and racism.

7. Culturally skilled counselors take responsibility in educating their clients to the processes of psychological intervention, such as goals, expectations, legal rights, and the counselor's orientation.

Sample Letters and Procedures
Related to Censorship

Sample Form Letter Expressing Concerns

[Inside address]

Dear (<u>principal</u>),

I am the parent of __student name__ who attends _____ School. Under U.S. legislation and court decision, parents have the primary responsibility for their children's education, and pupils have certain rights which the schools may not deny.

Parents have the right to be assured their children's beliefs and moral values are not undermined by the schools. Pupils have the right to have and to hold their values and moral standards without curricula, textbooks, audiovisual materials, or supplementary assignments.

Under the Hatch Amendment, I hereby request that my child NOT be involved in any school activities or materials listed unless I have first reviewed all the relevant materials and have given my written consent for their use:

- Psychological and psychiatric treatment that is designed to affect behavioral, emotional, or attitudinal characteristics of an individual or designed to elicit information about attitudes, habits, traits, opinions, beliefs, or feelings of an individual or group;
- Values clarifications, use of moral dilemmas, discussion of religious or moral standards, role-playing or open-ended discussions of situations involving moral issues, and survival games including life/death decision exercises;
- Contrived incidents for self-revelation; sensitivity training, group-encounter sessions, talk-ins, magic circle techniques, self-evaluation, and auto-criticism; strategies designed for self-disclosure, including the keeping of a diary or a journal or a log book;
- Sociograms, sociodrama; psychodrama; blindfold walks; isolation techniques;
- Death education, including abortion, euthanasia, suicide, use of violence, and discussions of death and dying;
- Curricula pertaining to drugs and alcohol;
- Nuclear war, nuclear policy, and nuclear classroom games;
- Globalism, one-world government, or anti-nationalistic curricula;
- Discussion and testing on interpersonal relationships; discussions of attitudes toward parents and parenting;
- Educating in human sexuality, including premarital sex, contraception, abortion, homosexuality, group sex and marriages, prostitution, incest, bestiality, masturbation, divorce, population control, and roles of males and females; sex behavior, and attitudes of student and family;
- Pornography and any materials containing profanity and/or sexual explicitness;
- Guided-fantasy techniques; hypnotic techniques; imagery and suggestology;

- Organic evolution, including Darwin's theory;
- Discussion of witchcraft, occultism, the supernatural, and mysticism;
- Political and/or religious affiliations of student or family;
- Income of family;
- Nonacademic personality tests; questionnaires or personal and family life attitudes.

The purpose of this letter is to preserve my child's rights under the Protection of Pupil Rights Amendment (the Hatch Amendment) to the General Education Provisions Act, and under its regulations as published in the Federal Register of September 6, 1984, which became effective November 12, 1984.

These regulations provide a procedure for filing complaints first at the local level, and then with the U.S. Department of Education. If a voluntary remedy fails, federal funds can be withdrawn from those in violation of the law.

I respectfully ask you to send me a substantive response to this letter attaching a copy of your policy statement on procedures for parental permission requirements, to notify all my child's teachers, and to keep a copy of this letter in my child's permanent file.

Thank you for your cooperation.

Sample Response to Form Letter Expressing Concerns

[Inside address]

Dear Mr. and Mrs. _____ ,

Mrs. (principal's name) , principal of _____ Elementary School, referred to me your request relating to the involvement of your children with activities and materials that you believe are governed by "U.S. legislation and court decisions."

The form on which you submitted your request is one which has been published in magazines, newsletters, and other media. It is based, as your letter notes, on the "Hatch Amendment." Unfortunately, the form letter contains many incorrect interpretations of the law and has produced widespread misunderstanding about the Hatch Amendment. The confusion reached the point that Senator Hatch himself felt obligated to make the following statement (Congressional Record, Feb. 19, 1985):

> On the other hand some parent groups have interpreted both the statute and the regulations so broadly that they would have them apply to all curriculum materials, library books, teacher guides, etc., paid for with state or local money. They would have all tests used by teachers in such non-federally funded courses as physical education, health, sociology, literature, etc., reviewed by parents before they could be administered to students. Because there are no federal funds in such courses the Hatch Amendment is not applicable to them.

Due to the incorrect legal assumptions inherent in your request form, I can not approve your request as presented. However, I would hasten to point out areas in which district programs and procedures are consistent with the views expressed in your request.

1. Parents are certainly welcome to review any instructional materials used in the district. If you wish to review specific material, please contact your child's principal. In some cases in which parents have concerns about materials or program, alternative assignments or an option not to participate can be provided. In other cases (such as state-adopted textbooks or state-mandated curriculum), an option may not be available.
2. Parental consent for your child's participation is required for any activity that is subject to the Hatch Amendment provisions (e.g., psychological testing). In addition, there are other occasions

for which provision for parental consent occurs even though parental consent may not be required by the Hatch Amendment (e.g., fifth-grade human growth and development program).

3. Many of the activities listed on the request form are not part of the district's instructional program.

Although these items represent major areas of compatibility between district programs and your request, I must, in all honesty, acknowledge that there are areas in which district programs are not compatible with your request. For example, your letter requests review and consent of "curricula pertaining to drugs and alcohol." Drug and alcohol education is part of state-required curriculum. Local districts would not have the option to waive such instruction. The state curriculum for biology includes evolution. Because biology is not a required course, students may choose not to take it. However, any student who enrolled in biology would be provided instruction in all curriculum components required by the state.

Some items listed are so vague or general that it is difficult to know what would be considered a problem. For example, "contrived incidents for self-revelation" could include compositions on "The Most Exciting Thing I Did This Summer," an assignment that has probably been given to millions of kids over the years. Teachers make other similar assignments. In doing so, they have an excellent track record of being nonintrusive and of meeting ethical and professional standards. In the rare event that an autobiography assignment is intrusive or otherwise inappropriate, corrective action can be taken with the individual teacher.

In summary, I am denying your request as presented, due to its incorrect legal interpretations, its vagueness, and its conflict with state curriculum requirements. You are welcome to review any instructional materials used in the district. You will have opportunities to exercise parental consent for your child's participation in certain activities. I would encourage you to bring any specific concern to my attention.

Sincerely,
Superintendent

Administrative Regulation

Subject: Response to Parents Expressing Concerns Regarding Developmental Guidance Program

To: Elementary Principals
        Elementary Counselors

Some parents have expressed interest in/concern about the content of the classroom guidance program. Most of these parents, after learning of the actual objectives of and materials used in guidance classes, have become comfortable with their children's participation in those lessons. A few have not.

The district's position is that although parents may choose to allow or not allow their children to participate in counseling, instruction in the guidance curriculum is part of the basic educational program. State-mandated "essential elements" and district-established instructional objectives are taught through the elementary guidance program. Students shall not be excluded from guidance classes solely on the basis of parental request, just as they are not excluded from math classes or physical education classes. In addition to the educational considerations, the logistical problems of supervision of the student during that class time are significant.

In the event of such expression, follow the procedure described below.

1st: When a parent expresses concern about the content of the classroom guidance program, the counselor should meet with the parent to (1) hear the specific concern of the parent and (2) describe the program at the child's grade level, the objectives taught, and the materials used. The principal or the Director of Guidance may sit in on this initial information-sharing conference if desired.

2nd: If the parent is still uncomfortable with the child's participation in the program, he/she must submit the specific concerns in writing to the Principal. The Principal may have a second conference with the parent to share and gather more information. The parent must be apprised of the problem of supervision of the student if the parent is requesting removal of the child from the guidance classes.

3rd: If the parent continues to request removal of the child from guidance classes, the request is to be forwarded to the Director of Guidance along with any information the counselor and the Principal have gathered.

4th: The Director of Guidance will meet with the parent and, after consultation with the Assistant Superintendent for Student Services, will decide the matter.

Date:
Originated By:

⌒ Appendix K ⌒

Public Relations Flyer

Presenting Your School Counselor

What Is Guidance and Counseling?

Guidance and counseling is an integral part of each school's total educational program. It is a comprehensive program that includes sequential activities kindergarten through Grade 12, organized and implemented by certified school counselors with the active involvement and support of parents, students, teachers, and administrators.

The program is designed to address the needs of all students by helping them to acquire competencies in career planning and exploration, knowledge of self and others, and educational and vocational development.

How Can Parents Help?

Active parental involvement in the activities of the guidance and counseling program is essential if students are to make informed choices. Parents can assist by encouraging their children to do their best in school and part-time jobs and by providing assurance that school subjects selected are tied to career choices. Parents are invited to contact their children's school counselor with any concerns, ideas, and requests for assistance.

What Do School Counselors Do?

Elementary School Counselors: assist students to learn the skills and attitudes necessary to be successful learners. They emphasize with students that the classroom is their first workplace and that communication, decision making, interpersonal, and career awareness skills are important to their success.

Middle School Counselors: work with students to address their career, personal/social, and educational needs and concerns. They provide students with expanded career awareness and career exploration activities to assist them in the development and utilization of short- and long-range education and career plans.

High School Counselors: work with students in acquiring guidance competencies that form the foundation for their next steps educationally and occupationally. They assist students to develop realistic education and career plans based on a clear understanding of themselves, their needs, interests, skills, and the realities and possibilities of the worlds of education and work.

School Counselors: foster excellence by helping all students to achieve their potential. They promote excellence through their work in four program areas:

- Classroom presentations and large-group activities such as career days and college nights to help students learn coping skills, career planning and decision-making skills, and to plan for the future.
- Individual student planning for academic and career success through the development of short-term and long-range education and career plans.
- Individual and small group counseling, consultation, and referral, related to helping students with personal goals and concerns, and with educational progress.
- Management activities to support the guidance program and other school programs.

Note. From *Presenting Your School Counselor* (flyer), by Missouri Department of Elementary and Secondary Education and Missouri School Counselor Association. Reprinted with permission.

⌒ Appendix L ⌒

Reassignment of Nonguidance Duties

The professional school counselor's time and task analysis has revealed all of the activities that professional school counselors are currently performing. A number of these activities are nonguidance and should not be part of the desired district's guidance program. A few of them are activities that all school staff members, including professional school counselors, take a turn in doing. These activities are fair-share responsibilities for professional school counselors and are included in system support. The nonguidance activities that are assigned to professional school counselors need to be reassigned so that professional school counselors can devote their time to fully implementing the district's comprehensive guidance program.

Budget constraints in many districts may preclude the instantaneous reassignment of nonguidance duties. To ensure that the transition to a fully implemented comprehensive guidance program is made systematically, however, it is critical that a written nonguidance activities displacement plan is developed as a part of the overall implementation plan presented to the board of education. A statewide task force of Missouri administrators and professional school counselors developed the ideas that follow for reassignment consideration. They identified nonguidance duties, grouped them into four categories, and then listed possible ways to handle the reassignment of them.

I. *Supervisory Duties*

A. Coordinating and monitoring school assemblies
- This is an administrative function and is not viewed as a part of guidance program responsibilities.

B. Hall duty, cafeteria supervision, bus loading and unloading supervision, and restroom supervision
- These duties could be shared equally among all staff.
- Teachers could be assigned to some of these duties as a regular part of their schedules.
- Volunteers could be assist with some of these tasks.

C. Chaperoning school functions and athletic event supervision
- These duties could be shared among the staff.
- Booster club members could assist staff with some of the athletic events.
- School staff could be paid extra to take on chaperoning duties

D. Substitute teaching
- Professional school counselors are not substitute teachers. On an occasional basis, however, professional school counselors could conduct guidance learning activities, particularly if teacher absences are known in advance.

II. *Clerical Duties*

A. Selling lunch tickets
  - Office support staff or cafeteria staff should do this.

B. Collecting and mailing out progress reports and deficiency notices
  - Sorting, stuffing, and mailing are clerical/secretarial functions. An individual could be hired on a temporary basis to handle sorting, stuffing, and mailing.
  - Conferences with students regarding progress reports are school staff functions, which includes but should not be limited to professional school counselors.

C. Maintaining permanent records and handling transcripts
  - Posting grades and test labels is a clerical duty. Part-time help could be hired if a full-time person is not available to handle these functions.

D. Monitoring attendance
  - Accounting for daily attendance is not a guidance program's function. However, it is appropriate for professional school counselors to meet with students who have chronic attendance problems.
  - Computer software packages are available to monitor attendance in a very efficient and effective manner.

E. Calculating grade point averages (GPAs), class ranks, or honor rolls
  - Computer software packages are available to efficiently and effectively perform these tasks.

F. Developing and updating the student handbook
  - This is an administrative function that the principal or assistant principal should perform.

G. Developing and updating course guides
  - Department chairpersons (teaching staff) have the responsibility for developing course descriptions and course guides.

H. Completing the paperwork related to changing students' schedules
  - The paperwork involved in changing schedules, balancing class loads, and processing student schedule cards are clerical functions. If full-time clerical assistance is not available, part-time clerical/secretarial assistants should be hired to help at key times during the school year. A wide array of computer software is available to handle the scheduling process including schedule changes and can be purchased to facilitate the completion of these important activities.

III. *Special Programs and Services*

A. Sponsoring class clubs and special programs
  - Sponsorship of these activities is a school staff function usually done on a voluntary basis. Professional school counselors should not be expected to as-

sume any more responsibility for these programs than any other person on the staff.
- Programs such as the Missouri Scholars' Academy should be the responsibility of administrative personnel or a committee of school personnel.

B. Coordinating and administering the school-testing program, which includes individual testing
- The overall coordination and administration of the school-testing program are the responsibilities of the administration.
- Retired teachers could be hired to handle this responsibility.
- School personnel could collaborate to accomplish the coordination and administration of the school-testing program.
- Professional school counselors assist in interpreting test data to teachers, administrators, parents/guardians, and the community; however, they should not be responsible for coordinating and administering the school-testing program.
- Professional school counselors use test data when working with students to help them monitor and manage their academic, personal/social, and career development.
- School psychologists and school psychological examiners are the professionals who are qualified to do individual testing.

C. Completing and managing Individual Education Plans (IEPs) and meeting other special education requirements
- Professional school counselors should not function as case managers for students with special needs.
- Professional school counselors could be members of the team involved in the diagnostic aspects of the IEP. However, they should not be responsible for the development, implementation, and monitoring of the IEP or the Individualized Vocational Education Plan unless they are funded by special education or by vocational education funds.
- Professional school counselors could take part in staffing and conferences when appropriate but should not coordinate or chair the staffings, conferences, or IEP meetings.

D. Completing and managing 504 Plans and meeting other 504 Plan requirements.

IV. *Administrative Duties*

A. Developing the master schedule
- This is an administrative function. Administrators can seek input from professional school counselors, but it is their responsibility to plan and develop the master schedule.

B. Acting as the principal of the day
- The professional school counselor should not fill the role of acting principal. Retired school administrators could be hired for this purpose.
- This responsibility could be assigned to teachers who have administrative certification.

- The superintendent or other central office administrators could be called upon to act as principal for the day.

C. Administering discipline
  - Administering discipline and assessing consequences for student actions are administrative functions, not guidance functions. However, it is appropriate for professional school counselors to meet with students who have chronic discipline problems.

D. Managing schedule changes
  - Students who desire or need to have their schedules revised are encouraged to first discuss the changes with the professional school counselor. The mechanics related to this process should be handled through administrative channels. Much of the process is clerical in nature. It is the responsibility of the administration to see that class sizes are appropriate and that sufficient staff members are available to accommodate students' needs.

Note. From *Missouri Comprehensive Guidance Program: A Manual for Program Development, Implementation, Evaluation, and Enhancement* by N. C. Gysbers, L. Kostek-Bunch, C. S. Magnuson, M. F. Starr, 2002, Instructional Materials Laboratory, Columbia, MO. Reprinted with permission.

Appendix M

Descriptors Related to Evaluation Categories

These descriptors are provided to counselors, their supervisors, and administrators as a means of enhancing communication about the nature of guidance and counseling and the specifics upon which to base sound evaluative judgments as to the proficiency of the school counselor. The specific items were generated by and large by Northside counselors, with some reaffirmation and augmentation from the guidance and counseling literature. They are offered to assist new counselors, experienced counselors, nonguidance-trained administrators, and guidance-trained administrators to have similar definitions for the skills and knowledge expected of our school counselors.

Specifically, the items provide more concrete descriptions for the performance indicators suggested for the areas that counselors are evaluated on. If it were laid out in one document, the format would be as follows:

Category	Performance Indicators	Descriptors
1. Implements guidance curriculum through the use of effective instructional skills	a. appropriate task analysis	1. selection of terminal objective 2. specification of learning increments 3. weeding out of nonessentials 4. instruction at appropriate level of difficulty 5. selection of learning sequence 6. explanation of unfamiliar or specially used terms
	b. effective use of lessons design . . . etc. . . .	1. focus 2. explanation

Still, this list is not all-inclusive, nor are all items necessarily mutually exclusive. It is not meant to be used as a checklist, but rather it is intended to make the school counselor's role more tangible.

1. *Implements guidance curriculum through the use of effective instructional skills, including*

a. *appropriate task analysis*
   1. selects terminal objective

    2. specifies learning increments
    3. weeds out nonessentials
    4. instructs at an appropriate level of difficulty
    5. selects learning sequence
    6. explains unfamiliar or specially used terms

b. *effective use of lesson design*
    1. focus
    2. explanation
    3. checking for understanding
    4. monitoring and adjusting
    5. modeling
    6. guided practice
    7. closure
    8. independent practice
    9. extensions
    10. corrections
    11. evaluation

c. *active involvement of students in the learning process*
    1. varies activities
    2. interacts with students in appropriate group formats
    3. solicits student participation
    4. extends students' responses/contributions
    5. provides "wait time"
    6. secures and maintains students' attention
    7. gives clear directions
    8. manages students' behavior
    9. uses effective teaching practices
    10. uses strategies to motivate students for learning
    11. maintains supportive environment
    12. provides materials and equipment needed for lessons ready for use at appropriate time

d. *selection of topics consistent with identified, high-priority student needs and district goals*
    1. implements instruction at appropriate level of difficulty
    2. assesses student needs formally and informally
    3. adheres to district guidance scope and sequence and curriculum

2. *Implements the individual planning system through the effective use of guidance skills, including*

a. *careful planning of sessions*
    1. performs appropriate task analysis
    2. effectively uses lesson design, with expanded use of guided practice
    3. guided practice
    4. uses of variety of guidance techniques
    5. has materials, audiovisual aids, and facilities ready for use
    6. understands/applies theories of vocational choice

b. *presentation of accurate, relevant, unbiased information*
    1. makes no significant errors
    2. presents information so that students can process/internalize it
        a. uses vocabulary appropriate to students
        b. explains content clearly
        c. presents appropriate amounts of information
    3. stresses important points
    4. clarifies students' misunderstanding
    5. uses accurate language
    6. identifies, selects, organizes, and makes accessible educational and career information systems; makes information resources available to students
    7. uses materials effectively
    8. is knowledgeable about the range of educational and career alternatives and the value of each of these

c. *involvement of students in personalized educational and career planning*
    1. helps students establish goals and use planning skills
    2. knows students' abilities, achievements, interests, and goals
    3. effectively uses consultation skills as needed
    4. encourages parental input into student planning
    5. correctly assesses students' educational and career aspiration and information needs
    6. makes appropriate and appropriately presented recommendations
    7. conducts activities with groups of sizes conducive to ensure effectiveness and efficiency

d. *accurate and appropriate test results interpretation*
    1. provides appropriate information to students, parents, and school staff in timely manner
    2. ensures that individuals know how to read reports of interest/use to them
    3. strives to guard against the over interpretation or other inappropriate use of test results data
    4. in presenting test results interpretation, attends to the confidential and private nature of individual test information
    5. (reference: item 2b above regarding accuracy of information)
    6. understands/applies basic statistical concepts essential in the use of appraisal instruments and data
    7. understands/applies basic concepts and principles of measurement and evaluation
    8. processes appraisal data appropriately for use in guidance and counseling
    9. makes effective use of appraisal data in counseling and guidance

e. *selection of individual planning activities consistent with identified, high-priority student needs and district goals*
    1. assesses student needs for planning assistance formally and informally
    2. presents needs-identification data to reflect data from follow-up studies of former students' actual educational and career progress
    3. provides information about important dates and tasks to be accomplished
    4. adheres to District Guidance Program Framework time frame and priorities

3. *Implements responsive services through effective use of counseling, consultation, and referral skills, including*

a. *proper identification of problems/issues to be resolved*
  1. uses effective intake procedures to properly discern problems/issues
  2. in counseling, assists students to define their problems
  3. in consultation, collaborates with consultee in problem definition
  4. in referral, understands and articulates the basis for referral

b. *selection of counseling, consulting, or referral interventions appropriate to students' problems and circumstances*
  1. recognizes own personal/professional limitations and organizes caseload appropriately
  2. accepts referrals in a competent and professional manner
  3. responds appropriately to requests for information

c. *uses counseling, consulting, or referral skills effectively*

  Counseling:
  1. uses a variety of techniques and procedures
  2. operates from a consistently applied and conscious awareness of own theoretical base
  3. is nonjudgmental of students
  4. understands the dynamics of individual behavior in the counseling relationship or in a group

  Consulting:
  1. has expertise to share
  2. shares information
  3. in problem specification, gathers as much information as needed to consult effectively and efficiently
  4. in goal setting, understands consultees' responsibilities and goals
  5. establishes credibility by being able to suggest a variety of options, alternatives, resources, or strategies
  6. coordinates the development and implementation of the consultees' behavioral plan of action

  Referral: (process: problem specification, evaluation of need for referral, resource identification, referral, and follow-up)
  1. is knowledgeable about sources for referral
  2. seeks out referral sources
  3. conducts adequate research about referral sources
  4. refers at appropriate time in helping process
  5. is able to explain the need for referral and the referral process
  6. provides minimum of three referral options to client

d. *conducts well-planned and goal-oriented sessions*
  1. sessions are effective: objectives are established and attained
  2. sessions are efficient: objectives are the focus of the sessions; however, sensitivity to divergent needs of the group/individual is imperative also
  3. materials, aids, and facilities are ready for use

e. *use of group and individual techniques that are appropriate to the topic and to students' needs and abilities*
  1. discerns when individual or group counseling would be most facilitative to the problem presented by the counselees
  2. uses group counseling when it is determined to be more effective than or as effective as individual counseling
  3. structures specialized groups as to topic and purpose as well as membership composition
  4. displays working knowledge of developmental tasks and coping behaviors or different age levels and the skills to use group techniques appropriate for client level

f. *actively involves counselees/consultees/referees in the process*

  Counseling:
  1. counseling results in students' acting to solve problems
  2. holds student-oriented sessions
  3. allows students to speak freely about problems
  4. assists students in exploration of affect
  5. assists students in goal setting
  6. assists students in establishing a concrete behavioral plan aimed at problem resolution
  7. ensures that plan is developed at an appropriate level of specificity
  8. avoids premature advice or superficial reassurance
  9. listens effectively

  Consulting:
  1. consulting results in consultee acting to solve problem
  2. encourages input from consultee
  3. facilitates communication between participants
  4. avoids premature, superficial advice or reassurance
  5. handles expression of conflict in a constructive manner
  6. is appreciative of ideas expressed by others
  7. promotes a spirit of compromise and cooperation
  8. listens effectively

  Referral
  1. exhibits skill in the art of referral such that person needing referral feels comfortable
  2. assistance results in client going to referral source
  3. initiates contacts between referral sources and individuals who have been referred

g. *timely follow-up*
  1. follows up with students and other clients as to their progress in implementation of the problem-solving action plan
  2. communicates with referral sources
  3. ensures communication between appropriate people
  4. prepares/maintains appropriate documentation, forms, records, etc., relevant to cases

   5. implements follow-up activities as recommended for clients by referral sources

   h. *provision of services consistent with high-priority, identified student needs and district goals*
      1. conducts formal and informal needs assessments
      2. determines needs and priorities as perceived by students, parents, staff, and administration
      3. recognizes situations that need attention
      4. attends to priorities established in the Guidance Program Framework and in other district memos

4. *Implements system support through providing effective support for other programs and by effectively enlisting support for the guidance program, such as*

   a. *providing a comprehensive and balanced guidance program*
      1. uses effective planning skills
         a. assesses program needs and priorities accurately
         b. establishes realistic program goals
         c. uses results of evaluation to improve program
         d. plans program and activities
         e. provides alternative plans
         f. determines suitable and workable time schedule
         g. plans an overview of the year
         h. writes program plan
      2. uses effective organizational skills
         a. establishes meaningful objectives
         b. sequences activities in a meaningful design
         c. sets time lines and follows them
         d. operates from a program calendar
         e. provides an appropriately balanced and comprehensive program
      3. uses resources effectively
         a. resources = materials, human dollars, equipment, facilities
         b. selects and creates sound materials
         c. manages equipment and facilities and budget effectively
         d. takes proper care/makes proper use of equipment
         e. assigns tasks or duties appropriately/delegates effectively
         f. considers strengths of human talent available
         g. seeks assistance if does not have adequate answers
         h. uses administration and other staff as appropriate
         i. uses available resources
         j. provides resource materials and information to students, staff, parents
         k. determines what personal and natural resources are available/needed
      4. evaluates program effectively
         a. systematically evaluates overall program effectiveness
         b. uses results of evaluation to improve program
   b. *selecting program activities that meet identified, high-priority student needs and are consistent with campus and district goals*
      1. bases campus program on student and community needs
      2. bases campus program on the district framework

c. *collecting evidence that students achieve meaningful outcomes from program activities*
   1. evaluates effectiveness of activities
   2. evaluates quantity and quality of student growth in guidance and counseling activities
   3. provides for a system of evaluating programs and activities
   4. plans, implements, and accesses systematic evaluation tools
   5. uses results of evaluation tools to reassess program goals, objectives, and strategies
   6. consistently evaluates program activities

d. *operating within established procedures, policies, and priorities*
   1. complies with letter and intent of regulations, directives, and instructions from superiors
   2. administers activities in accordance with district guidelines

e. *contributing to organizational solutions outside of assigned responsibilities*
   1. works as member of team in working to solve organizational problems
   2. accepts responsibility for helping others learn their responsibilities and is able to do this without taking over others' roles

f. *working cooperatively with school administrators to garner support for the guidance program*
   1. collaborates with administration in developing the campus guidance program goals and objectives
   2. seeks their support on matters of concern

g. *implementing programs that explain the school guidance program*
   1. explains the philosophy, priorities, and practices of the guidance program effectively and articulately
   2. has a campus PR plan for helping the parents as well as the students and staff understand the guidance program and its variety of activities
   3. uses a variety of strategies to communicate to parents, e.g., newsletters, columns, parent education sessions, open houses

h. *attending to ideas/concerns expressed regarding the guidance program*
   1. listens with an open mind
   2. accepts suggestions gracefully
   3. is not unnecessarily defensive with parents or community representatives; works to understand their concerns
   4. maintains professional detachment in circumstances where patrons are misinformed, mistrusting

i. *supporting campus administration policies and goals*
   1. establishes objectives that contribute to the goals of the campus administration
   2. complies with letter and intent of regulations, directives, and instructions from superiors
   3. supports administrative directives
   4. cooperates with campus administration in addressing campus goals

j. *supporting district policies and goals*
　　1. supports administrative directives, school board goals, and organizational policies
　　2. adheres to Guidance Program Framework
　　3. cooperates with district administration in guidance program improvement efforts

5. *Establishes effective professional relationships by building rapport with*

a. *Students*
　　1. demonstrates knowledge of, interest in, and understanding of the roles and responsibilities of the student
　　2. acts as student advocate appropriately and effectively
　　3. communicates effectively with and about students
　　4. exhibits sensitivity, empathy, and acceptance necessary for establishing rapport
　　5. encourages students to have respect for the rights, property, and opinions of others
　　6. primary commitment is to the student, yet keeps communications open with others
　　7. is student advocate and liaison for students/administrators/faculty/parents
　　8. knows the students' backgrounds
　　9. encourages students to assume responsibility for own behaviors, choices, and relationships

b. *Staff*
　　1. demonstrates knowledge of, interest, in, and understanding of the roles and responsibilities of the teacher and other staff members
　　2. works cooperatively as a team member with staff
　　3. communicates effectively with and about staff
　　4. exhibits sensitivity, empathy, and acceptance necessary for establishing rapport
　　5. works as a team member—educator, consultant
　　6. respects professional judgments of staff
　　7. seeks and respects ideas of others
　　8. is receptive to teachers' comments and suggestions
　　9. encourages teachers to adjust their programs to individual needs of students

c. *Parents*
　　1. demonstrates knowledge of, interest in, and understanding of the roles, responsibilities, and circumstances of the parent
　　2. cooperates with parents in problem solving
　　3. communicates effectively with and about parents
　　4. exhibits sensitivity, empathy, and acceptance necessary for establishing rapport
　　5. encourages parents to practice effective parents skills
　　6. communicates effectively with parents regarding students' progress and areas of difficulty and success

d. *Other counselors*
　　1. where there is more than one counselor on a campus: operates as a team member; works collaboratively in the development of goals and the implementation of the campus guidance program

2. cooperates with counselors from other campuses in the interest of serving students and the program better

e. *Administrators*
   1. demonstrates knowledge of, interest in, and understanding of the roles and responsibilities of the administrator
   2. works cooperatively as a team member with administrators
   3. communicates effectively with and about administrators
   4. understands and responds appropriately to the different roles/responsibilities of the campus and district administrators
   5. exhibits sensitivity, empathy, and acceptance necessary for establishing rapport
   6. plays the child advocate role appropriately

f. *Other in-school district specialists*
   1. demonstrates knowledge and understanding of the roles and responsibilities of other specialists
   2. communicates effectively with and about other specialists
   3. maintains positive working relationships with other specialists
   4. exhibits sensitivity
   5. seeks specialists' assistance when needed/beneficial to the student or other clients
   6. initiates communication when needed/beneficial to the student or other clients
   7. does not overrely on other specialists

g. *Community representatives*
   1. communicates effectively with referral agency staff
   2. maintains positive working relationships with PTA and other patron groups
   3. is interested in and understands roles/responsibilities of community agency representatives
   4. exhibits sensitivity, warmth, and openness for establishing rapport
   5. establishes harmonious relationships with referral sources commonly used
   6. informs community about total school and guidance programs

6. *Fulfills professional responsibilities by*

a. *seeking professional development*
   1. has adequate knowledge to be an effective counselor
      a. understands, applies, and can articulate own theoretical framework
      b. understands the organization and operation of the school and the district
      c. is knowledgeable of developmental characteristics of age group served
      d. has basic knowledge of
         —guidance content and theory
         —program model
         —school system organization and operation
      e. can articulate own theoretical framework with respect to guidance and counseling, psychology, and human dynamics
      f. understands and applies basic concepts of psychological theory, measurement and evaluation, group and individual techniques of counseling and guidance
      g. has an internally consistent approach to guidance and counseling

  2. plans for and engages in professional development
     a. monitors and evaluates own professional performance
     b. implements own Professional Growth Plan
     c. makes use of opportunities for improving skills and acquiring new and relevant knowledge
     d. has developed and is implementing a personal, professional growth plan
     e. attends professional workshops, conferences, and courses
     f. belongs to professional organization(s)
     g. invests personal time
     h. is selective in choosing programs
     i. participates actively in in-district in-service offerings
     j. assumes responsibilities for own professional growth
     k. seeks opportunities to improve skills and to acquire new knowledge
     l. maintains contact with current research and practice
     m. combines information from various sources to solve problems/to innovate
     n. attempts sound innovative and creative approaches to problems
     o. is open to new learning/is willing to learn
  3. demonstrates commitment to the counseling and education professions
     a. invests own resources in professional development—time and money
     b. volunteers to serve on committees or accepts other leadership opportunities as offered
     c. accepts leadership roles in professional associations
     d. shares, joins, serves
     e. encourages others to use new ideas
     f. takes pride in being a member of the counseling profession
     g. understands roles/responsibilities of the school counselor at own and at other levels
     h. applies research knowledge and skills to further the field of guidance and counseling

 b. *keeping records consistent with ethical and legal guidelines*
    1. keeps organized, accurate, legal, and ethically appropriate records
    2. interprets records to others as is consistent with ethical and legal guidelines
    3. keeps records in an organized and consistent fashion
    4. communicates and interprets accurately and openly
    5. monitors overall records procedure
    6. delegates appropriately
    7. supervises paraprofessional staff effectively
    8. ensures security, confidentiality, and legality
    9. is knowledgeable of proper procedures
   10. maintains adequate, differentiated records
   11. documents consultations, referrals, and other guidance and counseling events
   12. completes paperwork in a timely and efficient manner

 c. *maintaining professional work habits*
    1. performs responsibilities in an organized, timely, and dependable manner
    2. complies with district's standards for attendance
    3. is considerate of others' time
    4. completes required forms and reports
    5. attends/participates in required staff meetings

6. exercises professional judgment in absences from work
7. plans and uses time to best advantage
8. complies with established district work hours
9. is task-oriented
10. maintains a positive atmosphere for learning and growing
11. attends to detail

d. *practicing according to the profession's ethical standards*
1. observes ethical standards of the American School Counselor Association and the American Counseling Association
2. implements counselor's role as defined in the Guidance Program Framework and other district guidelines
3. adheres to district policies and legal guidelines
4. refrains from revealing confidential information inappropriately
5. does not impose personal value judgments on students, their families, or on school staff
6. demonstrates impartiality with respect to sex, ethnicity, or ability of students
7. is aware of own personal/emotional and professional limitations
8. maintains confidentiality within established parameters

e. *demonstrating appropriate personal characteristics*
1. demonstrates attitudes conducive to effective guidance and counseling; is:

positive	persevering	accessible/available
pleasant	genuine	supportive
cheerful	open-minded	receptive to change
accepting	future-minded	willing to share
realistic	enthusiastic	information and ideas
cooperative	optimistic	flexible
helpful	personally courageous	has vision

2. demonstrates attributes conducive to effective guidance and counseling:
   a. takes initiative
   b. is caring, kind, warm
   c. has a sense of humor
   d. demonstrates patience
   e. is sensitive to others; has empathy
   f. uses intelligence and creativity
3. holds values conducive to effective guidance and counseling
   a. demonstrates self-acceptance, -understanding, and -confidence
   b. holds positive regard for the worth, dignity, and uniqueness of each individual
   c. demonstrates belief in ability of others to change, grow, and accept responsibility for own actions
   d. demonstrates honesty and loyalty
   e. values own role as model to others
   f. demonstrates belief in the value of learning and schooling
   g. respects individual differences
   h. resists imposing conforming behaviors on individuals
   i. makes a commitment of primary responsibility to students while providing adequate communication to teachers, parents, administrators, and other referral sources without violating confidentiality of the counseling relationship

4. has high professional standards
   a. accepts constructive criticism
   b. adapts to unusual circumstances
   c. tolerates ambiguity
   d. maintains objectivity/professional detachment in problem situations
   e. seems informed and confident in expression
   f. has professional image with students, staff, and parents
   g. models expected social behavior, grooming, and courtesy
   h. maintains poise and emotional stability
   i. strives for excellence
   j. is motivated to achieve
   k. maintains good physical health
   l. provides a good moral example for students
   m. handles decisions of superiors appropriately
   n. recognizes own leadership role on campus and accepts the responsibilities of leadership on the campus

f. *demonstrating effective use of basic skills, e.g., communication, problem solving, decision making, educational*
   1. uses communication skills
      a. listens actively
      b. builds rapport
      c. is interested in others' messages
      d. uses appropriate vocabulary
      e. maintains a supportive environment
      f. speaks and writes professionally
      g. uses both verbal and nonverbal communication behaviors appropriately
      h. uses appropriate attending behaviors
      i. uses open-ended questions and prompts
      j. reflects feelings of communicator
      k. accurately paraphrases content of communicator's message
      l. uses interpretation skills effectively
      m. responds to verbal and nonverbal communications in meaningful ways
   2. problem solving
      a. diagnoses problems accurately
      b. prescribes appropriate remedies
      c. approaches problems with impartiality
      d. is able to think of multiple options for problem solution
      e. is able to envision consequences of various options
      f. handles dissenting individuals and groups
   3. decision making
      a. recognizes the need for a decision
      b. explores alternative choices
      c. predicts accurately the probable outcome of each choice
      d. assigns personal values to each choice
      e. determines the costs/risks attendant to each choice
      f. applies a variety of decision strategies
      g. makes a plan for decision implementation
      h. evaluates the outcome of decisions

4. educational skills
   a. imparts information effectively
   b. strengthens students' capacity to cope with life situations
   c. allows "wait time"
   d. maintains physical environment appropriate to the session conducted
   e. has materials, aids, and facilities ready for use for various activities
   f. maximizes use of time available for guidance and counseling
   g. manages student behavior, e.g.,
      —specifies expectations
      —uses techniques to prevent, redirect, or stop off-task, inappropriate, or disruptive behavior
      —applies rules consistently and fairly
      —uses reinforcement techniques effectively
   h. uses effective strategies to motivate students to respond to guidance and counseling
   i. displays a working knowledge of group dynamics, e.g.,
      —content and process variables
      —typical stage of group development
      —various leadership styles and their effective use
      —conditions for promoting healthy groups

Note. From *Guide to Counselor Performance Improvement,* by Northside Independent School District, 1987, San Antonio, TX. Reprinted with permission.

Observation Forms for Counseling, Consultation, and Referral Skills

Summary of Counselor Observation: Counseling Skills

Counselor _____ Date of Observation _____

School _____ Observation: From _____ to _____

General Information (theme, screening criteria, etc.)

    Grade level: _____ No. of students _____

    Session #: _____

    Goal of group: _____

    Objective(s) of session: _____

    Client(s)' descriptions: _____

	Observed? (Circle)		Indicators/ Comments:
I. *Results of Program Plans and Preparation*			
a. Selects group/individual needs appropriately for efficiency and effectiveness	Yes	No	_____
b. Uses appropriate procedures for group member selection	Yes	No	_____
c. Clearly articulates purpose and strategies of session	Yes	No	_____
d. Responds appropriately to requests for information	Yes	No	_____
e. Length of session is appropriate to plans	Yes	No	_____
f. Has materials, etc., ready for use	Yes	No	_____
g. Establishes environment conducive to counseling	Yes	No	_____
h. Selects strategies that are student-centered and appropriate to students' age level and problems	Yes	No	_____
i. Provides services consistent with high-priority student needs and district goals	Yes	No	_____

Comments:

	Observed? (Circle)		Indicators/ Comments:
II. *The Counseling Process*			
a. Provides focus for group	Yes	No	_____
b. Keeps group on task	Yes	No	_____
c. Facilitates students' problem definition and goal setting	Yes	No	_____
d. Gently encourages participation of each member	Yes	No	_____
e. Provides opportunity for student interaction	Yes	No	_____
f. Facilitates communication between participants	Yes	No	_____
g. Listens effectively	Yes	No	_____
h. Avoids premature or superficial advice or reassurance	Yes	No	_____

i. Handles expressions of hostility in a constructive
manner   Yes   No   _____

j. Checks for understanding   Yes   No   _____

k. Facilitates "guided practice" (if appropriate)   Yes   No   _____

l. Clearly states follow-up plans   Yes   No   _____

m. States independent practice/"challenges"   Yes   No   _____

Comments:

III. *Personal/Professional*

a. Protects confidentiality   Yes   No   _____

b. Leads without dominating   Yes   No   _____

c. Explains clearly and concisely   Yes   No   _____

d. Is genuine as opposed to "phony"   Yes   No   _____

e. Interrupts destructive interaction appropriately   Yes   No   _____

f. Discloses own feelings and beliefs in a constructive manner   Yes   No   _____

g. Is tolerant of ideas others express   Yes   No   _____

h. Treats individuals with respect   Yes   No   _____

i. Recognizes individuals within group   Yes   No   _____

j. Uses appropriate vocabulary   Yes   No   _____

k. Applies a sound theoretical base   Yes   No   _____

l. Operates within realistic limitations of school counseling
services   Yes   No   _____

Comments:

SUMMARY COMMENTS AND RECOMMENDATIONS:

Feedback Conference Date: _____ Time: _____

Observer: _____ Counselor: _____

(Signatures are for the sole purpose of documenting the conference.)

Summary of Counselor Observation: Consultation Skills

Counselor _____ Date of Observation _____

School _____ Observation: From _____ to _____

General Information—(context, participants, objectives, etc.)

Student grade level:

People involved in session:

Topic:

                                     Observed?   Indicators/

                                     (Circle)   Comments:

I. *Planning and Preparation*

a. Treats individuals with respect   Yes   No   _____

b. Makes objectives of session clear   Yes   No   _____

c. Is prepared for conference (e.g., has relevant information,
knows students' background, is focused on the problem/issue)   Yes   No   _____

d. Prepares appropriate documentation, forms, records, etc.   Yes   No   _____

e. Has knowledge of community resources and referral sources   Yes   No   _____

f. Demonstrates knowledge of school district policy   Yes   No   _____

g. Has established that consultation is an appropriate intervention   Yes   No   _____

Comments:

II. *The Consultative Process*
   a. Uses effective intake procedures to properly discern problem/issue — Yes   No   _____
   b. Collaborates with consultee in definition of problem and goal setting — Yes   No   _____
   c. Coordinates a specific behavioral plan of action — Yes   No   _____
   d. Listens effectively — Yes   No   _____
   e. Facilitates communication between participants — Yes   No   _____
   f. Suggests various options for problem resolution — Yes   No   _____
   g. Avoids premature, superficial advice or reassurance — Yes   No   _____
   h. Handles expressions of conflict in a constructive manner — Yes   No   _____
   i. Conducts session efficiently and effectively — Yes   No   _____
   j. States plan for follow-up — Yes   No   _____
   k. Summarizes conferences results accurately — Yes   No   _____
Comments:

III. *Personal/Professional*
   a. Protects confidentiality — Yes   No   _____
   b. Is genuine as opposed to "phony" — Yes   No   _____
   c. Is appreciative of ideas others express — Yes   No   _____
   d. Recognizes diversity of individuals' perspectives — Yes   No   _____
   e. Promotes a spirit of compromise and cooperation — Yes   No   _____
   f. Establishes professional credibility — Yes   No   _____
   g. Applies a sound theoretical base — Yes   No   _____
Comments:

SUMMARY COMMENTS AND RECOMMENDATIONS:

Feedback Conference Date: _____ Time: _____
Observer: _____ Counselor: _____
(Signatures are for the sole purpose of documenting the conference.)

Summary of Counselor Observation: Referral Skills

Counselor _____ Date of Observation _____
School _____ Observation: From _____ to _____
General Information—(context, participants, objectives, etc.)
   Student grade level:
   People involved in session:
   Topic:

	Observed? (Circle)		Indicators/ Comments:
I. *Plans and Preparation*			
a. Summarizes conferences results accurately	Yes	No	_____
b. Understands and articulates reason(s) for referral	Yes	No	_____
c. Is prepared for conference (e.g., has relevant information, knows students' background, is focused on the problem/issue)	Yes	No	_____

d. Prepares appropriate documentation, forms, records, etc.	Yes	No	_____
e. Has knowledge of community resources and referral sources	Yes	No	_____
f. Demonstrates knowledge of school district policy	Yes	No	_____
g. Has established that referral is an appropriate intervention	Yes	No	_____

Comments:

II. *Referral Conference*

a. Uses effective intake procedures to properly discern problem/issue	Yes	No	_____
b. Defines problem clearly	Yes	No	_____
c. Expresses rationale for referral clearly	Yes	No	_____
d. Outlines action steps for referral process	Yes	No	_____
e. Listens effectively	Yes	No	_____
f. Provides minimum of three referral options to client (if referral is nondistrict, program/specialists)	Yes	No	_____
g. Helps individuals referred to have realistic expectations of services available from referral source	Yes	No	_____
h. Helps individuals referred to understand their responsibilities and to make plans for action	Yes	No	_____
i. States own follow-up/coordination plans	Yes	No	_____
j. Summarizes conference results	Yes	No	_____

Comments:

III. *Personal/Professional*

a. Promotes confidentiality	Yes	No	_____
b. Is genuine as opposed to "phony"	Yes	No	_____
c. Recognizes feelings and thoughts of client(s)	Yes	No	_____
d. Promotes a spirit of cooperation and problem solving	Yes	No	_____
e. Establishes professional credibility	Yes	No	_____
f. Assists individual(s) referred to feel comfortable about referral	Yes	No	_____

Comments:

Summary Comments and Recommendations

Feedback Conference Date: _____ Time: _____

Observer: _____ Counselor: _____

(Signatures are for the sole purpose of documenting the conference.)

Note. From Northside Independent School District, San Antonio, TX. Reprinted with permission.

❦ Appendix O ❧

Missouri School Improvement Guidance Program Standards

6.9 *Guidance is an integral part of the instructional program.*

6.9.1. A districtwide guidance program has been developed and implemented in every building and contains:
- program objectives aligned with the CSIP [Comprehensive School Improvement Plan] and student performance data
- identified instructional competencies/learner objectives
- a Comprehensive Evaluation Plan

6.9.2. The K–12 guidance curriculum is in place and is systematically reviewed and revised. Modifications to the guidance curriculum are based upon student and school data and on needs assessment data, collected at least every three years. Instructional activities and resources are provided which allow for implementation of a K–12 guidance curriculum.

6.9.3. An individual planning system is in place (which includes the necessary forms and procedures) assists students as they develop educational and career plans. This planning is initiated no later than Grade 8 and includes:
- assessment activities
- advisement activities
- identification of long- and short-range educational/career goals including a 4–6 year plan that is reviewed and revised annually.
- collaboration with parents/guardians

6.9.4. Students have access to responsive services that assist them in addressing issues and concerns that may affect their personal, academic, social, and career development.

6.9.5. System support and management activities ensure full implementation and continued improvement of the district's comprehensive guidance program.

Note. From *Missouri School Improvement Program: Fourth Cycle Missouri School Improvement Standards,* by Missouri Department of Elementary and Secondary Education, 2005, Jefferson City, MO: Author. Reprinted with permission.

Appendix P

Standards for a Guidance Program Audit

There are eight standards against which a guidance program is audited:

1. The school district is able to demonstrate that all students are provided the opportunity to gain knowledge, skills, values, and attitudes that lead to a self-sufficient, socially responsible life.
2. The school district is able to demonstrate that students have acquired regular and timely information to enable them to make informed decisions.
3. The school district is able to demonstrate that all students have access to assistance in overcoming problems that are impeding their educational, personal, social, and/or career development.
4. The school district is able to demonstrate that a team of educators provides guidance to students within a supportive learning environment.
5. The school district is able to demonstrate implementation of a guidance program that reflects allocation of resources according to students' needs.
6. The school district is able to demonstrate that guidance program staff are used in roles reflective of their training and competence, and relevant staff development opportunities are made available.
7. The school district is able to demonstrate that the guidance program is developmentally sequential, structured comprehensively, designed to ensure appropriate program balance, and is an integral part of the overall educational program.
8. The school district is able to demonstrate that the guidance program is reviewed continually and renewed annually.

STANDARD 1: The school district is able to demonstrate that all students are provided the opportunity to gain knowledge, skills, values, and attitudes that lead to a self-sufficient, socially responsible life.

A school district meeting this standard has defined the content that all students should learn in a systematic, sequential way. The content goals are tied to those defined in the basic mission of the school district and are based on human development theories regarding individuals' personal, social, career, and educational development. The content is further defined in a scope and sequence that outlines the guidance curriculum. The implementation of the guidance curriculum component of a comprehensive guidance program entails teaching lessons and units designed to help students acquire the competencies outlined in the scope and sequence.

What the auditor expects to find:

- A developmentally appropriate guidance curriculum teaches all students the knowledge and skills they need to be self-sufficient and lead socially responsible lives.

- A guidance curriculum is articulated from elementary to middle to high schools.
- Priorities are established for acquisition of competencies and attainment of outcomes by students at each grade level.
- Sufficient curriculum materials support teaching the needed knowledge and skills.
- Yearly schedule incorporates the classroom guidance plan.
- Students in special education and other special programs receive guidance curriculum instruction.

Documentation:

- Guidance curriculum guides
- Guidance curriculum scope and sequence
- Teachers' and counselors' unit and lesson plans
- Yearly master calendar for the guidance program
- Curriculum materials

STANDARD 2: The school district is able to demonstrate that students have acquired regular and timely information to enable them to make informed decisions.

A school district meeting this standard has in place a system for guiding all students as they make and implement plans toward achieving their educational and career goals. In addition, students and their parents are assisted in understanding and monitoring the student's growth and development and in making thoughtful decisions. The individual student planning component of a comprehensive guidance program entails providing accurate and unbiased information at regular and developmentally appropriate times and guiding students and their parents through the use of that information. Activities included in this component include assessment, advisement, and placement assistance.

What the auditor expects to find:

- An individual planning system is in place and assists all students and their parents to understand and monitor the students' growth and development, to problem solve, and to make thoughtful decisions. The system includes assessment, advisement, and placement activities timed to meet students' developmental needs appropriately and effectively for planning, monitoring, and taking next steps in implementing their plans.
- Specific activities include individual and group guidance sessions designed to assist students with their educational and career planning, to assist students in making transitions from one school level to the next, and to assist students and parents make effective use of standardized test results.
- Information dissemination is conducted systematically and efficiently. Printed information is accurate, complete, and attractive.

Documentation:

- Individual planning system guides
- Guidance session plans
- Career guidance center schedule of activities and bibliography of information sources
- Test results and memos/handouts that indicate efforts addressed at making effective use of these results

- Standardized forms that reflect direct services to students and parent involvement
- Documents distributed through school orientations that provide information on test data interpretation, course content and selection procedures, promotion and graduation requirements, postsecondary educational and career options, financial aid information, and college testing information, requirements, and procedures.
- Individualized Educational Plans (IEPs) and treatment plans that reflect the inclusion of special education students into the activities that meet this standard.

STANDARD 3: The school district is able to demonstrate that all students have access to assistance in overcoming problems that are impeding their educational, personal, social, and/or career development.

A school district meeting this standard provides a variety of services for responding to the special needs and/or problems of students, their families, and teachers. The services that counselors/social workers are specially trained to provide include individual and small-group counseling, crisis counseling and response, consultation with teachers and parents, referral, and individual assessment. The responsive services component of a comprehensive guidance program includes preventive and remedial interventions that are planned in anticipation of recurrent student needs and are responsive when unanticipated needs arise.

Although at any given time all students are not in need of responsive services, these services must be available and accessible to all students. Ensuring equal access to the responsive services component entails guidance staff's outreach efforts and acceptance of students' diverse backgrounds and experiences.

What the auditor expects to find:

- A variety of responsive services—including individual and small-group counseling, crisis counseling, teacher and parent consultation, student assessment, and referral—are provided to students whose problems are interfering with their healthy development. Preventive and remedial interventions are available; services are planned in anticipation of student needs and are responsive when unanticipated needs arise.
- Counselors are readily accessible to students with problems.
- Efforts to reach out to students, teachers, and parents are made to ensure open access for those in need of services. In addition, procedures are in place systematically to identify students at risk and to implement strategies designed to decrease their level of risk.
- Teacher and administrator support teams are in place with counselor representation.
- Interdepartment and interagency linkages are in place to facilitate service delivery. Referral procedures are effective and clear.
- Record-keeping systems ensure confidentiality.
- Counseling staff adequately reflects the diversity in the community.

Documentation:

- Service delivery records that verify equitable service to all students regardless of race, ethnicity, socioeconomic status, ability/achievement level, gender.
- Critical documents that are multilingual and interpreter support that is available and provided as needed

- Crisis management plan
- Counseling session plans and notes
- Consultation session plans and notes
- Progress reports and evidence of their use
- Referral documentation forms
- Yearly/monthly/weekly schedules of activities
- Schedule of small group counseling offerings
- Letters of invitation and explanation; fliers
- Parents permission forms
- Referral source lists
- Case notes
- Multilingual, ethnically diverse staffing guidelines
- Counselor roster

STANDARD 4: The school district is able to demonstrate that a team of educators provides guidance to students within a supportive learning environment.

A school district meeting this standard knows that comprehensive guidance programs feature a team approach. Although professionally certified counselors/social workers provide leadership and are central to the program, all school staff collaborate in guiding students to attain educational success. Guidance staff collaborate with parents and community mental health services providers as well.

For a guidance program to be effective, the learning environment must be supportive and one in which relationships are characterized by mutual respect, trust, and open communication. Clients of the guidance program feel welcome, safe, and assured of their rights. Guidance program staff operate within ethical, legal, and professional standards.

What the auditor expects to find:

- Program delivery is the result of collaborative efforts among counselors, administrators, teachers, parents, and students.
- Building climates promote positive intra- and interpersonal relationships; i.e., relationships are characterized by mutual respect, trust, collaboration and cooperation, and open communications.
- To enhance the educational success of students, counselors are in partnership with parents—including PTA members as well as the parents of their counselees; with teachers as part of the educational team; with other school-based specialists as part of the specialist team; and with community mental health workers as part of the community mental health team.
- Communication mechanisms (e.g., staff meetings, case consultations, in-service training) are in place to facilitate these relationships.
- Opportunities are provided and taken for counselors to explain the guidance program to staff, parents, and the community at large.
- Counselors and others working within the context of the guidance program adhere to the ACA, ASCA, and other relevant ethical standards, which protect students' and families' rights to privacy, confidentiality, respect, and belief in their integrity, etc.
- The guidance program goals and objectives are understood and supported by district and campus administrators, teachers, and parents.
- Students and parents feel invited, welcome, and safe in the counseling office and when receiving counseling services.

Documentation:

- Staff meeting schedules and agendas
- In-service training agendas
- Counselors' meetings, newsletters, etc., with PTA
- Ethical standards readily accessible to each staff member
- Graduate follow-up information
- Climate studies or results
- School guidance committee philosophy statement/goals and objectives
- Student recognition process
- Natural helpers program plans
- Printed information regarding service offerings
- Documentation supporting parent involvement efforts

STANDARD 5: The school district is able to demonstrate implementation of a guidance program that reflects allocation of resources according to students' needs.

A school district meeting this standard has committed sufficient resources and channeled them to meet the identified, high-priority guidance needs of their students, and established a program implementation plan that focuses on meeting those needs most efficiently and effectively. Students' needs may be identified from the students' perspective as well as from that of the professional staff, the community, and other public policy entities. Consideration must be given to the demographics of the community served. The program's mission is articulated clearly to focus the allocation of resources. Resources include the guidance program staff, administrative support and rules and regulations, and access to students as well as budget, facilities, equipment, and materials.

What the auditor expects to find:

- The guidance program framework/plan is based on sound rationale; i.e., an assessment of students' and community's needs is done regularly and leads to the establishment of priorities for program delivery. The campus program is based on accurate information regarding the student body's demographic characteristics (e.g., race, ethnicity, socioeconomic status, parent educational levels, labor market).
- The program is based on a cogent theoretical perspective regarding student (human) growth and development and the contribution that the school-based guidance and counseling program makes to that growth and development.
- The mission of the program—its definition, goals and objectives, and organizational pattern—is stated clearly and is relevant to the district's overall mission.
- The program's implementation plan is clearly tied to the adopted program mission and established priorities and organized to meet these most effectively and efficiently.
- Actual program implementation reflects the plan.
- The resources appropriated are sufficient for the program staff to be held accountable for assisting students to attain high-priority outcomes. Resources include allocation of staff, sufficient access to students, budget appropriations, adequate facilities, equipment and materials, and appropriate regulations and procedures.

Documentation:

- Results of needs assessments

- Campus demographic data reports
- Statements outlining the theoretical basis (philosophy) of the program (the assumptions in the Gysbers model)
- Board policy providing the foundation for the program
- District's strategic plan
- Campus guidance program mission statements
- Written district and campus plans
- Adopted handbook/framework
- Master calendar of activities (planned and completed)
- Calendars and logs of program activities
- ESA/student ratio guidelines
- Itemized district and campus guidance program budgets
- Facilities standards for counseling offices and rooms, records and storage areas, classroom availability, etc.
- Inventory of equipment and materials
- Written procedures and regulations

STANDARD 6: The school district is able to demonstrate that guidance program staff are used in roles reflective of their training and competence, and relevant staff development opportunities are made available.

A school district meeting this standard has defined the appropriate roles various staff members play in the delivery of the comprehensive guidance program. School counselors/ social workers are the central guidance program staff; thus their job descriptions are such that students reap optimum benefit from their special skills (i.e., guidance, counseling, consultation, coordination, referral, assessment). The roles of other guidance program staff are also delineated and appropriate to their training. The relationships among the various staff members are clearly defined. The performance of guidance program staff is nurtured through a relevant and fair performance improvement system, which includes opportunities for supervision, performance evaluation, and professional development.

What the auditor expects to find:

- School counselors provide leadership to the guidance program, and within the program use their special skills—guidance, counseling, consultation, coordination and referral, and case management and assessment—at least 80% of the time. Their involvement in nonguidance tasks is kept to a minimum.
- Professionalism is evidenced in the adherence to professional standards, including the development and implementation of annual professional development plans.
- Other professional and paraprofessional staff with delineated roles in the guidance program are using their special skills; i.e., teachers teach, consult, and advise; administrators guide, consult, and advise; registrars maintain records; career guidance center technicians perform resource services; data-entry clerks do data-entry.
- Staffing patterns are defined and assignments are based on student-centered rationale.
- A counselor-appropriate performance improvement system is in place that is relevant to effective delivery of the district's guidance program. This system includes supervision and performance evaluation conducted by a trained counselor supervisor/evaluator. Clinical supervision also may be provided by peer supervisors/mentors/ coaches.
- Staff development is provided for regularly and on topics indicated as needed by the counselors and by program priorities.
- Professional induction activities are provided for new counselors.

Documentation:

- Professional certifications
- Staffing pattern/organizational chart
- Program definition with clarification of staff members' roles and responsibilities
- Position-specific job descriptions
- Staff members' professional development plans
- Clinical supervision schedules
- Program improvement goals
- Performance evaluation forms
- Staff development plan
- Staff development agendas and other materials
- New counselor orientation agendas
- Inventories of professional library resources

STANDARD 7: The school district is able to demonstrate that the guidance program is developmentally sequential, structured comprehensively, designed to ensure appropriate program balance, and is an integral part of the overall educational program.

A school district meeting this standard provides activities that are developmentally appropriate, i.e., they are based on the theory of human development previously described and are sequenced to ensure student development of prerequisite knowledge and skills. The guidance curriculum and individual student planning components are the basis of the developmental program; however, the responsive services component activities are based on awareness of the knowledge and skills students have/have not acquired.

A characteristic of the comprehensive guidance program is that program activities are organized according to the four delivery system components of guidance curriculum, individual student planning, responsive services, and system support. Between and within these components, priorities are established that direct the appropriate use of guidance program staff time and skills and identify the content to be addressed. In addition to having definitions of its own, the guidance program is integrated with other educational programs to better ensure students' acquisition and application of needed knowledge and skills.

What the auditor expects to find:

- The program is designed to provide students with a developmentally appropriate base of knowledge and skills from which to achieve a self-sufficient and socially responsible life. This basis is delivered to students through the guidance curriculum and individual student planning components.
- The foundation of the program is expressed in the rationale for, assumptions behind, and definition of the program.
- The program activities are organized to ensure implementation of the four delivery system components: guidance curriculum, individual student planning, responsive services, and system support, and of the priorities within each component.
- Priorities are established that direct the program balance, that is, provide the measure of appropriate allocation of resources.
- Fifty to 70% of the activities involve direct contact with students. An exemplary balance might be:

	% of Counselor's Time		
	ES	MS	HS
Guidance Curriculum	35–45	25–35	15–25
Individual Student Planning	5–10	15–25	25–35
Responsive Services	30–40	30–40	25–35
System Support	10–15	10–15	15–20
Nonguidance	0	0	0

- All staff participate in helping students achieve guidance program goals.
- The guidance program is integrated with other educational programs and has integrity as a separate program.
- Instructional goals are supported by the guidance department through such means as interpretation of standardized test results and other data regarding students' performance to teachers, administrators, and school board members.
- Communication mechanisms exist to ensure integration and understanding of mutual goals and plans—for example, guidance department head meets regularly with instructional department heads; guidance department head meets regularly with administration. Counselors are assigned as liaisons to each department.

Documentation:

- Curricular scope and sequence
- Guidance program framework/handbook, including priority topics by component by grade/school level
- Program balance charts
- Counselors' calendars and logs
- Staff familiarity with guidance program goals and objectives
- Curricular infusion bridge documents
- Staff roles and responsibilities statements
- Guidance program improvement goals and plans correlated to the campus goals and improvement plans
- Staff meeting schedules

STANDARD 8: The school district is able to demonstrate that the guidance program is reviewed continually and renewed annually.

A school district meeting this standard has in place a system for evaluating the effectiveness and efficiency of the comprehensive guidance program. The program is evaluated against the implementation standards that have been adopted (such as this audit). Evaluation is conducted to judge whether program changes are, in fact, program improvements. Finally, assessments are made of students' acquisition of the knowledge and skills taught through the program. The results of evaluations are used to redesign and thereby improve the program and for staff development. Reports of results are shared with appropriate audiences to ensure accountability of the comprehensive guidance program.

What the auditor expects to find:

- An annual process is in place for planning, designing, and evaluating the comprehensive guidance program with time appropriated for these activities and with mechanisms to ensure that evaluation data are considered in replanning the program.

- Evaluation is conducted regarding the effectiveness of program implementation, and students' attainment of priority outcomes.
- The process allows the guidance staff some autonomy in designing and implementing the program on the campus. An advisory committee provides meaningful input to the guidance program improvement efforts.

Documentation:

- Annual written evaluation of outcomes students have attained through the program
- Planning forms and evaluation reports
- Yearly, monthly, and weekly calendars
- Written reports analyzing actual vs. planned program implementation
- Program improvement plans based on evaluation findings
- Budget expenditures
- Counselor time accountability forms
- Data on effectiveness of program activities
- Advisory committee roster, meeting announcements/agendas, minutes of meetings

☞ Appendix Q ☜

Sample Memo Regarding Major Changes and New Program Recommendations

TO: Counselors and Principals
FROM: Director of Guidance
RE: Major Changes and New Recommendations in the Comprehensive Guidance
         Program Framework
DATE:

Client priorities
- Counselors' priority is students with needs for prevention/intervention services

Priorities for counselors' skill use
- Counseling
- Guidance program management
- Consultation

Guidance as a schoolwide responsibility
- Teamwork and collaboration between counselors, other staff members, and parents emphasized
- Administrators' and teachers' roles outlined
- Student advisory program for all students to extend the individual planning system
- School counselors' responsibilities for the quality of the total guidance program include consultation, support, and supervision

Parents' rights and responsibilities delineated
- Roles outlined
- Responsibilities for parent involvement clarified

Guidance program
- Recommended balance presented in ranges, leaving room for school-based decisions
- Teachers' role in guidance curriculum recognized
- Transition activities emphasized in individual planning system
- Responsive services emphasized for use of counselor time
- Each campus to set topic priorities for responsive services each year based on an assessment of student and community needs
- Counselors' responsive services outlined as a continuum: identification, appraisal, prevention/intervention, follow-up
- New priorities established for the time available to support other programs

- Special elements of the guidance program defined for better coordination with the basic program

Levels of service projected
- Minimum or possible numbers of activities specified for each component
- The numbers of students possibly served by a counselor in a specific program balance and with a given ratio calculated

Enhanced "Performance Improvement System"
- Roles related to program components
- Roles, competencies, indicators, and descriptors defined as basis of system
- Roles and responsibilities of specialist counselors detailed
- Supervision system recommended for elementary counselors
- Systematic staff development system implemented

Job descriptions established for guidance department paraprofessionals
- Nonguidance tasks take an undue amount of counselors' time (still)
- Recommendations: building test coordinator responsibilities be shared; "504" coordinator be an administrator; continue to pursue the addition of technical assistants at all three levels

Program management support
- Desired counselor–student ratio established at 1:350; reductions suggested in middle and magnet school head counselors' ratio
- Elementary: guidance classroom; flexible schedule; secretarial time

Index

D

N